TALES ARAB WOMEN TELL

TALES ARAB WOMEN TELL

and the Behavioral Patterns They Portray

COLLECTED, TRANSLATED, AND INTERPRETED BY
HASAN M. EL-SHAMY

INDIANA UNIVERSITY PRESS
BLOOMINGTON AND INDIANAPOLIS

This book is a publication of
Indiana University Press
601 North Morton Street
Bloomington, IN 47404-3797 USA

http://www.indiana.edu/~iupress

Telephone orders 800-842-6796
Fax orders 812-855-7931
Orders by e-mail iuporder@indiana.edu

The paper used in this publication meets the minimum requirements of American National Standard for Information Sciences—Permanence of Paper for Printed Library Materials, ANSI Z39.48-1984.

Manufactured in the United States of America

Library of Congress Cataloging-in-Publication Data

Tales Arab women tell and the behavioral patterns they portray / collected, translated, and interpreted by Hasan M. El-Shamy.
p. cm.
Includes bibliographical references (p.) and indexes.
ISBN 0-253-33529-9 (cl : alk. paper)
1. Women, Arab—Folklore. 2. Tales—Middle East. I. El-Shamy, Hasan M., date
GR268.A73T35 1999
398.2′082′0956—dc21
98-27710

1 2 3 4 5 04 03 02 01 00 99

CONTENTS

C. Siblings

SISTER AND SISTER

BROTHER AND SISTER

ACKNOWLEDGMENTS

Many friends and colleagues contributed generously toward the actualization of the present work. I am especially thankful to Mrs. Syd Grant, former secretary of the Indiana University Folklore Institute, for typing from my handwritten translations the majority of the tales in this collection, and for providing valuable advice on the readability and clarity of the translated texts.

I am also indebted to Joan Catapano, Senior Sponsoring Editor at Indiana University Press, for supporting the idea of a book addressing "Tales Arab Women Tell." Since I first discussed the project with Ms. Catapano in early 1984, she has enthusiastically welcomed the project and provided needed encouragement and moral support.

To the narrators of the tales selected, many of whom are my relatives and friends, no amount of thanks is sufficient.

A NOTE ON TRANSLITERATION[1]

THE TRANSLITERATION system adopted in this work is as follows:

’/a= ء	ḍ= ض
b= ب	ṭ= ط
t= ت	ẓ= ظ
th= ث	¿/ᶜ= ع[1]
g/j= ج	gh= غ
ḥ= ح	f= ف
kh= خ	q= ق
d= د	k= ك
dh= ذ	l= ل
r= ر	m= م
z= ز	n= ن
s= س	h= ه
sh= ش	w= و
ṣ= ص	y= ي

1. The ¿ sign is used here to designate the Arabic ᶜayn/ᶜain (ع). Although a number of approximations have been used to designate this Arabic letter in transcriptions (e.g., ᶜ, ^{C}, Σ, ?, &), the ¿ seems to be more practical, especially in computer-generated and -managed files. In comparison to the standard $\underline{^{C}}$/ᶜ (the letter *C* in superscript, usually italicized) as a ع, the ¿ is closer in form to the Arabic letter, and will not occur in other words (a quality that will facilitate some computer functions such as search-and-find). For a further discussion of this and related problems of transcriptions, see H. El-Shamy, “A Response [to Jason’s Review of *Folk Traditions of the Arab World* . . .],” in *Asian Folklore Studies* (1998), esp. pp. 351–52.

Short vowels:

a	*fatḥah*
i/e	*kasrah*
o/u	*ḍammah*

Long vowels:

â	aa
î	ee/ii
û	oo/ou/ô
ai/ä	*'imâlah*

PREFACE

In the summer of 1984, *Tales Arab Women Tell* was nearly finished: texts had been selected, transcribed, and rendered into English. Translations had been tested for clarity with native readers of English, and for fidelity to the Arabic utterances. Tale types and motifs had been identified according to available (but less than satisfactory) indexes. Annotations, comparative notes, and general conclusions concerning tales' meanings had been formulated under these prevailing conditions. For instance, three major deficiencies limit the applicability of the Aarne-Thompson Type Index of Folktales to Middle Eastern materials:

> First, only a fragment of the published collections from the Middle East was included. . . . Second, only a fraction of the tales which comply with the designated contents of the tale types in the works treated in the type index were recognized[. . .]. Third, in its present format the type index does not recognize the emotional aspects of a tale, nor does it handle adequately the symbolic significance of actors and their actions.[1]

Some of the early conclusions in the present work were subsequently reported. One of these findings reported demographic patterns of presence or absence ("distribution") of certain tales among social categories of the Arab World's populations, especially gender groups.[2] However, ensuing research undertakings and related circumstances resulted in numerous reevaluations of previously reached conclusions,[3] which consequently caused postponements in submitting the final manuscript to the Press for formal consideration and external refereeing. All the narratives included in the manuscript as it stood in 1984 are presented in this updated version of *Tales Arab Women Tell.* The changes involved adding a few tale texts,[4] and a more accurate, detailed documentation of a tale's belongingness to women's culture in the Arab World (which also encompasses ethnic groups and communities that speak languages other than Arabic, such as Berber, Nubian, and neo-Aramaic).[5] Full documentation of the tales given in the present work, and other tales of the folk narrative repertoire of that part of the world, will be forthcoming in *A Demographically Oriented Tale Type Index for the Arab World.* The demographic aspect of that index is represented by the fact that "Vital data about the narrators (e.g., gender, age, religious affiliation, and social status) will be provided when available; such data—typically ignored in previous works—is of considerable importance in the quest for the meaning, function and other significant aspects of a tale."[6] Also, considerable amounts of time and energy were dedicated to developing culture-specific themes, motifs, and tale types that allow for more precise identification of traditional culture materials and sentiments (emotions). Approximately 60 percent of the total motifs cited in this work are newly developed themes (see "Register of Tale Types," and "Register of Motifs," pp. 459, 467, below).

Nonetheless, some of the results of these efforts have been publicly attacked via the mass media in the Gulf Region by persons with insufficient familiarity with the issues involved, thus disrupting research schedules and requiring prolonged explanations in public forums and at governmental agencies. For instance, an unidentified "folklorist" in Kuwait, who apparently did not differentiate between formal religion and what El-Shamy labels "religion among the folk," declared that El-Shamy's "Brother-Sister Syndrome" theory attacks Islam and the Prophet Mohammad's grandchildren.[7] Coming at a time of war with sectarian overtones between "Sunni" Iraq and Shiite Iran, this accusation could have had more serious consequences than it actually did, had it not been addressed fully and openly in time. Yet, the negative effects of this disruptive affair still linger.

NOTES

1. Hasan M. El-Shamy, *Folktales of Egypt: Collected, Translated and Edited with Middle Eastern and African Parallels* (Chicago, 1980), p. 237. See Daniel J. Crowley's review of the work in *Research in African Literatures*, Vol. 12, No. 3, pp. 398–400; cf. Section I, note 5. The reference is to Antti Aarne and Stith Thompson's *The Types of the Folktale* (Helsinki, 1961) (first published in 1910, revised in 1928).

For evaluations of the efficacy of other relevant indexes, see H. El-Shamy, "A Type Index for Tales of the Arab World," in *Fabula*, Vol. 29, pt. 1/2 (Berlin and New York, 1988), pp. 150–63; and "Towards a Demographically-Oriented Type Index for Tales of the Arab World," in *Cahiers de Littérature Orale*, No. 23: *La tradition au présent (Monde arabe)*, Praline Gay-Para, ed. (Paris, 1988), pp. 15–40.

2. See "The Gender Difference," in Hasan El-Shamy, "Oral Traditional Tales and the *Thousand Nights and a Night*: The Demographic Factor," in *The Telling of Stories: Approaches to a Traditional Craft*, Morton Nøjgaard et al. (eds.) (Odense, Denmark, 1990), p. 83, and notes 98–99, p. 110.

3. For a case where major adjustments are reported, see introductory note to Tale No. 39 (Type 872B§); also see introductory statement to Tale No. 26 (Type 910K1§), where its presumed gender-orientedness had to be revised. Similarly, in pointing out "The Gender Difference," in the male-bound *A Thousand Nights and a Night* (*'alf laylah wa laylah*), it was concluded that "*ALL* 'formula tales'" were absent. (See El-Shamy, "The Demographic Factor," p. 83.) As will be shown in the forthcoming *Demographically Oriented Tale Type Index*, this conclusion must be revised to accommodate two formula tales: Type 2036, *Drop of Honey Causes Chain of Accidents* [bloody feud between villages ensues], (Victor Chauvin, *Bibliographie des ouvrages arabes ou relatifs aux arabes, 12 vols.*, VIII, 41, No. 9); and a combination of the amorphous Types: 2335, *Tales Filled with Contradictions*, and 2412§, *Unclassified Formula Tales* (Chauvin, V, 279, No. 16).

4. Five new tale texts were added, and the necessary serial rearranging and numbering of the book's contents were undertaken. The new texts were collected in the field during the late 1980s from Algeria (No. 8, also cf. résumé given in note 137) and the Gulf Region (Tales No. 11, 20, 34, and 49), and then added to the 1984 manuscript.

5. For a description of the parameters of "The Arab World" with reference to lore, see "Note on Data Presentation . . . ," in H. El-Shamy, *Folk Traditions of the Arab World: A Guide to Motif Classification* (Indiana University Press, Bloomington, 1995), Vol. 1, p. xxiii.

6. See El-Shamy, "A Type Index for Tales of the Arab World," p. 150. Also compare the data given on narrators' gender and meaning in Section I, note 43.

7. An outline of a religion among the folk is given under the title "An Islam-Based Worldview: The Supernatural Belief-Practice System in the Contemporary Folk Cultures of Egypt," in El-Shamy, *Folk Traditions of the Arab World*, Vol. 1, Appendix II, pp. 443–44, esp. part IV, "Deified Humans." It may be noted that the system is not labeled "Islamic." In such a folk system, numerous beliefs and corresponding practices perceived by laymen as part of a religion prove to be incongruent with the formal teaching of that faith (cf. Tale No. 18, note 412; also see Tale No. 9, note 177).

For examples of public clarifications, see "d. Ḥasan al-Shamî yuwaḍḍiḥ (Dr. Hasan el-Shamy Clarifies)," in *al-Qabas*, No. 5594, (Kuwait, Dec. 9, 1987); "tawḍîḥ ḥawla naẓariyyatih ¿an râbiṭat al-'akhkh wa al-'ukht min al-doktôr al-Shâmî (Clarification Concerning His Theory about the Brother and Sister Bond, by Dr. El-Shamy)" in *al-Qabas*, No. 5621 and No. 5622 (Kuwait, Jan. 6 and 7, 1988); and "radd ᶜalâ maqâl (A Reply to an Essay)," in *al-Mujtamaᶜ*, No. 855, pp. 40–41 (Kuwait, Feb. 9, 1988).

I

INTRODUCTION

Organizational Rationale

A NUMBER OF considerations governed the selection of texts and the formatting of data in this work. Foremost among these were the texts' *authenticity, accuracy,* and *representativeness.* These three criteria are especially critical for indicating the degree of validity of *any* "scientific" conclusion that a student of culture and society may offer. True (typical) folkloric performances, especially of intricate texts such as folktales, are practically never as perfect as publishers and readers wish them to be. The seemingly flawless texts that fill hundreds of published tale "collections" and anthologies are actually more indicative of their writers' re-creative abilities than of the characteristics of the hypothetical folk narrators of these literary texts. Subsequently, development of verifiable social scientific theories based on Arab folktales as they are lived in real life has been hampered by (among other things) the scarcity of available accurate texts, especially ones collected from females; and the prevalence of alterations, "improvements," and blatant forgeries and fabrications in published anthologies, even in some academic theses.[1]

The topical emphasis and arrangement of the components of this work reflect the postulates of El-Shamy's "Brother-Sister Syndrome" theory. The main premises of this theory are (1) that, contrary to prevailing academic views, the brother-sister relationship is of paramount importance in Arab cultures, and (2) that this relationship plays a decisive role in the generation, development, and continuation of a specific pattern of family structure and a host of other related social and cultural institutions. This phenomenon has been described as follows:

> Within the nuclear family the Brother-Sister Syndrome is manifested through brother-sister love, brother-brother hostility, sister-sister hostility, parents-children hostility, and husband-wife unaffectionate relations. The structure of sentiments in the larger kinship group is congruent with that found in the nuclear family; these sentiments include brother–sister's husband hostility, sister–brother's wife hostility, and child–mother's brother affectionate ties. The child's positive relationship with the maternal uncle is a product of the love a mother has for her brother, and the strong bonds of affection between a child and his or her mother (but not father).[2]

These aspects of familial interaction patterns can readily be seen as factors governing text selection, the sequence of tale presentation, and the grouping of tales into sections under kinship-bound labels (e.g., "Mother and Children," "Gaining a Wife," "Husband and Wife," "Brother and Sister").[3] Considering that a single text often discusses numerous familial ties, in a few cases determining the title under which a text is given is a matter of subjective judgment.[4] This format constitutes a significant departure from the usual grouping of tales according to genres, a system applied in the present author's *Folktales of Egypt,*[5] a work that introduced a number of changes in the general format and scope of coverage of the series in which it was published, but had to comply with the genre-bound arrangement of texts.[6] In terms of content, *Folktales of Egypt* sought to portray the major sociocultural institutions (e.g., familial, economic, religious), without sliding into overgeneralizations.

The above-cited pattern for the structure of learned sentiments[7] in Arab cultural expressions and social interactions is salient and recurrent. (See Attitudinal Systems, below.) Additionally, research on the various facets of the Brother-Sister Syndrome leads to conclusions that are incompatible with the basic tenets of the hypotheses of the Oedipus Complex theory. (See "The Systemic Qualities of Meaning," below.)

Research Orientation

The Texts: All texts included in this study are original, collected from the field from typical (nonprofessional) tale tellers, mostly by means of tape recording. Texts acquired in writing,[8] or in a language other than the narrator's mother tongue,[9] may be presumed to be of less verbatim accuracy in representing the actual narrative response elicited and performed by the tale teller. Care has been taken to retain the general characteristics of the original texts. Incidents of awkward sentence constructions, confusion, illogical syntax, conceptual errors, forgotten bits, and asides, were kept as such in the translations. In some texts,[10] these performance shortcomings were problematic, requiring numerous editorial clarifications; such extratextual additions are placed within brackets. Asides or clarifications given by the narrator are enclosed in parentheses. All interpretations of the meanings of texts are based on the original Arabic renditions rather than on the English translations presented in this work.

Theoretical Basis

Interpretations of the processes involved in the act of the narrating, and of meanings of texts and contexts, and the various conclusions proposed or affirmed, are based on the following theoretical perspectives: (1) cognitive learning principles; (2) the psychology of cognitive systems; and (3) the systemic qualities of meaning. These premises are interdependent, and require reliance on verifiable, observable facts as a research procedure.

First: The Texts as Cognitive "Folkloric Behavior"

The texts presented here may be said to have a high degree of traditionality manifested through transgenerational continuities, and spread among various cultural levels and social groups. This quality involves such factors as a tale's form, structure, contents, expressed sentiments, language or parlance (though altered here by translation into another language or speech level), medium of communication, direction of communication, and values. The most salient nontraditional component in most of the *narrating* processes involved in securing the present texts is that they were told by individuals acting in the role of informant to a tale collector, rather than in the role of an "operant" in typical daily living (which does not include tale collectors).[11] Whatever aspect of traditional behavior may be involved, it is a form of "folkloric behavior" which, by definition, is predominantly cognitive, and systemic. Simply stated,

> "Folklore" can be defined as a class of learned, traditional responses forming a distinct type of behavior. The individual must undergo the psychological process of learning in order to acquire the responses of folkloric behavior, and this learning process occurs under conditions determined by social and cultural factors. The fundamental factors involved in learning are: *drive, cue, response,* and *reward.* Secondary factors such as repetition, recency, and ego-involvement can contribute, but their presence is not required in the process of learning.
> . . . folklorists should initially concern themselves with *folkloric responses* (*narrating, believing, singing, applying* a proverb, or *dancing*) and relevant social and cultural factors before proceeding to the study of the folklore items themselves (narratives, beliefs, songs, proverbs, or dances).[12]

As components of the context, cues may be viewed as "social-stimulus situations." Assessing the role of these motivating situations in the eliciting of responses in folkloric behavior it was concluded that

> the relationship between an individual and a folkloric activity is a "contextual relationship," where "Emphasis on the relationship of parts within patterned wholes becomes indispensable in characterization of social-stimulus situations." The activity will be determined by every factor the operant can perceive: the status of the individuals involved, the nature of the folkloric activity involved, the time and place, and the nature of the objects involved.[13]

Subsequent developments in theoretical approaches and applications to the study of folklore designated as the "contextual," the "performance-centered," and the "ethnography of speaking," for example, involve emphasis on only some aspect(s) of "cultural behavior." As outlined above, the "folkloric behavior" approach is more inclusive, as well as systemic.

In folkloristic terms, the cognitive behaviorist system may be summed up as follows:

> what makes (stimulus and cues) a person (organism) tell (response) a tale (the measurement of the response) under which conditions (cues) and with what results (effect)? Naturally, the same is true of any other category of lore—material, kinesic, musical, and so forth.[14]

Critical aspects in the development of a person's sense of identity are the learning and consequent acquisition of the culture and social practices into which that person is born and/or in which that person is raised. The process involved is typically termed "enculturation" or "socialization"; it is different from schooling, which takes place at a later stage of life, usually starting when a child is about six years old. Among tradition-bound social groups and communities, regardless of social class, cultural traditions and related social practices are the basic means of raising children; these include practices associated with pregnancy and parturition, delivery through the aid of a midwife, a nurse shouting instructions to live by throughout life into the newborn's ears, and so on. At the time a child begins to be schooled in "classical Arabic," he or she will already have been communicating effectively in folk speech (the vernacular). Before being introduced at school to elite "poetry," the child will already have acquired a deep sense of the poetic from mother's lullabies and children's rhymes chanted during play or tale-telling sessions.[15] And before being schooled in the novel or short story (borrowed recently from the West), he or she will have developed a deep sense of "story" from repeated immersions in folk narration. These immersions occur in a relaxed atmosphere of security, trust, and acceptance—an affective state that tends to accompany tale-telling for the rest of the listener's life (cf. "conditioning").[16] Folkloric materials constitute distinct phenomena paralleling what individuals know of the physical natural components of their world (e.g., hills and towns); such materials "reach a child early in life, and influence him/her first. Primary impressions, other things being equal, are lasting impressions. . . . Lore is the instrument for enculturation."[17]

Lore and "Life Space"

Related to the process of enculturation and subsequent development of cognitive systems is the concept of "life space," introduced by psychologist Kurt Lewin. This concept may be applied to understanding the effect of early experiences on an individual's way of thinking. "Life space" may be characterized as the perceived world (from an individual's perspective), distinguished from the objective world, as these perceptions affect the individual's behavior.[18] "Life space" encompasses all the events that could actually or potentially affect an individual's past, present, and future; from a psychological standpoint, each of these three aspects of life can determine behavior in any single situation.[19]

Thus, lore and other early experiences governed by traditions may be viewed as major factors in an individual's "life space" and as lasting building blocks in that individual's cognitive system and "worldview." Regardless of whether a belief is "real" or "imaginary," and irrespective of how seriously or nonseriously a narrative is held by a narrator or taken by a listener, once known, that belief and that narrative become constituents of a person's "life space."[20] It is in this sense that a folktale, regardless of its generic qualities, generates far-reaching perceptual effects on individuals and social groups.[21] If a child is told that wolves swallow "kids" whole and live in old tombs, then an association is established between wolves and these acts and objects; for the child, this is what wolves really do and what happens at that site ("cognitive map"). (See Tale No. 1; cf. "bat's fang," note 44, this section.)

Similarly, through experiencing folk and other sorts of traditions, an individual develops multiple cognitions vis-à-vis a single object or act in accordance with the various referents to which that object or act is linked. Thus, a pitcher's spout, a pomegranate, a male snake going through a crack or a hole, a kneading tub, or a pendant, acquires additional signification such as suggesting parts of the human body or bodily functions. This quality may be labeled "multiplexity" of cognitive connotations. These connotations are part of an individual's "life space," and constitute shared symbolic systems among members of a social group.[22]

Second: Tales as Cognitive Systems and Parts of a Sociocultural System

Each folkloric item is treated as a *cognitive system,* and as a component of a broader sociocultural system.

> [A] tale *per se* is composed of two sets of components. The first set consists of the words, meanings and descriptions of actions which are organized in a form perceived as a narrative. The second set consists of the feelings which these words and these referents and actions generate in the tale teller and in the listener. Both the

> teller and the audience are fully cognizant of the majority of these words and acts, and of the feelings generated by these narrative components. Thus, the tale represents a cognitive system. Other non-cognitive components of the tale do presumably exist; . . . however, they lie beyond the scope of direct observation.[23]

Thus, the occurrence of an item of lore during the course of daily living, through being elicited by a tradition bearer, is viewed and treated as a cognitive response to specific cognitively perceived motivations in given contexts. The performance of the item is tied in part to the multiple social roles an individual must play within the context of communal norms and other regulators of individual and group behavior. Action with reference to these regulators constitutes the attitudes and social processes characteristic of the community and its culture.

Attitudinal Systems

Beside cognitions, another category within the cognitive system is that of attitudes.

> An attitude may be viewed as being composed of three major cognitive elements: a cognition, a feeling and an action tendency. Things such as a snake or a pigeon, kinship ties such as being a sister or a maternal uncle represent cognitions for an individual. How a person feels about these cognitions, such as the sentiments of hate or love, represent the feeling (affective) component. The action that the individual tends to take towards these objects represents the action tendency component of an attitude.[24]

Social processes (cooperation, competition, conflict, accommodation), which constitute much of the interaction between a narrative's characters (i.e., a tale's plot), a listener and narrator, or a collector and an informant, follow in the direction of these action tendencies.[25]

Among the multitude of components that make up a person's cognitive system and attitudes are his or her perceived *roles,* and the *norms* that govern the playing of these roles in real social life, a role being "a set of behavioral expectations" (of do's and don'ts). Typically, people play multiple roles in real life, some of which conflict, thus generating "role strain." Roles and norms are interdependent, roles being ascribed to certain individuals according to the social norms of a particular community. Thus, a "man" is not permitted to tell *Märchen,* for the group norms assign this type of activity to women, and his violation of the norms brings about punishment.[26]

> According to the "Law of Effect," the relationship between a certain motivation and a folkloric response (a response represents the *value attached to a genre,* such

> as the pronouncements that *Märchen* are "women's stuff," "songs are to be sung only to an appreciative, friendly audience," or "dancing is shameful") depends upon the type of reaction . . . [an] operant receives when he expresses the genre.[27]

Roles are acquired during the early phases of one's life, through enculturation (socialization), and are reshaped at later stages through *resocialization*[28] into the roles one is expected to play as "man," "woman," "good person," "respectable person," "provider," "consumer," "entertainer," and so on. Around puberty, the resocializing of girls into becoming women, and of boys into becoming men takes place. With reference to fantasy tales, both girls and boys experience them at an early age in a uniform manner, and mostly from the same female sources. As part of their proper role as women, girls continue openly to tell (and listen to) fantasy tales. Meanwhile, boys are instructed to inhibit feminine characteristics and display masculine ones; thus, fantasy tales are relegated to the status of "women's stuff" and not exercised (at least openly). Consequently, many women become "active bearers" of fantasy-tale traditions while many men become "passive bearers."[29] Whether "active" or "passive," childhood experiences have already become part of "life space" and influence the behavior of individuals and social groups.

Being a family's (or neighborhood's) tale teller and entertainer is a role governed by traditional communal norms.[30] This is the case with *all* the narrators in the present work, of whom *none* happened to be a professional narrator earning wages from telling prose tales by addressing an impersonally perceived general public as an audience.[31]

Women and the Telling of Fantasy Tales

A certain social category of a population is distinguishable from another by characteristic behavioral patterns and mannerisms ascribed to its members. Inclusion or membership in a social category is reckoned in terms of age, gender, religion, profession, and other significant factors, and is essentially a perceptual process of stereotyping: "Men do not do that," "This is children's stuff," "Only women tell 'women's-tales.' "

Narrating *truthful* stories is the only sort of narrative behavior endorsed by formal Islam (constituting ideal culture).[32] Within the realm of what is perceived to be "truthful," fantasy, exaggerations, and hyperbole are usually labeled *balâghah* (rhetoric) or *faṣâḥah* (eloquence), a cornerstone of classical Arabic literary expressions. Within the sphere of poetry, "lying" is taken as a necessary evil—or normal abnormality—and is not only tolerated but appreciated.[33]

Putting rhetoric to work in school curricula is termed *'inshâ*,[34] a word that literally signifies a construction or something built of separate constituents. The word signifies literary composition in classical, academic Arabic, not in the vernacular. Writing aids meant to assist pupils in developing the skill of *'inshâ* abound in the form of books offering lists of topics accompanied by impressive quotations, poetic passages, literary clichés, and the like, with which an essay is to be adorned (or "inlaid") and thus aesthetically constructed. Usually, an ascription, such as, "And in this respect The Lord states in His Holy Book," "As a poet has said," "A saying by the wise comes to mind in this connection," accompanies the quotation.[35] Imposing this *'inshâ* style on orally transmitted folktales is the literary re-creator's idea of salvaging the folk's verbal lore from its ungarnished vernacular language, and then upgrading it to a level thought to be worthy of being viewed as literature (*'adab*). Typical folk narration is free of these mental shackles, which are added as a matter of course to literary renditions of true folktales. This is the case with *The Arabian Nights,* and similar once orally transmitted folktales that were taken out of oral circulation and augmented with "literary" characteristics and other rhetorical devices.[36]

Emergence of Classification of Folk Traditions

Since the early stages of the history of Islamic cultures, lying has been associated with *quṣṣâṣ* (narrators of stories): a label restricted to those who interpret seriously held sacred beliefs through stories, outside formally acknowledged circles.[37] By contrast, fantasy tales, held from both religious and historical perspectives to be frivolous and of nonserious consequences, were labeled "*khurâfât*" (nonsense, nontruths, superstitions, "myths"), as opposed to "*qiṣaṣ*" (i.e., truthful or serious stories). Yet the term *khurâfah* also stood for "myth"—"myth" being a matter of faith considered to be the truth (usually in a sacred sense) by someone other than the person using the term, for whom the matter was not so.[38] Within this context, the cultural phenomenon labeled "women's talk," "women's say," "women's tales," or "old wives' tales" has been perceived and defined.

Although women poets, women priestesses and oracles (*kâhinât*), and women pseudo-prophets have been reported throughout Arab history, no differentiating characteristic mannerisms were reported as their culture specialty. Thus, the assigning of this "female-bound" aspect of cultural behavior—namely, the telling of *khurâfât* or fantasy tales—to a category of a given population in the Arab World may be seen as an early case of demographic orientation in the study of that population.

Perhaps the earliest student of Arab folk cultures and communities to report this phenomenon, in the eighth or ninth century A.D., was al-Jâḥiẓ (d. A.D. 868 or 869), a rationalist and promoter of the empirical, objective approach to the study of natural, social, and cultural issues. Also, it may be argued that he was the first Arab intellectual to present a folk narrative in its traditional folk style and dialogue.[39] He exhibited the qualities of rationalism, freedom from traditional, negative stereotypical views of women, and responsiveness to a female's right to self-esteem.

Attitudes of Moslems toward women stem primarily from the sacred Koranic accounts of the creation of Adam, his primacy and the subsequent creation of Eve as a derivative from and subsequent to Adam; also influential in the formation of these attitudes are the beliefs concerning the responsibility for the original sin of eating from the forbidden tree (or fruit) and consequent eviction from paradise. In spite of the fact that Qur'ân assigns responsibility for the commission of the sin to both Adam and Eve (Qur'ân 7:20–23) or even to Adam alone (20:117, 120–21), the prevailing view places much of the blame on Eve as the instigator and establishes a link between her and Satan (Eblis). This general perspective, formed loosely in reference to the sacred dogma, was elaborated on by early interpreters of the Qur'ân. According to these elaborations, God punished all creatures involved in this act: Adam, Eve, Satan, the viper (or the serpent); the severity of the punishment was proportionate to the degree of culpability. Thus it was reported that God meted out fifteen additional punishments to Eve and her daughters (i.e., women). Deficiency in mind and lack of religiosity were two of these punishments; and hence, the often quoted utterance, "*nâqiṣât ¿aql wa dîn*" (They [i.e., women] are deficient in mind and religion).[40]

Contrary to this central matter of faith, al-Jâḥiẓ saw both women and men as subject to the same environmental forces (cultural, social, and physiological).[41] He boldly proclaimed, "*A woman is of sound religion, sexual-honor, and heart, unless . . . [motivated by scruples or lust].*"[42] This declaration by al-Jâḥiẓ stands in sharp contrast to the assertion that "Women are lacking in mind and religion," which was also reported as a saying by the Prophet Mohammad (*ḥadîth*). Considering the fact that Qur'ân does not single out Eve for the blame, the judging of women involved seems to have been meant for a certain period or social situation under given conditions—as al-Jâḥiẓ stated. Yet, through males' interpretation of religious dogma, the utterance has come to be treated *as if* it were a divine (Koranic) creed stipulating that women were created with this condition of deficiency.[43] Applying his viewpoint in assigning given practices as characteristic traits of a specific category of a population, he wrote,

> With reference to the "say of women and the womenlike [i.e., womanlike, the effeminate] (*qawl al-nisâ' wa 'ashbâh-al-nisâ'*)" concerning bats, they claim that if a bat bites a boy, he [the bat] will not retract 'his' fang[s] from his [the boy's] flesh until 'he' hears the braying of a zebra. I will not forget my horror of a bat's fang and my apprehension caused by its being nearby, due to [my] faith in that saying, until I came of age.
>
> Women and the womanlike have *khurâfât* (superstitions/myths) . . . concerning this [belief] and [other beliefs of] its sort[;] perhaps we will mention some of them when we reach the [proper] spot ['if God wills'].[44]

Similarly, with reference to the *tinnîn* (dragon), al-Jâḥiẓ reported,

> Persians claim that [the multi-mouthed female supernatural being called] al-'Agdahânî is of greater [size] than a bull-camel, and that she may meet some people and swallow [many] a human being from each direction of a mouth [of hers].

He then concluded,

> This is of the talk of vendors and *al-¿ajâ'iz* (the aged, or old women).[45]

Of thieving animals, al-Jâḥiẓ mentions a certain type of mouse that hoards and plays with money. He gives an account of a story (probably a "legend") that tells of a mouse's treasure; it may be summarized as follows:

> A man from esh-Shâm spied [from a hiding place] a mouse bringing a *dînâr* (gold coin) from its ('his') hole. Knowing that the animal would bring out all its possessions, play with them, and then return them one-by-one back to the hole, he waited till it became evident that all the gold had been brought out, and the mouse had played, and began returning them by taking back the first piece. During its absence, the man took all the money and went back to his hiding place. When the mouse returned and discovered the loss, it began leaping into the air [in fury] and hitting itself against the ground until it died.

Al-Jâḥiẓ concluded,

> And this *ḥadîth* (report, account) is of women and the womanlike.[46]

By contrast, al-Jâḥiẓ characterized seemingly *individualistic reports* as "lies" (fabrications). Thus, he wrote the following account (a "memorate") concerning his professional fieldwork experience with reference to the two-headed viper:

> The author of *al-Manṭiq* (*Logic*, [i.e., Aristotle]) claimed that a viper with two heads appeared [(i.e., was reported to have been seen)]. I asked a Bedouin about that [phenomenon]; he claimed that this [report] is true. I said to him: "From which direction of the two heads does she *tas¿â* (creep forward)? And from which of the two does she eat and bite?" He stated: "As for creeping, she does not creep,

> but seeks her need [(i.e., reaches her target)] by rolling over, like little boys roll over sand. As for eating, she eats the evening meal with one mouth, and the noon meal with another. As for biting, she bites with both heads simultaneously."

Al-Jâḥiẓ judged his Bedouin informant in reference to this account: "Thus, he proved to be the biggest liar in all of creation. . . ."[47]

On the basis of the above, it may be concluded that as early as the ninth century A.D., the role of telling *fantasy tales* was assigned to women and the womanlike. This assignment still prevails today as a gender-bound "culture specialty." Until recently, collectors, with few exceptions,[48] have not paid sufficient attention to females as a source of Arab tales. Thus the absence of *Märchen* from early folklore studies and tale indexes was a result of inadequate collecting and careless surveying of the available literature. Theories with racial overtones, such as C. W. Von Sydow's on the origin of the *Märchen* as a genre and its presumed absence among certain unimaginative peoples, are a product of these ethnocentric attitudes.[49]

Third: The Systemic Qualities of Meaning, and the Role of Folkloristic Annotations

Determining the meaning of a tale (or part thereof) remains a focus for much theoretical speculation in folklore scholarship. An evaluation of the relationships among constituents of a narrative such as sentiment, genre, tale type, and meaning reveals that the message a narrative imparts to a narrator or listener is a component of the cognitive-behavioristic system of which the tale itself is also a part.[50] Other noncognitive components of a tale do presumably exist; however, they lie beyond the scope of direct observation.[51] Thus, meaning can be deduced and ascertained *only* in specific situations, and on the basis of all the tale's occurrences (or, minimally, of a representative sample of these occurrences) in a given community. This objective is to be reached through: (1) considering the tale in direct connection to its teller, and (2) a demographically oriented analysis of the tale's distribution among members of a population (rather than its distribution over a geographic stretch of land). Such an analysis would use the concept of tale type (and its correlate, the motif) as the identification device and unit of measurement for data under investigation. This approach has been described as follows:

> the meaning of an aspect of a tale is a part of a cognitive-behavioristic system whose components can be subject to verification. Such a system includes the expressed intent and sentiments of the narrator and audience, socio-cultural and other relevant factors, and *the verbatim text involved and its variants;* it also in-

> cludes the academic postulates pertaining to that text as perceived by the interpreter. Sentiments and other types of affective experiences are shown to be central constituents of a narrative. As perceived by the narrator and audience, these feelings add meaning to the structure of a tale by providing a sense of direction around which the tale coheres; they also strongly influence the meaning of the plot, through their association with social processes (e.g., cooperation, competition, [and] conflict) among the protagonists in a tale.
>
> The degree of validity of a certain interpretation depends on whether that interpretation demonstrates such systemic qualities as consonance (i.e., being in agreement with other components of the system), consistency (i.e., being applicable in other pertinent situations), and stability (i.e., exhibiting the same basic characteristics over a period of time).[52]

Regrettably, in folklore scholarship and related fields, such an approach is not fully developed and is often ignored. Interpreting the meaning(s) of a tale (or other items of lore) still depends largely on the prominence of academic authorities, and their theories, rather than on the verifiability of conclusions arrived at on the basis of data (evidence) objectively considered in broader sociocultural contexts.[53]

A recent publication that may be cited in this respect is Allen Johnson and Douglas Price-Williams's *Oedipus Ubiquitous: The Family Complex in World Folk Literature.*[54] As the title indicates, the work seeks to prove the universality of the Oedipus Complex, mainly by demonstrating the presence of the complex in 139 "folktales" (a subdivision of the broader field of "folk literature") representing the world (divided into six major regions). With reference to the vast region designated as the "Middle East and Africa," Johnson and Price-Williams build their case on the basis of *18* texts. A grand total of 4 texts represent Africa north-of-the-Sahara (Egypt and Sudan),[55] and a fifth text from "Persia" completes the evidence from the Middle East. These 5 texts cover the themes of brother-sister incest and parent-child incest (Oedipus). No texts are given from the entire Arabian Peninsula or from northwest Africa (the Maghreb: Libya, Tunisia, Algeria, and Morocco).

In addition to being plucked out of their "cross-cultural matrix,"[56] each of these precious few samples has been stripped of every bit of data that might connect it to a human narrator.[57] Considering that *Oedipus Ubiquitous* is a psychological study, the individual narrator—or the psyche that is postulated to be the depository for the Oedipus Complex—is conspicuously missing from the research equation. Also, despite the fact that the authors list Antti Aarne and Stith Thompson's *The Types of the Folktale* as one of their references, they make no effort to identify any of the tales according to Aarne-Thompson tale type numbers (save one: "The Oedipus story—specifically type 931"). They also express in the book's general index "difficulty in knowing how to index folktales in a meaningful way."[58] Consequently, the narratives are left un-indexed, leaving the reader with no ready means of verifying a motif or an idea in the tales. As a result, Johnson and Price-Williams's work is disconnected from major, readily available folkloristic literature on the folk narrative that may have contributed to their awareness of how a tale may be indexed and interpreted.[59]

Furthermore, none of the four folktales the authors provide from Africa north of the Sahara,[60] nor the text they give from Persia,[61] is an "Oedipus story." Although an incestuous theme is present in all the chosen texts, the Oedipus Complex (à la Type 931) fails to materialize in any of them. One of these tales in particular, "The Wife of the Prince's Son," in which actual incest takes place between a disguised mother and her unsuspecting son, seems to contain most of the elements of Oedipus. Yet, the gender of the narrators, who are almost exclusively adult females, tends not to substantiate the Oedipal interpretation.[62] Had it been an Oedipus tale, males would have been the ones with the irresistible urge to tell it. (On the failure of the Oedipal Complex to acquire systemic qualities in texts in *Tales Arab Women Tell,* see introductory notes to Tales No. 1, 5, 8, 10, 11, 15, 38, 41, and 42.)

Whether accurate folkloristic information and research methods could have affected the outcome of Johnson and Price-Williams's study is doubtful. There seems to be a general lack of academic appreciation for the intricacy of folkloric materials and folklore scholarship, especially on typology. Reviewing *Folktales of Egypt,* anthropologist Roger Joseph expressed the prevalent, but not frequently voiced, low rank that social scientists assign to many folklore studies. Thus, Joseph wrote, "The title of the book may dissuade Middle Eastern scholars from closely examining its contents. This is unfortunate because the book is filled with raw material upon which one can acquire some understanding of how a complexly organized society thinks and feels about the world."[63] Not only are Johnson and Price-Williams's data statistically insignificant in representing the "Middle East and Africa [north of the Sahara]," but the authors' treatment of opposing viewpoints lacks "neutrality." In citing El-Shamy's text entitled "The New or the Old?" they excluded the following assertion: "In spite of its incestuous nature, the tale should not be viewed as oedipal, for both the stepmother and the stepson belong to the same age group; the stepmother is thus not a maternal figure."[64] Like many psychoanalytically oriented scholars, Johnson and Price-Williams seem to have sought in folktale anthologies data that would support their point of view. Yet, true to Joseph's reservation, they did not find a folklorist's (collector's) thesis useful and omitted it without apprising readers of the exclusion or their reasons for it.[65] Furthermore, they made no use of the concept of tale type (Aa-Th 1563) to seek more information on their data.

If psychoanalytically oriented scholars seem too eager to perceive incestuous themes as Oedipus Complexes, they, along with others espousing nonpsychoanalytic viewpoints, seem to be immune to perceiving certain non-Oedipal types of incestuous cultural expressions. The incestuous elements in such expressions may be camouflaged[66] or blatant. An example illustrating the latter situation is Muhawi and Kanaana's treatment of a brother-sister erotic theme as it occurred in a tale entitled "The Golden Rod in the Valley of Vermilion."[67] The tale is given in the "Husbands and Wives" section; its initial part may be summarized as follows:

> A man marries three of his cousins, one cousin[68] after another; the first two exhibit suspension-evoking behavior (drugging the husband at night and leaving home by stealth on nocturnal journeys). Upon following each, the husband catches her sleeping with an abusive black paramour. The husband kills each paramour, takes a ghoulish token of the incidents (the first slain lover's nose and the second's tongue) to show to each wife later as proof of her infidelity. The husband bewitches each adulteress wife into an animal (a bitch and a fish with body half of stone, respectively). He subsequently marries his third cousin, and she exhibits the same mannerisms of the first two. Suspecting that his third wife is also faithless, the husband follows her. By magic, she opens a wardrobe and takes out a copy of the Qur'ân, "parts" sea waters, and opens an "arched door," till she reaches a place under the sea where she rendezvouses in a room with "a youth—handsome like a sweet basil plant." The youth addresses the wife as "sister," and she enters the youth's room.

The text of the narrative, being told as a personal experience by the deceived husband, proceeds as follows:

> [The husband continued,]
> "By Allah, she went inside with him. Setting the Qur'ân down they read until they had their fill. Then they talked, and he put the sword between him and her. They lay down and went to sleep.
> " 'By Allah,' I said to myself, 'he didn't do anything, and she didn't do anything. So, I'm going to bring back for her a small token that would cause him no harm.'
> "Waiting until they were asleep, I went inside. Since he had long hair, I approached and cut a small lock from the top of his head and tied it up in a handkerchief. As fate would have it, his soul was in that lock of hair, and he died. When she woke up, she wanted to bid farewell to her brother. 'Brother, brother!' she called out, but she found him dead. She beat her breast, tore her clothes, and left, taking the candle and the Qur'ân with her.
> "I stood aside until she had passed, then followed her.
> " 'Open, arched door!' she said, when she reached it. 'The lover will see his beloved no more!' "

Commenting on the ghoulish evidence the husband retained, Muhawi and Kanaana state,

> We cannot help observing the sexually oriented symbolic reference not only in the name of the tale and its hero, but also in the three items he removes from his wives' lovers (nose, tongue, and lock of hair)—all lend themselves comfortably to psychoanalytic interpretation.[69]

It is ironic that Muhawi and Kanaana felt they "cannot help observing" that these items in the tale had psychoanalytic (sexual) symbolism, yet they did not observe (or, perhaps, they could not help *not* observing) the sexual symbolism in *their own* inclusion of the brother among the "wives' lovers." For them, the brother was only reading the holy book with his sister in a hermetically secluded abode, while the other "lovers" were doing with the wives a great deal more than just worshipping the Lord. Also not observed are the symbolic significance of a host of elements that include passing through the arched door, the sister's 'holy' book that had to be opened so as to be read until they had their fill, and the brother's sword that was laid between himself and his sister when they went to sleep after having had their fill (evidently, the sister was in no hurry to return home to her husband after having exercised the 'sacred' ritual). Regardless of whether "he didn't do anything, and she didn't do anything" or whether he and she, like their predecessors, did have sexual intercourse, the entire incident is still an incestuous affair.[70]

Additionally, another aspect Muhawi and Kanaana did not observe is the fact that since the wife was the husband's "cousin" (most likely, a paternal cousin, *bint ¿amm*), the youth that was inadvertently killed had to be the killer's cousin and also brother-in-law.[71]

The irony in not observing all the "sexually oriented symbolic reference[s]" is even greater when we consider Muhawi and Kanaana's summation concerning "*Siblings.*" They write,

> Siblings of the same sex generally have relationships characterized by conflict, competition, and jealousy; among cross-sexual siblings, however, relationships of love, tenderness, and mutual cooperation prevail.[72]

If we substitute El-Shamy's "brother-brother" and "sister-sister" for Muhawi and Kanaana's "Siblings of the same sex," and his "brother-sister" and "sister-brother" for their "cross-sexual siblings," their statement, along with other "findings" (e.g., concerning husbands and wives, brothers-in-law, and so forth) proves to be surprisingly *identical* with the tenets of El-Shamy's "Brother-Sister Syndrome" theory. Evidently, the literature on the "Brother-Sister Syndrome" is another facet of fraternal relations Muhawi and Kanaana could not help *not* observing.[73]

The two cases sketched above indicate that in traditional Arab cultural expressions the existence of the Oedipus Complex, and the absence of the Brother-Sister Syndrome are, for the most part, a cultural fallacy or artifact. The existence of the Oedipus Complex is demonstrated by "theoretical" convictions that are predominantly a matter of faith, lying beyond the realm of objective verification, while the absence of the Brother-Sister Syndrome is caused by insufficient awareness of its characteristics. Both phenomena, however, are sustained by several negative factors; among these are the compartmentalization of research findings within academic departments and disciplines, partial presentation or total exclusion by some authors of critical data inconsistent with their convictions, and the lack of rigorous scrutiny and informed critical evaluations by academic referees and reviewers. Another factor contributing to both phenomena is a desire on the part of many Arab intellectuals, for various reasons, to be just "like the West." For example, reacting to the Brother-Sister Syndrome theme in a paper given at a symposium,[74] a prominent Palestinian literary and political figure found the thesis offensive; his reason (given here in a quotation, as recalled by the present writer) was, "It is people like you who give [the Israelis] an additional excuse to treat us [Arabs] in a manner inconsistent with '[Western] human rights' and then say to the West, 'They are not like us [and therefore, West European principles do not apply to them]!'" When El-Shamy asked, "Would you have felt better had I said that you have the 'hots' for your mother and would like to kill your father?" his answer was an immediate and unequivocal "Yes!"

Bearing in mind that for an adult, it is affection (kindness, sympathy), and togetherness in life, *not* incestuous impulses, that are the dominant facets of the Brother-Sister Syndrome, the following sequel to the exchange may be reported. Subsequently, the present writer understood from that eminent protester that his entire family fled Palestine in 1948, and that only he and a sister remain alone in the family home. This situation of "brother and sister left alone" is a recurrent theme in Arab lore, especially in *Tales Arab Women Tell*.[75]

NOTES

1. In 1991 a university press in the United States asked me to evaluate a "collection" of tales recorded from women at a site in Cairo, Egypt. The "collection" was a part of a thesis successfully submitted to a European university for a graduate degree in

anthropology, and had already been accepted for publication by a European press; the European publisher-to-be was seeking a copublisher in the United States. After careful examination of the texts, I concluded that *all* eighteen stories in the "collection" were fabrications, and that none had any existence in the oral or written traditions of Egypt, or any other Arab country. The supposed collector/editor of these texts was invited to provide a rebuttal to the reasons cited as proof of the texts' spuriousness, or show evidence of their authenticity; none was offered. (The U.S. press rejected the manuscript, but the thesis is out there in an academic environment ignorant of its misleading nature.) (Also cf. Roger Joseph's comment, below.)

Another academic publication reflecting comparable lack of authenticity of tale texts is Aki'o Nakano's *Folktales of Lower Egypt (1): Texts in Egyptian Arabic [1],* Studia Culturae Islamicae No. 18. Institute for the Study of Languages and Cultures of Asia and Africa (Tokyo, 1982). In this case, Nakano, who is clearly not a folklorist, seems to have been deceived by dishonest informant(s). Cf. al-Jâḥiẓ's experience with a "lying" informant cited in note 47, this section.

Although any writer may use lore to produce creative literary works, honesty in reporting sources is expected of all. Misleading claims of authenticity are harmful, especially to folklore scholarship.

For a description of this problem in collections of Arabic tales see "Contents, Syntax and Matters of 'Value,'" and "The Language and Other Stylistic Features," in H. El-Shamy, "The Demographic Factor," pp. 63–117, esp. pp. 73–83; also see H. El-Shamy, "Towards a Demographically-Oriented Type Index," pp. 15–40; esp. pp. 18–20.

2. Proposed to the Ford Foundation in 1970–71, and awarded a Social Science Research grant. The "Syndrome" was first introduced in "The Brother-Sister Syndrome in Arab Culture: A Preliminary Report," in *IX International Congress of Anthropological and Ethnological Sciences, Supplement* II, *Plan of Congress and Résumés of Contributions,* (Chicago, 1973), Abst. no. 1717.

Applications of the theses involved were undertaken in a number of studies which include the following: "The Traditional Structure of Sentiments in Maḥfouẓ's Trilogy: A Behavioristic Text Analysis," in *Al-ᶜArabiyya: Journal of the American Association of Teachers of Arabic,* Vol. 9 (October 1976), pp. 53–74; *Brother and Sister, Type 872*: A Cognitive Behavioristic Text Analysis of a Middle Eastern Oikotype* (Folklore Monograph Series, Vol. 8, Folklore Publications Group, Bloomington, Indiana, 1979), first read at the American Folklore Society Meeting, Portland, Oregon, 1974; "The Brother-Sister Syndrome in Arab Family Life. Socio-cultural Factors in Arab Psychiatry: A Critical Review," in *International Journal of Sociology of the Family,* Special Issue, *The Family in the Middle East,* Mark C. Kennedy, ed., Vol. 11, No. 2 (July–December, 1981) pp. 313–23, p. 320; and "Belief Characters as Anthropomorphic Psychosocial Realities," in *al-kitâb al-sanawî li-ᶜilm al-'igtimâᶜ* (Annual Review of Sociology), published by Department of Sociology, Cairo University, Vol. 3 (1982), pp. 7–36; Arabic Abstract, pp. 389–93 (paper read at "Symposium on Creatures of Legendry," held at the University of Nebraska at Omaha, Sept. 28–Oct. 1, 1978).

3. The current system, emphasizing kinship and other family ties in the grouping and subsequent treatment of tales, appears in some later works; see for example, Ibrahim Muhawi and Sharif Kanaana's *Speak, Bird, Speak Again: Palestinian Arab Folktales,* Foreword by Alan Dundes (Berkeley, 1989). See esp., "Afterword," pp. 111–14; cf. Dundes's evaluation of the "*Folktales of the World* series," cited in note 5, this section.

4. For examples, see introductory statement to "Zaynabu, 'Omm-Zmayyim, and Their Brother" (Tale No. 1–2, Type 123C§), and "The Sister and Her Brother and Moshsh, the Cat" (note 137, Type 312F§, and 327L§), below.

5. In his 1989 "Foreword" to Muhawi and Kanaana's work, Alan Dundes offers a number of "criticisms" of other tale collections and anthologies. Among these are the pronouncements that the tales are "presented with no cultural context or discussion of their meaning (we do not even know if their tellers were male or female)," that they lack "any scholarly apparatus linking the content of particular tales to the cultures from which they came," and that the texts are "accompanied by minimal comparative annotations" (p. x). Dundes finds "appalling" that these shortcomings, among others, apply even to "the highly regarded *Folktales of the World* series."

Compared to a European counterpart ("Märchen der Weltliteratur," which did not provide identification by tale type or motif, until the late 1960s or early 1970s), the University of Chicago series was indeed more academically oriented. R. M. Dorson, it may be added, was the general editor of the University of Chicago series, and contributed a Foreword for each of its various volumes; he was also a mentor to both Dundes and El-Shamy at Indiana University. Whatever the veracity (or fairness) of Dundes's statement concerning the University of Chicago series may be, all of the issues he raises have been pointed out and addressed in El-Shamy's *Folktales of Egypt,* a volume in that series. It is regrettable that Dundes seems not to be cognizant of this fact; yet, virtually every reviewer of *Folktales of Egypt* has commented on it (e.g., Daniel J. Crowley's assessment of the contributions of El-Shamy's volume, especially to the understanding of cultures of sub-Saharan Africa as well as Egypt; see reference in Preface, note 1). It is also regrettable that Dundes does not observe that a great many of Muhawi and Kanaana's findings concerning the culture from which the tales came are in total congruence with those offered by El-Shamy in several earlier publications, e.g., his study of "Maḥfouẓ's Trilogy" (1976), and *Brother and Sister, Type 872** (1974, 1979).

6. See Appendix, p. 511, which outlines the "Genres of the Folk Narrative" as applied in the works of the present writer.

7. For a clarification of the differences between "sentiments" (which are acquired) and "emotions" (which are genetically transmitted), see H. el-Shamy, "Emotionskomponente," in *Enzyklopädie des Märchens,* Vol. 3, Nos. 4–5, pp. 1391–95.

8. Tales No. 1–2, 4–1, 7–1, 7–2, 8, 9–1, 12, 17, 28, 31–1, 34–1, 40, 41, 46–2, 47–1; cf. résumé given in note 137, in reference to narrator of Tale No. 8.

9. Tales No. 9–1; 40; 47–1, rendered in English; cf. No. 8, learned in Berber; and No. 23, 25, learned in Nubian.

10. For examples of such texts, see "Pomegranate Kernels on Gold Trays," Tale No. 13; and "The Lovesick Husband," Tale No. 29.

11. On operant's motivation, and informant's motivation, see "Motivation and Folkloric Behavior," in H. El-Shamy, "Folkloric Behavior: A Theory for the Study of the Dynamics of Traditional Culture," Ph.D. dissertation, Indiana University, 1967, pp. 52–59. Also see Section II, note 66; and narrators' statements to Tales No. 3, 22, and 32.

12. El-Shamy, "Folkloric Behavior," Preface.

13. El-Shamy, "Folkloric Behavior," p. 64. On social-stimulus situations, see M.

Sherif, "Social Psychology: Problems and Trends," in *Psychology: A Study of a Science, Vol. 6: Investigation of Man as Socious: Their Place in Psychology and Social Sciences,* ed. Sigmund Koch (New York, 1963), esp. pp. 34–44. For an elaboration on the concept of context as a factor in performance and related part-whole perception and an individual's "adaptation level" see note 73, section II. Cf. data related to note 57, this section. For a concise assessment of the central issues presented here in current folklore studies, see El-Shamy: "Audience" (pp. 70–72), and "Context" (pp. 144–45), in *Folklore: An Encyclopedia of Forms, Methods, and History,* Thomas A. Green, gen. ed. (Santa Barbara, 1997). Also see El-Shamy, "The Demographic Factor," pp. 64–65.

14. El-Shamy, "Behaviorism and the Text," in *Folklore Today: A Festschrift for Richard M. Dorson,* Linda Dégh, et al., eds. (Bloomington, Indiana, 1976), p. 151.

15. For examples of such poetic expressions see Tales No. 1, note 16; 5; 27; 47; and 48.

16. The primacy of lore in forming an individual's patterns of thought has been pointed out in the narrative arts of Nagîb Maḥfûẓ, the Egyptian Nobel Prize laureate for literature. Maḥfûẓ's Trilogy (some 1500 pages) has been shown to manifest the same structure of sentiments and narrative pattern as Tale Type 872*, *Brother and Sister.* With reference to the attribution by some literary critics of Maḥfûẓ's narrating techniques to European sources, it has been stated:

> Perhaps it would be more appropriate to seek Mahfouz's literary roots in the folk narrative repertoires of his mother and the old family [woman]-servant Um-Hanafi, his two raconteurs. . . . Perhaps they did fill Kamal's (Mahfouz's) head with "medieval superstitions," . . . but in addition they instilled into him the forms and contents of his thoughts, feelings and expressions. (H. El-Shamy, "Maḥfouẓ's Trilogy," pp. 68–69)

On the effects of this relaxed atmosphere, see H. El-Shamy's "Foreword," in *The Tradition of Moses and Mohammed: Jewish and Arab Folktales,* B. L. Serwer-Bernstein, ed. (Northvale, New Jersey, 1994), pp. 171–77, esp. p. 171. Also cf. note 77, p. 56, this section.

17. H. El-Shamy, "Psychologically-based Criteria for Classification by Motif and Tale-Type," in *Journal of Folklore Research* Vol. 34, No. 3 (1997), pp. 233–34.

18. Winfred F. Hill, *Learning, A Survey of Psychological Interpretation* (New York, 1977), pp. 125–32, 136, 137, 142, 213.

19. Duane Schultz, *A History of Modern Psychology* (New York, 1975), p. 287.

20. See Hasan El-Shamy, "African World View and Religion," in *Introduction to Africa,* P. Martin and P. O'Meara, eds. (Bloomington, 1977), p. 208. For examples of the physical layout of "life space," see Tales No. 1, note 7; 14, note 319; 20, note 451; 22, note 471; 25, note 511.

21. Cf. "active bearers" and "passive bearers" of traditions, note 29.

22. For examples of this multiplexity, see respectively: section II, notes 74–75, and Tales No. 14, notes 316–18, and 18, notes 418, and 420; introductory note to Tale 33; Tale No. 14, note 325; Tale No. 17, note 399. On the concepts of "simplex" and "multiplex" systems as applied to lore, see El-Shamy, *Brother and Sister: Type 872*,* esp. p. 3.

23. *Brother and Sister, Type 872**, p. 3. It was noted that the "study is not concerned with subconscious mechanisms characteristic of . . . psychoanalytic approaches."

24. For applications of the concept of attitude to folklore materials see El-Shamy, "Folkloric Behavior," esp. pp. 162–66, and note 112, p. 165; El-Shamy, *Brother and Sister, Type 872**, p. 3; El-Shamy, "Belief Characters as Anthropomorphic Psychosocial Realities: The Egyptian Case," pp. 7–8; and El-Shamy, "Emotionskomponente," esp. p. 1393. Also see David Krech et al., *Individual in Society* (New York, 1962), p. 140; also cf. C. Sherif, M. Sherif, and R. Nebergall, *Attitude and Attitude Change* (Philadelphia, 1967).

25. On these "processes," see El-Shamy, "Emotionskomponente," p. 1393.

26. See "Social Factors and Perceiving Cues," in H. El-Shamy, "Folkloric Behavior," pp. 66–67; on multiplicity of roles, see pp. 63–64. For an application of the concept of role multiplicity, see El-Shamy's "Maḥfouẓ's Trilogy," esp. p. 55; cf. Mot. P7.1§, "Role strain (role conflict): effects of difficult choices between conflicting obligations."

27. El-Shamy, "Folkloric Behavior," p. 83; italics added.

28. Resocialization is essentially a process of changing one's own behavior from conforming to one set of social and cultural values into another within the same culture (e.g., from woman's to man's, from rural to urban, from membership in one family to membership in another). On the role of tales in resocializing male children, raised by women, into men's roles see "Traditions in Transition," in El-Shamy, *Brother and Sister, Type 872**, pp. 51–53; also see El-Shamy, *Folktales of Egypt*, p. lii, Tale No. 10, p. 75.

29. On the differences in psychological processes involved in "active" and "passive" bearing of traditions, see El-Shamy, "Folkloric Behavior," pp. 39, 95–96, 123, 138–39.

30. See "Attitudes Toward Narration," in El-Shamy, *Folktales of Egypt*, p. xlviii; also see Section II, "Profile of a Typical Household Tale Teller," below.

31. For an example of a professional balladeer's impersonal mode of communication aimed at the general public, see El-Shamy, *Brother and Sister, Type 872**, Variant No. 37, pp. 29–30. Also cf. Elisa Chimenti's *Tales and Legends of Morocco* (New York, 1965), which is derived from a professional narrator's performances.

32. El-Shamy, *Folktales of Egypt*, pp. xlii, xlvi.

33. A literary cliché states, "*'a¿dhabu al-shi¿ri 'akdhabuh* (The sweetest of poetry is that with the most lies)." On the viability of poetry despite Islamic prohibitions, see El-Shamy, *Folktales of Egypt*, p. xlvii. Also see "God's Language and Man's Parlance," in El-Shamy, "The Demographic Factor," pp. 65–67.

34. I.e., *'inshâ'-un.* Mot. Z1.0.1§, "*'inshâ*-style literary composition: constituted mainly from copied (memorized) famous quotations."

35. For examples of mild use of elements of *'inshâ* style, see introductory notes to Tales No. 41 and 45; cf. note 476, Tale No. 23.

This highly valued literary device is responsible for suppressing creativity and innovation, and promoting reliance on formulaic thinking and "authority." As a young pupil in elementary school, I witnessed and experienced punishments administered to pupils who opted not to make use of the *gumal wa ¿ibârât mukhtârah* (selected sentences and phrases) provided by Arabic-composition teachers. In college (in the late 1950s), Prof. ¿A. al-Quṭṭ, in a class on modern literature, recounted his own early experience as a teacher in assigning a nonformulaic topic: "Write an essay on a daily newspaper." Most students responded by writing on a "promenade in the countryside." Such a composition, I recall, would typically go like this:

> On a day whose sky was clear (. . . *ṣafat samâ'uh*),
> and air wholesome (*wa ṭâb hawâ'uh*),
> I was afflicted by a tedium (. . . *sa'âmah*).
> So, I went to the countryside
> so as to inhale the faint air (. . . *¿alîl*),
> along with the moist breeze (. . . *balîl*);
> with chirping birds (. . . *'aṭyâr*),
> and with blossoming flowers (. . . *'aẓhâr*). . . .

There, in that *formula-serviceable* environment (i.e., with a stock of available formulae), a *daily newspaper* was read; the reader concluded the day and returned to the city "*fariḥan mustabshiran* (in [a state of] mirth and optimism)."

Mot. X365§, "Humor concerning pupils and their answers"; J148.2§, "Memorization."

36. See "The Language and Other Stylistic Features," in El-Shamy, "The Demographic Factor," pp. 77–83. Concerning the use of poetry in *The Arabian Nights,* Enno Littmann observed that the poems/verses can be omitted with no adverse consequences to the prose text. Littmann, "Alf Layla wa-Layla," in the *Encyclopaedia of Islam,* 2nd ed. (Leiden, 1960), Vol. 1, p. 364.

37. El-Shamy, *Folktales of Egypt,* p. xlvii.

38. Mot. R113§, "Captives in fairyland (jinn-land) ransomed. (Khurâfah)"; Z62.0.1§, "'Khurâfah's report, [mythical, but is the truth].'"

39. The author is ¿Amr ibn Baḥr, nicknamed 'Abû-¿Uthmân (Uthmân's father), and al-Jâḥiẓ (Popeye) due to his protruding eyes (cf. Mot. F512.7§, "Popeyed person (*jâḥiẓ, 'buḥluq'*"). He was born in the year A.H. 150 and died in 255.

> A "Narrative's dramatic dialogue—(told as drama, as opposed to mere description)" is designated as Mot. Z18.0.1§. The story is an anecdote involving a debate between husband and wife; it contains the following motifs: J960.1§, "Man tries to persuade woman that elongated shadow of his limb (organ) on wall is indicative of his prowess"; U281.4§, "Merits and demerits of size (large or small, tall or short)"; U281.4.0.1§, "Size is unimportant—quality of performance is what counts." See al-Jâḥiẓ, *al-ḥayawân* (Animal[s]), ¿Abd-al-Salâm Muḥammad Hârûn, ed., 7 vols. (Cairo, 1938–45), Vol. 6, pp. 451–52.

40. Mot. W256.6.1§. For sample occurrences of this motif in contemporary lore, see references cited in El-Shamy, *Folk Traditions of the Arab World,* Vol. 1.

The accounts of paradise lost, in these literary interpretations, are quite similar to their Jewish and Christian counterparts. The following are some salient motifs of the reported events: A1275.1, "Creation of first woman from man's rib. [Adam's rib]"; A6.3.1§, "Eve created to relieve Adam's loneliness"; A63.5.1, "Satan seduces Adam to sin because he is jealous of him"; A63.5.3§, "Eblis vows to corrupt Adam's descendants";

A63.6, "Devil in serpent [(viper)] form tempts first woman (Satan and Eve)"; A1386.1.1§, "Eve serves Adam liquor till drunk (he obeys her sinful instigation)"; A1332§, "Accompaniments of paradise lost"; A1332.4§, "The forbidden paradise food (drink)"; A1332.1§, "Violation of food tabu in paradise results in need to defecate (assimilation of forbidden food is incomplete)"; A1371.5§, "Deviant women from Adam's 'crooked rib' "; A1372.9, "Why women are subservient to men"; A1231.3§, "Adam and Eve descend from sky"; A1650.5.1.1§, "Punishment of Adam: God's reconciliatory reprimand (*¿itâb*)"; A1650.5.1.10§, "Punishment of Adam: toiling and misery: the first to have his brow sweat from labor fatigue"; A1650.5.2§, "God's (fifteen) additional afflictions on women ('Eve and her daughters')"; A1650.5.2.1§, "Punishment of Eve: menstruation"; A1650.5.2.4§, "Punishment of Eve: deficiency in religion (faith)"; A1650.5.2.5§, "Punishment of Eve: deficiency in reason (mind)"; and A1650.5.2.16§, "Punishment of Eve: suffering defloration pains."

41. Mot. T9.0.1§, "Sexual frustration (deprivation)"; T271, "The neglected wife"; T201.1.1§, "Marriage fatigue: decreasing value of (affection for) a spouse with passage of time"; T317.2.1§, "Repression of lust by reading (reciting) holy book"; U248.4§, "Sexual desire (love) affects perception"; H631.4.1§, "What is strongest? Woman's resolve."

42. Al-Jâḥiẓ, Vol. 3, p. 291 (italics added); (Mot. V384.1.1§). This sweeping declaration is made in reference to actual social situations that seem to have motivated al-Jâḥiẓ to react to the negative stereotyping of women. One of these situations is presented in the form of a personal account given by a wise man describing how he used pigeons to solve a friend's marital problems; the narrative may be summarized as follows:

> A man married a fine maiden, but she was very shy. In spite of his affection, she refused to allow him conjugal relations. All his gentle attempts to approach her, including advice from women relations of his and hers, failed. He considered divorcing her, but a wise friend (the narrator)—who raises pigeons and is familiar with the birds' amorous nature—advised him to do the following: set the bride alone in a comfortable dwelling; provide her with all the necessities and many females' luxuries; assign a maid who does not speak the bride's language (Arabic) to serve her—so that they can have minimum communication but not a conversation; as she becomes lonesome, present her with a few pairs of pigeons (doves) as pets; she will watch them and will observe the satisfaction consensual tender mating bestows on both the female and the male; arrange for a wise woman to visit her and make sure that the link between gentle sexual intercourse and contentment is clearly understood; shortly afterwards, visit and converse with her; then try to get closer; if she is still resistant desist, and send the wise woman again.
>
> When the bride overcame shyness (or aversion), she "permitted him her self." Both emerged from [a state of] "*waḥshah* (apprehension/loneliness)" to [one of] "*'uns* (mirth/togetherness)" due to the pigeons' example. (al-Jâḥiẓ, Vol. 3, pp. 287–90)

This factual account belongs to a cycle of narratives on "The taming of a difficult person," (Types 901–9§); it is designated as Tale Type 904§, *Tender Persuading of the Shy (Innocent) Maiden (Bride, Girl, Virgin)*. It incorporates the following motifs: P529.0.5§,

"Refusal by wife to honor legitimate marital obligations"; T311.0.3§, "Overcoming aversion to conjugal relations through conditioning (psychotherapy, resocialization)"; T160.0.5§, "Tender defloration (first sexual intercourse)"; T311.0.3.1§, "Gentle arousing of bride's interest in sex"; F1043§, "Reaction to sensory deprivation"; U315.1§, "Seeking a conversation (social interaction)"; F951.3.2.1§, "Watching mating between lovebirds (pigeons, doves) arouses sexual desire"; J133.9§, "Kindness learned from example of animal's (bird's) kind behavior: imitated."

The prescribed treatment here is comparable to the "reorganization of the social system to accommodate the afflicted party," a technique applied by contemporary faith healers; in this case, both parties had to undergo changes, but the bride's refusal to honor marital commitments ("affliction") was accommodated. See El-Shamy, "Belief Characters," p. 21.

43. Mot. U248.5§, "Gender affects perception: males and females perceive different things (and view the same thing differently)"; and V384.1§, "Extreme interpretations of religious dogmas concerning females (social category)".

44. Al-Jâḥiẓ, *al-ḥayawân,* Vol. 3, p. 534. Mot. P611.3.1.1§, "Women's talk (superstitious ways, old wives' tales, old wives' medicine, etc.)"; W202.1.1.3§, "Indicator of femininity: women's superstitious ways (old-wives' tales, old-wives' medicine, etc.)"; B789.0.1§, "Bat fastens self with its fangs to victim's face"; B789.1.1.1.1.1§, "Bat releases victim upon hearing zebra's braying"; J29.2.1§, "Learning to overcome childhood fear."

It may be noted here that I learned about this belief (and another concerning frogs—which are perceived as feminine) from a young female cousin of mine, during one of my childhood visits to my family's home village (Aghûr al-Kubrâ) in Egypt's Nile Delta. This contemporary belief from Egypt varies only slightly from that reported by al-Jâḥiẓ from Iraq; it states that a "Bat releases victim only upon hearing country-style drumming" (Mot. B789.1.1.1.3.1§). The other belief (as practiced by the same girl-cousin) is designated here as Mot. D1794.1.1.1§, "Ability (by female) to utter trellis of joy (*'ẓaghrûṭah'/zaghrûdah*) magically acquired from kissing (licking) frog's belly)"; P790.1.2.1§, "Trellis (ululation) of joy. . . . (Typically voiced by women at a joyous occasion such as a wedding, pilgrimage, winning at law court, release from prison, etc.)."

These two motifs signify stable sets of attitudes: a negative one toward bats, and a positive one toward frogs. The latter belief is congruent with the ancient Egyptian belief in a female deity (Heket) with a frog's head; Mot. A132.17.1§, "Goddess in form of frog (Heket)."

The statement "['if God wills']" was added by ¿A. M. Hârûn, the contemporary editor of al-Jâḥiẓ's book, so as to amend an oversight on al-Jâḥiẓ's part; Mot. C51.9.1§, "Tabu: planning for the future without saying, *'in-shâ'-Allâh* (If God wills)'."

45. al-Jâḥiẓ, Vol. 4, p. 155. Mot. B15.1.2.6.1, "Seven-headed serpent"; also cf. B.15.2.1, "Six-mouthed serpent."

46. al-Jâḥiẓ, Vol. 5, pp. 301–3. This narrative is to be classified as a legend. In addition to formal and stylistic characteristics, its contents are possible, but—as al-Jaḥiẓ concluded—improbable. The story belongs to a cycle of tales affiliated with Tale Type 327L§, *Brother and Sister Possess Supernatural Animal's (Cat's) Treasure;* in which the magic animal suspects an organ of his of theft and beats it (himself) to death. (See introduction to Tale No. 8, note 137.) Mot. B277§, "Animal's own property (possessions:

field, crop, treasure, etc.)"; B778.1.2§, "Mouse (rat) as thief"; N534.1.1§, "Treasure discovered by following an animal"; F981.9.1§, "Animal kills self (commits suicide)."

47. al-Jâḥiẓ, Vol. 4, p. 156. Mot. B15.1.2.1.1, "Two-headed serpent. One head in front and one at rear." With reference to the fabricated information (*'intiḥâl,* or "fakelore"), compare the situation reported with reference to a contemporary dishonest informant employed by collector A. Nakano, cf. note 1, this section; also see El-Shamy, "The Demographic Factor," p. 76. The following are relevant motifs: K2250.2§, "Treacherous (dishonest) workman (hireling)"; P520.4§, "Unreliable testimony; witness's character suspected: truthfulness doubted"; J1215§, "Know-it-all person (*'Abu-el-¿urraif'*): a talkative fool"; W142.1.1§, "Person cannot bring himself to say: 'I do not know' "; X1370, "Lies about imaginary animals"; X1321, "Lies about snakes"; X1321.3, "Lies about remarkable kinds of snakes."

48. Among the relatively early collectors of the folktale (excluding the "personal narrative"), who were successful in acquiring "fantasy tales" from women are the female collectors F. Légey (1926) and E. Stevens (1931); other female fieldworkers seem to have collected tales only from men (e.g., W. Blackman [1927]). Male fieldworkers who collected from women include D. H. Müller (1902), J. Desparmet (1909–10), G. Bergsträsser (1915), and H. Schmidt and P. Kahle (1918, 1930). Aarne-Thompson's *The Types of the Folktale* largely ignores these anthologies.

49. See note 2, above. Also see the following by El-Shamy: "Folkloric Behavior," p. 108, 285; *Folktales of Egypt,* p. xlviii; "Sentiment, Genre, and Tale Typology," pp. 269–70; and "A Type Index for Tales of the Arab World," p. 152.

50. The study is an evaluation of the findings of four theoretical studies: psychoanalytic Freudian/Jungian (Type 326, *The Youth Who Wanted to Learn What Fear Is*), anthropological (Type 756C, *The Greater Sinner*), morphological (Type 91, *Monkey [. . .] Who Left His Heart at Home*), and classificatory-typological (Type 911*, *The Dying Father's Counsel*), in light of the methodology of positivism. See El-Shamy, "Sentiment, Genre, and Tale Typology."

51. I.e., emotions harbored in the subconscious, collective unconscious, etc. See H. El-Shamy, *Brother and Sister, Type 872*,* p. 3.

52. El-Shamy, "Sentiment, Genre, and Tale Typology" (1985), pp. 255–56.

53. On these folklore theories, see El-Shamy, "Behaviorism and the Text."

54. Stanford University Press, Stanford, Cal., 1996.

55. Their data were derived from two sources: Ahmad al-Shahi, and F. C. T. Moore, *Wisdom from the Nile* (Oxford, 1978); and El-Shamy, *Folktales of Egypt.*

Al-Shahi and Moore's collection comprises texts submitted in writing by pupils (presumably boys) who acquired them presumably from their families; as such it belongs to a category of collections described in the following manner:

> the overwhelming majority of tale anthologies give no information about their original narrators. Even recent "anthropological" studies employing tales collected in the field for analyzing "social and culture institutions" tended to ignore tale-tellers and perceive the repertoire of traditional narratives found in a certain

community as emanating from a relatively undifferentiated social mass to be designated under the generic rubric: "informants," without specifying who those informants happened to be. . . . Such is the case in studies based on tale collections by Daisy H. Dwyer, *Images and Self-Images, Male and Female in Morocco* [. . .], and by Ahmad al-Shahi and F. C. T. Moore, *Wisdom from the Nile* [. . .]. (El-Shamy, "The Demographic Factor," pp. 72, 106, note 44)

For more details on the texts used by al-Shahi and Moore, see note 60, this section.
On problems with such psychiatric studies, see El-Shamy, "The Brother-Sister Syndrome in Arab Family Life. Socio-cultural Factors in Arab Psychiatry: A Critical Review," in *International Journal of Sociology of the Family, The Family in the Middle East,* 313–23.

56. On the relevance of this "cross-matrix" to the study of a folktale, see El-Shamy, *Folktales of Egypt,* p. 237. For pertinent examples of applications of this factor, see notes 62, and 64, this section.

57. See Johnson and Price-Williams's "A Note to the Reader," p. xv. On the significance of the missing contextual data, see note 13, this section.

58. Johnson and Price-Williams, p. 339.

59. The exception is Alan Dundes, whom they quote on the "brother and sister" theme in the American movie *Star Wars,* and on his characteristic championing of the Freudian psychoanalytic theory. Cf. note 3, this section.

60. As listed in Johnson and Price-Williams, these tales are:
(1) No. 27, pp. 165–68 ("Muhammad Othman, the Sultan's Son," in al-Shahi and Moore, *Nile,* pp. 151–55). This narrative is a Middle Eastern subtype of Type 516, *Faithful John.* It has been designated as Type 516H§, *The Father Who Wanted a Share of His Son's Beautiful Wives.* He is killed with the help of the hero's friend. Twenty-eight texts are available from various parts of the Arab World; other renditions from the Sudan include: Kronenberg, *Nubische,* pp. 213–18, No. 44; Frobenius, *Kordofan,* pp. 179–92, No. 16; Frobenius, *Kordofan,* pp. 193–204, No. 17.
(2) No. 28, pp. 168–71 ("Fatma the Beautiful," in al-Shahi and Moore, *Nile,* pp. 110–14). This tale is often misclassified (see El-Shamy, *Folk Traditions of the Arab World,* Introduction, p. xvi, note 26); it belongs to Type 313E*, *Girl Flees from Brother Who Wants to Marry her.* For further information on this recurrent tale type dealing with brother and sister, see Section III, Tale No. 46, below.
(3) No. 29, pp. 171–73 ("The Wife of the Prince's Son," in al-Shahi and Moore, *Nile,* pp. 79–81). This tale is a Middle Eastern subtype of Type 705, *Born of Fish;* it has been designated as Type 705A§, *Born from Pregnant Man, Raised by Bird (Animal): The Falcon's Daughter.* For further information on this tale type, see Section III, Tale No. 5, below.
(4) No. 30, p. 174 ("The New or the Old?" in El-Shamy, *Folktales of Egypt,* pp. 222–23, No. 58). Tale Type 1563, "*Both?*" [Seduction by bearing false order]. For a cross-cultural study of this humorous anecdote and the nature of its erotic symbolism, see El-Shamy "'Beide?' AaTh 1563," in *Enzyklopädie des Märchens,* Nos. 1 and 2 (1977), p. 55–64.

61. In this Persian narrative, an ugly son murders his father in hopes of getting the father's young wife (stepmother). She, however, evades him, and no incest occurs.

62. This contextual (behavioristic) finding was reported repeatedly by the present writer. For further information on this tale type, see Tale No. 5 in the present work; also see El-Shamy, "The Falcon's Daughter," in *Tales Told around the World,* R. M. Dorson, gen. ed. (Chicago, 1975), pp. 159–63—text, tale types, motif identifications, notes, and theoretical conclusions are El-Shamy's. For a detailed worldwide analysis see El-Shamy, "Vom Fisch geboren (AaTh 705)," in *Enzyklopädie des Märchens,* Vol. 4 (1984), Nos. 4–5, pp. 1211–18; and El-Shamy, "A Type Index for Tales of the Arab World," "Appendix I B," pp. 161–62.

63. *Arab Studies Quarterly* (Summer 1982), pp. 273–74. Similarly, in his review of *Folktales of Egypt,* Francis X. Paz pointed out the merits of the work but found "that the Aarne-Thompson Type Index does not seem particularly useful or interesting in the context of this book," *Journal of the American Oriental Society,* Vol. 102, No. 1 (1982), p. 220.

64. El-Shamy, *Folktales of Egypt,* p. 222. The same viewpoint was emphasized earlier in a broader cross-cultural context; see El-Shamy "'Beide?' AaTh 1563," p. 56.

65. Thus, the study, wittingly or unwittingly, exercised what the present writer has designated as Motif A1698.1§, "'The Yorkshire syndrome': only Europeans can properly process raw materials from Third World countries (e.g., cotton, ore, myths, tales, etc.)." The core of this syndrome is a cultural tendency on the part of Europeans and "Third World" non-Europeans to accredit Westerners' products with originality and superiority of quality. The new motif complements Mot. A1667.1, "Why Europeans know more than natives." See also note 73, below.

66. See introductory note to Tale No. 46, note 774, below, where a text ("The Son of Nimêr") given by S. Hurreiz, *Ja¿aliyyîn Folktales* (Bloomington, Indiana, 1977), No. 8, pp. 83–85, is discussed in this respect.

67. Muhawi and Kanaana, No. 25, pp. 212–28, 365. For a similar text, with the theme of desire to commit incest with foster sisters, see El-Shamy's "The Sure News Is Up Ahead," in *Tales Told around the World,* Dorson, gen. ed., pp. 149–59. Also cf. Mot. R319.1.2.1.1§, "Incestuous brother and sister live inside closed tomb . . .".

68. Typically, the "cousin" is the father's brother's daughter, i.e., parallel paternal cousin (*bint ¿amm*).

69. Muhawi and Kanaana, p. 217, note 8.

70. Mot. P605.5.1§, "Sister and brother together asleep." On the theme of the "The sister in bed," see El-Shamy, "Maḥfûẓ's Trilogy," p. 58; also see *Brother and Sister, Type 872*,* p. 39. Also cf. Mot. T317.2.1§, "Repression of lust by reading (reciting) holy book," and T351, "Sword of chastity."

71. Mot. P263.3.1§, "Bad relations between a man and his cousin-sister's husband." See "Brother's Wife and Sister's Husband," in El-Shamy, "Maḥfûẓ's Trilogy," especially pp. 59–60, 62; also see "Relationship between Sister's Husband and Brother," in El-Shamy, *Brother and Sister, Type 872*,* pp. 59–61.

72. Muhawi and Kanaana, p. 111.

73. It should be noted that Muhawi and Kanaana cite El-Shamy *mostly* as a source

of field data. They list only his *Folktales of Egypt* as a source of tale variants; texts and studies by El-Shamy contained in a work under a general editor's name (i.e., Dorson) are accredited to the general editor, not to El-Shamy as the author of the contribution. See for example, Muhawi and Kanaana's No. 2, p. 330, "Egypt—Dorson (1975): 159–63 'Falcon's Daughter'"; and their No. 11, p. 341, "Dorson (1975: 164) cites other references from North Africa," etc. Cf. "The Yorkshire syndrome" (Mot. A1698.1§), in note 65, this section. Also, on the issue of El-Shamy's "different" ideas, see El-Shamy, "A Response [to Jason's Review of *Folk Traditions of the Arab World* . . .]," esp. pp. 353–54.

74. "Patterns of Sentiments as Expressed in Urban and in Rural Literatures." Paper read at the invitation of American Universities Field Staff, Center for Mediterranean Studies, Rome, Italy. A symposium on "Town and Country: Their Representation in Modern Arabic Urban and Folk Literature and Their Interaction," October 19–26, 1980. The proceedings were tape-recorded.

75. Mot. P254.0.1§, "Household composed of only brother and sister(s)"; and W129.1§, "Person who doubts a prediction (belief, claim, etc.) fails to see that he is living proof of its validity." See Tales No. 1–2; 8, note 137; 13, note 288; 37; 39; cf. Tales No. 43, 45, 46–3, 49, 50. Cf. El-Shamy, "Maḥfouẓ's Trilogy," p. 67, where the novel is shown to conclude with brother and sister left alone in the family home. Cf. Mot. T198§, "Return to parents' (father's) home after end of marital relations (divorce, or death of spouse)."

II

PROFILE OF A TYPICAL HOUSEHOLD TALE TELLER, 1969–72

Galîlah ¿A. is a young woman hailing from a village in the Nile Delta, and is employed as housemaid in Cairo. She is of medium height (about five foot, three inches), dark complected, heavyset, and soft-voiced. In the opinion of her friends and former employers, she is of "acceptable appearance"; that is she is neither pretty nor ugly. She is also viewed as honest, kind, good with children, dependable, and most important—"like a man."[1] This latter quality signifies that her sexual honor is irreproachable, especially in situations requiring close interaction with adult males outside of her immediate family circle. She can barely read and write.

I first met Galîlah in Cairo in September 1968, when she was employed by a young middle-class family of four (Mr. S., his wife, and two small sons); both husband and wife were university graduates, held full-time jobs, and left their home in Galîlah's care during the day. When I visited with that family in their residence in the Shobra district, Galîlah served us soft drinks in the parlor. I asked her whether she knew any *ḥawadît* (fantasy-tales);[2] she replied defensively, "No! My mind does not retain such things!" I argued that "these things" can often be very important, but Galîlah insisted that she did not know any. About a half hour later she returned and stated, "I can tell you a *masal* (story of wisdom)"[3] and hurriedly narrated while standing up the story of "The Man Who Threw Himself Off the Minaret" (Résumé No. 1, this section). She had heard her father tell this story to his friends several years before. I expressed my admiration for her story and asked for more, but she declined and claimed, "That is all I know."[4]

About one year later, in September 1969, Galîlah's employer and his family emigrated to the U.S., and Galîlah came to work for me and my family (my wife and one four-year-old daughter). She lived in our home, an apartment in the district of Maadi, Cairo, shared a room with our little girl, and visited her family—who dwelt in a nearby[5] suburb (al-Basâtîn)—on weekends (Thursday afternoon to Saturday morning). After the consummation of her marriage in the summer of 1971, Galîlah and her husband lived with her family and she commuted to work by bus.

The following is a brief personal-narrative account of Galîlah's life and network of social relations as she perceived them. She presented the majority of the data as replies to questions that I asked, as I interviewed her in July 1972 concerning my research on the Brother-Sister Syndrome. Galîlah's statements are given here verbatim (in translation), but the data were obtained in several sessions which took place over a period extending from January 1970 to July 1972. Two distinct phases of Galîlah's life are presented: those before and after the consummation of her marriage. The information was given in blocks, on specific issues. These blocks have been rearranged into their present sequence so as to allow for a more coherent account; the unity of each block, however, has been preserved.

The Informant and Her Household

My name is Galîlah ¿A.; I was born in the village of Sh., Munûfiyyah [Governorate]. I am twenty-two years old. I have three brothers. One, [Ḥ.], is married and lives [along with his own wife and children] with us here in Cairo; his wife hails from a hamlet near our village. He has three daughters and one son. My second brother is also married; he lives in the village. My youngest brother, ¿A., is eighteen; he attends the college of commerce [and lives with us here in Cairo also]. I have two sisters. The eldest is married and lives in the village. The youngest one of us, [W.], is twenty [and lives with us in Cairo, also]; she works [as a housemaid] for a German family here [in the Maadi District, Cairo].

My *kitâb* (marriage contract) was written down [and signed by my father and my husband-to-be] about six or seven years ago—[i.e., around 1964], but my father keeps postponing the *dokhlah* (consummation of the marriage) and keeps saying: "Next year!" [or] "Wait until your brother finishes college!"[6] I have told them that I would still help even after [the consummation of] my marriage; I would not leave them to be [financially] on their own, [but my father continues to put the consummation of my marriage off].

Presently my father is not working; he just stays home and yells [i.e., orders]: "More tea! More coffee! More smoke [i.e., cigarettes, tobacco]!"[7]

My fiancé,[8] [who is now in 1970 my husband, but only legally], was married before; he has a daughter [from the previous marriage], but she lives with his former wife. He has no [immediate] relatives. His salary is fourteen pounds per month [which is roughly the same amount as the cash portion of my monthly income].[9] He works as a janitor. He spends five pounds on cigarettes alone, and sometimes two or three on tea and transportation to and from his work. He says, "After we get married you'll have to [quit work and] stay home. We, [in my family], have no women who go out [i.e., we are conservative and don't allow our women to work outside the home]." I don't know to where these pompous airs[10] will lead us!

Living Quarters[11]

We live in an apartment which has three [bed]rooms and a *ṣâlah* (hall) [that serves as an entryway and a family room]; the contract is in the name of my elder brother [Ḥ.]. [Before the consummation of my marriage, in the summer of 1971], my father and mother occupied one room; my elder brother, his wife, and their youngest baby-[boy] occupied a second room; his three children [daughters], W. [my younger sister], and ¿A. [my youngest brother] slept in the third room. Every once in a while, especially in the summertime, when it would be hot, some of the younger children would sleep in the hall. As for me, due to the fact that I dwell with the people for whom I work, [when I went home on weekends] I would spend the Thursday and Friday nights with the children in their room.

[Within that room], my [eldest] brother's children [(three daughters)] sleep in the same bedding;[12] W. [my younger sister] and ¿A., my youngest brother, also share the same bedding.[13]

[In 1972, after the consummation of my marriage, and my husband's joining us in the apartment],[14] I, my husband, and our baby-boy sleep in one room—the one that the children of my brother used to occupy; my father, mother, sister W., and [younger] brother [¿A.] sleep in another room; my [eldest] brother, Ḥ., his wife and [four] children sleep in the third room.[15]

The landlady wants to raise the rent; she says, "Now you are three families living in the apartment." [My husband] says, "Let us move out and get a place of our own!" But I cannot do that until my brother finishes college. Besides, where are we going to find another apartment that we can afford?[16]

Uncles and Aunts

We moved to Cairo maybe twelve years ago [about 1958]; I was ten years old then. Before moving, my father had taken me to work for a family from our own village living here in Cairo; I was nine years old then. They did not treat me kindly. I left them and worked for Mr. S. [who emigrated], then for you. [We were a notable family in our village]; my father's father was a *¿umdah* (mayor, administrative head of village).[17] When my [paternal] grandfather died, he left a good deal of land for my father and his brothers [i.e., the grandfather's other two sons]. Because my father was a *'ibn-¿umdah* (mayor's son)[18] and used to being spoiled,[19] he wasted his [portion of the] land on showing off, tea and cigarettes. He sold his land bit by bit [until it was all gone].

Now, I have two paternal-uncles[20] both of whom are younger than my father, and two maternal-uncles;[21] they still live in the village. I [also] have paternal-aunts,[22] and I used to have four maternal-aunts;[23] only one [maternal-aunt] remains [i.e., is surviving]—she lives here in Cairo.

It seems to me that when it comes to *ḥinniyyah* (tenderness or kindness) [toward nephew or niece], both the paternal-uncles and the maternal-uncles are alike.[24] However, my *own* paternal-uncles are not kind—but my maternal-uncles are extremely kind.[25] It seems to me that the maternal-uncles are kinder than the paternal-uncles. Paternal-uncles, often, have jealousy when they find their brothers better than they are, or that the children of their brothers are better than their own children. . . .

During our last year [in the village, my father sold the land and then rented it from the buyer]. When my father began to sell his land, my older paternal-uncle was very pleased because he [thought that he would be the one] to get it by renting it from the man who was buying it (from my father). He (my paternal-uncle) kept on uttering insults at my father when he (my father) was unable to pay the rent. At the end of the year (my father) had sold all the land. [My paternal-uncle] kept on saying to him, "Get out of it, you 'son-of- . . . - [such and such]' "; he uttered insults at him until he got it [the land]. He took it and was very pleased that [he was able to] oust his own brother; he "stayed" in it. He took the land away from my father; my father had rented [the land back so as to plant] it, after he had sold it. He thought: "The crop will pay for the rent." The crop did not. My paternal-uncle was very happy because of this. Even before the person who had bought it came (to my father) to say, "Get off the land," he (my paternal-uncle) had come and said, "Get off it!" He stood there calling him, and the woman who begot him, [dirty] names—that is, his mother [who is also my paternal-uncle's own mother]. He kept on saying, "I am the one who will remain in it."[26]

Furthermore, my father had numerous children [i.e., too many to support].[27] That younger brother of his did not have [as many] children; he was married and had only one daughter. Her mother had died and she [the girl] inherited one acre [from her mother]. So, he was well-to-do, for he owned [i.e., controlled] one acre more [than each of his two brothers did]. Yet he ousted my father and took the land.

But God['s justice] pursued him. He remarried and ended up squandering all the land; he even squandered the house.[28] [Originally] he was married to his paternal she-cousin;[29] she died. He then married his maternal-aunt's daughter.[30] He used to have five acres, in addition to the acre [which his daughter inherited from her mother]: thus he had six acres, [but he squandered all of them]. Last year [1969–70] he came to Cairo in order to find a job for his son in the aircraft factory. He sold even the house. . . . However, [although we sold the land,] we did not sell the house [in the village].[31] He sold the house to his younger brother [i.e., to the youngest of all three brothers]. That youngest brother of his [who is also my youngest paternal-uncle] does not drink tea, nor smoke cigarettes, nor . . . [spend money on similar nonessentials]: his land is intact. This youngest paternal-uncle of mine is also not kind to us. Since we came to Cairo he has not visited us at all. Even when we go to the village he would come, like a stranger,[32] to greet us and leave [quickly]. He would not say, "Come stay with me for a while." [Also] when my father would go to [visit with] him, he would not insist that he should stay longer.[33]

The maternal-uncles are kind because they love the children of their own sister. . . . My older maternal-uncle had died while we were still little children; my second maternal-uncle—even after we got out of the village—still comes to us [in Cairo] regularly; he brings us gifts,[34] and stays with us for a long time [which is a good thing]. . . . As for my paternal-uncles, we have not seen their faces[35] since we came here from the village [which is not a good thing]. . . .

My father's sisters are okay (*kuwayyîsîn*) with him. I have one paternal-aunt[36] who is very close to my father; but my mother says she is two-faced![37] When she is with my father she shows one face, but when she is with my [older] paternal-uncle [her other brother], she would show another.[38]

Brothers and Sisters

A sister is kinder to her brother than he is kind to her. A sister always loves her brother very much and even if he were to do something wrong, she would not hate him. . . . A brother also loves his sister and is jealous *over* her[39] and loves her very much.

Brothers get jealous *of* one another.[40] If one of them or his children become better than the other's, that other [who is less fortunate] becomes jealous and feels offended. Sisters also get jealous of one another but not as [strongly] as brothers do of one another. If one of the sisters were to get something more than the other, that other would bear something in herself [i.e., have some jealousy].[41]

My older brother, Ḥ., and the youngest one, ¿A., are okay (*kuwayyîsîn*) with each other because we were raised to be okay with one another.[42] If one happened to be absent, for example, the other one would inquire about him. . . . But when it comes to money, the money (of my older brother) suffices him only—him and his children. True a he-person is kind to[43] his brother, but he would not like for his brother to be better than his own sons. . . . It is W. (my younger sister) and I who give ¿A. [our youngest brother], the money which he needs; this is so even after I got married.[44]

Every morning my older brother gives his children their pocket money. He is fully cognizant of the fact that his younger brother goes to college and needs money. Never would he give him any money, not even one piaster (ten cents). Only W. and I pay all the expenses for his education; whenever he needs a book, or the like, he would go to W. or would come to me (even after I got married in the summer of 1971). Just this past month [i.e., June, 1972], W. [my younger sister] had to pay ten pounds for groceries which they [the father, mother, and youngest brother] drew on credit from the grocer throughout the previous month. Before I or W. would go out of the house [to work], we would ask him [i.e., ¿A.] whether he needs anything. When we asked my elder brother [Ḥ.] to help in paying ¿A.'s [college] expenses, he said [coolly], "He does not have to finish. Let him find himself a job!" Even if he himself wanted to help, his wife wouldn't let him.[45]

Sometimes people become jealous of one another. Even Ḥ. [my elder brother—who works as a janitor at a public library—becomes jealous]. He would say, "Why should poor people have to go to [secular] schools and colleges [as is the case with ¿A., our youngest brother]! The government [by the Wafd Party, around 1950] made a mistake when it made education free just 'Like water and air!'" The first time I heard this [saying] was from the people for whom I worked first—that man from our village [who did not treat me kindly]; he used to curse all the time saying, "May God damn him [Ṭâhâ Ḥusain, the Minister of Education responsible for introducing the free-for-all, like-"Water-and-Air" Policy] who made education free and opened the doors to the lowly [to climb socially]!" He also used to say, "There is a Prophet's tradition that says, 'Don't teach *¿ilm* (gnosis, science) to the children of the lowly ('*safalah*') [(i.e., *siflah:* vile class; cf. mob)].'"[46]

But this [viewpoint] cannot be right! Nowadays, everyone must go to school—especially the poor.[47]

Sisters and Cousins

[My mother and father are related]: my father would call her father, "paternal-uncle."[48] My father is the son of my mother's father's sister.

A father's brother's son and a father's brother's daughter are like brother and sister. You have [for example] my elder brother [Ḥ.], who is married to that one [woman] who quarrels all the time. He could have married his *bint-¿amm* (paternal-cousin); she was very beautiful. We pressured him to marry her, but he refused and said, "No! She is just like a sister to me. I love her but like I love my sisters; I would not marry her!"[49] Instead, he went and brought into our family that scorpion![50] [Informant laughs.]

[He was deceived into that marriage]; someone said to him, "Come I will marry you a good bride; she is from the hamlet next to our village." When they—he and that friend of his—went to her house, she only appeared at the door [of the room where they were seated] with her head shawl[51] covering her face. Before my brother could get a good look at her she disappeared [as a sign of bashfulness and modesty]. He sent my mother to look her over . . . , but she also came to my mother all wrapped up [in flowing gowns and a head shawl]. So my mother could not get a good look at her. My mother said, "Instead of breaking their pride,[52] I will let the matter pass." She [the bride] turned out to be—(away from you)[53]—horrid![54]

When the brother [of a girl] gets married, of course his wife takes him away from his family. If his sister or mother were to visit him, his wife couldn't bear [even] to see them. You have [for example], the wife of my [elder] brother [Ḥ.] who is living here; she would like to see us all dead.[55] [Based on] all I have seen (in my family and elsewhere), a brother's wife never *could like* her husband's sister or mother.

If a woman's husband and her brother happened to get upset with each other[56] her brother would have priority for her.[57] The first time I heard the proverb, "A[nother] husband is available; a[nother] son would be born; [but] the brother is irreplaceable,"[58] was from that quarrelsome wife of my [elder] brother [Ḥ.]. Once she was repeatedly saying: "I love my brothers very much!" I asked her, "Do you love them more than you do your husband?" She replied [by citing the proverb (with syntax error)]: "A[nother] son would be born. . . . "

The Neighbors

Since we came to Cairo we have been keeping to ourselves. Everyone [around us] is preoccupied [with making a living].[59] The landlady lives on the second floor [of the apartment building where we live]; she is married to a man named ¿I. He works as a laborer in the [limestone] quarries [in the Muqqaṭṭam Hills ṇear Cairo]; he breaks stone off the mountain.[60] She has children [by her present husband], the eldest is a boy of 17 or 18 years of age. She and her husband quarrel all the time. The apartment building is owned by her [and is registered in her name].[61] She has a bad character trait:[62] any day on which her husband is without work she would not give him a single *millime* (penny), cause him to be angry, hide the food from him and not feed him or [do] anything else for him.[63] So he would go to his own family and would stay there for six or eight months at a time.[64] Her money is for her; she gives him nothing and saves her money in order to build more apartment buildings. Very recently, she had a second one built.[65]

The landlady says that she is possessed by a line of *zâr*-jinn.[66] When her husband is mad at her [and becomes menacing], she would say to him [in a warning tone]: "Get away from me: my body is not un-attached [i.e., not free]!"[67] He would leave her alone [due to fear of the possessing-jinn]. Occasionally, out of vexation, he would beat her up [and would take some money from her by force].[68] Then she would say to him, "Go! May He [God] bring [calamities] and heap [them] upon you,[69] O you ¿I.-Son-of-Ẓarîfah—[your mother]!!" [Informant is amused and laughs].[70]

Concluding Event (told by El-Shamy, the present writer)

Upon our departure from Egypt in the summer of 1972, my wife and I recommended Galîlah (with some reservations concerning her inability to communicate in English and her fear of dogs) to a young American couple working for a major Western corporation in Egypt. She was hired for her honesty and housekeeping abilities, and was given a substantial raise in wages. The new employers lived in a large home (a two-story villa) and had no children, but they had a dog. Galîlah was confident that she would be able to overcome her fear and care for the pet, and the new employer (who was studying Arabic at college) was confident that she could communicate with Galîlah in Arabic. (Regrettably, we learned later from friends that Galîlah lost her job a few weeks after starting, due to her failure to care properly for the dog.) That was the last we heard of Galîlah and her family.

During the 1981–82 period, I returned to Egypt for an extended stay and made numerous attempts to locate Galîlah—short of traveling to her home village, but I was not successful. All the persons who I knew had knowledge of her had lost contact with her several years before then. Significantly, upon informing one of my own women relatives of my futile attempts to locate Galîlah, and asking whether she had heard any news of her or her family, the relative replied: "What is there for you to seek to know!? Either her husband has already divorced her, or he has married another 'over her,' . . . !"[71] Although not a verified fact, this 'guess' is quite indicative of a woman's expectations, based on the harsh social realities that the Arab woman in general, and the Muslim in particular must face especially with reference to marriage and divorce.

Narrating Tales outside the Normal Context

Following my initial September 1968 inquiry concerning folk narratives, I repeatedly requested tales from Galîlah, but she consistently denied any further knowledge of "these things." After she had been with us for several months, she was accidentally placed in a position where she had to admit knowing some additional tales. She explained, "They are not [of] much [value]; these are things [only] for the household, or for children before they go to sleep. Here, [among the urban middle class in the city], many parents like you [i.e., the present writer, or 'the educated'] do not want their children to hear these [backward] things." I assured her that I would accept whatever she could tell me and that I wanted these things exactly as they are told, even though some people might think they are not nice. Finally, on August 7, 1970, Galîlah decided to tell me a sample of the *ḥawadît* (fantasy-tales) that she knew; she, however, asked that I not tape-record them. Nervous and often visibly embarrassed, she told me the *ḥaddûtah* (fantasy-tale) of "The Ostrich of the Sultan's Son,"[72] and a few others. I expressed my satisfaction and asked her to permit the recording of the tales on tape; she was very hesitant and finally consented.

Acting as an "informant," motivated by an atypical request for information from an outsider, rather than as an "operant," responding to typical motivations in her daily life, Galîlah's tape-recorded renditions proved to be defensively narrated and somewhat "cleansed."[73] She spoke rapidly and was obviously embarrassed when presenting materials that were overtly or symbolically of an erotic nature. Her discomfort was particularly observable with reference to an episode in the tale of "The Ostrich of the Sultan's Son," where the water bottle[74] rolls "herself" downhill over the pottery pitcher[75] and broke "his" spout; symbolically, a water bottle represents a female whereas a pitcher represents a male. Similarly, in outlining "The Green Sparrow" (Type 720, see Résumé No. 4, this section), Galîlah dropped the word "pimp" from the verse chanted by the Green Sparrow [a metamorphosed slain boy]. Also in the humorous anecdote titled "The [Miserly] Husband and the Leg of Lamb" (Résumé No. 9), she substituted the word "ear" for the indecent "anus"; thus the phrase "until *fat* has oozed out of his *anus*" was changed to "until *parsley* has grown out of his *ear*."

Galîlah's main text, "The Girl Who Fed Her Brother the Egg" (Résumé No. 14), was even more carefully guarded. After she had told a tale containing a similar theme in which a sister is slandered and eventually vindicated (Résumé No. 3), I inquired about the tale of the sister who raised her brother. Galîlah first stated, "I don't know it." Upon my introducing the main elements of the plot, she remarked, "Maybe I had heard it, but I don't remember it." It was quite accidentally that I learned from W.—Galîlah's younger sister, when she came to visit her at our home—that Galîlah did know the tale and that she had recently told it to their brother's daughter.

The Learning of the Tales

Galîlah explained the manner in which she had acquired her repertoire:

I have heard these tales maybe a hundred times and perhaps more.[76] The person who told me all the fantasy tales (*ḥawadît*) I know is my grandmother, my father's mother; she was living with us in the village until she passed away. After all the housework and chores were done, the animals put in the zareba (farm animals' enclosure) and everything else finished—everything—we, my brothers and sisters, would go to our grandmother and say, "Tell us a *ḥaddûtah!*" So, she would. Sometimes, when she happened to be ill or very tired, she would say, "Not tonight!" Then we would go to my mother. If my mother happened not to be busy, she would tell us a tale; but this happened only once in a while. Her tales were the same as my grandmother's. My [maternal] grandmother, my mother's mother, died before I was born.

[In the village], other women or older girls who were our neighbors would sit in the lane beside a wall, or on the *maṣṭabah*[77] [in front of the house] and tell *ḥawadît* to children, especially after the grown-ups had gone to bed or gone out some place. Or someone would say, "Let us converse," so women and children would sit down and talk.[78] Their stories were also the same as those of my grandmother and my mother. My older sister also told tales to us. When no adult woman or older girl was available, children narrated these tales [to one another] but, of course, they did not tell them well. When an adult narrated there would be [only] two or three tales [in a session]; but when children narrated, there would be five or six of the same [repertoire of] tales, but they would be shorter. Occasionally I listened to men narrating [to one another], but their stories are different [from those narrated by women and children].[79]

After my elder sister got married [and moved out to her husband's], I began telling those tales to my younger brother and sister. Now [after we moved to Cairo] I tell only two or three of these tales to the children of my elder brother [Ḥ.]—the eldest of whom is a 14-year-old girl, a senior in junior high school this year.[80]

Since I came to Cairo, I have not heard any [new] *ḥawadît* (fantasy-tales), but I hear [factual reports and personal experience narratives and legends] about what happens [to people] every day and everywhere, even while on the bus [as I commute to work]![81]

Galîlah's Narrative Repertoire: Tales and Conversational Narratives (Nontales)

As a household tale teller, rather than a recognized community raconteur, Galîlah's repertoire and narrating skills are modest. In this respect her repertoire is like those of the majority of tale tellers, where fragmentary, incomplete, and distorted texts are common occurrences. These performances of modest quality are the most frequently told and, consequently, more influential on young listeners.

For the narrator, conversational narratives, e.g., "The Changeling,"[82] "Why the Kite Always Attacks the Crow,"[83] and accounts of possession, healing, marriage and divorce, etc., are "neither *ḥawadît* (fantasy-tales) nor *qiṣaṣ* (serious or philosophical 'stories')"; they are simply "things that happened [i.e., facts]."[84] In addition to numerous such accounts (or social reports), Galîlah eventually presented the following folktales:

Résumé 1. The Man Who Threw Himself Off the Minaret[85]

A poor man became sick and tired of life; he jumped off a minaret. He found himself in a different world. They [i.e., people there] told him that he may acquire anything for "prayers on behalf of the Prophet." He found several tents, with several earthenware water bottles[86] in front of them. He chose the largest tent and the prettiest bottle and drank from it. They told him, "That belonged to the king's daughter; if you marry her you may not ask any questions about anything you see here." He agreed. They got married; but he could not stay home. Each time he went out he saw a strange thing: the first time he saw a man picking ripe and unripe watermelons off their vine. He could not resist. "Why don't you wait for the little one to ripen?" When he went home, the king's daughter said to him, "I have been divorced from you!" He begged and they gave him a second chance. Still he went out. He saw something (I do not remember now what it was); he asked about it and his wife became divorced. Still he begged and got another chance. The third time he saw people on opposite sides of the riverbanks, pulling a houseboat towards themselves—in opposite directions. He could not resist and still he asked. They told him, "This is the third and final time!" They explained: "The first was the angel of death harvesting lives—young and old must go; the second was something similar to that; the third was the world: everyone wants it, but no one gets it." He was cast out and lived in regret.

Résumé 2. The Ostrich of the Sultan's Son (Type 898. For the full text, see Tale No. 14)

Résumé 3. The Girl Whose Father Had Only Her and His Two Men-sons[87]

A man had one daughter and two sons. He said the girl should not stay with her male brothers; she should stay in a house by herself so that she may watch over workers and slaves [as they worked]. She was very good to poor people. There was a poor man who used to come to see her; she would give him "whatever to drink." One day he came but the outside gate was closed. He climbed over the fence and went to her. (She was predestined [to be] for him.) As he was getting down from that thing (i.e., climbing down the gate)—she had not told him there was a well (a fountain in the garden)—he fell in it. She went to help him get out but she too fell in. A slave told her father [i.e., slandered her]. The man [the father] almost went crazy [with rage]. He went to her brothers and said to them, "You must take her to the hills and kill her [for she has committed fornication]!" They had compassion for her and let her loose. She went around begging. Our friend who used to come and beg from her found a treasure and bought himself an estate. She met him; he recognized her but she did not recognize him. He told her his story. In order that he might "correct his mistake," he married her. She bore him three sons. The children grew up and whenever they went out to play, the other children would twit them saying, "You have no family (no maternal-uncle, I mean)." She said to the man [i.e., told her husband] to go bring [i.e., steal] things from her father's. When her brothers came looking for these things, she said to her children, "Go get those people here by any means." She greeted them with drinks [i.e., offered them tea or coffee] and sat with them with her face masked. She told them her story. They recognized the story to be their own. She revealed her identity and sent for her husband and said, "This is him." They cried and she cried, and kept on crying. They went to their father and told him the story. Her father, mother, and her maternal-uncles all came. And of course all the neighbors knew the truth.

They lived in stability and prosperity and begot boys and girls.

Résumé 4. The Green Sparrow[88]

There is a tale about a boy and his sister. His stepmother killed him and cooked him. His sister buried his bones. (I don't remember it well), but he became a green sparrow and would chant:

> I am the green sparrow, the green.
> I walk on top of the wall with a waggle, with a waggle.
> My stepmother slaughtered me, slaughtered me.
> And my father . . . [the pimp] ate my flesh, ate my flesh.
> And my dear sister gathered my bones, my bones.
> And my dear sister buried my bones.

He put needles in his father's mouth and his father died; and did the same with his stepmother.

The tale ends with that.

Résumé 5. The King Who Had Three Daughters[89]

A king had three daughters. The elder two flattered him. He became angry at the youngest daughter for claiming that it is God who is the cause of her prosperity, not her father. At the suggestion of her elder sisters the father gave her away to a beggar. She forced him to work—(by getting a soft twig and beating him up whenever he stayed home, or would not work). [Also] eventually she discovered a pot of gold in their hut. The father became poor and roamed the world with her brother.[90]

She recognized them, disguised herself in man's clothing and invited them. After dinner she told them a story. The father recognized the story to be that of his daughter and expressed his sorrow. She revealed her identity and gave the father money to restore his kingdom. And they lived in stability and prosperity.

Résumé 6. The Three Sisters, or Khushayshbân [Woody][91]

A man and a woman begot three girls and died. The elder sister took over, and she would divide household work among them. One day the youngest went out to get matches from their neighbor woman [(actually an ogress)]. She saw that the neighbor was cooking meat in a pot on the stove. The youngest girl ate the meat and pushed the neighbor's little son into the pot and left. The boy's mother came looking for him and found him in the pot; she lost her mind [i.e., became outraged]. She bought some chewing gum, needles and thread and went around saying [to the girls], "Have some [of my goods and in return] tell me about your troubles and sorrows since the day your mother died." Everyone would tell her, "I haven't got any" until she met that girl. The girl told her about pushing her son in the pot. She took the girl with her to her home [under the pretense of giving her some gum]. She left her with her [other] son and went away to get the butcher's knife so as to slaughter her. The girl bribed the son with a piece of gum and escaped. She disguised herself as a man in a wooden costume and worked as a herder for the king's geese. Every day she would kill a goose and eat it. The king's son wondered why the geese were quacking so loudly. One day he hid in a tree and saw her take off her wooden cover and bathe in the fountain. The geese quacked, "fair-complected and stout, fit for the one with the big turban." The king's son ordered that the gardener [i.e., the goose-herd] bring him his meal to his room. She claimed not to have the dexterity but is finally forced to do so. The king's son forced her to take off her covering. They got married.

Résumé 7. The Girl, Her Brother and Their Mother's Cow[92]

A man and a woman had a girl and a boy (daughter and son); the mother died. Their father married another woman who had an ugly daughter. Before their mother died she left them a cow. The stepmother hit them constantly and gave them no food, while giving her own daughter no work and the best food. She also forced them to sleep in the zareba (cattle enclosure). The girl and her brother used to weep every night; the cow talked to them and gave them good food to eat. They grew fatter [i.e., healthy and pretty], while the stepmother's own daughter remained meager. The stepmother sent her daughter to spy on the children; they let her share their food but she betrayed them. The stepmother feigned illness and agreed with a man (to pretend to be a doctor and) say, "Only the liver of the cow will cure her." The father of the children agreed to have it slaughtered, but it could not be slaughtered until the girl said to her [it], "My cow, get slaughtered." Then the cow would not cook until the girl said to it, "Get cooked." When the others began to eat its meat it was bitter in their mouths, but sweet in the mouths of the girl and her brother. The girl took the bones of the cow, for the cow had told her to do so, and buried them. A good tree with all sorts of fruits grew out of the spot, and they ate from it.

That is all. And they lived in stability and prosperity.

Résumé 8. The Cow [Statue] (Type 510B. For the full text, see Tale No. 10)

Résumé 9. The [Miserly] Husband and the Leg of Lamb[93]

A miser had a lamb. He would not buy any meat for his wife. Whenever she asked him to slaughter it for them to eat he would say, "Not until parsley has grown out of its ear."[94] Upon the recommendation of a neighbor woman, she stuck parsley ([fat]) inside the ear [rear] of the lamb. Thus, the husband could not avoid slaughtering it. The wife gave the neighbor woman a leg as reward. The husband demanded to know where the leg went and the wife insisted that the animal had only three. He left home and roamed around. He took the king's newborn son out of the crib, put himself in its stead, and pretended to be the baby. The nurse took him to her home. His wife visited with the nurse and revealed the trick. The king had him executed.

Résumé 10. The Girl and Her Father's Wife[95]

A man was married to a woman. They had a daughter. The woman died. At the suggestion and insistence of the daughter, the father married a neighbor woman, who herself happened to have one daughter. The stepmother mistreated her husband's daughter. In order to get rid of her, she sent her to the ogress to borrow a sieve. On her way the stepdaughter saw a rose, a jasmine, a palm tree, and a crow who were thirsty; she was kind to them and each conferred upon her his or her own attribute in the right place: rosy cheeks and lips, jasmine-white skin, raven-black eyes and hair, and palm-tree-length hair. She was also kind and obedient to the ogress and was rewarded with lavish gifts of money, garb, and other valuables. The king's son saw her and wanted to marry her. The jealous stepmother sent her own daughter. She was unkind to the same objects and creatures, and received their attributes but in the wrong place: red eyes, white hair, black face, and palm-tree-length legs. At the ogress's she was unkind and disobedient. She was punished by being covered with filth, scorpions, and other creepers.

The king's son asked the girl's father for her hand. On the wedding day the stepmother imprisoned her and put her own daughter in her place. A cat—which the heroine had—went at the head of the marriage procession shouting, "Moon-face is in the storeroom; crow-face is in the howdah!" People took notice. The king's son checked the matter and the deception was discovered. The heroine was rescued, and her stepsister and her mother were killed.

Résumé 11. Truth and Falsehood[96]

Truth and Falsehood are brothers; they were going together in the street. Falsehood was riding a donkey while Truth was walking—(No! It was Truth that was riding and Falsehood that was walking). The donkey belonged to Truth. Falsehood said

to Truth, "Let me ride for a while." Truth dismounted, and Falsehood mounted. Falsehood would not let Truth ride anymore and said, "Let us ask people as to who should ride?" People replied, "Falsehood should ride and Truth should get out of town (the country)."
(This story is just like what happened to my father [with his brother]).

Résumé 12. The Kite and the Crow[97]

People sent the kite to God to request that He return the dead to life after three days. The crow met the kite; he offered to take the message himself. The crow told God, "People say, 'Don't bring back whoever dies, ever!' " God granted people their wish. That is why kite and crow are enemies.

Résumé 13. If the Sultan Were to Marry Me, I'd Do Such-and-such for Him[98]

There were three girls, sisters. Each one of them was saying, "If the sultan were to marry me . . . " (I don't remember exactly how it went, but) only the youngest of them was able to beget for the sultan a girl and a boy. The children's hair [was] of gold and silver; when the girl cried, it would rain, and when she smiled, the sun would shine. Their maternal-aunts threw them in the river and put a cat and a dog in their place.
(But God did not forget them. They grew up together and did many good things. At the end, the girl and her brother found their mother and father).

(It is a very long tale, but I don't remember how it went).

Résumé 14. The Girl Who Fed Her Brother the Egg, While She Ate the Shell[99]

Woman begot boy and girl in answer to prayer. Before dying, she asked the girl to care for the boy. The sister cared for her brother: she would boil an egg, feed him the inside and eat the shell herself. When he showed maturity, she handed him their parents' wealth, and advised him: "Do not get married except when I marry you [off]." But he married without her consent.

The brother's wife pretended to like the sister. She, however, tried to set her husband against his sister by accusing her falsely of many misdeeds. The brother always forgave his sister. The brother's wife starved the sister, and then fed her an omelet made with pregnancy eggs. The sister's stomach started rising.

As the brother was once beating his wife; she taunted him with his pregnant sister. To test his wife's claim, he asked his sister to pour water for him; she got dizzy and the pitcher fell; he touches her stomach (supposedly accidentally) and realized it was quite high. He took her to the hills to kill her, but couldn't do so; he abandoned her and returned home.

Jinn, upon hearing her sad story, built her a palace surrounded by a garden. One day she sneezed: out of her nostrils came two pigeons. The birds flew to their *khâl* (maternal-uncle) and harassed his wife. She cursed them; they retorted.

The brother overheard the exchange and followed the birds. The sister masked as man and invited him in, and—as the host—provided a story to entertain the guest. He learned the truth: he rushed to her hands, kissing them and crying, "Forgive me! For I have made a grave mistake." They hugged each other and kept on crying together.

He went back home and killed his wife by setting her on fire (assisted by the community). Jinn transferred the sister's palace to the site of the old home; she and her brother lived in it.

And they lived in stability and prosperity and begot boys and girls.

General Remarks on Galîlah's Life Accounts and Tale Repertoire

As mentioned above, Galîlah's repertoire and narrating skills are modest. It will be noted that the overall pattern of sentiments expressed in her portrayal of her own life, and those expressed in her tales are congruent with the Brother-Sister Syndrome theory. It may also be noted that, in the texts she was not able to recall in full (Résumé 4, Type 720, and Résumé 13, Type 707), the components dealing with "brother and sister" were clearly remembered. The assumption in this respect is that the retention of these themes is due to such psychological factors as her ego-involvement, or the cognitive salience that characterizes these themes in her life space, or to both factors since they are mutually interdependent.[100]

Attempting to ascertain the sentiments and attitudes embedded in a verbal account, real or fictitious, is not an easy task. Human feelings expressed verbally are too intricate to lend themselves readily and consistently to reduction by an external observer to a single adjective (positive, negative, neutral, mixed, ambivalent, etc.). For example, the refusal of Galîlah's elder brother (Ḥ.) to marry his father's brother's daughter due to the fact he felt she is just like a sister, cannot be readily characterized as positive, negative, or mixed. Likewise, assessing the intensity of the feeling component and the variations in that intensity would require intricate psychological testing and measurement procedures that lie beyond the scope of the current research.[101] It may be concluded that the various components of the Brother-Sister Syndrome are present in Galîlah's life, and in her performed verbal lore—both being aspects of her cognitive behavior.

The following table (see p. 50) diagrams in a general manner the overall uniformity between the sentiments expressed in the young woman's real life and those expressed in the tales she habitually tells. The same conclusion had been reached several years earlier with reference to a mature novelist's description of his own life, and tales he had heard during his childhood.[102] There are, however, two notable exceptions in the present case. The first is Galîlah's relationship with her younger sister (W.); from Galîlah's descriptions, this sister-sister relationship seems to be free from overt hostilities. This may be due in part to the fact that they have been living and working apart since childhood (Galîlah was nine, and W. would have been seven). The second exception is that, in spite of Galîlah's open resentment toward her father, there seem to be no negative overt feelings between daughter and mother. This may also be attributed to Galîlah's absence from the family circle, except when she visited during weekends. Nonetheless, in a number of situations Galîlah expressed the view that her mother was as "helpless" as she herself was in bringing about any significant change in her husband (Galîlah's father), especially with reference to his deferment of the consummation of Galîlah's marriage and his lacking of gainful employment.

Sentiments in Narrator's Social Life and in Her Tales
Signs: + =Positive; – =Negative; ± = Mixed; **ø** =Neutral; **?** =Ambivalent

Relation	Personal Feeling		Feeling in Tale	Rés. No.
Brother–Brother	–		–	04
•				
Brother–Sister		+		04
Brother–Sister			+	07
Brother–Sister			+	14
•				
Brothers–Sisters		+		03
•				
Daughter–Father	–		–	03
Daughter–Father			–	08
Daughter–Father			±	05
•				
Daughter/foster–Father/foster			±	02
•				
Father's Brother's Son–Father's Brother's Daughter	+/?			00
•				
Father's Brother–Nephew/Niece	–			00
•				
Father's Sister–Niece	±			00
•				
Mother's Brother–Sister's Child		+		03
Mother's Brother–Sister's Child			+	14
•				
Mother's Brother's Wife–Husband's Sister's Child			–	14
•				
Mother's Sister–Niece	ø		–	13
•				
Mother/Grand–Child/Grand	+			00
•				
Mother (maternal) figure			–	02
•				
Mother/step–Children			–	07
•				
Parents–Children	±		–	04
•				
Sister–Sister	±/ø		–	02
Sister–Sister			–	05

Relation	Personal Feeling	Feeling in Tale	Rés. No.
Sister–Sister		–	13
Sister–Sister		ø	06
•			
Sister/step–Sister/step		–	10
•			
Sister–Brother's Wife	–	–	10
•			
Wife–Husband		–	01
Wife–Husband		–	09
Wife–Husband	±	±	05
Wife–Husband		±/?	03
Wife–Husband		+/?	13
•			
Wife–Husband's Sister		–	02

NOTES

1. Mot. W201.1.1.2§, "Indicator of manliness: powerful manners (being assertive, firm, resolute)"; cf. Mot. P149.0.1§, "Manly woman, or girl (*marah-râgil/'imra'ah rajul*)—resolute, serious, businesslike (no-nonsense gal)."

2. Sing.: *ḥaddûtah;* i.e., *Märchen,* fairy-tale, magic tale.

3. I.e, *mathal,* lit., proverb—a story of wisdom; a philosophical, serious, or didactic narrative; also labeled *qiṣṣah.* The prose fantasy-tale, unlike the ballad and the *sîrah* (epiclike romance), is typically told while sitting down.

4. This situation, where a female narrator *defensively* offers this "story of wisdom" in response to a collector's request for "fantasy tales," may be seen as a display of self-worth (Mot. W164.1.3§, "Display of wisdom [knowledge] as promoter of self-esteem"). A nearly identical occurrence was reported from the Egyptian immigrant community in Brooklyn, N.Y., in 1961 (see H. El-Shamy, "Sailor," pp. 27–34, No. 2). The female narrator of that text (age thirty-seven, and a recent emigree to the United States), stated that she learned the story from an elderly lawyer, a brother of a courtier to King Farouk, whose family is related to hers by marriage (Mot. P3.2§, "Social connections [friends] as indicator of social status"; cf. P3.2.1§, "Name-dropping . . . "; and U90.0.1§, "Some are perceived as credible, others are not. . . . "). She explained that she had left her [(husband's ??)] home "angry" and went to the home of these relatives (Mot. T198.3.1§, "Angered wife . . . "). There, the "fatherlike" host told her the story in a manner that was "something like preaching" (p. 33). It may be presumed that the "preaching" (*wa¿ẓ*) involved the nature of life, the manifest theme of the story, as well as a wife's role as an agent of her own family, implicitly endorsed in the narrative.

5. Since money is scarce while time (required to cover a certain distance) is perceived to be ample, distance is often reckoned in terms of monetary cost. Thus, when asked "How far from here is your home?" Galîlah answered, "A piaster" (i.e., the equivalent of ten cents, or, "Not far"). Cf. Mot. U303.4§, "Distance is relative."

6. Lit.: 'entering;' Mot. T160, "Consummation of marriage"; cf. Mot. T164.2.1§, "Loss of daughter's income (labor) as an obstacle to consummation of marriage."

During a visit to the home of the author by Galîlah's father and younger brother (¿A.), to express their appreciation for a monetary gift and some men's clothing presented to ¿A., the issue of the deferment of her marriage came up. The father expressed reservations that the family needed more time to prepare for the actual wedding (Mot. T132.3§, "Bride's family prepares furnishings, clothing, etc., for bridal residence"). But the fiance (like Galîlah) had been impatient (Mot. T132.3.1.1§, "Groom-to-be becomes impatient of waiting") and had declared that he wanted only his bride "with only the garment she is wearing" (Mot. T101.1.0.1.1§).

As Galîlah's employer, the writer assured the father that no effort would be spared in accommodating Galîlah's commitments to her family after marriage (shorter work hours, fewer days, and so forth); but the father remained unpersuaded. He agreed, however, that the situation was unfair to her (and to her husband-to-be), and added, "*lakîn hiyya maqdûr ¿alaihâ*" (i.e., she can be made to endure the injustice for the time being), Mot. U46.2§, "Ready unfairness, deferred fairness. . . . "

7. Mot. P209.4§, "Sister as provider"; and P209.3§, "Daughter as provider."

8. *khaṭîbî.*

9. Beside her cash stipend of fifteen pounds per month, Galîlah's additional earnings included room and board, surplus food which she took home, clothes, cash gifts on religious and national holidays, and medical care. Her total income (then) exceeded that of a university graduate's staring government stipend. Cf. Mot. P209.2§, "Wife as provider."

10. *nafkhah kaddâbah;* Mot. W165.0.1§, "Improper pride (pomposity)"; W201.1.1.1§, "Indicator of manliness: controlling women"; W165.2§, "Man ashamed of working woman, though her honest earnings support him (or feed family)."

11. Mot. P605§, "Living (sleeping) arrangements within the household."

12. *maṭraḥ:* spot, place, location.

13. Mot. P605.5§, "Brother(s) and sister(s) share sleeping quarters."

14. Mot. T109.3.2§, Temporary residence in bride's parents' home (as means of helping daughter consummate marriage).

15. Mot. P605.2§, "Parents and children share sleeping quarters."

16. Mot. P525.0.2.4.1§, "Demand that terms of set contract (agreement) be changed." The implication here is that another apartment's rent would be too high; whereas apartments with "old" rent are considerably cheaper. The law then did not allow for readjustment of old contracts.

17. I.e., we suffered a reversal of fortunes for the worse; Mot. L405§, "Rich (high) becomes poor (low)."

18. The folk expression "mayor's son" or "mayor's daughter" indicates a person receiving preferential treatment; it may also designate a profligate or wasteful person (cf. Mot. W131, "Profligacy").

19. *dala¿*. Mot. T603.1§, "Pampered son(s)."

20. *¿ammain,* two father's brothers.

21. *khâlain,* two mother's brothers.

22. *¿ammât,* father's sisters.

23. *khâlât,* mother's sisters.

24. It should be noted here that, with reference to paternal and maternal uncles, the speaker is citing a value of "ideal culture": things as they ought (or are presumed) to be (Mot. J6§, "'Ideal culture.' . . . "). This phenomenon characterizes almost all assessments by informants of their own situation as atypical. Thus, they are implicitly stating: "Don't judge by my own case because it is not the rule;" Mot. U1.1§, "Pluralistic exception ('pluralistic ignorance'). . . . "

25. *'i¿mâmî ('a¿mâmî) mish ḥinayyinîn, lakîn 'ikhwâlî ḥinayyinîn khâliṣ*. Mot. S71.2§, "Cruel paternal-uncle (*¿amm*)"; P293.2.0.1§, "Kind *khâl* (mother's brother, maternal-uncle)."

26. Mot. P761.1§, "Division of inheritance causes conflict"; W183§, "Pleasure (rejoicing) at another's misfortune (*shamâtah*)"; W183.1.2§, "Brother pleased with his brother's failure"; cf. J885, "Clever person's defeat pleases inferior [*shamâtah*]."

Cf. Type 613A§, *Who May Remain in Town: Truth or Falsehood?* (See Résumé No. 11, p. 46).

27. Mot. T503.1§, "Complaint about too many children (dependents)."

28. Mot. Q552.18.5§, "Ill-gotten property 'sweeps away' usurper's own."

29. *bint ¿amm,* father's brother's daughter.

30. *bint khâlah:* maternal-cousin. Mot. T105.1§, "Endogamous marriage preferred"; T131.0.2§, "Endogamy. Marriage (only) within the group."

31. Mot. P3.3.4§, "Owning own dwelling (house) as 'status symbol.'"

32. *zayy eḍ-ḍaif:* lit.: "like a guest."

33. I.e., he does not even carry out the formalities of being a courteous host. Cf. Mot. P324.0.2§, "Providing welcome (conversation, entertainment, 'greetings') is host's responsibility."

34. *ziyarât:* lit.: "visits"; i.e., presents born by the visitor, usually edibles from village crops or cuisine.

35. *mâ-shufnâsh wishshuhom:* an unfriendly mode of expressing the idea of "not seen."

36. *¿ammah,* father's sister.

37. *bi-wishshain,* lit.: "with two faces," i.e., a hypocrite. Mot. W171, "Two-facedness"; P264.1§, "Bad relations between wife and husband's sister."

38. Mot. P253.13.2§, "A caring sister between her two feuding brothers"; P7.1§, "Role strain (role conflict) . . . "; P294.0.1.2.2.1§, "Paternal-aunt reserved (cool) toward her brother's daughter: thinks niece is allied with her own mother (i.e., the wife of the aunt's brother)."

39. *yeghîr ¿alaihâ:* i.e., feel jealousy when she is seen or approached by another man—a requirement of maintaining one's sexual honor as a man; cf. Mot. P253.1.1§, "Brother as guardian of his sister's chastity (sexual honor)."

40. *yeghîro min ba¿ḍ;* Mot. W181, "Jealousy"; W195, "Envy."

41. *tishîl fî nafsahâ:* i.e., suppresses feelings of resentment vis-à-vis the sister.

42. In spite of this positive self-concept, the eldest brother, as indicated in the next paragraph, seems to harbor feelings of resentment toward the youngest's college education. Cf. Mot. W195.6§, "Social status (influence, authority) envied."

43. *ḥinayyin ¿alâ,* lit.: tender toward.

44. This financial commitment on the part of a wife toward her family generates resentment in her husband toward her and her family; Mot. T277.3.1§, " 'A woman would ruin her husband's home in order to make her father's prosper.' " See El-Shamy, *Folktales of Egypt,* No. 41, esp. pp. 176–77.

45. Mot. cf. W155.0.1§, "Apathy (social insensitiveness, indifference to the plight of others)."

46. Mot. P502.2.1.1.1§, "Promise: free education for all: 'like water and air' ('Ṭâhâ Ḥusain's Policy')"; P752.5§, "Social class strife (conflict)"; P752.5.2§, "Educating the lower social classes (through free education) criticized."

47. Galîlah stated in a different context that she had heard from a cleric in the village that "The Prophet said: 'He who teaches [an illiterate] person, even a slave, reading and writing would enter paradise.' " Mot. Q50.1§, "Reward for teaching the nonliterate how to read and write"; Q172, "Reward: admission to heaven."

48. "*yâ ¿ammî*" i.e., 'father's brother.'

49. Aversion to cousin-marriage (*'ibn-¿amm and bint ¿amm*); Mot. T416.5§, "Aversion to cousin-marriage: incestlike. Cousin (paternal or maternal) refuses marriage to cousin."

50. *'itgawwiz-linâ el-¿aqrabah di:* lit.: 'He married for us that scorpion;' cf. Mot. P262.1.1§, " 'A mother-in-law is a fever, a husband's sister is a deadly scorpion,' " expressing from a wife's perspective the same negative attitude toward a husband's sister.

51. *ṭarḥah;* Mot. K1305.2§, "Man is deceived into marrying an ugly woman: the veiled (bashful) female."

52. *'aksar nifsohom:* lit.: 'breaking their spirit;' i.e., disappoint them in a humiliating manner. Mot. W10.3.3§, "Poor arrangement (deal) tolerated so as not to injure pride of the other party"; cf. W164.2§, "Injured pride."

53. *'ib¿id ¿annak.* Mot. Z13.9.1§, "Speaker wards off evil effects of own speech (words)."

54. *mezaffitah:* lit.: 'tarred'; i.e., 'like tar.'

55. I.e., disappear.

56. *yiz¿alû ma¿a ba¿ḍ:* i.e., have a falling-out.

57. *yîgî el-'awwall:* lit.: would come first. Cf. Mot. P7.1§, "Role strain (role conflict) . . . "; P211.0.1§, "Wife chooses her brother's side in feud"; and P253.3.1§, "Sister favors brother over her husband."

58. *el-goaz mawgûd, we-l-'ibn mawlûd, we-l-'akhkh mafqûd;* Mot. P253.3, "Brother chosen rather than husband or son.' See Tale No. 45.

59. Mot. P725.8.3§, "Weak neighborly ties in the big city"; P305.6§, "Weak relations between neighbors."

60. Mot. P410.1§, "Unskilled laborer."

61. Mot. P210.1§, "Wife's own property."

62. *khiṣlah.*

63. Cf. Mot. W111.4.1§, "Wife punishes (beats, refuses to feed) lazy husband."

64. Mot. T198.3.4§, "Unhappy (angered) husband leaves marital ('his') home." This is the reverse of the prevailing social pattern: it is the wife who typically goes to her family's home when she is *za¿lânah/ghaḍbânah* (angry); evidently, the situation in this account is an outcome of the wife's economic independence (cf. Mot. P209.2§, "Wife as provider").

65. Mot. J706, "Acquisition of wealth"; J707.1§, "Property preferred to marital amity (peace in marriage)"; J708.2§, "Acquisition of property (real estate) leads to wealth."

66. *"¿alayya ṣaff 'asyâd":* i.e., I'm ridden by several *zâr*-spirits, related to one another. Mot. F381.0.4§, "Possession by a clique of jinn (*ṣaff 'asyâd*)."

67. *'anâ gittitî mish-khâlṣah:* i.e., my body is occupied by jinn; I am not responsible for what may happen. Mot. F385.2.4§, "Possessing *zâr*-jinn placated by appeasing (mollifying) person whom they possess"; cf. K2092§, "Spirit possession feigned in order to gain pity (sympathy)."

68. Mot. T205.1§, "Wife-beating"; T277.1§, "Husband robs (steals from) his wife."

69. *yigîb we yuḥuṭ ¿alaik;* Mot. M440.2.1§, "'May He bring [calamities] and heap [them] upon . . . [someone].'"

70. As a female's given name, Ẓarîfah (i.e., Cutie) is uncommon; cf. informant note to Tale No. 7–1. It carries humorous links to a male and female pair of comic characters: Zaqzûq *wi* Ẓarîfah (i.e., Slippery and Cutie, Messy and Neat, or the like); they constitute marital disharmony, an odd couple, or two stooges (Mot. Z130.1.1§, "Marital disharmony personified—the odd couple").

In supernatural practices, as in the case of the present curse (Mot. M411.20.2§, "Curse by wife"), identification by maternal descent is required for effectiveness (Mot. T149.1§, "Mother's name required for supernatural . . . ritual)."

71. *'iggawwiz ¿alaihâ.* Cf. Mot. P529.0.3§, "Man entitled to more than one wife at a time."

72. Also known as "The Three Girls of Whom One Inherited a Hen That Laid Golden Eggs," "*Sit* Ṭaṭar," and "The Ogre's Daughter;" (Type 898). See full text, Tale No. 14.

73. On "operant" and "informant" motivations, see Introduction, note 11.

These variations in presenting the same data (to a collector, in the present situation) may be viewed as a product of the "adaptation level," or the influence of the frame of reference upon perceiving an object such as, in the present case, the narrator's judgment of certain words as obscene (Mot. U300§, "Relativity of perception: 'adaptation level' [judgment depends on circumstances, objects of comparison, frame of reference]"; U304§, "Relativity of perceiving quality"). For a similar situation involving adaptation level, see Tale No. 25, note 507.

For additional information on this perceptual phenomenon, and the "Adaptation-Level Theory" advanced by psychologist Harry Helson as it applies to the study of lore, see El-Shamy, *Brother and Sister: Type 872**, pp. 83–84, note 32.

Also see Harry Helson "Adaptation Level Theory," in Sigmund Koch, ed., *Psychology: A Study of a Science,* Vol. I, *Sensory, Perceptual, and Physiological Formulations* (New York, 1959), pp. 565–621; see also H. Helson, "Current Trends and Issues in Adaptation-Level Theory," in Gerald M. Murch, ed., *Studies in Perception* (Indianapolis, 1976), pp. 219–36.

74. *qullah* (f.): porous pottery water bottle, cooler; Mot. Z139.9.3.2§, "Water jug (jar, bottle, inkwell)—female (vagina, womb)." See Tale No. 14, notes 316–17.

75. *'abrîq/'ibrîq:* pottery water pitcher, with a spout; Mot. Z186.5§, "Symbolism: pitcher's spout—penis." See "multiplexity of cognitive connotations," section I, note 21.

76. *yiṭla¿ mît marrah, wi zyâdah,* lit.: "[If I were to count, the result] would turn out to be a hundred"; idiomatic for "far too many times to remember exactly how many." Mot. Z93§, "Formulas of numbers [i.e., denoting numbers]."

77. The *maṣṭabah*-[porch] (to be differentiated from the funerary 'mastabah') is a folk architectural feature comparable to a house's front porch in size and function. A platform that ranges from one to three feet in height, it is built of adobe at the street-side entrance of a country-style house. It is used for sitting and for social gatherings, *with the house door open;* thus these social activities take place in the lane or narrow street and constitute an invitation to passersby to join. Cf. Mot. Z70.5.1§, "Mastabahs-talk (relaxed, informal, careless, not binding, etc.—like that uttered while sitting on a mastabah-porch)"; P3.3.4.2§, "Living in house with 'open door' as indicator of social status"; P610§, "Homosociality: social relations between persons of the same sex"; P320, "Hospitality"; U315.1§, "Seeking a conversation (social interaction)"; P790.0.1.1§, "Having a conversation (interesting social talk)." Cf. "closed door" in Tale No. 1, note 11. Also cf. "relaxed atmosphere," in note 16, p. 21, above.

78. "*yallâ nitḥaddit/nataḥaddath* (lit.: Let us converse), or *ta¿âlu nuq¿ud nitkallim* (Let us sit and talk)"; Mot. P790.0.1.2§, "Invitation to have conversation."

79. When asked, "How different?" Galîlah replied, "I do not know; but they are different." She then cited the first tale as an example of "men's stories," and added, "I had not told it to anyone before telling it to you [in 1968]." (See Résumé No. 1).

On the generic traits of these narrative categories, see "Classifications of Traditions," *Folktales of Egypt*, pp. xliv–xlvi; also cf. Appendix, p. 511.

80. *f-el-'i¿dâdiyyah:* i.e., preparing for the middle/junior high school national examination.

81. Cf. "conversational narratives" in note 340, informant note to Tale No. 15.

82. Mot. F321.1, "Changeling. . . . " For the full text, see El-Shamy, *Folktales of Egypt*, No. 43.

83. Actually, a folk belief accounting in a narrative manner for the origins of death; see Résumé No. 12.

84. These accounts may be characterized as belonging to the genre of belief legends. See "*kalâm* (talk or chatter)" as a category of narratives in El-Shamy, *Folktales of Egypt*, pp. xliv–xlvi. Also see "other [sorts of] stories" in informant note to Tale No. 15.

85. Type 470C§/801A§, *Man in Utopian Otherworld Cannot Resist Interfering: He Is Expelled.* ("It Serves Me Right!"). Mot. P215§, "At her husband's home, wife is viewed as representative of her own blood relations (father)"; S57§, "Husband cast out of wife's home by his in-laws"; T198.2§, "Man returns to parents' home after end of his marriage"; cf. T197§, "Wife's relatives (father, brother, etc.) force her divorce from husband without her consent."

86. *qulal*, pl. of *qullah;* Mot. Z139.9.3§, Pot (jar, water bottle) as symbol of female—(general); and Z139.9.3.2§, Water jug (jar, bottle, inkwell)— female (vagina, womb).

87. Type 883A, *The Innocent Slandered Maiden.*

88. Type 720, *My Mother Slew Me; My Father Ate Me. The Juniper Tree.*

89. Type 923B, *The Princess Who Was Responsible for Her Own Fortune;* 986, *The Lazy Husband.*

90. The inclusion of a brother in this tale is atypical and seems to be an error on the part of the narrator. This theme typically occurs in Type 883A (Résumé No. 3), where brothers act as compassionate executioners.

91. Type 327G, *The Boy at the Devil's (Witch's) House.* The daughters are to cook him, but are killed by him; 533A§, *Beautiful Maiden in Hideous Disguise.* She is detected by the prince. (Khushayshibûn, Khashabân, Galadânah, Gulaidah, etc.). Cf. 327, *The Children and the Ogre;* 1119, *The Ogre Kills His Own Children.* Places changed in bed (nightcaps).

92. Type 511A, *The Little Red Ox.* [Cow helps orphans (brother and sister.)]

93. Type 1653A*, *Pretended Corpse at Practice Funeral.* [Priest kills pretender]; cf. 1313D§, *Death Feigned to Discover Who Had Consumed the Food. . . .* Mot. K289.1§, "Artificial (deceptive) compliance: 'Wait until fat (parsley) has oozed out of the ram's anus (ear).' "

94. Narrator admitted later that the anecdote, as it is typically told, states, "Not until fat has oozed out of his anus!"

95. Type 480, *The Spinning-Women by the Spring. The Kind and Unkind Girls.*

96. Type 613A§, "*Who May Remain in Town: Truth or Falsehood?*"
On another occasion, the narrator commented on the similarities between the story and her father's experiences with his own brother and his leaving the village.

97. Type 774M1§, *Origin of Death: Bad or Careless Messenger;* cf. 200C§, *Careless Animal (Bird) as Messenger;* Mot. A1335.1.1, "Origin of death: wrong messenger goes to God." For the full text, see El-Shamy, *Folktales of Egypt,* No. 28.

98. Type 707, *The Three Golden Sons* [Castaway Brother(s) and sister reunited with their parents].

99. Designated as Type 872A§, *The Pregnancy of the Virgin Sister by Treachery.* For the full text and analysis of this tale type within the context of "The Brother-Sister Syndrome," see El-Shamy, *Brother and Sister: Type 872*,* pp. 6–8, "Text 0."

100. On the roles of these factors in the processes of learning and retention see "Ego-involvement and the Law of Exercise: Memorization as a Function of Ego-involvement," in H. El-Shamy, "Folkloric Behavior," pp. 160–73; also see "Emotionskomponente," pp. 1391–95.

101. See "valence," in El-Shamy, *Brother and Sister, Type 872*,* pp. 68; 86 n. 60; 61.

102. I.e., N. Maḥfouẓ; see El-Shamy, "The Traditional Structure of Sentiments in Maḥfouẓ's Trilogy . . . ," pp. 68–69; also cf. Introduction, note 2.

III

TALE TEXTS

A. PARENTS AND PATERNAL FIGURES

MOTHER AND CHILDREN

❖ 1 ❖

THE NANNY GOAT WITH THE IRON HORNS[1]

(EGYPT)

NARRATED IN NOVEMBER 1969 BY SAYYIDAH D., A FIFTY-FIVE-YEAR-OLD GRANDMOTHER FROM THE VILLAGE OF AGHÛR AL-KUBRÂ, QALYÛBIYYAH GOVERNORATE, NILE DELTA. "THIS IS A FANTASY-TALE FOR THE LITTLE ONES (*ḤADDÛTAH LI-Ṣ-ṢUGHÂR*). I'VE HEARD IT, SAY, MAYBE ONE HUNDRED TIMES, PERHAPS MORE, WHEN I WAS A LITTLE GIRL; I'VE TOLD IT JUST AS MANY TIMES. THE CHILDREN OF MY SON ¿ABD-EL-Ḥ . . . , OR OF MY DAUGHTERS—WHEN THEY VISIT, WOULD COME TO ME AND SAY, 'GRANDMOTHER, TELL US A TALE!' ONCE IN A WHILE CIRCUMSTANCES WOULD ALLOW, AND I WOULD TELL THEM ONE OR TWO! THEY LIKE THIS TALE VERY MUCH."

The roles of a mother as teacher and protector of her young[2] *are central themes in this tale; she is also the provider, a role* ideally *reserved for the father.*[3] *Typically, the tale depicts a single-parent family headed by a mother; a father for the children—who would also be the husband to the children's mother—has not been reported as part of this narrative as it occurs in the Arab World. However, in most renditions from the Sudan,*[4] *the tale deals with a brother who plays vis-à-vis his sisters the roles played by the mother vis-à-vis her "sons" in the present text.*

The character that swallows the "kids" is most often a wolf—a male figure; less frequently an ogress or other female cannibalistic being is the culprit. The agents who, usually unwittingly, aid the swallower are predominantly adult males (e.g., blacksmiths, masons, builders). Consequently, while the tale presents the mother as a source of affection and security, it indirectly reinforces the notion that a father is aloof and usually absent from his child's daily activities. Thus, a mother perceives her influence as a centripetal force and the father's power as centrifugal. As expressed by our present narrator in another context with reference to her eldest son, "A mother draws in, a father drives out."[5]

Action in the tale takes place within the confines of familiar social and physical settings: encounters with the blacksmith, masons, oil vendor; payment in kind; the pool[6] *and the old cemetery (both sites within the village boundaries), and the dammed mouth of an irrigation ditch (*barbakh*) are all parts of the daily experiences of rural life. Such a familiar environment (or cognitive map) constituting a part of life space*[7] *lends a measure of symbolic realness and credibility to the tale and helps generate a more intense empathetic affect in the young listeners. (See also introductory note to Tale No. 20.)*

The parlance used, especially in performing the rhyme with which the mother goat addresses her kids, is characteristic of the playful, warm, and endearing exchanges that a human mother has in daily life with her children. The effect of using the diminutive feminine-plural form—e.g., bizâzâtî *(my little boobies), and* qurûnâtî *(my little hornies)—parallels the use of the diminutive form in the English language (e.g., birdie, doggie, piggie); though grammatically incorrect, it is a pleasantry that denotes endearment and is typical of "women's parlance," and "parlance of the little ones" (baby talk).*[8] *Adult males refrain from using such speech, especially in the presence of strangers.*

It is significant to observe that in spite of the absence of a father, and negative sentiments toward adult male figures, no Oedipal tendencies are detected in this tale. The reunion is always between the mother and all her sons. A reunion between the mother and only one son, without the other siblings, does not occur. (Cf. introductory note to Tale No. 1–2, where the brother-sister(s) reunion seems exclusive.)

ONCE there was a nanny goat who had three little billy-goats; the eldest was Ḥâz, the middle Bâz, and the youngest Yiḍrab bi-l-¿Ukkâz.[9] Every day she would go out to the fields in order to get food for them, and she would leave them at home. When she would return she would say (calling aloud, in chant):

> Open for me, O my kiddi-i-i-es:
> milk is in my boobi-i-i-es [i.e., little udders],
> and grass is on my horni-i-i-es![10]

When the little kids would hear her say that, they would be flying for joy (*ṭâyrîn mi-l-faraḥ*). They would open the door and their mother would get in; they would eat, drink, and thank the Lord. [They lived in this manner]: their door is closed after them, and they do not interact much with others,[11] thus they were living peacefully.

One day a wolf came and saw the mother leaving and her young ones following her. She pushed them into the house and said to them, "Wait, don't open the door to anyone!" He stayed there waiting to see what will happen and [thinking out-loud]: "Maybe, one of these baby-goats will come out, so that I would eat him." But the day passed and their mother came. He heard her say what she had been saying:

> Open for me, O my kiddi-i-i-es:
> milk is in my boobi-i-i-es,
> and grass is on my horni-i-i-es!

Then the door was opened and the little goats jumped up and down for joy. He stayed there in ambush until the morning. After their mother had left, he went to the door and knocked.

"Who i-i-is it?"

[The wolf answered in a husky voice]:

> Open for me, O my kiddi-i-i-es:
> milk is in my boobi-i-i-es,
> and grass is on my horni-i-i-es!

When the little kids heard that, they jumped up and down for joy and ran to the door to open it. The youngest one—Yiḍrab bi-l-¿Ukkâz (the one who strikes-with-the-staff)—was clever, but the other two were naive and did not understand; he said to them [in a warning voice], "Wait! This is not the time our mother returns. This is not her voice. This [voice is] too husky." So they replied, "No! You are not our mother! Our mother's voice is not coarse like this [voice of yours]!"

The wolf went away. He thought, "Boy, how can you make your voice nice? Boy, how can you make your voice sound nice?" So, he went to the blacksmith; he took with him a few eggs and two, maybe three ears of corn [to pay the fee], and said to the blacksmith, "I want you to make my voice sound like that of the bleating of a nanny goat." The blacksmith said to him, "All right!" and took the stuff that the wolf had brought him for a fee. He said to the wolf, "Your tongue is too thick. I'll file it for you so that your talk will be light!" He said [with relief], "That is my hope!" The blacksmith got his file [Narrator imitates the movement of a hand using a file and applying pressure]: file! file! file! until the wolf's tongue became thin and light and sweet.[12]

He went running to the house of the kids and their mother. He waited until she left and shouted, [Narrator depicts the wolf's attempt to imitate a female's voice]:

Open for me, O my kiddi-i-i-es:
milk is in my boobi-i-i-es,
and grass is on my horni-i-i-es!

When the little kids heard their mother's voice they were very happy. They ra-a-a-a-an to the door to open it, but Yiḍrab bi-l-¿Ukkâz yelled at them, "Wait, you idiots! Our mother has just left. Look through the gap underneath the door and see who it is!" They looked through the gap underneath the door and saw the feet of the wolf. Yiḍrab bi-l-¿Ukkâz said to him,

"You are not our mother!"

"I am your mother! Even look for yourself. I have milk in my udders and grass on my horns for you."

Yiḍrab bi-l-¿Ukkâz said, "No, your legs are black, our mother's legs are white!"

The wolf went to some masons building a house; they had lots of lime piled up in the place where they were working. He waited until they were busy and bounced into the lime. The lime stuck to his hands and legs [i.e., four paws] and they became white. He went to the kids while their mother was away. He yelled [in a feminine voice]:

Open for me, O my kiddi-i-i-es:
milk is in my boobi-i-i-es,
and grass is on my horni-i-i-es!

When the little kids heard this, they thought it was their mother's voice and they were very happy. They ran to the door to open it, but Yiḍrab bi-l-¿Ukkâz yelled at them, "Wait, you [stupid] donkeys! Our mother has just left. Look through the gap underneath the door and see who it is."

They said, "It is our mother; her legs are white!"

He said, "Wait, don't open the door. Look through. . . . " Before he could finish what he was about to say Ḥâz and Bâz opened the door! The wolf [Narrator speaks with excitement] leaped in and caught Ḥâz. In one gulp he swallowed him whole,[13] and in one gulp swallowed Bâz whole. But when he came to swallow Yiḍrab bi-l-¿Ukkâz, he ran into the oven. [As the wolf chased after him] he would enter through the fire chamber (*miḥmah*)[14] and would get out through the baking chamber (*sharûqah*),[15] he would enter through the fire chamber and would get out through the baking chamber, he would enter through the fire chamber and would get out the baking chamber, until the wolf got tired of chasing him. Finally, when the wolf got very tired and became breathless, and it was time for their mother to return, he left. Yiḍrab bi-l-¿Ukkâz remained hidden inside the oven.

A while later their mother came and said:

> Open for me, O my kiddi-i-i-es:
> milk is in my boobi-i-i-es,
> and grass is on my horni-i-i-es!

Yiḍrab bi-l-¿Ukkâz got out and opened the door for her. She asked him [with considerable anguish], "Where are your brothers?"

"O mother, the wolf came and swallowed them whole. I told them not to open the door but they did not listen to me!"

When she heard this, she said to him, to her youngest son, "You stay here. Don't open the door to anyone!" She went to look for the wolf and for her children. She met an oil vendor (*zayyât*); she said to him:

> O paternal-uncle, oil-man,
> haven't you seen a wolf who passed by and got away,
> with seven kids in his [big] potbelly?[16]

He answered her, "No, lady, I have not seen him!"

Then she came to some men, brick-[making] men (*ṭawwâbîn*), who were mixing adobe; she said to them:

> O paternal-uncle[s], you and him, brick-[making] men,
> haven't you seen a wolf who passed by and got away,
> with seven kids in his [big] potbelly?

They answered her, "No, lady, we have not seen him!"

She asked many [persons], but every one would say, "No, lady, I have not seen him!"

Finally, she went to the cemetery where wolves live—to the old cemetery. It was getting to be nighttime. She knocked at the first tomb. She heard something saying [in a scraping, husky, threatening voice],

> Who is that who is knocking at my tomb,
> while I am snatching away at my piece of meat!!?[17]

She said [with determination], "It is I: Mother-of-Ḥâz, Bâz, and Yiḍrab bi-l-¿Ukkâz! Come out and bring my children back to me!"

He [the wolf inside] said, "Lady, I have a dead chicken. I have not seen your children!"

She went to the next tomb. She knocked on it and she heard something say [in a scraping, husky, and threatening voice]:

> Who is that who is knocking at my tomb,
> while I am snatching away at my piece of meat!!

She said, "It is I: Mother-of-Ḥâz, Bâz, and Yiḍrab bi-l-¿Ukkâz! Come out and bring my children back to me!"

He [the wolf] said, "Lady, I have a dead field-rat. I have not seen your children!"

She went to the next tomb. She knocked and heard something saying [in a scraping, husky, but muzzled voice issuing through a mouth full of food and a bloated belly]:

> Who is that who is knocking at my tomb,
> while I am snatching away at my piece of meat!!

She said, "It is I: Mother-of-Ḥâz, Bâz, and Yiḍrab bi-l-¿Ukkâz. Come out and bring my children back to me!"

He [the wolf] said, "No! And if you don't go away, I am going to eat you too!"

She said to him, "Come! Let us have a wrestling contest (*khushsh-lî bâṭ*),[18] if you win, you eat me up; but, if I win, you give me back my children!"

He said [asked], "Over what are we going to have the [wrestling] contest?"

She said, "Let us see who of us can drink the *nash¿*[-pool] dry."

They went to the *nash¿*[-pool]. He was parched (due to all the meat he had gulped down). He kept on drinking and drinking until his belly became like an inflated skin [in which milk is processed into butter]. As for her, she only pretended to be drinking, and would only stick her muzzle into the water and snort. When she saw that he was not able to drink all the water (for she knew that he could not), she said [slyly], "Come! No one can win this [contest]. Let us have a ramming contest!"

The wolf said [in protest], "You have horns, [but I do not]." She replied, "These horns [of mine] are made of dough. You can have horns too. You can make them of mud."

When the wolf heard that he became very happy. He went and got himself some mud, fashioned it into two horns and stuck them on top of his head. She went and got some flour and made some dough. She pasted the dough over her horns to make them longer. The two met. She said to the wolf [slyly]—(Narrator reaches over her head and pretends to be crumbling a cookie), "See, my horns crumble like shortbread would (*zayy el-ghurayyibah*)!"

She backed up, backed up, and backed up [some more]; then she came charging at him. And he [came charging] at her! She aimed her horns at his belly. He rammed her first. His horns crumbled. But when her horns hit his belly, it went "Wû-û-û-sht" [i.e., made the sound of an inflated skin rupturing]. All the water he had drunk came out gushing like that of a dammed mouth of an irrigation ditch (*zayy el-barbakh*). Her children, Ḥâz and Bâz, came out yelling: "Mâ-â-â', mâ-â-â'" [bleating: "B-a-a"]. She took them and went home. They lived in contentment.

That is all. And I was there and just returned.

❖ 1-1 ❖

THE MOTHER-OF-THE-TWO-KIDS[19]

(SAUDI ARABIA)

NARRATED IN THE WINTER OF 1977 BY A MOTHER FROM SAUDI ARABIA WHILE VISITING HER SON, WHO WAS STUDYING IN THE UNITED STATES. THE NARRATOR WAS MIDDLE-AGED, NONLITERATE, AND RESIDED IN DAMMAM. A FEMALE RELATIVE OF THE NARRATOR WROTE DOWN THE TEXT IN ARABIC.

The initial act in this Saudi version of the tale indicates the ease with which a human character may be perceived by a narrator—and consequently, by the listeners—as animal, and vice versa.[20] *Although this text expresses the same set of attitudes present in its Egyptian counterpart, the threat to the nuclear family comes from a female.*

The phrase "to enter upon," which appears in this text, often designates an encounter between a stationary person or character (in a certain mental or physical state) and a moving one whose advent is expected to produce noticeable changes in the stationary person's condition. (Also see pp. 150, 212.)

THERE was a woman named Mother-of-the-two-kids, who had four young children. She used to go out to the pasture lands (prairies: *al-barr*) in order to cut the grass and mow the herbs, then sell these [greens and herbs] in the market and [buy] eggs, butter, and bread that she brought back to her children to eat. She used to instruct them to open the door for no one.

One time a vixen[21] came to them and said, "Open the door for your mother." They replied, "Stick in your tail so that we may see whether it is smooth or rough." She stuck her tail in [through a gap in the door]. They yelled, "Rough! Rough! You are not our mother!" She asked, "What does your mother do [to make her tail smooth]?" They answered, "She shampoos her tail with butter and eggs."

The next day the vixen shampooed her tail with butter and eggs and went to them and said, "Open the door for your mother." They asked her to stick her tail in, so she did. They said, "This is our mother because her tail is smooth." [They opened the door.] She entered upon them (*dakhalt ¿alayhum*) and they realized that she was the vixen rather than their mother. One of them hid under the staircase, another hid inside the kohl jar, the third in the oven, and the fourth in the chest. She could only find the one that hid under the staircase. She ate him up and returned to her home.

When the mother [of the kids] returned she found her youngsters sad. She asked them, "What is with you?" They answered, "The vixen came and ate our little brother." So, the mother went and shouted, "Vixen, open up." She replied, "Wait until I've finished eating my little porridge!"

She [the mother] said, "Vixen, open up!"

She replied, "Have patience until I've licked my little pots and pans."

She [the mother] said, "Vixen, open up!"

She replied, "Wait until I've buried [hidden] my little keys."

Then the vixen went out to her. The Mother-of-the-two-kids said to her, "Come on, let us have a wrestling match." Each of the two wore two horns and they wrestled until the Mother-of-the-two-kids slit the belly of the vixen and took her child out of it.

The tale (*ḥikâyah*) has ended.

❖ 1-2 ❖

ZAYNABU, 'OMM-ZMAYYIM, AND THEIR BROTHER

(SUDAN)

NARRATED IN FEBRUARY 1970 BY A HOUSEWIFE AND MOTHER, AGED FORTY-NINE, FROM DONGLA, SUDAN. AS A LITTLE GIRL, SHE HAD HEARD THIS TALE FROM HER GRANDMOTHER (*ḤABBÛBAH*). MISS Z.B., A RELATIVE OF THE NARRATOR, WROTE DOWN THE TEXT IN ARABIC FOR THE PRESENT WRITER.

The present text belongs to a regional subtype (designated as Type 123C§) of the "Wolf and the Kids." In the present variation, children are cared for by a male relative; all available renditions from Sudan designate a brother in this role. (In sub-Saharan Africa, a father is also cited.) Within this narrative context, our tale may be seen as depicting a brother's motherly *functions toward his sister(s). Thus, from a psychological perspective, the narrative belongs to the "Brother and Sister" category (Tales No. 36–47). Yet, except for the theme of a brother as rescuer of his sister(s), the plot is identical to that of the two previous texts depicting the mother as savior of her* male *children.*

The names of the two sisters are commonly cited, as in this skeletal rendition, as the tale's title. Our text is ambiguous on the fate of 'Omm-Zmayyim, the other sister; there is no explicit mention of her joining the reunion of her two siblings. Consequently, it may be argued that she seems to have been dropped out of action, thus allowing for an exclusive reunion between the brother and only one sister. (Cf. introductory note to Tale No. 1, where the mother-children reunion is inclusive.)[22]

A man and his wife begot children, [a boy and two girls]. When they [the children] grew up some, their father and mother died, and left the boy and Zaynabu and 'Omm-Zmayyim without any one to care for them. The brother took the two girls and built a hut on top of a large, tall tree; they lived on top of that tall tree. They got to the hut by means of a rope.

Every morning, he [the brother] would go out to catch something for them to eat, bring back that [game as] food. When at the tree, he would sing a song that they had agreed on, then Zaynabu and 'Omm-Zmayyim (his sisters) would throw down the rope. He would climb up with whatever he had caught that day. One day, an ogre-hyena ("*ghûl-ḍab¿*") saw him doing that, and said, "I will eat these two sisters." He (the ogre) went to the tree [after the brother's departure], and tried to sing the song. His voice was bad and scratchy. He went and sat on an ant-nest; the ants went upward through him, got out via his mouth, [thus clearing his throat]. When he sang this time, Zaynabu and 'Omm-Zmayyim [were deceived and] said, "Our brother came back early." They lowered the rope, and he climbed up and swallowed Zaynabu.

In the evening, their brother came back, and learned of what had happened. He went to the water hole; all animals used to come to drink from that spot (because there was no other place with water). He put all the water in his water skin and hung it on top of a tall tree; he then, [supernaturally], made the tree rise up very high, so as to [place the water skin] out of reach. All animals came to drink—small ones [i.e., young] first—but found no water. He would ask, "Who ate Zaynabu?" The [small] animals would answer, "We are too small [to have been able to do so]; ask the bigger ones." Finally, the hyena-ogre came to drink. He asked the ogre, "Where is Zaynabu?" The ogre answered, "In my belly." The brother waited until the ogre was parched, he then pierced the skin and let the water flow down. The ogre, due to his being very thirsty and [having] a full belly, drank it all; his belly burst and all the people he had inside it [whom he had devoured], came out. Zaynabu came out whole. Her brother finished the ogre off; all the people that came out of the ogre['s belly] stayed on the spot at that water hole and it became a village where people live. He (the brother) took Zaynabu [and returned] home. He became king over the [people of the] village.

After that, people lived safely in the village and prospered.

❖ 2 ❖

THE TWO SISTERS AND THE OGRE'S TREASURE

(SAUDI ARABIA)

NARRATED IN FEBRUARY 1977 BY A LITERATE TWENTY-YEAR-OLD HOUSEWIFE FROM DAMMAM, SAUDI ARABIA, WHILE IN THE UNITED STATES. SHE WAS THE MOTHER OF TWO SMALL CHILDREN AND ACCOMPANIED HER HUSBAND DURING HIS UNIVERSITY STUDIES IN THE UNITED STATES. THE NARRATOR HAD HEARD THE STORY BACK HOME FROM HER MOTHER, AND HAD TOLD IT TO OTHER RELATIVES. SHE HAD NOT YET HAD THE OPPORTUNITY TO TELL TALES TO HER CHILDREN BECAUSE THEY WERE TOO YOUNG. THE NARRATOR WROTE DOWN THE TEXT, AFTER HAVING TOLD IT ORALLY; TYPICALLY, SHE FELT IT WAS IMPROPER TO HAVE HER VOICE TAPE-RECORDED BY A MALE WHO WAS NOT A CLOSE RELATIVE OF HERS.

The following fantasy-tale (sabḥûnah) *was given under the title* "'as-sa¿luww *(The Ogre)"; yet, this character is presented later as a jinni (see this tale, note 28).*

The narrative portrays the negative feelings between two sisters who are also mothers: one is rich while the other is poor. The cruelty of the rich woman toward her less fortunate sister is congruent with the negative role the rich woman plays as a maternal-aunt toward her sister's children.[23] *In both poor and rich households, the role of the husband (the children's father) is marginal and his presence is not required for the continued existence of the family. In the case of the poor mother whose husband has died, the family has persisted; but in the case of the rich woman, her death causes the "collapse" of the family in spite of the fact that her husband is alive.*[24]

This tale represents a female-bound variation of its male-bound counterpart involving two brothers. Perhaps the best known example of the male sibling rivalry in this context is the literary narrative of "Ali Baba and the Forty Thieves" of The Thousand Nights and a Night.[25]

ONE day there were a mother and three children without a father to look after them. This poor family had a maternal-aunt (*khâlah*)[26] who was very rich. She owned a large palace, inside of which there were many children and a father who looked after them. But that maternal-aunt was without feelings [hardhearted]. She did not think of her sister and her children, nor did she ever happen, out of kindness, to grant them some of her great wealth.

Time passed, and that widow raised her children on what people gave them as alms. One day [while] she was asleep, she sensed something in the image of a human being, resembling her [late] husband, saying to her, "I thank you because you cared for my children and did not [cause them to be] dispersed in the streets [as vagabonds]. In return, I will make you comfortable for the rest of your life."

She interrupted him saying, "My beloved husband, never leave us [again]; we need you. Where have you been? And how could you have led us to believe that you had died!"

He interrupted her saying, "I am not your husband, but I am the jinni[27] who killed your husband because I had fallen in love with you and wished that these children were my children. Before killing your husband, I was a jinni. I felt and lived just like a typical human being would. It is because of this that I decided to kill your husband and to take his place because you have taken over my heart and soul and I cannot live without you. But unfortunately for me, after I killed your husband my jinn family took revenge on me, [punished me for my evil deed:] they made me live without [the senses and functions of] touch, hearing, eating, or drinking, and made me [able to] talk only once a year. I beg of you to forgive me [for having] lusted after you and your beauty. If you happen to have forgiven me, you will accept this gift from me that will make you very rich. [The gift is] that you take your children and go to the house of *es-Saȝluww* (the ogre); he is the king of the jinn.[28] It is essential that you go during daytime, for if you were to go during nighttime, he will see you and will devour you. When you get there, the only thing you need to do is to make a [small] cut on one of your fingers; the door [to the house of the ogre] will open, for the door does not open unless it sees blood."

She listened to his [the jinni's] words and after he had disappeared, leaving a trace of smoke in his path, she took her children along and went to the house of the ogre so that she might get the jewels, the camels, the sheep and the cows. When she arrived, she wounded one of her fingers and suddenly the door [swung] open. She saw all the livestock and a special room containing the remains of all the women, children, and men that he had devoured; these were in the form of hanging-down skeletons. When she saw that scene she became fear-stricken, had a violent trembling, and fainted for a brief while. She, however, came to upon hearing her children cry. She hurried up and took all she wanted.

When she reached her home she sent her children to their maternal-uncle [error: i.e., aunt] to [borrow] the gold scale in order to use it [in weighing her find]. But she [the maternal-aunt] ridiculed them and kicked them out. So the mother herself went and told her the whole story. She warned her [sister] against going during nighttime.

The following day her sister went in order to get for herself the same wealth which her [poor] sister had gotten. However, she did not believe her sister, and went during the nighttime. When the ogre saw her, he devoured her and hung her skeleton up [with the others].

[Thus] she left her children behind—[they became] orphans—after having lost her. Luxury and wealth [that they had enjoyed] collapsed due to her greed and not believing her sister.

MOTHER AND SON

3

MOTHER'S LIVER

(EGYPT)

CITED IN JUNE 1970 BY (MRS.) LAṬÎFAH H., AGED FIFTY-FIVE, A LITERATE HOUSEWIFE AND GRANDMOTHER. SHE HAILED FROM A VILLAGE IN THE NILE DELTA BUT HAS LIVED IN CAIRO MOST OF HER ADULT LIFE. SHE ATTENDED ELEMENTARY SCHOOL BUT WAS NOT ALLOWED BY HER CONSERVATIVE FATHER TO FINISH THE FOURTH AND FINAL YEAR, AND HAD HAD TO STAY HOME AWAITING MARRIAGE.

DURING A GATHERING OF FAMILY MEMBERS AND CLOSE NEIGHBORS IN ORDER TO MEDIATE A FAMILY DISPUTE INVOLVING LAṬÎFAH, OUR PRESENT NARRATOR, AND HER ELDER SON'S WIFE, SHE (AS AN OPERANT) ALLUDED TO THE STORY IN A PROVERBIAL MANNER: "DON'T THEY SAY, 'FOR THE SAKE OF HIS WIFE, THE SON ASKED HIS MOTHER TO GIVE HIM HER HEART SO THAT HE MAY GIVE IT TO HER [HIS WIFE], AND SHE CONTENTEDLY GAVE IT TO HIM!'" MOST OF THOSE PRESENT, INCLUDING INDIVIDUALS FROM SOUTHERN EGYPT AND THE SUEZ CANAL AREA, KNEW THE STORY TO WHICH SHE WAS REFERRING. AT A LATER DATE I ASKED LAṬÎFAH TO TELL ME THE STORY. SHE DID NOT REMEMBER FROM WHOM OR WHEN SHE HAD FIRST HEARD IT, BUT ADDED, "THESE ARE THINGS THAT ONE NATURALLY KNOWS. . . . MY MOTHER USED TO MENTION IT OFTEN."

Although all conversational references to the story spoke of "heart," the narrative itself cited "liver." A liver is perceived, especially among women, to be the place of residence for empathy—chiefly in situations that generate acute feelings of pity, compassion, and similar sentiments connected with pain and sorrow.

*This moralistic story (*mathal*)*[29] *is a hyperbolic illustration of a mother's perception of how a married son is expected to behave when he has to choose between his mother and his wife. The narrator added, "'My heart ruptured [from compassion and love] over my son; but over me, my son's heart is rock.'"*[30]

Another female relative responded in an emphatic manner, "Yes! Children forget their fathers and mothers once they are married"; she then elaborated by citing a truism emphasizing the power of sex: "'The one whom he takes under him [in bed] would not be [considered by him] to be like his mother or sister'";[31] *that is, through sex, a wife has more coercive, or coaxing, power. This notion is typically referred to by allusion; sometimes, however, it is illustrated hyperbolically. According to a Saudi tale told by a female, a stepmother wanted her husband to get rid of his children; she adorned her vagina and told her husband: "Choose! Either* 'denaidesh'[32] *or your children!"*

It is worth noting that the son's wife, a university graduate and a career woman, described her husband as "a toy in his mother's hands ('ibn-'ommoh*)."*[33]

THEY say that a woman had a son; she had no one but him. Although she was young and pretty, she [chose to] remain a widow solely for his sake.[34] She raised him, taught him, deprived herself of [essential] things so that he may get what he desired, until he grew up and became a man to be counted among men. When he grew up and became a man—after he had been just a little boy—she searched for a bride for him until she found some girl suitable for him. In short, he married her—that one whom his mother had brought [chosen] for him; and the bride came to their home. His mother received her well and made her lack nothing. She did not let her do any household work and she [the bride] remained being treated and acting ladylike (*misssattitah*),[35] [with] her hand not even coming close to [laundry or dishwashing] water.

But still she [the bride] was not content. She would say to her husband—after his mother would have cooked [the food], prepared [all other things], and done everything—[she would hide the food and say], "Your mother ate it all. She left us nothing!" He went to his mother [and said, sternly], "Why didn't you leave some [food] for us?" She answered him [in an accepting tone], "Never mind (*ma¿lish*), son! Forgive me for I am an old woman [who does not know any better]!" She did not want to say to him, "Your wife is a liar!" or anything else that might ferment troubles (*khamîret-¿aknanah*).[36]

Everyday [matters went on as follows]: "Your mother says, 'Do [such and such]!'" "Your mother says, 'Do [such and such]!'" And, "Your mother says, 'Do [such and such]!' I can't do a thing [on my own]." [Then he would go to his mother and inquire:] "Why, Mother, did you say, 'Do such and such'? Here are [the consequences of your misdirections]: The livestock are dying, and the house is [getting] ruined."

[Then his mother would reply, in a totally accepting tone of voice:] "Your wife is right, son. From now on, I will not speak at all!" And she uttered no word [from that time on].

"Your mother is crowding things up!"

"Mother, why are you crowding things up?"

"Your wife is right, son. She is a bride and needs lots of room (*baḥbaḥah*).[37] I'll sleep in the oven room!"[38]

[Pause] . . .

"Your mother is [still] crowding things up!"

"Mother, you are still crowding things up!"

"Your wife is right, son! I'll sleep on the housetop!"

[Pause] . . .

"And still, your mother is crowding things up!"

"Mother, you are still crowding things up!"

"All right, son. I'll move out of the house. But where to?"

He went to his wife and said to her, "To where should she go?"

She said to him, "Brother, is she going to live through her own lifespan and that of others!?[39] Make her die and give us some rest!"

He went to his mother: "Mother, I am going to make you die!"

She replied [readily], "What is wrong with that, son? You are right! And she [your wife] also is right!"

He—(the more distant one, *el-'ab¿ad*)[40]—got up and cut up his mother into pieces. He put her into a large pottery water jar (*zal¿ah*).[41] He carried the jar and went running to his wife. As he was running he stumbled and fell. [The jar also fell and its contents were scattered around.]

His mother's liver screamed [in anguish], "O my very dearest (*yâ-kibdî*)! May God's name be upon you [so as to protect you] (*'ism-'Allah ¿alaik*)!"[42]

❖ 4 ❖

THE MOTHER'S TONGUE

(EGYPT)

NARRATED IN JULY 1972 BY ZAINAB Ḥ., AGED FIFTY-THREE, A LITERATE MOTHER OF EIGHT CHILDREN, WHO LIVED IN A NORTHERN CAIRO SUBURB. SHE HAD HEARD THE STORY FROM HER OWN MOTHER, WHO ALLUDED TO IT FREQUENTLY. ZAINAB GAVE THE STORY TO EXPLAIN HER OWN ROLE AS A MOTHER AND TO JUSTIFY HER SEEMINGLY INCESSANT ADMONITIONS, REBUKES, AND CRITIQUES OF HER CHILDREN'S ACTIONS.[43]

"The mother is the school (el-'omm [hiyyah el-] madrasah*)," "Everything [a person does] emanates from the mother* (kulloh mi-l-'omm*)," and "The foundation is the mother* (er-rakk ¿a-l-'omm*)"*[44] *are folk truisms often cited to account for a person's behavior. Other sayings, such as "Upset the jar on her [its] mouth, a girl grows up to be like her mother,"*[45] *reinforce this viewpoint and countervail the classical Arabic literary cliché, "He who takes after his father has committed no injustice,"*[46] *which has very limited circulation and is confined to accounting for a male's behavior.*

The following didactic story (qiṣṣah*)*[47] *gives a graphic example of the pivotal role a mother plays in the socialization of her children.*

IT is said[48] that a woman had a son. They were poor and of limited means.[49] One day, when the boy was still little, he came back home to his mother [saying with excitement], "Mother, mother, I found an egg!" She said [with apparent joy], "Show me, sweetheart (*yâ roaḥ 'ommak*)."[50] She took the egg, and kissed her son. So whenever he found a small thing: an egg, an ear of corn, or the like, he would bring it home to his mother.

After he grew up somewhat he came home to his mother, "Mother, Mother! I found a chicken!" She said to him, "Show it to me, sweetheart!" She took the chicken and kissed him. So whenever he would find any thing—such as a chicken, a rooster, a duck, a goose, or the like, he would bring it home.

After he grew up some more, he came home to his mother, "Mother, Mother. I found a goat!" She, as before, said to him, "Show it to me, sweetheart!" And she took the goat. So whenever he would find something similar to a goat [in value or size], he would bring it home.

Things went on like that during the boy's life, [from boy, to youth, to man]:[51]

"Mother, Mother, I found a donkey!"

"Show it to me, sweetheart!"

"Mother, Mother, I found a camel!"[52]

"Show it to me, sweetheart!"

The boy became a man; he has become a thief (*ḥarâmî*),[53] then a highwayman,[54] then head of a band of robbers (*shaikh manṣar*).[55] One day as they were robbing cattle from a zareba of a rich man in a village, the police came and they were captured. Naturally, during the course of his robberies he had to commit murder: policemen, nightguards, and owners of things. So, he was sentenced to death.

As he was on the gallows, and ¿Ashmâwî[56] [the hangman] has put the noose around his neck, they, [as required by custom], asked him:

"What do you desire (*nifsak fî 'aih?*) [as a last wish]?"

He answered, "I want to see my mother!"

They said, "All right. Bring in his mother!"

When his mother came, he said to her, "I want to kiss your tongue!"

"Why, son?" [she asked].

"I just want to kiss your tongue. That is all!"

She let her tongue out and he—[narrator bows to show how he reached down from the gallows, with the noose around his neck, so as to reach the mother's tongue]—and [narrator speaks abruptly and snaps her jaws shut to illustrate the surprise] grabbed her tongue with his teeth! He bit so hard until it came off between his teeth!

Everyone was taken by surprise, and stunned by this deed of his. They asked him [in disbelief]: "Why!?"

He replied, "Had this tongue said to me, 'No! *ḥarâm* (It is sinful [to steal!])' when I first brought the egg home, I would not be standing here now!"

❖ 4-1 ❖

THE TONGUE OF THE SHROUDS-THIEF MOTHER

(SOMALIA)

RENDERED IN WRITING (IN ARABIC) IN 1973, BY NASÎM, AGED THIRTY-FIVE, A SOMALI WOMAN WORKING AS A NURSE IN DOHA, QATAR. SHE HAD HEARD THE STORY FROM HER MOTHER IN SOMALIA, AND TITLED IT "THE WOMAN SHROUDS THIEF." THE NARRATOR-WRITER WAS RESPONDING TO A REQUEST FOR TALES BY ANOTHER WOMAN (ASSISTING EL-SHAMY).

In this Somali version, the mother's guilt is greater than mere failure to scrutinize her son's actions; she provides a model, and the child takes after the parent.[57] *The text is fairly elaborate and includes the themes of "the chivalrous thief" (cf. Robin Hood), and the "master thief" or fragments from* Rhampsinitus,[58] *which do not normally appear in this tale type. The conclusion represents a greater punishment for the bad mother, but a less severe one for the misguided son.*

HÂBU was a widow; she had lost her husband while she was pregnant. Four months after the death of her husband, she gave birth to a child and named him Hayân. Hâbu used to steal the shrouds off the dead, during the night. And in this manner she lived and supported her only son. Hâbu used to take along her son when she went to the tombs during the night while she stole the shrouds; she took him along in fear that he might cry during her absence—were she to have left him to sleep at home—and perhaps he would wake up, cry, and thus alert the neighbors to her absence and her ghastly deeds. She therefore preferred to take him along.

It was in this manner that Hayân grew up and received the arts of thievery. When he reached being five years of age, Hayân started stealing. He stole an egg from their neighbor, Egwâ the old woman, and took it to his mother. His mother was very happy and said to him, "This is a fine deed, son. But you should have stolen two eggs." A few days later Hayân stole two eggs and brought them to his mother. But she said to him, "You should have stolen the hen so that it may lay eggs for us." So Hayân did that, and stole the hen.

Hayân kept on stealing whenever he found an opportunity to do so until he reached the age of ten. One day as he was on his way to steal he overheard their neighbor, the sheikh, saying to his wife, ¿Abarû, "Do you know that the Prophet—(May prayers and peace be upon him)—has instructed us to be kind, and to take care of our neighbors, [especially] those who live next door to us, as far as seven doors away." The sheikh was recommending charity toward the neighbors to his wife and children.

Hayân was touched when he heard the sheikh's words. So he bought a hen and two eggs and gave them to their neighbor, Egwâ, from whom he had stolen two eggs and a hen. From that day on, he was resolved not to steal from neighbors but practiced that profession of his away from the lane [where he lived]. It was in this manner that Hayân grew up and became twenty years of age, strongly built. He asked his mother to stop stealing. As for himself, he robbed [only] the rich; as for the weak and the orphaned, he was kind to them and gave them alms.

One day he wanted to steal from the house of the viceroy [governor] (*wâlî*). That house was surrounded by guards and had a tall fence around it and there was no [easy] way to enter it. So Hayân climbed up a tall tree that had spreading branches; he went on a branch, descended inside the wall. He stole whatever money he could find. He waited until the guard, who was at the door, fell asleep, then he went out through the door. In this manner Hayân robbed the governor's house each night for a month, until much of the governor's money was gone. The governor tightened security around his house and increased the number of the guards, but in spite of that Hayân continued to steal from the governor's house. However, instead of going out through the door [as he did earlier], he dug himself a long tunnel near the wall; one end was inside the wall and the other on its outside. He placed some straw on the entrance and used to sneak through this passage until he would reach the palace [i.e., the governor's house]. As soon as he would get hold of the money, he would exit through that tunnel.

One night the governor was awakened by the movement in [his] room and looked around. Hayân was afraid that the governor might seize him, so he stabbed the governor with his dagger and ran away. But before he could reach the tunnel entrance he fell on the ground. The guards were alerted and seized him. They led him to prison to await receiving his due. The following day the governor sentenced him to death. It was supposed that they would execute him on Friday. On Thursday morning, they sent him a guard; the guard said to him, "They will execute you tomorrow; therefore, you may have one wish and the governor will fulfill it for you." Hayân answered, "My wish is to see my mother and that the governor would allow her inside my cell."

The governor fulfilled that wish for him. They brought his mother to his cell. Hayân asked his mother to open her mouth so that he may see her tongue. She did so. Suddenly Hayân bit his mother's tongue [to the extent] that he cut it in two. Then Hayân called the guard and said, "Now I shall die with my mind at ease, after having cut off my mother's tongue!" The guard told the governor about what had happened. The governor ordered that Hayân be brought to his court (*dîwân*). When Hayân came, the governor asked him, "Why did you bite [off] the tongue of your mother (*wâlidtak*)!?"[59] Hayân answered, "The mother is the school for the child. It is the lessons that my mother gave me which brought me to prison, then to the gallows!" The governor asked him to tell about his life and how he received those lessons about which he had spoken.

Hayân told the governor his story. The governor forgave him and ordered that he be sent to the shop of the blacksmith and said to him, "Learn the ways of a craft so that you may do without ill-gotten money and so that you may earn [your livelihood] by the sweat of your brow."

Hayân learned ironwork and became a skilled blacksmith and a straight young man. After that he learned [of] the sweetness of life. And thus Hayân advised all those who came his way to work and earn a legitimate livelihood.

As for Hâbu, Hayân's mother, she died instantly due to the effect of that bite.

❖ 5 ❖

THE DAUGHTER OF THE *KHUDDÂRÎ*-BIRD[60]

(SUDAN)

NARRATED IN FEBRUARY 1971 BY FÂṬIMAH KH. B., AGED SIXTY-THREE, A WIDOW AND THE MOTHER OF EIGHT SURVIVING SONS AND TWO DAUGHTERS,

"IN ADDITION TO OTHERS WHOM GOD REMEMBERED [I.E., WHO ARE DECEASED)." NONLITERATE, SHE HAILED FROM THE ENVIRONS OF OMDURMAN CITY, IN WEST CENTRAL SUDAN, WHERE SHE HAD LIVED FOR SOME FIFTY YEARS.

THE NARRATOR HAD HEARD THIS FANTASY-TALE (*ḤUJWAH*) WHEN SHE WAS A GIRL AND BEFORE MOVING TO THE CITY AFTER HER MARRIAGE, FROM HER MOTHER AND OTHER WOMEN IN THE VILLAGE (*ḤILLAH*). FOR HER, THE TALE WAS "FOR WOMEN," AND SHE ADDED, "WE HAVE NOT HEARD OF AN ADULT MAN (*ZOAL*) WHO PAYS ATTENTION TO [SUCH] WOMEN'S PASTIME CONVERSATIONS (*WANASÂT AN-NISWÂN*)."[61] IN THE PAST, THE NARRATOR USED TO TELL TALES TO THE YOUNGSTERS IN HER FAMILY; MORE RECENTLY NOT MANY OPPORTUNITIES FOR TALE TELLING HAD ARISEN. YET, SHE STILL REMEMBERED MOST OF THE TALES SHE HAD HEARD AS A CHILD.

The following is one of the relatively infrequent cases in Arab traditional culture where the Oedipal situation seems to be explicitly verbalized. From the outset, a mother displays hostility toward her yet-to-be-born daughter[62] *and partiality in favor of a son; incest occurs between* another *mother and* her *unsuspecting son, with no mention made of the son's father. The geographic pattern of distribution for this component of the tale indicates that its presence is confined to the texts from the easternmost tier of the Arab world, along a line extending from Somalia to Syria, especially in the Nile Valley. However, the pattern of* demographic *distribution of the tale tends not to substantiate this Oedipal interpretation. The mother-son incest in the present narrative traditions appears among various age, ethnic-racial, social class, regional, economic, and religious groups, but fails to appear under normal narrating conditions among adult males in these groups. There is evidence that when adult males narrate this story, the components dealing with son-mother incest are completely absent.*[63]

The tale is typically narrated by females, and—occasionally—by young males who have not been fully resocialized into the subculture of adult male groups. Thus, it revolves around a highly stable core of sentiments expressing a wife's *hostility toward the domineering role of her mother-in-law, rather than an adult male's sexual attraction toward his own mother.*

*In the present text, the "heroine" marries the brother of the girl who was her "circumcision-mate" in the clitoridectomy ritual (*ṭuhûr*),*[64] *and she was treated by her future husband's mother "as if she happened to be her own daughter." This act may be viewed as another form of expressing the theme of "the sister in bed," a recurrent mental image (fantasy) in Arab literature.*[65]

The violent punishment meted out to the incestuous mother in this tale stands in sharp contrast to the absence of any punishment for the equally incestuous sister in the story entitled "¿Azîz Son of His Maternal-uncle" (Tale No. 49).[66]

A married woman remained for a year, two, or three—four, and ten—without having any offspring (*khilfah*). She did everything and visited the domed shrines [of saints] (*gubab*),[67] but still she did not become pregnant. One day a fakir saw her coming [repeatedly] to a shrine, day after day after day.

He asked her, "What is your request?"

She said to him, "[To have] an offspring."

He said to her, "Get a young lamb and a dog's puppy and roast them. Before it is time to be with your husband, feed him the lamb, and you eat the puppy!"

She went to her home and did as the fakir had told her! But [before she could eat her share], her husband came, lifted the cover off the pot and found roasted meat! He said [to himself], "That woman! She feeds me porridge (*¿aṣîdah*) everyday, while she eats roasted meat!!"

[narrator speaks with emphasis.] He ate the meat! It turned out to be the puppy, that his wife was going to eat for pregnancy. He became pregnant! [Narrator laughs.] His wife said to him, "Stay at home until the time [for delivery] comes!"

When his time came, she said to him, "Go to a spot far away from people and do what is necessary! If it is a boy, bring him home. And if it is a girl, leave her on her spot!" The man went to a faraway place, and out of his leg—after he cut it open with a dagger—he took out a baby girl. He wrapped her in leaves and straw and left her where he had dropped her, and he returned [to his home].

Now, Our Lord does not forget anyone; that girl—God caused a bird to be in her service:[68] the *khuddârî*-bird. He [the bird], picked her up and put her on top of a very tall date palm tree. He kept on feeding her and giving her to drink, raising her, and looking after her until she grew up.

After a number of years, it came to be the time for the girl's circumcision. The *khuddârî*-bird heard that the sultan's wife was about to circumcise her [own] daughter. He (the bird) said to her, "I will carry you to the sultan's palace. You say to them, 'I am an orphan and my circumcision is due; I've heard that you are having a circumcision [ceremony of your own].' The sultan's wife will say: 'You [may] be circumcised along with my daughter!'"

She [the girl] replied, "Will do." The bird carried the girl to the [top of the] sultan's palace; and when the sultan's wife went up she [found the girl and] asked her, "Who are you? What brought you here? What do you want?" The girl replied, "I am an orphan; my circumcision is due; would you, by God, let me be circumcised along with your daughter?" She replied, "Certainly![69] Orphans are God's beloved!"

On the day of circumcision the sultan's son saw the girl lying on the bedding (*¿angarîb*). He said to his mother, "I want to marry her." Meanwhile, the bird came and carried the girl and returned her to [the top of] the date palm tree. Now, Wad-an-Nimair,[70] the sultan's son, came to look at the girl again but did not find her. He asked, "Where is the girl who will be my bride?" They told him, "We have not seen her. She ran away!" He became very sad and put on airs of unhappiness. They said to him, "Outstanding girls are plenty (*Ḥawwâ wallâdah*)![71] Choose from among [all] the girls of the kingdom." He said, "No one but that girl will I wed!"

In order to forget [her], he said, "I will go out with the merchants!" They traveled and they went around until their trade was done. On their way back they chanced to pass by the place where the girl was—by that tree. They sat down underneath the date palm tree to rest. The girl began to drop dates on them. [She dropped ripe dates on Wad-an-Nimair and unripe ones on his companions.] They wondered: "How come the ripe dates are falling only on Wad-an-Nimair and the unripe ones on us?" He said, "I will climb up the tree to see what the matter is." When he reached the top he looked and saw no one, but as he was about to climb down he caught a glimpse of the girl's fingers, then he saw her face [reflected on the water surface] in the well below. He went down and said to the merchants, his friends, "There is nothing up there." And after they have had their rest they left.

Wad-an-Nimair said—after they had traveled some distance—"Oh, I forgot my ring under the date palm tree! You go on and I'll catch up with you." He returned to the spot and yelled, "O daughter of [good] people (*yâ bint an-nâs*), climb down!" But she did not say anything. So he climbed up and brought her down with him. He took her to the palace and she was wed to him. People came with drums, and women kept on making ululations [of joy] (*zagharîṭ*)[72] so as to celebrate the wedding. And when everything was completed, they became bride and groom.[73]

Now, after some time, Wad-an-Nimair wanted to travel with the traders again. He left his wife at home and said to his, mother, "I appeal to you by the Prophet,[74] O mother, that you take care of my wife during my absence!" And he left.

Now, his mother hated his wife. She called one of the slaves in the palace and said to him [in a commanding tone], "Take her, kill her and bring me a bottleful of her blood!"

The man was an old, good-hearted man. He took the girl and said [to himself], "What sin has she committed? She has done nothing!" So he caught a turtledove, slaughtered it and put its blood in a bottle; he left the girl in the wilderness, and went back to his mistress and said to her, "Here is the blood!" She gave him some money and said to him, "If you tell anyone I'll chop off your head!" As for the girl, she kept on going until she came to an island in the middle of a river. God made the island flourish for her sake; after being barren, it became green.

Now the mother of Wad-an-Nimair dressed herself like his wife, [narrator speaks with considerable hesitation], . . . , and pretended to be the girl. When he returned, she received him and said, "Your mother died! Your absence and the death of your mother have made me [look like] a grey-haired woman." She showed him a spot where she had buried a sheep and said, "Here is your mother's tomb." He did not think of the matter much. They slept together . . . [pause] . . . and she became pregnant. She craved [the cooked dish of] *molokhiyyah.*[75] They said to her, "This is not the season for *molokhiyyah;* it is not summer time [when it grows]!" But she kept on craving it and saying, "I want *molokhiyyah!* I want *molokhiyyah!*"

Someone said, "There is a girl on the island who has a garden with every plant growing in it." Wad-an-Nimair sent a slave to ask for some *molokhiyyah.* The slave went to her and said [in rhyme],

> O our lady, [pause] O our lady,
> . . . [pause]
> Wouldn't you give us some *molokhiyyah,*
> for the craving-woman whom we have.[76]

(Narrator: "I can't remember all the song! But it is longer.")
[Evidently the slave recognized her, and she realized that he did].[77] She replied,

> Shame! Shame!
> My mother craved me and my father was pregnant with me.
> Wad-an-Nimair made his mother pregnant;
> and her craving hits [afflicts] me!
> O Scissors, clip off the slave's tongue,
> and return back to me.[78]

The slave went back to Wad-an-Nimair, but he could not speak and went, "A-a-a-a!" They sent a second slave and a third slave, but the same thing happened to them. Now Wad-an-Nimair decided to go himself. When he asked for the *molokhiyyah,* she answered him,

> Shame! Shame!
> My mother craved me and my father was pregnant with me.
> Wad-an-Nimair made his mother pregnant;
> and her craving hits [afflicts] me!
> O Scissors, clip off the slave's tongue,
> and return back to me.

But when the scissors flew at him, he avoided them and they went astray. He asked her for the story. She told him about what had happened. He went home and told the people of what had happened. They brought four camels, two hungry and two thirsty. They tied his mother to them and placed fodder and water before them. When they [the camels] pulled to get to the fodder and the water, she was torn apart.

Wad-an-Nimair took his wife to the palace. And they lived in God's safe-keeping.[79]

MOTHER AND DAUGHTER

❖ 6 ❖

"MOTHER, SEE WHAT I'VE GOT FOR YOU!"

(PALESTINE)

NARRATED IN MARCH 1969 BY 'OMM-SA¿ÎD (I.E., SA¿ÎD'S MOTHER), A YOUNG PALESTINIAN WOMAN IN HER EARLY TWENTIES, FROM BAIT RÎMA, A VILLAGE NEAR RAMALLA. SHE WAS A HIGH SCHOOL GRADUATE, RECENTLY WED, AND THE MOTHER OF AN INFANT SON.

THE NARRATOR HAD OVERHEARD THIS FANTASY-TALE SOME TEN YEARS EARLIER WHEN A MAN, WHO WAS A GUEST IN THEIR HOUSE, TOLD IT IN JEST TO HER FATHER AND OTHER MEN IN THE PARLOR. SHE REMEMBERED THAT HER MOTHER AND OTHER WOMEN IN THE HOUSE COMMENTED THAT THIS MAN WAS A BUFFOON, EFFEMINATE, AND UNRESPECTABLE FOR TELLING SUCH A TALE, ESPECIALLY AT A FAMILY'S HOME.

The wished-for child, born to a childless couple—or less frequently, to only a mother—is a recurrent theme. Such a character usually has the form of a bird, animal, or—as in the present case—an object. When in human form, this character is often born with physical deformity, such as being a half person or being the size of a thumb.[80] *The tricky character in the present tale is a water jar, typically perceived in feminine terms and referred to as* "her"*; a proverb cited by the narrator states, "Upset the jar on her [its] mouth, a girl turns out to be like her mother."*[81]

A message implicitly expressed is the economic benefits a daughter may bring her parents.[82] *In a number of variants, such wealth is fraught with the danger of exposure to "sexual shame," or the tarnishing of the "sexual honor;"*[83] *the jar returns to "her" mother with "something" that a man has deposited in "her." It is this concluding adventure (and acquisition) by the water jar that seemed to constitute humor for the male guest whom the narrator had first heard relating the tale. Presumably, she eschewed this theme for reasons of modesty.*

THERE was that woman. She gave no birth. She prayed to her Lord to grant her [an offspring]: "O Lord grant me a boy or a girl, even if she happened to be a *baṭṭiyyah* (water jar).[84] Our Lord heard from her, and granted her. She became pregnant and completed [her pregnancy term]. After nine months she begot: she gave birth to a water jar. She was very happy with her [(the jar)] and dressed her up just as [if the jar were] a little girl. O day, go! O day, come! [time passed],[85] Baṭṭiyyah[86] grew up and started to go out [of the house], and to get around.

One day she found her mother sad, [and asked], "Mother, why are you saddened?"

"Because we are poor. The Lord willed that we [only] would be of good repute."[87]

One day Baṭṭiyyah went out with the youngsters of the neighborhood; they went to the ravine to wash. At the ravine they took off all their jewelry, [then wondered], "Where shall we keep them [until we are finished]! Where shall we keep them!"

Baṭṭiyyah said to them, "Keep them here!" . . . [pause].

She said to them [pointing to herself], "Keep your gold, your earrings and all here!"

The girls, right away, placed their things—rings, earrings, ankle bracelets—inside Baṭṭiyyah and went to do the wash. They finished and went to open the Baṭṭiyyah, but Baṭṭiyyah would not open up. They tried; but she would not open up. Evening came! They became afraid and left for their homes in order to tell their mothers and fathers. Baṭṭiyyah got up and rolled herself [all the way] to her mother [yelling], "Mother! Mother! Open the door! Open the door! Open up your Water Jar and see!"

Her mother came trotting, "May God make it good![88] What is the news?" She found Baṭṭiyyah standing before her. She opened her and [narrator speaks with astonishment] found all sorts of God's boon:[89] this is gold, this is silver, and that is carnelian (*¿aqîq*) and the like! She took the stuff and lived off it.

Now, O day, go! O day, come! the money was exhausted. Baṭṭiyyah went out again. She went to the meadow [or garden] around the well (*bayyârah*); there, she found some shepherds. They had killed a small goat (*sakhal*) in order to have dinner, but then had no pot in which to cook their goat. Baṭṭiyyah came to them and said [pointing to herself], "Place your food here!" They were happy. After the meat was cooked, they tried to open that pot (*ha-ṭ-ṭanjarah*) but she would not be opened!! "What do we do!? What do we do!?" [they wondered]. They sat down for a while, and finally decided, "May God compensate [us] (*ye¿awwaḍ-Allâ[h]*)!" [(that is: they gave up).] Baṭṭiyyah rolled herself home: "Mother! Mother! Open the door and see what I've got for you!" [she yelled]. Her mother opened her and found the [goat] meat, cooked and ready.

O day, go! O day, come! Baṭṭiyyah went out again. She found a neighbor woman spreading wheat out to dry. After the wheat got dry, she looked for a vessel in which to carry it. Baṭṭiyyah went to her. "Place your wheat here," [pointing to herself]. The woman was happy and said to her, "May [the Lord] bring you happiness!" She put her wheat in Baṭṭiyyah and carried her home. When she tried to open her, she would not open; she tried until her fingers became bloody, but there was no use. She left her. Baṭṭiyyah rolled herself home to her mother. "Mother, mother, open the door and see what I've got for you!" The woman opened her and found the wheat. She ground it, kneaded the dough, and baked.

O day, go! O day, come! Baṭṭiyyah went out again. She rolled herself to the river bank. She found a man wishing to bathe. He had taken off his clothes . . . , [narrator pauses, hesitates.][90]

She did with him as she did with the others, then went to her mother. "Mother! Mother! Open the door and see what I've got for you!" Her mother opened her. When she saw what was inside—[narrator pauses, her companions giggle], she [in rage] got hold of Baṭṭiyyah and smashed her against the floor. Baṭṭiyyah broke up into pieces.

And the bird flew; may He [The Lord] make your evening good.[91]

EL-SHAMY: What did the man put in Baṭṭiyyah?
NARRATOR: Something that belongs to men.
EL-SHAMY: Like what?
NARRATOR: [Embarrassed]. Anything, and that's all!

[A male listener stated, later, that the object in question was a penis.]

❖ 6-1 ❖

SHE-SPARROW

The Cumin Guard[92]

(EGYPT)

NARRATED BY MERVAT Ḥ., A THIRTEEN-YEAR-OLD SCHOOLGIRL, FROM THE CITY OF EL-SINBILLAWAIN, IN NORTHEASTERN EGYPT. SHE HAD HEARD THIS "CHILDREN'S TALE" FROM HER PATERNAL GRANDMOTHER AND OLDER SISTER.

Children are typically viewed, especially in rural areas, as a source of economic gain and future security against old age; they constitute a significant part of the labor force. The responsibilities of a child's work assignment often generate tension and place the child in conflict with adults since the task is often arduous, or even impossible. In a number of variants of this tale, the task is to guard a tamarisk shrub. The heroine of the present tale exemplifies this dual role: she is a reluctant mother's helper and at the same time a source of wealth.

The theme of a she-swallow guarding a precious tree seems to hark back to Egyptian antiquity (Plutarch's Mythological History of Isis and Osiris), where the goddess Isis is reported to have played this role vis-à-vis a tamarisk tree which grew to enclose the casket containing Osiris's corpse.[93]

PRAY on behalf of the Prophet.

There was once a woman who did not beget any children. She said [in an imploring tone], "O Lord, I [wish to] beget, even if a she-sparrow." The Lord responded to her plea and she begot a she-sparrow. Her [the she-sparrow's] mother was happy with her and her father owned a field of cumin. He said to her, "She-sparrow, go and guard the cumin field!" So She-sparrow went to guard the cumin field. Someone came to take [by stealth] some cumin. She said [angrily, in chant],

Take your hand off, may your hand get cut off!
[May what is] above you [become] underneath, and [what is] underneath [become] above,
you and your master![94]

Immediately, the man became upside-down, and he went running away. Another man came and the same thing happened; she would say,

Take your hand off, may your hand get cut off!
[May what is] above you [become] underneath, and [what is] underneath [become] above,
you and your master!

And the man would become upside-down.

Her story spread in the village. A pasha heard the story and said [to himself], "By God, I will go and bring some cumin!" [So] he went to the field, and took along his horse-attendant. [When he got to the field], he said [in a commanding voice], "Carriage driver, get down and bring some cumin!" The driver got down and went to bring some cumin, but when he reached out with his hand in order to get the cumin, he heard a voice [She-sparrow's] saying,

Take your hand off, may your hand get cut off!
[May what is] above you [become] underneath, and [what is] underneath [become] above you,
you and your master!

He looked [only] to find[95] himself [immediately] upside-down. The driver became scared and ran away. The pasha stepped down, out of the carriage and went to take some cumin. He was listening, and when he heard her, she who was saying,

Take your hand off, may your hand get cut off!
[May what is] above you [become] underneath, and [what is] underneath [become] above you,
you and your master!

He [quickly] put out his hand [in the direction of the voice] and seized her; she kept on chirruping,

Mother, don't think that I am guarding the cumin.
I am in the pasha's hand, going to Constantinople.[96]

The pasha was very pleased with her voice and said to her, "Say it again!"

She replied, "I won't say [it] until you put me in your big pocket."

He put her in his big pocket. She said,

Mother, don't think that I am guarding the cumin.
I am in the pasha's big pocket going to Constantinople.

While in his pocket, she swallowed his money; she kept on swallowing the money, picking it up with her beak and swallowing it.

The pasha said to her, "Say it again."

She answered, "I won't say [it] until you put me in your watch pocket [of the vest]." He took her out of his big pocket and put her in the watch pocket.

She said [in chant],

Mother don't think I am guarding the cumin.
I am in the pasha's watch pocket going to Constantinople.

While in the pasha's watch pocket, she took his gold watch.

The pasha said to her, "Say it again."

She answered, "I won't say [it] until you put me on the tassel of your fez."[97] [So] he placed her on the tassel of his fez. As soon as she found herself on the tassel of his fez, she [narrator speaks in tone denoting abruptness and surprise] fle-e-ew away, and said,

Take your hand off, may your hand get cut off!
[May what is] above you [become] underneath, and [what is] underneath [become] above you,
you and your master!

The pasha became upside-down. Then she flew to her mother. She pecked at the door with her beak and said, "Mother, open. I am She-sparrow, mother."

Her mother replied [in a reproaching voice], "You are neither my daughter, nor do I know you. Where have you been?!

She[-sparrow] replied, "Open, mother. I was in Constantinople and I have brought you fine things."

Her mother opened the door and she flew inside. She kept on throwing up the gold [coins] that she took from the pasha's pocket. Her mother was happy with her, after having been angry at her for leaving the cumin field without telling [or asking the permission of] anyone.

And that is it. And bit by bit, the tale is over.[98]

❖ 7 ❖

FUṬMAH AND THE PICKLED FISH HEAD[99]

(EGYPT)

NARRATED IN JANUARY 1970, BY SA¿DIYYAH A., AGED THIRTY-EIGHT, A WIDOW AND THE MOTHER OF FOUR CHILDREN—THE ELDEST "A MARRIED MAN WITH A JOB, AND THE YOUNGEST IS A GIRL WHO WAS JUST ABOUT TO ENTER SCHOOL [I.E., A SIX-YEAR-OLD]." SA¿DIYYAH WAS A NATIVE OF RURAL GÎZAH, IN THE SOUTHERN ENVIRONS OF CAIRO. SHE WORKS AS A BUTCHER AND SPECIAL-ORDER MEAT SELLER, SUPPLYING FRESH "COUNTRY-STYLE"[100] MEAT TO A FEW WOMEN BROKERS[101] TO DELIVER TO CLIENTS IN CAIRO, WHERE THIS COMMODITY IS IN DEMAND. SA¿DIYYAH REFERRED TO HERSELF AS A "CITY GAL,"[102] AND A *TÂGRAH* ("SHE-MERCHANT") WHO WAS "MAKING A LIVING THROUGH LEGITIMATE OCCUPATION."[103] SHE IS ADDRESSED IN THE SOUK (MARKETPLACE) AS "SHE-BOSS" (*MI¿ALLIMAH*).

AFTER HAVING TOLD ME THIS TALE, HER ELDEST SON—WHO IS ABOUT TWENTY YEARS OLD AND WORKED AS A MINOR CLERK IN A GOVERNMENT-OWNED FACTORY—WALKED IN. HE BECAME QUITE UPSET AT MY PRESENCE AT HIS MOTHER'S HOME. FOR HIM, IT WAS ALL RIGHT THAT HIS MOTHER INTERACT WITH MEN IN THE SOUK, FOR IT IS A PUBLIC DOMAIN AND HER DEALINGS THERE WERE A MATTER OF "MAKING A LIVING"; BUT SITTING DOWN WITH AN ADULT MALE—A STRANGER—AND SPEAKING NONSENSE[104] CONSTITUTED AN ACT OF INDECENCY (*¿AIB*).[105] THE RECORDING SESSION HAD TO BE TERMINATED.

Conflict between mother and daughter is the pivotal theme for this fantasy-tale. Dissociative relations develop over the consumption of food, and a mother's role as disciplinarian. A mother's constant nagging is viewed as a customary punitive measure for the rearing of children; by contrast, a father's approach is usually depicted as stern, abrupt, and decisive.[106]

Miss Y.M.—the narrator of another rendition of this tale[107]*—provided clues as to why the tale seems to be more ego-involving and some of its components more cognitively salient, and thus more memorable, for a female. She stated,*

> *I heard this tale some fifteen years ago from a servant girl named Mabrûkah; she hailed from Bani-Swaif [in middle southern Egypt], and was then about fourteen years old. She used to tell a number of tales, but this is the one that got glued to my mind. Sometimes I think of Mabrûkah and I'd remember this tale of hers. But the thing that really is glued [in my memory] is the mother . . . saying to her daughter [narrator imitates the mother's nagging tone of voice and menacing facial grimace], "O Faṭmah, have you eaten the pickled fish head and the two loaves of bread! O Faṭmah, have you eaten [. . .]!"*

Miss Y.M. added, as she laughed, presumably at this typical aggravating situation that recurs in daily family living,

> *Another thing that is stuck in my mind is when Faṭmah was sitting on the balcony with her husband and the tree [that grew out of the mother's grave and] had little, little [i.e., "itty-bitty"] women—all looking exactly like her mother—and saying [in a hissing, whispering, yet still menacing tone], "O Faṭmah, have you eaten the pickled fish head and the two loaves of bread! O Faṭmah, have you eaten [. . .]!"*

Neither of these two narrators—a married woman and a maiden—expressed feelings of sympathy, pity, or sorrow at the "death" of the nagging mother.

Another salient aspect of the tale for Miss Y.M. is the wife's claim that her husband's beard reminded her of the besom[108] *and broom at her father's home. Although for Miss Y.M.—who could not stop laughing—this element was very comic, it depicts the precariousness of a wife's position in "her husband's home," and warns that a wife may be turned out with absolutely no gain from her married years.*[109] *Consequently, a wife's status is, to a large measure, tied to that of her own family.*[110]

The theme of a grateful dog as helper is relatively frequent in Arab lore. Formal Islam views dogs as unclean animals and permits ownership of a dog only for the purposes of hunting, shepherding, and guarding property; yet, folk attitudes toward dogs do not always comply with the formal dogma.

ONCE there was a man and a woman; they were married and had a daughter whose name was Fuṭmah. The man died and left behind his wife and that daughter of his: Fuṭmah. They were very poor; they owned nothing in this world except the little shed in which they lived.

What will they do? The woman started going out [begging] and saying, "'Alms, for God's sake, Ye benevolent!'" People gave her whatever they could.

One day someone gave the woman a head of a pickled fish, and two loaves of bread—(before, people gave her only bread). The woman became very happy and ran home to prepare for a feast. [Narrator laughs.] She said to her daughter, "Fuṭmah: keep your mind on the pickled fish head and the two loaves of bread until I return." The girl said, "Will do, mother!" Her mother went back [to the streets], but no one gave her anything else.

While she [the mother] was away, a dog came by; it was a very old dog, sick and dying of hunger. Fuṭmah said [to herself]: "Hey, kid! why don't you give him a morsel of bread. Maybe he would eat it and benefit from it." She took a pinch off a very tiny crumb and gave it to the dog. The dog gulped it down. One crumb, after another, after another [Narrator laughs while imitating the pinching off of the bread crumbs with her own fingers], the two loaves were gone. The dog revived a bit but he still looked very hungry. She thought: "Maybe a little of the smell of the pickled fish head would help him." As she brought the head close to the dog's mouth, he [with an abrupt snapping head movement] gulped it. Now: no two loaves of bread, and no pickled fish head! [Narrator laughs.]

Her mother came, naturally expecting [to have] a feast.

"O Fuṭmah! Bring the two loaves of bread and the pickled fish head so that we may eat."

"By God, mother, a sick dog came by and I gave him the two loaves of bread and the pickled fish head" [she replied].

"Oh, what a ruinous thing for me (*yâ-â-â kharâ-â-â-bî-î-î*)! No, you ate them!" [her mother yelled in anguish].

"By God, mother, I did not eat them. I gave them to the dog."

"You ate the two loaves of bread and the pickled fish head!"

"By God, mother, I fed them to a dog."

The woman became crazy; she kept on hitting her daughter [and shouting], "You ate the two loaves of bread and the pickled fish head."

"By God, mother, I gave them to a dog."

"You ate the two loaves of bread and the pickled fish head!"

"By God, mother, I gave them to a dog."

"You ate the two loaves of bread and the pickled fish head!"

"By God, mother, I gave them to a dog."

Finally, her mother said to her, "Because you are a liar, and for you a dog is more preferred than your mother, get out of here [leave home]."

[Narrator speaks with great sympathy], the girl—(oh, what a pity: *yâ ¿ainî*)[111]—left home. She kept on walking and walking until she came to a palace. There was a fence [around it] and a garden. She sat down next to the trash cans. She kept on searching [for something to eat] in the trash: a clean morsel of bread she would eat; a dirty morsel of bread she would set aside. A clean morsel of bread she would eat; a dirty morsel of bread she would set aside.

Now who saw her? One of the servants saw her doing so. He went to his master, [the king's son], and said, "My master, there is a poor girl outside. She is going through the trash: a clean morsel of bread she would eat; a dirty morsel of bread she would set aside."

The king's son looked out the window and saw her; he felt sorry for her. He said to the servant, "Go and bring her in. Among the servants, she will be another servant, [she will not be an additional burden]." They brought her in. She lived with the servants, (and of course ate well—naturally, she ate the remnants of royal cuisine). She flourished and blossomed fast.

One day as the king's son was inspecting the palace, he saw her. In his eyes, she looked pretty.[112] He said to his mother, "I want to marry this girl." She answered [in a reprimanding tone], "We know nothing about her: neither origin nor class or status!"[113] He said, "Mother, I want to marry her." In short, [after arguing] from here to there, his mother said [with great reluctance], "All right, son. May God lead us [to do what is good]."[114] They made the wedding celebration and the king's son married Fuṭmah the beggar. She lived in the palace in royal luxury.

Fuṭmah's mother came one day to the palace—she did not really come to the palace—but as she wandered, begging, she chanced by the palace where her daughter was now living. With whom? [With] the king's son. Her daughter saw her coming. Of course she [the mother] was poor: her clothes were all torn and dirty and things like that. She sat down next to the garbage and started doing what her daughter, that Fuṭmah, had done earlier: eat the clean bread morsel but set aside the dirty morsel.

Fuṭmah saw her. She said to a servant, "Go to that beggar woman, bring her in, feed her all she wants, give her the best clothes and place her in the guest room." They [the servants] did as she told them to do.

The following day Fuṭmah went to see her mother. She, of course, did not recognize her at first because she was dressed in royal clothing, and royal jewelry, and . . . and . . . and . . . [she looked completely different]. She said to her,

"O mother, I am your daughter. I am Fuṭmah!"

As soon as the woman heard this, she said [narrator speaks with great excitement],

"O Fuṭmah, you ate the pickled fish head and the two loaves of bread."

"By God, mother, I gave them to the dog."

"You ate the pickled fish head and the two loaves of bread."

"By God, mother, I gave them to the dog."

"You ate the pickled fish head and the two loaves of bread."

[(Narrator laughs and comments, "There are [some] people who are just like that: never cease nagging[115] nor complaining.")]

The girl left her mother in the guest room, in utmost comfort—(but still buzzing)—and said to the servants, "Make her lacking in nothing."

She [the mother] lived in the palace in utmost comfort but whenever she would see Fuṭmah, she would say [reproachingly], "You ate the pickled fish head and the two loaves of bread, Fuṭmah."

Finally, when Fuṭmah became fed up (and of course she feared that her husband may find out about her origin: a beggar) she said to a servant, "Take this woman, kill her, and bury her in the garden [next to the balcony]." They seized the woman and—(away from you: *bi¿îd ¿annak*)—killed her and buried her where her daughter had said. On the spot where they buried her, a tree came out.

One day, as Fuṭmah and the king's son were sitting on the balcony, Fuṭmah heard a voice [narrator whispers]: "O Fuṭmah, you have eaten the pickled fish head and the two loaves of bread." When she looked in the direction from which it came, she saw little, little, little women [narrator holds out the tip of her index finger to indicate the women's size]: all of them looked exactly like her mother. This little woman would say, "O Fuṭmah, you ate the pickled fish head and the two loaves of bread!" and that little woman would say, "O Fuṭmah, you ate the pickled fish head and the two loaves of bread!" and this one would say "O Fuṭmah, you . . . ," and that one would say "O Fuṭmah, you . . . !"

When she saw that sight and heard all these little women saying this, she broke out in laughter. Her husband, the king's son, was not paying any attention. He just saw Fuṭmah laughing, and laughing and laughing. He [in puzzlement] said to her, "What are you laughing about?"

"About nothing."

"'About nothing!?' You must be laughing about something!"

"No! About nothing."

"'About nothing!?' You must be laughing at me."

"No, by God! About nothing."

(Of course, as you know, laughter for no reason is impoliteness.)[116]

He said to her, "Either you tell about what you are laughing at, or you take [only] whatever you brought with you into my home and go."

She thought quickly—(what is she going to say?) She said, "I was looking at your beard. It reminds me of things. Oh, I just was reminiscing about my father's palace. [There] the [strings of] my father's besom were pearls, and [the bristles of] my mother's broom were gold. Your beard reminded me of them."

The king's son wondered [at what she had just said]: 'My father's pearl besom and my mother's gold broom!' He said to her [in amazement], "Oh my! You must be a daughter of kings. These [things] I must see. Your origin and class must be like my own origin and class.[117] Take me to your father's palace so that I may see your father's pearl besom and your mother's gold broom!"

(Now, what is she going to do?) She [secretly] packed up her things and left the palace without anyone knowing about it. She kept on walking until she got tired and night was overtaking her. She sat down to rest; she took out some food, which she had taken with her. A dog came by; she gave him some of her food and remembered the pickled fish head and the two loaves of bread; so she cried.

The dog spoke! He said to her, "Why are you crying?" She told him her story from its beginning to its end. He said to her, "Don't worry. You go back to the palace and say to the king's son, 'Tomorrow morning—if God wills—we go to my father's palace to see my father's pearl besom and my mother's gold broom.' I will walk ahead of you [to show the way]."

She returned to the palace and spent her night preparing for the trip. In the morning she said to the king's son, "Let us go."

They got into the carriage and she said to the driver, "Go this way! Go that way!" (Of course, the dog was running ahead of them so as to show her the way.) They finally came to a palace much bigger and more beautiful than that of the king's son. The dog entered, and they entered after him.

As soon as they stepped in, they looked and saw a besom, its threads were beaded with genuine pearls:[118] that big [(the size of an egg)]! And [they also saw] a broom: the bristles of that broom were twenty-four-karat gold. She said to her husband [in a relieved tone], "Here is what I was laughing at."

The king's son said, "True! Your origin and class are like my own origin and class."

The dog [took her aside and] said to her [in a whisper], "I am the same dog to whom you had fed the pickled fish head and the two loaves of bread."

When she returned to the palace where she and the king's son were living, she ordered the gardener to cut off the tree (the one with the little women on its branches). They chopped it off.

That is all. And bit by bit, the tale is over.

❖ 7-1 ❖

THE PICKLED FISH HEAD

(EGYPT)

NARRATED IN 1972, BY BAṬṬAH (I.E., DUCK, PROBABLY A NICKNAME), AGED FORTY-EIGHT, A GRANDMOTHER, LIVING IN CAIRO, HER MOTHER CAME FROM BANI-SWAIF AND HER FATHER FROM QINA, IN SOUTHERN EGYPT. SHE HAD HEARD THE TALE SOME TWENTY-FIVE YEARS EARLIER. THIS TEXT WAS COLLECTED AND WRITTEN DOWN IN ARABIC BY MISS ZAYNAB EL-BAKRÎ.[119]

THE PRESENT NARRATOR IS NOT A RACONTEUR. ALTHOUGH HER MOTHER HAD TOLD HER NUMEROUS "LONG FANTASY TALES" (*ḤAWÂDÎT*), SHE HERSELF PREFERRED TO POSE RIDDLES (*FAWÂZÎR*), "BECAUSE THEY ARE SHORT AND CUTE (*ẒARÎFAH*)." IN RESPONSE TO THE COLLECTOR'S REQUEST FOR FANTASY-TALES, THE NARRATOR PRESENTED SIXTY RIDDLES—AN UNCOMMONLY LARGE NUMBER—BUT NO NARRATIVES. WHEN THE COLLECTOR REPEATED HER REQUEST FOR TALES, THE NARRATOR MANAGED TO COME UP WITH ONLY THREE BRIEF "PHILOSOPHICAL" NARRATIVES AND EXPLAINED THAT HEARING FANTASY TALES AND SEEING OTHERS PLAY CARDS MAKE HER DROWSY. CLEARLY, THIS EFFECT IS A PRODUCT OF CONDITIONING.[120]

THE PATTERN OF THE TALE'S DISTRIBUTION, AND PRESENCE OF CHARACTERISTIC ELEMENTS FROM THE "NORMAL FORM" IN WHICH IT IS TYPICALLY TOLD—GIVEN IN TALE NO. 7, ABOVE—INDICATE THAT THE PRESENT TEXT IS LIKELY TO HAVE BEEN LEARNED IN THAT DOMINANT FORM. EVIDENTLY, IT IS A TRANSFORMED RENDITION THAT ACQUIRED THE GENERIC CHARACTERISTICS OF A PHILOSOPHICAL NARRATIVE. THE TRANSFORMATION SEEMS TO HAVE TAKEN PLACE THROUGH STANDARD FACTORS DEPENDENT ON THE NARRATOR'S MENTAL SET, AND PROCESSES INVOLVED IN PERCEPTION, LEARNING, RETENTION, RECALL, AND FORGETTING.[121]

A daughter's responsibility toward her aging mother,[122] *the power of habit, and poverty as a state of mind are the focal points for this atypical rendition of the story.*

THERE was a poor woman who had a daughter. They were poor. [The woman used] go to the pickled fish shopkeeper (*fasakhâni*). When she would get there, she would take the heads of the pickled fish after he had cut them off [and cast them away because they are inedible and, therefore, had no value]. Later her daughter became rich [apparently through marriage to a rich man, and moved out to her husband's home]. She said to her [mother], "Mother, doing such a thing is a disgrace. Come [stay with me]. I'll feed you and give your beverages." [The mother agreed and moved in with her.] But [in spite of all the food and drink] her [powerful] habit (*ṭab¿*),[123] used to overcome her, and she still would bring in the head[s] of the pickled fish. Her daughter told her that her husband would divorce her if she [the mother] were to continue to bring home the head of the pickled fish. She [the mother] left the house angry and kept on going from door to door begging morsels of bread.

[Finally, she went back to her daughter's home, and][124] she entered; they bathed her and dressed her [in proper clothes]. They gave her fine food and put her up in a private room. [Nonetheless], she locked [herself inside] the room, brought a pillow, stacked the morsels of bread [that she had gotten by begging] and kept on saying, ["Give me alms] for God's sake! [Give me alms] for God's sake! Alas, what a great loss the head of the pickled fish was!"

People entered her room [and saw what she was doing]. They wondered, saying, "Indeed, she was made rich, but she did not cease to be needy." She stacked the pillows [on top of one another] and begged, "Give me [alms] for

God's sake!" [She was doing this] in lieu of begging for the head of the pickled fish.

(This tale says that a person who has a powerful habit cannot give it up).

❖ 7-2 ❖

[THE POT OF MEAT]

(KUWAIT)

NARRATED IN AUGUST 1970 BY RUQAYYAH B., KUWAITI, AGED FIFTY-NINE. THE BLACK, FORMER SLAVE HAD HEARD THE TALE FROM HER GRANDMOTHER AND HAD RECENTLY TOLD IT TO HER DAUGHTER'S DAUGHTER. THE TEXT WAS COLLECTED AND WRITTEN DOWN IN ARABIC BY MISS 'ILHÂM KHALÎL.[125]

The following is an example of a regional subtype (recurrent mostly in North Africa), where the theme of a helpful animal testing his master's gratitude plays a major role. The conflict in the present text is with father and sisters over meat. Significantly, the heroine's real father is dropped out of action; he, presumably, continued to live with the other two daughters. The heroine marries a nonpaternal figure, who had to ask his own father for permission to marry her.[126]

The humiliating punishment of the heroine by her husband, and his subsequent forgiveness, illustrate the husband's role as his wife's disciplinarian.

THERE were three girls, sisters, living with their father. They were very poor. One day, their father bought them [some] meat and brought it home so that they might cook it. They put the meat in a pot over the fire. However, due to the severity of their hunger, each one of them went [repeatedly] and ate a piece of meat from the pot before the meat was done. The young[est] sister became vexed; she lifted the pot off the fire and ran with it outside. The father, her two sisters, and their dog ran after her. She kept on running, and they would run after her until she managed to get them lost [i.e., lose them]—she and the dog [that joined her]. When she got tired, she sat down to rest next to the fence of a big palace. She fell asleep while sitting down due to the excessiveness of fatigue. After a while, a big carriage drawn by six horses halted in front of the [palace] door, and the prince[127] got out of it. As soon as he saw her, he felt pity for her;[128] so he asked the guards to take her into the palace, upstairs. The guards took her upstairs and dressed her well [in fine clothing]; they also took her dog along with her. [Upon seeing her], the prince admired her beauty very much. He asked his father—[the king—to allow him] to marry her. The king refused. But due to his son's persistent pleading, he consented, and permitted his son, the prince, to marry her.

The prince married the girl; she, along with her dog, lived with him in the palace in luxury and contentment. One day, as she was sitting with the prince, she remembered the pot, the meat, and the days of poverty and hunger. She laughed. The prince asked her as to the reason she was laughing. She said to him, "The reason is that your beard reminds me of the broom in my father's house." Upon hearing this, the prince took offense, and [his displeasure] showed. However, she answered quickly and said to him, "This means that [it is made of gold and pearl beads:] a gold bead [next to] a bead of pearl." The prince became happy when she said that, and became determined to learn who her father [happened to be:] the one who has a broom of gold and pearl beads. He [the prince] began to ask about him.

The princess [his wife] was afraid that the prince, her husband, might learn of her secret, and learn that she used to be poor. [She kept on searching without success for a solution.] But one day, her dog came to her and said, "Do not worry. I also have been searching. At long last I found a very rich man who is dying; while on deathbed, he confessed to his children that he has a daughter by another mother [other than theirs], whom they do not know. This man is very rich. As soon as he dies, you go and say that he was your father. And [thus] the problem would be solved."

The princess became happy. She went and said to her husband (after the [rich] man had died) that her father died and that she must go console her brothers.[129] The prince went with her. As soon as the [dead] man's sons saw her, and [as soon as] she told them that he was her father, they welcomed her very much. The prince was pleased because he, at last, got to know who her father was. While he was sitting with the princess and her [assumed] brothers, he looked at a corner [of the room only] to find a broom [made of gold and pearl beads:] a gold bead [next to] a bead of pearl; he became certain that this [dead man] is the father of the princess, his wife.

After a number of months, the dog wanted to test the princess's love for him. He pretended to be sick. The princess left him [alone] and ignored him completely. When his illness became more intense, she told the servants to keep him downstairs in the kitchen; she did not ask about him at all. One day, the dog pretended to be dead; and the servants told the princess that he had died. She told them to take him and throw him outside the palace. When the dog realized that [that would be his reward], he became very unhappy, got up, and went to her. He told her that, formerly,[130] he was a man, but a sorceress bewitched him into a dog; and that he thought that the princess loved [i.e., liked] him and was kind to him; but since she is treating him in that [ungrateful] way—[especially] after he had toiled in her behalf, helped her escape her father, assisted her in hiding her secret from her husband—he will avenge himself [on her by] going to the prince and telling him everything.

Indeed the dog went to the prince and told him [the story] from the beginning [to the end]. The prince got very angry and very offended that his wife had been lying to him. He kicked her out of the upper stories, and made her go down to the kitchen [on the lower floor to stay] with the rest of the servants.

The princess went down [to live] in the kitchen; she came to wear old clothes, cook, wash floors, and clean, just like the rest of the servants. She, however, looked after her dog more than [she did] in the beginning. Later on it happened that the dog became sick indeed. She would carry his food to him, sit beside and try to cheer him up. She was truly sad that he is sick. After the illness became too great, the dog died; she was very saddened and refused to throw him outside the palace [as is the case with dead pets]. She took her clothes out of the chest and she laid the dog inside it.

Days passed. The prince kept on thinking of his wife and wished she would come back to him.[131] Finally, he could not maintain his patience any longer,[132] so he went to her in the kitchen and asked her to come back to him, and that he had forgiven her. The princess was very happy with this [development]; but she asked that she bid farewell to (*tiwadda¿*) her dog that was [still] in the chest. She went and opened the chest; to their surprise—hers and the prince's—she found that the dog's body has been transformed to gold, and his eyes turned into two large very precious gems.

After this, the princess went up[stairs] anew with the prince; they lived in happiness and contentment. She always was kind to all animals, especially dogs.

❖ 8 ❖

MORE BEAUTIFUL THAN THE MOON[133]

(ALGERIA)

NARRATED IN MARCH 1989 BY Ḥ. M. ABOUT TWENTY-SIX YEARS OLD AND A UNIVERSITY GRADUATE, MISS H.M WORKS AS A RESEARCHER IN A GOVERNMENT RESEARCH CENTER. SHE HAD LEARNED THE TALE IN HER NATIVE KABYLE-BERBER LANGUAGE, FROM HER MATERNAL GRANDMOTHER. THE PRESENT WRITER MET THE NARRATOR WHILE PARTICIPATING IN AN ACADEMIC SYMPOSIUM HELD IN ALGIERS. THE NARRATOR COMMENTED ON THE WRITER'S BROTHER-SISTER SYNDROME THESIS IN THE LORE OF THE ARAB WORLD, BY CITING A NUMBER OF EXAMPLES EXPRESSING THIS THEME IN MAGHRIBIAN TRADITIONAL CULTURE.[134]

THE NARRATOR SPOKE IN THE FORMAL, BUT LESS EXPRESSIVE, CLASSICAL ARABIC, WHICH SHE ACQUIRED AS A SECOND LANGUAGE AT SCHOOL AND FROM HER FATHER AT HOME, INTERSPERSED WITH SOME FRENCH[135] WORDS USED FOR CLARIFICATION. SOME COLLEAGUES OF HERS VIEWED HER INTERACTION WITH THE PRESENT WRITER AS IMMODEST, AND WERE DISPARAGING OF IT.[136] A SECOND INTERVIEW, IN WHICH THE NARRATOR WAS TO TELL IN DETAIL THE TALE OF "THE SISTER AND HER BROTHER, AND MOSHSH—THE CAT,"[137] WHICH SHE HAD OUTLINED EARLIER, DID NOT MATERIALIZE. THE PRESENT TEXT WAS WRITTEN DOWN AS THE NARRATOR TOLD IT.

Jealousy between a mother and her daughter concerning physical attractiveness is a cardinal component in this tale. Significantly, the plot develops to replace this *initial Oedipal theme with one in which brothers compete for marriage to their foster sister. (This latter theme is recurrent in narratives designated as Type 885**,* The Foster Children.*) There is no mention of the heroine's father.*

Other salient themes include the mischievous she-cat, henna as marriage test, the importance of a maternal-uncle for a child, the heroine's reunion with her adoptive ogre-brothers, and the marriage of these "brothers" to daughters of a defeated ogress.

ONCE there was some woman. With every sunset, that woman would go to the housetop and ask the moon, "O moon, is there someone prettier than me?"[138] The moon would answer her, "I am pretty, and you are pretty, but no one is prettier than you!" One day that woman became pregnant, she gave birth to a little girl, she [the mother] had no [other children] but this little girl. The girl was very beautiful—and her mother was beautiful also; but the girl was prettier than her mother. The girl had a [natural] beauty mark on her chin; she was named *Lalla* ¿Ayshah el-Khaḍrah.

After the birth, the woman went up to the top of the house and asked the moon, "O moon, is there someone prettier than me?" The moon answered her, "I am pretty and you are pretty, but *Lalla* ¿Ayshah el-Khaḍrah is prettier than everyone!"

The woman became jealous. "How can I be that pretty, and my own daughter be prettier than me!" She asked the moon, "Shall I kill her?" The moon answered, "Yes, but not yet. Wait until she has finished [the stage of] breast-suckling."

A year passed and the woman asked the moon again, "O moon, is there someone prettier than me?" The moon answered her, "I am pretty and you are pretty, but *Lalla* ¿Ayshah el-Khaḍrah is prettier than everyone!" She said, "Now that she is not suckling, shall I kill her?" But the moon answered, "No, wait until she is a little girl that can walk and run."

Years passed and the woman asked the moon again, "O moon, is there someone prettier than me?" The moon answered her, "I am pretty and you are pretty, but *Lalla* ¿Ayshah el-Khaḍrah is prettier than everyone!" She said, "Now that she is a little girl, shall I kill her?" Still the moon answered, "No, wait until she learns how to cook."

A year or two later, the woman asked the moon again, "O moon, is there someone prettier than me?" The moon answered her, "I am pretty and you are pretty, but *Lalla* ¿Ayshah el-Khaḍrah is prettier than everyone!" She said, "Now that she can cook, and take care of a household, shall I kill her?" Still, the moon answered, "No, wait until she learns how to sew."

By that time *Lalla* ¿Ayshah el-Khaḍrah had grown up, and reached the age [of being a young woman], her mother said to the moon, "O moon, is there someone prettier than me?" The moon answered her, "I am pretty and you are pretty, but *Lalla* ¿Ayshah el-Khaḍrah is prettier than everyone! She is old enough to get married and beget children! Kill her now; and if you don't, I will kill you!"

She [the mother] decided to kill ¿Ayshah—her own daughter—so that she would remain the prettiest one. So, she went to the butcher and gave him some jewelry, and said to him, "I want you to take my daughter to the forest, kill her, and bring me a flaskful of her blood so that I may drink it!"

The man took the money [jewels], along with *Lalla* ¿Ayshah el-Khaḍrah and went to the forest. He could not bring himself to kill the innocent girl. Every time he looked at her he thought, "What sin has she committed. She is the Lord's creation! How could a young woman like this be slaughtered!!?"[139] He left her at that place—with the [wild] beasts; he thought, "God will carry out His plan for her." He slaughtered a ewe, filled a flask of its blood, and took it to *Lalla* ¿Ayshah el-Khaḍrah's mother. She drank the blood.

Lalla ¿Ayshah el-Khaḍrah waited for the old man [the butcher] to return, but he did not. She had neither food nor drink with her. In order to protect herself from the beasts, she found a cave and crawled into it. After a while, she passed out. The mother went up to the top of the house and said to the moon, "O moon, is there someone prettier than me?" The moon answered her, "I am pretty, and you are pretty, but no one is prettier than you!"—(that is because *Lalla* ¿Ayshah el-Khaḍrah was not on the surface of the earth). Upon hearing this [answer from the moon], the fires of jealousy went out of her heart.

Meanwhile, *Lalla* ¿Ayshah el-Khaḍrah came to. She heard noises, and saw seven ogres surrounding a carcass of an animal that they had killed, and were devouring. She was about to die of horror, and she remained in hiding. After the seven ogres had finished their meal, their youngest shouted out, "I smell an odor of a human." His six brothers said, "You are too young, and don't know. Since we left our parents' home, no one has come here!" (Those seven ogres were human beings—seven brothers who had run away from their [human] parents, and have lived like wild beasts in the forests.) But the youngest insisted, "I smell an odor of a human." They searched the cave, but could not find anyone. They said to the youngest, "See there is no one." They all went to sleep. When they were in deep sleep, *Lalla* ¿Ayshah el-Khaḍrah crept out of her hiding place, ate a little food and drank a little water, then she went back into the place where she had been hiding. In the morning, the youngest ogre shouted, "There is a human being here: someone has eaten from my food and has drunk from my water." Again they searched but found nothing.

Finally, they yelled, "If there is someone here, [let him] come out and he will be safe." They swore that they would not do any harm to that person. She came out; and they were stunned by her beauty and innocence. They said to her, "You are our sister!" She stayed with them, dear to them, and each one of them was trying to do what would please her. She remembered that she had learned cooking and sewing: she tailored some clothes for them, and cooked their food. She also cleaned them up: cut their hair and their beards and clipped their fingernails; they became human again. Every morning, they would go out to hunt, and return home before sunset with whatever they had caught. *Lalla* ¿Ayshah el-Khaḍrah would cook the meat and feed them. They all lived in the forest, and she became very dear to them.

Meanwhile, her mother went up to the top of the house and asked the moon, "O moon, is there someone prettier than me?" The moon answered her, "I am pretty and you are pretty, but *Lalla* ¿Ayshah el-Khaḍrah is prettier than everyone!" She was shocked [and wondered]: "My daughter *Lalla* ¿Ayshah el-Khaḍrah is dead, I drank a flask of her blood! How can this be!?" The moon still answered, "I am pretty and you are pretty, but *Lalla* ¿Ayshah el-Khaḍrah is prettier than everyone! She is with her seven brothers in the forest!" Out of vexation, the woman went "B-o-o-o-o-om!" [i.e., (burst)] and died.

But they [the seven foster brothers] all fell in love with *Lalla* ¿Ayshah el-Khaḍrah and began to quarrel with one another; each would say, "I will marry her!" The eldest said, "I am your eldest, and I [deserve to] marry first!" The youngest replied, "And I—your youngest—am the one who saw her first [therefore, it is fair that I would be the one who would marry her]." She thought of a trick to rid herself of this situation; she said to them, "Don't quarrel. I will marry the one in whose hands henna is the reddest!" She brought some henna and [pretended to] put it on their hands; she wrapped their hands in cloth until the next day. When she took the wrappings off, no one had henna on his hands—for she had not put real henna on their hands, but some other [herbs]. She said, "No one gets to marry me! I am a sister to each one of you." And they continued to live as before.

One day the seven brothers went out to hunt; but—contrary to their habit—they did not return at sunset. She, while waiting for them, became very hungry; [as a snack], she began to munch on some beans that they had. The she-cat came and said, "You ate my bean!" She gave her some beans but she [the cat] refused them and said, "I want my [very own] bean!" She emptied the entire sack of beans before her [the cat], but the cat still said, "I want my bean!" But her [the cat's] bean was gone. So the cat [in anger] said, "If you don't give me my bean back, I will punish you!" She answered, "Your bean is gone! I ate it!" So, she [the cat] went to the fire and went to the toilet [i.e., urinated] on it; the fire went out. Now the house had no fire. How is she [*Lalla* ¿Ayshah el-Khaḍrah] going to cook or keep warm? She thought she would borrow a spark from their neighbors and went out to look for fire, but they had no neighbors. She wandered about in the forest looking for fire till she saw a fire at a distance—(that was the fire in the house of the ogress). She went in the direction of the fire and arrived at the ogress's house. The ogress gave her some embers on a piece of potsherd, but she [the ogress] put much ashes along with the embers. The ashes dripped along the trail in the forest, and the ogress followed them to where the girl lived. When it became very late and her husband and her brothers had not returned, *Lalla* ¿Ayshah el-Khaḍrah fell asleep. The ogress sneaked in and stuck seven needles in ¿Ayshah's head; she drove them into her head very deep so that no one could see them beneath her hair, which was so long and thick. *Lalla* ¿Ayshah el-Khaḍrah became as if dead. The ogress sneaked out and went back to her house.

When her brothers returned, they found her in that condition; they thought that she was dead. They cried and cried, and said, "If we bury her, maggots will devour her!" So they put her on a horse's back and let the horse loose. The horse traveled for days, finally it stopped near a town. The king's son was out hunting: he saw the horse with *Lalla* ¿Ayshah el-Khaḍrah on its back. He drove his filly toward it, chased it until he got hold of the reins. He took the horse, along with its load, to his palace. Everyone marveled at the beauty of *Lalla* ¿Ayshah el-Khaḍrah, and was very sorry that she was dead. The king said to his son, "This girl must be buried." His son said, "But, sire, she does not look dead." But the king insisted that she be buried.

They handed her over to the undertaker to wash her body for burial. As one old woman was passing her fingers through her hair . . . , [that is] as she was combing *Lalla* ¿Ayshah el-Khaḍrah's hair, she felt something strange. When she looked, she found the needles and pulled them out. *Lalla* ¿Ayshah el-Khaḍrah—by God's will—opened her eyes and came back to life. Everyone rejoiced, especially the king's son because he had fallen in love with her. But alas! when they asked *Lalla* ¿Ayshah el-Khaḍrah about her name and what had put her in that condition, she could not answer: she had become dumb!!

The king's son insisted on marrying her. They said to him, "But we know nothing of her, or whether she [even] has a family!" But he insisted on marrying her, and his father and mother said, "All right. As you wish." They set up the wedding celebrations; and they got married according to God's edict, and His Prophet's.[140] *Lalla* ¿Ayshah el-Khaḍrah became pregnant and gave birth to a boy, but she remained unable to speak.

Years passed. The boy grew up and was once playing in the garden with the vizier's and the judge's sons. They had a dispute and quarreled. The sons of the vizier and the judge said to the boy—the son of *Lalla* ¿Ayshah el-Khaḍrah and the king's son, "Your mother has no origins!" So he went to his mother and cried, "You have neither a father nor a brother!" The poor child wept and wept. He ceased to go out of his room. He would neither eat nor drink, until he became very ill. His mother would look at him with great sorrow, and would not know what to do. One day, as her son was laying between life and death in his room; she—by the Lord's Power—spoke up! "You have seven maternal-uncles! Tell your father 'Papa, I want to go see my maternal-uncles!' When he tells you, 'I found your mother on a horse in the prairies!' you say to him, 'I want to go with my mother to look for my seven maternal-uncles!' " The child, [who had been re-activated by his mother's talk], went to his father and said what his mother had told him to say.

Lalla ¿Ayshah el-Khaḍrah and her child, along with servants and soldiers, set out to search for her brothers. She led them in the direction of the forest where her ogre-brothers lived. After a few days of travel, she caught a glimpse of seven shadows [silhouettes of persons] at a great distance walking, with their heads hanging down [in sorrow]. By their silhouettes, she suspected (*shabbaḥathum*)[141] that they might be her brothers. She sent the soldiers after them, and said, "Invite these poor people for a meal [in our camp]." (In reality they were her brothers roaming the surface of the earth in search of her corpse, which they had placed on the horse's back.) The soldiers returned with the seven; she immediately recognized them as her brothers and was very happy. She told her son, "At meal time say to me, 'Mother, tell me a story,' and when I say, 'Not now,' you cry and say, 'All little boys have a story told to them before they go to sleep!' "

After the guests had had dinner, and the trays lifted, it was tea-time. The child said to ¿Ayshah el-Khaḍrah, "Mother, tell me a story," and things went as she had instructed him to say. She replied, "Not now!" He wept and said, "All little boys have a story told to them before they go to sleep!" Then, ¿Ayshah el-Khaḍrah said, "Once there was a woman who used to ask the moon, 'O moon, is there someone prettier than me?' And the moon would answer her, 'I am pretty, and you are pretty, but no one is prettier than you!' Then, she begot a little girl whom she named ¿Ayshah el-Khaḍrah. . . . " She told her entire story from the day she was born to the night she went to the ogress's house for fire. Her seven brothers [recognized she was their sister], stood up, and all embraced one another.

Her brothers, all seven, went to the ogress's house, killed the ogress, and set her afire. There they found seven young maidens, who were the ogress's daughters. ¿Ayshah el-Khaḍrah told them [her brothers] not to cause them any harm. They all went to her home. She married her seven brothers to the seven daughters of the ogress.

And we went there and returned, may the Lord have mercy on our parents—concerning what we have said or forgotten [to say].[142]

FATHER AND DAUGHTER

9

FATHER OF SEVEN JOYS AND FATHER OF SEVEN SORROWS

(EGYPT)

NARRATED IN OCTOBER 1969 BY NABAWIYYAH M.Y., ABOUT FORTY-FIVE YEARS OLD AND A HOUSEWIFE. SHE WAS THE MOTHER OF FIVE GROWN CHILDREN, AND A NATIVE CAIRENE, DWELLING IN THE SOUTHERN SUBURB OF GÎZAH. SHE REFERRED TO HERSELF AS AN "URBAN-GAL (*BINT-BALAD*)."[143] I MET NABAWIYYAH AT A GOVERNMENTAL OFFICE AS SHE WAS BEING INTRODUCED TO A PROSPECTIVE EMPLOYER LOOKING FOR A MAIDSERVANT. HER AGENT WAS A DYNAMIC SIXTY-EIGHT-YEAR-OLD WOMAN NAMED AMNAH, WHO HAILED FROM THE CITY OF EL-MINYA IN SOUTHERN EGYPT AND WAS SELF-EMPLOYED AS A BROKER (*DALLÂLAH*).[144] THE WOULD-BE EMPLOYER REFUSED TO HIRE NABAWIYYAH ON THE GROUNDS THAT SHE WAS "STREET-SMART (*DÂYRAH*),"[145] "TOO CLEVER WITH WORDS (ARGUMENTATIVE: *GHALABAWIYYAH*),"[146] AND "WOULD NOT BE STARED DOWN (*¿AINHA QAWIYYAH*)."[147] LATER, NABAWIYYAH SORROWFULLY STATED, "I WAS WELL-TO-DO. . . . BUT I SQUANDERED A LOT OF MONEY ON *ZÂR*-[RITUALS FOR APPEASING POSSESSING-JINN], AND THE LIKE. NOW THAT ALL THE MONEY IS GONE, SO ARE THE '[*ZÂR*]-*'ASYÂD*'[148] [WHO USED TO POSSESS ME]!" A NUMBER OF DOMINANT PRINCIPLES, EXPRESSED IN PROVERBLIKE UTTERANCES, SEEMED TO GOVERN NABAWIYYAH'S VIEW OF THE ROLES OF THE FATHER AND MOTHER WITHIN A FAMILY; ONE OF THESE IS THAT "A MAN IS TO BRING [(PROVIDE)], A WIFE IS TO MANAGE [THE ENTIRE HOUSEHOLD]."[149] HOWEVER, DUE TO THE CHANGING ECONOMIC AND SOCIAL CONDITIONS, SHE HAD MODIFIED HER VIEWS: "IF WHAT THE MAN PROVIDES IS INSUFFICIENT, THE WIFE [SHOULD] PROVIDE TOO."

THE NARRATOR, WHO HAD REFUSED IN AN EARLIER SESSION TO TELL TALES, RELISHED NARRATING THIS STORY. AS A WOMAN WHO HAD TO WORK FOR A LIVing, she saw herself as comparable to the tale's heroine, who won "honestly with the sweat of her brow, and brains."

Nabawiyyah had heard the story when she was twelve or thirteen from other neighborhood women during bread-baking sessions; such gatherings "brought together at least three women . . . every two weeks . . . ; and we spoke about everything." Bread baking at home began to decline in urban centers during the 1950s; the taste of commercially produced bread is preferred.[150]

Āmnah, the narrator's elderly companion, sponsor, and agent, was a chatterer and seemed not to allow others to dominate the scene. She was reluctant to surrender the central stage to Nabawiyyah for the duration of the performance of the lengthy tale. She interrupted several times to interject comments. Her observations pointed out conceptual differences between the two women as to "the way the tale is told." Each had in mind a slightly different variant. Yet, when asked to tell the tale herself, Āmnah managed to present only a sketchy and incoherent rendition; evidently she was a "passive bearer" of folktales: capable of recognizing that which is told, rather than recalling what she had heard.[151]

Events in this realistic tale portray a set of complementary attitudes considered characteristic of the structure of sentiments within the traditional Arab family, and value systems. These include the rivalry between male siblings, intimacy between mother and son vis-à-vis the son's intimate personal concerns,[152] *and a father-daughter closeness with reference to matters that are largely nonpersonal and not of an intimate nature.*[153]

The conflict between a girl and her paternal-cousin ('ibn-¿amm*),*[154] *who ideally would be her preferred marriage partner, is unusual. This deviation is, nonetheless, congruent with the fact that—one being the youngest and the other being the eldest—considerable age difference is assumed to separate the two paternal-cousins, and with the fact that in most variants they do not get married to each other.*

The tale also challenges the universal Arab ethos of highly valuing sons and distrusting daughters; a daughter is perceived as vulnerable to temptation and, thus, a constant threat to her family's sexual honor (¿irḍ*).*[155] *A father's viewpoint is expressed in a lyric folksong(s) (*mawwâl*) from Egypt recurrent among males:*[156]

Night is like a predatory beast, and everyone fears it:
And the girl said to her father, with no bashfulness toward him [i.e., shamelessly],
"The garment wore out, O father, and the bosom showed through it!"

O father of daughters, be early and find yourself a market.
[If you] sell at the cheapest price, the market will have been profitable for you.
The begetting of girls is an evil, that will bring upon you infamy and harm.[157]

From a mother's perspective, although sons are preferred, the negative attitude toward female offspring is countervailed by the usefulness of a daughter as a mother's helper. The narrator expressed this view in a traditional aphorism: "She to whom time [fate] is kind, would beget her girls before her boys."[158]

The tale also reflects a number of gender-bound themes. Among these are: the disadvantageous position (e.g., raising capital, choice of roads) in which a girl—as a matter of course—is placed; pseudo-homosexual attraction,[159] *and the feminine experiences associated with menses.*[160] *In one variant told by a woman from the Gulf Region, the disguised heroine "stuck her finger into her self [so as to dip it in blood], and wrote with her [blood-stained] finger" a message to her admiring young host.*[161]

THERE were two brothers; one was rich while the other was poor. That rich one had seven "male sons,"[162] while the poor one—(Oh, what a pity!)[163]—had seven daughters. Every morning the poor one, the father of the seven daughters, would say to his rich brother—who is the father of the seven sons, "Good morning, father of seven joys!"[164] He would reply [coolly], "[And a] bright morning [to you, too],"[165] father of seven slumps."[166] Consequently, the poor one became depressed and silent. He would think to himself, "No ability [except for the power of] God.[167] [Is it possible that] he is my brother and I would greet him in the morning by saying, 'Good morning father of seven joys,' and he would respond to me in such a manner!" He [the poor brother] would thus suppress his feelings[168] and be depressed!

One day, his young[est] daughter saw him very saddened and [he seemed to be] suppressing things. She said to him, "What is the matter, Papa?"[169] He replied [in resignation], "Nothing, daughter! Nothing is the matter!"

She said [earnestly] "Just tell me! Tell me about that which is saddening you! Have we [daughters of yours], God forbid, done something bad, or something shameful, or . . . or . . . ?"

He said to her, "No, daughter! [The matter is that] I would say to your paternal-uncle (*¿ammik*), 'Good morning, father of seven joys!' and he would respond to me by saying, 'Bright morning, father of seven sorrows!'"

(All these matters about begetting boys or girls are only God's. No one can choose what he wants.)

So the girl said to her father [with affection], "O papa, don't be saddened. We, with God's permission, will cause you to hold your head high.[170] You should go to my paternal-uncle and cast upon him the morning greeting, as you are used to. When he replies to you, 'Bright morning, father of seven sorrows,' you should say to him, 'Come, let us send your eldest son and my youngest daughter Fuṭnah[171]—(or Zainab, for example—whatever her name happened to be)—on a trade-[mission]. And let us see who of the two of us has got the joy and who has got the sorrow.' If he were to reply, 'All right,' then let it be [a contest]; but if he were to say 'No!' then you should say to him, 'If that is so, we shouldn't be [reproaching each other by] saying, "Joys" and "Sorrows".' And [conclude by advising him,] 'May the Lord shield everyone'[172] [from infamy]."

The man stood up on his feet [i.e., erect and proud]! He went to the father of the seven sons—who is his brother:

"Good morning father of seven joys," [said he, in a tone denoting anticipation].

"Bright morning [to you, too], father of seven sorrows!"

"By God! Instead of your telling me 'joys' and 'sorrows,' come let us send your eldest son—'Mḥammad' [(Muḥammad)] (for example)—and my youngest daughter, Fuṭnah, on a trade-mission. And let us see who of the two of us is the 'felicitous one' (*'abu-es-sa¿d*) and who is the 'failed one' (*'abu-l-waks*)!"

His brother responded to him [sarcastically], "My! My! My![173] What kind of talk is that! Is there a little girl who could beat a [grown] man in trade-[matters]. Go your own way, [you silly] man, and 'pray on behalf of the Prophet' [i.e., calm down, wise up]!"

From here to there [after arguments], they agreed that they send the eldest boy and the youngest girl of his paternal-uncle [on a trade-mission] and see [how things turn out].

That was it! That man—the father of the seven sons—got with it: he prepared [things]; he brought [merchandise]; he spared no effort or expense;[174] he loaded that son of his, 'Mḥammad,' with stacks [of merchandise] that had neither a beginning nor an end. What for!? For him to set out so as to conduct commerce and show profit. As for that poor fellow [father of seven daughters], (oh, what a pity!), he owned nothing. He went and said to his daughter [in an apologetic, weak tone], "Daughter, [things are] as you can see: matters are plain and simple,[175] [we possess nothing]!"

She said to him [in a reassuring, warm tone], "Papa, don't worry. Our Lord will not forsake us, or let our [honest] labor go to waste!"

She went ahead and made herself into a "broker"—(narrator laughs and nods her head toward her own companion and employment agent stating, "Just like Āmnah, here"). She went to her women neighbors: Mother-of-he-So-and-so and Mother-of-she-So-and-so, Daughter-of-he-the-aforementioned, and Daughter-of-she-the-aforementioned.[176] She said to them, "I am setting out on a trade-mission; the one of you who would like to get in partnership with me will be a partner in profit [only, but] not in loss."[177] This one would give her an earring, this one would give her a bracelet, this one would give her a [copper] cooking pan,[178] and maybe that one chanced to have a little money—two or three pounds—(for they were all poor like her). She took all these things and hawked them at some merchant—one of those who loan money: [thus] she raised for herself a little capital.[179] She relied on God and set out to conduct the trade.

Now, here was much ado and boisterous festivity, while there, [matters were] hush-hush:[180] her paternal-uncle's son was setting out from his home [accompanied] by drumming, pipe playing, and much ado and boisterous festivity, while she was setting out from her home in hush-hush. The two met at the roads—(I mean the two reached a spot where you might say)—the road branched out. One branch had "The Road of Safety" inscribed on it, another had "The Road of Regret," and yet another had "The Road of He-Who-Goes-Doesn't-Return."[181]

The boy jumped and said to her, "I will take The Road of Safety."

She replied [with assuredness], "And I will take The Road of He-Who-Goes-Doesn't-Return! And let us meet here after a year—(for example)—and each of us would [then] find out how his brother had fared." He said to her, "Well, okeydokey (*mâshî*)!"

He, along with his people, servants, porters, and other [helpers] went down his path, The Road of Safety. And she, solely, went down her path, The Road of He-Who-Goes-Doesn't-Return.

She kept on going until she came to a [strange] country: people other than the people and a country other than the country [she was used to]. She arrived in that country and looked here and there [narrator moves her head to the right and to the left] only to see people going and people coming. Due to fatigue, she sat down; she came next to a shop and sat down [on the ground] to catch her breath. As she looked, she saw a tailor—one of those country-style tailors[182]—seated in his shop stitching, [narrator imitates the movement of sewing with a needle and thread]. But every now and then—[narrator speaks with astonishment]—he would reach into his bosom, take his wallet or his cloth purse[183] out of the pocket of his vest, take out something small—(as small as this—[narrator indicates how small, using the thumb against index finger to indicate about a finger joint in length]). He would lick it, then put it back into the wallet, then put the wallet back into the pocket of the vest. He kept on doing this for an hour, maybe two. She wondered, "What is that thing that he has in the wallet and he licks?" She went to him.

"Peace be upon you."

"And upon you be peace."

"I am a merchant who is a stranger in your country. I've just arrived. . . . " ([Aside]: I have bypassed you with my talk;[184] she had put on the clothing of a man—a young man, I mean—and called herself Ḥasan el-Bahbahâni,[185] and passed herself as a [man] merchant.)

She said, "My name is Ḥasan el-Bahbahâni; I am a merchant from the city of Such-and-such (I mean: Cairo, Alexandria, for example)."

"Oh, welcome, welcome. Please be so kind as to have some coffee; please be so kind as to have some tea."

She sat next to him and he ordered [from a coffeehouse] for her the [drink of] greeting.[186] Of course he thought she was a man, [but] he ordered nothing for himself. After a while he reached into his bosom and took out that thing which he had been licking. She said to him [in an inquisitive tone], "You have greeted me with the drink, but you did not drink along with me: [Hopefully, the reason for this is] good, if God wills!?"[187]

He answered her, "Good [it is]!: We, here in this country, have no salt! So, if we were to drink much water, we would slobber. If I were to slobber, I would ruin [with my saliva] the clothes of the customers. So, we must lick salt [to prevent that from happening]. That salt pebble, that you saw me take out of my wallet, is more expensive than [its weight in] gold."

She said to him, "May you prosper[188] [i.e., Thank you];" and "Peace be upon you [i.e., goodbye]."

"And upon you be peace."

She went. . . . She had saddlebags (*khurg*), or maybe a cloth bag,[189] out of which she took her travel supply of salt: a goodly sum, I mean—(for in olden times when people traveled, they used to take along rations and salt in plenty so as to preserve the food from going bad [by salt curing], but this is not done nowadays). She set out for the ruler of that country. She sold him the amount of salt that she had. At what price? For its weight in gold!

The king of the country had her for a guest. That king had a son, an only child: with no other [offspring] but him.[190] They placed that Ḥasan el-Bahbahâni in the visitors' room,[191] or, in the guesthouse (*maḍyafah*), and the king's son stayed with him in order to keep him company and welcome him. They sat together. Of course they were youthful: maybe they played cards, maybe they played backgammon, maybe they conversed; but the king's son would look [closely] at him. The eye [of the host] would meet the eye [of the guest]. He could not figure him [the guest] out.

The king's son went to his mother saying, "O mother, the mouth is the mouth of a lass (*bunayyah*),[192] the eyebrow is the eyebrow of a lass, the glances (*laḥẓ*)[193] are the glances of a lass; but the willpower (*¿azm*) is the willpower of men."

His mother said to him, "Son, maybe he is a lass dressed as a man."

"Mother, I don't know about him! If he is a lass, I am in love with her."

His mother said to him, "Son, why don't you invite him for dinner and see how he is going to eat. If he falls behind and lets you and the other invited men sit down ahead of him—(I mean does like a woman would do among men)—then he is a woman. See whether he will 'eat in the manner camels eat, and quit [the table] ahead of the [other] men!' "[194]

The king's son went to say to that Ḥasan el-Bahbahâni, "You are invited for dinner today, . . . "—(that you might say was a Friday)—"after the Friday prayers [at noon in the mosque]."

ASIDE

[Āmnah interrupts and disputes the accuracy of the tale.]

Āmnah [disagreeing]: Invited for dinner, what!? How can that be!? It is said [in the tale] that he is already in the guesthouse! Wouldn't one feed his guests: breakfast, dinner, and supper; or what!?*

Narrator: That is it; the tale is told this way.

Āmnah: No, sister, it is told [in the following manner]:

His mother said to him, "Bring some *ḥawâdiq* (salties, i.e., salt-cured foods): pickles, *fesîkh* (pickled fish), and the like; because women go for salted stuff."

Narrator: What salty foods!? It is said that salt with which [various] salted things—*ṭorshî* (pickled vegetables), *mishsh* (pickled cheese), *melûḥah* (pickled Nile-fish) are made—is more expensive than gold, and that they keep it in their wallets. How could they then have salt-cured foods!?

Āmnah [defending her viewpoint]: Isn't he the king's son [i.e., rich and can afford it]; and isn't he an only child?

Narrator [concluding]: No, it is not like that. Your story must be another [different] one.

Āmnah remains unconvinced.

---

*Āmnah addressed this question to the present writer, thus implying that she and the narrator, being his guests, should be treated to dinner.

[Narrator continues:] They prepared the dinner: fowl—(chickens, pigeons, and the like),[195] and meat—(lamb, beef, and the like) and sent the tray [carried by servants into the guesthouse]. She was alert[196] and clever; she detected the ploy. She didn't do as women would: wait until men have finished eating [then eat]. She [promptly] sat down, rolled up her sleeves, and said, "In the name of God," and she grabbed the fowl—say: a fried tom-duck (*ḍakar baṭṭ*, i.e., drake) or tom-turkey (*dîk-rûmî*)[197]—tore it apart, and gave each [guest] his share: "You take the breast (*sidr, ṣadr*), you take the drum (*ṭablah*) [which is the fatty part of the tom-turkey's breast], you take the thigh, you take . . . , and you take . . . !" She herself ate her share in two or three gulps: 'in the manner of camels.' [Narrator laughs.] That was all. His ploy did not work out; he looked at her (like this: [with a stare of disbelief]). Whenever his eye would meet hers he would wonder: "I don't believe it! The mouth is the mouth of a lass, the eyebrow is the eyebrow of a lass, the glances are the glances of a lass; but the willpower is the willpower of men!"

So, his mother said to him, "Maybe she detected the ploy. Take him and show him your father's treasury; show him what is in it and find out what will appeal to him. If he be a lass, he will go for women's things."

He [the king's son] said to him, "Come, let us look at my father's treasury"—(the king's treasury, that is). [So, they went]:

"Look! This is a pearl necklace," [said the king's son].

. . . . [Silence].

"Look! This is a snake[-shaped] bracelet."

. . . . [Silence].

Of course, the girl was alert, so she said to him [in a reprimanding tone], "What bracelet! And what necklace! Enough! Look at this sword; it is from India [where good swords are to be gotten], isn't it! And look at that dagger! And that small handgun (*ferfir*)! And that . . . , and that . . . !"

He went running to his mother and said to her [in a sad tone], "I still don't believe it. He has chosen the swords and the daggers and did not [even] look at the necklaces or the bracelets!"

His mother said to him, "Perhaps she detected the ploy. Now you say to her, 'You-[girl] come[198] . . . ,' (I mean): 'You-[man] come[199] let us go to the palace's garden so that we may climb up the palm trees and bring date fruits off the palm trees,' then see what she will do."

. . . . [Narrator pauses.]

ASIDE

Āmnah asks [slyly]: Why have you become silent? You have already said it! [i.e., what you are reluctant to say now].

Narrator [to collector]: But, it is . . . (May God's name protect your status.)* [i.e., it is indecent].

El-Shamy: That is perfectly all right!

* *'ism-Allâ ¿alâ maqâmak,* lit.: God's name is on your status. In the present context, this phrase signifies that consideration for the listener's social position is holding the speaker from using improper language. Cf. Mot. W44§, "Proper bashfulness (*ḥayâ'/khafar, kusûf/khajal*). [. . .])"; W44.2§, "Bashfulness at indecent (obscene) words."

[Narrator continues:] She went. . . . She said to him, "All right." She went and got two doum[-nut]s,[200] . . . [narrator giggles nervously] and something like that which men have—(say: a cucumber, a carrot: any thing in that form [which resembles a phallus])—and she tied them to herself [thus giving the appearance of having the organs of a male].

He climbed up the palm tree first and brought down a single stalk (*sham-rûkh*) of dates. Then she climbed up while he kept on gazing at her climbing upwards: [narrator raises her eyes gradually upwards, as if observing a person climbing a tree]—and would find her having those things of men! She brought down a whole bundle (*ṣubâṭah*)![201]

He went to his mother [complaining]: "Mother! She has men's things! I still don't believe it: the mouth is the mouth of a lass, the eyebrow is the eyebrow of a lass, the glances are the glances of a lass; but the willpower is the willpower of men!! Mother! He brought down a whole bundle [of date stalks]!" His mother said to him [with a little despair], "Invite him to go bathing in the river,[202] . . . , tell him that the two of you should go and bathe your horses at the river. Naturally, you [two] will take your clothes off; [then] you will see." [He did as his mother suggested].

When the two of them went to the riverbank, each one of them holding his horse, she came—(like this: [narrator whispers out her words to denote stealth])—to the rear of the animal (no offense: *'lâ-mu'âkhzah'*) that he was holding. She had brought with her some black pepper (or hot red pepper, or something like that); as he was not paying attention, she put the hot pepper—(no offense)—in the animal's rear. [Narrator speaks with emphasis and abrupt transitions between sentences.] So the animal—(May God's name protect your status)—bolted! And ra-a-a-a-n! It dragged the king's son [who was holding the reins] on his face [(i.e., on his stomach or belly)] for some distance! Then it broke the reins! It ran far and fast; and he flung himself after it.[203]

Our friend—the girl—splashed around (*balbaṭet*) in the water for a while, took a dip, bathed her horse, and sat down waiting for him [to return]. When he returned, tired and worn out, he said to her, "O Ḥasan, O Bahbahâni,[204] let us bathe ourselves." He [the girl] answered, "I [fear I] might catch cold. I've already taken a bath and bathed the horse!!"

He [the king's son] returned—vexed and desperate. He told his mother about that which he had been saying every time, "Everything: the face, the eyes, the mouth, the body-figure (*el-kasm*),[205] everything is feminine (*ḥarîmî*);[206] but the willpower is the willpower of a man."

After a number of days, her—(no offense)—menses (*el-¿âdah [esh-shahriy-yah]*)[207] came. She looked around; (naturally she did not have with her any of the feminine things [that she would have needed for this situation]). So, [since it is important for a woman to have her hair covered during her period], she wrapped her head with the turban-shawl [which she wore as part of her male disguise]. (She used the shawl of the turban as a head-kerchief in lieu of a woman's pompon-fringed head-kerchief[208] so that her hair would not fall out and get into things [especially food].)

His mother said to him, "Take two [freshly cut] bundles of sweet basil (*reḥân*)[209] or [fresh] green mint (*ni¿nâ¿ 'akhḍar*). During the night place one on the quilt on his bed and the other on yours! If—in the morning—[you find that] his bundle has withered, then [this is proof that] he is a lass. He did as she said; he got two bundles of mint, placed one on her bed, and the other on his. ([Aside:] And, as you know, [fresh] mint looks bright (*mezahzah*); but if a woman is menstruous, she should not step into fields of eggplant, cucumbers, and the like . . . for she would cause it [supernaturally] to wither and die.)[210]

She got up during the night and found the bundle of mint placed on her quilt; [it was] withered. She sneaked over and placed her [withered] bundle on his quilt and took his fresh-looking bundle and placed it on her own quilt, and she slept till midmorning. He got up early in the morning supposing that he was getting up first: "O-o-o-ps! What happened? Mine is withered but hers [i.e., his] is fresh!" [he wondered. He went and told his mother].

His mother told him, "'I am at my wit's end'![211] Maybe, son, he is [really] a man!!"

Meanwhile, she [the girl] had been carrying out [some] trade, and turning profit until she became [one] of the biggest merchants. She went and said to the king's son . . . , ([narrator explains:] during that period, and due to [their intimacy through] togetherness-in-life (*¿ishrah*),[212] for they were in each other's company for some time, her heart leaned toward him), she went and said to the king's son, "I must go back to my country."

ASIDE

Āmnah comments: *¿ishqituh: mish bint-bnût, we-yilzamhâ eg-gawâz!?* (She fell in [erotic] love with him: isn't she a young-virgin, and [as such] doesn't she need marriage!?)

[He answered, with considerable concern], "Why! Here, you would become the head of the [guild of] merchants.[213] Remain with us."

[She replied], "No, I have in my trust[214] things [shares of the capital and of profits] that belong to poor people and orphans. I must return them!"

"All right! But you must return!"

"If God wills (*'in-shâ'-Allâh*)!"

They prepared for the trip: horses, camels, carts, and . . . , and . . . , all loaded with goods and gifts, in addition to the servants and entourage. Wow! Very impressive (*dunyâ*)![215] In the middle of the night, after all had gone to sleep, she got up and wrote [a letter stating]: "My name is So-and-so, daughter of So-and-so,[216] from such-and such a place, and if you want me you [should] come for me in my country."

ASIDE

Āmnah interjects: [She—the heroine—wrote],

"'*in kont ¿âshiq wi mushtâq,*
ḥaṣṣalnî f-blâd el-¿Irâq"
("If you are in love and yearning [for me],
catch up with me in the countries of Iraq.")*

Narrator: No! This [statement] is in a different tale.

---

*A statement (Mot. R134.1§) typically uttered by the departing supernatural wife at her human husband in Arab renditions of Type 400, *The Man on a Quest for his Lost Wife.*

Now, where did she arrive? [She] arrived at that place at which she and her paternal-cousin had agreed to meet. She got there first. They [the servants] unloaded the burdens off the animals, and erected a pavilion (*ṣuwân*)[217] for leisure: something of pomp and splendor![218] Not too long afterwards someone came: in ragged clothes, barefooted, and his condition—(the more distant one) (*el-'ab¿ad*)[219]—[was] sheer misery. She recognized him [to be her paternal-cousin] but he did not recognize her for she, naturally, was still dressed in men's clothing.

"Peace be upon you!" [said the newcomer].

"And upon you be peace," [she replied].

"Haven't you got something [for me]—alms—for God's sake, for I am hungry and naked."

"Yes, we do! But, would you work [for it]?"

"Yes, I would!"

"What can you do?

"I am a merchant, I had with me a heck of a lot of merchandise![220] But time [i.e., fate] finished it off! I was not careful with myself. I squandered my money over frivolous indecent fun and shameful conduct,[221] and my trade expedition was bankrupted!!" [he replied with great sorrow].

She said [with caution], "All right. What would you say if I were to put you in charge of this trade expedition of mine. You deliver it to my home, and you would receive a fee of such and such—(say: a thousand pounds, for example)?"

When he heard this, he cheered up and said, "No reason why not to." (That is he, her paternal-cousin, is saying to her "There is no reason why not to.")

[She said with slyness], "But, of course I must stamp you on . . . [narrator hesitates] . . . on your back [stating] that you are one of the slaves of Ḥasan el-Bahbahâni!"

[He replied with hesitation and reluctance], "All right! No harm in this. I'm your man and this is your merchandise."

That was it! She got up and took out the seal and stamped him: "This is one of my slaves. [Signature:] Ḥasan el-Bahbahâni."

That friend of ours [her paternal-cousin], now said to himself: "Relief has [unexpectedly] come!" He got hold of the entire business [caravan] and [commanded]: "Let us go (*yallâh*)!" To where? To his own home, at such and such a place.

Before arriving at his home he sent messengers to announce that "I am coming home with my business caravan!" The entire town—its old and its young—went out to look at the arrival scene. [Much] drumming, pipe playing, trellises of joy (*zaghârîṭ*), and dancing—(for this was the custom in olden times). He went to his father and said, "See, here I am. I have returned to you with [great] profits. I have brought back [such and such], and I have brought back [such and such], and . . . !"

"Well! But where is the daughter of your paternal-uncle (*bint ¿amm*)?"

[He replied, sarcastically,] "She failed! Maybe you will find her cast away in the streets, somewhere. Or, maybe she is a. . . . She probably ended up in a . . . [place of ill repute]." [He continued, speaking in a contrived tone of piety,] "Never mind! May the Lord shield our women-folk[222] [from a similar fate]!"

When her father [who, evidently, was among the well-wishers] heard that, life turned black to his eyes. He extracted himself out [stealthily] from among the men. His brother shouted at him with malicious joy (*bi shamâtah*), "O father of seven sorrows, have you now seen [for yourself]!"

The man [the girl's father] extracted himself out and silently left for his home. Naturally he felt dishonored and would say, "O earth, [please] open up and swallow me [so that I may be spared the humiliation]!" Due to [good] luck (*bakht*), he returned home and found his [youngest] daughter also at home.

[He said with great amazement and anguish], "Oh my! When did you return? What did you do? Where did you go? And from where did you come back?"

She said to him, "By God, Papa, I've dispatched my servants and my slaves ahead of me, accompanied by my trade caravan. Haven't they arrived?"

[He answered with great suspicion] "O my daughter, what servants, what slaves, and what trade caravan! Your paternal-cousin arrived accompanied by drumming and pipe playing, while here you are: arriving in hush-hush, just like a person guilty of malfeasance!"[223]

She said to him, "Papa, all those things [that he brought back] belong to me and are my property. I want you to go fetch the judge, the ruler of the country, and all the people so that they may judge [the case] between us."

He said to her [in a skeptical tone], "Daughter, what judge and what ruler! Let the shame that is not known to people remain as it is."[224]

She said [imploringly], "Papa, just do that which I am telling you to do!"

From here to there, the man, her father, acquiesced. They went to the judge. He, her father, said—(No! [I forgot]; before they went to the judge)—she had said to her father, "You, Papa, should say to the judge that your brother's son owes you something that has been entrusted to his honor[225] for delivery to you. When the judge asks you for the witnesses, you leave the rest up to me."

They went to the judge and her father spoke to him as she told him to: " 'This [accused] is my brother's son,' " and that " 'There is something of mine entrusted to him,' " and that " 'He has not delivered the things entrusted to him to their rightful owners.' "

When the judge heard that he said, "Bring him [the accused] here."

They brought him, and the judge said to him, "This man says that he has something in your trust!"

He replied [with surprise], "Not at all! True that he is my paternal-uncle but he has nothing placed in my trust!"

"He says that a merchant sent with you merchandise to [be delivered to] him!"

"Never. I saw no one, neither a seller nor a buyer! All the goods I brought back home are things that I have earned by the sweat of my brow."

The judge looked at the man [the girl's father] and asked him, "Do you have any witnesses or proof?"

Here, the girl, his daughter, still dressed in men's clothing, spoke out from among the crowd [that had gathered], "Yes, Your Honor,[226] I am his witness!"

"Who do you happen to be?" [the judge asked].

"I happen to be Ḥasan el-Bahbahâni—[one] of the biggest merchants! I am the one who sent the merchandise to this man [pointing at the girl's father] with this person [pointing at the girl's paternal-cousin]. This person is one of my slaves; he has betrayed the trust and [unlawfully] taken the merchandise. If you were to check his back you will find my seal: This [person] is one of the slaves of Ḥasan el-Bahbahâni!"

The judge, in front of all the people of the town, said to the guards, "Seize him and check his back!" (Or, "Check the spot where that seal was.")[227] [So, they did.] They found the seal exactly where Ḥasan el-Bahbahâni had said it would be, and saying exactly what he said it would state.

The boy broke out in tears and confessed that he lied, that he cheated, and that he stole, and that he . . . , and that he . . . ; he told them everything. Now the judge said to him [sternly], "You stole. You committed perjury. You betrayed trust. To what shall I sentence you? [I sentence] you to return the merchandise to its owner: Ḥasan el-Bahbahâni. And, [from now on], you are one of his slaves; [he may] dispense with you as he pleases and as he sees [fit]!"

Here, the girl revealed herself. She said [declaring]: "I am So-and-so, daughter of So-and-so. This man is my father, and I am his young[est] daughter; this man is my eldest paternal-cousin. His father, [who is] my father's biological brother,[228] used to call us [me and my sisters] 'seven sorrows.' Now, you Judge, and you people of the town [can] judge for yourselves as to who of the two is the 'father of seven joys' and who is the 'father of seven sorrows!' "

Thus, everyone knew that a girl can be more adroit than a boy.

(I had bypassed you with my talk.) When the king's son—the one who fell in love with her and was trying to discover her secret—found the letter that she had written [stating] that, "I am a girl! And if you want me, come to our home and ask my father for me [in marriage]," he [felt as if] he was flying for joy. He went to his mother and said to her [with excitement], "Haven't I told you that this Ḥasan el-Bahbahâni is [in fact] a girl!" He asked [and received] permission from his father and mother to go searching for the girl.

He [set out and] kept on asking about her father's house until he found it; good-hearted people showed him the way and told him, "They are at the judge's!" It chanced that he arrived [in her town] while they were at the judge's.

When the judge asked [the girl's father], "Do you have any witnesses?" and the girl replied, "Yes, I am Ḥasan el-Bahbahâni, and . . . , and . . . , and . . . !" the king's son [spoke up and] said, "And I testify that this Ḥasan el-Bahbahâni was in our country, and [was] our guest, and we saw nothing from him except [every aspect of] good manners and perfection [in conduct]!"[229]

When the girl revealed her true identity, that was all [that was needed]. He asked her father for her hand. Her father said, "If she were to say 'Yes,' I also would say 'Yes!' "

They set up the wedding celebrations, and the fine [joyous] eves:[230] forty days and forty nights.

Āmnah [adds]: She went back with her husband; she went back to live in his father's country, and she became queen. And it came to be that when her father would say to his brother, "Good morning father of seven joys," his brother would answer him: "May He [the Lord] make your morning blissful,[231] you father of the seven felicitous ones (blessings)."

❖ 9-1 ❖

SEVEN GIRLS AND SEVEN BOYS

(ALGERIA, BERBER)

NARRATED IN JULY 1982 BY AN ALGERIAN MAN IN HIS MIDTWENTIES AND OF KABYLE-BERBER ETHNIC AFFILIATION. THE TEXT WAS COLLECTED AND WRITTEN DOWN (IN ENGLISH) BY ¿ABD-AL-QÂDIR ¿ARBÎ-ZÂZOU, A YOUNG MAN OF THE SAME NATIONAL AND ETHNIC AFFILIATION AS THE NARRATOR. AT THE TIME OF THE COLLECTING, BOTH WERE STUDENTS AT A COLLEGE IN THE UNITED STATES.

In this brief rendition, the heroine wins by sheer luck (or fate): her cousin lives and dies by the sword,[232] while she benefits from "unintentional" deception ("cleverness") in the marketplace. This text also seems to be of an overtly didactic nature. "It is told to adults to teach them that one should not laugh at [i.e., slight] a woman . . . ," the narrator explained.

THE story goes like this: "There were two married brothers. One had seven boys and the other had seven girls. During some gathering, the one who has seven boys humiliated his brother because he has girls only in the house. The humiliated man went back to his home ashamed. His children saw him so depressed, they asked him what the matter was. He told them. The youngest girl said to him the following: 'Go to your brother and ask to get his smartest child [son] so that I and him [he] go for an adventure.'

Their father went to his brother and told him. They agreed. The smart boy and the young girl went for an adventure on horseback. The girl had a young greyhound with her and the boy had a sword. They went until they reached a certain place that had two ways to go. They each chose a way. In the middle of his trip, the boy was killed by bandits. The girl on her way met a shepherd. He liked the greyhound and asked the girl if she wanted to exchange her dog for a sheep. She agreed and continued on her way. The greyhound escaped to be with its owner, that is, the girl. In another place she met another shepherd who liked the dog too. The girl exchanged her dog for a cow and left. Since the greyhound liked her, he escaped again and followed her. On her way back home, the cow gave birth. She returned to the village where everybody was waiting. She told them that her cousin was killed.

Her father was proud and excited. His brother was ashamed and cried in public," [i.e, was humiliated].

❖ 10 ❖

THE GIRL INSIDE THE GOLDEN COW[233]

(EGYPT)

NARRATED IN JULY 1971 BY GALÎLAH ¿A., AGED TWENTY-FOUR, A HOUSEMAID FROM THE VILLAGE OF SH., MUNÛFIYYAH GOVERNORATE, IN THE NORTHERN NILE DELTA. SHE LEARNED THE TALE IN THE VILLAGE FROM HER PATERNAL GRANDMOTHER. (SEE SECTION II—PROFILE, P. 42.)

This text is a skeletal rendition of the narrative as it is commonly told. Although it contains all the basic episodes found in fuller renditions, it lacks elaboration, dialogue, and background events. It is not clear whether these qualities are the product of defensive mechanisms on the part of the narrator due to the incestuous nature of the tale, or simply due to "forgetting." The narrator's ability to provide narrative details is demonstrated in her renditions of other tales.[234]

This narrative is one of the relatively infrequent cases in Arab lore where an Oedipal theme is overtly presented. It may be argued that a narrator's perception of a father wishing to marry his daughter is an externalization of the narrator's own subconscious desire. Thus when told by a female (i.e., a daughter), the tale may be viewed as a case of projecting[235] *this socially unacceptable behavior by attributing it to the father. When narrated by a male (i.e., a father), the tale may constitute an expression of incestuous tendencies on the part of that male toward his daughter.*

Yet, here, as in the overwhelming majority of similar depictions of incestuous situations involving father and daughter, the Oedipus complex fails to crystallize and is subsequently dissipated. Typically the daughter succeeds in escaping from her father, and the separation is total and final. She usually marries the son of a patriarch, a person of her own age group. Thus the girl's actual husband may not *be identified symbolically as a father figure.*[236]

ONCE there was a man who had only one daughter. He went on pilgrimage, and brought back from Hejaz a single ankle bracelet.[237] He said, "Whosoever it fits, I will marry." So he toured all the entire country in order to put it on this one and on that one, so as to find out whom it would fit. It fit only his daughter. He said, "I must marry her!" Naturally, his daughter—upon learning of this matter—ran away. She went to a man, a carpenter, and said to him, "Make me a statue of a cow, (or something like that), so that I can enter into it. It should [be big enough to] hold me inside of it!" [So he made her a statue of a cow; she took it home and entered into it.] The man [her father] kept on searching for the girl, and kept on touring around [looking for her], but he could not find her. He found only the statue of the cow.

Because the statue belonged to his daughter, it was very dear to him. Finally, he said, "Whosoever would give me its weight in gold will be the one to take it." The king's son came, paid its weight in gold, and took it [to the palace] into his own room [on the upper floor].

Afterward, whenever they would take the food upstairs to him—I mean in the place where he would have his meals, next to the statue, she would come out [while he was gone], eat the food, then would go back into [the statue] and lock herself in. [Upon discovering that the food was missing], they would be very puzzled. "What is it that causes the disappearance of the food! It must be the slave who takes the food up, or the cook, who is the one who eats the food!" [they concluded.]

One day, their son, [the king's son], slipped in between the bed mattresses and hid there in order to catch the cook as he ate the food after carrying it upstairs. He looked [only] to find this one [the girl] opening [the cow], getting out, and eating up the food; for as soon as the food was brought up, she would come out and finish it off. He realized that it was she who had been eating the food all along.

He married her after that.

EL-SHAMY: Did he [the king's son] do anything to her father [as punishment]?
NARRATOR: [No.] Her father realized that he was at fault in that respect, and that she has married the king's son.

❖ 11 ❖

MARYAM, OF COOL AND COQUETRY[238]

(BAHRAIN)

NARRATED IN THE SUMMER OF 1986 BY ¿AYSHAH/'OMM-Ḥ., A SEVENTY-YEAR-OLD, NONLITERATE WIDOW, FROM BAHRAIN. SHE REFUSED TO GIVE HER FAMILY NAME OR OTHER INFORMATION CONCERNING HERSELF OR THE TEXT. HER NARRATING STYLE WAS CHARACTERIZED BY SHORT SENTENCES, ALL UTTERED IN THE SAME TONE OF VOICE.

THIS TEXT WAS COLLECTED WITH THE ASSISTANCE OF K. AL-Ḥ., A LITERATE DIVORCEE OF ABOUT FORTY-FIVE YEARS OF AGE. SHE CAME FROM BAHRAIN AND WORKED AS A CUSTODIAN AT A GIRLS' SCHOOL IN DOHA, QATAR, WHERE SHE LIVED WITH HER BROTHER AND HIS FAMILY.

Fear (or anxiety)[239] *concerning father-daughter incest, an animal paramour, relations between a white mistress and her black slave-girl,*[240] *disguise by wearing someone else's hide, and marriage between two males are salient themes in the following fantasy tale. It is a regional subtype of the narrative given in Tale No. 10, and seems to be confined to the Arabian Peninsula.*

In lieu of the incestuous father, a father's stallion or bull camel is the source of the daughter's fear.[241] *As such, an initial Oedipal theme is less overtly expressed. Still true to the pattern, the Oedipal situation is unfulfilled: the daughter marries a sheikh's son, not a paternal figure. Also of interest is the use of the kinship appellation:* ¿ammah *("paternal-aunt") to designate a slave-mistress relationship.*

A man has a stallion: a thoroughbred (*'aṣîl*) that he kept well. He made a living off that stallion: he sold molasses and butter; this was his trade. [He also had a daughter named Maryam.] One day, as the man was gone, [narrator addresses the daughter directly:][242] O Maryam—you who are his daughter—get up, open the door a crack, and peep at the stallion. When that one [the stallion] saw her, his heart sank; he began to neigh and trot around, neigh and trot around. He neither ate nor drank; neither defecated nor urinated. He became emaciated, for the stallion fell in love with the girl and became lovesick.

Maryam's father came back; [he saw the stallion in that condition, and moaned], "My capital is this stallion! What am I to do! Without him I can neither sell nor buy. What am I to do?!" He said [to Maryam], "Daughter, pack up yourself and leave. I will hold him back for three days."

She packed up her personal belongings, took along her slave-girl (*¿abdah*) and departed. She went on and she went on. Days passed; she said, "My slave-girl, wear some kohl [so as to sharpen your eye-sight] and go up and look."

The slave-girl wore some kohl, climbed up a hill, and looked. She said, "I see something on the horizon; he is as big as a fly."

They kept on going.

A day later, she said: "My slave-girl, wear some kohl and go up and look." The slave-girl wore some kohl, climbed up a hill, and looked. She said, "I see something on the horizon, he is as big as a chicken."

They kept on going.

A day later, she said: "My slave-girl, wear some kohl and go up and look." The slave-girl wore some kohl, climbed up a hill, and looked. She said, "I see something on the horizon, he is as big as a camel."

They kept on going.

[She kept on saying], "My slave-girl, wear some kohl and look!" "My slave-girl, wear some kohl and look!" "My slave-girl, wear some kohl and look!"

[And the slave-girl kept on answering], "O my paternal-aunt [i.e., mistress],[243] I see something of this size!" "O my mistress, I see something of that size!" "O my mistress, . . . !" [narrator gestures with her hands to indicate the increasing size of the creature seen].

All of a sudden he [the stallion] was on top of them [about to seize them]. She found a high date palm tree, and the two of them climbed up to its crown. Upon seeing Maryam, the stallion went crazy. He kept on neighing, bolting back and forth, and rearing up. He began to ram the palm tree [with his head], ram the palm tree, ram the palm tree, as he went around it staring [with his eyes fixed upward at Maryam]. She threw her clothes into his mouth; he swallowed her clothes. She threw her gold [jewelry]; he swallowed her gold. She threw every thing into his throat but with no avail; he would not quit or calm down! She [finally] found a pair of scissors, she threw the scissors into his throat; the scissors landed crosswise. The stallion went into convulsions and fell [dead] to the ground.

She remained on the palm tree for some time. Her slave-girl would say to her, "O my mistress, let us get down." She would answer her, "I fear he might revive, get up, and attack us." [They remained up there] until the stench from the stallion's odor was too strong to bear. She climbed down, slit his belly and retrieved her belongings. They left his carcass on the ground and went on.

During the night it became very cold; [they saw light from a fire at a distance]. She said to her slave-girl, "My slave-girl, go get us a spark so that we may have ourselves a fire."

The slave-girl went to get the fire. She came upon some people (who were [actually] not people). She said to them, "My mistress bids you well and begs of you a spark." They answered, "Where is your mistress?"

"Over there at a distance," [she replied].

They got hold of the slave-girl, slaughtered her, flayed her, and ate her up. They stretched her skin over the fire-pit to dry. Then they went after Maryam, her mistress.

When she saw them coming, she ran and hid inside the carcass of the dead stallion. They looked for her everywhere and could not find anyone. They said, "The slave-girl was lying. There is no mistress here." They kept on going, so as to look for Maryam elsewhere. [Meanwhile], she got out of the stallion's carcass, went to the fire to look for her slave-girl, and found the skin stretched over the firepit. She took her clothes off, put on the slave-girl's skin, and departed before they got back.

[She posed as a black boy, and called out], "Who would like a boy [servant]?" "Who would like a boy [servant]?" "Who would like a boy [servant]?" Some people replied, "Go to the sheikh's house, they need a boy [servant]." At the sheik's house, they asked her, "Yes, we need a boy [servant]. Do you herd camels?" She replied, "I can herd camels and livestock."

The first day, she took the camels to pasture on the sheikh's lands. She came to a spring; there were [fruit] trees all around it. She took off the slave-girl's skin and went into the spring to swim; she would splash around in the water and chant,

"Before, I [used to be] Maryam: of cool and coquetry!
Today, I've become a camel-herd!
O peaches, blossom out, and you pomegranates, clap your hands,
for Maryam the daughter of the sultan's son!"[244]

One she-camel exclaimed, "¿A-a-a-a-a!"

She [Maryam] retorted,

"May an arm-length knife strike you,
leaving on you neither bone nor meat!!"[245]

The she-camel dropped dead. Maryam gathered her things, put on the skin, and left for home. [When she got there, she yelled],

"Where is my master? Where is my master?"

"What is with you, boy?" [the master replied].

"A she-camel died today!!"

"Well, that is her fate!"

The following day, she took the camels back to the same spot to pasture. She went to the place and took off the slave-girl's skin and went into the spring to swim; she would splash around in the water and chant,

"Before, I used to be Maryam: of cool and coquetry!
Today, I've become a camel-herd!
O peaches, blossom out, and you pomegranates, clap your hands,
for Maryam the daughter of the sultan's son!"

Another she-camel exclaimed, "¿A-a-a-a-a!"

[Maryam] retorted,

"May an arm-length knife strike you,
leaving on you neither bone nor meat!!"

The she-camel dropped dead. She—Maryam—took her things, put on her skin, and left for home. [She yelled],

"Where is my master? Where is my master?"

"What is with you, boy?" [the master replied].

"Another she-camel died today!!"

"Well, that is her fate!" [the master replied with some suspicion].

The third day she took the camels back to pasture. She went to the spring, took off the slave-girl's skin, and went into the spring to swim; she would splash around in the water and chant,

"Before, I used to be Maryam: of cool and coquetry!
Today, I've become a camel-herd!
O peaches, blossom out, and you pomegranates, clap your hands,
for Maryam the daughter of the sultan's son!"

Yet, another she-camel exclaimed, "¿A-a-a-a-a!"

[Maryam retorted:]

"May an arm-length knife strike you,
leaving on you neither bone nor meat!!"

The she-camel dropped dead. She—Maryam—took her things, put on her skin and left for home. [She yelled],

"Where is my master? Where is my master?"

"What is with you, boy?" [the master replied in apprehension.]

"Another she-camel died today!!"

"Well, that is her fate!" [the master replied with exasperation]. But this time he thought to himself: "Something is the matter. Tomorrow I will go there myself in order to find out what is going on at that spring."

Early in the morning, before anyone was up, he went to the spring. He hid himself among the branches, and he waited. Before the sun was up, she came, went to the spring, took the slave-girl skin off, and began to comb her hair: long, silky locks reaching down to her waist. Like before, she went into the spring to swim; she would splash around in the water and chant,

"Before, I used to be Maryam: of cool and coquetry!
Today, I've become a camel-herd!
O peaches, blossom out, and you pomegranates, clap your hands,
for Maryam the daughter of the sultan's son!"

Yet, another she-camel exclaimed: "¿A-a-a-a-a!"

[Maryam retorted:]

"May an arm-length knife strike you,

leaving on you neither bone nor meat!!"

The she-camel dropped dead. She—Maryam—took her things, put on her skin, and left for home. [She yelled],

"Where is my master!? Where is my master!?"

"What is with you, boy?" [the master replied in apprehension].

"Another she-camel died today!!"

"Well, that was her fate! You go have your supper and rest," [the master replied in a consoling tone].

The sheikh, [the chief's son], went to his mother and said, "Mother, I fell in love with that herder. I want you to give him to me in marriage[246] this [very] evening!"

His mother replied [in shock], "We marry a man to you! This is a herder: a man, like yourself! You are a sheikh, son of a sheik! What a disgrace!"

He replied [defiantly], "Herder or no herder, man or no man, I want you to marry him to me, this evening!"

The end of it is that she thought, "Maybe he has seen in that herder something of which we have no idea! Let us see how this matter is going to end up."

She spoke to her [the herder]: "This evening, we will write down the contract of my son's taking you in marriage."

She replied [in astonishment], "This can't be. I am a man! A man just like your son! How could a man marry a man!"

"Man or no man, my son is bound and determined!"

They set up the wedding for them; and he entered upon her [so as to consummate the marriage]. Once the two were in the [bridal] chamber, he ordered,

"Take off your skin!"

"How can one take off his own skin? I am a man, like you!"

"Don't play satanic tricks on me.[247] Take off your skin. I have seen you with my own eyes at the spring!"

He began to slit her skin. She kept on screaming, "I am a man, like you! I am a man, like you!"

The black skin of the slave-girl fell off, and he saw Maryam: beautiful, Glory be to the Creator for His creation, [an unsurpassed dazzling beauty].[248]

They gave her to him in marriage, according to God's edict, and His Prophet's.[249]

And they remained [i.e., lived happily].[250]

❖ 12 ❖

LADY KÂN[251]

(SYRIA)

NARRATED IN 1971 BY GALÎLAH F., OF ALEPPO, NORTHERN SYRIA, AND LIVING IN CAIRO, EGYPT. A GRANDMOTHER IN HER SEVENTIES AND A CHRISTIAN, SHE HAD LEARNED THE TALE SIXTY YEARS EARLIER IN ALEPPO FROM HER SYRIAN MOTHER, AND HAD NOT NARRATED IT FOR SOME FORTY YEARS PRIOR TO THIS RECORDING. THE TEXT WAS COLLECTED AND WRITTEN DOWN IN ARABIC BY MONÂ ḤANNÂ FAHMÎ, THE NARRATOR'S GRANDDAUGHTER.[252]

A man's hatred for female offspring, intended infanticide,[253] and anxiety over father-daughter incest are central themes in this realistic fantasy-tale. Incestuous tendencies are expressed in a father's love-hate relationship with his daughter, and the potential exposure of a daughter's privates to her father—one of the rare instances in which this theme occurs in Arab folk literature.[254] The daughter marries a king's son, a nonpaternal figure.

Especially significant is the tale's presentation of "role strain," represented here by a woman's role as a mother protecting her daughter from her husband (the daughter's father) and at the same time as a powerless wife trying to appease her cruel (and perhaps incestuous) husband.[255] Other cardinal themes include a husband's capriciousness, a wife's precarious position in her husband's home, and the tragic death of lovers.

ONCE there were a man and his wife. The man did not like girls (*al-banât*) [as daughters]. When his wife became pregnant, he said to her, "Today, I am going to travel and leave you behind; if you beget a girl, slaughter her, and put her blood in a bottle so that I may drink it." She became very unhappy because her husband does not like daughters and would like to drink their blood.

Indeed, her husband traveled away. After some months she was granted a girl who was very beautiful. She [the mother] felt pity for her;[256] so, she decided to kill a she-pigeon, put her [its] blood in a bottle, and raise her daughter at the neighbors'. Four years later, the man returned. He saw the bottle filled with blood; he drank it, then he entered his home to greet his wife. At that time, the maiden (*al-fatâh*) was at the neighbors'.

A few days later, the neighbors said to the mother, "We will try every way we can to make the father like[257] his daughter." The mother agreed. So, one night the neighbors dressed the little maiden[258] in a pretty white dress, handed her a lighted candle, and said to her, "Go downstairs, [put out the candle], then place it at the neighbors' door; in order to light it up again, knock at the neighbors' door, and ask for matches with which to light up the candle."

The maiden went down and did what they asked her to do. When she knocked at the neighbors' [her parents'] door, her father opened the door. He was astonished at the beauty of that young maiden who was very politely asking him for matches. He lighted her candle for her and greeted her; she returned to her home at the neighbors'. Meanwhile, he entered upon [went to] his wife, and told her about the maiden. She replied, "Have I not told you that maidens are beautiful," and she kept silent.

The following day, they dressed the maiden in a blue dress and asked her to do the same thing. Sure enough, her father opened the door for her, lighted her candle for her, and asked her to stay for a short while; but she—in all politeness and good manners—excused herself [on the grounds that] she must return home. He entered upon his wife and said to her, "I've begun to like (*'uḥibbu*)[259] this young maiden." She answered him, "This maiden is the exact age of our daughter whose blood you have drunk," then she became silent.

She told the story to the neighbors; they became delighted and told her that they will tell him the truth on the third day. Indeed, on the third day, they dressed the maiden in a blue[260] dress and told her to do the same thing. When she knocked at the door and her father opened the door for her, and insisted that she enter [his home] and sit down for a while with him, she agreed provided that she would call her family [to join them]. He agreed as well [as she had agreed to sit down]. All of them sat down together; signs of pleasure and happiness for seeing the maiden showed up on him. So, they told him the truth, and he became very happy and decided that the maiden should remain with him and live with her mother and with him.

At night, the maiden slept in the same bed as her mother and father did, in their midst. But the mother's heart was not feeling comfortable for she was afraid that her husband might revert to what he used to be in the past,[261] [and] kill the girl so as to drink her blood.

That particular night, the mother fell in deep sleep after [all that worrisome] thinking. Sure enough, her fears[262] were realized. The father woke up during the night, awakened his daughter, and said to her, "Lady Kân, get up; only you and I are going to a big party" (for her name was Lady Kân). Thus, Lady Kân agreed, and went along with him, but, her heart also was not feeling comfortable. The two of them went out—the father [had] taken with him a long rope; they kept on walking during the night till they went out to [the outskirts of] the desert. Lady Kân became tired, and fear showed up on her. She said to him, "O father, I need to go to the toilet."[263] Her father tied her up to the rope, held its end in his hand and said to her, "If you are bashful of me, you [may] distance yourself a little from me." Sure enough, the maiden went very far, untied the rope, and leaped to the top of a tree [and hid]. Her father kept on looking for her, but to no avail. [So, he left.]

A short while later, a horse, with the king's son ("the prince")[264] mounted on it passed by. The horse halted in front of the tree. The prince was astonished and got off the horse, [because] he heard groaning sounds of suffering (*'anîn*) coming from the treetop. He called up in a loud voice, "[Are you] human or jinn?" and [at the same time] he saw the maiden. She answered him, "I am human, of the best humans."

The prince asked the maiden to get down; she did. The prince was dazed by her fascinating beauty.[265] He asked her to ride [his horse] in front of him[266] so that she might go to the palace [with him]. There [in the palace] he said to his mother, "This young maiden is my lot [in life]. So you—all—welcome her and consider her as if your own daughter, because I will marry her when she grows up."

A few years later, when the young maiden has become a beautiful, elegant-bodied young woman,[267] the prince decided to marry her. He built a large palace so that he might live with her alone [in privacy]. And indeed, they got married after a huge celebration.

After a few months, the prince came to his wife and said, "I must travel [and remain away for] thirty days. Take those thirty hazel nuts made of gold; each day place one nut in this box. When the box is full with the thirty nuts, I will have returned." His wife agreed, took the thirty gold nuts, greeted him [farewell], and he departed. She did as the prince, her husband, asked her to do. But on the thirtieth day, the princess [the wife] placed the last nut in the box and awaited her husband; it became nighttime, but he had not arrived. She thought that he had died and she became very sad over [having lost] him. She asked the slave-girls and the servants to change the color of everything in the palace into black color [as sign of mourning]. Indeed [they did], and the palace became black on the outside and on the inside. She entered her room, put on the black slip, and lay down in the black bed with a black mosquito net on it. She told her maidservant, "My husband has died. If it so happened that he returns—thus it would have become clear that he has not died—come and tell me before he enters [my] room." She fell asleep because she was tired.

Sure enough, about midnight, her husband returned from the trip. He was surprised to see the palace [draped in] black. The maidservant saw him [and was about to go and awaken her mistress], but he held her by the hand and said to her, "Wait. I will go into the room ahead of you." He entered and saw the room all black, and his wife asleep on the black bed. He approached her, spat on her face, then exited and left the palace.

When she, the princess, woke up in the morning, she asked the maidservant whether her husband had come. She answered her, "Yes. The prince did arrive, but he prevented me from entering [your room] while he himself went in, came out, then left the palace." The princess noticed that her face was wet. She understood the matter [for what it actually was], became very sad, and began to cry. A few days later, as she was promenading in the [garden of the] palace, she saw a large chest; she opened it and saw inside it a very old ring. The ring was quite dirty, so she began to rub it with her fingers. Suddenly a huge man [a jinni giant] appeared before her, telling her that this ring is Solomon's Ring; then he said to her, "I am your obedient servant: bliss is between your hands [at your fingertips]."[268] The princess understood that this ring is the ring of kingship,[269] and that anything she may want she could ask for, and that it [the ring] would cause everything to materialize for her. She asked him [the jinni] to build for her a very luxurious palace, far more luxurious than the king's palace, provided that he builds it in front of the king's palace, and that he transports her along with her entourage there.

Indeed, in seconds all of them were in a beautiful palace facing the king's palace. She, dressed in luxurious clothes and [smoking] a water pipe, sat in the balcony. The prince—who was at his father's palace—was astonished at the beauty of this young woman; he did not realize that this [woman] was his wife. He kept on looking at her every day as she sat on the balcony smoking the water pipe and dressed in luxurious clothes. He fell in strong love with her and asked his mother to go to her and to give her three diamond bracelets as a present. The mother agreed and went to the princess, but the princess did not receive the queen in a manner befitting her [rank]. When the queen gave her the bracelets as a present, she [the princess] did not thank her, but she called on her she-kitten and put the bracelets on her. The queen was taken aback by this reception that was not befitting her rank. When she returned home, she told her son about that reception. He asked her to be patient [tolerant] and to take with her next time a diamond necklace. She consented. A few days later the queen went to the beautiful princess and gave her the necklace; she received her in a slightly better manner than she did the time before. When the prince learned of this, he was glad and said to her [his mother], "Next time tell her that I want to marry her." Sure enough, the queen relayed that message to the princess. The princess agreed, provided that he should cover [the ground] from her palace to his with roses. The prince agreed. He bought all the roses in the country, and laid them down [like a carpet] on the grounds between the two palaces.

At the appointed time, she stood at [her] palace door, and he stood at his palace door; whenever he went down one step, she would go down one step: he would go down one step, she would go down one step. Suddenly, she cried out, "*'u-mâ-â-ân!*[270] A thorn pricked me." She ran back to her palace and closed the door. The queen came to her and asked, "With what should we cover [the ground] for you now?" The princess answered her, "Roses have thorns. I want tamarisk." The prince agreed, and covered [the ground] with tamarisk. At the appointed time, she appeared at [her] palace door, and he at his palace door; he began to go down one step, and she one step. Suddenly, she cried out, "*'u-mâ-â-ân!* A thorn pricked me," and she escaped back to the palace and closed the door. [She remained there] until the queen came to her; the princess said, "This time, I want jasmine because it has no thorns." The prince agreed.

But the princess asked the queen to tell the prince,

> I am the lady, Lady Kân.
> Abandon [your] family and homelands,
> and catch up with the lady, Lady Kân.[271]

The prince realized that this [princess] is his wife, he became even much happier, and hurried up with the wedding [for he was going to remarry her]. He covered [the grounds] for her with jasmine. At the appointed time, she appeared—dressed in the most beautiful clothes—at the door of her palace, while he [stood] at the door of his palace. They kept on going down the steps until they met at midway. She said to him,

> O moon[-like in beauty], the day you die, I die [too].
> I'd go to the wood market, and would craft a casket:
> [with] a nail of pearl, [next to] a nail of [red] ruby.
> People of the kingdom would wonder, "Two sweethearts in one casket!"[272]

At this moment they hugged each other and they fell down on the jasmine. The two of them died together.

PATERNAL FIGURES

❖ 13 ❖

POMEGRANATE KERNELS ON GOLD TRAYS[273]

(EGYPT)

NARRATED IN 1970 BY SAMÎRAH SH., A SIXTY-YEAR-OLD COPT FROM ṬÛKH-WALKAH, A SMALL TOWN IN MUNÛFIYYAH GOVERNORATE IN EGYPT'S NILE DELTA. SHE WAS MARRIED AND THE MOTHER OF A NUMBER OF CHILDREN, MOST OF WHOM WERE UNIVERSITY GRADUATES. SHE HAD RECEIVED "VERY SIMPLE SCHOOLING," TO THE EXTENT THAT SHE COULD READ A NEWSPAPER. THE RECORDING TOOK PLACE IN THE VISITORS' ROOM IN HER APARTMENT IN SAKAKÎNÎ DISTRICT, CAIRO, IN THE PRESENCE OF ONE OF HER SONS. THE SON WAS ABOUT FORTY YEARS OLD, A UNIVERSITY GRADUATE, AND DID NOT TELL TALES BUT AS A PASSIVE BEARER COULD RECOGNIZE SOME OF HIS MOTHER'S TALES AS SHE TOLD THEM; HE ALSO PROVIDED SOME CORRECTIONS (COMPARE INFORMANT NOTE TO TALES NO. 9 AND 33-1).

THE NARRATOR HAD HEARD "THIS AND ALL OTHER TALES FROM WOMEN IN THE FAMILY." SHE USED TO TELL A FEW TALES, BUT INFREQUENTLY, TO HER OWN CHILDREN. HOWEVER,

> TIMES HAVE CHANGED AND THERE IS NO OPPORTUNITY TO TELL NOW [IN THE 1970S]. CHILDREN GO TO THE MOVIES, WATCH TELEVISION, OR PLAY IN THE STREETS UNTIL THEY ARE EXHAUSTED. IN OLDEN DAYS [SUCH ACTS] WOULD NOT HAVE BEEN TOLERATED: THE RADIO WAS ON ONLY WHEN THE MAN OF THE HOUSE WAS IN . . . , GOING TO MOVIES WAS CONSIDERED INDECENT, AND NO KIDS COULD RUN ABOUT AND YELL IN THE STREET, ESPECIALLY PAST SUNSET TIME.

THE NARRATOR COMPARED THESE OLDER CONDITIONS THAT SURROUNDED A CHILD WITH THE EXPERIENCES OF THE HEROINE IN THE PRESENT TALE:

> IN OLDEN TIMES, UNLIKE NOWADAYS, CHILDREN HAD TO ADDRESS THEIR TEACHER BY [THE TITLE] "MASTER" OR "SIRE" (*SÎDÎ*, OR *SAYYIDNÂ*),[274] OR—[IN COPTIC

SCHOOLS]—"FATHER" (*'ABÛNÂ*);[275] [WHEN ORDERED TO DO SOMETHING, THEY WOULD RESPOND BY]: "YES, SIR," AND "RIGHT AWAY,"[276] JUST LIKE . . . [THE HEROINE DOES] IN THE TALE. CHILDREN FEARED THE TEACHER, AND USED TO FIGURE HIM INTO [THEIR PLANS],[277] AND HAVE AWE (*RAHBAH*)[278] TOWARD HIM.

ALTHOUGH THE NARRATOR IS CHRISTIAN, THE TALE'S ACTIONS OCCUR WITHIN AN ISLAMIC CONTEXT. THIS TEXT WAS COLLECTED JOINTLY WITH MISS HODÂ BUQṬOR.[279]

Until recently, instruction in kuttâb-*(preschool)*[280] *was routinely carried out through fear and physical punishment.*[281] *For a child, the lower cleric-instructor (*¿arrîf*)*[282] *represented fear and pain. The equating of a cleric-instructor with an ogre seems to derive from these practices, and consequently may be viewed as a "conditioned response."*[283] *Frequently, a father shares this uncomplimentary image with the teacher.*[284] *Although these religious preschools were coeducational, severe physical punishment was reserved for boys. Significantly, the overwhelming majority of renditions of the following tale concerning an "ogre schoolmaster" report a boy as his victim.*

One of the possible symbolic interpretations for this ghoulish act is sodomy, an accusation often leveled at the male instructors at these traditional schools. Although overt expression of male homosexuality is virtually nonexistent—with a few exceptions, in fantasy-tales, and realistic and philosophical tales[285]*—it constitutes a major theme in cycles of jokes and humorous anecdotes about teachers of little boys; such instructors are often labeled "[sodomites] of little boys."*[286] *Curiously enough, the tale's "normal form" does not include punishment for the ogre schoolmaster, a fact that perhaps is reflective of its scarcity in real life, especially in law courts.*

The present text contains an episode that seems not to appear frequently in other renditions; it deals with the latent "competition" between a father and his son over marriage to the same female who belongs to the son's age group, and, consequently, may not be identified as a mother figure for the boy.[287]

The concluding episode results in a reorganization of the familial unit: the father is reunited with the children's mother, the eldest son marries the father's bride-to-be, and a brother and a sister remain unwed. Thus the triadic relations among the three siblings—two brothers and a sister—are transformed into dyadic sets in which the brother and sister closest to each other in age are left together. This latent (unverbalized) experience is congruent with the Brother-Sister Syndrome in Arab cultures.[288]

ONCE there was: [and] there was plenty, O generous gentlemen; talk would not be sweet except by mentioning Our Lady Mary, may the most honored greetings be upon her.

There was a family of middle-[class] standing.[289] But God had not given her [the lady of the family][290] any children. So she would ask of God, "O God, grant me [a child]! O God, grant me!" God answered her and she begot a girl; she named her Pomegranate Kernels. ([Narrator hesitates and explains:] The girl—I mean—was named Pomegranate Kernels, not the mother.) She named her daughter Pomegranate Kernels. Later, the girl. . . . There was a *kuttâb*-preschool in town; the girl went in order to learn in it. [That] school had boys and girls; she was the youngest. The cleric-instructor (who is the sheikh of the *kuttâb*-preschool) said to them, "The one who will get me a turnover[291] early in the morning [tomorrow], I will like . . . and will pay attention to!"

The girl went to her mother and said to her, "O mother, the sheikh wants a turnover from me!"

She answered her [readily], "Certainly! Will do!"[292]

"And he said to me, 'Bring it early!' "

"Fine."

She got up early in the morning and made the turnover for her and gave it to her in order to take it [to the sheikh]. [It happened that] a boy had heard the same word from the sheikh, who wanted what? [A turnover]; he [had] said, "The clever one is the one who will bring me a turnover early in the morning!" He [the boy] also said to his mother, "Make me a turnover; the sheikh wants a turnover!" She said to her. . . . She [like the girl's mother] said to him, "Fine," and she got up early and made the turnover for him. The boy took the turnover and [happened to have] arrived there ahead of the girl.

(The girl—until she had taken the turnover. . . . Oh, [I forgot to say that] the [girl's] mother had put a gold ankle bracelet around her daughter['s ankle] due to the girl's dearness to her. She put around [her daughter's ankle] her own gold ankle bracelet. She [the girl] took the turnover.)

The boy had arrived there ahead of her! She entered [the preschool]; as she entered, she found the sheikh holding the boy and was eating him. The girl was horrified. She dropped the turnover and ran. While she was running, the ankle bracelet got caught—in spite of her—on the doorstep. She left it and ran. She ran. Due to her bewilderment,[293] she got lost; she could not return to her home. She got lost. The girl got lost and roamed aimlessly, not knowing anything. She walked [through] towns; and countries, and countries.[294] And [various] people met her [and asked her]:

"What are you, daughter?"

She would answer them, "I don't know!"

"From what country?"

"I don't know!"

They took her to the governor of the town [and said]: "This girl . . . ; we found her lost. We don't know of anyone related to her. In your capacity as the most trustworthy person in the town, keep her at your place until someone related to her appears; then we can give her [back] to him!"

He [the governor] took the girl. (She was, say, eight years, ten years of age.) She stayed inside the house. That king—that viceroy (*wâli*)—that governor of the city, happened to have a son, but he was [absent] on a trip abroad.

The girl grew up in their house, in their company. Of course she was staying in the kitchen. She was staying with them, got educated, and became a fine [person]. The girl was [also] pretty good-looking and of good descent;[295] in addition, she was brought up well. . . . The girl. . . .

(One day—her son [the viceroy's wife's son]). . . .

The girl had grown up and become a young woman of marriageable age.[296] The king's son—(I mean: the sultan's son)—arrived; he returned from the country in which he was. He entered [his parents' home] and found her; [he exclaimed in a tone of admiration and surprise]: "God! [i.e., Wow!] What is she, Mother!?"

She answered him, "Son, this is a girl that we found; she has been here for a number of years, ever since you traveled away. She has been with us for [maybe] five, seven, or eight years."

He asked her, "What is she? Why did you bring her, and why was she brought [here]?"

[The mother answered], "Because when we found her . . . , when the town's people found her, they said, 'You are the most trustworthy family. Keep her with you until some relatives of hers appear.' Since that day no relatives of hers appeared."

He said to her, "This girl is very beautiful, Mother. She appeals to me."

She answered him, "No! How could this be! She is neither of your rank nor is she of your status.[297] This is [a girl] from the street!"

He said to her, "No [i.e., yes, maybe she is from the street], but she seems to be fine."

She said [with uncertainty], "What shall we do now! How could it be that you wish to marry her!"

He answered her, "By God, Mother, I desire to marry this girl!"

She kept on arguing hard against him,[298] but he did not become convinced.

In short, talk rebutted by [other] talk; she [finally] said to him, "Son, as long as this is your infatuation (*gharâmak*), then suit yourself."[299] He said to her, "In any case, I'll leave her with you during my travels."

He married her . . . [pause], (I mean) he consummated the marriage,[300] and they set up the wedding celebrations, and the fine [joyous] eves: forty eves, less an eve. He entered upon her [and they lived as husband and wife]. Then what? The girl became pregnant and gave birth to a boy. [Meanwhile], he had already gone on a trip; she gave birth during his absence.

After she gave birth, the eve of the celebration of the seventh day of birth (*subû¿*) came upon them, while they were happy. They set up decorations and beat the drums in town. [But the sheikh] came to her . . . [pause]. [Narrator speaks in a tone denoting surprise and apprehension.] She looked—at night-time—to [suddenly] find that person, [the sheikh], coming out through the wall at her. He said to her,

> O Pomegranate Kernels on Gold Trays,
> What of the wondrous have you seen,
> when you left an ankle bracelet of yours at the threshhold?[301]

She replied [submissively],

> My lord, you were teaching the boys and the girls,
> teaching them gnosis and manners.[302]

He took the boy away from her, and smeared her hands, her mouth, and all her face with blood, then he went out. [When] the servants and slaves entered [her room], they looked [only] to find that atrocious scene. They shrieked and yelled, "The girl ate her son! The girl ate her son!" The entire kingdom[303] was stirred up; so was the city and the world. They sent [a messenger] and brought her husband back from the trip.

> "Why did you do so, Pomegranate Kernels?" [he asked her].
> . . . . [Silence].
> "Why did you eat your son?"
> . . . . [Silence].

She would not answer them at all. They would hurl insults at her, mockingly belittle her, and abuse her but to no avail. She [still] would not answer.

The man [her husband] looked around. What is he going to do? [Narrator speaks in a kindly tone.] . . . He felt pity for her.[304] [He pleaded,] "Do not abuse her. Be patient with her a little more. Who knows what are the circumstances: what might have happened to her!" He kept on trying to conciliate her.[305] God granted her; again, she became pregnant. She begot a second boy, while her husband was away on a trip.

The very same thing that happened with the first [infant], happened with the second: [the sheikh came through the wall, and asked her the questions, she gave him the reply, but] he still took away the boy from her, smeared her with blood, and went away!

They said, "No! That one shouldn't remain inside the house. She is a an ogress." They abused her plenty and put her in the kitchen; they kept on slapping her face as they went to and fro. They were afraid of her.

The man, her husband, returned from his trip. He, however, felt sympathy for her;[306] he loved her somewhat [i.e., liked her], for he saw that she was powerless and miserable (*ghalbânah*). He still took her in, and married her, meaning he again entered upon her.[307] She, again, became pregnant. She begot a baby girl; the newborn turned out to be a baby girl. Still he [the sheikh] came to her during that very customary night, and said to her,

> Pomegranate Kernels [on Gold Trays],
> what of the wondrous have you seen,
> when you left an ankle bracelet of yours at the threshhold?

She replied [in total surrender],

> My lord, you were teaching boys and girls,
> teaching them gnosis and manners.

He took away the [baby] girl and the same situation [that he had created before was repeated]; he did her [i.e., smeared her] with blood and he left.

They said [in despair], "N-o-o-o-o-o! That's it! This one may never remain [among us], this ogress, lest she should turn around and also eat us up." They sent her down [to the kitchen], and ran her down by [having her do menial] services in the households.

Meanwhile, the man [her husband] had traveled and was absent for "numerous years," long years—(for in olden times they traveled, in order to earn money). When he returned with money and things like that, he said [in a petitioning tone] to her, "Mother, I want to marry!" She replied, "Go get married!" So they looked around in the country for a suitable bride—the vizier's daughter, or the like. [When a bride was found,] they set up the wedding celebrations throughout the city. Meanwhile, she, the girl [Pomegranate Kernels] remained speechless. Her mouth would not be opened; she only signaled [with her hands] like this: [narrator shows how].

One night, a few days before the wedding would be affixed [and actually take place], she—the girl [Pomegranate Kernels]—as she was lying down, looked [only] to find the wall splitting like before and he [the sheikh] popped out of it. He said to her,

> Pomegranate Kernels [on Gold Trays],
> what of the wondrous have you seen,
> when you left an ankle bracelet of yours at the threshhold?

She answered him [submissively],

> My lord, you were teaching the boys and girls,
> teaching them gnosis and manners.

He said to her [with amazement and admiration]: "Oh, my (*yâ-â-â salâ-â-â-m*)!! All the insults that you have seen, and all that has happened to you! Still you never did betray my secret. You have been made homeless, [made] to leave your children, and [in spite of] all the abuse and all that has happened, [still] you have not let out [the secret]. You are a fine [person]. Here are your children: well disciplined, educated, ready [to go]—twenty-four karats [i.e., fully]!"

She said to him, "Well, what do I do now? What do I say to them? He [my husband] is going to marry!"

He replied, "I brought your children back . . . and I have taught them what to say. As for you . . . you [will] have nothing to do with the matter, [take it easy]."

They—on the day of the wedding celebration—the bride was entering. . . . (I had forgotten to say that they had named the first boy Shaddâd, the second boy Boghdâd. . . .) [Narrator pauses.]

ASIDE

Narrator's son correcting his mother: "No! [The second was named] Raddâd."

On this aspect of the narrating process, see the "law of self-correction," in El-Shamy, "Folkloric Behavior," pp. 12, 15–16, 107–8.

[Narrator corrects her statement:] No! [not Boghdâd, but] Raddâd, and the girl Boghdâd! (The [second] son was Raddâd, and the girl was Boghdâd.) In short, when they [the people in the wedding procession] came to enter the palace with the bride[-to-be]—the palace was all doors. Shaddâd stood at the door and made his arms like this [narrator stretches out both arms horizontally to signify a complete blocking of the doorway], . . . [He chanted],

> I am Shaddâd, my brother is Raddâd, and my sister is Boghdâd!
> [I swear] by the head of my father, the king,
> that the bride will not enter tonight upon my mother and make her sad![308]

[People in the procession said], "Come on fellows. Come on fellows. To the other door!" [People kept on wondering:] "What is this! What is that! What is that who is standing by, over there, [blocking our way]." So they went to the other door. [There, they found someone else blocking it too.] He said,

> I am Raddâd, my brother is Shaddâd, and my sister is Boghdâd!
> [I swear] by the head of my father, the king,
> that the bride will not enter tonight upon my mother and make her sad!

They left for the third door. [Their sister was standing there blocking it.] She chanted,

> I am Boghdâd, my brother is Raddâd, and my brother is Shaddâd!
> [I swear] by the head of my father, the king
> that the bride will not enter tonight upon my mother and make her sad!

Meanwhile, the girl [the children's mother] had entered [the bath and] bathed, tidied herself up, and prepared herself in the best manner; she put on the most luxurious clothes, that she happened to have—(that is, while she was set aside in the kitchen, as she spoke not). She stood by the [fourth] door like this [narrator—while still seated—shows how: stance of defiance]. She blocked her [the bride-to-be's] entrance and chanted:

> I am the mother of Shaddâd, the mother of Raddâd, and the mother of Boghdâd!
> [I swear] by the head of "my father," the king,[309]
> that the bride will not enter upon me tonight. Never!

[Her husband wondered, with excitement and pleasure:] "What is it? It is you! You [can] talk! You are [finely] attired! You are bathed! What, then, had caused you to be the way you were? Come on here, 'sister' Pomegranate Kernels. What is with you? What is your story?"

She said to him, "My story is such and such"; [she told it] from its beginning to its end.
He declared, "This [new] bride is sinful for me, but legitimate for[310] my son Shaddâd."

They wrote the marriage contract between the incoming bride and the boy, her [Pomegranate Kernels's] son. Meanwhile, he [the boy's father] reinstated his own lady [as his wife],[311] while Shaddâd took [in marriage] the new bride.

And they lived in stability and prosperity. And I was there and just returned, even supper I did not have.

❖ 14 ❖

THE OSTRICH OF THE SULTAN'S SON

(EGYPT)

NARRATED IN JULY 1971 BY GALÎLAH ¿A., A TWENTY-FOUR-YEAR-OLD HOUSEMAID. SHE HAD HEARD IT FROM HER PATERNAL GRANDMOTHER (SEE SECTION II, "PROFILE," P. 42, AND INFORMANT NOTE TO TALE NO. 10). SHE ALSO KNEW THE TALE UNDER THE TITLES OF "THE THREE GIRLS OF WHOM ONE INHERITED A HEN . . . ," "THE OGRE'S DAUGHTER," AND "*SIT* ṬAṬAR."

*A number of familial situations and related sets of attitudes are portrayed in this text of a fantasy-tale (*ḥaddûtah*). First is sibling rivalry among three sisters that occurs over economic matters; yet, in the majority of renditions this initial theme does not recur, and the culprit sisters are not punished. Second is the authoritarian foster father's interaction with his adopted daughter; in this case, the paternal figure is an ogre who imposes tabus without providing reasons for the interdictions. Third is a husband's relationship with his wife and the antagonism that emerges between a wife and her rivals for the husband's attention; these rivals are the husband's sister(s)—as is the case in our text, his female parallel paternal-*

*cousins (*banât ¿amm*), who are also potential wives for him, or the husband's other wives (i.e., the heroine's co-wives, or* ḍarâyir*).*[312] *Notably, a husband's mother has not been reported as his wife's rival in this situation. A parallel situation is the jealousy and consequent antagonism that had developed between the pet ostrich*[313] *of the sultan's son and the heroine.*

The heroine's name, Ṭaṭar, appears abruptly; it has not been reported in narrative contexts other than the present tale type. Although the word may suggest "the Tatar,"[314] *it has not been reported as a given name among Arab groups; for the narrator the word is nonsensical. Similarly, the relationships among the words "Ṭaṭar" and "Maṭar" (rain), and "Sun" and "Moon" are not clear.*[315] *The emphasis placed on the necessity for the husband to call his wife by her name in conjunction with her mother and father (i.e., bilaterally), seems to countervail the prevalent practice in traditional communities of the husband not addressing his wife by name, but by the euphemism: "daughter of [good] people (*bint en-nâs*)," by her child's name as: "Mother of So-and-so," or namelessly. Yet none of the available texts gives a reason for the interdiction; thus, this absence constitutes the "normal form" for the tale in Arab cultures.*

The earthenware qullah[316] *(water bottle)* without *a spout, and* 'abrîq[317] *(water pitcher) with a spout symbolize female and male respectively, and are so designated by the pronouns "she/her," and "he/his." The act of breaking the pitcher's spout may symbolize castration or an illicit sexual act. The narrator experienced observable embarrassment while presenting this episode.*[318]

Latent, unverbalized aspects of the tale may be revealed by the two sites constituting the stage (or cognitive map) for its actions.[319] *The first is the heroine's own house, which overlooks the backyard of the ogre's house; the second is the ogre's house, which overlooks the backyard (or garden) of the house of the sultan's son. A narrator's (or listener's) perception of the physical boundaries of the residential space designated by this layout would be that the heroine did not wander far from her own home; and perhaps that she returned back to her own home. The heroine marries a youth of her own age group, a sultan's son.*

THERE was, and there was plenty (*kân, [wi] yâmâ kân*).

Once there were three girls whose parents had no children but them. Then their father became deceased[320] and their mother[321] too. They, the three girls, remained by themselves. Each one had a hen; the youngest one [also] had a hen all to herself. Naturally because she was the young[est] and [because] God deprived her of her elders (*'ahl*),[322] He granted her something so as to compensate her for having been deprived of her parents: she [the hen] began to lay a gem egg. Every day she [the girl] would take the hen['s egg] and would sell it to the sultan's son for one hundred pounds.

Her sisters became jealous of her [and wondered], "How come this one earns one hundred pounds every day while we earn nothing?" So they ganged up against her [and conspired] to drop her hen into [the yard of] the ogre's house; thus, they immediately dropped her hen [into the ogre's yard]. [This happened] while she had gone in order to sell the egg to the sultan's son. When she returned, she asked about it [the hen]. They said to her, "We lost the hen unintentionally,[323] it fell in the ogre's house!" She wondered, "How am I going to get it back?" They [the two elder sisters had thought], "Well! We should lower her [off the top of our house, into the ogre's yard under the pretense] that she may get back the hen. After lowering her in, we will leave her for the ogre to eat her up!" So they said to her, "Come on! We will tie together our head-scarves[324]—(those scarves that fellahin[-women] wear), and [use them as rope to] lower you in."

They did, and they lowered her in. After she grabbed the hen, they let go of their head-scarves (*ṭuraḥ*) and she fell! She was at a total loss as what to do (*lâyṣah*). What was she to do!? She became afraid that the ogre would come and eat her up, so she hid herself under a [pottery] kneading tub (*magûr*).[325]

As soon as the ogre entered [his house] he wondered, "Do I smell the odor of a human not of our race?"[326] Of course, she did not answer. [He searched his home but did not find the source of the odor.] He finally said, "If you are a maiden you will become my daughter; if you are a boy you will become my brother, and if you are a grown-up lady (*sit*) you will become my wife!" (. . . He also said other such things.) Immediately, she came out and said [with relief], "I am your daughter!" He said to her, "Well, you will be my daughter!"

[She cooked and cleaned the house for him]; after a period of time, he put her in charge of the household. He said to her, "Here, take the keys to all the rooms [in the house—you may open them all] except for this one!" He [also] said to her [in a warning tone], "This room, you don't open at all because it contains important things. You don't open it at all, and you will have nothing to do with the neighbors who live next to it [and over whose backyard the window opens]!"

She began to wonder as to how it was that her papa[327] had left her with all these things [in her trust], but forbade her to enter that room!

One day she waited until he went out. She got the key and opened the room! She opened the room, looked [and saw a window overlooking a garden] and saw the she-ostrich of the sultan's son standing before her in the garden.

As she was saying to her [the ostrich], "Good morning, you ostrich of the sultan's son." She [it] answered her, "May He make your morning blissful,[328] O ogre's daughter, you whom the ogre is raising, fattening, then will in the end devour!"

She became sad; she kept her sadness to herself and became afraid of the ogre. Whenever he spoke to her, she would become scared of him, thinking that he was going to eat her up! [Thus she became ill and lost much weight. Her father, the ogre, noticed that and asked her why she was losing weight and looking ill, but she would not give him a satisfactory answer.] Finally, he said to her [in a threatening tone], "Are you going to tell me the reason that caused you to lose weight in such a [drastic] manner, or shall I boil water in a [cooking-]pot and dip you in it!!?"

When she saw that he acted in that [menacing] manner, she told him [about the she-ostrich]. He instructed her that when she [the ostrich] would say that you . . . ,[329] "When you say to her, 'Good morning, O ostrich of the sultan's son,' and she replies, 'May He make your morning blissful, O ogre's daughter, you whom the ogre is raising, fattening, and will later devour!' you [should] say to her, 'He will raise me and fatten me for the sultan's son to marry. [For my wedding], he will make your feathers into brooms for me, your blood into henna for me, and your skin into a strap for my clogs.' "[330] [Narrator chuckles.]

Later on, she said so [to the ostrich]; the ostrich went crazy; she began to pluck out her hair [i.e., feathers] and consume herself with frustration.[331] The sultan's son went to look at her [the ostrich], for he was used to looking at her every day. He found her to have no feathers. He found her in a sad condition. ([Narrator is amused; she laughs and explains:] This is the way the tale goes.) So he asked her about the reason. The ostrich told him, "It is the ogre's daughter! She said to me [such and such] and she said to me [such and such]!" So he went and hid [in the garden] and found out about the ogre's daughter. He discovered that this one [the girl] was saying to her [the ostrich], "Good morning, you ostrich of the sultan's son." She [the ostrich] replied, "May He [the Lord] make your morning blissful, you whom the ogre is raising, fattening, then will in the end devour!"

She replied [to the ostrich with confidence], "He will raise me, fatten me for the sultan's son to marry me; he [the ogre] will make your feathers into brooms for me, your blood into henna for me, and your skin into a strap for my clogs!"

When he [the sultan's son] saw her, he fell in love with her and wanted to marry her. What will he do? He kept on going daily to the ogre in order to do what? In order to ask for her in marriage [but the ogre kept on turning him down]. Finally, he [the ogre] said to him, "All right, but you will not consummate the marriage until you have learned her name!" He [the sultan's son] replied, "All right!" They agree on that condition. So he took her to his home (to the house of his family, I mean). She remained in a room by herself and she did not allow him to enter until he had learned her name.

She used to practice some magic. She had a pottery water bottle and a pottery water pitcher with a spout that used to get water for her daily from the river (for she had learned some magic from the ogre).

The sultan's son kept on asking around [about her name, but to no avail]; after two years he became desperate. He used to send his sisters to spy on her. But whenever one of them would come [the ogre's daughter would play magical tricks on her], she would turn her fingers into bananas and peel them. When they would go back and try to do as she did, and cut off their fingers, they would die, for [in their case] it was for real.

Finally he became desperate and thought, "Maybe I will have to go and kill the ogre, or even kill her, if she does not tell [me her name]!!"

As he was on his way, he looked and chanced to see the bottle and the pitcher going to the river to get filled. The bottle filled [herself first] and was climbing [up the riverbed to the bank] while the pitcher was climbing behind her. She [the bottle] rolled herself down and fell on top of him [the pitcher] and broke his spout. [Narrator giggles and is embarrassed.] [The pitcher said,] "By God, I'll go tell your mistress that you have [deliberately] fallen on top of me and broke my spout!"

He [the pitcher] went to the mistress. As he was entering—angry and quarreling as he was entering [the house]—he said to her,

> O Lady Ṭaṭar, O Lady Maṭar,
> you whose mother is the sun and father is the moon,
> the bottle broke my spout.[332]

He [the sultan's son] was standing outside by the door. No sooner had he learned the name than he entered [her room]. He knew her name. And he entered her room and said,

O Lady Ṭaṭar, O Lady Maṭar,
you whose mother is the sun and father is the moon,
answer me, for my heart has ruptured.[333]

[She broke her silence.] They repeated the wedding celebration from its beginning.

And they lived in stability and prosperity and begot boys and girls. [Narrator giggles.]

B. COURTSHIP AND MARITAL RELATIONS

GAINING A WIFE

❖ 15 ❖

THE DAUGHTERS OF THE BEAN VENDOR[334]

(EGYPT)

NARRATED IN APRIL 1971 BY TAḤIYYAH M., KNOWN AS *ES-SIT* TAḤIYYAH *EL-KHAYYÂṬAH* (LADY TAḤIYYAH THE SEAMSTRESS). SHE WAS ABOUT FIFTY YEARS OLD, MARRIED, AND A MOTHER, AND HAD RECEIVED ELEMENTARY RELIGIOUS EDUCATION.[335] SHE WAS BORN, RAISED, MARRIED, AND STILL LIVING IN THE SAME HOUSE IN A DISTRICT OF THE CITY OF ZAQAZIQ, SHARQIYYAH GOVERNORATE IN NORTHEASTERN EGYPT. DUE TO THE SUCCESS OF HER BUSINESS (AND A CLIENTELE OF ONLY WOMEN AND CHILDREN), SHE RETAINED BOTH HER BUSINESS AND HER RESIDENCE AFTER MARRIAGE (I.E., HER HUSBAND JOINED HER AT HER PARENTS' HOME). THE RECORDING TOOK PLACE AT HER WORKSHOP—A LARGE ROOM IN HER HOUSE—WITH HER TWO YOUNG FEMALE APPRENTICES AND YOUNGEST DAUGHTER (A TWELVE-YEAR-OLD) LISTENING.

IN OLDEN TIMES NARRATING AND WORKING USED TO GO TOGETHER. NOW WE HAVE THE TELEVISION AND THE TRANSISTOR [RADIO] GOING ON, AND BUSINESS IS NOT AS [BRISK AS IT] USED TO BE; PEOPLE WEAR READY-MADE. . . . TWENTY OR FIFTEEN YEARS AGO, I USED TO HAVE FIVE, SIX, OR MAYBE SEVEN GIRLS [WORKING FOR ME]. DURING BAIRAMS, ESPECIALLY THE LITTLE-BAIRAM,[336] WORK WOULD BE VERY HEAVY, BECAUSE EVERYONE WOULD BE WANTING TO HAVE A NEW OUTER-GARMENT (*GALABIYYA*),[337] A LADY'S DRESS-UP DRESS (*FUSTÂN*); PAJAMAS (*BEJÂMAH*),[338] OR ANYTHING ELSE. WE USED TO STAY UP UNTIL DAWN. THIS HOUSE [WHERE WE ARE NOW] DID NOT HAVE ELECTRICITY THEN; WE WORKED ON [THE LIGHT OF] NO. 10 [KEROSENE] LAMPS. I WOULD SCISSOR THE CLOTH AND PIN THE PARTS TOGETHER, ANOTHER [GIRL] WOULD LOOSELY STITCH (*TISHATTIK*) THE CLOTH TOGETHER, ANOTHER WOULD BASTE (*TISARRAG*) [SO THAT IT COULD BE EASILY UNDONE IF NEED BE], ANOTHER WOULD SEW TIGHTLY (*TIMAKKIN*),[339] ANOTHER WOULD BLIND HEM (*TISHALLIL*) . . . AND SO ON. WE MAY STAY UNTIL DAWN AND MAYBE UNTIL SUNRISE.

WE USED TO TELL FANTASY-TALES (*ḤAWADÎT*) AND OTHER STORIES (*ḤIKAYÂT TÂNYAH*)[340] [SUCH AS]: "HAVE YOU HEARD! SUCH AND SUCH A THING HAS HAP-

PENED," "SO-AND-SO, FROM OUR LANE OR OUR NEIGHBORHOOD,[341] IS GETTING MARRIED AND SHE RECEIVED SUCH-AND-SUCH [GIFTS]," [OR] "SO-AND-SO—(AWAY FROM YOU)[342]—WAS TAKEN TO THE HOSPITAL," AND THINGS LIKE THAT.

THE TALE OF THE DAUGHTERS OF THE BEAN VENDOR USED TO COME UP ALL THE TIME. THE GIRLS LIKED IT VERY MUCH AND WHENEVER IT WOULD COME TO AN END THEY WOULD SAY, "O LADY-MENTOR, BY THE PROPHET,[343] SAY IT AGAIN!" DUE TO THEIR INSISTENCE, I WOULD TELL IT AGAIN, AND AGAIN. I HEARD IT WHEN I WAS A LITTLE GIRL FROM A GIRL NAMED BASHAWÂT WHO USED TO LIVE IN THE LANE HERE. SHE WAS OLDER THAN ME AND NARRATED IN A FANTASTIC WAY,[344] AND ONE COULD NEVER HAVE HER FILL OF HER TALK.

*Verbal sexual harassment (*mu¿âksah*),[345] clandestine rendezvous, and "marriage for spite"[346] are central themes in this realistic tale. Except for the limited interaction among close relatives (e.g., cousins), and occasionally among very intimate family friends and neighbors, traditional Arab cultures do not provide institutionalized means for courtship or premarital friendship (Mot. T380§, "Heterosociality"). Consequently, countercultural practices in this regard develop and persist. Although sexual harassment is universally condemned as a "violation of a female's modesty,"[347] it is a common daily occurrence.*

From an ideal culture perspective, if "love" between a man and a woman is to develop, it is supposed to be only after marriage.[348] Thus, marriage is more of an association between two families via two of their members than it is a union of a couple. The tale's main male character marries the heroine in order to gain control over her and, consequently, over her family. In real life, a father referred to the power that his daughter's husband holds over him by citing a proverbial phrase, "He is seizing me by my tender-hand";[349] thus, the father was indicating that any pressure applied by the husband on his wife would inevitably be felt by the wife's father.

*Other typical social scenes and roles depicted in the tale include: the powerless bean vendor, the seamstress as a marriage broker or messenger between lovers, and a sister as the chaperon of her other siblings. The act in which the heroine disguises herself as a puppet seems to be a combination of the image of the "Prophet's-Birthday [Sugar] Doll,"[350] and the *qaragoaz.[351]

None of the available renditions of this tale includes a mother for the girls (i.e., a wife for the bean vendor). Affectionate relations between the father and his daughters, especially the youngest, are expressed; yet no Oedipal factors seem to be present.[352]

STATE the oneness of God.

Once there was a man who was a bean vendor, one of those people who sell fava beans and cooked wheat[353] for people to eat at breakfast; he had three daughters. One was the eldest, another was the middle, and one was the youngest.

Those three used to go to a seamstress in their neighborhood to learn sewing. Every morning while they were going to the seamstress they would find the sultan's son sitting on a chair in front of his father's palace and blocking their way in order to tease-flirt with them. That sultan's son would come to the eldest and would say to her, "Daughter of bean vendor, how are your father's beans?" She would reply [softly in a friendly tone],

> My father's beans were well cooked, well cooked;
> family and close friends ate [some] from it.[354]

So, he would say to her, "All right, you may kindly go ahead." Then he would come to the middle girl and would say to her, "Daughter of bean vendor, how are your father's beans?" She would reply [in a friendly tone],

> My father's beans were well cooked, well cooked;
> family and close friends ate from it!

So, he would say to her, "All right, you may kindly go ahead!" Then he would come to the youngest and would say [slyly and provocatively], "You, damned one,[355] who are the youngest, how are your father's beans?" She would reply [firmly and with some anger]:

> My father's beans were well cooked, well cooked;
> family and close friends ate from it!
> What concern of yours is it, you son of a clog!?[356]

The sultan's son would hear this and would become vexed at her and would say [in a threatening tone], "By God, I'll show you!"

One day he went to the seamstress—(where the girls worked, I mean)—and said to her, "I would like you to keep the youngest girl at your house tonight!" and he gave her a pound, or something. She said to him, "Will do!"

At sunset when it was time for the girls to return home, their tutor (*'ublit-hum*) said, "Who would stay with me [overnight] for we need to bake [bread] tomorrow [at dawn]?"

The eldest girl said [with enthusiasm], "I would, my tutor!" She answered her, "No! You will not do." The middle girl said, "I would, my tutor." She answered her, "No! You will not do." The two [girls] said, "All right." So she looked toward the youngest. She [the youngest girl] said [without zeal], "I would stay overnight with you, tutor!" The tutor [readily] said, "Oh yes, you cutie![357] You sugar! You stay with your tutor and help her bake. You are the one who impresses me!"

The two elder sisters went home while she stayed with that tutor of hers. Whenever she asked, "Where is the flour?" the tutor would say, "We've got it!"

"Where is the yeast?"

"We've got it."

"Let us start early so that we can finish early."

"O sister, there is plenty of time; it is still too early."

Things kept on going like this until the girl fell asleep. Naturally she was tired and she did not feel anything around her. After a little while, her tutor put out the light (one of those No. 10 kerosene lamps of older times). The sultan's son came—for that was the sign they had agreed on. She had told him, "When it gets dark, come to my place when the light is turned off." He cleared his throat at the door, and she opened the door for him.

When he got inside, he kept on hugging and kissing the girl. She would wake up and see nothing. She would say to her tutor, "Tutor of mine, what is this that hugs and kisses?"[358] The tutor would say, "Sleep, sleep, there is nothing; it is [only] a nightmare!"[359] After a while the sultan's son went home. In the morning, when the girl woke up, she asked the seamstress, "We haven't done any baking, tutor." She answered her, "We changed our mind, maybe tomorrow."

The following day, as she and her sisters were going to the seamstress's house, they found the sultan's son, as he was used to, in front of his father's palace. He asked the eldest girl, "Daughter of bean vendor, how are your father's beans?"

She answered him, "My father's beans were well cooked, well cooked, and family and close friends ate some."

He would say to her, "All right, you may kindly go on."

Then he asked the middle one, "Daughter of bean vendor, how are your father's beans?"

She answered him, "My father's beans were well cooked, well cooked, and family and close friends ate some."

"All right, you may kindly go on!"

[Narrator speaks emphatically.] Then, what next? He came to the youngest. He said to her [with a hint of sarcasm], "Daughter of bean vendor, how are your father's beans?"

She [defiantly] answered,

My father's beans were well cooked, well cooked;
family and close friends ate from it!
What concern of yours is it, you son of a clog!

He said to her [in a twitting manner, and imitating a female's voice], "'O my tutor, what is this that hugs and kisses?' 'O [girl], sleep, sleep! There is nothing, it is only a nightmare!'"

That was it!! She said [in anger], "That was you!!"

He replied, "Yes! [It was] I."

She said to herself, "Well, well, well. I must get even!" She thought and thought; she went to the tinsmith and said to him, "I want you to make me ten cones to fit my fingers, [at the end of each cone there should be a holder for] a candle." He said to her, "Will do! And come back at such and such a time!"

She waited until midnight [narrator speaks in a low tone denoting secrecy]; she put on a black outer-garment (*galabiyyah*), covered her face and head with a black shawl, with two holes for her to see through. She fitted ten candles into the candlesticks at [the end of the tin] cones and lighted them. She went to the sultan's palace, where the sultan's son happened to be. As soon as the gatekeeper saw her, he became frightened and asked [in a fearful, trembling tone], "Who is there?"

She answered [in a husky, eerie tone], "I am Little Azrael [angel of death]; Big Azrael sent me ahead of him, and he will follow, in order to seize the soul of the sultan's son."

As soon as the guard heard this, he placed his tail between his teeth and flew away [thus fleeing in a hurry, like a scared dog is thought to do]. The same thing happened with every guard and doorkeeper; they all ran away. She, finally, reached his room and found him asleep on the bed. [She hissed at him in a quivering tone:] "I am Little Azrael! Big Azrael has sent me ahead of him to seize the soul of the sultan's son!!" He [the sultan's son] opened his eyes like this [narrator opens her own eyes slowly in a slumbering manner]. He bounded up from his sleep; naturally he saw those ten flaming fingers and the black thing. He was about to—(may God protect your status)—wet the bed! [Laughter.] She said to him, "Prepare yourself for death!" He replied [in an imploring tone], "I am too young to die. Take my money; take my belongings; take my father's palace! Take everything!! Just let me be!" She said, "No! Utter the [death] Testimony over your soul:[360] prepare yourself for death!"

He kept on begging her for mercy, and she kept on saying, "No!" until finally, he plucked off his own beard—(from fright, he pulled his own whiskers out).

Whether he fainted or passed out, I don't know what; when she left, he was finished. His servants came and revived him. His condition was very bad and he kept on [mumbling], "Little Azrael is here and Big Azrael is following him! Little Azrael is here and Big Azrael is following him." They soothed him until he was calm again. But, still, he did not change.

The following day he sat in front of his father's house. When the bean vendor's daughters passed by, he stopped them and asked, "How are your father's beans, you eldest?"

She answered him, "My father's beans were well cooked, well cooked; and [our] family and close friends ate some!"

He asked the middle one, "How are your father's beans?"

She answered him, "My father's beans were well cooked, well cooked, and [our] family and close friends ate some!"

He asked the youngest, "How are your father's beans, you damned one, who are the youngest?"

She replied,

> My father's beans were well cooked, well cooked;
> family and close friends ate from it!
> What concern of yours is it, you son of a clog!

He retorted [sarcastically, in a girl's voice], " 'O my tutor, what is this that hugs and kisses!?' 'Oh, sleep, sleep; it is a nightmare!' "

She retorted [in an eerie voice], " 'I am Little Azrael; Big Azrael will follow. I've come to seize the soul of the sultan's son.' [In an imploring, frightened tone,] 'I am too young to die! Take my money, take my belongings. . . .' "

The sultan's son [interrupted and] exclaimed [with considerable bitterness], "*'Â-â-â-kh-kh-kh!*[361] Was that you!!?"

[She answered defiantly,] "Yes, that was I!"

He realized that he will not be able to get anywhere with her. So he decided to get to her through her father. He sent a messenger to the bean vendor to say to him, "The sultan's son wants you." When he [the bean vendor] went to him at the palace, he [the sultan's son] said to him, "Tomorrow I want you to come here, riding-walking. If you do not, I will do to you—(distant one: *el-bi¿îd*)—such and such [evil things]."

The man became very confused, and he returned to his home saddened. The girls asked him, "[May it turn out to be] a good thing! What is the matter, Father? Why are you sad?" He told them the story, and that the sultan said to him—the sultan's son (I mean) said to him, "'You must come here tomorrow, riding-walking!'"

The youngest said, [in an unconcerned tone], "Don't be afraid, father! Our neighbor has a burro that has just given birth to a little one; get it from him and ride it. Your feet will be dragging on the ground [while] you will be seated on its back; you will be 'riding-walking!'"

He did as his daughter, the youngest, told him to do and went to the sultan's son: riding the little donkey, with his feet dragging on the ground. When he [the sultan's son] saw him coming in this manner, he said to him [in a disappointed tone], "*Â-â-â-h* [I see]! This [idea] is not of your own doing; it is your youngest daughter's!" [Pause.] [The sultan's son continued in a commanding voice,] "Since this is the case, tomorrow you must come here attired-naked!"

The man, saddened, returned home to his daughter. She said to him, "What happened, Father? Didn't the little ass work out?" He answered [in despair], "Daughter, it worked out, but the sultan's son said, 'This [solution] is not yours! Tomorrow I want you to come here attired-naked!'"

She said [in a reassuring tone], "Is that all? Go to our neighbor So-and-so, the fisherman; borrow his net and wear it like a mantle. You will be dressed and you will be naked!" (Narrator giggles and adds, "May God's name protect your status.")

The man did as his [youngest] daughter told him to do; he went to his neighbor the fisherman and said, "Father of So-and-so, by God, lend me an old net of yours." The man said, "More than gladly!"[362] The bean vendor wore the net and went to the sultan's son "attired-naked." The sultan's son became extremely vexed, for he knew that it was all the work of the bean vendor's young[est] daughter. He said to him [angrily], "Tomorrow I want you to bring me your three daughters: pregnant!" He [the bean vendor, in a pleading tone] said, "Sire, how can that be! They are virgins!" He [the sultan's son] said [in an uncompromising tone], "This is no concern of mine. Bring them here pregnant, tomorrow!"

The man returned home to his daughters saddened, more [so] than before. They asked him, "What is the matter, Father?" He said to them, "Nothing!" (Of course he was ashamed to tell them that the sultan's son told him, "I want you to bring me your three daughters pregnant.") The youngest asked, "Didn't the net work out?" He replied, "[Yes], it worked out. But now the sultan's son is saying to me, 'I want you to bring to me your three daughters: pregnant!'"

She thought for a while and said, "Simple! Go buy lots of lentil, and we will cook it with lots of fried minced onions (*taqliyyah*)." [Narrator laughs repeatedly and interrupts her story until she is able to continue.] "And you know . . . , after we drink that lentil soup our stomach[s] will get inflated and bloated (*baṭninâ titnifikh wi-tibangar*), . . . and we will be . . . pregnant-and-virgins!!" [Laughter.]

The man did as his daughter had told him. They bought lots of lentil. They cooked it, [then] diced lots of onions and fried them in oil, and they *ṭashshû* (sizzled)[363] the fried onions [onto the lentil]. They kept on drinking, drinking, and drinking that lentil [soup]; they didn't even use any bread. Before morning time came, their stomach[s] became that high [narrator laughs, and places the palm of her hand in front of her stomach to indicate how high]—as if [their pregnancy was in its] ninth month.

The man took his three daughters and went to the sultan's son: "Here are my three daughters: pregnant and virgin!"

The sultan's son said, "No, they are not pregnant! How do we know that they are pregnant?"

The young[est] girl said, "Pregnant ones crave!"

So the sultan's son said to the eldest, "What do you crave?"

She [immediately and simple-mindedly] replied, "Apples!"

They got some apples for her; she sat down in total absorption in[364] [devouring] them.

Then he asked the middle-one, "What do you crave?"

She [immediately and simple-mindedly] answered, "Pears."

They got some for her; she sat down in total absorption in [devouring] them.

He said to the youngest, "And what about you, damned one—you who are the youngest!?"

She replied [emphatically], "I want a male radish planted in the heart of stone."[365]

He [the sultan's son] asked his servants, and his guards—(his people, I mean)—to fetch for her what she has requested. They said to him, "We don't have her request[ed item]!" He said to her, "Ask for something else!" She replied [defiantly], "No! This is what I want!" He said to his soldiers and guards, "Find what she has asked for!" They answered him, "Impossible. How can a radish be planted in [solid] stone?!" So he turned to the girl and said to her, "What you have craved is impossible: there is no 'male radish planted in stone!'"

She immediately [in a taunting tone] retorted, "How could it be, then, that you want virgin girls to have become pregnant without a male!"[366]

She said to her father and the other two [sisters], who were still immersed in their total absorption[367] [with eating their apples and pears], "Let us go home!"

And she left the sultan's son sitting there—(of course she confounded him[368] in front of everyone). He became more vexed with her.

So, what did he say [to himself]? He said, "I must marry her in order to break her spirit,[369] and bring her nose [down] to the ground[370] just like she brought my nose to the ground!" So he went to her father and said, "I wish to marry your [youngest] daughter."[371] The man said, "No!" He, [the sultan's son], said to him, "Just consult with her and find out what she might say!" [When her father asked her,] she said, "Yes, father, I would marry him; I agree to marry him. You tell him that you [also] agree."

Her father went to the sultan's son, and they agreed on the marriage. Meanwhile she had gone to the sweets man[372] and said to him, "I want you to make me a [sugar] doll: in my size, looks like me, and with strings which when pulled would cause her [it] to move her head, eyelashes, arms, waist, . . . I mean move exactly like a [living] human being!"

ASIDE

A child comments: "Like a 'Prophet's-Birthday doll' "; see note 350, this section.

[Narrator continues, repeating listener's comment:] Just like the doll of the Prophet's Birthday celebration, but very much bigger and with moving hands, head, and everything.

When the time came for the actual consummation of marriage (*dukhlah*), she went into the room of the bride and groom before anyone else was there. She set the doll on the bed, covered her [the doll] with the [lace] shawl, put out the lights, and hid inside the wardrobe; (and of course, she held the strings in her hands). The sultan's son entered the room: [he was] bent on getting even with her, for all what she had done to him. He held the sword in his hand and said to her [in a taunting tone], "Do you remember the time you [insulted me by] saying 'You, son of a clog!?' Do you remember, or have you forgotten!? And do you remember the time you did to me [such and such]!?, And Do you remember . . . ?!" He unreeled before her (*karr-e-lhâ*)[373] all she had done to him.

Meanwhile, she pulled the strings and the doll kept on winking, fluttering her eyelashes (*titrammishsh*), and swaying her body coquettishly (*titqaṣṣaʿ*)—like this and like that. [Narrator, while sitting on a cushion on the floor, shows how it is done.] Every time he would say to her, "Do you remember the time you did such and such to me?" she would pull the strings, and the doll would keep on winking (*titghammiz*),[374] fluttering her eyelashes, and swaying her waist. He became more and more vexed and said to her, "This is the end for you!" He struck her with his sword. The doll broke up into a thousand pieces and scattered everywhere. One piece flew into his mouth; he found it to be sweet. [Suddenly] he was saddened and said, [in a sorrowful voice], "Your beginning [in this affair] is bitterness (enmity), but your end is sweetness!"[375]

That was it! She got out of the wardrobe, and said to him, "There need not be bitterness [between us]. I am your wife: legitimate for you."

And they repeated the wedding celebration [in a more joyful manner].

And they lived in stability and prosperity and begot boys and girls.

> EL-SHAMY: How could they live together after all that has happened?
>
> NARRATOR: That which happened between the two of them took evil and went away [with it].[376] When something bad (away from you) happens, this is what we would say. With marriage, they will have to get along.

Two years earlier, Nabawiyyah M.Y. (see Tale No. 9), the narrator of another variant of this tale, gave the following answer to the same question:

> Of course, now that she is a married woman, she will have to relax the tension [of her pride] somewhat; she will have to obey her man. Or, maybe he will not be so uptight: [because] "a pillow would not carry two [of a kind]."[377] A man and his wife cannot be too much alike; for if both are handsome, proud, or moody, both will be demanding; neither will yield to the other and there will be no give and take.

❖ 16 ❖

THE SPEECHLESS [BRIDE]

(SYRIA)

NARRATED IN APRIL 1981 BY 'ĀMÂL Q., THIRTY-FOUR YEARS OF AGE, MARRIED AND THE MOTHER OF A NUMBER OF CHILDREN. SHE HAILED FROM A SMALL TOWN IN SOUTHERN SYRIA, WHERE SHE RECEIVED AN ELEMENTARY SCHOOL

EDUCATION. DUE TO HER GOOD LOOKS, SHE HAD BEEN ENGAGED TO A RELATIVE AT THE AGE OF NINE; HER FATHER HAD INSISTED THAT SHE SHOULD NOT GO INTO THE NEXT LEVEL AT SCHOOL AND "REMAIN AT HOME" UNTIL SHE GOT MARRIED. SHE HAD HEARD THIS *ḤICHÂYEH* (FANTASY-TALE) WHEN SHE WAS STILL A GIRL, FROM HER MOTHER. I MET THE NARRATOR WHEN SHE WAS VISITING RELATIVES IN THE MA¿ÂDÎ DISTRICT OF CAIRO, EGYPT. THE RECORDING TOOK PLACE IN HER HOST'S SITTING ROOM; A NUMBER OF EGYPTIAN AND SYRIAN FRIENDS AND RELATIVES WERE PRESENT AND LISTENED INTENTLY.

Forced marriage between a young woman and an old man, the young woman's feelings concerning her need for the tenderness of a husband of her own age group, and a wife's resentment of unwanted sexual intercourse (Mot. T183§) are central themes in this tale. Also illustrated are the qualities of fertility, and being a mother to numerous children as major factors in establishing the status of a new wife in "her husband's household."[378]

Ridicule—by mimicking (Mot. Q477.1§), in our present text—is a traditional means of exercising social control.

YOU listeners, state the oneness of God!

Listeners: There is no god but God.

There was a king—(and no one is King but God). That king had a daughter; he had no children but her: [She was dear to him and he gave her whatsoever she wished for]. One day that lass (*bunayyah*) was seated and combing her hair. As she looked [at the fine-tooth comb] she saw something she had never seen before:

"What is this?"

"This is a louse!" [someone answered her].

She cried in disbelief, "A louse!! A louse!! Tell my father, the king: 'Your daughter has a louse in her hair!'" They took the louse to the king, and said, "King of [this] epoch,[379] your daughter found a louse in her hair!" They showed him the louse. He said, "Put it in the well and cover it until we rule on its fate!"

O day, go! O day, come! [time passed], and the matter of the louse slipped the king's mind. He traveled away [on some business] and returned; he went about his normal business for some time.[380] One day he remembered the louse. He called on the slaves: "Where is the louse [that had been placed] in the well? Bring it!"

They lifted the cover [off the well] and found the louse to have grown to be that big—as big as a cow!!! They tied it with a rope and dragged it to the king. He wondered, "Is this a louse or a cow?" They said to him, "A louse. It is the louse that your daughter [had] found in her hair." He [the king] said, "Do not tell anyone! Slaughter it, skin it, and bring me the skin! [But tell no one about it.]" They did as the king told them to do. They slaughtered it—(as a cow or a ewe would be slaughtered), skinned it, and took the skin to the king. He sent [criers to declare] in the city: "Whoever can guess what type skin this is, I'll give my daughter [in marriage]!"

He who lived faraway, and he who lived nearby came, [people came from everywhere and guessed:]

"It is a cow's skin!"

. . . [No!]

"It is a ewe's skin!"

. . . [No!]

"It is a camel's skin!"

. . . [No!]

"It's a wolf's skin!"

. . . [No!]

No one could say. Finally, an old man (*'ikhtiyâr*), who was very, very old, came. He could walk only with a cane and by dragging his feet. He said [in a quivering, feeble voice], "The skin is the skin of a louse!"

"Ah-h-h! That goner of an old man (*l-ikhtiyâr el-fânî*) guessed that it was a louse!" [exclaimed the audience].

The old man said, "Give the king's daughter to me in marriage!"[381] The girl—being too young—cried and wailed. [But] her father said to her, "I have given my word, and a king's promise is irrevocable.[382] Prepare yourself and go with him. Wheresoever he takes you, you go!"

What will she do? She went with that old man: *hai-hai-hai* [walking very slowly and with great difficulty] until he got to that old hut: dirty and empty, with nothing but a mat [on the floor] and a broken pot. He used to go—(he was a beggar who went from town to town)—begging and take her with him. Now he said to her, "You must carry me [in a basket] on top of your head!" What could she do! She carried him and they kept on going around from one town to another. This one—('Omm-Aḥmad—for example) would give him an end-of-the-bunch loaf of bread,[383] and that one—(like *ed-daktoar* [Dr.] Ḥasan [the collector], for example)—would give him something else, for God's sake.

At the end of each day he would take her to his hut. When it was time . . . [narrator hesitates] to go to bed, he would say to her:

"Let us go sleep, O you bag of bones!
Oh, how my heart languishes, [craving] the fair-complected, fleshy ones."[384]
She would hear him talk and get [more] saddened.

ASIDE

An Egyptian listener comments, "We have a proverb that says: *reḍîna be-l-hamm, we-l-hamm mâ-rḍîsh bîna* (We reconciled ourselves to grief, but grief did not reconcile itself to us)."

Narrator: By God, this is true; we, too, have it [in Syria].

The girl was hungry and naked [insufficiently dressed]; that old man caused her grief constantly. She became ill and pale; she became weak and thin. One day an old woman passed by the hut and saw her crying; she said to her, "Why are you crying, daughter?" She replied, "My husband is a goner of a man. I carry him in a basket [but] he says to me:

Get up, so that we may go to bed, you bag of bones!
Oh, how my heart languishes for the fair-complected, fleshy ones!"

The old woman said to her, "When he says that to you, you reply:

[Wait] till I recuperate [from the last time],
you [who are a] bag of carnelian [i.e., crunched glass]!
Oh, how my heart languishes for [craves] a tender-mannered young man!"[385]

The old woman left. The old man—[the husband]—came home. After a while it became nighttime. He said to the king's daughter:

Get up, so that we may go to bed, you bag of bones!
Oh, how my heart languishes for the fair-complected, fleshy ones!

She replied [narrator speaks with apparent sense of pleasure]:

Wait till I recuperate,
you bag of crunched-glass!
Oh, how my heart languishes for a tender-mannered young man!"

He heard this talk and [with bafflement] said, "Ah!! This is not your own talk [not of your own thinking]. Who put you up to this?" She answered him, "A woman, [just] a woman of God's creatures!"[386] He said [in despair], "Ah! A town in which women have figured you out is a town in which there is no more living for you!"[387] [He ordered], "Woman, carry me in the basket [on your head] and let us depart!"

She carried him and walked from town to town; she would go up a mountain and go down a mountain. Things continued like this until she was about to be finished. She said to him, "I am thirsty." He replied, "There is no water!" They came to a well; she put him down [on the ground] and tried to reach the water, but she could not reach it. He shrieked at her, "Get down the well!" "I can't!" [she replied, faintly]. He took her scarf, tore it up into strips, and tied them together; he got to the well and he was lowering the strap into it [to reach the water]. He fell! "Pull me out, O So-and-so!" She pulled! [The strap] broke. The strap was wet and she squeezed the water [out of it] into her mouth. [Meanwhile] he was still shrieking at her, "You who are [such-and-such], You who are [such-and-such], get me out!!" She said to him [with determination], "Remain where you are!" He said [cursing her], "May God bring you disgrace; and may your tongue disown you."[388]

She kept on going, going, going!! (She is in pitiful shape: emaciated, starved, and thirsty.) She [finally] came to a spot where she found a spring—a little lake, and trees with fruit. She ate and said, "Thanks are due God [for his boon]!" Then she heard [narrator speaks in a manner denoting childlike mimicking and ridiculing of an adult, with a shrill but muted voice and a pendulumlike movement of the head]:

"Thank God!" [a mysterious voice echoed].

"Oh!" [she wondered].

"Oh!" [the voice echoed].

"What is this?" [she wondered].

"What is this?" [the voice echoed]. [Narrator laughs.]

Every word she said, that tongue—[that later proved to be that of her husband who evidently died in the well]—repeated in a manner that [would have] made everyone laugh! What was she to do? She pretended to be speechless.[389]

The king's son came to that spot and found her:

"Who are you?"

She did not utter a sound.

"What [type of a person] are you?"

She did not utter a sound.

"Are you a human or a jinni?"

. . . [Silence.]

The point was that she did not say a word, neither a good word nor an evil word. He saw that she was not [feeling] well, seemed hungry and emaciated; [but still] she seemed to be of good descent. He took her home to his mother and said to her, "I found this dumb one lost. Take care of her."

In the king's house she regained her health and looked beautiful (for she originally was of royal descent).[390] He [the king's son] saw her and said to his mother, "Mother, I want to marry her!" She said to him [in a reprimanding tone], "Son, she is dumb! We know nothing about her descent!"

The point is that he married her. When [i.e., after] he married her, she begot three children [two boys and a girl]: Sa¿d,[391] Sa¿îd, and Sa¿diyya. Still she did not utter a word. He [the husband] got fed up.[392] He said to his mother, "Mother, I want to marry another, in addition to the dumb one."[393] She answered him, "Before you are the daughters of your paternal-uncle (*banât ¿ammak*), and the daughters of your maternal-uncle (*banât khâlak*)." She affianced (*khaṭabat-luh*) for him his paternal-uncle's daughter.

They said to the speechless one [in a taunting tone], "He will marry someone else in addition to you!"

She said nothing.

They said, "He affianced his paternal-cousin!"

She said nothing. On the day of the wedding celebration they said to the speechless one, "Get up and bake!" She burned the bread. They said to her, "Get up and cook (for the bride and the wedding celebration)!" She ruined the food. She put a kantar [a huge amount] of salt in the food.

She said to her children, "Go to the bride. Whatever she would say, you say [it, mimicking her]." The children, the two boys and their sister, dressed up in royal clothing and . . . went to where the women [in the celebration happened to be]. They served the bride some food [from the wedding banquet]. She took a first bite and yelled [in disgust], "Yak-k-k!! [It is pure] sa-a-a-lt!"[394] The children said, [in a mocking manner, with a grimace on the face and moving the head like a pendulum], "Yak-k-k! Salt! Yak-k-k! Salt!" The bride, his paternal-cousin, said [cursing], "May He [God] terminate [the life of] the speechless one and terminate her children!"[395] So the children said [mockingly], "May God terminate the speechless one and terminate her children!" The bride said, "Get me some water! The salt is in my mouth!"

The children said [mockingly], "Get me some water. The salt is in my mouth!"

The bride cursed, "May God terminate the speechless woman and terminate her children!"

The speechless woman spoke [abruptly] and said:

> I've begotten Sa¿d, Sa¿îd, and Sa¿diyya,
> [yet] never has the king's son heard a bad word out of me![396]

The old man's tongue came out and said [mockingly]:

> I've begotten Sa¿d, Sa¿îd, and Sa¿diyya,
> [yet] never has the king's son heard a bad word out of me!

The new bride tried to do like she [the speechless woman] had done. She started to say, "I've begotten . . . !" Before she could finish, the tongue got hold of her! [Narrator laughs.] It got hold of her and said [in mimicking manner] everything she said. [Narrator laughs.]

The king's son heard of what had happened. His first wife proved not to be speechless. He divorced his paternal-cousin and reinstated as wife the deserted one (*ṭallaq bint-¿ammuh we radd el-mahjûrah*).

And the bird flew away. Good evening to you.[397]

❖ 17 ❖

THE GIRL WITH A DANGLER

(PALESTINE)

NARRATED IN 1971 BY MRS. N.N., THIRTY-SIX, BORN TO A TURKISH FATHER AND PALESTINIAN MOTHER IN AL-RAMLAH AL-BAYḌÂ, PALESTINE. SHE WORKED AS A CLERK AT A WESTERN ESTABLISHMENT IN CAIRO. THIS TEXT WAS COLLECTED AND WRITTEN DOWN IN ARABIC BY MISS HODÂ Ḥ. FAHMÎ.[398]

The risqué title of this tale, "'Omm-mi¿lâq," *is based on a pun. The word* mi¿lâq *denotes a piece of jewelry or an ornament that "dangles down" when worn (e.g., a pendant).*[399] *It may also refer to the male organ that "dangles" or "hangs down." The naive heroine uses the word in both senses.*

Conditions generated by the segregation of gender groups constitute the core of this humorous fantasy-tale. Masking as a woman in order to gain access to women's quarters, or a harem, is a recurrent theme in Arabic lore.[400] *The fostering of homosexuality—pseudo-lesbian attraction*[401] *in the present text—is one of the outcomes of such segregation. Under these conditions, the role of "safe" individuals who are allowed access to women's quarters (e.g., a eunuch, or a "middle-woman" or female marriage broker,*[402] *as is the case in the present text) as go-between is vital. The tale illustrates this role of procuress, and mocks the "morality" of prominent "upstanding" families.*

THERE was that king. That king had one lone son, with whom he wanted to become happy with him and wed him to [some girl]. The prince thought, and wished that he himself could see the bride whom he was going to marry. But he was unable to do so (because in older times they used to cover their faces with a certain type of cloth). So, the prince thought that he would accompany the [marriage] broker as she toured the homes, so that he might test the manners of the bride whom he would select. He sent for the broker and had her brought to him. He said to her, "Pretend that I am your daughter, and take me along with you to every home you enter." She replied, "Whatever you command, my lord."

He changed his looks, and masked himself in girl's clothing; the first day, he went with her to the vizier's home. After the broker and her daughter (the prince) had stayed there for a while, she [the broker] said, "By the Prophet, sister, keep my daughter with you; I will pick her up on my way back [from my trip]." (The broker intended to be gone for some time, for this was an agreement between her and the prince.) [The vizier's family agreed.] When it was sunset-time, they served her [the disguised prince] supper, and said to her, "Please be so kind as to go to sleep." Naturally, he did not sleep and stayed awake during the night. He [awaited a moment] when the people of the house were inattentive and slipped himself underneath the bed of the vizier's daughter. About midnight, after everyone in the house had gone to sleep—including servants and the entourages—he heard a light knock on the [house] door. The truth of the matter is that the vizier's daughter had someone for a lover. She opened the door for him and led him into her room. Naturally, between the two lovers there was kissing, hugging, horsing around (*hiẓâr*),[403] laughter, conversation, and reconciliatory reprimand (*¿itâb*). At dawn, the paramour sneaked, and slipped out the door. The following day the broker stopped by to pick up her daughter (the prince), and she left [along with him].

Following that, the broker began to take him to the homes of the notables of the country: the head of the merchants,[404] the governor of the city, the head of the police. He [the disguised prince] found out that every girl in these homes had a paramour; [moreover], all girls were haughty and arrogant—they did not meet the broker with [adequate] welcome.

At long last, the broker took him to the home of a subdued (*ghalbân*), poor man, who had a sole daughter; she was pretty and her mother was dead. She received the broker and her daughter with courtesy; she repeatedly stated, "Hello," and "Welcome" to them.[405] She also was very glad that the broker was going to leave her daughter to "sleep with her" [i.e., spend the night]. When it was nighttime, she [the poor girl] got up and served supper and they ate supper. After supper, she brought a drum, and kept on drumming and singing; then she said to the broker's daughter, "Take the drum, so that each of us would dance in turn."

The prince fell very much in love with the girl, because of her simplicity (*basâṭah*)[406] and beauty. He wished to see all her body. So, as she was dancing he asked her to take off her clothes (. . . [??]). At first, she was too bashful, but he said to her, "We are girls, we are alike." The girl went along [with his wish]: he kept on drumming for her, and she [kept on] dancing as she took the clothes off, until she became stark naked.[407] Then she put on her clothes. Now it was the turn of the broker's daughter—(the prince). He kept on dancing, and taking his clothes off until he became stark naked. The girl gasped when she saw his appearance. She asked him, "Sister, what is this?"—as she was pointing at his body; she was astonished because she had never seen a man['s organ]. He answered her—going along with her simplicity, "This is a dangler (*mi¿lâq*)."[408] The girl said, "Consequently, I shall call you 'The-girl-with-a-dangler!' " Afterward, they became tired, they finished their nighttime fun (*sahrah*),[409] and they fell asleep.

When the broker came back the following day to pick up her daughter, the girl got hold of her [the daughter], and pleaded, "Maternal-aunt, by the Prophet, let your daughter stay with me." The prince stayed with her for three nights; each day they would stay up late and dance. He fell in love with her, because he sensed that she honestly loved him,[410] and that she was good-hearted and beautiful.

When he returned to his family in the palace, he insisted that he will marry that girl. He told his father about her [good] characteristics, and about the [bad] characteristics of the other girls each of whom had a he-friend [paramour]. His father consented, and capitulated (*khaḍaʿ*) to the wish of his son the prince, because he felt that he [the son] will be pleased.

The wedding celebration was made; and when the eve of the [consummation of] the marriage came, the bride was surprised. She struck her chest [in disbelief] and exclaimed, "So, it was you: the one with the dangler; and I did not know."[411] He answered her, "I fell in love with you." He told her everything. They lived in stability and prosperity, and begot boys and girls.

HUSBAND AND WIFE

❖ 18 ❖

"WHO WILL ENTER PARADISE FIRST?"

(EGYPT, EASTERN DESERT)

NARRATED IN JUNE 1972 BY 'OMM-SHINDÎ (SHINDÎ'S-MOTHER), AGED SIXTY, A SETTLED BEDOUIN, OF THE ṬARABÎN ARABS, OF THE EASTERN DESERT, EGYPT. SHE HAD BEEN MARRIED FOR FORTY-EIGHT YEARS AND BEGOT HER FIRST CHILD, SHINDÎ, TWELVE YEARS AFTER HER MARRIAGE. SHINDÎ, THE FAMILY PROVIDER THEN, ACCOMPANIED HIS MOTHER DURING THE RECORDING. ALTHOUGH HE GAVE HER HIS PERMISSION TO CITE HER NAME, SHE REFUSED TO DO SO, AND WAS VISIBLY VERY UNCOMFORTABLE WITH HIS INSISTENCE.

THE NARRATOR HAD LEARNED THE STORY AT HER HOME; SHE STATED,

> I HEARD THIS STORY FOR THE FIRST TIME FROM MY MOTHER WHEN I WAS STILL A BRIDE (*¿ARÛSAH*) [I.E., NEWLYWED]. THERE WAS SOME DISAGREEMENT BETWEEN 'ABU-SHINDÎ [MY HUSBAND] AND ME. . . . SO, MY MOTHER SAID TO ME, "THERE IS A RELIGIOUS STORY[412] . . . THAT SHOWS YOU THAT A WOMAN MUST OBEY HER MAN TO THE UTMOST." THEN SHE TOLD ME THIS STORY. LATER ON, I HEARD IT FROM THE SENIOR PEOPLE (*EN-NÂS EK-KUBÂR*).

SHINDÎ, WHO HAD TWO FEUDING WIVES, AGREED FULLY WITH HIS MOTHER'S STORY AND COMMENTED, "I WISH THERE WERE SOMEONE WHO COULD TELL THIS STORY TO MY FIRST WIFE [¿AZÎZAH]. SHE LISTENS TO [I.E., OBEYS] NO ONE!"[413]

Formal religious dogma specifies that one of a husband's rights is that his wife must obey him in whatever he may ask for, provided that no sin is involved.[414] *The present folk narrative gives a vivid example of this ideal principle of marital interaction. In literary traditions, stories that express this theme abound.*[415]

In the late 1980s, the present writer asked Mrs. X (a mother and a bright young career woman: a university graduate, married to one of her peers, and both em-

ployed in the Gulf region) whether she knew the narrative. She was visibly irritated and stated sternly, "Are you going to tell me that you believe [in the moral expressed in] this story!" She went on to explain the reasons for her resentment of the mere mention of the narrative:

> *Women here [in the Gulf region] always bring up this story so as to justify [their enduring] the abuses by their husbands! [They say] that the wife of the firewood man would always stand before him, with a stick in her hand, and she would say, "Better that he would take his frustration out on me than on people outside!"*[416]

Clearly, Mrs. X did not find many women who shared her resentment of the "moral" of this moralistic story.

The role assigned to Fâṭimah, the Prophet Mohammad's daughter, in this folk narrative is highly atypical, in that she deliberately seeks to sow discord between a happily married husband and wife. According to Islamic doctrines, "sowing discord" is a cardinal sin. The story, however, still maintains the innocence of the outcome, and reiterates Fâṭimah's primacy and higher status within the stratified community of the inhabitants of Paradise.[417]

The symbolic association between a pitcher with a spout and a male is clearly depicted in the story.[418] *This association recurs in folk expressive contexts, as well as in actual life. A historian, for example, reported that the guardian of the "house of women fakirs"*[419] *prohibited the use in bathrooms of pitchers with spouts.*[420]

FUṬMAH [i.e., Fâṭimah],[421] the Prophet's daughter, was once asking her father, "Father, is there someone who is going to enter Paradise ahead of me?" He—(may prayers on his behalf and greetings be)[422]—said, "Yes!"

She asked [in astonishment], "Who, father!?"

He replied, "The wife of a poor firewood man (*ḥaṭṭâb*)!"[423]

"How could this be! I am the Prophet's daughter! And I am the mother of el-Ḥasan and el-Ḥusain! And I am the mother of *'es-Sayyidah*[424] [Zainab]. And I am . . . ! And I am . . . !"

Her father said to her, "This is what will be!"

"How could that be?" [she still wondered]. She thought, "I must go to that wife of the firewood man and see what she does; how she is living, and how she manages [her life]."

She went to the hut of the firewood man and knocked [on the door].

"Who is it?"

"I am Fuṭmah."

"Fuṭmah who?"

"Fuṭmah, the Prophet's daughter."

"What do you want?"

"I want to talk with you. Open the door so that I may enter."

"[Wait] until I consult with my husband. Come back tomorrow."

Her husband returned from picking up the dry stalks for fire-stuff, dusty and haggard (*m¿affar w-mjaffar*). As he entered, she was awaiting with a water pitcher for him to wash for ablution. Before he was done with the sunset prayer (*maghrib*), she had already set the food. She served him food, gave him drink, and made him content. As he was sitting [relaxing] she said to him, "Fuṭmah, the Prophet's daughter, wants to come [and visit]." He replied, "Nothing wrong with that, woman. Let her come!"

The following day, Fuṭmah the Prophet's daughter came. She knocked.

The firewood man's wife said, "Who is it?"

"Open up, I am Fuṭmah, the Prophet's daughter; with me is el-Ḥasan [my older son]."

"You may come in, but el-Ḥasan may not."

"How can that be?"

"He must wait until I've consulted with my husband. He said, 'Fuṭmah [may] visit with you,' but he did not say 'el-Ḥasan may enter!' " [Fuṭmah and her son left.]

Her husband returned from picking up the firewood, dusty and haggard. She poured water for him to wash for ablution, and he did the [sunset-] prayer. After he had eaten, drunk [water], and got comfortable, she asked him, "Fuṭmah, the Prophet's daughter, came, along with her son el-Ḥasan. Shall I let the two in?" He replied, "Nothing is wrong with that, woman! Let her come; let him [el-Ḥasan] come, and let el-Ḥusain [the younger son] come too!"

The following day the door knocked.

"Who is it?"

"Fuṭmah, the Prophet's daughter; with me are el-Ḥasan, el-Ḥusain, and their sister Zainab!"

"You, and el-Ḥasan and el-Ḥusain, may get in, but their sister Zainab may not!"

"How can that be?"

"She must wait until I consult my husband!"

Her husband said, "Woman, let them all: the three—or the four—in!"

The following day Fuṭmah, the Prophet's daughter, came with her three children, the two boys and the girl. She let them in; she welcomed them and gave them to drink. At sunset time, her husband [the firewood man] returned. His wife received him. She poured water [out of a pitcher] for him to wash up and do the ablution; he did the prayers of sunset-time. She had set his food, his drink, and everything. (Now, Fuṭmah was watching.) When the firewood man was about to go out [of the house], his wife brought him his light footwear (*madâs*),[425] handed him his rope and ax, and prayed that he should return safely. Now Fuṭmah watched all this and wondered, "What a dusty, scruffy man!" [She said to the wife,] "How can you stand living with such a dusty, scruffy man! There are men who are much better than he is! What does he get for you?" She kept on talking to her like that and egging her on against her man[426] until the woman hated him. [Fuṭmah then left.]

When her husband returned she remained where she was. He went to wash for ablution; she remained seated.

[He said,] "Get up and get us the food, woman!"

[Pause.] She did not reply.

"Hand me the water!"

[Pause.] She did not reply.

From here to there, they started quarreling. She took her clothes and headed for her father's home. On her way she saw an old man crying and wailing. [When] that old man saw her coming, he wailed more loudly and bitterly.

"What is the matter with you, father hajji?" [she asked].

"O my daughter, I had a pitcher. He [i.e., it] fell and broke into pieces!"

[In amazement,] "Is that all? Buy a new one!" [she answered].

[He replied with incredulity,] " 'Buy a new one!' How can that be!? I have had that [broken] one for all my life. My private parts have been exposed to it.[427] It has kept my private matters confidential (*sâtir ¿alayyah*).[428] How can I expose myself to a new pitcher. It is togetherness-in-life (*¿ishrah*)!"

She [the wife of the firewood man] thought of her husband and she said [to herself], "By God, O daughter-of[-good-]people, this [old man] is a man, and he is crying over his old pitcher. He does not want to expose himself to a new pitcher. What about you [i.e., me], you are a woman; how could you marry another man and expose your [privates] to him!"

So she went back to her husband and told him the story. He said to her, "I forgive you, and may God forgive you [too]!"

Now Our Master (*sayyidnâ*)[429] Muḥammad asked his daughter [in a reprimanding tone], "Why did you do that?" She answered, "So that she may not enter Paradise ahead of me!" He said to her, "You give up jealousy and you [too] will enter Paradise. She [the wife of the firewood man] will enter Paradise first, [but] holding the bridle of your camel, [the camel on which you will be mounted]!"

EL-SHAMY: Who was that old man?
NARRATOR: That was an angel from heaven; God put him to the task of showing her [the right way], so he appeared to her in that form.

❖ 19 ❖

"SEVEN OVERBOILING CAULDRONS FROM A SPARROW'S SIDE!"

(EGYPT)

NARRATED IN MAY 1982 BY 'OMM-EL-¿IZZ, A FORTY-YEAR-OLD PEASANT WOMAN, A POULTRY VENDOR FROM THE VILLAGE OF EL-QINAYÂT, SHARQIYYAH GOVERNORATE, NORTHEASTERN EGYPT. SHE WAS NONLITERATE AND THE MOTHER OF THREE. AT THE TIME OF THE RECORDING, SHE HAD JUST BEEN FORMALLY DIVORCED "AFTER [ALMOST] THIRTY YEARS [OF MARRIAGE], AND BEING TURNED OUT: WITH ONLY THE GARMENT [SHE] WORE."[430] SHE HAD TAKEN UP "BUYING AND SELLING" SO AS TO PROVIDE FOR HERSELF AND HER CHILDREN. THE CHILDREN, WHOSE AGES RANGED FROM FIVE TO FIFTEEN, ARE STAYING WITH HER BECAUSE THEIR FATHER WAS TOO BUSY WITH HIS NEW WIFE WHOM HE MARRIED A YEAR EARLIER.

Conflict between husband and wife over economic matters, symbolized here by the consumption of food, is the central theme for this humorous anecdote. Although food is of considerable importance, complaining of its lack or of being hungry is seen as shameful (see also introductory note to Tale No. 21). A man who chooses to keep his wife needy is viewed—usually by women—in very negative terms. A truism states, "Shit son-of-shit is he who can provide but renders the woman (wife) needy!!"[431] *A variation on the present tale type describes the dilemma of few choices that a wife faces in such an abusive marital relationship:* "Wife Escapes her Miserly Husband to Find her New Fiancé More Miserly; She Returns to the First" *(designated as Subtype 1407B§).*

*For our narrator, the story is told as a fantasy-tale (*ḥaddûtah*), and as a joke (*nuktah*, i.e., a merry tale) as well. She had heard it while still a little girl, from her mother and other "grown-up women" in the village. 'Omm-el-¿Izz stated that she had not told this or any other tale for years, due to the fact that "the weighty concerns of life (*humûm ed-dunyâ*) have left me no mind (*bâl*) [for such matters]."*

When asked about whether she would remarry, the narrator answered with the proverb: "'O quince, what shall I remember of you: every bite brought a tear!'"[432] *(I.e., like a quince, marriage at first seems radiant and fragrant, but it proves to be extremely sour.) Significantly, in our present tale the widowed wife does not remarry.*[433]

STATE the oneness of God.

There was once a man and a woman. They had three daughters. They were living in contentment. One day someone came to ask for the eldest girl [in marriage]. They said to him, "Wait until we ask [about you]." He said, "I will pay such-and-such: one hundred, two thousand [pounds as dowry]—as much as you wish." They said to him, "Wait until we ask."

He was a big merchant who had money and gold [that can be measured] by the kantar. And what else was he? He was an old man; he had married many a time before but not a single wife lasted long with him. They [the parents] thought, "We have three daughters and [as for] the man: no [major] faults are to be found in him (*mâ-yit¿ayyibsh*). We should give him the eldest girl."

They [the old merchant and the girl] got married and she went to his home to live. She entered the house to find it empty: neither food nor drink; neither rations nor edibles (*lâ zâd walâ zuwwâd*).[434] What is she to do? She kept this [secret] to herself and she suffered through. Whenever she would say, "O Father of So-and-so, we need to buy annual rations (*khazîn*),"[435] he would answer, "It is not the season for rice! It is not the season for butter, wait until winter [comes]. It is not the season for onions. It is not the season for . . . !" The girl got—(away from you)—ill and died. [He buried her secretly.]

He went to her father and mother and said [slyly], "Your daughter caused me an infamy (*faḍaḥitnî*).[436] She ran away from home (*ṭafashit*)." They said to him [in a voice denoting shock], "How could that be!!" He replied [bluntly], "That is what happened! Maybe she ran away with some other man! Give me her sister [in marriage] so that we can hide the disgrace (*fiḍîḥah*)!!" They said, "[We leave] our affairs up to God. [Daughter] So-and-so, get up and go with him!"

He took the middle girl and went to his house. What happened to the eldest [girl], happened to the middle: she found neither food nor drink, neither rations nor edibles! What is she to do? Just as her sister had done; she was too ashamed to say, "I am hungry!" She suffered and did not speak up. Just like her sister, she got ill and died.

He [the husband] gathered himself and went back to her father and mother and said [slyly], "Your second daughter turned out to be worse than the first. She too ran away."

"How could that be!!!"

"That is what has happened!"

. . . [Silence.]

"Give me your youngest daughter so that we may hide the disgrace!"

They implored him, "May God guide you! We have no one else but her now!" He said, "Never! Give her to me in lieu of her sisters who caused me disgrace!"

The girl was listening. She said, "Mother, I want to go with him. Marry me off to him."

"Why, daughter!? For what reason!?"

"For no reason."

They gave her to him. He took her and returned to his home with her. Once she set her foot inside the house and saw how [empty] it was, she said to herself, "Ah! So, this is the story!"

When it was time for supper he placed some bread morsels and a few salt pebbles in front of her and said [in a commanding voice], "Eat!" She replied [in contrived astonishment], "What is this? Why are you so extravagant! All this food for two!"

"How much [of that food], then?"

"Half of it, or one half of the half. 'Verily, God likes not those who are extravagant!' [the Qur'ân states]."

When he heard this [kind of talk] from her, he thought, "This is the one who will last [with me]." He relaxed his guard,[437] and kept on doing his business. He would go down to the market, sell and buy, and would return at the end of the day. She kept on waiting—she pretended every night to be asleep. She kept on waiting to learn where he hides his money. She kept on waiting until one night he got up, slipped out of the room, and went up the stairs to the roof. [Narrator speaks with a sense of secrecy.] She followed him on the tips of her toes. She saw him get to a grain bin (*ṣomaʿah*),[438] which he had sealed with mud mortar.[439] He broke the seal, and lifted the cover. [He lifted some grain that was on top], took off his cummerbund, and lowered it into the bin; gold pounds went down: "Clink, clink, clink!"—one fistful after another (*bi-l-kabshah*)! When he finished, he put back the grain on top [of the gold], put the lid back, and sealed it with mud. And he went back to the [bed-]room. He looked and saw the girl in deep sleep.

The following day, when he left, she said to him, "Don't buy any more bread or salt. What we have is plenty!" As soon as he departed, she went upstairs to the roof, looked at the bin with the seal [and wondered], "O my girl, what are you to do?"—(for she could not break the seal; he would know [if she did]).

She went downstairs and got a [long-handled] baking poker. She stood on top of a kneading-tub right underneath the bin and [narrator imitates driving a poker into a solid ceiling) drove the poker into the ceiling. Gold coins came down: clink! clink!! She got as much as she wanted and sealed the hole with some mud.

Now the girl went and bought whatever her heart may have longed for: chicken, meat [beef], butter, sweets, and . . . , and . . . , everything! She would eat as she pleased, [but] when he would come, she would put the bread crumbs and the salt on the [dinner] tray.

One day she said to him, "O hajji! O Father-of-So-and-so!"

He replied [dryly], "What?"

She said, "I would like to give an eve-feast for the sake of God's people[440] and invite our neighbors and my mother and father. . . . "

He [interrupted in horror], "Have you gone mad, woman! Have you gone mad! What 'eve,' what 'neighbors,' and what other absurdities!?"[441]

She said [calmly], "For God's people. All I am requesting from you is your permission. I've caught a sparrow. I cooked one side of it for you tonight. [As for] the other side and the broth, I will cook for the guests during the eve-feast."

He said, "As long as this is what it is, [go ahead and] cook. But don't you dare make this into a habit."

She went ahead and bought two or three rams, a calf, ten pairs of chickens, two sacks of rice, two jars of clarified butter (*samnah*),[442] apples, pears, and . . . , and . . . , and . . . , everything that one may wish for! (All that [food] is only a bit of what you, [listener], do have.)[443] She made rice with liver [topping], stew, and *fattah;*[444] she prepared fried [foods], baked [foods], boiled [foods], and stuffed [foods] of every sort and color:[445] [stuffed] grape leaves, cabbage, eggplant, zucchini. Seven cauldrons on the stoves were boiling over. Neighbors and the poor were everywhere: eating, drinking, and thanking God.

When he arrived he looked and saw all that crowd, all those people. He went running to his wife [panting and yelling in a tone of great agony and anguish]:

> O woman! O woman!
> Seven overboiling cauldrons;
> from one side of a sparrow![446]

He realized what had happened. And: "Uh-h-h-h!" [narrator utters an inhaled deep extended guttural gasp]: he gasped and—(the more distant one)—dropped on the ground motionless! [He was dead.][447]

She gave her mother and father enough money to live comfortably for the rest of their days; she also gave money to the poor. As for her, she lived in contentment [presumably in her own new house].

❖ 20 ❖

¿ALI AL-¿ABDALÎ

(OMAN)

NARRATED IN MAY 1986 BY NÔRA BINT-J. FROM ṢALÂLHAH, OMAN. SHE WAS A DIVORCEE OF ABOUT SIXTY YEARS OF AGE, AND WORKED AS A CUSTODIAN IN THE FEMALE WING OF A HOSPITAL. SHE HAD HEARD THE TALE IN HER CHILDHOOD FROM WOMENFOLK IN THE FAMILY AND NEIGHBORHOOD. WITH REFERENCE TO THE OIL BOOM, THE NARRATOR REMARKED:

> IN OLDER TIMES [BEFORE THE OIL BOOM], OUR MEN: FATHERS, BROTHERS, HUSBANDS, . . . USED TO TRAVEL AND STAY AWAY FOR MONTHS OR YEARS AT A TIME. THEY WENT TO BOMBAY [INDIA], IRAQ, ZANJBÂR [ZANZIBAR], AND WHEREVER ELSE

MAKING A LIVELIHOOD WOULD HAVE TAKEN THEM. WOMEN GOT TOGETHER AND WOULD NARRATE.[448]

SHE ADDED SORROWFULLY,

NOW WITH ALL THAT MONEY, OUR MEN ARE GONE [FROM FAMILY CIRCLES], AND OUR NESTS HAVE BEEN DESERTED. THERE IS NO TIME TO TALK, AND THERE IS NO ONE TO TALK TO. AND IF THERE WERE, THEY WOULDN'T WANT TO LISTEN.

The role of a woman's mother-in-law, especially under rules of patrilocal residence where a wife joins her husband's household, is the central theme of this "true story." Also of significance is the endogamous marriage that is always preferred by family patriarchs for economic and power interests. The importance of having an offspring, the "curse" of childlessness, and their effect on the husband-wife relationship are dramatically depicted. Also depicted is the effect of rumor mongering (Mot. K2107.3§).

The tragic ending of the narrative is typical of Arab perceptions of "great love."[449]

*The tale's simple formulaic beginning (*hâdhî*: This is) is a regional equivalent to Once there was, Once upon a time, and the like; its presence adds an element of concreteness and realness to the story by generating in the listener a sense of being there.*[450] *In this respect its dramatic effect is similar to the use of familiar objects in the physical environment (or cognitive map).*[451]

THIS is a woman: dear to her man. But she would not get pregnant, nor bring forth children. The point is: he stayed with her [in spite of that].

Now the man has his mother, who has her brother and her brother's daughter [the mother's niece]. She [the mother] would say to him [in pleading tone], "My son. Your wife does not get pregnant! What are you waiting for?"

He would answer her, "By God, mother, I saw nothing but goodness from her. She never disappoints me! As she wishes,[452] leave her be!"

She said, "Here you have your *bint ¿amm* (paternal-uncle's daughter)."

He replied [in a curt manner], "I don't want her!"

She said, "Here you have your *bint khâl* (maternal-uncle's daughter)."

He replied [in a curt manner], "I don't want her!"

She said, "Here you have *banât ¿ammâtak wi banât khâlâtak* (daughters of your paternal-aunts and daughters of your maternal-aunts)."

He replied [in a curt manner], "I don't want them!"

He traveled—(in older times, our men: fathers, brothers, husbands, . . . used to travel and stay away for months or years at a time: they went to Bombay, Iraq, Zanjbâr, and wherever else making a livelihood would have taken them [. . .]). He traveled and left his wife with his mother.

The point is [narrator addresses the mother directly]:[453] O you, mother of his, get up and bring your brother's daughter, dress her in man's clothing: dress her up in a [man's] gown (*thawb*), dress her up in a [man's] mantle (*bisht*), dress her up in a [man's] head-scarf (*ghutrah*), dress her up in [man's] head-scarf cord (*¿igâl*),[454] dress her up in . . . , dress her up in . . . , until she gets to look exactly like a man. Now take her and deliver her to your son's wife.

That girl [the niece] said [to the wife], "Let us have coffee!"

She [the wife] did not think much about the girl's clothes; she thought: "Youth's play."

Now, O you old woman: get up and run to the neighbors, and run to the imam of the mosque (*mṭawwa¿*),[455] and run here and run there saying [in a taunting tone], "My son's wife! My son's wife! A man has entered her room! Her husband is away and she has been having men in her room!!"

The women [of the neighborhood], and the imam, too, said, "We have seen her [commit adultery]! We have seen her!"

Her husband returned. He went [first] to the [men's] gathering place [parlor].[456] [Meanwhile], she got [the house] ready for him: she arranged, cleaned, polished, and hung up flowers;[457] she sat down awaiting his entering.

She, [the mother], sent their slave to him in the men's gathering place. The slave went to him. [Upon seeing him the master inquired,] "So-and-so, [what brings you here], did my mother die?"

"That would have been lighter!" [the slave answered].

"Did my maternal-uncle die?"

"That would have been lighter!"

"Did the daughter of my maternal-uncle die?"

"That would have been lighter!"

"Did my wife die?"

"That would have been lighter!"

"Then, quickly, tell me what brings you here!"

He told him [that his wife has been unfaithful].

[Meanwhile, as her husband was in the men's gathering place], you [wife] get up, go to him in the men's gathering place, and say:

> I've looked for you till [my] heart felt sorrow, and folded,
> for every early shepherd has returned home [but you did not].

If it is a guest, keeping you too busy to see us:
I'm the daughter of the [hospitable]-one who-finds-excuses-for-guests.
And if it is a treacherous one, having now sown discord between us;
what is the use: the attempts of the treacherous are doomed.[458]

[He replied curtly, by addressing her by her first name:]

O Ghuṣainah,[459] you who have betrayed and fallen:
[living with you], O Ghuṣainah, is a loss.
Clear away from us at tomorrow's sunrise.
Let morning light not fall on you [at our home].[460]

[He continued:] "Go! [You are] divorced (*rûḥî: ṭâlig*)!"

She loaded and packed up [on a camel]; she took along her men slaves and women slaves, and when the sun was up, she was already at her family's home.

The mother of her husband was happy, she affianced to him the daughter of her brother. He [the son] took the daughter of his maternal-uncle [for a wife].

Now, O you maternal-cousin of his: get pregnant and do not beget a little boy, but get pregnant and beget a little girl. [Meanwhile], that other one [his former wife, Ghuṣainah], was taken [as a wife] by her paternal-cousin. She became pregnant and begot a little boy.

[One day], he [¿Ali] was cuddling up the little girl—(like this [narrator shows how]). She [his mother] asked him, "Do you love the girl, my dear (*yâmmak*)?"[461]

"Yes, by God, I do love the girl."

"Do you love Ghuṣainah [the first wife]?"

He answered [with considerable pain], "Yes, by God, I do love Ghuṣainah. But, that which she did to herself . . . , [faithlessness, I cannot forget]!"

She said, "By God, my dear little son (*yâ wildayyh*),[462] I wish to be absolved from a sin (*dhanb*) [committed]. Your first wife was more pure than the doves [in the holy shrine in] Mecca![463] I have never seen a [thing that may] blemish her [honor]. She was pure (*ṭâhrah*).[464] But I wished you would marry someone else, so that you may have a daughter or a son."

[He retorted, in disbelief,] "Does this mean that all that you have told me about her, 'One man going in and another man coming out,' is a falsehood!"

. . . [Silence.]

[He exclaimed in pain,] "All that you have told me about her is a falsehood!"

He handed the girl over to her, got on his she-riding-camel (*dhalûl*) and went looking for her [his first wife] and her family. He reached her country, and came to her palace. Under her [window], he halted. He kept on staring at her [window]. Tears filled his eyes.

Her slaves went and said to her, "There is someone outside staring at the palace!"

She looked, and found him. When she saw him, she said [in poetry recitation style]:

You, herder of thoroughbreds, that have become [so numerous that the moving herd looks like] waves,
may God [pardon??]; it is a cursed day when you weep for long.
If in debt, [payment of] your debt is with us;
and if owing blood vendetta, we will transfer the blood [you owe to us].
But, if you want me in the manner things used to be,
your desire has gone astray, for [your] sweetheart has become dour toward you![465]

He bit on his finger [due to rue]; he dropped dead from sorrow and regret, right under her room. Upon seeing that, she shrieked and leaped from the height over his corpse: she died right next to him.

❖ 21 ❖

THE CRUEL MOTHER-IN-LAW

(IRAQ)

NARRATED IN JUNE 1970 BY SALMÂ Q. SHE WAS FORTY-NINE, FROM BAGHDAD, MARRIED, AND LITERATE. THE RECORDING TOOK PLACE WHILE SHE WAS VISITING WITH RELATIVES IN CAIRO. (ALSO SEE INFORMANT NOTE TO TALE NO. 35.)[466]

This humorous narrative is a hyperbole of the powers exercised by a mother-in-law, in her capacity as the administrator of a household, over the incoming wife of her son. A separate residence seems to be the practical solution for a wife's problems at her in-laws' home. The story also reflects the value of food, and the fact that it is shameful to complain of its lack, or of hunger. (See also introductory note to Tale No. 19.)

A woman had an only son who became grown up and had not been married yet. She wanted to find him a bride, but he always told her, "Later, not now," and things like that. One day his mother said to him, "Listen, my son, I've grown old and become tired of household work. You must get married before I die [so that your wife may help me]."

He said to her, "Well!! Find me a good-hearted girl from a good family."

She searched until she found him a girl from one of the most notable houses in their town and he married her.

When the wedding [celebration] was over and after seven days or so [had passed], he went back to his shop to work. Meanwhile, his mother stayed home as before, [but now she was] with his wife. His mother said to his wife [sternly], "Listen, in this house [you] don't open that which is closed or close that which is open, nor uncover that which is covered or cover that which is uncovered, nor fold that which is unfolded or unfold that which is folded. Do you understand?"

The girl, his wife, said [submissively], "I understand, Mother!"

Days passed with matters going on as [the mother] has instructed. His mother is everything in the household; his wife works all day while her mother orders her around. When the man would return home his mother would call him before he would enter his room and would take whatever he would have brought home with him—food, pastry, or [good] things like that. His mother would set the dinner for him and if he were to say, "[Let us] call So-and-so [his wife] to eat with me," she [his mother] would answer him, "This can't be (*mâ-yṣîr*)! She is still new in the house. She would get bold [fresh] with us (*tiṭṭâwal ¿alaina*)! Wait for a few more days."

After a few more days her son would say, "Mother, let her come and eat with me."

His mother would say, "She hasn't been broken to our house yet. She does not need to eat for she has been eating all day."

He would say to his mother, "May God extend His grace upon us. Let her eat as much as she wants," and he used to eat only until he would become half-full and leave some of the best food for his wife. His mother would hide it and give her only dry bread and water.

The girl was not used to that; she had been raised in a household of plenty.

She grew sicker and weaker by the day. Her color faded and she became as yellow as saffron (*kurkum*). Whenever her husband asked her, "What is the matter with you?" she would answer, "Nothing."

One day he said to one of his friends at the shop, "By God, father of So-and-so, my wife is becoming sick. Every day she is getting sicker and pale. I don't know what to do. I am afraid she doesn't want me. Ever since she set foot in our house and she . . . , she doesn't speak to me and she is always sad."

His friend said to him, "I'll tell you what to do to find out whether she wants you and wants to stay in your house, or whether she hates you and would like to return to her father's home. After dinner swear by God she join you and your mother for the coffee, then break wind. If she laughs at you, she doesn't care for you and you should send her back to her father's home." [Listeners laugh.] "If she doesn't, then she is ill."

That same day after the man ate his supper and thanked God, he said to his mother, "Call So-and-so [his wife] to have coffee with us."

His mother said to him, "O Mḥammad, O my son, wait! If you treat her like this, she will have no awe of you!"[467]

He swore by God, and his mother went to call her. As they were drinking their coffee, he broke wind. His mother laughed, but his wife didn't and kept on drinking until she finished her cup.

The following day he told his friend about what had happened. His friend said to him, "Your wife is hungry. Your mother is starving your wife!"

When he went back home that day, he said to his mother, "We will have guests for dinner. Cook good food for ten persons." His mother went to the souk and bought everything: meat, chickens, vegetables, rice, and fruit and prepared a huge dinner.

When the meal was done, he said to her, "Mother, my friends are not coming. By God, call my wife and let us all eat this food."

His mother said to him, "You eat and leave the rest; I'll take it to her later."

He swore [that his wife come]. His mother got up to call the girl, his wife, and said, "You will spoil her. No one does this. She will not respect you after that!"

He answered, "That is all right."

His mother said [in a warning voice], "If she eats too much, she will mess up the bed!" [Audience laughs.]

He said, "That does not matter."

His wife came, sat down, and ate, and ate, and ate, while his mother was saying all the time [growling], "I told you. From now on, she will have awe for no one. She will get sick from too much eating. She will do it in bed!"

After she finished eating, they went into their room while his mother stayed outside boiling with anger. When he got up for dawn prayers, his mother slipped into the room and defecated in the bed and ran out. [Roaring laughter from audience.] She waited. When he went back into the room, he saw [the bed and understood] what had happened. He took a gold dinar out of his pocket and walked out.

His mother was waiting and shouted, "Didn't I tell you! Now what are you going to do?"

He answered, "Mother, God made us rich; this is a blessed girl. Look what she has defecated—gold! A gold dinar, and there are more."

His mother shouted, "That is not her! It was I who did it in your bed. This gold is mine."

He replied, "True, Mother! It is yours. Now go clean up the mess you have made."

He built a new house for his wife and moved out of the old one. He got his mother a servant.

❖ 22 ❖

"A SON'S WIFE, EVEN WHEN A STICK"[468]

(SYRIA)

NARRATED BY (MRS.) ʾĀMÂL Q. (SEE INFORMANT NOTE TO TALE NO. 16) AS AN ASIDE, SO AS TO EXPLAIN A PROVERBIAL TRUISM WITHIN ANOTHER TALE. DURING HER TELLING OF THE TALE ENTITLED "MY DAUGHTER IS MY SON'S WIFE" (TALE NO. 44), A LISTENER INTERRUPTED TO EXPLAIN A TRUISM (THE TITLE OF THE PRESENT STORY) THAT OCCURRED IN THE CONTEXT OF THAT TALE. ʾĀMÂL

(AS AN OPERANT) INTERRUPTED THE INTRUDER, TOLD THE PRESENT TALE IN FULL, AND THEN RESUMED TELLING THE MAIN NARRATIVE. SHE HEARD THIS "PROVERB AND STORY" FROM HER MOTHER.

This etiological narrative with a humorous twist illustrates the ideal conduct of a son toward his aging mother. It also views sympathetically the apprehensions of a man's mother concerning his marriage and bringing into the household a new person who may challenge her own position. Although a mother-in-law's excesses toward her daughter-in-law are recognized, the tale suggests that a good son should, ideally, avoid placing his mother in such a trying situation.[469]

[THE explanation of the proverb is as follows:]

A young man had a mother; he was a dutiful son[470] and refused to bring a wife into his home as long as his mother was still alive. [But] she was getting old and wanted to see him married with children. She kept on telling him, "I will not rest and have peace of mind until you marry, and I see your children!" One day he told her, "Will do, mother." He brought a stick, dressed it ["her"] like a woman and placed her in an upstairs room in the house, and said to his mother—[who was staying downstairs], that he got married, brought the bride home, and placed her upstairs: "So that she would not quarrel with you."[471]

A week or so passed, then one day he returned from his shop, and found his mother a little bit upset,

"Mother, why are you upset?" [he asked].

"Your wife cursed me!" [she answered].

"I will speak to her" [he replied].

The following day, he came home from the shop and found his mother very upset.

"Mother, why are you very upset?"

"Your wife cursed me and cursed my ancestors!"

"No! This may not be faced with do-nothing. I will teach her good manners (*'arabbîhâ*)."[472]

The day after, he came home from the shop and found his mother crying,

"Mother, why are you crying?"

"Your wife hit me!"

"I will teach her good manners and send her back to her father's home. Come upstairs with me so as to witness [the execution of the punishment]."

He carried his mother upstairs—for she was very old and could not climb up the stairs; he opened the door [to the room of the supposed wife], and said [pointing at the stick], "Mother, is this the son's-wife that cursed you, and cursed your father, mother, and grandparents!? Is this the son's-wife that hit you!? As you can see for yourself, she is nothing but a stick!"

She answered, "'[A] son's wife [is injurious], even when [she happens to be only] a stick.'"

He replied, "This is what I mean [by refusing to marry now]."

He remained with his mother, looking after her in her old age until God remembered her [i.e., she passed away]. Then he married.

❖ 23 ❖

THE SULTAN OF THE UNDERWATER

(EGYPT, NUBIA)

THIS FANTASY-TALE (*KUMMAH*) WAS NARRATED IN 1969 BY KUNÛZÎ NUBIAN FANNIYYAH[473] M.G. A FORTY-FOUR-YEAR-OLD, NONLITERATE, BILINGUAL WIDOW, SHE LIVED IN DAHMÎT—A NUBIAN VILLAGE IN SOUTHERN EGYPT. FANNIYYAH, A RACONTEUR, WAS VISITING RELATIVES IN CAIRO WHEN MR. ¿U. KHIḌR AND I VISITED HER IN ORDER TO COLLECT TALES. KHIḌR—A FOLKLORIST, TALE COLLECTOR, AND RE-CREATIVE WRITER OF FOLK NARRATIVES, HAILING FROM THE SAME ETHNIC REGION—PROVIDED ARABIC TRANSLATIONS AS THE TALE WAS BEING TOLD. FANNIYYAH CORRECTED HIS TRANSLATIONS OCCASIONALLY, FOR SHE KNEW ARABIC VERY WELL. HOWEVER, UNLIKE MANY OTHER BILINGUAL NUBIANS,[474] SHE REFUSED TO NARRATE IN ARABIC. FOR HER, KUNÛZÎ NUBIAN[475] IS THE LANGUAGE FOR TELLING TALES: "I HEARD THE TALES IN NUBIAN AND I TELL THEM IN NUBIAN," SHE EMPHATICALLY STATED, AND ADDED, "ARABIC DID NOT COME EASILY OR NATURALLY" TO HER IN TALE TELLING.[476]

FANNIYYAH WAS QUITE SHY AND RELUCTANT TO NARRATE FANTASY-TALES FOR TWO REASONS. THE FIRST WAS THE PRESENCE OF AN ADULT MALE

STRANGER (THE PRESENT WRITER), FOR SUCH NARRATIVES ARE MEANT FOR WOMEN AND CHILDREN ONLY, WITH THE POSSIBLE "EXCEPTION OF A [NARRATOR'S] BROTHER." SECOND, IT WAS ELEVEN O'CLOCK IN THE MORNING AND TALE TELLING SHOULD TAKE PLACE AT NIGHT. ALSO, THE NARRATOR REFUSED TO NAME HER SOURCES FOR THE TALES SHE TOLD, "BECAUSE THEY WERE WOMEN." SHE CONSIDERED IT IMPROPER TO CITE TO AN OUTSIDER THE NAMES OR OTHER PERSONAL CHARACTERISTICS OF THESE WOMEN. HOWEVER, KHIḌR REPORTED THAT FANNIYYAH HAD LEARNED HER TALES FROM HER ELDER SISTER (ZAINAB M.G.).[477] THIS NARRATIVE WAS COLLECTED JOINTLY WITH MR. KHIḌR, WHO ALSO PROVIDED THE ARABIC TRANSLATION ON THE BASIS OF WHICH THE PRESENT TEXT IS GIVEN.

A wife's patience, endurance, and ability to curb her inquisitiveness toward the private affairs of her husband are central themes in this tale. A woman whose behavior exhibits these traits toward her husband will reap—the story promises—the rewards for her good conduct.[478] *The fantastic image of the husband's body as containing a secret "otherworld" out of which the wife is locked seems to be a euphemistic expression of that marital state. Marriage by proxy, often a form of arranged marriage, is a legal practice and occurs in real life.*

The tale also portrays the attitudes of a husband's sisters toward their brother's wife, and the crucial role that giving birth to a son plays in the process of integrating a wife into her husband's family. The elder sisters of the husband, who are presumed to be closer to him in age, are the ones who display the real hostility toward their brother's wife; this aspect of the tale is congruent with the "Brother-Sister Syndrome."[479]

A woman could not give birth to any children. She went to the river [(Nile)] bank, and there near a large stone she prayed, saying, "God, give me a daughter and I promise to fulfill my vow concerning her."

God answered her plea and she had a daughter. The girl grew up. Whenever she went to the Nile to play near that stone, the stone pinched her and said, "Tell your mother to fulfill her vow."

One day while the girl's mother was bathing her, she discovered that her body was all bruised. She asked her, "What's this?"

The girl replied, "Every day I go to the Nile to play and I sit on that big stone. It pinches me and says, 'Tell your mother to fulfill the vow she owes.' "

The mother took the girl one day, went to the Nile bank and placed her on that stone. No sooner had she done this than the stone sank with the girl on top of it. It turned out that this stone was a slave. He took the girl to the king of the underwater. They came to a palace in the midst of the water.

Every night the slave gave the girl a glass of water that she drank, and she became unconscious. Of course every night the sultan came and visited her.

A few days later the girl heard a crow cawing. She asked the slave, "What is it saying?"

He answered her, "He's saying, 'Your mother died.'"

When the sultan came that night he heard the girl sobbing in her sleep. He asked the slave, "What happened?"

The slave said, "The crow told her that her mother died."

The king said, "Take this purse of gold and accompany her to her mother's. I am sure her mother will advise her well." (Her mother will tell her to be good to her husband and things like that.)

The slave took her to her mother's to stay for three days. Women neighbors made fun of her saying, "Is this black slave your husband?" And they all giggled: "*hi'-hi'-hi'!*"

But her mother advised her, "Be good to your husband. Don't pay attention to what these women might say."

After three days they went back to the water. Time passed and again the girl heard the crow cawing: "Kâ-â-k, kâ-â-k!"

The girl asked the slave, "What is it saying?" and he answered, "It is saying 'Your mother died!'"

When the sultan came that night, he heard the girl sobbing again. He asked the slave, "What is the matter?"

The slave answered, "The crow told her that her mother died."

The sultan said, "This time when you accompany her do not let her alone for even one step, for women are going to spoil her about her husband. This time she will have no mother to set her straight."

This time women really pressed her hard. "Is this your husband? He's a slave! He's black!" and things like that.

They asked her, "How do you live?" and she said to them, "Every night after I eat my supper, he gives me a glass of water that I drink, then I become unaware of myself [pass out]."

They told her, "Clever one, when you get back, do not drink this water. Pour it into your bosom and find out what will happen to you."

That night she poured the water as they told her and went to sleep. Of course she wasn't asleep. After a while a tall, broad sultan, handsome and fair-complexioned, walked in. When the sultan went to sleep next to her, she got up and looked him over. On his thigh she found a door with a lock on it with a key in it. She opened the door and went in.

Inside she found goldsmiths working on jewelry.

"What is this?"

"It is for she who is patient and wins in the end."

She also found upholsterers making mattresses and things.

"Whose are these?"

"It is for she who is patient and wins in the end."

She also found cabinetmakers working on cabinets and things.

"Whose are these?"

While she was inside, the sultan woke up and found her inside. He plucked her out [narrator demonstrates] yelling, "Get out! Get Out! Get Out!" and he kicked her away.

She went out tired and hungry. She kept on walking and walking and walking until she came to a palace. She sat down underneath it. The servant was taking out the garbage, and the girl started searching through the garbage for something to eat. The servant ran inside, "Mistress, Mistress! I know you might kill me for this, but there is somebody outside who is more beautiful than you are!"

The mistress came out and when she realized who the girl was, she said, "You are my brother's wife. Ever since he came across you, we hardly ever see him!" and sent her away.

She kept on going until she came to a second palace. The same thing happened. The sultan's middle sister said to her, "Don't you ever come here!"

She went until she came to a third palace. It belonged to the sultan's youngest sister. The third sister took pity on her and said, "Oh, how wrong my brother is!? Where is he sending you? Come here, come here."

While the girl was at the sister's house, she gave birth to a baby boy that looked exactly like his father.

In the meantime, the sultan missed his wife and went out to look for her. He went to his oldest sister. She said to him, "She was here, but I kicked her out."

He said to her, "From today on, you are not my sister."

The same thing happened with the second sister. He told her, "From today on, you are not my sister."

And finally he came to his youngest sister. She said to him, "First why don't you sit down and drink a glass of tea and eat some dinner; after that, we will look for her together."

He sat down, drank the tea and ate. His sister said, "I need to get some water. Why don't you hold this baby."

The sultan looked at the baby and found the door on his thigh. He said, "Ah-ha! This is my son! Where is the mother of this child? [Truly] you are my sister!"

His sister reproached him, "How could you have done this to her? She is a stranger here and has nobody to go to!?"

The sultan drowned [showered] his sister in gold, took his son and his wife, and went home.

And they lived happily.

❖ 24 ❖

THE EARS THAT DIDN'T HEED THE WIFE'S FEARS[480]

(EGYPT)

NARRATED IN APRIL 1971 BY *ES-SIT* TAḤIYYAH, THE SEAMSTRESS (SEE INFORMANT NOTE TO TALE NO. 15). SHE HEARD THIS TALE FROM HER MOTHER, "BUT THE ONE WHO NARRATED IT BEST WAS AN OLDER NEIGHBOR GIRL NAMED BASHAWÂT." TAḤIYYAH ADDED,

> MY APPRENTICES LIKE THIS TALE ALSO [AS THEY DO THE DAUGHTERS OF THE BEAN VENDOR]! WE TELL IT [OFTEN]—BUT I WOULDN'T TELL IT WHEN IT IS TOO LATE AT NIGHT AND THE GIRLS HAVE TO WALK BACK HOME. THE STREETS WOULD BE DARK AND ABANDONED; THEY GET SCARED. SOME OF THEM WOULD BE UNABLE TO GO TO SLEEP, OR WOULD HAVE NIGHTMARES.

A folk truism recurrent in Egypt states that "A he-man, son-of-a-he-man, is the one who never consults a woman."[481] *Some elements of formal religious literature express a similar attitude.*[482] *However, this traditional value is largely confined to the woman in her role as a wife or—less frequently—as a friend or lover, but seldom in her roles as a man's sister, or mother.*[483] *The use of the pejorative word* marah *(used mostly in Egyptian vernacular Arabic to denote a "broad") tends to substantiate this viewpoint; in such a context, a mother or a sister may* not *be commonly labeled* marah. *This fantasy-tale presents an opposing viewpoint. It portrays life in a nuclear family whose head is a poor provider and foolish. Willingly, adamantly, and against his wife's stern warning and sound advice, he endangers the lives of the entire family. Only due to the wife's perceptiveness and resourcefulness is disaster averted, but not for the mindless husband, who finally declares that he should have listened to his wife. Interestingly enough, the man's declaration that his wife has been right is uttered in the feminine baby talk (see this tale, note 501).*

From the perspective of a wife, the ogress—who poses as the husband's sister—may be viewed as symbolic of the husband's real sister in actual life.[484] *The affectionate ties between a man and his own sister threaten the wife and, consequently, her children. The antagonism between the wife and the alleged sister is further illustrated by the wife addressing her as "maternal-aunt (*khâlah*)," a title of address indicating social distance and respect, but* not *affection or friendliness.*[485]

The conclusion of the tale indirectly reinforces the notion that the death of the husband (the children's father), though regrettable, does not cause the collapse of the family.[486] *Also noticeable is the narrator's dwelling on the scene of the husband's demise (cf. leaping and lingering, Mot. Z12.3§).*

THERE once was a man and his wife. They had begotten ten kids, but the man was jobless and would stay home all day long. His wife said to him, "Why don't you go out of the house and buy and sell! I mean get something and sell it. Maybe [you will make a profit, then] we will have something to eat."

He said, "What shall I sell?"

She answered, "Sell anything. Sell fish, from the stream!"

So he went and caught himself some fish—catfish [which have long whiskers]—and put them in a soft basket (*maqṭaf*)[487] and went around calling [in the manner and tone of peddler's cries]:

> Close your doo-oo-oo-rs,
> the Whiskered-One[488] has come after you!
> Close your doo-oo-oo-rs,
> the Whiskered-One has come after you!

Naturally people became afraid [and thought] that this meant that the Whiskered-One came to raid their homes. [Narrator laughs.] So people closed their doors and no one came out; no one bought anything from him. He kept on going around all day long without making a sale of even one millime-worth [i.e., pennyworth]. When he became tired he went home, without having sold a thing. So his wife took the fish and cooked them; they—and the children—were able to have supper that night. She asked him, "How come you didn't sell anything?" He answered, "I kept on calling, 'The Whiskered-One has come to you! The Whiskered-One has come to you!' And no one came out to buy." His wife said to him [in a reprimanding tone], "You idiot, you should have said, 'Seven of the big ones, and eight of the little ones [sold at the same price]!' " He said to her, "All right."

He went out and caught some more fish. This time he caught bluegill-type fish (*mishṭ*),[489] and went around calling, "Seven of the big ones, or eight of the little ones [for the same price]! Seven of the big ones or eight of the little ones!" As he was going through the streets, there happened to be a funeral, and people were carrying the bier. Of course they were crying and saying "There is no god but God," and things like that—all the things that are said at a funeral. Our friend—[narrator laughs heartily]—kept on yelling, "Seven of the big ones or eight of the little ones! Seven of the big ones or eight of the little ones!" One of the people in the funeral procession came to him and said [in a reprimanding tone], "Brother, you shouldn't say that! Say, 'May God have mercy on him,' and 'May long life be yours!' " But our friend kept on shouting, as his wife had instructed him, "Seven of the big ones, or eight of the little ones! Seven of the big ones, or eight of the little ones!" So, of course, people in the procession thought that he was wishing that more people would die. So they turned around and started beating him up. He ran away from them.

He ran until he reached another district of the town. He began yelling, " 'May God have mercy on him!' " and " 'May long life be yours!' " It chanced that there was a wedding procession passing by: the bride was ["dolled up"] wearing red and white [cosmetics], drummers drumming, pipers playing pipes, dancers dancing, and the like. [All that was going on] while our friend kept on yelling, "May God have mercy on him!" and "May long life be yours!" "May God have mercy on him!" and "May long life be yours!" [Narrator laughs.] The bride's family came to him and said, "Brother, this is a wedding! Don't say, 'May God have mercy on him,' nor 'May long life be yours,' but say, 'Congratulations! [May it be] with prosperity and [begetting] sons.' "[490] But he kept on following them and yelling, "May God have mercy on him! May long life be yours!" They ran after him to beat him up. So, he left his fish, placed his tail between his teeth [like a scared dog is thought to do], and ran [as fast as he could] home to his wife.

When his wife opened the door and saw that he had neither the basket nor the fish, she thought that he had sold them; she was very happy. She asked him [with anticipation], "How did you do? How much have you earned?" So he told her, "People beat me up and threw the fish away." And of course, he told her about the funeral procession, the wedding procession, and all that. That night, they slept with their stomachs utterly empty.[491]

The following day his wife said to him, "Well, why don't I get you some lupine; do not go around. All you have to do is stand in the street in front of the courthouse or the [train] station and call, "O lupine, you are [like] pistachios! O lupine, you are [like] pistachios!" So, they got some dry lupine—(and as you know . . . , soaked it in the river [until it became soft and its bitter taste washed away])—then he stood at the train station calling, "O lupine, you are [like] pistachios!" So people would buy for one millime, or maybe for two—(in olden times a millime had some worth)—and they [the vendor and his family] kept on living like this [in poverty] for a while.

One day he went out to sell the lupine, but no one would buy. He kept on walking and walking and walking until he got out of the town, and still kept on walking and walking until he reached the cemetery [at the edge of town]. Still there was no one [to buy]. He kept walking and walking until he finally came to two or three, I mean a few houses: a small hamlet, but there was no trace of a child of Adam [a human being] around. He came next to a wall and sat down and all of a sudden some woman appeared. When she saw him, she said to him [with excitement and warmth], "O my brother! My beloved brother, where have you been? It has been so long since I have seen you!" The man looked at her and wondered, " 'My brother?!' 'My beloved!' Lady, I have no sisters!" She said, "Oh, no! Our parents died when we were little, and after that we got separated from each other. O my beloved brother, where are you now?" So the man said to her, "Oh, I am married; I have ten kids. I am very poor and my wife sent me out to sell fish, then to sell lupine and—as you know—this [state of affairs] is God's will." She said to him [with contrived sympathy], "How can that be: that you would have a sister and suffer like this, be poor, married and have children, and I would not even know about it! O my beloved brother, you go get your wife and get your ten kids. You're staying with me. I have this [property], and I have that, and I have food, I have houses and I have land, I have cattle, and I've got sheep; I've got everything. God has been generous to me. How could it be that you would have a sister in this world and would suffer like this?"

Of course, the man didn't, at first, believe this. Then he took up his little tray full of lupine and dumped it on the ground and ran home. He banged on the door and his wife opened. He said to her [with great excitement], "Wife, I've got everything! Bring the kids! I've found my sister! We are going to live with my sister. She is going to take care of us." The woman, that is his wife, said to him [with amazement], "What happened to you, man? Have you gone crazy, or what? I have known you for maybe fifteen, twenty years; you have been a limb cut off a tree. All my life I have not heard of your having a sister or your having a father or your having a mother!" He said to her [with great excitement], "Oh, no! I have a sister. We were separated when we were little. Now she is going to take care of us. She owns such and such and she has got houses and she has got enough food for all of us!"

So the woman gathered her children and said [with suspicion], "As it is said [in proverbs], 'Stay with the liar as far as you can go, then the truth will out.' "[492] They kept on walking—she and he and the ten kids. When they got there his sister got up and received them with, "Welcome! Welcome! Welcome to my brother—my beloved, my brother's wife, and my brother's children," "[Children], come here to your paternal-aunt," and things like that. She went and killed a sheep or a ram for them and kept on feeding them. Every day she would prepare different types of foods—foods of all types and colors. Of course, they were not used to a life of luxury. [Now] they didn't have to work; they slept most of the day and of course, they had comfortable beds and mattresses and quilts and things like that. One day after another and one week after another they became, all of them, obese with [quivering] flabby fat.[493] ([Narrator comments with amusement:] Of course, they were living in luxury.) One day, as they all were asleep [narrator speaks in a tone denoting mysteriousness], his sister came stealthily. [Narrator indicates tiptoeing by using a closed hand, pointed down, and slowly moving the middle and index fingers backward and forward.] And once she was inside the room, she started feeling them on their parson's nose (*zalamukkah*)[494] [narrator laughs] and would say [growling], "Hmmm, I raise you, I fatten you, and then I turn around and devour you. Hmmm, I raise you. Hmmm, I fatten you, and then I turn around and devour you!"

Now, who heard her? The woman! Of course, she became very scared but she didn't make a movement. His sister turned around and went out saying, "Tomorrow I start with the biggest one!" (the biggest kid, that is).

In the morning the woman, his wife, went to him and said [secretively], "Man, that's not your sister; this is an ogress. She wants to eat us. I heard her last night saying, 'Hmmm, I raise you, I fatten you, and then I turn around and devour you!' " He said to her [in a slighting and inattentive manner], "Woman, go away! What are you talking about? Have you gone crazy or something? This is my sister; she loves us and her heart is on us [i.e., sincerely concerned]. She is feeding us. She is clothing us. She is giving us of the good livelihood that God has granted her! Now you come and say she is an ogress! Don't say that!" The woman said to him, "I swear by God that she is an ogress. Last night she came in and said, 'Hmmm, I raise you, I fatten you. . . . ' " He [interrupting] said, "Woman, shut up! Don't talk like that about my sister: my beloved!"

So the woman, of course . . . what's she going to do? The man, her husband, was not going to believe her. So, she decided to escape with her children. She said to him, "Tomorrow . . . I'm not going to stay another day. Tomorrow morning before anyone gets up, I am leaving." He answered her [in an uncaring tone], "[Whether you] leave or don't leave, stay or don't stay, I am staying. I am staying with my sister: my beloved."

The following morning the woman got up very early, at dawn. She woke up her children and they started going out, tiptoeing. She woke up her husband [in a pleading tone], "I say, man, come with us. She is an ogress." He said to her [in a slumbering tone], "Woman, I told you I'm not going. I'm staying here with my sister."

As the woman was about to leave she opened the door [narrator imitates opening the door in a very careful manner] and as she stepped out of the room, whom did she find? [Pause.] She found the ogress sitting, crouching, right next to the door and she [the ogress] said to her [with fake friendliness], "O wife of my brother, where are you going?" She said to her, "Oh, I am not going, [my] sister. We have just been eating and sleeping and we got tired of this luxurious life. I thought that maybe there is some work around the house that we could do." She said to her, "Oh, no! No wife of my brother will do any work. You just sit here endeared and honored and don't even raise a finger of yours."

What would the woman do? She said to her, "All right, but there is something. Ever since we came here we have been eating that which is fried and that which is broiled:[495] chicken, mutton, and [beef]-meat, and the like. We are really getting a little nauseated; we need something that would harshen up the stomach (*tiḥarḥash el-mi¿dah*). We want a meatless (*qurdaiḥî*) meal. Why don't you prepare for us some bean mash!?"[496] So his sister said to her, "Whatever you wish."

That day, she fixed them a huge pot of bean mash and of course, the woman brought her ten children and they kept on eating. And she would say, "Kids, eat! Kids, eat!" And of course—(as you know)—they don't like bean mash.

ASIDE

A listener's voice declares: No one likes bean mash!

But their mother kept on saying [anxiously], "Eat! Eat!" Of course, with bean mash one eats onions, and one eats leeks, and [other gas-giving] things like that." [Narrator laughs.] The woman kept on force-feeding[497] her children until their stomachs became that high: ([narrator places her open hand about a foot away from her own stomach]). Also, while the ogress was not looking, she took some bean mash [narrator giggles] and put it in their underpants; [. . .] she smeared the behind of each child [with the stuff]. Then she said [shouting], "Whoops! Now, sister of my husband, look! The kids have messed up themselves. What are we going to do?" She [the ogress] replied, "Bathe them [here]." She said, "Well, things will get awfully messy here. We need to go to the river. All of us need to take a dip and wash ourselves well." So the ogress said, "All right. Go, but don't stay too long. Take this tambourine with you; it will make sounds so that I will know that you're all right, that you have not drowned or gotten lost, I mean."

So the woman took the tambourine and the ten kids; she went to her husband and said [in a warning manner], "Man, she is not your sister; this is an ogress! Come with us." He said [in a slighting tone], "No, I'm not coming with you. I'm staying here with my sister." So the woman said to him [in an uncaring tone], "All right, suit yourself."

She took her children and kept on going until they reached the river. And of course, they leaped into the water. The tambourine all the time was making noise. Of course, the ogress was listening and every time she would hear the jingling of the tambourine she would realize they were still around. The woman was clever and smart. She tied the tambourine to a tree branch; every time the wind would blow, the branch would hit the tambourine and it would make sounds and the jingling that a tambourine makes.

It chanced that a [large freight]-boat was passing by. So the woman said, [yelling, in an imploring tone], "O paternal-uncle, boatman, won't you do us a favor for God's sake and take us across?" The man said, "All right, come on." He brought his boat closer to the bank and the woman pushed her kids into the boat and the boatman took them across. He said to her [in amazement], "What were you doing here? This is the ogress's country! Thank God that you got away with your skin."

The woman went back to her home. She and her children stayed in the town where they had been [living as] poor before.

Now, to whom do we return? To his sister, to the ogress who had been saying, "I am your sister." She kept on listening and hearing the tambourine [jingle]; but an hour passed, and two hours passed; then it became the afternoon time and [still] she kept hearing the tambourine. She began to smell a rat.[498] She placed her tail between her teeth and flew [went running] to the river; she found no one. She [exclaimed with great sorrow], "Akh-kh-kh!" [narrator bites on the index finger of her right hand to simulate the ogress's reaction]. "You son-of-a-dog! You got away from me." And, of course, she became angry, and she went back running to where? To her home.

That friend of ours—who did not listen to his wife—saw her coming, with her eyes crackling out sparks. He said [with great sorrow], "Akh-kh-kh! My wife was right! She is an ogress!!" He became afraid and kept on looking for a place in which to hide: "Where shall I hide? Where shall I hide?" [he wondered]. He hid in the grain bin. She came in and kept on saying [forcefully], "Where are you, you son-of-a-dog! Where are you, you son-of-a-dog! Oh, where! Oh, where! They got away! They got away! The fattest and youngest got away! . . . " ([Narrator giggles and explains:] Of course, she wanted the tender-tasting young (*barâbir*);[499] as for the tough-fleshed old (*el-¿agûz el-mikhanshar*), she did not want. The most tender and youngest got away.)

The ogress kept on calling: "Where are you? Where are you; you who . . . ?" She kept on looking from this room to that room, in the closets, under the beds. Finally she found him—(Oh what a pity!: *yâ ¿ainî*)—hiding in the grain bin. From fear, he messed up himself: he did it in his underpants.[500]

She said to him [while growling], "Come here! From where shall I eat you?"

He replied [in a remorseful tone], "Eat me from my earsies which did not heed the words of my wifie!"[501]

That was it. She descended upon him: "Hmmm, hmmm, hmmm (*ḥatatak batatak*)"; she devoured his flesh and munched on his bones, and finished him up—flesh along with bones.

Now what? That ogress . . . , the ogress . . . [narrator hesitates] did not want to lose the others: the woman and her ten kids, that is. So she said, "By the

Prophet, I will go look for them." Of course the man [had] told her where they were living and all that. So, she went and bought herself some fine-tooth combs (*fallayât:* delousers), earrings, bitter-gum (*libân ḍakar*),[502] needles, and . . . ([she kept on naming] things: women's things, things that women and girls buy). She put them in a stick-tray (*mishannah*)[503] and went around from street to street, lane to lane, pretending to be what?: A she-vendor! [Narrator imitates a vendor's cries:] "O gi-i-i-rls! Earrings! O gi-i-i-rls! Fine-tooth combs! O gi-i-i-rls! Needles! O gi-i-i-rls!" and I don't know what else. [She finally reached their house.]

The woman's oldest daughter said to her [in a tone denoting suspicion], "By the Prophet, mother, this vendor woman who is selling fine tooth-combs and chewing gum looks like my father's sister—the ogress!" The woman said to her [in a slighting tone], "No, my daughter, that can't be!" But the girl would [still] say [in a pleading tone], "By the Prophet, mother, it is her! Look at her eyes, look at how she is looking at us as if she wants to eat us up with her eyes!" Of course the woman looked and scrutinized. She [the mother] said [exclaiming], "By God, yes! She is the ogress!" [Pause.] The woman said to her daughter [with resolve], "By God, we must play a trick on her! Just as she ate your father up, we must kill her." So very quickly [narrator speaks with a tone denoting speed], they heated a pot of water until it was boiling—on their mud stove (*kanûn*), or something like that—for in olden days they did not have [kerosene] stoves, bottled gas, or things like these.

The point is: they called on her, "O lady! O gum-vending lady! Come here! We would like to buy some fine-tooth combs and chewing gum! But our door would not open [it is jammed]! Creep through underneath." (Of course, as you know, the door of those people—poor people, and in villages—would be nothing but a few wooden boards, with a gap that high: [a palm's span (*shibr*)][504]—(narrator indicates with the palm of her hand fully stretched how wide the gap would be). Naturally, the woman [ogress] was very glad; she was going to get into their house and eat them all. She said, "All right! How can I get in?" They said, "Just set your basket beside the door and come in through the gap underneath the door." As soon as she stuck her head in, they poured the hot water on it! She died on the spot!

The woman gathered her ten kids and they went to the ogress's house. They lived there in contentment. Everything that the ogress owned became theirs. Plenty of God's boon. They brought people into the town and populated it.

That is all. And bit by bit, the tale is over.

❖ 25 ❖

THE MAN WHO SEVERED HIS OWN THING

(EGYPT, NUBIA)

THE FOLLOWING TALE WAS RECORDED IN CAIRO, IN MARCH 1969, FROM ¿U.K, A KUNÛZI NUBIAN. THE NARRATOR WAS ABOUT THIRTY-FIVE YEARS OF AGE, SINGLE, AND WORKED AS SCHOOLTEACHER; HE ALSO WAS A COLLECTOR OF TALES AND A CREATIVE WRITER. ¿U.K. REPORTED, "I HAVE HEARD THIS TALE REPEATEDLY FROM ¿aYSHAH M[. . .] (WHO IS NINETY YEARS OLD), ZAINAB M.G.,[505] FANNIYYAH M.G.,[506] AND OTHER [KUNÛZÎ NUBIAN] WOMEN." WHEN APPROACHED BY THE PRESENT WRITER FOR THIS TALE, BOTH LATTER WOMEN RACONTEURS SUMMARILY REFUSED EVEN TO ALLOW ANY MENTION OF THE NARRATIVE TO BE MADE IN THEIR PRESENCE. THE PRESENT WRITER'S QUEST FOR A WOMAN'S RENDITION PROVED FUTILE: NO WOMAN WOULD TELL THE TALE TO AN ADULT MALE OUTSIDER; ZAINAB M.G. WAS EVEN OFFENDED BY THE TELLING TO AN OUTSIDER (EL-SHAMY) IN HER PRESENCE OF A TALE THAT INVOLVED ATTEMPTED FATHER-DAUGHTER INCEST (TYPE 510B, SEE THIS TALE, NOTE 505). HOWEVER, TWO RENDITIONS OF THE PRESENT TALE WERE RECORDED BY THE WRITER FROM MALE NARRATORS.

A NOTEWORTHY ASPECT OF THE PERFORMANCE OF THIS TEXT IS THE NARRATOR'S ASCENDING "ADAPTATION LEVEL"[507] VIS-À-VIS THE COLLECTOR (THE PRESENT WRITER) AND THE "OBSCENE" WORDS. THE PRESENTATION BEGAN WITH THE ACADEMIC: "PHALLIC ORGAN," FOLLOWED BY THE EUPHEMISTIC: "SUBJECT," AND "THING," AND WAS CONCLUDED WITH THE EXPLICIT AND INDECENT "PENIS."

This folktale harks back to Egyptian antiquity; it is the second part of "The Tale of the Two Brothers" Batu and Anubis. Due to the cognitive salience and related affective experiences associated with the theme of a man severing his own penis (e.g., ego-involvement), this component of the ancient story—it may be argued—seems to have been retained (in memory) and told by narrators as an independent story. In the ancient text, the restoration of the severed organ is accomplished by "the seven Hathors"; in the present tale, it is done by the vaguely defined "shadow."[508]

Marriage preference, a wife's perfidy, barrenness, impotence, relations among "men whose wives are sisters (¿adâyil),"[509] *and sexual prowess are major facets of the present tale. The narrator of the text explained:*

> *Nubian men are usually absent from home for periods of years at a time—working in distant cities; they, therefore, prefer not to marry a beautiful woman. In the absence of their husbands, women occasionally narrate erotic tales. One such narrative is this tale of "The Man Who Severed. . . . "*

The narrator's opinion that women in his home region "are usually not very beautiful" seems to be a case of "The grass is always greener on the other side of the fence. . . . " (Mot. U118§). However, his report on men's fear of a woman's beauty is supported by some folk traditions in the region. A local historical account (legend) recurrent in neighboring Sudan provides a vivid illustration of such a fear. According to the narrative, entitled "Tâjûj" after its tragic heroine, armed conflicts broke out because of that woman's excessive beauty. Although innocent, she was murdered by a person who sought to restore sanity among men by removing the cause of the irresistible temptation.[510]

A woman, a very beautiful woman. . . . (Aside: In our homeland, [Nubia,] women usually are not very beautiful; when a woman is very beautiful, she causes fear, [thus, a man would not choose a beautiful woman for a wife].)

A girl turned out to be very, very, very beautiful! Her eyes were beautiful, her thighs were beautiful, her body was beautiful and fair-complected; her breasts were large and she looked very beautiful. When men would see her, they would be afraid to marry her. (There is no apparent reason [for such fear]!) Now, what did they used to do? They used to make passes at her. When these men got together, this one might say, "I was with her!" that other one might say, "I'm going with her!" and that one might say, "She winks at me," and that one might say, " . . . " [a similar thing]. Even little boys used to tell stories about her. In the middle of all this commotion there was an old woman who said to that beautiful girl, "You are going to marry the master of men." So, naturally, she was waiting for that master of men. Whenever a [suitor whom she considered a] vagabond would propose to her she would turn him down.

Because she was very beautiful people were going crazy over her. One man came along [and decided to marry her]; he went to her father directly and said, “I want to marry your daughter.” He replied to him [with great relief], “Enough said! Take her!”

He got married to her. They got married and he was happy. He loved her and she loved him. They lived a love story. They remained four or five years without her belly rising or swelling [as sign of pregnancy]. People started saying, “By God, she doesn’t beget.” People started saying to him, “Fellow, is there anyone who would live with a barren woman? The woman was created so that she could bear children for the man and work for him. You are spoiling her. She bears you no children and she does nothing for you!”

In spite of all that [reproaching], he was in love with her. The important thing is that he continued to live with her. One day he looked [only] to find her becoming ill. Of course, he was very much in love with her. He hurried to the doctor. He brought her a doctor from Cairo, faith-healer sheiks from Southern Egypt,[511] and went to those in the south [in Sudan] and brought magicians who made amulets or incantations—(because, as you know, an amulet or incantation from southern Sudan is believed to be very, very great: second to none). There was no use; she was ill and she was dying. After that. . . . Here she was dying; his luck was like tar [extremely bad]. She was losing [her fight with death]. She kept on saying to him, “Tomorrow you will forget me and marry someone else.”

He replied to her [by uttering the divorce pledge], “‘May divorce befall me [from you, if I were to remarry].’[512] I will not remarry, ever!” and [he promised other] things like that. She remained dying and crying. When he would ask her, “Why are you crying?” she would answer him, “Tomorrow I will die and you will remarry.”

“My lady, I will not remarry.”

She would reply, “You will remarry.”

He said to her, “How [can I convince that I will not remarry]?”

She said to him, “Cut it off!”—(that is: to cut off his phallic organ).[513]

She kept on saying to him, “If I were to die without somebody loving me, I will not find myself [and be lost] in the hereafter. But if you truly love me, we will meet in the hereafter.”

ASIDE

Narrator (commenting on the notion of not finding oneself in the hereafter): “I don’t know from where this [uncommon] idea came to them [Nubians], or from where it came to the [Nubian] person who told it to me.”

It should be noted, however, that meeting family, friends, foes, etc. in the hereafter is a basic Islamic belief; it is part of the final trial and judgment, and the rewards and punishments of the Day of Judgment; cf. note 253, this section.

The important thing is that the man saw that she was dying and that she kept on pleading with him: "If you love me, cut it off."

He was very much in love with her. So, he went and got a razor and chopped it off; he fell down right next to her and thought, "[Let us] die together." When he came to, he wondered, "Will I be burying her, or [has she recovered] and I will not have to bury her!"

He found that thing; he found his thing, thrown beside him and that woman fast asleep. One day passed, two days passed, she got up. His wife got her health back and he was very happy. People said to him, "Paternal-uncle, have fun; for you are going to enjoy her again and you will be happy again. Be satisfied!"

He thought to himself, "She was the one who asked for it [(my emasculation)]; she will not defame me." The girl recovered and was cured and was more vigorous than before and more beautiful than before. Now she started asking for the affair (*el-ḥikâyah*)[514] [i.e., sexual intercourse]. He said to her, "O daughter of [good] people, you know the story and you are the one who demanded it."

She started treating him rudely, insulting him and ridiculing him. One night she said to him, "Listen, two women may not sleep in the same bed. You should find another town."

He said to her, "I [leave] my affairs up to God." He gathered himself together and disappeared from that town. He got out of that town and kept on walking and walking and walking. He reached another town. He found no one in it: "By God! [he wondered.] Where did the people go?" He looked and found a blind old woman: "Maternal-aunt,[515] what is the matter? Where are the people?" [he inquired.]

She replied, "Son, for what reason are you standing here?" She kept on feeling him [with her hands]. She said to him [in bewilderment], "Your day is black [miserable]! You are a man!" She kept on touching his face (like this—[narrator closes his eyes and pretends to be feeling a person]).

"You are a youth! Catch up with them! Catch up with them!"

"What is the matter?"

"Run to the square, the king has summoned all men."

"What for?"

"The girls. . . . The king has three daughters and has declared: 'I will choose a groom for each one of my girls. Every girl should choose whomever she likes from amongst all the males of the country.' "

He said to her [in hesitation], "But I mean, I am . . . !"

She replied, [sharply], "You are what."

He said (naturally he did not want to reveal his secret), "But I am a stranger!"

She replied to him, "This shouldn't matter. Men have come from the end of the world for this event. The girls are very beautiful. May God reward you by getting the eldest one. The eldest is [as beautiful as the] moon."

He said to her, "All right! But if—what would happen if I do not go?"

She said, "You would get slaughtered!"

After that the young man, with the old woman dragging her feet behind him, went into the lineup. He went there and it turned out that he was the very last one to arrive. When he entered the city [square] he found that others had formed a very long line. He stood in the line with the rest of the men: old and young, big . . . [and small].

The princess . . . each princess, would throw her handkerchief over whichever suitor appealed to her; thus he [the selected suitor] would become her groom and a prince. He was afraid and said, "O God, safeguard [us]!" (because a princess might throw her handkerchief on him, thus he might become a groom).

He was thinking, "All these [men in the lineup] have got their own credentials! As for me . . . !" (He hasn't got any! How is he going to become a groom!)

The important thing is that the first princess threw her handkerchief [over one of the men]; all [the women] made ululations [of joy]; the second princess did the same. Suddenly a handkerchief fell over his face. And he fainted! The drumming [to declare the marriage] started. He fainted and they carried him away. Where did they take him? They took him to the bride's house! When they got there, they made the wedding celebration. He thought, "My affairs are up to God! What may happen, will happen."

On the night of the consummation of the marriage (*dukhlah*)—now he is married to the eldest girl, the eldest princess, the prettiest one—on the night of the consummation of the marriage, they performed the wedding procession and now he is a groom. They made him enter upon her. He sat down crying [in the bridal chamber]. She said to him, "What's the matter, kid? Don't I appeal to you or what?" He replied, "You appeal to me, but—I mean—may God ruin your house, [you who . . .]"—(meaning that woman who caused it to be severed off)! She said to him [kindly], "What is the matter?"

He told her the story. He said to her, "I was very much in love with some woman, and married her. When she was dying she said to me, 'You will remarry after I am gone.' She made me cut it off!" She [the bride] replied, "Is it only with that mess and sad stuff (*nîlah we sukhâm*) that people can live! Does this mean that one cannot live without it [sexual intercourse]!? [Of course one can do without!]"

He asked her, "Will you not defame me [by revealing my secret]?"

She replied, "Of course not!"

The important thing is that he stayed with her and they lived together. No one knew their secret. The princess was happy with him. The girls, the other two [sisters of the wife] had their bellies rise [repeatedly], then they would deliver, but not this [eldest] one. She lived—(dear friend [listener])—for ten years without him touching her. Of course, he was treating her very well.

One day he said to her, "Now listen daughter of [good] people. That sad stuff, you must taste it before you die. I will take you and run away or escape with you from this country. I'll take you to another country and claim that you are my sister and marry you off to another person so that you get a taste of that business."

She said to him, "Don't say these things. This is the second time [that you make this offer]" and things like that. "As for that affair, I don't want it at all."

Now, who overheard them? A slave: one of the slaves overheard [the whispering between the two of] them. He ran to the husbands of the girls—(of her *silfât*, that is).[516] [The slave said with excitement], "Can you imagine! The husband-of-your-wives'-sister (*¿adîl-kum*)[517] hasn't got a thing!"

He [one of the brothers-in-law] replied, "What a black day! That is why she hasn't begot any children during all this time."

They went to the king, "Can you imagine! Your daughter's husband hasn't got a thing!"

He replied, "Unbelievable!"

They said to him, "By God, that is it!"

[He inquired], "How is that?"

The youngest girl liked her eldest sister. She went and said to her, "Hurry up, for they are. . . . They have agreed. . . . " (What had they agreed upon?[518] They had agreed that they would take the boy, that boy [the husband of the eldest sister] to the river and undress him and check him up; as if what? As if they were going swimming! If they were to find him like all the others, then this one [the brother-in-law] is a liar. But if they found him to have no thing, they would kill him. And of course the king was very sad.)

The [youngest] girl went to her [eldest] sister saying, "Can you imagine they said such and such about your husband and they will [take him for a] dip in the river and check him out."

[The husband of the eldest princess said to her], "Now we must run away!" He gathered himself and took some gold and [he alone] ran into the hills. He went deep into the hills. He saw a shadow;[519] it appeared to him out of the middle of the hills, as he was sitting down. He wondered and said, "What? What do you want, shadow?" She [the female shadow] said to him, "My, my! I want the business."

He said to her, "Now, you [women] son[s] of a bitch, all of you gather around me after it has been lost. Why couldn't it have been like this from the beginning?"

She said to him, "Just try. Maybe!"

He said to her, "But there is nothing at all."

She replied, "Just, just try!"

He said to her, "Come on."

He hugged the [supernatural] shadow tightly. He found out that the subject (*el-mawḍûʿ*)—his subject—dropped out just like it used to be; perhaps, a little better. He gave her a good one . . . ; [but before doing so, and in order to show off his recovered possession], he went down the hills trotting, with his outer-garment lifted up. . . .

ASIDE

One man who told me this tale used to say, "He lifted up his clothes, like this*—and ra-a-a-a-n down. . . . "

* Narrator—wearing trousers—stands up and demonstrates how his own source for that version of the tale—who wears a long outer-gown—had enacted this scene.

His wife said to him [with great apprehension], "Why did you come back? They will kill you!"

He said to her, "Look!" He grabbed her to his bosom and gave her one, a very perfect one: perfecting on perfection (*tamâm et-tamâm*).

ASIDE

El-Shamy [interrupts]: What was the nature of that shadow? Was it an angel or what?

Narrator: No, the shadow was the image of the girl, his wife herself [i.e., a personification of the wife's good deeds], because she was a good-hearted girl who kept his secret (cf. Mot. Z125, "Virtue personified"; also see note 508, this section).

Now he gave her a very, very good one and got ready to meet the other princes.

Now—(my friend)—the other princes took him and pushed him into the water. When they took him out and stripped his clothes off so as to find out whether the subject was there or not, they found out that his subject was there, "My! My! My!" [they exclaimed]. They found that his subject was perfect. They saluted him [in a military manner]. They went back and slashed the throat of the slave. [Then], and for the first time, he went back to live with that blossom of his, [his second wife], and was happy with her and begot children from her. And with her he forgot that other nymphomaniac (*labwah*)[520] who had made him cut off his penis.

And they begot children, and lived in stability and prosperity.

❖ 26 ❖

"A LOST HOUR OF FUN CANNOT BE MADE UP FOR"[521]

(EGYPT)

NARRATED IN APRIL 1971 BY LADY TAḤIYYAH, THE SEAMSTRESS (SEE INFORMANT NOTE TO TALE NO. 15). SHE HAD HEARD THIS TALE WHEN STILL A GIRL, FROM AN OLDER GIRL NAMED BASHAWÂT WHO "WAS A NEIGHBOR." TAḤIYYAH TELLS THIS STORY OCCASIONALLY TO HER APPRENTICES AS THEY WORK.

A distinct category of tales deals with advice that represents a philosophy of life derived from the worldview of a social group; consequently tales in this category are held by such a social group to be wisdom stories and to represent behavioral models. There is evidence indicating that tales belonging to the narrative cycle of "The Good Precepts" were told during the Middle Kingdom (about 2350 B.C.E.*) in ancient Egypt. Numerous motifs found in the cycle appear as wise advice given by parents and viziers. The teachings of the vizier Kagemni, for example, are concluded in the following* narrative *manner:*

> *Then the vizier had his children summoned after he had comprehended the manner of mankind. And he ended up by saying to them:* As to all that is written in / this *papyrus roll, heed it, just as I have said it to you[. . . .] So they proceeded to live accordingly.*[522]

Relativity of beauty, balance between merits and demerits of opposites (black and white),[523] *and a wife's faithlessness are basic themes in our present tale of "good precepts." The tale's title is a common truism; yet, this piece of advice stands at sharp variance with the dominant cultural ethos emphasizing solemnness, and avoidance of frolic and play. Students of Egyptian culture have observed that the ancient inhabitants of the land "enjoyed" life to the fullest; for them "an hour of fun" must have been a cherished experience. By contrast, modern Egyptians, on the whole, do not value this approach to life. For the majority, life is to be endured rather than enjoyed. To describe someone as a "fun-loving person ('*ibn-*ḥaẓẓ)," is virtually synonymous with condemning that person as frivolous, or even worthless.*

According to a folk belief, when a person has had "fun," he should expect a mishap to take place. Much laughter is often followed by the supplication: "May the Lord make 'it' [i.e., (what will follow)] a good [thing]!"[524]

Although this rendition is narrated by a female who had learned it from another female and tells it only to females, and in spite of assurances from several informants that it is a "women's tale," this tale type seems to be more male-bound. (See Section V, Tale No. 26, "Occurrences," p. 436; also cf. Preface, p. xvii, note 3.) The following childhood experience by the present writer may shed some light on the process of collecting this tale:

> *When I was about twelve years of age (in the early 1950s), I was dispatched one evening prior to a bairam to* sit *Taḥiyyah in order to bring home some garments that she was sewing for my family. Upon arriving at her home, I was told that some finishing touches still had to be made, and was asked to wait for a few minutes. As I sat in the parlor, adjacent to the work area, I overheard* sit *Taḥiyyah narrating parts of our present tale (but with numerous interruptions) to her girls. I was somewhat disappointed when the work was completed and I had to depart in the middle of the tale. Later, as a folklorist, I sought this tale, and inquired about it during my extended fieldwork in*

the Arab community in Brooklyn, New York (in 1961–65). Numerous female narrators remembered some of the tale's themes (especially the episode of the giant jinni with two women seated on his shoulders), but were unable to tell it in a meaningful manner; men narrators reported that it was a woman's tale. Consequently, one of the tasks after returning to Egypt in the summer of 1968 was to hear the tale from the person whom I knew would tell it well: sit *Taḥiyyah. I traveled to Zagazig, the town where she lived and where I grew up. Her 1971 rendition is given below.*

PRAY on behalf of the Prophet.

Once there was a rich man—(and no one is rich but God). That rich man died and he had only one son. He left all his wealth to that son of his. The boy went wild with his father's money; that which took his father a year to earn took the boy a day to spend: the income was tiny while the expenditures were huge.[525] After a short while the boy had only three hundred pounds left. He thought, "What am I going to do? What am I going to do?" He said, "I will go to the souk and buy and sell as my late father used to do!"

He went to the souk. He looked around and saw a man sitting there without anything to sell: no basket, no stick-tray[526] [to hold merchandise]; everyone in the souk was selling something or buying something except this man. There was nothing in front of him to sell. The boy went to him and said:

"What are you doing, paternal-uncle?"

"I am selling," [replied the man].

"Selling! What are you selling?"

"I am selling talk."

The boy said [in amazement], "In life, talk is more plentiful than grief on the heart! How much is a word [piece of advice]?"

The man replied, "One hundred pounds a word."

"One hundred pounds!"

[Coolly:] "One hundred."

The boy thought, "One hundred pounds: to be added to the grand total[527] [that I have already squandered]." He took a one-hundred-pound [bill][528] out of his pocket, gave it to the man and said, "Give me a word, paternal-uncle."

The man took the one hundred and said, " 'The beautiful one is the person whom you love, even if a slave as black as Noah's [raven]'."[529]

The boy replied, "That we know already! Give me another word; here is another one hundred."

The man took the hundred and said, " 'Do not betray him who places trust in you, even if you are a betrayer!' "

The boy replied, "This also, we already know! Here are the last one hundred. Give me a third word."

The man took the last one hundred pounds that the boy had remaining from his father's wealth. Now the boy became cleaner than a china [plate] after it has been washed: he did not own even a millime [penny]. The man said to him, " 'A [lost] hour of fun can never be made up for!' "

The boy took the three words and left. He had no place to go. He kept on walking until [when it was late evening and dark,] after *¿ishâ*-prayers-time, he came to a town. He knocked on a door of one of the houses—it was a house of good-hearted people; they were well-to-do. They asked, "Who is it?" He answered, "A stranger, tired and thirsty." They opened the door for him; he entered. They fed him supper, and he spent his night there.

In the morning the owner of the house asked him, "To where and from where?"

The boy answered him, "By God, paternal-uncle hajji, I have no place to go. I squandered the fortune that my late father had left me; now I am looking for work."

That man, who has taken him as a guest, looked at him and saw that traces of gracious living were still showing on him; so he asked, "What can you do?"

The boy replied, "I never worked before."

The man said to him, "By God, son, there is no work in this town. I am a merchant and I have a mill that is idle; I hired many a man to operate it, but everyone who ran the mill for a day was found dead the following morning. . . . " Naturally—(as you know, and you are the master of the knowledgeable[530])—the person who runs the mill, whom we call the miller, sleeps in it in order to guard it. [The man continued:] "We don't know why they die, nor from what they die, but we find them in the morning—(away from you)—smashed and in pieces."

The boy said to him, "Let me work the mill for you."

The man said to him [with compassion], "No, son! You are a stranger, traces of gracious living still show on you, and too young to die. Find yourself another place. You are entitled to three days of hospitality. Stay here for those three days; afterward find yourself a job elsewhere!"

[After arguing] from here to there, and after [the boy's imploring,] "for the Prophet's sake! and for the saint's sake!"[531] the man agreed to let him run the mill. The man said [in resignation], "We surrender [entrust] our affairs to God!"

The boy opened the mill, blew its whistle [to announce that it was open], and ran it. People, lots of people, came from every direction, for the mill had been closed for years. At the end of the day everyone went home except the boy. He swept and sprayed the ground [so as to settle the dust], cleaned the machine, and made his bed in a corner of the mill and went to sleep.

During the night—at midnight—he heard rumbling and a great noise. He—(away from you)—woke up frightened. He looked around and saw the wall of the mill split open and out of it came a giant jinni (*mârid*) with two women sitting on his shoulders. On this shoulder [there was] a woman who was white, white, white, as white as milk, her hair yellow, and her eyes green; her beauty was indescribable![532] On that shoulder [there was] another woman—a slave woman, [who was] black, black, black: Noah's [raven] black; (*¿abdah, soadah,* [. . .]: *sawâd nûḥî*), her hair was kinky, and her lips [drooping down] to here [narrator points to her lower chin, and laughs].

The giant jinni said to the boy, "I am divided between these two women. I want to marry one of them but can't make up my mind as to which one is the more beautiful: the white or the black? You tell me! If you are right, I will let you go; if you are wrong, I will—(away from you)—kill you!"

The boy was frightened and did not know what to say: before him there were two women: one white and beautiful, the other black and ugly. As he was about to say, "Marry the white one, for she is the beautiful one," he remembered the words which he had bought from that old man in the souk, those three pieces of advice which he had bought for three hundred pounds. So he said, "'The beautiful one is the person whom you love, even if Noah's [raven]-black!'" It happened that the giant jinni was in love with the black woman. Everyone had been telling him, "Marry the white woman because she is the one who is beautiful!" That is why he had killed all those other men who were running the mill. Everyone told him, "Of course, the white woman is the beautiful one! You should marry the white woman." Then, as soon as that giant jinni would hear them say so, he would get angry and would smash them against the wall.

He said [with apparent relief] to the boy: "May you find contentment in what you have been granted [by God]!"[533] And he went back to where he had come from, and the wall returned to its original form.

In the morning the man, the owner of the mill, came with the shrouds under his arm; the undertaker also came along in order to prepare the boy for burial, because they were sure to find him smashed like those who preceded him. They found him still alive; they were pleased. The man, the owner of the mill, said, "Son, what happened?"

The boy told him: "By God, paternal-uncle hajji, a giant jinni came out of the wall with two women on his shoulder, and . . . , and . . . , and . . . , and . . . !" He told him the whole story.

The man said to him, "From now on you stay here, you run the mill and take care of things for me; God has not granted me any children. You will be like a son to me."

The boy operated the mill; all people came to it, instead of taking their grain to be milled in another town. God blessed the mill for them and their business prospered.

One day the owner of the mill said to the boy, "I, if God wills, will go to Hejaz [on pilgrimage]. You will be in charge of everything: my home, the mill, and everything until I return."

The boy said to him, "May God bring you back safe to us. Rely on God, and have no concerns."

The man left and the boy took care of everything. The wife of that hajji was not a good woman. She began calling the boy, "O So-and-so, fetch this for me." He would say, "Will do," and would get her whatever she asked for but would not enter the house [as rules of good conduct require]. She kept on saying, "Get me this! Hand me that!" and things like that. Of course the boy was not aware of what she was after. One time the woman got bold; she went to the mill one night and got hold of him. She said to him—(away from you), "Let us go. . . . Let us go. . . . " [Narrator hesitates, and seems to be quite embarrassed.] "My husband is not here; he is an old man. I am young and pretty. And I am [such-and-such], and am . . . ," and [seductive] things like that.

The boy was tempted. Satan urged him to betray the trust. But just before he was about to say "Yes!" he remembered the second word that he had bought: "Do not betray him who places trust in you, even if you are a betrayer!"

He immediately pushed her away and said to her, "Shame! Your husband entrusted his family, his honor, and his possessions to me. He trusted me! How could it be that I would betray him! Never!"

The woman was put to shame and started crying. She said to him, "Don't tell my husband."

He answered her, "Promise that you don't do again what you had just done and I promise you that I will not tell anyone about what happened!"

She said to him, "I promise you. And I've repented at your hands."

The fire of grudge broke out inside the woman. She wrote a letter to her husband: "You must return immediately. The one to whom you entrusted your family and your honor—(meaning whom!? Meaning the boy!, that young man who said to her, "Shame on you! Fear God!")—tried to do such and such a thing to me, but I did not enable him to get what he wanted."

As soon as the man received the letter and read it the world became black to his eyes; he cut his pilgrimage and returned to his hometown. He went directly from the train station to his home; of course the boy was at his work in the mill. The woman told him, "You must get rid of the boy. You took him out of the street, gave him refuge, fed and clothed him, and put your trust in him. You took him as a son to you, and [in spite of all that] he tried [seduction] with your wife. This boy must be killed!"

The man believed her. He had a friend—a very dear friend—who was a butcher. He went to that butcher and said, "So-and-so, someone from my house will come to you and say, 'Deliver to me what was entrusted to you.' [When this happens] I want you to kill that person." (This man [the mill-owner] was, as you might say, a king or a mayor in that town of his; I mean a ruler of that town and people had to obey him.) The butcher said, "Will do!" and did not inquire, "Who?" nor "For what [reason]?"

The man, or the ruler, went to the boy in the mill. He thought he should try to find out about what had happened.

"Peace be upon you."

"And upon you be peace, father hajji. A thousand thanks [to God] for your safe return to us."

"Did something happen while I was gone?"

"No! Nothing happened. Everything is safe: your money, your mill and your home [i.e., wife]."

"Is that so?"

"That is so!"

The boy, of course, as he promised the woman, did not tell. So the man said to him, "I want you to go to So-and-so, the butcher, and say to him, 'Deliver to me what was entrusted to you.' "

The boy said, "Will do," and he left immediately.

On his way to the shop of that butcher, he heard drumming and pipe music, trellises [of joy by women] (*ẓagharîṭ*), and much jubilation. He followed the sound until he saw a procession for a boy to be circumcised. Everyone was singing and happy. He thought, "I should go on that errand right away." But he remembered what!? He remembered the third word for which he had paid his last one hundred pounds: A [lost] hour of fun can never be made up for! So he joined the procession and went along with all the others to the home of the circumcised-to-be [boy]. He drank the punch (*sharbâṭ*)[534] and ate the food along with all the others who were there. They sang and danced; the hour of fun did not pass him by.

Now, to whom do we return? To the man and his wife. The man went home and told his wife, "So-and-so, the butcher, will kill the boy. He will send the corpse to us so that we may—(away from you)—bury him!" She waited, but no one came from the butcher's. It was getting late. So she said to herself, "Go to the butcher and see. Get the corpse yourself!" She did not tell her husband, "I am going somewhere," or anything else. When she got there, she said, "Deliver to me the thing that my husband entrusted to you."

That was it! The butcher got hold of her and—(away from you)—slaughtered her. He put her in a sack and sent it to her husband. The man looked for his wife but did not find her. So he put the sack in the corner.

Now who arrived at the butcher's a short while after this had happened? The boy! He said to the butcher, "Deliver to me what was entrusted to you." The butcher replied, "That which was entrusted to me has already been delivered." The boy went home. As soon as the man saw him he was stunned. He ran to the sack and opened it. When he opened it he found his wife['s corpse]. He said to the boy, "Sit down here and tell me exactly what happened."

The boy told him the story from hello to goodbye [i.e., from beginning to end]:[535] how his father died and left him the wealth; how he squandered all his money, how he bought the three words for three hundred pounds; and how the giant jinni really wanted the black woman; how he refused to give in to [the seduction of] that man's wife; how he followed the circumcised boy's procession; and how he went to the butcher; and how . . . , and how. . . . [He concluded,] "And here I am standing in front of you."

The man said to him, "You did not waste your father's wealth, [because] you have just earned back all you had squandered, and more. The three words you bought are worth all the money in the world. From now on, you are my son and I am your father. I will get ready to go for my own reward.[536] Therefore, I'll be spending the rest of my days in prayers and fasting. My home and possessions are yours."

❖ 27 ❖

THE VIRGINS' LOUSE

(EGYPT, EASTERN DESERT)

NARRATED IN JANUARY 1982 BY MAJÎDAH F., ABOUT FORTY-FIVE YEARS OLD, A MOTHER OF SIX CHILDREN, WHO HAILED FROM THE ṢALḤIYYA DESERT REGION, SHARQIYYAH GOVERNORATE, NORTHEASTERN EGYPT. SHE WAS OF BOTH PEASANT AND ARAB (BEDOUIN) DESCENT; HER PEASANT MATERNAL GRANDMOTHER WAS MARRIED TO AN "ARAB SHEIKH" FROM THE TRIBE OF AL-DAWÂGHRAH, WITH NEARBY DESERT CAMPS. AT THE TIME OF THE RECORDING, MAJÎDAH AND HER HUSBAND—HER PATERNAL COUSIN—WERE RESIDING IN SUEZ CITY WHERE HE WORKED AS A TRUCK DRIVER.

MAJÎDAH, OR 'OMM-MḤAMMAD (MOTHER OF MUHAMMAD)—AS SHE IS TYPICALLY CALLED—HEARD THIS TALE WHEN STILL A CHILD IN HER VILLAGE; HER SOURCE WAS "WOMEN IN THE HOUSEHOLD," ESPECIALLY HER MATERNAL GRANDMOTHER WHO, HAVING BEEN ESTRANGED FROM HER BEDOUIN HUSBAND, HAD RETURNED TO HER PATERNAL HOME IN THE VILLAGE.

THE NARRATOR SPOKE ARABIC WITH A BEDOUIN ACCENT TYPICAL OF THE DIALECT OF THE REGION OF HER CHILDHOOD, WHERE HEAVY BEDOUIN INFLUENCE IS NOTICEABLE.[537] SHE HAD TOLD TALES TO HER CHILDREN OCCASIONALLY, BUT NOT MUCH SINCE RADIO AND TELEVISION CAME TO THE HAMLET, AND ALL OF THEM HAD GONE TO SCHOOL.

MAJÎDAH LABELED THIS NARRATIVE A "LITTLE FANTASY-TALE" (*ḤIJJAIWAH*);[538] IT IS ALSO A "JOKE" (*NUKTAH*),[539] "BECAUSE IT MAKES ONE LAUGH," AND IT IS A "PUZZLE" (*ḤIZR*)[540] AS WELL, "BECAUSE NOT EVERYONE CAN TELL IT [SKILLFULLY]."

The husband-wife relationship, sympathy among various elements of the environment, and means of expressing grief are salient themes in this humorous formula tale. The comic aspect is represented by the marriage between the two parasites, and by the disproportionate grief that a wife exhibits over the death of her husband. The cumulative effect of the plot reaches a climax through the presenting of a human situation which parallels that of the two insects. The human husband, who represents wisdom and sanity, perceives the louse's grief as unjustifiable since a husband can be readily replaced.[541] *The tale is typically concluded with the human husband divorcing his wife because of her foolishness. In both situations, marriage is perceived in the tale (i.e., by the narrator) as fragile and easily dissolved either by death or by instant divorce.*[542]

PRAY on behalf of the Prophet.

Once there was a [she]-louse and a [he]-flea; they were married: to each other (I mean). The flea was named Hajji Abu-¿Ammâr, and the louse was named Virgins' Louse.[543] One day the flea—that [Hajji] Abu-¿Ammâr—was returning home from the field, tired. He found his wife, the Virgins' Louse, sitting in front of the oven: keeping its fires going and baking [bread]. He said to her, "O woman, hand me a hot loaf." She replied, "Be patient for a while, it is still doughy." [Irritated], he [snapped and] said, "Move aside!" She said to him, "O Man, be patient for a while!" He hopped to get himself a loaf! He fell! He fell in the oven. [Narrator laughs.] He was—(away from you)—burned. He died!

That Virgins' Louse, [as a sign of grief], undid her hair [and let it down in an unruly manner],[544] slit her gown[545] [all the way down] to the ground, and wailed: "Oh, what a disaster for me! Oh, what a ruin for me!"[546] Over what!? Over what!? Over what!? [one may ask]. [The answer would be, "Over the fact that] Hajji Abu-¿Ammâr died!"

She kept on wailing,

> I am the Virgins' Louse;
> my hair is undone,
> over Hajji Abu-¿Ammâr
> who hopped and fell in the fire![547]

The crow-of-ill-omen[548] met her as he had his wings spread out and asked,

> What is the matter with you, Virgins' Louse,
> [so that you have] your hair undone!?[549]

She replied,

I am the Virgins' Louse;
my hair is undone,
over Hajji Abu-¿Ammâr
who hopped and fell in the fire![550]

The crow-of-ill-omen heard this; he [immediately] plucked out the [feathers in his] two tails. [Narrator laughs.] He flew to the top of the date palm tree. The palm tree asked him,

Why is it, crow-of-ill-omen,
[that] you've the two tails [of yours] plucked out?[551]

He replied,

I am the crow-of-ill-omen,
I have plucked out the two tails [of mine],
for the Virgins' Louse
has her hair undone,
and Hajji Abu-¿Ammâr
hopped, and fell into the fire![552]

The palm tree heard [this] and said, "Droop, droop!"[553] She let her palm branches droop down, and their fronds shed off. The well below [narrator raises her eyes upward, as if she were the well looking up at the palm tree] asked,

What is the matter with you, palm tree of dates,
[that] your branches are droopy, droopy!?[554]

She replied,

I am the palm tree of dates,
my branches have become droopy, droopy,
over the crow-of-ill-omen,
who has plucked out the two tails [of his].
and the Virgins' Louse
has her hair undone,
and Hajji Abu-¿Ammâr
hopped and fell into the fire.[555]

The water heard this and immediately became murky.[556]

The sheep came to drink. They looked and saw the water murky. They asked,

> What is the matter with you, well water?
> you have become murky, murky![557]

The water said,

> I am the well water,
> I've become murky, murky,
> over the palm tree of dates,
> with her branches, droopy, droopy,
> over the crow-of-ill-omen,
> who has plucked out the two tails [of his],
> and the Virgins' Louse
> has her hair undone,
> and Hajji Abu-¿Ammâr
> hopped and fell into the fire.[558]

When the sheep heard that, they shed their fleece and did not drink. The shepherd came [and exclaimed],

> What is the matter with you, young sheep?
> You have become lean, lean![559]

They said to him,

> We are a few young sheep,
> we have become lean, lean,
> over the well water;
> it has become murky, murky,
> over the palm tree of dates,
> with her branches, droopy, droopy,
> over the crow-of-ill-omen;
> he has plucked out the two tails [of his],
> and the Virgins' Louse
> has her hair undone,
> and Hajji Abu-¿Ammâr
> hopped and fell into the fire.[560]

When the boy [the little shepherd] heard this, he broke his stick—(with which he drives the sheep)—and sat down. His sister came carrying [midday] dinner. She found him sitting down on the ground and his stick broken. She said to him,

What is the matter with you, Naṣṣâr, my brother?
Your stick is broken, broken![561]

He replied,

I am your brother, Naṣṣâr;
my stick is broken, broken,
and my sheep [are] young, young;
they have become lean, lean,
and the well water,
has become murky, murky,
and the palm tree of dates,
her branches [became] droopy, droopy,
over the crow-of-ill-omen,
who has plucked out the two tails [of his],
and the Virgins' Louse
has her hair undone,
And Hajji Abu ¿Ammâr
hopped and fell into the fire![562]

When his sister heard that she got hold of the dinner and poured it over her own head and face. . . . (They had sent the boy a dish of bean mash.)[563] She went home; her mother said to her,

What is with you, daughter, Zahrat an-Nawwâr?
you are covered with bean mash![564]

She answered her,

I am your daughter, Zahrat an-Nawwâr;
on me is bean mash, bean mash;
over my brother Naṣṣâr;
his stick is broken, broken.
and his young, young sheep,
have become lean, lean,
and the well water,
it has become murky, murky,
and the palm tree of dates,
her branches became droopy, droopy,
over the crow-of-ill-omen,
who has plucked out the two tails [of his],
and the Virgins' Louse
has her hair undone,

and Hajji Abu-¿Ammâr
hopped and fell into the fire![565]

The woman, when she heard this, she had . . . , she had a spindle in her hand and was spinning. She—(away from you)—stuck the spindle in her own eye and punched it out.[566] After a short while her man [husband] came. He said to her,

What is with you, woman,
one-eyed, one-eyed!?[567]

She said to him,

I am your wife, Ḥamâmit el-'Asḥâr;
I've become one-eyed, one-eyed,
and my girl Zahrat an-Nawwâr,
she is smeared with bean mash, bean mash,
and her brother Naṣṣâr,
his stick is broken, broken,
and his young sheep, young sheep,
have become lean, lean,
and the well water,
has become murky, murky,
and the palm tree of dates,
her branches [became] droopy, droopy,
over the crow-of-ill-omen,
who has plucked out the two tails [of his],
and the Virgins' Louse
has her hair undone,
and Hajji Abu-¿Ammâr
hopped and fell into the fire![568]

The man heard this and was about to go crazy. He said [with vexation], "Is this something to be done, you idiot of a woman! You punch your eye out! The girl will wash her face and become clean; the boy will soon get himself another stick; the sheep will soon grow fleece anew; the water will soon become clear again; the palm tree will soon grow branches; the crow-of-ill-omen will soon grow another tail; and the Virgins' Louse will soon find another husband; as for Hajji Abu-¿Ammâr: to hell with him[569] . . . ! As for you: how are you going to get another eye? Go! You are divorced! Go to your father's home!

THE WIFE IN A POLYGYNOUS COMMUNITY

❖ 28 ❖

SHE WHOSE REASON COULDN'T BE MADE TO SLIP[570]

(EGYPT)

NARRATED, ON THE PHONE, IN 1972 BY IQBÂL A.H., SIXTY-FIVE YEARS OLD, A WIDOW FROM CAIRO, OF TURKISH UPPER-CLASS ANCESTRY. SHE HAD HEARD MOST OF THE FOLKTALES SHE KNOWS FROM A NANNY IN HER HOUSEHOLD CALLED 'OMM-¿ABDUH, WHO CAME FROM SOUTHERN EGYPT. THE NARRATOR TOLD THE STORY TO HER SON'S DAUGHTER IN RESPONSE TO THE GRANDDAUGHTER'S REQUEST FOR TALES FOR HER FIELDWORK PROJECT IN A COLLEGE FOLKLORE CLASS. THIS TEXT WAS COLLECTED AND WRITTEN DOWN IN ARABIC BY MISS MÂGDÂ ZUHDÎ.[571]

A man's honor is reflected in the conduct of his sister and mother; his wife's conduct reflects on the honor of her own family (usually, the paternal line). A number of Bedouin honor cries, shouted in battles, use the sister's name: "I am he-So-and-so, brother of she-So-and-so!"[572] The present realistic tale is a fictitious portrayal of this value. Marriage for spite[573] provides a rationale for the tale's plot.

Also presented are basic aspects of social interaction between two racial groups, whites and blacks, within an urban household. Significantly, there is no punishment for the black male slave for having had a sexual relationship with the white wife of his presumably white master. This reaction contrasts sharply with the severe and unforgiving attitude toward a black female slave consorting with a white male.[574] Such feelings of animosity toward and rivalry with a black woman seem typical of a female's perceptions—as reflected in her narration—in a community where she has to compete with a black woman for the attention of the male.

THERE once was a man and a woman [who had] begotten a girl and a boy. They [the parents] left a good deal of wealth for them [when they died]. That girl was very wise and the boy loved her; for him the weighty[575] oath was, "[I swear] by my sister, whose reason no one can slip."[576] Whenever he would go to a place, he would keep on swearing by that [oath].

Once someone got irked at him and said [to himself], "What does that sister of his amount to? By God, I will make her reasoning slip!" That man was a big merchant and he was rich. He went and got a mosquito net [i.e., a canopy] adorned with gems and little [crystal light]-cups; he set it up under her window [and lighted the crystal lights]; the mosquito net lighted up the whole street. [When] she looked, she saw something that was attractive, adorned with gems, and beautiful. So she told the nanny (*dâdah*) to go down [and ask him] to sell it to her. He replied, "I'll sell it to her for free, [but only] if she shows me a hand-finger[577] out a window." He was a married man but he wanted to lay a trap for her brother. She realized that he was trying to make her fall, so she went and got a [head of] large mild radish (*figlah rûmî*).[578] She adorned it like a finger and she put it through [the lattice work of] the window. [When the man saw it,] he wondered, "If the finger of her hand is such: [light and crisp] like palm-tree sprouts (*zayy el-gummâr*)[579] and pretty, then how beautiful would her face be!!"

The following day he went ahead and brought for her a mosquito net more beautiful [than the first one], and set it [in front of her house, under her window]. The nanny went down to buy it. He said, "I'll sell it for free only if she looks out the window and shows me her face!"

She happened to have a European maid;[580] so she made her look out the window. He wondered: "*Y-â-â-âh!* (Oh, my!) If her face is as such, then how would her body be! How would her beauty[581] be! And how would a repose in her arms[582] be!" He gave her the second mosquito net.

The third day he came with a third [and more beautiful] mosquito net and set it up. The nanny went down to buy it. Meanwhile that third net was so pretty and lavish that she [the sister] went crazy over it and wanted to buy it. He said, "I'll give it to her for free, but only if she lets me in, and lets me sleep and stay up late with her tonight." [When she heard this] she said [to the nanny], "Tell him to come at ten o'clock at night, after my brother has gone to sleep, and I will open [the door] for him. But he should come through [the door of] the basement (*badroam*)."

Meanwhile, she prepared a room in the basement, furnished it and said to the [Abyssinian] slave-girl (*gâryah*),[583] "You must meet him and spend the night with him, but do not speak with him at all. Before daybreak, you leave him and say to him, 'Go, lest my brother wake up and see you!' " She also gave her a piece of paper and said to her, "Fasten it to the tassel of [his] fez, but do not let him see you [do so]!"

Indeed, [everything went according to plan, and] during the night she [the slave-girl] fastened the paper to the tassel of the fez. Naturally her voice [accent] would have been recognized as that of a black slave-girl, so she did not make any attempt to speak and she told him that she had a cold [and therefore could not talk]. He slept in her arms and he enjoyed himself.[584] Early in the morning she woke him up and said to him [in a disguised voice], "Wake up lest my brother should wake up!" She let him out of the house and closed the door.

In the morning, all of them got up. The brother went to the coffeehouse and suddenly he swore by his sister as he was talking with someone. Then that merchant got up and said to him, "Man, go blow![585] 'By your sister' what! I have spent the night with her yesterday." As he was speaking [other people in the coffeehouse noticed the paper fastened to the tassel of his fez]; they said to him, "Wait, wait! There is a piece of paper fastened to the tassel of the fez!" When they read [it] they found out that the letter or that piece of paper was saying, "The finger [was] a radish-head, the face [was] the face of a European maid, and the repose was the repose [with] an Abyssinian slave-girl. There is no way, you son of a dog, that you can reach me!"

Thus her brother was relieved, emerged victorious, and said nothing. As for the merchant, he was vexed because he had paid [lost] a lot of money. He thought, "I am going to ask for her in marriage and avenge myself on her!" So he went and proposed to her. The brother told his sister, "He is the one who tried to make you fall. [Any family in] the entire town would wish him [to be a husband or an in-law of theirs]! What do you say?" She consented and said to him, "I am your sister, [the one] whom no one can cause her reasoning to slip." They signed the marriage contract; he married her, and the bride went to the groom's house.

Now he wanted to return the trap [and get even]. He, his [first] wife, and his children were [living] on the upper floor. He also had a slave, among his [other] slaves, named Surûr. He said to him, "Surûr, I am bestowing upon you this [woman—the bride]." (Meaning that it would be legitimate (*ḥalâl*) for Surûr [to enjoy her sexually]).

Naturally, Surûr used to sleep in the basement. ([When she joined her husband] she went to him, along with her three mosquito nets that she had taken from him.) She went with Surûr down to the basement. Then he [sensing aloofness on her part] said to her, "Aren't you coming so that we may sleep [together]?" She replied, "After a rest [for] I am tired." A while later she undressed but she would not lie down until he had cleaned, swept, and washed the room. [Being a basement room and a storage room, it was very dirty and crowded.] Surûr kept on washing and sweeping [the floors] all night long until daybreak. [In the morning] his master asked him, "What have you done, Surûr?" He replied, "By God, master, all night long [she kept on telling me], 'Lift here, stick [it] here!'[586] until my waist got busted [from exhaustion]." His master [thinking that Surûr was talking about sexual intercourse] said, "Good for you. Keep it up!"

Then, the following night, he [Surûr] said to her, "Now, let us." She answered, "Let us what!! The basement still has a foul odor and is dirty." He said to her, "Okay" and kept on cleaning up, lifting the barrels that were in the basement, cleaning the carpets, . . . until daybreak. He went upstairs to his master in the morning and he [the master] asked him, "What did you do, Surûr?" He replied, "By God, master, all night long: 'Stick [it] here!' 'Lift [it] from here!,' until my waist got busted." He replied, "Good for you. Keep it up!"

The third night she could not find an excuse [not to go to bed with her new owner—Surûr]. What should she do? She got a mosquito net and set it up in the spot that they had cleaned. [She did so] before the lady living upstairs [the co-wife] would go to sleep. [When she saw it] that lady went crazy [over it] and wondered "[How can] the wife of the slave sleep inside a [lavish] mosquito net like this one, while I sleep inside a [mere] tulle mosquito net!!" So she sent to ask her for it.

She [the new wife, the girl] said, "I will give it to you free, [on the condition that] you come down and spend the night in my place, while I go upstairs and spend the night in your place!" So, this one [the first wife] went down and spent the night in the place of that one. She [the girl] entered [the room], slept with him [the merchant] and became pregnant as of the date of that night. Meanwhile, the lady who went down [to the basement] became pregnant by the slave. She [the new wife] rose up early in the morning [while the two men were still asleep], went downstairs and said to her [the first wife], "Go upstairs while it is still early, before your husband wakes up."

Soon the merchant traveled away and was absent for two years. [Meanwhile his first wife gave birth to a black boy, and the second gave birth to a white boy.] She [the new wife] never consented to sleep with the slave. When the bey [the merchant] returned, the slave went to await his master at the station; he was carrying the black child on his shoulder—the one who was [thought to be] the bey's son—and holding the [hand of the] white child. [When the master saw that] he struck the slave and said to him, "You son of a dog! [How dare] you carry your son on your shoulder and let my son [stand] on the ground!" He replied, "Bey, this [white one] is my son, and this [black one] is your son!" The bey exclaimed, "Unbelievable!" and he went home and asked his [first] wife, "Is it true that my son is this one, the black?" She answered, "Yes! This is the way God's creation is!" The slave went downstairs to that other one and said to her, "Go upstairs, greet the bey." She went upstairs carrying her son. He said to her, "It is strange that your son [should] be the white one [when his father is black]." She replied, "Indeed, he is [my son]." And she told him the entire story. He was very pleased and stated, "Truthful was your brother [when he said] that no one could cause your reason to slip!"

He cast away (*ramâ*) his old [i.e., first] wife to the slave because her reason slipped due to a mere mosquito net [canopy], and he took [as a wife] the [new] bride.

And they lived in stability and prosperity and begot boys and girls.

❖ 29 ❖

THE LOVESICK HUSBAND

(EGYPT)

NARRATED BY FÂTIMAH K., AGED FIFTY-SIX, A HOUSEWIFE FROM CAIRO. SHE HAD HEARD THIS TALE FROM HER ELDER SISTER. FÂTIMAH WAS A RACONTEUR AND POSSESSED A RELATIVELY LARGE REPERTOIRE WHICH SHE PRESENTED WITH CONSIDERABLE SKILL. THE PRESENT TEXT WAS COLLECTED JOINTLY WITH MRS. F. ṬAMMOUM.[587]

This realistic tale portrays a case of happy polygyny, a recurrent theme in Arab tales. Here, a man's father's brother's daughter plays two distinct, but fused, roles: that of his wife, and that of his friend and helper—or as the character in the tale puts it, his "sister." She helps her husband reach the maiden whom he truly desires.

When asked what she would have done had she been the cousin character in the tale and experiencing the same "role strain," the female narrator of another rendition[588] *stated with resignation, "Isn't that a man's right? God allowed him to do so. I can't forbid it!" However, when asked whether she personally would allow her own husband to marry another woman, she confidently stated, "He can't! I have a [magical] fix*[[589]] *put on him." Yet, a third female narrator suggested a different approach to the problem. She explained, " 'A woman trusting men['s fidelity], is a woman trusting water [to remain] in a wide-meshed sieve!' "*[590] *Then she followed this proverbial simile by a practical female aphorism: "Clip your bird['s wings] lest he mate with another,"*[591] *which urges a woman to squander her husband's wealth so as to ensure that he has no financial means to acquire another wife.*

The country of esh-Shâm, the stage for much of the tale's action, refers to the Levant Coast Arab culture area (Syria, Lebanon, and Palestine).

STATE the oneness of God.

Once there was, and there was plenty; talk would not be sweet except with the mentioning of the Prophet, may prayers on his behalf and peace be.

There was someone who was the king of Egypt, and there was someone who was the king of esh-Shâm [(Syria)]. The king of Egypt wished to set out [on pilgrimage] to Hejaz, [so he did]. And, likewise, the king of esh-Shâm set out to Hejaz, without either one knowing [about the other's trip]. The one from esh-Shâm had a daughter, and the one from Egypt had a son. Each official caravan[592] [was] carrying draperies and the gifts from the state [government] to the Kaaba, [the holy shrine], in Mecca. The Egyptian one and the *shâmî* (Syrian) one accidentally traveled side by side. The camel [on] which the king of Egypt—(his son, I mean)—was riding, was right in front of the camel [on whose back] the daughter of the king of esh-Shâm was mounted [inside a howdah]. By chance, the son of the king of Egypt opened a little window in the howdah in which he was, and also by chance, the daughter of the king of esh-Shâm opened a little window in her howdah. The two faces met: he looked at her and she looked at him. They did not know each other nor did either know who [the other one] happened to be.

She waved at him [gesturing]. She placed her hand on her head. [Narrator shows how.] [Then she placed her hand on her breast], then she removed her hand [. . .] and placed it on her eye, then removed her hand from her eye and placed it on her navel, then she removed her hand from her navel and got hold of [the hem of] her dress with both hands and fanned it twice,[593] then she closed the window. He also closed the window [of his howdah]. He became preoccupied with her, but he knew not who she was, nor from where [she is], nor whose daughter she happened to be. They did not meet again after that [event], and each one returned home—the girl preoccupied with the boy and the boy preoccupied with her.

After the pilgrimage the lad became ill and did not want to speak to anyone. They would bring him doctors but the doctors would state, "There is nothing wrong with him!"

[His family would wonder], "Then, what's the matter with him?!"

Someone advised them to find him a wife. Then what? They went and affianced to him a king's daughter to be his wife. They got married. But when he entered upon her [in the bridal chamber], he said to her, "Why are you sitting here?" She answered him, "They have married me off to you." He said to her, "And who told you that I want to get married? Do you know where your father's home is? Go to it [i.e., Get lost]!"

His father was upset with this prank (*faṣl*).[594] A few days later they advised his father that he should marry someone else to him. So, they affianced to him a vizier's daughter. What he did to the first one, he did to the second, and his father became too embarrassed to engage anyone else to him.

It happened that he had a girl paternal-cousin (*bint ¿amm*), raised in the same house. At that time, she had come of age; so they said, "Let's marry her to him." On the wedding day he said to her the same thing that he had said to the others: "Do you know where your father's house is?" She answered him, "I do know." He said to her [curtly], "Hit the road!"[595] She said, [in an astonished tone], "And what's the difference between my paternal-uncle's home and that of my father? This one here [pointing to the ground] is our house." He replied, "O lady, I don't want to marry." She replied, "Never mind marriage, and let me be your sister. Only tell me about what is making you upset and has caused such a change in you." He said to her [in a slighting tone], "And what do you know about my distress?" She replied, "Perhaps I can help you." He said, "I know that you can't help me. Get away from me and leave me alone." She kept on insisting and saying, "Tell me the story. What is the reason that since the day you returned from Hejaz you have been shutting yourself up in such a manner? What . . . ?"

When he got fed up with her nagging at him, he said to her [curtly], "My lady, the day I went off to Hejaz a very handsome lass met me. She was on pilgrimage and she had her window open and I also opened the window of my howdah. We were face-to-face opposite each other and I have become preoccupied with her since that day." She asked him, "Did you speak with each other?" He replied, "I wish . . . !" She asked, "Do you know whose daughter she is?" He replied, "I wish . . . !" She asked him, "Haven't you waved at each other?" He replied, [in despair], "And what good could waving do?" She answered, "It could do plenty." He said, "I didn't learn anything from the waving." She said to him, "Well, why don't you tell me about it, perhaps I will know." He said, "She placed her hand on the top of her head. [Narrator shows how.] She removed her hand [from her head] and put it on her eye. Then she removed her hand from her eye and placed it on her left breast. Then she removed her hand from her left breast and placed it on her navel. Then she removed her hand from her navel and she picked up the tail of her dress with both hands and shook it off [as if to dust it off or to fan a fire]. Then she closed the window. Since that day I have been in this condition: preoccupied with her and with her waving which I did not understand."

His girl paternal-cousin said to him [in a self-assured tone], "She spoke to you and got her fill [of talk]." He said to her [in a perplexed tone], "How??" She said to him, "I will tell you: the placing of her hand on top of her head means [that she is] the daughter of a king or a chief; the placing of her hand on her eye means [that she is] from a town called Buṣra[596] ["eyesight"]; the placing of her hand on her left breast means [that] beside their palace, to the left, there is a fruit stall; the placing of her hand on her navel means [that] their house is in the center of town;[597] the placing of both of her hands on her dress and fanning it means [that] in front of their house there is a tailor. And that is the meaning of all that signaling [by her at you]."

He [in excitement] sat up and said to her [with great expectation], "And how do we reach her?" She replied, "Say to your father and to your mother that I looked appealing to you and that we would like to travel to spend the honeymoon in esh-Shâm [countries], so that we may have a change of air [and relax]. You should also greet them in the morning when you get up just as you used to do before. When it is time for us to depart, we should take with us some untailored cloth and I should take a wrapping-mantle."[598]

They got ready for travel and took with them sufficient amounts of money, and a little more. They rode until they reached Buṣra in esh-Shâm [i.e., in Iraq (see note 596, this section)]. They rented an apartment close to midtown. She told him to take the piece of cloth and give it to the tailor in front of the palace in order to make him a suit. She also told him, "After he has taken your measurements and has said to you, 'Congratulations!' you should hand him ten pounds [as a tip]. He will be very happy with that tip and will get loud and will order in a loud and far-traveling voice, 'Boy, get a chair! Boy, get coffee!' As soon as the coffee arrives you should give [the boy] a pound [as a generous tip]. The two of them will become more boisterous. As for you, during that loud commotion, you keep your eyes on the window at the king's palace."

[He did as she instructed him.] When they [the tailor and his assistant] became boisterous, he looked at the window and found the very girl [whom he had seen in the howdah]. She looked at him, and brought a yellow shawl (*maḥramah*) and spread it across the [open] window, she removed it and placed a rose-color shawl. Then she went inside and closed the window. He stayed for a short while after she had closed the window and went home to his girl paternal-cousin. She asked him [with anticipation], "What have you done?" He answered her, "I haven't done a thing. I saw her, and that was all." She said, "Did she talk to you?" He answered, "No!" She asked, "Did she wave?" He answered, "No, she did not wave but she placed a lemon-color shawl on the window sill, and removed it; then she placed a rose-color shawl [on the sill]." She said to him, "This means that she has spoken to you." He asked, "How come?" She said, "Meaning that since the day she had seen you her color has become as yellow as a lemon [a sickly color], and when she saw you, blood ran into her face and she became of rose color [healthy pink]." He asked her, "Then what?" She said, "Take another piece of cloth and return to the tailor. As soon as he sees you, he will get boisterous. You still tip him ten pounds. He will get louder and you keep your eye on the window."

[He did as she instructed him.] When he looked at the window he saw that she had placed a shawl with a drawing on it—it had the drawing of a clock stopped at seven o'clock. It also had the drawing of her father's garden and her father's fountain—with her beside the fountain, and he [the youth] was also portrayed right next to her. She then removed the shawl, went inside, and closed the window. He went to his girl paternal-cousin and told her about what had happened. She instructed him, "Dress up and go meet her at the spot about which she had told you." He said to her, "I will go ahead of the appointed time." She said, "All right. When you get there early, be careful not to fall asleep for the garden is full of nice fragrances and a beautiful breeze that makes one drowsy." He snapped, "How could I fall asleep? I have been waiting for this rendezvous for a long time!"

He went a little bit early, sat in the garden, but sleep overcame him without his knowing it. She arrived while he was asleep and couldn't find it in her heart to wake him up. She wrote [a message] on a piece of paper, in which she told him:

A lover who falls asleep deserves the spilling of his blood;
for having dozed off without waiting for his sweetheart.

She put the paper in the little [change] pocket of his jacket; then brought an apple from a tree, wrote the same words on it, placed it in his big pocket, [and she left]. He woke up later and did not think that he had fallen asleep; he waited long until it was much later than the appointed time. When she did not show up, he went home sad.

His girl paternal-cousin said to him, "You must have fallen asleep." He answered her, [with assuredness], "Neither did I fall asleep nor anything [of the sort]." As he was taking his jacket off, the apple fell out. She exclaimed, "And you have also eaten apples!" He replied, "I have neither eaten apples, nor [anything of the sort]!" She wondered, "How could that be? It has writing on it!" He said, "Perhaps you are the one who wrote on it." She said, "Search your pockets, maybe you will find something else." He found the paper and [upon reading it] he became very distressed. His girl paternal-cousin said to him, "Don't be sad. Take another piece of cloth, return to the tailor [and do as you did before]. When he becomes boisterous, look at the window and see what will happen."

[When this happened], she [the king's daughter] looked out the window and placed a shawl on which she had a drawing [conveying the message] that he should meet her at the fence outside the palace. He went to his girl paternal-cousin and told her. She said, "When the two of you meet each other, the two of you will fall asleep." He asked, "How can that be?" She answered, "Just like the time before." Then she added [if this were to happen . . .], "The money is with you. If the two of you fall asleep they will take the two of you to the police station. Naturally, since she is a king's daughter, they are going to confine you [both] in a room overlooking the street. As soon as they put you in confinement, you should look out the window. Cast this purse of money at anyone who happens to be passing by and give him another purse with three pounds in it, then ask him to go to such-and-such a place [where I will be], and let me know your whereabouts. The man should yell, 'Owner of the yarn, your yarn has become entangled'—that's all. And I will have things readied [for your release]."

After her paternal-cousin had left, she got up, prepared very good food, placed it on a tray, and put on her mantle; she was ready so that as soon as she would hear somebody yelling: "Owner of the yarn . . . ," she would leave immediately. A while later she heard [that call]. She took the tray and left immediately for the police station. She met the guards and said to them [softly], "Good evening to you. I, by God, have a celebration for the sake of the poor [or the saints][599] and thought that I would bring you some of it since you [have been too busy and] have not eaten because of that incident that took place." After they had eaten, she said to them, "She [the king's daughter] had already eaten at her father's home." (Narrator adds: Oh! I forgot to say that the guards have told her that there was an Egyptian man who was caught along with the king's daughter. So, she told them, "She [the king's daughter] has already eaten at her father's home. As for him, he is poor and deserves pity—all that may be done is done for God's sake. Let me in so that I may give him a little morsel to eat and may God's reward be yours.") They answered, "Please go ahead."

She walked into the prison room [cell] where they were. She took the clothes off the king's daughter and put them on herself and gave the king's daughter her own clothing along with the mantle. She instructed her, "Take this tray with you and throw it in the river on your way. Go to your father's home. When they ask you 'What happened?' you should reply [defiantly], 'Where is that Egyptian with whom I have been accused?' "

The king's daughter performed this ruse and said to her father, "I must see that person and I am ready to marry him since I have been accused [of having sinned] with him."

The important thing is that the king's daughter got out of prison and the other one [the girl paternal-cousin] remained there in her stead. She said to her paternal-cousin, "When they ask you about me, tell them that I am your sister and that we have come to this country for recreation and that as we were walking we found a nice spot next to the king's palace, we thought we might take some rest. We fell asleep and suddenly found the guards right there and that they took us into custody."

In the morning the king found his daughter greeting him, as was her custom. He asked her, "Oh, have the guards released you?" She answered him, with astonishment [pretended innocence], "Who are those who were supposed to have released me!!!" He told her about what he had heard the previous night—that the guards had caught her with an Egyptian man and that he instructed them, "Keep them in jail until morning." She replied, "I want to see the two they have arrested."

They were brought from prison and their story was heard. The young man said, "I am the son of the king of Egypt [and told him the rest of the fabricated story]. And since they have slandered us in this manner, I am ready to marry her!" She [the king's daughter] declared, "And I also am ready to marry him."

The king set up a wedding celebration for them that lasted for forty days. After that he [the son-in-law] asked permission of her father, the king [of esh-

Shâm], and left for Egypt. In the middle of the road his girl paternal-cousin said to him, "Come on, divorce me and live with your bride." He refused to divorce her and said, "Had it not been for you I couldn't have reached her. For me, the two of you are exactly alike."

And they lived in stability and prosperity and begot boys and girls. And bit by bit, the tale is over. Was it sweet or draggy?[600] If sweet, you owe a song; if draggy, you owe a story.

❖ 30 ❖

THE SON OF SEVEN [MOTHERS][601]

(SYRIA)

NARRATED IN APRIL 1981 BY ʾĀMÂL Q. (SEE INFORMANT NOTE TO TALE NO. 16.) SHE HAD HEARD THIS TALE WHEN A YOUNG GIRL FROM HER MOTHER.

To be "like co-wives"[602] *is a proverbial simile indicating that two persons—typically females—are in perpetual acute conflict. The intensity of this conflict is occasionally perceived as second only to that among women whose husbands are brothers. A truism states, "The ship of co-wives sailed, but the ship of wives of brothers foundered."*[603]

Our present story gives a dramatic example of how co-wives—as partners in misery—can cooperate so as to confront the danger presented by a new bride for their husband: a co-wife—who is destructive like "a locust"—and refuses to share the husband with the rest. The reunion between the reinstated wives and their cruel husband is nonexclusive; it simply restores matters to their previous state before the advent of the ogress bride.[604] *Thus, no one wife has exclusive right to their husband.*

Of interest here is the fact that the child of one co-wife refers to his father's wives (i.e., his stepmothers, his mother's co-wives) as khâlât *(maternal-aunts). Equating* *maternal-aunt with co-wife or stepmother is congruent with the negative roles assigned to both a woman's sister and a woman's co-wife (*ḍurrah*).*[605]

Other significant aspects include the wisdom of an ogress sister,[606] *and the generally unaffectionate relations between an ogress and her son.*

THERE was and there was plenty, O you who are listening to this narrating and talk: should we fib [by telling nonsense fairy-tales] or should we sleep?

There was one day a king—(and no one is King but God)—who had seven women [as wives]; [these women were almost] brides. He married them one [shortly] after another until they reached seven [in number]. One day that king went out to promenade and do as kings do (hunt beasts or [do] something similar). As he was in a parklike forest[607] he came to a creek; he saw a young woman swimming in the creek. She was beautiful. Her beauty was [so great it] was indescribable. He became enamored with her! He said to her, "I am the king and I wish to marry you." She answered, "I agree, but on one condition!" He asked, "What is it?" She said to him, "The condition is that I be the endeared one (*ma¿zûzah*)!" He replied [instantly and with enthusiasm], "And I agree!"

He took her to the palace where his [other] women were, [but] she couldn't bear [being with] them—(for she was an ogress [*ghûliyyah*], and wanted to kill them). She said to the king [in a commanding voice], "Divorce them!" He replied [readily, by uttering the divorce oath at his wives]: "You are divorced!" Then he turned to the new [wife and said], "They have been divorced!"

They took them and cast them away in the kitchens of the palace (where cooking and storing away rations are done). They [the women] kept on crying and wailing, while she [the new wife] stayed endeared to the king. The king forgot about his wives—those seven—and lived with the new one. But she did not forget [about them]. She went to them, took them, and placed them in a room underneath the ground; it had neither a door nor a window [a dungeon]. She took them and lowered them [into the dungeon], closed the lid, and left. She left them there with neither food nor water; neither light nor candle. They kept on weeping and wailing: "What shall we do!" (There is nothing they could do!) They surrendered [entrusted] their affairs to God.

O day, go! O day, come [time passed,] and they became very hungry and thirsty. One day, she [the ogress wife] came to them with a tray (*ṣadr*) full of food and with flasks of water. She lifted the lid of the dungeon, [looked down] and said to them, "Are you languishing away for food?"

"Yes, by God! Give us some for we are about to perish!"

"[If you want this food], I will pluck out your eyes and place them on that tray [and you get this food]!" [Narrator points with her finger, as if pointing to the food on the tray.]

Poor women; they were hungry, tired, and had no hope. They agreed. She pulled out their eyes, and she did not give them all the food or the water [that she had]. She threw them a little food and one flask of water. And she put the lid back. [Then she put the eyes in crystal cups and took them to her own crystal palace, where she kept them.]

It turned out that they, those seven women, the wives of the king, were pregnant. The first got labor pains before the others. She lay down and the [six] others helped her deliver: a baby boy. They handed him over to her saying, "God sent you a boy!" She got hold of him, but she was hungry; she had not tasted any kind of food whatsoever for maybe a month! She . . . , she. . . . ([Narrator is visibly uncomfortable and states:] The responsibility is the teller's!)[608] She reached to her child, slaughtered him, divided him up into seven pieces and gave each a piece! They ate some . . . [pause], and saved the rest for the following days. A month later, the second got labor pains—(for the king had married them, each a month apart from the other; each became pregnant the day she married). The others helped her deliver: a baby boy. She did the same thing as the first one—for the food was all gone. She divided her child into seven pieces and gave each a piece. A month later, the same thing happened to the third. A month later, the same happened to the fourth, until it was the turn of the seventh. She had not been eating her share, but she had been saving the share[s] she had received from the others. When it was time for her to deliver, she gave birth to a baby boy. The others helped her deliver and handed her the baby. She hid him—of course all of them were blind and could not see—and took out the piece[s of flesh] that she had gotten from them and gave them each a piece and said, "Here is your share [of my own child]!"

She raised the boy, [whom she named Mister Aladdin],[609] on whatever they happened to have. The boy grew and started poking around. One day he was holding a bone from one of his [slain] brothers in his hand and was going like this. (Narrator imitates the motion of scratching into a wall.) [A small piece of] the wall crumbled. He [swiftly] kept on scratching with that bone and soon he could see sunlight. With God's help he scratched a hole [big enough for him] to pass through. When he got out he saw a world he had never seen before! It happened that he emerged inside the garden of the king—(who is his father). He stood by the kitchen door. When they took out the garbage, he went through it, took out the leftovers: bread, rind of watermelon (*gabas*), and whatsoever [may be eaten]. He took these and went to his mother and his "maternal-aunts"[610] [i.e., stepmothers]. They ate and thanked God. The following day the boy went out again, went to the kitchen, and went through the garbage. And the following day, and the following day. Who was watching him? The king's cook. He saw him come day after day and go through the garbage. His [the cook's] heart felt for the boy.

He asked him, "For whom do you take the food, son?"

"To my mother and my maternal-aunts! They are hungry! [They are] naked! They are miserable!"

The cook said, "Would you work in the kitchen to assist me?"

He replied, "I'll ask my mother!"

He went to his mother and said, "Mother, the king's cook wants me to be his helper!" [All seven] women feared for his safety. His mothers said to him, "The king is your father. His wife did this to us. She will kill you too!" He said, "I will not tell them who I am." His mothers said to him, "God be with you! But if your father's wife knew about you, she will cause your destruction."

He went to the cook and the man took him to the kitchen to assist him. At the end of the day he would give him [as pay] some food, some old clothes, and the like. One day the king saw the boy. His heart felt for him. He asked the cook, "Cook, whose son is this [boy]?" He replied, "He is an orphan, My Lord. He is assisting me, for I am getting old." [The king] said, "Good. Take care of him and let him bring me my food." He replied, "Whatever you order will be carried out!"

One day, as the boy was carrying the food from the kitchen to the king, his stepmother saw him; she noticed that he resembled his father!

"Boy, come here!"

"Yes, maternal-aunt!"

"What are you doing here?"

"I help So-and-so, the cook. I am an orphan."

She realized that boy was the son of her husband and one of the wives of her husband. She thought, "If the boy and his father get together, then I will have lost everything!" She got some saffron, boiled it and put its water on her face [so that it would yellow]; she also got some bread, toasted it, and placed it under her mattress [so that it would crackle whenever she moved]. She said [in a weak voice], "I am ill!" The king, her husband came to visit her. He saw how yellow her face was and how her bones [the bread] crackled whenever she turned to the right or to the left. She pretended to be [almost] dead. She said [in a feeble voice], "I need the heart and the liver of the ram that is in the Garden of Pearls and Coral, that is in the country of ogres."[611] The king replied, "Who can go there: to the land of ogres!" She said, "Aladdin" (meaning that the boy, her stepson, is the only one who can get it).

The king went to the cook and said to him, "My wife is ill; only Aladdin can get the medicine prescribed for her." The [cook] replied, "I will ask him." The cook told the boy. The boy said, "Let me consult my mother." When his mother and his maternal-aunts heard about the request, they cried and wailed and said to him [in anguish], "Your father's wife wants your destruction! She is sending you [to that place] so that you may never come back!" He replied, "With God's permission, I'll finish her off. I must go!" He left them crying and wailing; he went to the cook and said to him, "I will go but I need a horse and a sword." The cook told the king and the king said, "Give him whatever he needs."

Aladdin set out, carrying rations . . . to look for what? For the Garden of Pearls and Corals! He kept on going and going until he came to a spot [on the road where it branched out into three roads]: The Road of Safety, The Road of Regret, and The Road of He-Who-Goes-Doesn't-Return. He took The Road of He-Who-Goes-Doesn't-Return. He kept on going and going. O day, go, O day, come! O month, go, O month, come! O year, go, O year, come! [Years passed], until he finally came to a [populated] place. He saw an old man (*'ikhtiyâr*) sitting on the ground in front of his house. His beard was [down] to here [narrator, with the palm of her hand turned upward, touches her knee with the inner edge of her palm]; his fingernails were that long [about three joints on the index finger], and he was dusty and soiled. Aladdin said, "Peace be upon you." He replied, "Had your greeting not overcome [preceded] your speaking, I would have munched on your flesh along with your bones! What do you want, Aladdin?" He replied, "The Garden of Pearls and Coral, I seek it!" The old man—who was an ogre—said, "You are in the country of ogres; better go back! Your mother needs you."

Aladdin sat beside him. Beside him [the old man] there was a razor and other things used for shaving. He trimmed the [old man's] beard, clipped his fingernails, and cleaned his face. The old man said to him, "May God bless you. Go to my sister: She is a month older than I, [but] an epoch['s worth] more knowledgeable.[612] Suckle her breast and say to her,[613] 'I have suckled your breast and have come to be like [one of] your children.' "

He went on until he came to a woman standing in the middle of the road.

She had one foot in the East and one foot in the West, one breast hanging down in the front and one breast thrown over her back. [Narrator giggles.] He did as the old man had told him: he r-a-a-an to her, suckled her breast, licked some [granulated] sugar that was beside her, and said [in a hurry], "Peace be upon you, Mother Ogress![614] I've suckled your breast and I've become like [one of] your children!" She answered him, "Had your greeting not overcome your speaking, I would have munched on your flesh along with your bones! What do you seek, Aladdin?"

"I seek the Garden of Pearls and Coral!"

"Go back to your mother; between you and the Garden of Pearls and Coral, [there are] epochs' [worth] of travel."

"By God, I must get there!"

She said, "My son will be coming soon. He can take you there but he hates the race of humans (*jince el-'unûce*). If he sees you here, he will kill you, and devour you!"

She bewitched him into a pomegranate, and placed it on the table. When her son came home, he started sniffing around and saying, "I smell a human being." She—his mother—answered him [in anger], "[May] a human being [get stuck] between your molars, and [may] a sword cut off your head!"[615] [No such a being is here, damn it!] He sat down to rest and saw the pomegranate. He took it and before his mother could snatch it away from him, he had cracked it and sucked in all its seeds. One seed fell down on the floor and his mother hid it. He laid down and placed his head on his mother's knee [who sat down cross-legged]. She said to him—after he had quieted down—"If your brother were to visit you and ask a favor of you, what would you do?" He replied, "I would give him whatever he would ask for." She immediately turned the pomegranate seed into Aladdin and said, "He suckled my breast and has come to be [like] my son!"

He, the ogre, asked him, "What do you seek?"

"I seek the Garden of Pearls and Coral!"

"This is something that no person can reach. Between you and it [there] are years of travel. The garden is [annexed to] the crystal palace; the palace is on [the peak of] a high mountain; the palace and the mountain used to be inhabited by an ogress named Jundubah [i.e., She-grasshopper].[616] She devoured all its inhabitants. Those whom she did not devour ran away from her! Now she has assumed the form of a beautiful woman, and is married to a king. And if my knowledge is truthful, that king is your father, you are his son, and Jundubah the ogress is the wife of your father!"

He [Aladdin] said, "I want to get the ram that is in the garden. My father's wife is ill and she wants to eat its liver and heart."

He [the ogre] replied, "The ram's liver and heart will cure any ailment. But the ram is an ogre—he is asleep for a year, awake for a year.[617] You strike him once and he will die, but he will say to you, 'Repeat!'[618] You [should] reply, 'My mother did not teach me [to do so]!'[619] If you strike him again he will come back to life and will finish you off! As for Jundubah, her soul is in a crystal flask inside the palace. If you break the flask, she will die. Nothing else will kill her!!"

[The ogre gave him a stick with which to strike the palace, in order to drive it home.] Their mother, the ogress, said to them, "[Go] in God's safety!" He carried Aladdin on his back and [in a short time] placed him before the palace gate.

He [Aladdin] placed his hand on the gate, [suddenly] everything: the door, the bricks, the crystal, the trees, the birds—everything, everything began to shout, "A stranger! A stranger!" It chanced that the year of sleep was just about to elapse. The ram woke up quickly and came charging at him; he [Aladdin] struck it with his sword—with the side of the sword. The ram fell down snorting, and said, "O Aladdin, second it!" He replied, "My mother did not teach me [to do so]!" The ram dropped dead. As soon as it died, the palace door opened and everything started singing. He went in, looked for the flask until he found it in a safe. He also found the eyes of his mother and maternal-aunts in glass jars. He took all of them. He got the stick. (Oh! I had bypassed you with my talk.) The ogre had given him a stick and said to him, "When you get in, strike the floor of the palace with this stick and say:

> O you palace, that has chimed its [own] bells,
> and departed, and its inhabitants have [also] been gone,[620]
> Take me home!

The palace, the entire palace—all lighted up: its grounds, its gardens, its bells—all of it, all of it, all of it—began to move! It went from there to his home country, with its bells chiming!

When Aladdin arrived in his palace, he went to the kitchen and told the cook. The cook told the king, and the king came out to get the heart and liver of the ram. Aladdin told him the whole story. The king was very happy and said to him, "Truly, you are my son!"

He went to his mother in the dungeon. When she saw him—I mean when she heard him, she became thrilled. He put her eyes back [into their sockets] and placed some of the ram's liver and heart on them. Her eyes became like they were before. He restored the eyes of his mother and his maternal-aunts. He sprinkled the resuscitation water[621] on the bones of his brothers, whom their mothers had eaten. All of them came back to life. He went to Jundubah, the ogress. When she saw him, she became furious and went toward him [to attack]. He held the flask up and said, "Your soul is in my hands, you cursed one!" Before she could do anything, he smashed the flask on the floor. Jundubah dropped dead and [her corpse] evaporated like smoke.

His father reinstated his wives and they lived the rest of their live[s] happy and pleased, and may you, listeners, be safe [and well].[622]

[As for] the tale: we have narrated it, and in your bosom we dumped it![623]

❖ 31 ❖

FINGER JOINT[624]

(EGYPT, EASTERN DESERT)

NARRATED IN APRIL 1969 BY ¿AZÎZAH M.¿I., THIRTY-EIGHT YEARS OF AGE, ORIGINALLY A BEDOUIN, MOTHER OF A GIRL OF THREE, WHO LIVED WITH HER HUSBAND, THIRTY-TWO, AND HIS SECOND, YOUNGER AND FAVORED WIFE, IN AL-BASATÎN, A DISTRICT NEAR MA¿ADÎ, A SUBURB OF CAIRO, EGYPT, BORDERING THE EASTERN DESERT. SHE HAD HEARD THE TALE FROM HER MOTHER.

THE RECORDING TOOK PLACE IN THE PRESENT WRITER'S LIVING ROOM, IN THE PRESENCE OF ¿AZÎZAH'S HUSBAND AND THE WRITER'S WIFE. THE HUSBAND INSISTED ON THIS ARRANGEMENT SO THAT THE ACTIVITY WOULD BE A FAMILY AFFAIR. HE STATED, "WITH US [BEDOUINS], IT WOULD BE A GREAT DISGRACE FOR A WOMAN TO ENTER A STRANGER'S HOUSE OR TO SPEAK TO A MAN!" ¿AZÎZAH ENJOYED TELLING THE TALE AND WAS VIVIDLY EGO-INVOLVED IN ITS EVENTS. SHE USED TALE TELLING TO ATTRACT HER HUSBAND TO HER QUARTERS.[625]

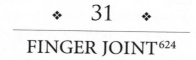

This fantasy-tale revolves around the rivalry between co-wives. A belief that plays a major role in the tale is that of the ṭulbah *(prayed-for child: an abnormal, usually physically deformed, child born in answer to prayer). As both the narrator and her husband asserted, a* ṭulbah*'s wishes are always answered by God, "just because of being a* ṭulbah *[handicapped]."*[626]

Yet, action in the tale occurs within a fairly realistic frame of reference and stage. The tale also contains an element of humor that evoked laughter repeatedly on the part of the narrator. This humor, however, seems to be of an esoteric nature and is meaningful mainly to a person with the narrator's real *experience as a co-wife for it accurately reflects her negative sentiments and hostile attitudes toward her younger and more attractive rival (co-wife) in real life.*

Religious laws (sharî¿ah) *concerning polygyny require a man to be utterly equitable, but adds: "Ye are never able to be fair and just as between women, even if it is your ardent desire" (Qur'ân, 4: 129). In congruence with the latter view, the tale demonstrates that the equal treatment by the husband of each of his two wives still did not prevent jealousy and hostility from developing between them. The equal treatment is also portrayed by the symmetrical structure the tale assumes when listing what "this one" wife received as compared with what "that one" wife received.*

It is interesting to note that the tale, and consequently, its narrator, reward the younger, aggressive, and tricky, but favorite wife. From an affective viewpoint, the attitudes the tale expresses toward the older, passive, and naive wife are exactly those that cause chagrin to the narrator in real life. Yet the narrator identified—or at least seemed to do so—with the younger wife, judging by observable events during the narrating process. Such an experience is typical vis-à-vis trickster tales.[627] *The narrator's husband—who would prefer to keep only the new wife—concluded, "I must [continue to] live in this misery" (cf. Mot.W14.8§).*

ONCE there was a woman who did not get pregnant. Finally she prayed to God, "God reward me with a girl child even if she happens to be as big as a finger joint."

God granted her a daughter that was as big as a finger's joint. When she grew up, she took the water jar and went to fill it with water [carrying the jar on top of her head]. Of course the jar was right next to the ground. [Narrator laughs.] One man was passing by and saw the jar and wondered, "Is this water jar moving by itself? Or is there somebody carrying it?"

They said to him, "No, there is somebody carrying it."

The man said, "Fine, I'll follow her and I'll marry her."

They said to him, "She is only a *ṭulbah* (prayer-child). She is as big as a finger joint. How are you going to get married to her?"

He said, "I'll just marry her and that's final."

He followed her to her house and sat down with her father, and said to him, "I wish to be of your relations by marriage" (*nasîbak*).

The father wondered, "Through whom!?"

He said, "Through your daughter."

He [the father] said, "I have no daughters! We prayed for her so that she may only serve us. She's as big as a finger's joint. Could such a thing get married?"

He answered, "I'll marry her and that is final."

He handed the father the money [for the dowry] and put her in his saddle-bag—for he was an Arab [Bedouin]. He put the saddle across the donkey's back and left. When he got home he reached for a window (like this one) and put her on its sill. She wasn't a real woman, so he just put her on the windowsill. After he put her on the windowsill, her co-wife (*ḍurrah*) came looking for some eggs in that window. She had—(do not blame me)—a chicken that used to lay eggs on the sill of that window. She reached into that window and Finger Joint said to her:

> Take your hand off
> May your hand get cut off!
> For I am your co-wife,
> and I'm here to make your life bitter.[628]

The woman said [narrator looks around], "Where is that co-wife?" She looked here and there; she didn't find anybody. Finally she saw her in the niche. She said to her, "Sister, why should you make my life bitter? You are welcome." So they lived in the same house.

One day he [the husband] brought this one twenty okes[629] of flour and that one twenty okes of flour. Finger Joint, the following morning, was eating her bread; she had already baked and had everything ready while the other one hadn't even started yet. (For Finger Joint was a prayer-child; whatever she wished for got done.)

Her co-wife came to her and asked, "What did you do!? How did it get done so soon?"

She answered her, "I prepared the dough and said, '*Bessssss, bessssss-bessssss,' and 'Kish-kish-kish,'*[630] so the cats and dogs came and baked it for me." ([Finger Joint said so because] she wanted to trick the other one [her co-wife]).

The other one, being so dumb, prepared the dough and called the dogs and the cats and shut them inside with the dough. [Narrator laughs.] Every time they fought with each other over the dough: "Ne-y-o-o-w! [Mew! Mew!]," Finger Joint would say to her, "Here you are, now they are baking. They are even toasting the bread for you!" The other one entered the room only to find the dough tray wiped clean; nothing in it. The cats and dogs were unable to move for they had their bellies so full. [Laughter.] Now she shrieked, "They didn't bake!"

Finger Joint said to her, "That's because you did not invite their chief! Had you invited their chief, he would have ordered them to work. He would have hit them and made them work. Now they have become disorganized, without a headman."

She said, "All right!"

The husband brought this one a jar of cheese and a jar of honey, and brought that one a jar of cheese and a jar of honey. In the morning Finger Joint had her door painted—(like this one). [Narrator points at a door in the collector's living room.] The other one asked her, "What did you do to the door?" She said to her, "I mixed the honey and cheese with my feet and splashed it [the mixture] on the door. That made it shiny."

The other one being so dumb, did as she told her. She splashed the door and the walls. All the flies in the world landed on it. [Narrator laughs.] She said to her, "How come my door is not like yours? What happened?"

Finger Joint answered, "That's because you did not mix it well. Had you mixed it well, flies wouldn't have gathered on it."

Now this one became pregnant—that is: this one got a loaded belly and that one got a loaded belly.[631] Finger Joint completed her months and delivered, and the other one completed her months and delivered. After delivery, Finger Joint's son was already saying, "Mother! Father!"

The other one asked her, "Sister, your baby is [already talking and] saying 'Mother! Father!' How come?"

She answered her, "You are not clever. Already I have prepared the oven and heated it well, put the baby in it, and baked him inside. He came out saying 'Mother! Father!'"

She said, "All right."

The other one, being so dumb, went, prepared the oven, heated it, cleaned it, and inserted her baby in it. The kid—(poor little thing! *yâ ¿ainî!*)—turned into a piece of coal.

She said [to Finger Joint], "Where is the kid, lady?"

She answered, "Maybe you did not prepare the oven properly. What could I do for you [you are hopelessly stupid]!"

Now the husband came home and found out about what had happened to his son. He beat the first wife and ordered her, "Go to your father's home!" He lived with Finger Joint in stability and prosperity and they begot boys and girls.

And I was there and just returned.

C. SIBLINGS

SISTER AND SISTER

❖ 32 ❖

ZLAIZLAH AND 'OMM-ZABA¿BA¿[632]

(EGYPT, WESTERN DESERT)

NARRATED IN APRIL 1982 BY KÂMLAH A. FROM BÂRÎS OASIS, WESTERN DESERT, EGYPT. SHE IS ABOUT SIXTY YEARS OLD AND A FARMER. KÂMLAH (AS AN OPERANT) WAS SEATED ON A MAT IN FRONT OF HER HOUSE, SHORTLY AFTER SUNSET, SURROUNDED BY FOUR YOUNG ADULT FEMALES AND ABOUT FIVE OR SIX YOUNG BOYS AND GIRLS. ONE OF THE WOMEN IN THE AUDIENCE WAS BREAST-FEEDING AN INFANT. IN THIS RELAXED ATMOSPHERE, SHE WAS TELLING TALES TO THAT TYPICAL AUDIENCE. KÂMLAH'S GRANDSON—A UNIVERSITY STUDENT, AND MY HOST IN THE OASIS—SECURED HER CONSENT TO PLACE A SMALL TAPE-RECORDER BESIDE HER AS SHE TOLD HER TALES. MY YOUNG HOST AND I WATCHED FROM A SHORT DISTANCE. THE NARRATOR STATED THAT SHE HAD LEARNED THIS TALE FROM AN ELDER WOMAN NARRATING TO THE YOUNG, AS SHE PUT IT, "[IN THE SAME MANNER] AS I AM TELLING IT NOW."

Sibling rivalry among stepsisters is the focal point of this tale. Obedience, conformity, and flattery of authority are presented as the means for success. A balanced view toward various objects in one's environment is portrayed; thus things that are typically viewed as evil are still accorded some positive value.[633] *Evidently, this consideration is not extended to a stepmother or stepsister. In this tale, as in numerous others, the father is powerless and is assigned no real role.*[634]

THERE was a woman whom God had not compensated by [granting her] any children. She prayed to God, "O God, my Lord, grant me a child; if it happened to be a girl, I will dress her in silk and undress her in silk!" God accepted [her plea] and granted her a baby girl. She raised her in luxury; she dressed her in silk dresses. Whenever a dress got soiled she would not wash it, but would use it to wipe her daughter['s feces] and would throw it out in the [neighbor's] yard. That woman neighbor collected these dresses; she took them, washed them, and kept them until she had a full bolt.

When the girl grew up—that girl's name was Zlaizlah—she went to visit their neighbor (that woman who had been taking the diapers, with Zlaizlah's stuff in them). That woman was a seamstress. She had a daughter, [but] her daughter was ugly; her name was 'Omm-Zaba¿ba¿. That woman said to Zlaizlah, "Look at that silk dress!" Zlaizlah said to her, "By the Prophet, maternal-aunt, let me try it on!" She answered her, "If you want to have it, close the [lid of the] chest that you have at your home on your mother's neck. If you do that, I will give you the dress!"

The girl went home and as her mother was getting something out of the chest—(like this, [narrator illustrates how far one's head and neck would be inside a chest when reaching to its bottom])—the girl, her own daughter who is her own flesh and blood, rushed and slammed the lid shut on her neck. The woman fell down without making a sound. The girl—(of course, she was young and did not understand)—went to that neighbor woman and said, "I did as you told me, now give me the dress!" She said to her, "First, say to your father, marry our neighbor so that she may serve us. After [you have done] that, I will give you the dress!"

Zlaizlah went to her father and said, "Father, marry our neighbor." He replied, "Girl, your mother has not been dead for a [full] week yet! Her blood hasn't dried up yet in her grave! And you want me to marry!" She answered, "Our neighbor is a fine woman; who will grind and bake for us? Who will look after you?" She said to him all these things which that seamstress neighbor had told her to say. The man said, "All right, since this is what you want!" He married that neighbor woman of theirs.

When the woman moved in she could not bear the sight of her husband's daughter. She finally said to him, "It is either I or she." The man couldn't say a thing. The father's wife kept on feeding her oat bread while she fed her own daughter wheat bread and cookies.

Her mother had left her a heifer. The heifer gave her whatever [food] she wished for. The other girl, the daughter of her father's wife, pretended to be ill; they brought *figî* (Qur'ân recitalist, preacher)[635] and gave him something [a bribe] in order to say, "Her medicine is in [eating the meat of] this heifer!" The girl [Zlaizlah] cried and cried, but the heifer told her, "Don't cry. Take [some] of my skin, flesh, and bones and bury them. I will grow for your sake (*'aṭla¿-lik*) in the form of a cat. I will provide for you even better than the heifer did!"

The other girl, the daughter of her father's wife, kept on saying to her mother, "Mother, I can't stand the sight of her!" Finally she [the stepmother] decided to get rid of her. She sent her to Mother Ogress and instructed her, "Go to Mother Ogress and say to her, 'My father's wife wants the wide-grid sieve,[636] the whip,[637] and the chains of the mighty'."[638]

ASIDE

A girl in the audience explains: "She wanted to get rid of her husband's daughter."

She went down the road to the house of Mother Ogress. On her way she saw two date palm trees, a male and a female, quarreling: the female would say [narrator speaks in a tone denoting contention], "I am the female. I bear fruit!" Then the male would retort, "No, I am the male. I am better!" When they saw her, they asked her, "Who is better, I, the female, or he, the male?" She replied [narrator speaks in a conciliatory tone], "You are the female; you yield fruit that is good for us, and he is the male that yields pollen[639] that we use to make you bear fruit. You can't do without him, and he would be worthless without you!" When the two palm trees heard that they said to her [in a tone denoting contentment], "Go, May God make our length in your hair and not in your legs!" So her hair became long. After a while she met two birds—a [white] she-dove and a raven—quarreling; the she-dove would say, "I am better than you are!" and the raven would say, "No! I am better than you are!" She said to them, "You, she-dove, are good, and he, the raven is also good! White is fine, like milk; black is also fine; without the black [pupils] of the eye, we would not be able to see! You, [she-dove] give us baby chicks to eat, and you [raven] clean up the place [by eating rats and dead animals]. So, you are good and he is good." The she-dove said to her, "Go. May God make my whiteness in your face, not in your hair!" And the raven said, "Go. May God make my blackness in your hair, not in your face!" [Thus, her face became white and her hair black.]

She continued [going] down the road. She met two—a rose and a bee arguing. The rose would say, "I am better!" and the bee would retort, "No, I am better." She said to them, "You, the rose, are red and fragrant, and you, the bee, give us sweet honey!" The rose said to her, "May God make my redness in your cheeks and not in your eyes!" And the bee said, "May God make my honey['s sweetness] in your mouth [words], and my sting not in your tongue!"[640]

Then she came to two threshing grounds; one was a sesame threshing ground, while the other was . . . [pause] (that thing from which they make oil . . . , 'May God pray on behalf of the Prophet!').[641]

ASIDE

A little girl in the audience replies: *gurṭom!* (i.e., *qurṭom,* safflower!).

[Narrator continues]: " . . . the other was safflower!" They also were quarreling. She reconciled the two of them.[642] The sesame and the safflower said to her, "Take some [sesame] from me," "Take some of my safflower oil."

That was it, of course, she became beautiful, with long black hair, white complexion, black eyes, rosy cheeks and a honey-dripping tongue. She reached the house of Mother Ogress. When she reached the house of Mother Ogress, she [the ogress] asked her, "What do you want?" She answered, "May God give you health. My father's wife sent me and said, 'Go to Mother Ogress and say to her, My father's wife wants the wide-grid sieve, the whip, and the chains of the mighty!'" Mother Ogress said to her, "All right! [Before I do so] go dirty the house up, move the [farm] animals into the sun and starve them, dirty the [cooking] utensils, soil the children, and pierce their eyes!" She [Zlaizlah] said, "Will do, Mother Ogress!" She found the house dirty; so she swept it clean and sprinkled water on the [earthen] floor, dusted off the furniture. She went to the cattle enclosure (zariba, *zerîbah*) and found all the animals tied up in the sun, and the feeding platform (*madwid*) empty; so she moved them into the shade, cleaned the feeding platform and filled it with [fresh] chaff (*tibn*), beans and barley. [She went back into the house and found the cooking area dirty.] She cleaned up the mud stove (*kanûn*), and put fresh fire-brush (*ḥaṭab*) beside it, took the copper [utensils], cleaned and polished them. She found the children dirty and their clothes ragged; so she bathed them, changed their clothes, and put kohl in their eyes: [thus] a house cleaner than that [of Mother Ogress] was not to be found. When she [Zlaizlah] finished, she went to Mother Ogress and said, "Mother Ogress, I am done! Now give me the wide-grid sieve for my father's wife!" She said to her, "Come and louse me (*fallînî*)." Zlaizlah got the fine-toothed comb (*fallâyah*) and sat down [behind the ogress]; every time she ran the comb through, lice would come out by the heap. She [Zlaizlah, who had sesame seeds in her pocket] would take one sesame seed [place it on the nail of the thumb of one hand and squash it against the nail of the thumb of the other hand], put the squashed sesame in her mouth and say [in exclamation], "O Mother Ogress, your lice are delicious!"

That was it! Mother Ogress took her and placed her in the [magic] well, and said [in a commanding voice], "O well, O well! Dress her in plenty of silk [clothes]! O well, O well! Adorn her with plenty of gold and ruby [jewelry]! O well, O well! . . . and O well, O well . . . [do such and such for her]!" When she [Zlaizlah] came out, she had become beautiful—(and no one is beautiful except [Prophet] Mohammad!)—and had everything: dresses, gold, and whatever one desires. She [the ogress] gave her the wide-grid sieve, [the whip], and the chains of the mighty. She took them and went home.

When she knocked on the door—of her father's house—the wife of her father opened the door, [she struck her chest and exclaimed:] "Oh, what a calamity for me (*yâ-â-â lahwitî-î-î*)! Where did you get all these things? You must have murdered someone!" She replied, "No, by the Prophet! Mother Ogress gave them to me!"

The father's wife said [shrieking in a subdued voice:] "Hey, you! 'Omm-Zaba¿ba¿! [Audience giggles.] You unnameable [thing]![643] Come here! See what your father's daughter got from Mother Ogress! Go do like she did and get [some] of what she has gotten!"

'Omm-Zaba¿ba¿ said [in a grumbling tone], "And what business of mine is it (*wa-nâ mâlî*)!?[644] I will not go!"

Her mother pushed her out the door and said [in shouting], "If you don't go to Mother Ogress, ask her for the wide-grid sieve, the whip, and the chains of the mighty, and bring back [fine things] like those your father's wife's daughter has brought, your day will be black!"

'Omm-Zaba¿ba¿ went down the same road as did her sister. ([Narrator explains:] I had bypassed you with my talk. As Zlaizlah came home, she told her father's wife and her daughter about what had happened between her and the male palm tree and the female palm tree, the black raven and the white she-dove, the rose and the sesame—[she told] of all of it.)

ASIDE

A young girl in the audience comments: "*¿ashân yatîmah w-bint ḥalâl!*" (Because she [Zlaizlah] is an orphan and of legitimate birth [i.e, in spite of suffering deprivation, she remained good-hearted, and thus, deserving of God's reward]). Cf. Tale No. 14, note 322.

(Now, to whom would our resumption of the tale take us? To 'Omm-Zaba¿ba¿!) She met the two palm trees—the male and the female. They were still reconciled and leaning [narrator indicates with a movement of her hands that they leaned to and fro] against each other. She ['Omm-Zaba¿ba¿] said to them [in a disgruntled, sour voice], "My, my! By God! Aren't you two [too] tall, and your height is blah (*mâsikh*). You, male! You are good for nothing except for making brooms and baskets [out of your fiber and fronds]. The two palm trees became vexed and said to her [cursing], "Go! May God make our height in your legs, not in your hair!" [Audience laughs.]

She went down the road. She came across the she-dove and the raven. She said to them [in a sour voice], "You she-dove, you fly about inside our house and make droppings all over. Besides you are all white and your whiteness is vapid! And you raven, you are a snatcher and your face brings disaster [a bird of ill omen]; [besides] you are black and your blackness is vapid!" The she-dove and the raven became vexed with her; the she-dove said, "Go! May God make my whiteness in your hair, not in your face!" And the raven said, "Go! May God make my blackness in your face, not in your hair!"

She went down the road; she met the bee and the rose. She said to the bee, "By God, bee! You are a buzzer and your buzzing is vapid. You sting. Who needs you! As for you rose, your presence is like your absence; your thorns hurt and there is no benefit in you [you are inedible]!" The bee said to her, "Go! May God make my sting in your tongue, not in your walk [in a brisk manner]!" And the rose said to her, "Go! May God make my redness in your eyes, not in your cheeks!" Now she had become—(away from you)—something! A disgrace: palm-tree-length legs, black face, white short hair, poison-dripping tongue, red eyes, and could hardly move.

When she reached the house of Mother Ogress she said to her, "My mother wants the wide-grid sieve, the whip, and the chains of the mighty!" (She did not say [as good manners require], "Peace be upon you!" or "May God grant you health!" or anything [of that sort]!) Mother Ogress said to her, "All right! Go dirty the house up!" 'Omm-Zaba¿ba¿ [quickly] replied, "I am not your servant! Do it yourself!" Mother Ogress said, "Move the [farm] animals from the shade into the sun!" She replied, "Are you crazy! You keep the animals in the shade!" But when she went to move them, the jackass kicked her and sent her reeling on the messy ground [listeners roar with laughter]. Mother Ogress said to her, "Clean up the kitchen!" She replied, "I am not your servant. Do it yourself!"

"Bathe the children!"

"I am not your father's servant! Bathe them yourself!"

"Get me some firewood for the fire-pit!"

"I am not your father's servant! Are you a cripple!? Or are you a cripple!? Get it yourself!"

That was all! Mother Ogress said to her, "Come here!" She took her and put her inside the well and said [in a commanding voice], "O well, O well, cover her with plenty of dung beetles! O well, O well, dress her in plenty of snakes! O well, O well, heap [evil things][645] on her; . . . and—(away from you)—when she came out, she was "something that no one would wish [even] on a worst enemy!" [Audience is clearly delighted.]

As she went home people would take one look at her and say, "Close the doors! Shut the windows!" When she reached home to her mother, she knocked at the door. [Her mother answered], "Who is it?"

"I am 'Omm-Zaba¿ba¿, mother!" [Audience laughs.] "Open up for me." Her mother opened the door and (shrieked in horror), "Oh, what a calamity for me!" [Audience roars with laughter.] "Out! Out!" She kicked her out, and—(away from you)—got a broom and started sweeping off all the things that she had on her body.

It chanced that the emir's son had seen Zlaizlah while she was returning from the house of Mother Ogress. He wished to marry her. He sent [emissaries to her father] to say, "We want your daughter for the emir's son!" He replied, "Good and blessed." They wrote the marriage contract and set the day for the carrying away [of the bride to her husband's home] (*esh-shailah*).[646] On the carrying day, the mother of 'Omm-Zaba¿ba¿ got hold of Zlaizlah, tied her up, and forced her into one of those small grain bins [on the roof of the house]. She dressed her own daughter in the bridal gown and placed the [bridal] veil on her face.

The groom's family, and of course the groom, came to get their bride. The emir's son said, "I want to see my bride!" The woman—who is the mother of 'Omm-Zaba¿ba¿—said [in feigned shock], "Oh, no! What a disgrace. When she gets to your home and becomes your wife you may look at her all you want!" The procession went on: drumming, pipe playing, and ululations [of joy by women], and, naturally, the camel carrying the bride in the howdah was up front.

The cat [that Zlaizlah had] went in front of the wedding procession saying, "The crow-faced [girl] is on the howdah, [while] the moon-faced [girl] is in the grain bin!" People stopped and wondered, "What is this cat saying?" The woman [mother of 'Omm-Zaba¿ba¿] would say, "Nothing; it is only a cat! Are you going to listen to a cat! Are you crazy!"

The procession went on, but the cat kept on saying, "The crow-faced is on the howdah, but the moon-faced is in the bin!" Finally, the emir's son said [emphatically], "By God, I must see who is in the howdah!" He made the camel kneel. When he took the veil off the face [of the fake bride], he found—(away from you)—something that could not be looked at. They all went to Zlaizlah's home and found her tied up and crammed inside the grain bin.

They said, "He who loves the Chosen Prophet would set that witch and her daughter afire."

Zlaizlah married the emir's son, and she went to live with her man.

And they lived in stability and prosperity.

❖ 33 ❖

PEARLS-ON-VINES[647]

(EGYPT)

NARRATED IN APRIL 1971 BY *ES-SIT* TAḤIYYAH, THE SEAMSTRESS (SEE INFORMANT NOTE TO TALE NO. 15). SHE HAD HEARD IT FROM AN ELDER NEIGHBOR GIRL NAMED BASHAWÂT SOME FORTY YEARS EARLIER; SHE NARRATED IT OCCASIONALLY TO HER APPRENTICES DURING WORK.

The affective core of this fantasy-tale is rivalry among sisters. At first, they vie for the father's attention; then jealousy and conflict develop over a supernatural lover, who is not a paternal figure. No mention is made of a mother for these daughters.

*The image of a male snake ('*ḥanash*') going through a crack or a hole in the wall—adorned, perfumed, and flowered—into a maiden's chamber and causing her enviable pleasure symbolizes an act the narrator found too risqué to verbalize. Within the context of folk beliefs, reports of intimate liaisons between a human and a jinni of the opposite sex are quite common.*[648]

The drastic punishment dealt the two elder sisters is an even match to the fate of black slave-women who compete with a "white" woman for the attention of her man.[649]

ONCE there was, and there was plenty, a king—(and no one is King but God). That king had three girls; his daughters, one that was the eldest, a second that was in the middle, and the third was the youngest. One day the king wished to go to Hejaz. So, he called the eldest daughter and said to her, "I—if God wills—will set out on pilgrimage; what do you wish I bring back with me for you?" She replied [in a greedy excessive tone], "I want the moon and the stars!" He said to her [in a resigned tone], "All right, eldest daughter of mine!" He then called the one who was in the middle and said to her, "I am setting out for pilgrimage to visit the Prophet"—(may the best praise and greetings be upon him)—"What do you wish I bring back for you with me?" She replied [in a greedy, excessive tone], "I want you to bring me a mortar [and a pestle] that people in the countries of Sind and India can hear." He said to her [in a disappointed tone], "All right, middle daughter of mine!" After that he called the youngest one. She was the sweetest [or, the prettiest] of all three. Just as he asked the first two, he asked that one, who was the third, "What do you wish I bring back for you from Hejaz?" She replied [in a soft tone indicating compassion and modesty], "O Papa, I want nothing except your safety, [to see again] the [dignity of the] wrapping of [the of the shawl around] your turban, and your sitting home in the way to which you are used!"[650] As soon as the king heard her say that, he was very pleased and said to her, "Well, daughter of mine, may God bless you. You are the one [who is the best] among them!"[651] And he left the room.

The following day, her two sisters went to the king (who is their father) and asked him [in a sly manner], "What did our young sister ask for?" He replied to them [in admiration], "She asked for nothing except my safe return and said to me, 'I want nothing except your safety, the wrapping of your turban, and your sitting at home in the way to which you are used!' " The two said to him [narrator speaks in a sly, mischievous manner], "A-a-a-h! That youngest sister of ours! By God, she wants—(away from you)—your death; it is the custom that when someone is going away on a long trip to ask him for something so that he may return with that something. Our sister asked for nothing so that you may not return! She must ask for something!"

When the king heard that talk, he became very angry and went to the youngest one and said [in a resolute tone], "You are wishing that I never return! You must ask for something!" The girl replied, "But I already have everything that I [may] wish for!" He said to her, "There is no use [dodging the issue]; you will ask for something!"

The girl stayed in the room and kept on weeping; she thought and thought and thought: she was not in need of anything. She looked out of the window, still thinking, while her tears were rolling down her cheeks. Her tears fell. It chanced that a very old woman was passing underneath the window. That old woman had a plate full of henna on top of her head; the tears of the king's daughter fell on the henna and turned it into a paste [thus ruining it]. The old woman looked upward and saw that girl looking out the window with her tears coming down her cheeks. "You, young woman—are you in love or crazy?" She, replied [in despair], "I am neither in love nor crazy. Keep going on your own path and leave me in my [own sorrowful] condition!" The old woman said to her [in an imploring and compassionate voice], "Just tell me about your grief, maybe I can help you." So, the girl told her, "My father is setting out for Hejaz and wants me to ask him for something to bring back. I told him, 'I want nothing except your safety, the wrapping of your turban, and your sitting at home in the way to which you are used!' He became angry and said, 'You want my death!' "

The old woman said to her [in a tone indicating how simple the problem is], "Do not occupy your mind [with this matter]. When your father comes again and asks you 'What shall I bring back for you?' say to him, 'I want the Pearls-on-Vines. And I will take nothing else except that!' "

The girl heard that talk of the old woman; she ceased weeping. A short while later her father came and said, "What is the thing you want me to bring back for you?" She immediately answered him, "I want you to bring back for me Pearls-on-Vines!" He did not say anything and left.

When the time for his trip came, all the people [in the kingdom] went out to say to him, "Peace be with you." (You see, in older times people used to travel to Hejaz by boat or on camelback; some even traveled on foot. It used to take, maybe, six months or even a year for a person to go on pilgrimage and return.)

When he got there—of course, after he had finished his pilgrimage—he went to the souk and got the dress with the moon and the stars for his eldest daughter, and he got the mortar [and the pestle] that could be heard in Sindland and India. Naturally these things cost him plenty. But when he asked about Pearls-on-Vines, merchants would answer him, "We have this and we have that!" [No one would speak to him about what he was asking for.] He kept on inquiring until the market day was over and everyone returned home. So, he said [to himself], "I have done what is expected of me. After all, she did not want anything." And he packed up his things and boarded the ship.

So the ship sailed—two or three days later, the salty sea became turbulent and wavy; the ship—the one with the pilgrims who were returning home—was about to sink, naturally it was loaded because everyone had with him plenty of God's boon, that he was taking home [as presents] to his family and neighbors [as the custom requires]. The captain shouted [narrator speaks in a tone denoting distress], "You, God's worshippers! Has any one of you sinned? Has any one of you left [Hejaz] without paying a debt? Has any one of you forgotten a promise? We will have to lighten up the load!"

When the king heard the words, "Has any one forgotten a promise?" he said to the captain [apologetically], "A-â-â-âh! It is I who am the cause of this distress. I did not get Pearls-on-Vines for my daughter!" That was all; they put him on a boat and set him at sea in the direction of land. As soon as they had done so the wind subsided and the sea quieted. The ship went in one direction, and the boat went in the other.

When the king reached land, he kept on asking whomever he met, "Can you tell me [anything] about Pearls-on-Vines?" But no one would tell him anything: this one would say, "No, by God, I know nothing!" That one would say, "Paternal-uncle, keep away from me for I have children [to support]!" And that one would say, "If you want pearls, you go to the gold market!" Finally, after he had grown dizzy of going around, he sat down next to a tree in the desert; he [laid down], rested his head on his elbow, and fell asleep. In his sleep he saw a green snake. He [the snake] spoke to him [narrator speaks in a tone portraying a short-tempered person], "I hear that you have been asking about me! I am Pearls-on-Vines! What do you want from me?" The king replied, "My youngest daughter asked me to bring back for her Pearls-on-Vines. She said, 'I will take nothing but that.'" He answered, "Has your daughter seen me?" The king replied, "No!" He said, "I am the one whom she wants. I am Pearls-on-Vines, the son of the king of the Moslem jinn! Tell your daughter to bore a hole in the wall of her room, sprinkle it with rosewater, and cover it with roses. I will come to her when the time comes!"

The king awoke and returned to his home. When he got there, of course, all the [people in the] kingdom went out to receive him, along with drumming, pipe playing, and trellises of joy [made by women] (*zagharîṭ*). He gave his eldest daughter the dress adorned by the moon and the stars; he also gave the mortar that when pounded can be heard in Sind-land and India. The eldest wore her dress and kept on walking around [coquettishly] in a waggly manner; the middle one got her mortar and kept on pounding it—people in Sind-land and India heard her pounding—until everyone got headache from the noise. [Narrator laughs.]

Now, to whom do we turn? To the youngest! Her father said to her [in mild anger], "The thing that you asked for was about to sink the ship! Pearls-on-Vines says to you. . . . " He [her father] told her what Pearls-on-Vines had told him to tell her—that: "You should make a hole in the wall of your room, sprinkle it with rosewater, and cover it with roses . . . " and everything. She did what her father told her, what that Pearls-on-Vines had said.

One night, as she was in her room, she heard a sound and saw the roses—the roses that were covering the hole—stir. She looked [only] to find a snake creeping inside the room and: Oo-oo-ps!, with the power of the Almighty—he became an Adamite [i.e., a human being] standing in front of her. She looked and saw a young man who was beautiful (and no one is beautiful except Our Master, Mohammad). That was all. She appealed to him, and they fell in love. He kept on coming to her through that hole in the wall; they would pass their time together in what? . . . [Narrator does not answer this question.]

Now to whom do we return? To her two sisters: one wearing the dress with the moon and the stars, and the other pounding her mortar that is audible in Sind and India.[652] [Narrator laughs and comments: (that was what they had chosen).] They kept on asking their youngest sister, "What did you get?" (I had bypassed you with my talk: the son of the king of the jinn, who is [in the form of] the snake, had said to her [in a warning and ominous tone], "If you were to tell anyone about me, that I am the son of the king of the jinn, or that I assume the form of a human, you will never find me.")[653] So, she would tell them, "Nothing! I am still waiting!"

O day, come, O day, go! O month, come, O month go! O year, come, O year, go! [Days, months, and years passed.] The two older sisters wondered, "How could it be that our youngest sister got nothing and she looks happy. She is always in her room with the door locked! Something must be the matter!"

They hid in the garden to see what was happening. One night they saw that green snake coming through the garden and creep into that hole. They looked through the hole; they saw the snake turn into a young man; [he was] handsome! handsome! handsome! (And no one is handsome except Mohammad.) That was all! Fire of jealousy was ignited—(away from you)—in their hearts. They said, "How could that be? We are the older and still remain unmarried! She is the youngest! We must find a way to get rid of that snake!"

They went and got some bottles and pounded them until the glass became like powder; they put that pounded glass inside the hole through which the snake went into their sister's room. In the morning, as the snake was leaving, he crept through the hole; the glass—(away from you)—slashed every spot of his body. He howled and disappeared.

Our friend [i.e., the youngest sister] waited for the son of the king of the jinn to return, but he did not. She waited and waited but neither a sound nor a piece of news [reached her]. Her two older sisters kept on poking at her: "O our dear youngest sister, why do you seem to be so sad?" "Have you gotten what you have asked our father for?" And things like that. But she did not reveal the secret of the snake, who was the son of the king of the jinn. Finally, when her waiting became too long, and her patience overflowed (*fâḍ bîhâ*), she went to someone—one of those people who tell fortune, open the Book (*yiftahû el-kitâb*) [i.e., the Holy Book], and other things like that. She said to him, "Tell me about the thing that is occupying my mind!" He opened the Book (or did whatever these people do to tell fortunes), and said to her, "You will not find the one for whom you are waiting except after searching for seven years, seven months, seven days, seven hours, seven minutes, and seven seconds!"

She went home and asked for rations to be prepared for her; she wore men's clothing, and set out to look for the son of the king of the jinn. [Narrator speaks in a tone denoting fatigue and sorrow.] One country would carry her, and another would put her down.[654] She kept on asking about the son of the king of the jinn, but no one knew anything about him. She asked about Pearls-on-Vines. People ran away from her (not knowing, naturally, that she was not a man).

One day as she sat beneath a tree, it was midday and it was midsummer and very hot, she heard sounds coming from the top of the tree. She listened and heard two cooing-doves[655] talking. One said to her sister [in a tone denoting secrecy], "O my sister cooing-dove, did you hear about Pearls-on-Vines, and what happened to him?" The other said [in an inquisitive tone], "No, my sister cooing-dove, what happened?" [The first said,] "He fell in love with a human girl. She betrayed him and put broken glass in his path. The glass slashed his body. Now he is lying in bed in his father's palace between the seven seas; [he is] between life and death. He has sworn that as soon as he is well again, to go and kill that human whom he had loved!" The other cooing-dove asked, "Will God cure him?" The first answered, "No one knows! But all the doctors have given up. But, you know, the only cure for him is my liver and yours! If they were to take my liver and yours, roast them, pound them till they become like powder, and sprinkle it on the wounds of Pearls-on-Vines, he would be healed!" The other one said [with concern], "Sister, spit [that] out of your mouth [i.e., wish that you never said what you've just said]. Someone may hear us!" The first said, "No one is here except you and I."

Our friend, sitting down there, heard all that. She did not [even] breathe. Because of the heat, and because it was noon, the two birds went to sleep. Our friend climbed the tree [narrator whispers the words so as to denote caution] until she reached the two birds [narrator reaches out with her hands], and she stretched her hand and: Oo-oo-oo-oo-ps! [Narrator simulates the swift movement of a hand snatching a bird.] She got hold of the two. She mentioned God's name over them[656] and slaughtered them; she took their livers, roasted them and pounded them until they became powder. She traveled until she reached that place "between the seven seas." She came to a palace with a huge gate. Guards were standing at the gate of that palace. She said to them, "You have an ailing man; I am a doctor. The remedy for your ailing man is with me only!" The guards did not doubt the news[657] and ran to their master to tell him, "Master, there is a man outside; he says, The remedy for your ailing man is with me only." He [Pearls . . .] said, "Let him enter!"

When she entered his room, she found him on his bed; his mother was crying over him. His body was all slashed up and he was saying [in a sorrowful and threatening tone], "O you Adamite girl, I have forsaken my own people for you. I fell in love with you and revealed to you my secrets. You betrayed me! I make a pledge (*nadr*) that as soon as I am healed, I will find you and kill you in the same way that you tried to kill me!"

She said to him, "Before I begin to heal you—and only God is the Healer—you must promise me something. You must promise not to leave this room until you have heard a story that I will tell!" He said [in a tone denoting resignation and weakness], "I agree. Give me your medicine."

She took out that medicine—the livers of the two cooing-doves, and looked at his body. His body—(away from you and me)—was all slashed up and glass was still stuck to the wounds. She cleaned it and sprinkled powder on it. And she waited. In a day his wounds crusted, in another the crust fell off, and on the third he was as before. He immediately jumped out of his bed and shouted [narrator imitates the tone and intensity, but in a low voice, the tone of a prince giving commands] "Get me my sword! Get me my dagger! For I am going to kill her." She—still dressed in a man's clothing—said to him [in a reprimanding tone], "But you promised to wait until you have heard the story that I will tell to you!" He replied, "Hurry, say it!"

She began by telling him, "There were three sisters; their father wanted to go on pilgrimage and he asked each one, 'What would you wish me to bring back for you . . . ' " and, and, and how the older sisters became jealous and put the glass, that they had pounded, in the hole which Pearl-on-Vines passed through, and . . . , and . . . , and . . . , [she told him the whole story]. When she finished, he exclaimed, "How do you know all that?" [Narrator pretends to be taking off the man's outer-garment.] She replied, "I am the youngest, and I am the one who asked for you and the one with whom you fell in love. Now, if you wish to kill me, kill me."

They went to the king, who is the girls' father. They told him the whole story. He ordered, "He who loves the Chosen Prophet would set these two [wicked sisters] afire."

They held a forty-day and forty-night wedding celebration. She married Pearls-on-Vines.

And they lived in stability and prosperity and begot boys and girls.

❖ 33-1 ❖

WITHOUT A TITLE

(EGYPT)

NARRATED IN 1972 BY *MUSTASHÂR* (SUPERIOR COURT JUSTICE) M.Z., FORTY-FIVE YEARS OLD; HE WAS LIVING WITH HIS FAMILY IN CAIRO, BUT HAILED FROM THE VILLAGE OF BENÎ-ḤUSAIN (NEAR ZAQAZIQ—HOME OF THE ABOVE RENDITION OF THE TALE, NO. 33), SHARQIYYAH GOVERNORATE, NORTHEASTERN EGYPT. HE HEARD THE TALE FOR THE FIRST TIME "MORE THAN THIRTY-FIVE YEARS EARLIER," FROM HIS LIVE-IN NURSE ṢIDDÎQAH. HE HAD NEVER TOLD THE TALE UNTIL THEN, WHEN HIS DAUGHTER ASKED HIM FOR A *ḤADDÛTAH* (FANTASY-TALE) AS PART OF HER COLLECTING PROJECT FOR A COLLEGE FOLKLORE CLASS. THIS TEXT WAS COLLECTED AND WRITTEN DOWN IN ARABIC BY MISS MÂGDÂ ZUHDÎ.[658]

The following is an idiosyncratic rendition, a fragment, constituting an adult male's recollection of the female-bound tale given under No. 33.[659] *Significantly, the rivalry among sisters is dissipated, and transformed into a political conflict (war). The attitude expressed toward an "ugly" slave-girl is devoid of the hostility characteristic of females' attitudes toward slave-girls (Mot. P187§, "Inherent rivalry between mistress and young female slave"), and is replaced by legal or ethical considerations (keeping a promise).*

In a follow-up, the present writer summarized the tale as it is typically told, and asked the narrator for his reaction to that text. In a written reply, the narrator pointed out that he recognized as "familiar" the oral formulas uttered by "the youngest sister as she replied to her father"—[a father's dream as to how a daughter should be], the dialogue of the two pigeons, and the general plot.

The loss of the original data on the part of our present narrator may be due to any of a number of factors: being a child who has undergone resocialization into becoming a "male" (whereas a female child does not undergo such a process),[660] *mere forgetting due to the passage of time, inhibition or suppression of knowledge and sentiments perceived as "women's stuff," or elite education that condemns feelings of jealousy and conspiracy.*

THE sultan had a son whose name was Clever Ḥasan. It happened that the sultan's enemies wanted to lay a snare for him. One day the sultan's son, Clever Ḥasan, went to the [public] bath to bathe. So they pounded glass into tiny pieces that entered into his entire body, and he got to be sick. He remained ailing for a long time and his body[661] would not heal. The sultan was at a loss; he brought doctors from "Sind, India, and countries [whose inhabitants] ride elephants."[662] He would ask whoever came [to treat his son] to wish for a grant [to be given in case he cured the ailing son]. All [of those who came] kept on treating him, but he would not be cured.

The sultan had a slave-girl (*gâryah*) to whom no one paid any attention because she was not beautiful and [she was also] ugly. So she was always bemoaning her luck, sadness-ridden, and keeping to herself in isolation whenever she had nothing to do.

One day—as she was sitting under a tamarisk tree, while her tears were running down her cheeks because no one was paying attention to her—she looked and found two cooing-doves perched on a tree. She heard them saying, "O sister cooing-dove, do you know what [medicine] will cure the sultan's son?" She [the other cooing-dove] replied, "[No!] What?" She [the first] said, "My liver in addition to yours, my gizzard in addition to yours, and my lungs in addition to yours; [all] are to be toasted dry, pounded [into powder], and distributed [i.e., sprinkled] on the body of the sultan's son. He would then be immediately healed, with permission of the Compassionate [i.e., God]."

The slave-girl thought about that talk. And with deliberate, slow, stealthy steps[663] she extended her hand slowly and grabbed the two cooing-doves. She went to the kitchen, slaughtered them and took the lung[s], the liver, and the gizzard of the two cooing-doves; she roasted them and prepared them and went to the sultan. She said to him, "I have the treatment for my sire, Clever Ḥasan!"

He [the sultan] scoffed at her and said, "No one left but you, ugly one!"

She replied, "Try me, and if he is not cured, put me to death."

So the sultan—after [such an] attempt on her part—agreed to her [request] and said, "And if he were to be cured at your hand, my kingship would be at your feet,[664] and Clever Ḥasan will be your lot [in life]."

She uttered the name of the Compassionate, took off all Clever Ḥasan's clothes, and anointed his body [with the medicine]. Glass started falling out, piece by piece. He began to get well and was healed. When he got on his feet, completely sound, the sultan brought her and said to her, "An honorable person's promise is a debt.[665] I made a promise to you: Clever Ḥasan [as husband]." He married her to him and set up wedding celebrations for forty nights less a night.

And they lived in stability and prosperity and begot boys and girls.

❖ 34 ❖

THE FISHERMAN'S DAUGHTER

(OMAN)

NARRATED IN JUNE 1986 BY NÔRA BINT-J. FROM ṢALÂLHAH, OMAN. SHE IS A DIVORCEE, ABOUT SIXTY YEARS OLD, AND WORKS AS CUSTODIAN IN THE FEMALE WING OF A HOSPITAL. SHE HAD HEARD THE TALE IN HER CHILDHOOD FROM WOMEN IN HER FAMILY, AND FROM THE NEIGHBORHOOD.

A basic form of the Cinderella tale type, based on the key motifs of slipper test (H36.1) and lowly heroine marries prince (L162), seems to have its roots in a his-

torical event reported from ancient Egypt. In her The Egyptian Cinderella *(1989), Shirley Climo reports,*

> *The tale of Rhodopis (ra-doh-pes) and the rose-red slippers is one of the world's oldest Cinderella stories. It was first recorded by the Roman historian Strabo in the first century* B.C. . . .
>
> *What is fact is that a Greek slave-girl, Rhodopis, married the Pharaoh Amasis (ah-may-ses) (Dynasty XXVI, 570–526* B.C.*) and became his queen.*

According to that ancient report, an eagle (which Climo replaced with a falcon in her re-telling) stole the slipper of a Greek slave-girl and brought it to the attention of the Pharaoh, thus setting off his search for its owner (Mot. N353§).

In our present indigenous Arab rendition of Cinderella, the heroine's name is not given. The focus for the tale is the stepmother's cruel treatment of her stepdaughter and the ensuing conflict among stepsisters over marriage to the same man; typically that man is not *a paternal figure. This affective component parallels that of a brother imitating his brother with reference to marriage to a girl who is not a maternal figure.*[666]

Of interest here is the theme of "the four women," that evidently represents a local belief in helpful supernatural beings comparable to the ancient Egyptian "seven Hathors."[667] *In the majority of renditions, the helper is a Faskarah (diminutive: Fsaikrah or Efsaichrah), a label signifying a small fish about the length of an index finger, with a yellow stripe on each side.*[668] *Typically, the heroine's father is helpless.*[669]

PLUMP [and] silvery she is; if a flea were to walk on her cheek, he [it] would mess it up.[670]

He who loves the Prophet should pray on his behalf.

A fisherman (*ḥawwât*)[671] married a woman. She begot for him a daughter. The mother died. So the man brought up his daughter. When the girl became nine years of age, she said to her father, "Father, why don't you marry? Marry someone who would give you comfort." He answered her, "I will not marry. I am afraid for you! If I were to marry, I fear that a stepmother[672] would cause you trouble." She replied, "No! Just you marry, and don't fear for me!"

The man, that fisherman, married a woman and she begot for him a girl! The girl grew up. That woman loved her own daughter and hated the daughter of her husband. She made her work: gather firewood, sweep, wash, and the like.

At night she made her sleep next to the cooking area,[673] and the father had no knowledge [of his own daughter's misfortune].

One day, it was the day for the circumcision of the sultan's son. The sultan held a party,[674] and all the people went there! The fisherman's daughter wanted to go there also to see the playing and the drumming, but her stepmother said, "No! You do not go. You would dishonor us!!!" Then she gave her a sack full of wheat and said to her, "Grind it!" and seven buckets and ordered, "Fill them from the well!" She and her [own] daughter went to the party for the circumcision of the sultan's son.

The fisherman's daughter: poor she! She sat down and cried. She cried and cried. Finally, she picked up the first of the seven buckets and went to the water well. She lowered the bucket while her tears were still coming down. The four women [evidently jinn or ogresses] came out to her and said, "Do not cry. Your stepmother and her daughter have gone to the celebration for the circumcision of the sultan's son; and they left you to grind wheat and fill seven buckets with well water. You too must go there!"

She said, "My stepmother would kill me [i.e., beat me severely]." The four women replied, "Don't be afraid! Just you go. Here take this dress of silk, these earrings and necklace of pearls and coral.[675] Wear them. Also, take these: a sack full of gold [coins] and [a sack full of] camel dung. Scatter the gold over the guests and spray the dung over your stepmother and her daughter!"

She went to the celebration. There she saw the sultan's son in the middle [of the dance circle]. She danced until she had her fill. All the people there were fascinated by her beauty. When she was satisfied (with dancing), she wanted to leave, but all the people followed her; so she was unable to leave. She took out the sack of gold coins and went: *whoosh-sh-sh-sh* [i.e., cast them out of the sack with such force that they made a whooshing sound]. All the people rushed to pick up some gold—including the sultan's son, and were bending with their faces down. She then took out the sack of camel dung and sprayed [its contents] over her stepmother and her [step]sister. And during the commotion, she r-a-a-a-an to the house.

When she got there, she found everything ready: the wheat was ground, the seven buckets full, the floor swept, the dishes washed . . . everything. Her stepmother and her stepsister returned, covered with camel dung and dirt. The stepmother shouted, "Did you grind the wheat!"

"Yes, stepmother!"

"Did you fill the seven buckets!"

"Yes, stepmother!"

"Why did you not wash the dishes?!"

"They have been washed, stepmother!"

The stepmother went to find out. She saw that everything was clean and in its place.

The daughter of the fisherman's wife [her stepsister] came to her and said [in a taunting tone], "At the sultan's son's, there was that beautiful girl. She danced and sang, and then threw gold coins over people. When they bowed down to pick up the gold, she disappeared. No one knows who she is, or whose daughter she may be!"

[It happened that] the sultan's son, [after picking up some gold coins]—when he looked up at her, he could not see her; she had gone!! He said to the guests, "Enough today. Come back next week. We will resume [the celebration] like today [i.e., the same day] next week!"

On the appointed day the stepmother and her daughter got ready. She, the stepmother, prepared her daughter: silk clothes, gold [jewelry], perfume, and made her [look like] a doll [or, like a bride]. As for her husband's daughter [i.e., her stepdaughter], she gave her rags to wear and a loaf of oats [i.e., poor bread]. She said to her, "Things [that you did last time] were no good! This time do things well. Here are three sacks of wheat [mixed] with rice (*¿aish*) and fourteen buckets. Separate the wheat from the rice, then grind the wheat; fill the fourteen buckets with water from the well!" Then she took herself along with her daughter and went to the celebration.

This time the sultan's son was determined not to pick up any gold. He said [to himself], "I'll not take my eyes off that girl who was here last time and threw gold over us!"

She sat alone in the house and cried. The four women appeared to her and said, "Don't cry. Don't be sad! You go to the celebration and do not worry!" They did for her as they did the time before. They gave her a silk dress, earrings, necklace, perfume and everything [including two sacks: one filled with gold coins, the other with camel dung].

She went to the celebration, and as the time before, there was a circle and in the middle was the sultan's son. She danced [along] with those who danced and she had her fill. The sultan's son did not take his eyes off her. Now when she had her fill and wanted to go home, she took out the sack of gold and: whoosh-sh-sh!, she scattered [its contents] over people's heads. A commotion ensued; the old and the young trotted to pick up some gold. Her stepmother and her stepsister also ran to get some for themselves, but she took out the sack of camel dung and: whoosh-sh-sh!, she scattered it over those [two]. She went home and found everything done: the rice in one heap, clean and ready [for cooking], the wheat in a heap, the buckets full of clean water, the dishes washed, the floor swept, and the house fumigated with incense.

The sultan's son, during the commotion—for people ran with all their strength toward [the place where the] gold [had fallen]—lost sight of her. She disappeared. He ran in this direction and in that direction but to no avail! He became sad and said to the guests, "Come back this day next week!" They left.

The stepmother went home with filth and stench covering her up from foot to head, and her daughter likewise! They washed up and said to her,

"Did you prepare the rice and the wheat?"

"Yes, stepmother!"

"Did you fill the buckets?"

"Yes, stepmother!"

To everything she [the stepmother] asked, "Did you do?" she answered "Yes, stepmother!"

The woman said [in a reprimanding tone], "No good! Everything is [done] poorly!" Again, she gave her rags to wear, and a loaf of oat bread [to eat], made her sleep next to the fire pit. Her [step]sister came to her and said [with some joy], "At the celebration of the circumcision of the sultan's son there was a beautiful girl. She danced and played, then scattered gold coins over the guests and fled. The same thing that happened the previous times, happened this time; the sultan's son said to the guests, 'Come back this day next week!' "

[Again there was another party.] The stepmother did to her as she did the previous times, and worse. She gave her sacks of wheat, rice, and fava beans (*fûl*) [mixed together], and twenty-one buckets, and—as before—told her to separate the wheat, rice, and the beans from one another, and to fill the buckets. She and her daughter went to the celebration of the sultan's son. Again—(poor thing)—she sat down and cried. The four women appeared to her and said the same thing they had told her the previous times. This time, they gave her things more beautiful and expensive than before.

She went to the celebration. This time the sultan's son had prepared himself for her [visit]. After she had danced and played as much as she wanted, then scattered the gold pieces [over the guests] and the camel dung over her stepmother and her daughter and ran away, he was ready on horseback. She ra-a-a-an and he galloped [his horse] after her. But she dodged him and returned home. While running, an ankle bracelet (*ḥijl*)—one that the four women had given her—caught on something and she lost it. The sultan's son took it and found it to be like no other he had seen before!! He went to his mother and father and said, "I want to marry the girl to whom this ankle-bracelet belongs."

Every girl in the sultanate kept on saying, "It is mine! It is mine!" But the sultan's son would say, "Show me its match [the other one of the pair]!" Naturally, no one could bring its counterpart, for it was from the four women; they were from underneath the ground [i.e., jinn].

They began going around the Sultanate—the women folk (*ḥarîm*) of the sultan's house—would go into a house and try it on all the women and the girls [in a household]. This one: "No! It is too large" [they would say]. This one: "No! It is too little!" They did that for thirteen days. On the fourteenth, they entered the house of the fisherman. The stepmother said, "I'll try it on!" It did not fit. [Then] she said, "It fits my daughter!" But it did not fit. One of the women of the sultan's household caught a glimpse of the fisherman's daughter, with her clothes in rags and [face] soiled! She said, "Try this girl." Her stepmother shrieked, "This is a slave-girl. A sultan's son marries [only] a[nother] sultan's daughter! She is not suited for him, for she is a slave-girl!" They tried it on [anyway]. It fit perfectly. They told the sultan's son, "It is the elder daughter of the fisherman!" He came and said, [holding the ankle bracelet in his hand], "Do you have its match!?"[676] She replied, "Yes! Its match I do have!" She showed them its match. The sultan's son said to his mother and father, "I want to marry this girl!"

They said to the fisherman, "We want your daughter for our son."

"Which one?" [the fisherman inquired].

"The elder one!"

"All right!"

They agreed on the bride-wealth (*mahr*),[677] and the day for the writing of the marriage contract (*katb al-kitâb*).

On the day of the consummation of the marriage (*'dakhlah'*), the fisherman's wife went to her husband's daughter and said to her, "This heap of beans you will eat!"

"O stepmother! O stepmother!" [she pleaded] but the stepmother was determined.

The poor girl sat down and ate the heaps of beans. Any time she would relax a little, her stepmother would say [yelling], "Eat! Eat!" She ate until her stomach became like a drum. And they took her [apparently without a wedding procession] to her husband's home. When she was in the [bridal] chamber, the four women appeared to her. They said [in a soft, kind, reassuring tone]: "Don't be afraid! Don't be afraid!" They got hold of her, slit her belly, took the beans out and put in their stead pearls and coral [i.e., red precious stones]. After they took the beans out of her stomach and filled it with pearls and coral, they put the belly together; it returned exactly as before!

Her bridegroom entered upon her [i.e., entered the room]! During the night she said, "I want to defecate (*'atghawwaṭ*)." Her groom said, "It is late [you should not go out for that]. Here is my head-scarf (*ghutrah*). Go on it!" She did. In the morning he called the servants and ordered them to take the head-scarf and wash it. The [woman] servant came back [yelling in excitement], "There are pearls and corals! There is no 'dirt' in your head-scarf, but [there are] God's grants! There are pearls and corals!" The sultan's son was astonished. He told his mother and father, the sultan. He [the father] exclaimed, "What a blessing!"

The younger brother of the sultan's son heard that his brother's bride defecated pearls and coral! He went to his mother and father and said, "I want [to marry] her sister!" They brought the fisherman and said, "We want your younger daughter for our other [younger] son!!" He replied, "The younger one: the say concerning her is with her mother![678] Ask her [mother]!" They brought her mother [and said]: "We want your daughter for our son!" She agreed and was happy.

But the fisherman's wife had heard that her husband's daughter was defecating pearls and coral. She thought that this was due to the beans she had fed her before the wedding. She got hold of her own daughter and stuffed her up with beans; then took her along with a great procession to the palace of the groom.

The sultan's [younger] son entered upon her [i.e., entered the room]. He kept on waiting for her to speak up. During the night she said, "I want to defecate!" Her groom said, "Here is my head-scarf." [Narrator laughs and pauses]—but the odor was unbearable. In the morning he found the filth everywhere!

His mother asked him, "How is your wife?" He replied [with sorrow and disgust], "She defecates in bed!" They asked her, "Why did you do that?" She answered, "My mother gave me a large serving tray (*ṣafriyyah*) full of beans and said to me, 'Eat it; it will make you drop pearls and coral!' "

The sultan brought the fisherman's wife and said to her, "For what purpose did you do so?" And they beat her severely,[679] and sent her daughter back home with her!

34-1

FSAIJRAH

(QATAR)

RENDERED IN WRITING IN JUNE 1973 BY A NARRATOR IDENTIFIED ONLY AS A "QATARI PRINCESS" (QATARI ROYALTY IS TYPICALLY LABELED *SHAIKH* OR *SHAIKHAH*, CF. NOTE 755), PROBABLY IN HER TEENS. THE NARRATOR-WRITER WAS RESPONDING TO A REQUEST FOR TALES BY ANOTHER WOMAN (ASSISTING EL-SHAMY).

This rendition is skeletal and incomplete. Yet, it includes all the basic constituents of the tale plot. It ends abruptly, presumably because the narrator-writer ran out of paper space. Like other written texts, the present rendition sought to make use of literary Arabic. The word "shaikh" *in the present context may signify a "prince" or an older man.*

NO one has come to you except[680] a girl whose name is Fsaijrah.

A woman had two daughters: one her [own] daughter, and the other is the daughter of her husband [i.e., stepdaughter]. She gave her husband's daughter [some] fish in order to [clean and] cut up at the sea[-shore]. The girl went with it to the sea[-shore]. After she was done with cutting [the fish up], there remained one little fish. The fish said to her, "Let me go and I will make you rich." The girl answered her, "I am afraid of my father's wife."

The fish slipped out of her hand and dove into the sea. The girl went back home with the [cut up] fish to her father's wife. Her father's wife said [to her], "Show me the fish." The girl answered, "One got away from me unintentionally (*ghaṣb ¿annî*)." Her father's wife deprived her of [midday] dinner and of supper. After they [the rest of the family] were done eating, they gave her the rest to throw into the sea. When she went to the sea[-shore], she saw in front of her the little fish with beautiful food [tray set] before her; it contained pure fish and Qatari clarified butter (*samn*) [which is more delicious than clarified butter from other lands].

A few days later, there was a drums party in their district. Her father's wife went to the party along with her [own] daughter; but she left behind the man's daughter to labor and work at home. Her friend, the fish, came to her, dressed her in all [sorts of] party dresses, and took her to the party without her father's wife knowing about it. She [also] put on her diamond footwear ("*maydâs mâs*")—[or] slippers (*ni¿âl*). After the party was finished, the girl (Fsaijrah) returned home so that they would not know that she had gone to the party. Due to the girl's speed [in returning] home, her shoe (*ḥidhâ'*) fell in the well. The *shaikh* [and some companions] came to the well; they saw the shoe glittering. . . . So, the *shaikh* sent the shoe to the town in which they [happened] to be; and declared, "Whomever it fits and whose foot would enter the shoe, I will marry."

The daughter of her father's wife [tried, but] the shoe did not fit her;[681] as for the girl (Fsaijrah), the shoe fit her foot. The *shaikh* affianced her for himself.

Her father's wife said, "For her [bride-wealth], we want radish, pickled fish, and dates."[682] [When these were delivered], they [the stepmother and her daughter] said to her, "Eat them."

The little fish [that she had released] came, adorned her, and dressed her in the prettiest of dresses; she [also] put in her stomach pearl and [red] coral (*murgân*) [which she, later, let out in the bridal chamber].

As for the daughter of her father's wife: luck was not her ally.[683]

❖ 35 ❖

THE MATERNAL-AUNT

(IRAQ)

NARRATED IN NOVEMBER 1970 BY ¿Â'ISHAH AL-Ḥ, FROM BAGHDAD, IRAQ. SHE WAS IN HER FIFTIES, LITERATE, AND THE MOTHER OF FIVE SONS AND DAUGHTERS. SHE HAD LEARNED THE TALE WHEN A CHILD FROM HER PATERNAL GRANDMOTHER. I MET THE NARRATOR IN CAIRO WHILE SHE WAS ON A VISIT TO

HER YOUNGER BROTHER, WHO WAS THEN WORKING AND RESIDING WITH HIS FAMILY IN A CAIRO SUBURB. WHEN ASKED, "DO SISTERS DO THESE SORTS OF THINGS TO EACH OTHER AND TO DAUGHTERS OF THEIR SISTERS?" THE NARRATOR REPLIED, "THESE ARE THINGS OF THE IGNORANT PAST. NOWADAYS, PEOPLE ARE ENLIGHTENED." HOWEVER, SHE ADDED, "BUT IGNORANT MOTHERS AND FATHERS CAN SOW SEEDS OF HATRED AMONG THEIR CHILDREN BY BAD [CHILD-] REARING PRACTICES."

*Being a sister to a sister, and being a maternal-aunt (*khâlah*) to that sister's children—a daughter in the present case—are two interdependent kinship roles that determine the direction of action in the plot of the following tale. In both situations, the character playing these two roles is portrayed as extremely and consistently cruel. As pointed out by the narrator, the father of the two sisters fostered the rivalry between them.*

The abused sister's husband—who is also the heroine's father—is powerless and plays no significant role (see also Tale No. 2).

The themes of "eyes exchanged for food" and "eyes successfully replaced" harken back to Egyptian antiquity and are recurrent.[684]

HERE is . . . ! Here is . . . ! And [only] on God reliance is to be.[685]

A merchant in a town—(one might say) in [in the city of] Mosul—he was rich and had two daughters: one older and one younger. He used to ask them, "From where did my riches come?" The older one would say to him [in a flattering tone], "From you and your labors, father!" [but] the younger would say, "From God! It is the Lord who gives, and it is the Lord who deprives."[686] He would be happy with the elder one and upset with the younger. He put the older one . . . , when he felt that his life span (*¿umruh*) was about to elapse, for he was old and became very sick, he put the older one in charge of his money and possessions. He gave her in marriage to one of his associates in the trade (business). He [the father] died. Immediately after the funeral and his burial, the older sister took over everything in the home and left nothing for her younger sister. She put her [the younger sister] to do the household work for her, her husband, and her children: knead and bake, wash the clothes, sweep the floors and—at the end of the day, after sunset—would sleep in the animals' stall.

One day a beggar came to the house. He knocked at the door [saying], "[Give me something] for God's sake, O ye benevolent!"[687] The older sister said to him, "Here, here is a wife for you!" She gave away her younger sister to the beggar!! The man took the girl and left. He married her according to God's edict and his Prophet's: legitimately.[688] And the two lived in his hut.

Day after day, she became pregnant and craved watermelon (*raggi/raqqî*). She sent her husband to her rich sister: "O Lady, your sister is about to have a child. We have nothing to eat at home; she is craving watermelon!" The sister replied, "I don't have any! Whatever we have is [barely] enough for me and for my children." (Of course she was lying.) It was summertime [i.e., the season for watermelon]. She had plenty, but she—out of intense begrudging hate (*ḥiqd*) and envy (*ḥasad*)—would not give to her destitute sister.

While the man was away, labor pains came to his wife. Poor thing!! No mother, no sister, not even a neighbor woman to stand by or help her. [Narrator speaks with intense empathy, as if she were the one in labor:] The hurt (*al-'alam*)! The labor pains (*ṭalq*)! The hunger (*al-jû¿*)! She cried out, "God, O Lord, You are the One who grants and withholds!"[689] God responded to her plea and angels from heaven came down to her so as to help deliver the newborn. By God's power the delivery became very easy, no pain, and—[excuse me]—no blood, no placenta: something divine!!! She gave birth to a baby girl. The angels said, "This blessed newborn. . . . When she smiles the sun will shine. When she speaks gold and green emeralds will fall out of her mouth, and whatever spot she will step on, jasmine and narcissus flowers will grow [out of it instantly]." They wrapped the child in a silk shawl and left her beside her mother. And they ascended to heaven.

When her [i.e., the child's] mother came to [for evidently she had passed out before the descent of the angels], she found that baby girl beside her: Glory be to the Creator for His creation [i.e., unsurpassed, dazzling in beauty].[690] Jasmine and narcissus flowers were shooting up from underneath the infant. She got off the delivery bed and bathed the child. When she threw the water away, she found gold coins and emeralds in it. She took them and thanked God: "Truly You are the One who gives and takes away," [she exclaimed in reverence, as she raised her face toward heaven]!!! She named her Zahrat an-Narjis (Narcissus Flower).

Her husband returned, tired and haggard. He said to her [in a desperate tone], "I did not find watermelon. Your sister—may God send her her due—would not give me anything and drove me away!!" She [smiling] said to him, "God has been merciful to us. Come and see your daughter!!" She gave him some of the gold she got from the child, and said to him, "Go to So-and-so, the goldsmith; sell these and come back to me." He did! With the money, she had a palace built and they lived in it: with plenty and they were content.

The girl, Zahrat an-Narjis, grew up. One day the sultan's son was coming back (I mean, was traveling,) from a hunt. He passed through the town where the girl (Zahrat an-Narjis) was living. It chanced, due to destiny, that she was looking out of the window of the palace. The eye of the king's son fell on her! Immediately he fell in love with her. He asked about her and learned who she happened to be, and who were her parents. When he reached his home, he sent emissaries to ask for the hand of Zahrat an-Narjis. A magnificent procession of viziers, aides to the sultan, and royalty left loaded with gifts and the like. They arrived at the home [of Zahrat an-Narjis] and asked for her hand in marriage. Her mother and father gave their consent. (Of course in such an occurrence, the bride's family prepare their daughter, then send her to her husband's home.) They said, "We will prepare her and will send her to the sultan's son!" The guests left.

When the maternal-aunt heard that her sister had become rich and that her [the sister's] daughter was going to marry the sultan's son, the fires of jealousy and intense hate ignited inside of her! She had a daughter; she was ugly and ill-mannered. [She wondered:] "How come the daughter of my [once] poor sister marries the sultan's son!! By God, my own daughter is more deserving!!!"

She ran to her sister and [in a contrived affectionate tone] said to her, "My dear sister, we have no one [to rely on] except each other. I have always looked after you. May the Lord forgive the past!! Let me escort my beloved niece to her husband!!" Her good-hearted sister agreed.

The maternal-aunt took her own daughter along. Of course, there were other people, but one by one, she sent them home. After a while only she, her daughter, and her sister's daughter, Zahrat an-Narjis, remained. She kept the food and the water away from her [i.e., her niece] until she was about to starve to death. The girl implored, "O my maternal-aunt, give me some food, for I am about to die!" She answered [sternly], "For your right eye!" The poor girl agreed. She took out the girl's right eye and gave her a morsel of bread!!! A day or two later, the girl, "O my maternal-aunt, give me some water for I am about to die of thirst!" She answered her, "For your left eye!" and the poor girl consented. She took out her left eye and placed both eyes in a flask that she had carried with her. The maternal-aunt left Zahrat an-Narjis alone in the marshlands, hoping that a beast would devour her or that she might drown, and she proceeded with her own daughter to the sultan's son.

When they arrived [at the sultan's son's palace], they were received with great festivities, but when the time came for the groom to see his bride, he lifted the veil off her face and [to his surprise] found out that she was not the one he had seen before. "What is this?! This is not the one whom I had seen!!"

The girl's mother replied [in a devious tone], "What are you talking about?? This is the girl, Zahrat an-Narjis, only she is changed due to the long [harsh] trip!!"

The girl spoke but stones and bricks came out of her mouth. No jasmine or narcissus grew around her. "Where is all that? Where are the jasmine and narcissus?"

Her mother replied, "It is not the season for jasmine and narcissus! Just be patient!!"

The sultan's son reluctantly kept quiet.

Now talk takes us back to whom? To the poor Zahrat an-Narjis! Now she is blind. She waited in the wilderness for a while. God sent a fisherman her way. This old fisherman saw the lost girl. "Who are you?" [he asked]. She told him her story. The man said [in an unbelieving tone], "No ability or power except with God's [aid]! [i.e., What a shame!]" He said to her, "Come and live with my daughters. You will be the seventh" (for he had six daughters). She went with him to his home. His wife and six daughters received her well and welcomed her. And she stayed with them in comfort; they were poor but generous and good-hearted.

One day the fisherman came and said that the maternal-aunt [of Zahrat an-Narjis] was looking for jasmine and narcissus flowers—for her daughter, so that she can claim that she produces jasmine and narcissus wherever she steps. Zahrat an-Narjis produced some jasmine and gave them to her [foster] father and said, "Take these to her, but accept no money. Say, 'The jasmine's price is the right eye,'"[691] [which her maternal-aunt was still keeping in a flask].

He took the jasmine and went to the palace and cried out, "Jasmine out-of-season! Jasmine out-of-season!" The maternal-aunt heard him and asked him in. "For how much?" [she asked].

"For the right eye!" [he replied].

She gave him Zahrat an-Narjis's right eye and took the jasmine. He took it [the eye back] to Zahrat an-Narjis; she placed it in its place and prayed to God to restore it as it used to be! With God's will, it returned as it used to be!! Then she produced some narcissus flowers and gave them to her [foster] father and said, "Father, sell these but accept no money. Say, 'The flowers' price is the left eye.'"[692] The same thing that happened with the [selling of] the jasmine happened with the narcissus. He got her the left eye, she placed it in its place and prayed to God, and with God's will it returned to its original condition. She regained her eyesight and her beauty.

She gave her father some gold and emeralds and said, "I must leave to meet my own fate!" They said to her, "Stay with us. You are our daughter now!" and the like. But she insisted [on leaving]. They said to her, "Peace be with you!" and she left them.

Zahrat an-Narjis went to the palace of the sultan's son. ([Pause.] No! before this. . . .) She went to a man who was making mats—making mats out of palm fronds. She said to him, "Make me an outer-garment from these palm fronds; and here is a gold piece as your fee!" The man was very happy with the fee and made her the garment. She put it on, and covered her golden hair with an old ragged turban and went to the palace of the sultan's son. She went to the chief of the guards and said, [in an imploring tone], "I am an old man looking for a place to stay. Won't you allow me to work in the garden just for my food." The chief of the guards felt pity for her [i.e., for the old man] and said, "Welcome!"

She stayed in the garden and every spot she stepped on blossomed with jasmine and narcissus [flowers]. The sultan's son noticed that the garden was blossoming; it was blossoming with flowers out of season! He wondered, "This never happened before. Where is the gardener?" The chief of the guards brought the gardener to the sultan's son.

"Old man, why are flowers growing out of season?" [the sultan's son asked].

"God's will!" [answered the gardener]. The sultan's son said to her [i.e., to him], "Stay here in the palace. For you are a blessed man!" She stayed in the palace and watched what was happening.

One day . . . [pause]. The sultan's son had given her a ring when he went to affiance her. One day the sultan's son had a feast. Of course there was much baking and cooking. She—[disguised as an old man wearing a garment of palm fronds]—went to the [woman] baker and said to her, "Let me carry the turnovers (*faṭîrah*) to the sultan's son!" The woman said, "All right!" As she was carrying the turnovers, she put the ring in the largest one, placed it on top [of the bunch], and took the turnovers to the sultan's son. When he tried to tear the top one with his hands, the ring fell out of it!!! He recognized it to be the one he had given his fiancée. He brought the baker, and asked her, "From where did you get this ring?" She said, "I don't know anything about it, but the gardener was the one who carried it to you." They brought the gardener. "Old man, where did you get this ring?" He [i.e., the gardener] said, "[First], give me the kerchief of safety [i.e., assurance that no harm would come to me]."[693] The sultan's son said, "The kerchief of safety is with you!"

She told him the story from beginning to end: how her maternal-aunt stole the inheritance of her [own] sister; how they lived in poverty, and how her maternal-aunt tricked her sister and escorted her to her husband, and how her maternal-aunt sold her food and water for her right and left eye . . . , and how. . . . After telling all, she said, "I am Zahrat an-Narjis, your legitimate wife!!!"

He [the sultan's son] learned the truth and said, "You are my wife!" He told his father, the sultan, and his mother. They sentenced the maternal-aunt and her daughter to death.

(This is the tale, and had our house been near by, I would have gotten you a load of raisins.)[694]

❖ 36 ❖

THE COW OF THE ORPHANS

(EGYPT)

NARRATED BY SAYYIDAH D. (SEE INFORMANT NOTE TO TALE NO. 1); THIS IS ANOTHER OF A FEW TALES THAT SHE TOLD REPEATEDLY TO HER GRANDCHILDREN.

For the Egyptian fellah, no farm animal—with the possible exception of the water buffalo—is more valuable and treated with greater care than the cow. In spite of the fact that the camel and the horse are also held in high esteem, neither animal seems to have replaced the cow as a helpful animal in our present tale.

The role of the cow as protector of orphans harks back to religious beliefs of Egyptian antiquity. The goddess Hathor, depicted as a cow, provided safety and nourishment for the orphan boy deity Horus, and to others including Amenhotep II.[695]

In keeping with the pattern of reorganization of the social environment, the orphaned brother and sister who are forced to face a hostile social environment end up together with no paternal scrutiny (or abuse). Our text's formulaic ending tends to reinforce this recurrent narrative feature. A Berber text is concluded in the following unformulaic manner expressing the same notion:

> *The young girl grew up, [. . .], the sultan married her. Subsequently, her brother himself took the sultan's place.*[696]

PRAISE the Prophet.

Once there was a man and woman; they had a boy and a girl. They had a cow; they milked and drank the milk of that cow. After a while, the mother of the children became ill. She called her children and said to them, "I am going to die. Take care of the cow; she will feed you and she is the one who will protect you."

After a few days their mother died. Her children used to take the cow to pasture; she would eat the grass, then the children would say to her,

> O, You, [who are] our mother's milk-producing cow!
> You, who are protecting us from fire and wolves,
> Provide us with your goodness, for we are poor orphans![697]

The cow would give them milk; they would drink until full.

Their father married another woman. She hated the children of her husband. She begot a boy and girl; after several years they grew up. Their mother would give them the best food, and dress them up in the best clothes; she would give the children of her husband only two dry morsels of cornbread (*¿aish-ḍurah*),[698] and ragged clothes of her own children. The [original] children would eat the morsels and, as usual, they would take the cow to pasture. They would say,

> O, You, [who are] our mother's milk-producing cow!
> You, who are protecting us from fire and wolves,
> Provide us with your goodness, for we are poor orphans.

Then, the cow would give them milk until they would become full.

Their father's wife noticed that they were growing up while her own children were weak and nothing [of the good food she gave them] was showing on them. She said, "These children must be doing something [wrong]!" She said to her son, "Go with them and see what they do. Take these two morsels of bread to them [in the field] and see what they do!"

When dinner time came [at noon], they ate the two dry morsels that their father's wife sent them; they remained hungry. They said to the son of their father's wife, "If we make you full, would you swear not to tell anyone!" He said to them, "Yes!" They went to the cow and said,

> O, You, [who are] our mother's milk-producing cow!
> You, who are protecting us from fire and wolves,
> Provide us with your goodness, for we are poor orphans.

She gave them enough milk for all of them to drink and be full.

When the boy went home his mother asked him, "What did they eat?" He did not tell her anything.

The following day, she sent her daughter, and told her the same thing she had told her brother. She went to the field carrying the dinner: the two morsels of bread. They ate the two morsels of bread but remained hungry. They said to her, "If we make you full, would you swear not to tell anyone?" She said to them, "Yes!" They did with her as they did with her brother. But the girl, while drinking the milk, poured some milk on her dress. When she went home her mother said to her, "What did they eat?" She, replied [slyly], "Instead of interrogating me and making me swear, ask my dress!" The woman felt the dress and found milk on it; she realized that the girl and her brother—(her husband's children)—were drinking the cow's milk.

She pretended to be ill and dying: she put [yellow] saffron dye on her face, and dry bread under the mattress [so as to produce the sounds of crackling bones]. She said to her husband [in a weak voice], "I will not be cured unless you get me the liver of a cow that is red and white [in color]!" The man kept on searching for a cow, as his wife had described, but could not find any. He found that only the cow of the orphans was red and white. So he decided to slaughter it. The cow heard him telling his wife that he will slaughter the orphans' cow. She said to the girl, "They want to slaughter me; but I will not be slaughtered unless you and your brother say to me, 'get slaughtered.' After they slaughter me, take my bones and bury them; [still] I will feed you, you and your brother!"

When the man, their father, tried to slaughter the cow, the knife would not cut her throat. The knife broke. They got another knife, but it would not cut her throat (of course the girl and her brother were standing [there] crying). Finally, the girl said,

> O, You, [who are] our mother's milk-producing cow!
> You, who are protecting us from fire and wolves,
> Get slaughtered!

So the cow got slaughtered.

When they tried to cut her up, she would not be cut up. The girl said,

> O, You, [who are] my mother's milk-producing cow!
> You, who are protecting us from fire and wolves,
> Get cut up!

So she got cut up. When they tried to cook her meat, the meat would not get cooked. The girl said:

O, You, [who are] my mother's milk-producing cow!
You, who are protecting us from fire and wolves,
Get cooked!

So she got cooked! When they tried to eat the meat, it became [as bitter as] aloe in their mouths; but the girl and her brother refused to eat.

After they finished off the cow's meat, they threw her bones away. The girl and her brother gathered them and buried them in the field. From the bones of the cow a tree came out; it grew very quickly. The girl and her brother ate from the fruits of the tree; she [the tree] gave them everything they asked for.

(That's all.) And they lived in stability and prosperity.

❖ 37 ❖

THE GREEN HE-SPARROW

(EGYPT)

NARRATED BY SAYYIDAH D. (SEE INFORMANT NOTE TO TALE NO. 1).

*The strong bond between sister and brother is portrayed in this narrative, which typically carries this tale's title (*el-¿aṣfûr l-akhḍar*), or* ed-dîk l-khḍar *("The Green Rooster" or "The Green Cock"). An acute indignation is leveled at the children's father, presumably for being a slave to his wife's whims. The characterization of a father as a "pimp," though intolerable in actual social life, seems to be permissible in this narrative context, as well as in folk psychodrama in healing rituals.*[699]

The reincarnation in the form of plant or animal of a woman's murdered brother has its counterpart in the ancient Egyptian belief account ("myth") of Isis and Osiris.[700]

Again, the pattern of reorganization of the social environment is present: with the violent elimination of parents, the brother and sister end up together. The formulaic close of the tale states that "they begot boys and girls."[701]

SIT-EL-ḤUSN[702] and her brother, Clever[703] Mḥammad. Their mother died and their father married another woman; that woman could not give birth, so she became jealous of Sit-el-Ḥusn and her brother, who is Clever Mḥammad.

One day the boy went to the field with his father; as they were walking beside an irrigation ditch,[704] they saw a catfish.[705] The man plunged into the water and caught that catfish, gave it to his son and said, "Take this catfish and say to them at home, 'My father says cook this catfish for our dinner.'" The boy said, "Will do, father."

As he was going home, the boy—Clever Mḥammad—became thirsty; so, he descended to the [water level of the narrow] rivulet to get a drink. The [slippery] catfish glided out of his hand into the water and disappeared. When he went home he told his father's wife about what had happened. She, due to her vexation,[706] said to him, "Lie down and rest." When he fell asleep, [narrator speaks with considerable sympathy], she got up and brought a knife and slaughtered him; she cut him up into little pieces, put him in a cooking pot and cooked him.

When his father returned home from the field at the sunset, he was hungry. She brought him, without him knowing it, the [cooked] flesh of his son. They sat down to eat. He said, "Where is the boy?" She said [in a careless tone], "Outside, playing with the boys in the lane!" As they were eating—(I mean: as they were about to start eating)—his sister, Sit-el-Ḥusn, found the little finger [pinkie] of her brother in the stew. She said, "I am not hungry! I will go call my brother in!" And she did not eat. The man and his wife ate until they were full. His [the boy's] sister went out looking for him. She realized that the meat was her brother. She kept on crying, but she could not tell their father, because she was afraid of her father's wife: she would slaughter her as she did slaughter her brother.

Sit-el-Ḥusn, during the night, went and collected all the bones, her brother's bones; and—(Oh, me!)—the tears of her eyes were coming down her cheeks like rain. She took all the bones and buried them in front of the house. The following day a tree grew out of that spot, a big tree. On top of that tree there was a green he-sparrow. The sparrow and the tree came out of the bones of her brother. The sparrow said,

I am the gree-ee-ee-n sparrow, the gree-ee-ee-n!
I walk on the wall and wa-a-a-ggle, waa-a-ggle!
My stepmo-o-o-ther slaughtered me, slaughtered me!
And my pimp father ate my fle-e-e-sh, ate my fle-e-e-sh!
And my dear sister buried my bo-o-o-nes, my bo-o-o-nes!![707]

A vendor—(one of those wandering vendors who go around villages selling things)—passed by; he heard the sparrow. He said to him [with amazement], "What are you saying, Sparrow?"

He [the sparrow] replied, "What are you selling?"

He said, "Pins and needles."

He said, "Give me some and I will tell you!"

The man said, "Here you are! What were you saying?"

He said,

I am the gree-ee-ee-n sparrow, the gree-ee-ee-n!
I walk on the wall and wa-a-a-ggle, waa-a-ggle!
My stepmo-o-o-ther slaughtered me, slaughtered me!
And my pimp father ate my fle-e-e-sh, ate my fle-e-e-sh!
And my dear sister buried my bo-o-o-nes, my bo-o-o-nes!!

The man heard that talk and left saying [in a sorrowful voice indicating pity and helplessness], "No ability or power except with God's aid!"[708]

A while later another vendor came by. He heard the sparrow. He said to him, "What are you saying, Sparrow?"

"What are you selling?"

The vendor said to him—(away from you!), "Poison!"

"Give me some and I'll tell you."

[He gave him some:] "Here you are! Now tell me."

He said,

I am the gree-ee-ee-n sparrow, the gree-ee-ee-n!
I walk on the wall and wa-a-a-ggle, waa-a-ggle!
My stepmo-o-o-ther slaughtered me, slaughtered me!
And my pimp father ate my fle-e-e-sh, ate my fle-e-e-sh!
And my dear sister buried my bo-o-o-nes, my bo-o-o-nes!!

This poison vendor heard that talk, and like the one before him left saying, "No ability or power except with God's aid!"

A while later another vendor came. He heard the sparrow.

"What are you saying, Sparrow?"

"What are you selling?"

"Candy!"

"Give me some and I'll tell you."

"Here you are, now tell me."

He said,

> I am the gree-ee-ee-n sparrow, the gree-ee-ee-n!
> I walk on the wall and wa-a-a-ggle, waa-a-ggle!
> My stepmo-o-o-ther slaughtered me, slaughtered me!
> And my pimp father ate my fle-e-e-sh, ate my fle-e-e-sh!
> And my dear sister buried my bo-o-o-nes, my bo-o-o-nes!!

Like the two before him, the candy man left saying, "No ability or power except with God's aid!"

Now, his stepmother came by. She heard the sparrow saying what he had been saying. She asked, "What are you saying, Sparrow"?

He replied, "Open your mouth and I'll tell you." The woman opened her mouth. He threw the pins and needles into it; she dropped dead on the spot (*ṭabbat sâktah*)!

After a while his father came and heard the sparrow saying what he had been saying. He asked, "What are you saying, Sparrow?" He answered, "Open your mouth and I'll tell you!" The man opened his mouth; he threw the poison into it. The man dropped dead on the spot.

Now his sister came, and said, "O my brother, O Mḥammad, what are you saying?" He answered her, "Open your mouth and I'll tell you." She opened her mouth and he put the candy in it, and said,

> I am the gree-ee-ee-n sparrow, the gree-ee-ee-n!
> I walk on the wall and wa-a-a-ggle, waa-a-ggle!
> My stepmo-o-o-ther slaughtered me, slaughtered me!
> And my pimp father ate my fle-e-e-sh, ate my fle-e-e-sh!
> And my dear sister buried my bo-o-o-nes, my bo-o-o-nes!!

That is all! (It ends with this.)[709]

And they lived in stability and prosperity, and begot boys and girls.[710]

❖ 38 ❖

BROTHER DEER[711]

(LIBYA)

NARRATED IN JUNE 1970 BY ZÎNAH (OR, ZAYNAH) D., A MIDDLE-AGED WOMAN (PROBABLY ABOUT FIFTY YEARS OLD) FROM THE LIBYAN BRANCH OF ¿ALI AL-'ABYAḌ TRIBE. SHE WAS LIVING NEAR TOBRUK, LIBYA, AND HAD RELATIVES—(THE FAMILY OF MR. ṢÂFÎ ¿A.)—LIVING NEAR ALEXANDRIA, EGYPT.[712] SHE HAD HEARD THE TALE FROM ṢÂFÎ'S WIFE. FOR THE NARRATOR, THE TALE SHOWED "HOW AN ELDER SISTER MUST CARE FOR HER BROTHER; [. . .] EVEN WHEN SHE IS MARRIED, WITH CHILDREN, AND IS UNDER THE RULE OF (*FÎ ḤOKM*) HER HUSBAND." THIS VIEWPOINT REPRESENTS A CHARACTERISTIC WOMAN'S ATTITUDE TOWARD HER BROTHER, AND CONSTITUTES ROLE STRAIN.[713]

A brother and a sister who are persecuted by the social system are the cardinal characters in this fantasy-tale. Children sealed inside their home may be seen as indicative of potential conflict with society or the outside world (cf. notes 439 and 716, this section). The wailing exchanges between the drowned sister and her transformed brother may be viewed as symbolic of a female's role strain: a woman wanting to be a dutiful wife to her husband and a good mother to "his son" (and hers), and at the same time be a loving sister to her helpless brother. The use of the diminutive form, "my little sister" and "my little brother" ("khayyitî" *and* "khuwayyî"*) signifies endearment.*[714]

In the present rendition, the young sister—contrary to the dominant pattern in other narratives—marries a "sultan" who is already married to other women. Thus, although the age of the sister's rescuer was not specified, it may be postulated that he may represent a paternal figure. *Consequently, the tale may harbor some underlying Oedipal elements. Yet, no affection is expressed between the sister and her patriarchal husband.*

By contrast, the sister's affectionate relationship with her brother is amply portrayed; the brother and sister at the spring, the sister's comb, the brother's horn, drinking from the forbidden water—all are powerful erotic symbols. The rendition from Iraq (cited in Section V, Tale No. 38, no. 11, p. 447) introduces the element of incest initiated by the husband's own disguised sister and her unsuspecting brother (who is the heroine's husband). Although the occurrence of this motif is atypical in the context of Type 450, its appearance complements the erotic implications of the brother-sister relations postulated here for our present text.[715] *Additionally, the sister's reunion with her husband is not inclusive, for she must share him with other culprit wives (who were not divorced).*

On the significance of the tale's formulaic beginning for the process of narrating, see notes to Tale No. 20.

HERE there is that girl and that boy. Their mother and father wished to go to Hejaz. So they said to the girl, "Take care of your brother!" And they said to the boy, "Take care of your sister!" They brought provisions and left some for the children and kept the rest with them. They sealed the house with [a plaster made of] water and dirt and said to the neighbors, "Keep an eye on the children."

O day, go! O day, come! and the girl and her brother were inside the house. Her brother said, "My sister, why don't we go out to promenade. We have been here for months and days!!" She said to him, "Our mother and our father have sealed us in with mud mortar and they have said to the neighbors, 'Keep an eye on the children!' "

O day, go! O day, come! O month, go, O month, come! and their food ran out. What did they do? They dug a hole in the plaster, and got out of the house. They looked around and found no one. They walked about, here and there; it got dark and the night overtook them and they could not go back home. Then they slept out in the wilderness[716] under a tree. The boy would say to his sister, "O my sister, I am hungry!" And she would say, "O my brother, wait until morning, for daytime has eyes."

In the morning, the two—the girl and her brother—got up and saw that the date palm tree was bearing fruit. They ate some, took some along, and thanked the Lord. They kept on going. The boy said to his sister, "O my sister, I am thirsty!" (due to their having eaten unripe dates [which dries up the mouth and causes one to be very thirsty]). She said to him, "Be patient!" And they kept on walking until they came to a well.

"O my sister, I am thirsty!"

"Descend into the well and get some water."

Her brother went down the well, and he was about to drink [narrator speaks with excitement; she cups the palm of her hand and imitates the movement of dipping one's cupped hand into water and raising it to the mouth]. As he was about to drink they heard a voice saying, "He who drinks from this well will become a dog!" His sister immediately yelled at him, "Don't touch the water!" and he climbed out without drinking. They kept on going.

"O my sister, I am thirsty!"

"Be patient!"

"O my sister, I am thirsty!"

"Be patient!"

They reached another well,

"O my sister, I am thirsty!"

"Go down the well and drink." That which happened at the first well happened at the second. Just before he would drink, a voice said, "He who drinks from this well will become a donkey!" His sister immediately yelled at him, "Don't touch the water!" And he climbed out without drinking.

"O my sister, I am thirsty!"

"Be patient!" They kept on going until they came to a well . . . (I mean) a spring (*¿ain*).

"O my sister, I am thirsty!"

"Go down and drink . . . !"

He went down to the water; as he was about to drink [like this] they heard a voice saying, "He who drinks from this spring will become a deer!" His sister immediately yelled to him, "Don't touch the water!"

"Oh! But, sister, I am thirsty. I am about to die of thirst!"

She said, "Let us bathe, but don't you dare drink!"

They bathed and cleaned themselves. The girl and her brother sat down. . . . She took out a comb that she had and combed her hair and tidied herself up. They rested . . . and after they rested they left. A short while later the girl is saying [with concern], "My brother, I forgot the comb at the spring. Wait here. I'll go get it and I'll come back!" He said to her, "No, sister, I'll go get it for you. Wait here and I'll be back quickly."

[She warned him,] "Let the spring be! Don't you dare drink."

"Will do, sister!"

He ran to the spring and found the comb. But he—for he was very thirsty—disobeyed his sister's talk and took one gulp of water. [Narrator talks with a sense of surprise.] He looked [only] to find himself [transformed into] a deer. He picked up the comb with his horns and galloped back to his sister.

[Once] his sister saw him, she broke out crying and wailing, "Why did you drink from the spring!! O my brother. Haven't I told you . . . [not to drink]!"

In short (*quṣr el-kalâm*), she collected herself and kept on going and he—her brother, the deer—trailed her. They walked and walked—one land carried them and another land put them down—until they came to a spot where there were trees and springs: oasis (*wâḥ*), but with no people. They lived there for a while.

One day the sultan went out hunting. God willed that he get to that spot where the girl and her brother were living. One of the people with the sultan saw her with the deer. He told the sultan and the sultan chased her [on his horse]. She ran and her brother was trailing her, until finally she could not run any longer and he, [with his horse], cornered her:

"Are you a human being or a jinniyyah?" [he inquired.]

"Human, of the best humans!"

"What are you doing here in this desolate spot?"

"God's will!"

"No one lives here. You [must] come with me to the inhabited part!"

She answered, "I don't move anywhere without the deer!"

The sultan placed her on the horse behind himself and returned [to his hunting party]. All the time she would cry and the deer [trotting after them] would cry too. He, the sultan, took her to his palace, placed her with the servants (at first!). She and her brother lived in the garden and her brother would come in and go out [of the palace] as he pleased.

One day the sultan saw her in the garden. She appealed to him and he wanted to marry her but she refused; she said, "No!" Day after day she became more beautiful and the sultan became determined to write [a formal contract of his marriage] to her,[717] but whenever he asked her, she would say, "No!" Finally, she consented but on the condition "That the deer must stay with me at all times!" The sultan said, "And I agree!"

They got married; he entered upon her [i.e., consummated the marriage], and she became pregnant by him.[718] The sultan's [other] wives became jealous of her. One day when the sultan was away, they said to her [slyly], "Come, let us promenade in the garden!" They had arranged for a slave-girl to place a mat on the mouth of an [old dry] well in the palace garden. They said to her, "Slave-girl, place a mat over the well." They said to her [the new bride], "Come, you are the one who is special. You sit in the middle!" While she sat down [narrator speaks abruptly] the mat took her and fell down into the well. They went back into the palace. No one [else] saw, and no one knew.

The deer would come to the well and would weep and wail! The Lord willed that when she fell in the well she would not get hurt. One day passed! On the second day she delivered a baby boy. Her hair grew long and covered her up. By God's will she would nurse her child inside the well. Her brother would come and constantly hover around the well and would wail and cry until the servants in the palace began to inquire, "Why is this deer crying?" [Now, fearing that their crime would be revealed, the sultan's wives drew up a plan to get rid of the deer.] One of the sultan's wives pretended to be ill and said, "I must eat the liver of this deer [in order to be cured]!" The sultan said, "All right!" (For they had told the sultan, after he had returned home, that his new wife had run away.) So he [the sultan] said, "All right! Slaughter her deer!"

When the servants went out to slaughter him, he galloped to the well and wailed (*nawwaḥ*),

O Budûr, my [dear]-little sister!
O Budûr, my little sister!
They have sharpened the knives,
and heated the cauldrons;
for your little brother, Ṣûr![719]

And she replied [in an anguished tone],

O Ṣûr, my [dear]-little brother!
O Ṣûr, my little brother!
My hair is undone and is covering me up,
while the sultan's son is in my arms.
And I have no means to reach out for you![720]

[He wailed,]

O Budûr, my little sister!
O Budûr, my little sister!
They have sharpened the knives,
and heated the cauldrons;
for your little brother, Ṣûr!

[And she answered,]

O Ṣûr, my little brother!
O Ṣûr, my little brother!
My hair is undone and is covering me up,

while the sultan's son is in my arms.
I have no means to reach out for you!

Who was listening to all this? The servants who were to slaughter him, slaughter the deer. Tears would flee away from their eyes [i.e., they wept in spite of themselves] and they were unable to catch him for he kept on running away from them. But when they looked into the well, they could see nothing except the hair of the girl, his sister—[which had grown to such a length as to allow for] covering the [inside of the] well; and they would think that it was something that grows in water [i.e., water weeds]. They would go to the sultan's wife and say, "He [the deer] ran away from us! We couldn't catch him!" Then the sultan's wife would become wild [with anger], beat them up, and say, "Go back! If you do not slaughter the deer, I will have the sultan slaughter you!" and things like that.

One day, at dawn, as the boy [i.e., the deer] was standing at the edge of the well saying [in a wailing tone],

O Budûr, my little sister!
O Budûr, my little sister!
They have sharpened the knives,
and heated the cauldrons;
for your little brother, Ṣûr!

and his sister [was] replying,

O Ṣûr, my little brother!
O Ṣûr, my little brother!
My hair is undone and is covering me up,
while the sultan's son is in my arms.
I have no means to reach out for you!

it chanced that the sheikh of the mosque [(i.e., the imam)] was passing by on his way to call for the dawn prayers. He said, "In the name of God the Merciful, the Compassionate! Is this well haunted [by jinn],[721] or what!?"

He called, "Are you [of the] humans or the jinn (*'ince 'aw jince?*)?"

She said, "I am a human, of the best humans."[722]

"What are you doing here? Who did this to you?"

She told him the story: "I am the sultan's wife; my co-wives (*ḍarâyrî*) threw me in the well; they said to me, 'Come let us promenade in the garden.' They placed a mat on the well and said, 'Sit here in our midst!' And here I am in the well:

My hair is undone and is covering me up,
while the sultan's son is in my arms.
I have no means to reach out for my little brother Ṣûr!"

As soon as the sheikh heard this he went running to the sultan. He told him the story. They went and brought her out, she and her son, and took them to the palace. And the deer [was trotting] after them.

That other woman, her co-wife, was still lying in bed, pretending to be ill, and was saying [in a fake, weak voice], "Did you bring the liver of the deer?" They said to her, "Get up! Receive your due!" He [i.e., the sultan] sent her back to her father's house and said to her, "You are thrice divorced (*ṭâliq bi-t-talâtah*) [i.e., irrevocably]!"

And they lived in happiness.

EL-SHAMY: What happened to the other wives?
NARRATOR: Whatever may have happened.
EL-SHAMY: I mean, didn't their husband do something to them [i.e., punish] them too? Weren't they all partners in the conspiracy to kill her [his new wife]?
NARRATOR: I know the story only like I told it.
EL-SHAMY: What about the deer: her brother?
NARRATOR: He remained with his sister in the palace.
EL-SHAMY: [As] a deer!?
NARRATOR: Who could attain![723]

❖ 39 ❖

AN IVORY BED AND A GLASS BED[724]

(YEMEN)

NARRATED IN APRIL 1982 BY MISS ¿A. AL-SH., AGED TWENTY-TWO, A UNIVERSITY STUDENT FROM SANAA, YEMEN, STUDYING IN CAIRO, EGYPT. SHE HAD HEARD THE TALE REPEATEDLY DURING HER CHILDHOOD FROM HER MOTHER, WHO CAME FROM SOUTHERN YEMEN. FOR THE NARRATOR, THIS IS ONE OF THE

"OLD-WIVES' TALES,"[725] OF WHICH SHE "WOULD RATHER NOT THINK MUCH DUE TO THEIR NAIVE AND SUPERSTITIOUS NATURE."

Killing for sexual honor (sororicide), repeated reincarnation, mystical bonds, the sister in bed, and sex flirtation by the sister (incestuous foreplay) are salient facets of this regional subtype of the "Brother and Sister" tale cycle. Unlike Type 720 (see Tale No. 37), it is the sister who is murdered, then reincarnated, and a reorganization of the social setting is introduced.

In 1974 and 1979, the present writer concluded that a Yemenite text of our present tale, in which the sister was actually murdered and then reincarnated, represented an idiosyncratic rendition of an "individualistic nature." Consequently, it was argued that "to allow for the reunion [between the brother and his sister], the narrator, an adult female, introduced the atypical *theme of the [re]incarnation of the murdered sister."*[726] *The following tale, and other recently located texts, demonstrate that this conclusion—arrived at on the basis of then available data—is incorrect; the reincarnation theme constitutes the* typical *core for this regional subtype of the tale.*

TWO living together: a girl and her brother. They had no one else in the world to look after them or be kind to them [except each other]. Every day he would go out to his work, while she would stay at their home and take care of the household work. They lived like this ever since their mother and father died. One day the brother said to his sister, "I need to take a wife!" His sister answered him, "Good, if God wills." She searched in the town and found a lass, someone she thought would be a good wife for him. He said to her [i.e., to his sister], "I [will] marry this girl." She replied, "Good, if God wills!"

The wedding [ceremonies were] completed and the girl came to live with them in their home. His sister was very happy that he found a wife and tried to make her [the bride's] life in their home comfortable to the utmost; she helped her with the cooking, cleaning, and with all other household chores. [The sister did] all that for the sake of the happiness of her [own] brother.

But God willed it that the girl [that the brother took for a wife] was of no-good origins. She became jealous of the sister, and her heart harbored hate for her; she tried through all possible means to get her brother [i.e., the woman's own husband] to hate her too, so that she alone would remain in the house, and she alone would have all the attention and the [power of] dispensing with [household] matters. She went to her brother [i.e., to her own husband] and said to him, "Your sister is getting to be an old maid! Why don't you marry her off to someone? Your sister is jealous of me; she is trying to imitate me [in acting like a married woman]. She is wearing rouge and powder, and . . . and . . . !" Naturally, at first the brother did not pay attention to what she was saying about his sister. But gradually he began to rebuke his sister: "You, why do you not help with the housework? You, why have you taken off the mantle of modesty [and are acting brazenly like a married woman, instead of the maiden that you are]!"

His sister would hear all this and would not utter a word. Finally, when her brother's wife found out that [her accusations were to] no avail, she decided to get rid of her [once and for all]. So she began to change her tune and display concern and affection [or love] for the girl until he became convinced that she was concerned about his sister, about her health and about her [good] reputation.

That woman was able to perform witchcraft (*siḥr*). She got the eggs of an ibis-bird (*¿ardân*) and gave them to the sister of her husband. . . . (I mean she gave them to her after she had cooked them.) The girl ate them, and after a month or two she began to look pregnant: every day her stomach got higher, her appetite for food was gone, her face became pale and she became weak and unable to stand upon her feet.

The woman, her brother's wife, went to him and said, "See what you sister has done! I told you that 'there is no good in her [i.e., she is no good]!' See the sexual dishonor (*¿âr*) that she has brought upon us. She is illegitimately pregnant!" At first he did not believe her, but she told him, "A woman knows when another woman is pregnant. All you have to do is look and see for yourself!" He became enraged! He went to his sister's room and saw her in bed. She looked exactly as his wife told him [i.e., pregnant]. He charged at his sister and shook her violently, shouting, "Tell me who is the criminal, your lover! Who! Who!" Of course the poor girl could not utter a word. In his rage he grabbed her neck and strangled her! All of that was happening while his wife was standing next to him, egging him on to finish off his sister.

When the girl died, they wrapped her in her bedding and carried her out of the house to the field. They buried her next to a creek, and they returned to the house.

A period passed and a little date palm tree grew out of the spot where the body of the sister was buried. With God's will, the palm tree grew quickly; in a few days it was higher than any other tree. Women used to come and do the laundry at that spot and spread it on the rocks to dry. But the palm tree bent itself for them, until its branches touched the ground so that they could place their laundered clothes on it. When the clothes got dry, the palm tree would bend down again for them to pick the clothes off its stem. When her brother's wife heard of that new spot, she took her clothes to that place. She washed them and when she tried to hang them, the palm tree leaned [all the way] to the ground. She placed the clothes on it[s stem], but the palm tree threw off the woman's clothes and kept the clothes of the brother! And she [i.e., the palm tree] straightened again! The woman was so angry and ashamed; her clothes fell on the dirt and she had to wash them again. The same thing happened several times until she [the brother's wife] became exhausted. Finally, the palm tree kept her clothes and did not throw them off to the ground. But when it was time for her to pick them off, the palm tree refused to lean. The woman was naked. All other women of the region got their clothes back except her! She began to cry and curse the palm tree. Everyone who was passing by saw that woman—naked—trying to get her clothes off the palm tree. And they would laugh. Someone told her husband, "Your wife is naked at the creek." He took some clothes and went to her. He asked her [in anger], "What is the matter woman! Why are you naked!" She replied, "The palm tree would not give me my clothes back!" When he turned to the palm tree, she leaned to him and stayed until he got all the clothes off, then she straightened herself up!

The woman returned to the house humiliated! She said to her husband, "I want you to cut down this palm tree. This palm tree is not a palm tree, I want you to cut it down." He asked her "Why?" She said, "Because it is haunted (*mutajannisah*)!"[727] He took a saw and went to the palm tree. The moment he laid the saw on her, she moaned [in pain], "Ayy-yy-yy!!!" He stopped; then he began to saw again. She said, "Ayy-yy-yy . . . !" He stopped; then he began to saw again. The palm tree said,

> O sawer, for what reason do you saw?
> You're sawing my bones off with the saw![728]

When he heard this, he stopped! But his wife wrapped a shawl around his ears so that he would not hear the moaning. He sawed the tree off; it fell down, and they went back to the house.

An old woman, who was used to going around from one field to another to gather whatever fruit might have fallen off the trees, happened to come by that felled palm tree. She looked around and searched the ground. She saw one date fruit (*tamrah*); she picked her up, and put her in a basket [she was carrying on her head]. [As she walked back to her home] she felt the basket getting heavier

[and] heavier! She finally reached her home and placed the basket down. She found out that the small date, that she had found on the ground, had grown to be the size of a watermelon; she kept on becoming larger and larger until she burst open. Out of it came a little girl: Glory be to the Creator [i.e., of unsurpassed dazzling beauty].[729] The old woman became very happy for she had no one in the world [as family]. The little girl, by God's will, grew quickly and in a matter of days she became a young woman of thirteen, fourteen years of age. Her [foster-]mother, the old woman, concealed her inside the house; because of her beauty, she was afraid to let anyone see her. But one day, she [the girl] went to the top of the house [narrator speaks with excitement] at the time her brother [chanced to be] looking out of the window of his house. He saw her beauty and her modesty and bashfulness (*jamâlhâ wa ḥayâ'hâ*). He fell in love with her: but he did not know then that she is his sister. He went to the old woman and said, "By God, mother,[730] I want to marry your daughter!" She replied, "I have no daughter!" He said, "Then I want to marry your relative!" She replied, "I have no relatives." He said, "Then I want to marry the girl who is visiting you." She answered, "I have no visitors!" He returned home sad.

The girl, when she knew that there was a visitor in the house, stood behind a door and eavesdropped. The moment she heard the voice, she recognized her brother! But she said nothing. He did not despair; he went back to the old woman and insisted on looking through the house for the girl: so he pretended to need to go to the toilet;[731] but in reality he searched the place—as he went through the house, he looked here and there. He found her standing there: right behind the door. The old woman said to him [in a warning tone meant to dissuade him], "Her bride-wealth[732] is too high for you; it is two purses: one [full of] gold and one [full of] silver!" He said, "I will pay!" And he paid her the bride-wealth.

But the girl said, "I will not marry him until he has brought me one ivory bed, and one glass bed. Without these two beds I will not marry him." He—after much searching and travels—brought all that they had asked him to bring, and the wedding celebration took place. On the eve of the consummation of marriage, the two went into their [bed]room; he sat on one bed while she sat on the other. When he came to her bed, the bed spoke up and said,

> An ivory bed, and a glass bed:
> how could marriage between a brother and his sister be legitimate![733]

He asked [with surprise]: "What is that? Who said that?"

But no one answered him. He again approached his bride and they moved to the other bed. When he was about to come close to her, the same thing happened:

> An ivory bed and a glass bed:
> how could marriage between a brother and his sister be legitimate!

He realized that something was the matter. He asked his bride about her story. She told him, "You are my brother and I am your sister. Your wife set up her wiles for me, until you got to hate me and you strangled me." They hugged each other and kissed each other and he said to her, "How truthful you are! You are my sister and I am your brother!"

He went to their home and divorced his wife. He and his sister lived in the home of their parents and grandparents.

And they remained [i.e., lived happily].

❖ 40 ❖

SNAKES IN THE SISTER'S BELLY

(ALGERIA, BERBER)

RENDERED IN WRITING IN ENGLISH, IN JULY 1982, BY BELKACEM [ABU-AL-QÂSIM] Z., AGED TWENTY-FOUR, A UNIVERSITY STUDENT WHO WAS STUDYING IN THE UNITED STATES; HE HAILED FROM THE REGION OF "KABYLE," IN THE ATLAS MOUNTAINS, A HUNDRED MILES WEST OF ALGIERS. HE HAD LEARNED THE TALE FROM HIS SISTER SADIA [SA¿DIYYAH] AND ASSIGNED IT THE TITLE, "THE BROTHER AND SISTER."

A father's cruelty, a mother's conflicting roles resulting in the ultimate self-sacrifice,[734] *a sister raising her infant brother on the bone marrow of their dead mother, and the importance of the maternal-uncle are characteristic themes of this subtype of the "Brother and Sister" tale type. The order in which the pigeon, the wife, and the daughter are cited by the narrator (writer) indicates his perception of the primacy of the pet bird in that man's life in his roles as husband and father.*

LET my narrative be beautiful and roll like a long thread.

[A] long time ago, there was a man who had a pigeon that was dearer to him than anything else in the world. He had it in a cage. He was the only one who fed this bird and nobody was to see it. This man was known to be cruel, and he let everybody know that he would harm anyone who would have anything to do with the pigeon. Also, this man had a wife and a daughter.

One day the daughter insisted on seeing the bird, so the mother tried to show it to her. The bird flew away. Aware of the consequences, the mother told her daughter, "We have to leave and disappear at once before your father gets home."

With some provisions in a basket, the mother left with her daughter. Also, the mother was about to have another baby. At the end of the day they were deep in the forest. They had to find a place to hide because the forest was full of wild animals. They climbed a huge tree and settled for the night. But, deep in the night, the animals that smelled the human odor gathered around the tree. At the same time, the girl told her mother that she needed to relieve herself.

"Wait, my girl!" replied the mother.

"Can't hold it!" [the daughter warned].

But the girl could not [wait]. So the mother offered her ears, one after the other to the girl [so as to urinate in them]. A drop fell on the lion's mustache [i.e., whiskers]. The lion asked the ant to go up and see what was going on. But it was killed by the mother. The animals waited and waited for a long time, then a snake volunteered to climb the tree, and downed her [the mother]. As the animals were going to devour the corpse, the mother rabbit asked the lion, "Sir king, may I ask you to spare the baby in the belly of the mother?" The lion carefully opened her belly and took out the baby fetus and gave it to the mother rabbit.

The animals ate the mother. When the morning came there were only bones left. The mother rabbit looked in the tree and asked the girl to come down. She also gathered all the bones; [. . .] she [cracked the bones] open, got the marrow out, and put it on the biggest bone. Then she gave the baby to the girl and told her: "During your trip, give the baby some marrow when he cries and say, 'O God, let my brother stand up and start walking.' The second time you feed him say, 'O God, let my brother be an adolescent.' You will see an adolescent in front of you. The last time you feed him say, 'O God, let my brother be an accomplished man.' Then you will have a very handsome man in front of you." With all these recommendations well sunk in her brain, the girl took her brother in her arms and started her long journey. She did exactly what the mother rabbit had told her to do, and by the time she got out of the forest, her brother was a man. At dusk, on one day, they entered a village. They knocked on [a] door and an old woman opened it. They told her their story and that they wanted to find a place to live. The old woman offered them her house, saying that she didn't have anybody to take care of her. They lived happily until the old woman died. Then, the sister told her brother that he should get married. He replied, "My sister, why should I get married? We are very happy." The sister insisted so much that he gave up [attempting to dissuade her] and got married.

Soon, the spouse realized how dearly her husband loved and respected his sister, and became jealous. One day, the young spouse found snake eggs in the woods and fed them to the sister. The eggs opened [i.e., hatched] inside the sister's belly, and her stomach started to inflate. They [the brother's wife and her cohorts] did not waste any time telling the brother about it. He would not believe her at first, but it became so obvious that he had to do something about it. The next morning he asked his sister to come with him to the woods and do some work. When they got there he pushed [her] in a hole he had prepared for a cache. He came back home and left her there screaming. A hunter, hunting [near]by, heard her screams and pulled her out. He took her to his house where she told him her story. To find a solution to the problem, the hunter went to the man of the village, full of wisdom, who told him this: "You have to get the snakes thirsty. To do this the woman has to eat a lot of salt. After this hang her by the feet over a bucket of water that you will splash. Then the snakes will fall one by one, attracted by the water." The hunter went to his house and did exactly what the old man had said; the snakes fell.

The sister became healthy, and the hunter married her. After one year, they had a son. The son grew and became a handsome infant. One day his mother asked him to cry when his father gets home and tell him that he wants to see his maternal-uncle. The hunter understood that his wife missed her brother. He gave them permission and they left. At dark, they got to the brother's house and asked for shelter for the night; they did not recognize her because she was very poorly dressed. Before leaving her house she had instructed her son to ask her to tell him a story before he goes to bed. When bedtime came the son started crying and asking his mother to tell him a story. She started narrating her own story since the pigeon sequence. As she narrated her own story, her brother and his wife sank into the ground beneath them. She took her brother by the head and pulled him out of the ground [but she let his wife be swallowed by earth].

My narrative is like a river. I narrated it to nobles.

❖ 41 ❖

CLEVER ḤASAN'S SISTER

(SYRIA)

NARRATED BY GALÎLAH F. (SEE INFORMANT NOTE TO TALE NO. 12); SHE HAD LEARNED IT IN ALEPPO, SYRIA, SIXTY YEARS EARLIER FROM A SYRIAN FEMALE FRIEND. THE NARRATOR TOLD THE TALE TO HER GRANDDAUGHTER—A UNIVERSITY STUDENT—AND STATED THAT UNTIL THEN, IT HAD BEEN SOME FORTY YEARS SINCE SHE HAD LAST NARRATED THIS TALE.

THIS TEXT WAS COLLECTED AND WRITTEN DOWN BY MISS MONÂ ḤANNÂ FAHMÎ.[735] THE STYLE OF THE WRITTEN TEXT REFLECTS THE INFLUENCE OF THE *'INSHÂ*-STYLE ("ACADEMIC ARABIC COMPOSITION") OF THE COLLECTOR-WRITER (RENARRATOR).

Spouses in the likeness of one's sibling and premarital sexual intercourse and consequent pregnancy are among the salient themes of this tale. The story also includes the infrequent motif of a brother's wife as helper of her husband's sister. In his role as a brother to his sister, the hero is totally trusting and forgiving. Significantly, the tale is concluded with the husband's sister moving out of the household to join her own husband. This move is usually the device by which amity is maintained between the two women with reference to each one's interaction with the same man in his roles as brother to the first and husband to the latter.[736]

A repeated error in this written text, with reference to the identity of the male character involved in the act of impregnating the heroine (Clever Ḥasan's sister), is the confusing of "king's son" with "king."[737] *This confusion may suggest Oedipal undercurrents in the tale. Yet, there is no other evidence that might further support such an Oedipal interpretation.*

CLEVER Ḥasan had a sister who loved him and wished to wed him to a beautiful girl. Clever Ḥasan's [only] condition concerning his future wife was that she must be completely identical in looks with his sister. So, his sister kept on looking in all houses and homes until she found a maiden (*fatâh*) who looked exactly like herself, and she wedded her to her brother [Ḥasan].

The sister dwelt in the ground floor [of their house], while Clever Ḥasan and his wife dwelt on the second floor. One day, Clever Ḥasan traveled to India; upon his return, he brought back two presents, for his sister and his wife. The present[s] were two [identical] pieces [of cloth] of red silk embroidered with gold thread.[738]

The sister used to go [up] every evening to her brother and his wife; they would stay up late and play until sleep time comes, then she would go down to her apartment. One day, when the sister went down to her apartment as usual, she noticed that one of the staircase slabs was broken. She looked at it, and saw underneath it large stairs. She went down these stairs, and saw a very large palace whose inside was furnished with regal furniture, and a dining table crowded with delicious foods—but covered up. Clever Ḥasan's sister ate [some] from each plate, then she climbed up the stairs and went to her home [(apartment)]. The sister did not know that this was the palace of the king's son, to which he came every night; he had built it underground intentionally so that he would not be disturbed by people. When the king's son came, he noticed that bits of the foods on the plates were missing. He became angry because people were not leaving him in peace. He decided to wait for the intruder the following night so that he may know who he may be.

The following day, when the sister came down after the customary visit [to her brother and his wife], she removed the slab, went down the staircase, and began to eat. The king's son was watching her from a distance. He admired her, went to her, and they became engaged in a conversation. They spent the night together, but he feared that she might give him the slip; so, he tied her dress to his outer-garment (*bi gilbâbih*).

In the morning, her brother's wife went down [to the sister's apartment] but did not find her home. She saw the [broken] slab and the staircase [to the palace of the king's son]; she descended and searched in all rooms until she saw them asleep together in one bed. She said to her,

O mistress of the beauties! O mistress of the beauties,
the night is gone, and dawn has come.
When will the returning home be done?[739]

Clever Ḥasan's sister woke up very disturbed, and pleaded with her, "Untie me. Untie me, I beg of you." The wife of Clever Ḥasan looked for scissors until she found them; she clipped the dress off, and they ran home before the king's son would wake up. Clever Ḥasan's sister asked his wife not to tell him anything; she [the wife] agreed provided that the sister does not go to the palace again. Clever Ḥasan's sister asked her, "What shall I do about the dress?"—for that dress was [made from] the present her brother had brought from India. Her brother's wife answered her, "Take my dress and wear it."

When the king's son woke up, he did not find Clever Ḥasan's sister beside him: he became very sad.

One of the wondrous coincidences was that Clever Ḥasan happened to be a friend of the king's son since childhood; he also kept him company every night at the coffeehouse. That night, the king's son began to narrate the wondrous [i.e., bizarre] story to Clever Ḥasan; he put his hand in his pocket and said [as he pulled out the piece of clipped-off cloth], "Look. This red cloth is a piece of her dress." Clever Ḥasan was astounded for he knew that this cloth was from India, and that only his sister and his wife have this cloth. He returned home and asked his sister, "O my sister, where is the red dress? Why do you not wear it these days?" The sister went to her room [in her apartment], and put on the dress her brother's wife had given her. He was puzzled and exclaimed, "Many things in the world seem alike!"[740]

Nonetheless, the following day the sister went down the staircase anew, met with the king's son, and they spent the night together. He feared that she might give him the slip, so he tied her hair-braids around his arms. But her brother's wife came in the morning and kept on untying all the hair-braids off the arm of the king's son. Only one knotted braid remained; she clipped it off with scissors. In the evening, Clever Ḥasan met with the king's son, who began to tell him the story, and said to him, "Look at that beautiful hair-braid!" The brother was amazed because the hair-braid resembled exactly his sister's hair. He returned to the house and said to his sister, "O my sister, your hair is beautiful. I want to see your braids."

Her brother's wife had repaired her hair for her, so that Clever Ḥasan should not notice anything. And indeed [he did not]; he wondered much, and exclaimed, "Many things in the world are alike!"

The third night, Clever Ḥasan's sister went to meet the king's son. They slept together. But the king['s son] smeared [the bottoms of] her clogs (*qubqâb*) with tar, so that he may follow her to her place. But, in the morning, her brother's wife [came to awaken her and] noticed the tar; she prevented her from wearing them [the clogs].

However, there was a catastrophe: the sister was pregnant by the king['s son].[741] She told her brother's wife, and began to weep. The wife of her brother—who knew that her husband was a friend of the king's son—went to Clever Ḥasan [her husband] and told him that his sister was very ill, and must rest. She suggested to him that he should ask the king's son for the key to one of his palaces so that she and his sister would go there for rest [and relaxation]. Her husband consented, and—consequently—the king's son consented. The two [women] went to the palace; and there, after nine months, Clever Ḥasan's sister raised one leg [(thigh)], lowered one leg, and brought forth a [baby] boy the size of a calf.[742]

The king's son was unaware that he was in love with [a girl who was actually] Clever Ḥasan's sister. One day he asked one of his maidservants to go to the palace where Clever Ḥasan's sister and wife were [staying], and find out from a distance who those people whom Clever Ḥasan had brought happened to be—only out of curiosity.[743] There the maidservant saw Clever Ḥasan's sister with an infant boy[744] in her arms; [she was] screaming and weeping,

> You, child of a night and of three nights,
> The first night of the three, he tied my dress to his!
> The second night of the three, he wrapped my hair around his arm!
> The third night of the three, he smeared tar on my clogs![745]

The maidservant went and conveyed all that talk to the king's son. He realized that Clever Ḥasan's sister is his sweetheart, and that he has a son by her.

A month later Clever Ḥasan's sister decided to go back to her house. She placed her son in a small basket, filled it with roses and jasmines, and asked one of the servants to give that basket full of roses to the king's son. The king's son became happy and realized that this baby is his son. In the evening, when he met with Clever Ḥasan, he said to him,

> A she-bird flew from your dove-cotes to ours.
> The she-bird begot, and her chicks are with us.
> Will you join the she-bird with the he-bird,
> or will you clear your chicks away from us?[746]

Clever Ḥasan was astounded. He repeated what he had heard to his wife. She said to him, "Go to the king's son and say to him,

> The sheikh is worth two [money] bills.
> The paper is worth two quarters [??].
> And we would find the she-bird on the he-bird."[747]

[He did so.] The king['s son] answered Clever Ḥasan, "I wish to marry your sister." Clever Ḥasan understood the entire affair. He married them to each other.

And they lived in stability and prosperity, and begot boys and girls.

❖ 42 ❖

ONE GARMENT FOR A MAN AND HIS SISTER

(SUDAN)

NARRATED IN FEBRUARY 1971 BY FÂṬIMAH KH. B. (SEE INFORMANT NOTE TO TALE NO. 5). SHE DID NOT REMEMBER WHERE OR FROM WHOM IN THE SUDAN SHE HAD HEARD THIS STORY FIRST. HOWEVER, SHE WAS CERTAIN THAT IT IS "TRUE."

Unquestioning faith and unqualified acceptance of one's fate are overtly expressed in this "religious narrative."[748] *The intent of the narrator was didactic: to illustrate that "even when God wills trouble for people [and they accept fate], matters still turn out well."*

Regarding the fact that this rendition deals with brother and sister rather than husband and wife (as some variants of this narrative do), the narrator cited the following Sudanese truism: He who has no sister is an orphan.[749]

Significantly, the Oedipal motif of son and mother has not been reported in this narrative context.

A man and his sister owned nothing in the world except one shirt.[750] When he would go out he would wear it, and when she would go out she would wear it. They were living like this. One day *sayyidnâ* (Our Master) Moses visited them; he entered their home—their hut.[751] They asked him, "Where to? God willing!" He replied, "To the Mountain to worship God." They said to him, "All right, would it be possible that you ask God as to when our condition will improve?" He answered them, "All right. I will, if God wills!"

As Our Master Moses was speaking with God—(Might and Glory are His)[752]—he asked Him, "My Lord, there is a man and his sister; they are poor and do not own [anything] except one outer-garment. When he would go out he would wear it, and when she would go out she would wear it. When will their condition improve?" God—(Praise is due Him, and Loftiness is His)[753]—[said to him] [narrator speaks in a forceful, resolute tone]: "O Moses, their condition will remain the way it is!"

Our Master Moses naturally took these words and conveyed them as they were said: "Our Lord—(Praise is due Him, and exaltation is His)—says to you, 'your condition will remain the way it is!' " The two, the man and his sister replied at the same time, "We thank God."

One day, that man left [home]; as he was walking he saw a heap of firewood. He looked and saw a cloth purse (*kîs*); he opened it and found in it a [large] sum of money: twenty pounds. He looked here and there and saw the owner of the heap standing nearby. [He asked him], "Paternal-uncle, I found this cloth purse with that sum of money on that heap of firewood of yours!" The man replied, "The firewood is mine, but not the cloth purse, nor the money!" (Meaning what? Meaning the twenty pounds!) He looked for anyone else to whom that sum of money may belong, but he saw no one.

He took the sum of money and consulted with his sister: "Sister, what should we do with that money?" They agreed to buy a horse to assist him in carrying firewood—(for he, too, was a firewood-man). One day he went to gather firewood. The horse came to a spot in the hills and began to scratch the ground with his hoof. Our friend went to see and found a chain; when he pulled it, a box full of gold, silver, and other similar things of God's grants [to man] appeared. They became rich.

That brother and sister built for themselves a palace on the spot where they had the hut and lived in it. A year went by and Our Master Moses was going back to the mountain to speak with His Lord. He stopped by that brother and his sister. Naturally, he expected to see them in the hut, in the same condition in which he had seen them before. Instead, he found them in a palace.

"Peace be upon you!"

"And upon you be peace, Our Master Moses!"

"Aren't you the same people whom I visited last year?"

"Yes. God has improved our condition, Thanks to God."

Our Master Moses was astonished. When he spoke to Our Lord—(Praise is due Him, and exaltation is His)—he said to him [narrator speaks with a tone denoting submission and awe], "My Lord, allow me to ask one question! I had asked you about the condition of the brother and sister who were poor and owned only one garment. You stated, 'Their condition will remain as it is.' Now, I have visited them and found them in a palace; now they have, and they have [plenty]. What is the reason?"

God—(Praise is due Him, and exaltation is His)—answered him: "O Moses, their condition changed because they thanked me, [even when they] knew well that they will remain poor and that their condition will not improve. The reward for their thanks [is that] I improved their condition."

(As you know it is said, "Thanks are due God, who is the only One that is to be thanked for an affliction").[754]

❖ 43 ❖

THE DEATH OF *SHAIKHAH*[755] SHAFÎQAH'S BROTHER

(EGYPT)

NARRATED IN MAY 1982 BY MISS SANÂ' W., AGED NINETEEN, A UNIVERSITY STUDENT, FROM SALAMOAN, NEAR THE CITY OF MANṢÛRAH, DAQAHLIYYAH GOVERNORATE, EGYPT. SHE HAD HEARD THIS "TRUE EVENT" FROM OTHER GIRLS IN HIGH SCHOOL, AS A "MIRACLELIKE MANIFESTATION (*KARÂMAH*)" BY THE WOMAN SAINT. "THIS [MANIFESTATION] WAS ALSO WRITTEN ABOUT IN NEWSPAPERS AND MAGAZINES," THE NARRATOR ADDED.

The mystical bond between brother and sister, madness due to a brother's death, and a vanishing (uncontrollable) corpse are at the core of this "local saint's legend." Implicit in the narrative account is the assumption that the husband and infant son were forsaken for the dead brother; (cf. Type 985, Brother chosen . . . , *Tale No. 45, below, esp. note 768). Also expressed is the theme of a sister's nudity (in the room of the dead brother), and the saintliness of the insane.*

A close parallel of this contemporary social legendary event is given by al-'Ibshîhî (ca. *1388–1446) in his* al-mustaṭraf *(Vol. 1, p. 149), as an undertaker's personal labor reminiscence. According to this fifteenth-century account, one day a "youth of beauty," who knew the time of his own death—which is a saintly trait—contracted the undertaker to prepare him for burial; the youth died the same day. The youth's sister, who resembled her brother greatly, kissed her dead brother and promised to join him soon. She asked the undertaker whether his wife could prepare her for burial as adroitly as he had her brother. Upon the undertaker's return accompanied by his wife to the brother and sister's house, the sister declared that only the wife may enter. The undertaker's wife found the young woman facing the Qiblah (Mecca) and deceased. She performed the corpse-washing on her, and* "'anzalathâ ¿alâ 'akhîhâ *(lowered her upon her brother [in his grave])."*

[Thus, the brother and sister, who may be assumed to have lived alone together, were buried together in one grave.] (See Section V, Tale No. 43, "Other Renditions," variant no. 4, p. 450.)

WE have, in Salamoan, a lady saint. Her name is *esh-shaikhah* Shafîqah; there are some people who call her [by the nickname of] 'Omm-¿Ali (Mother-of-Ali). This lady saint was married [and living with her husband] in a town—that might have been Faqqûs, or Esh-Shoabak in Sharqiyyah [Governorate]. She was married to someone who was rich: a man of means. During her youth, she was very beautiful; they say she was the most beautiful one in our town and her father married her off to that man from Sharqiyyah [Governorate] and she went with him [to live in his hometown].

God willed that her brother should die. She had only one brother and two sisters. Her brother died—she was the immediate younger.[756] When they were about to entomb him, he [i.e., the corpse] adamantly refused to be buried. They kept on placing him on the bier and taking him to the cemetery, but whenever they would look for him, they would find the bier empty. They would return home and look [only] to find him laid [on his back] in his room. People kept wondering: "Why is he refusing to be buried? He was neither indebted nor did he owe or was owed; also, he did all the [required] fasting and praying."

It happened that his sister Shafîqah had not arrived [for the funeral]—that was before she entered the ranks of saints (*qabl ma-titmashyakh*) [by becoming a recluse with diminished mental faculties, but with enhanced spiritual capacities]. She arrived . . . ! She entered upon him and cried silently over him.

They [the undertaker and bier bearers] came back, placed him on the bier anew, and went to the cemetery; they placed him down, buried him and returned. [This time he remained in his grave.]

His sister entered his room and—(we appeal to the Merciful, i.e., God: *fassarnâ bi-r-Raḥmân*). She suffered some mild diminished mental capacities (*luṭf*).[757] She remained naked; she would not allow a piece of clothing to touch her body. She would not eat, nor drink, nor speak, nor . . . , nor. . . . She remained in this condition for a long while—say six or seven months. [It happened] that she was still a bride—one full year had not gone by [since her marriage]. She had given birth to a baby boy from that husband of hers. He tried many a time to get her to return with him [but did not succeed, for] she had become [i.e., entered] in[to] another world (*¿âlam tânî*)!!

They force-fed her; they pushed food down her throat. She remained in her room with whatever garment that happened to cover her; she adopted the dervish ways (*'iddarwishit*), and the saints' way (*'itmashyakhit*). She said nothing without it turning out to be true. Many miraclelike manifestations (*karâmât*) appeared at her hands. Some people say, "The Veil[-of-gnosis] has been lifted off her[758] [i.e., she became clairvoyant, can see the Divine sphere]." Many a person did she heal! And many a [sinful] person forswore sin due to her.

❖ 44 ❖

MY DAUGHTER IS MY SON'S WIFE

(SYRIA)

NARRATED BY 'ĀMÂL Q. (SEE INFORMANT NOTE TO TALE NO. 16). SHE HAD HEARD THE STORY AND THE PROVERB REPEATEDLY FROM HER OWN MOTHER AND OTHER "LADIES FROM PROMINENT FAMILIES" IN SYRIA. RELATIVES OF THE

NARRATOR WHO WERE PRESENT AGREED THAT THE *MABDA'* ("PRINCIPLE," I.E., CORE THEME) OF THE PROVERB IS WELL KNOWN.

One of the forms of adults' playful interaction with children is to pose to a child the possibility of brother-sister marriage: "Would you marry your sister?" "Would you marry your brother?" or "We will marry you to your brother!" Though didactic in nature—labeled: a mathal *(proverb, example)—the following story is an elaboration on this hypothetical incestuous theme. It may be viewed as a fantasized legitimation of the brother-sister marriage.*[759]

THERE was a woman who had a son and a daughter. Her husband had died when her children were young, and it was she who raised them until they grew up and reached the age of marriage.

One day her son told her that he wanted to marry, and asked her to look for a suitable wife to live with them in the[ir] house. The mother agreed and searched here and there, and in houses and households—among suitable families (I mean), but she did not find the right girl. She wanted to marry her son to someone who is like her [own] daughter in beauty, manners, character—(I mean) of good breeding. She began to search in neighboring towns and villages and provinces, but she found no trace of a young woman who would resemble her own daughter and whom she could consider to be precisely like her own daughter. She did not want to find someone else, for the daughter-in-law (*kunnah*) causes so much trouble [for her husband's family], if she happened to be from a not-so-good family.

So, the mother decided to marry her own daughter to her son, (I mean to marry the sister to her [the sister's] brother).[760] When she told her son about it, he said, "[This is] the best you could have done!"[761] He agreed—because by marrying his [own] sister there would be no annoyances, no quarrels, no [situation that could be described as], "His wife is unhappy [and has left for her father's home] (*maratuh ghaḍbânah*)." This would be so because his sister is the one who will become his bride: [she would be] from them and into them.[762]

ASIDE

An Egyptian listener comments: "We [in Egypt] say, '*zaitnâ fi-dqiqnâ*' (Our [own] oil, into our [own] flour)"—(Mot. T105.1.1§).

Narrator [responds]: "We, too, have this [saying in Syria]."

Cf. Aside, p. 317.

[Narrator continues main story.] For it is said, "[A] son's wife [is injurious], even when [she happens to be only] a stick."

ASIDE

A listener attempts to explain this truism; but the narrator presents its story in full. (See informant note to Tale No. 22, and note 468, this section.)

[Narrator continues main story.] (Where were we?—May God pray on behalf of Our Master Muḥammad.[763] Oh yes: the woman was going to wed her son to her daughter.)

And, indeed, she married the sister to her brother.

In the morning following the consummation of the marriage (*ṣabâḥiyyah*), the bride woke up. She went out of the bridal chamber to make the morning tea for her groom and herself. As she was coming out of the kitchen, she met her mother and said to her [in a disgruntled manner]: "Good morning."

The woman [mother], turned around and said [in bewilderment]: "Amazing![764] The face is that of my [own] daughter, but the huff is that of [a] son's-wife!"[765]

❖ 45 ❖

SON, HUSBAND, OR BROTHER?

(YEMEN)

NARRATED IN APRIL 1982 BY ¿A. AL-SH., AGED TWENTY-TWO, A UNIVERSITY STUDENT, FROM YEMEN. (SEE INFORMANT NOTE TO TALE NO. 39.) SHE HAD *READ* THE STORY TWO OR THREE YEARS EARLIER IN A MONTHLY MAGAZINE (*AL-¿ARABÎ*) PUBLISHED IN KUWAIT. THE NARRATOR'S STYLE FOR THE TELLING OF THIS SERIOUS STORY (*QIṢṢAH*) REFLECTS THE STYLISTIC DEVICES OF CLASSICAL ARABIC (*'INSHÂ*-STYLE, PRESUMABLY PRESENT IN THE PRINTED LITERARY

SOURCE); ALSO, THE TEXT IS PRESENTED LESS DRAMATICALLY, WITH RELATIVELY FEW DIRECT QUOTATIONS FROM THE STORY'S CHARACTERS.

This rendition of a literary narrative represents what may be described as latent folk traditions *brought forth into the overt expressive realm (folklore) via a popular or academic culture channel of communication. The traditionality of the value of the narrative's contents is evidenced by the recurrence of the expression of the strong affective bond between brother and sister. As a* folk narrative, *the present text demonstrates the high degree to which a "latent tradition" is readily embraced by an individual who is cognitively and affectively apt to perceive and identify with its contents.*[766] *Tyranny in this text is assigned to al-Ḥajjâj ibn Yûsuf (d. 714), one of the most faithful and ruthless partisans of the Omayyad regime.*

The dilemma of having to make difficult choices between close relatives constitutes the affective core of this literary explanatory (etiological) narrative. The proverb with which the tale is concluded is recurrent in oral traditions, yet the story associated with it seems to exist only in older literary books. Ms. 'Â.R. al-Ḥamdân, a Kuwaiti folklorist, commented on the present writer's inquiry about the tale by pointing out that the proverb is used in Kuwait as a dirge: women lament the death of a brother by stating: "A[nother] child would be born, [. . . but] the fire of [losing] a brother burns without fuel."[767]

Implicitly, the pattern of reorganization of the social environment is present in our text: with the inescapable elimination of husband and son from a woman's life, she—as a sister—ends up with her brother (with no other men in her family, as is the case in the present text). (Also see Tale No. 49.)

The Arabness (and womanness) of this choice is further demonstrated by the fact that in neighboring sub-Saharan African communities, with value systems different from Arab ones, variations on this tale type appear as dilemma tales with no socially institutionalized choice or answer.[768]

AL-ḤAJJÂJ was a tyrant (*ṭâghiyah*), a dictator (*diktâtoar*), I mean. It is said that he killed and imprisoned thousands upon thousands[769] of innocent [people] who resisted the Omayyad State. One day there was an uprising and al-Ḥajjâj was ordered by the caliph to extinguish it. Of course, he dealt with the rebels ruthlessly and put down the uprising. Naturally his army brought back captives. He ordered that all should be placed in detention, interrogated, and then executed.

A woman came. She was in a hysterical state, crying and shrieking, with her gown slit, head uncovered, etc. etc.[770] She stood by the gate of al-Ḥajjâj's palace and started demanding in a very loud voice to see al-Ḥajjâj. The guards tried to drive her away but she would not leave or stop yelling. It was a big commotion and people from everywhere gathered to see what was happening. Finally, it chanced that al-Ḥajjâj heard of the matter and ordered that they let her in. When she was taken to him he asked her what the matter was and why she was causing such a commotion. She said to him, "Your soldiers have under detention (*taḥt al-'i¿taqâl*) three persons from my family: my son, my husband, and my brother! They are now in your jail awaiting execution. Yet they are innocent of what they are being accused. These are the only men left in our family!"

Al-Ḥajjâj felt pity for her—(and that was unusual, for he was very cruel and his heart knew no mercy); he decided to allow her to choose one of the three [to be pardoned], and he set the condition that the person to be set free would never rebel against the caliph again! So, he told her to choose one. She [readily] said, "I choose my brother!" Al-Ḥajjâj and all his assistants were stunned. He asked her [in amazement], "Why did you not choose your son or your husband?" She replied: "'A[nother] son would be born; a[nother] husband would be found, and a brother would be lost.'"[771]

Al-Ḥajjâj asked her about the meaning of her statement; so she said, "I am young, if my son dies I can give birth to another son. I am pretty; if my husband dies I can always find another husband. But how will I ever be able to replace my brother, or find someone who would be a substitute for him!? The brother is irreplaceable."

Al-Ḥajjâj was amazed. He said to her, "Take your brother and go!"

❖ 46 ❖

FAIR FÂṬMAH[772]

(SUDAN)

NARRATED BY FÂṬIMAH KH. B. (SEE INFORMANT NOTE TO TALE NO. 5). SHE HAD HEARD THIS *ḤUJWAH* (FANTASY-TALE) "IN THE SAME MANNER AS ALL THE OTHER TALES—WE ARE ALL WOMEN, ALONG WITH OUR CHILDREN."

The following fantasy-tale illustrates a girl's flight to avoid the advances of her incestuous brother, who has become infatuated with some or her physical attributes.[773] *Yet, the separation between brother and sister is often temporary (see the variants, below) and/or the girl marries a person who may symbolically be equated with her brother. This situation is most vividly illustrated in another Sudanese text entitled "The Son of Nimêr," narrated by a fifty-year-old widow:*

> *The son of Nimêr once took his horse to the river. There he found a lock of hair with which he could [have been able to] tie his horse. He said, "I'll marry the girl to whom this lock of hair belongs even if she happened to be my sister, Fâṭimah."*
> *[. . .]*
> *[The sister ran away and hid inside an old man's skin. She was captured in that disguise by] the son of Nimêr.*
> *[. . .]*
> *They started playing [a game . . .]. In the end the son of Nimêr beat the old man and tore the garment of dry skin that Fâṭimah had, and there was a beautiful girl. They . . . got married.*[774]

Although the assumption is that the two characters named "The Son of Nimêr" are unrelated, the psychological implications are evident. The same unintentional (noncognitive) "error" is manifested in the Egyptian variants cited below through the use of the formulaic ending, "And they lived in prosperity and stability and begot boys and girls," thus indicating the same affective implications.

Other salient themes in this Sudanese text include: masking as another person by hiding inside that person's skin (the disguised flayer), ogress's mash, obstacle flight, and crocodile ferry.

ONCE boys were swimming in the river. After they finished swimming and went away, girls came and swam, then went home together—young maidens, seven or eight of them. After that boys came again and got into the river. As they were splashing and playing about, one of them found a hair floating. He pulled it out of the water: he pulled, pulled, [and] pulled. The hair was entangled in something at the bottom [of the river]; [finally] he managed to disentangle it. It was so lo-o-o-o-ng! He screamed, calling his mates; they gathered around him. He showed them the hair and said, "I will marry the girl from whose head this hair came!" Another boy said, "Let [each one of] us measure it against [his . . .] sister's!"

The boy went home and told his mother and father about the hair and his agreement with the boys. They were glad that their son was going to get married. The woman [his mother] looked at the hair and took it to the village's girls [in order to match it against their hair]. She found no one whose hair was that long or that beautiful. She returned home and said to her daughter, "Faṭmah, hold this hair beside yours." She held it. The match was perfect!! The woman told her man. They agreed that they would marry their daughter to their son. The boy's sister—Fair Faṭmah (*es-samḥah*)—came in[to the room], with her father, her mother, and brother [already in it]. She was carrying a heavy load on her head:

"Help me carry it down, mother."

"Don't say 'Mother!' Say: 'My mother-in-law (*yâ nasîbtî*)!' "

"Help me carry it down, father."

"Don't say 'father!' Say: 'My father-in-law (*yâ nasîbî*)!' "

"Help me carry it down, brother."

"Don't say 'brother!' Say: 'My groom (*yâ ¿arîsî*)!' "

Faṭmah understood. She dropped her load and ran outside [the house]. She ran and went to all her girlfriends: "Girls, your brothers are planning on marrying you! There is no more staying [living] for us in this country!" During the night, every girl smuggled herself out of her home and all of them left.

They walked all night and all day; they became tired and hungry, [for] they had with them neither food nor drink. Finally, they saw [at a distance] two fires: one on this side [to their right], the other on that side [to their left]. Faṭmah said, "Girls, this [right-side] one is the Arabs' [camp] fire; if we were to go there, we will be safe but get no supper. That one is the ogress's fire;[775] if we were to go there, we will not be safe but will get supper!" They argued with one another for a while, and finally settled on going to the ogress's fire. Faṭmah said to them, "Before you eat anything of hers, look at me and see what I will be doing and do like me."

[They went to the ogress's house.]

"Mother Ogress, greetings!"[776]

"Greetings to you, Fair Faṭmah, and to your companions; and greetings to [i.e., blessed is] the day you were led here!"

The ogress made them comfortable, gave them [water] to drink, and immediately began to prepare supper for them. She prepared porridge of ground [human] bones and milk from her own breast—(this is the ogress's mash:[777] whoever eats from it becomes crazy). When she was done, she said to them, "Come on, girls. Eat!"

Faṭmah said to them, "Girls, this is ogress's mash—whoever eats from it becomes crazy! Do not eat!" The girls did like Faṭmah told them to do: each one would put a morsel in her mouth, then when the ogress was not looking, she would spit it in her own bosom. But there was one idiot girl (*hablah*); she would swallow her morsels, and exclaim: "Oh, your cooking is tasty, Mother Ogress!" But Faṭmah would poke her [with her elbow in the ribs], and shake her head so as to warn her. But the idiot girl would cry out, and complain, "Mother Ogress, Faṭmah is hitting me!" The ogress would ask, "Why are you hitting your sister?" and Faṭmah would reply [slyly], "I saw her dozing off; I wanted only for her to . . . 'Be alert!' " (You see, she was still warning the idiot girl without the ogress becoming aware of that.) But that idiot girl paid no attention, and did not understand [the hint].

After a while, they all went to sleep. All the girls, due to their being fatigued, went into the seventh sleep [the deepest sleep]. The ogress also went to sleep; but she was only pretending, for her eyes were closed—(when ogres go into deep sleep their eyes would be open). The ogress got up quietly and began to sharpen her knives and axes. Fair Faṭmah pretended to be getting up, "A-â-â-ah, it is morning already!" The ogress said, "No, it is only the moonlight! Go to sleep!" and went on with what she had been doing: sharpening her axes and preparing to eat the girls. A short while later Faṭmah woke up again, "A-a-a-ah, it is morning already!" and, again, the ogress said, "No, it is only the moonlight! Go to sleep!" [This same thing happened repeatedly:] Faṭmah would wake up, "A-a-a-ah, it is morning already!" and the ogress would say, "No, it is only the moonlight! Go to sleep!" Faṭmah would wake up, "A-a-a-ah, it is morning already!" and the ogress would say, "No, it is only the moonlight! Go to sleep!" Faṭmah would wake up, "A-a-a-ah, it is morning already!" and the ogress would say, "No it is only the moonlight! Go to sleep!"

Finally the ogress shouted, "Faṭmah, why don't you sleep? Fish in the river have gone to sleep; birds in the sky have gone to sleep! Why don't you sleep!?" Faṭmah replied, "I am thirsty, Mother Ogress!"

The ogress got up and brought her water from the vat (pottery water tank).[778] [But] Faṭmah said to her, "For all my life I've never been given jug-water to drink; I drink [only] water from the seventh sea: fetched in a sieve, [served] in an uncut [whole] gourd[779] [as drinking cup]!"

The ogress went to the seventh sea. With a sieve that she had with her, she tried to get the water; but every time she would lift up her sieve, all the water would have seeped away. She kept on trying from sunrise till noon: but to no avail. Finally [she had an idea], she began to wring the sieve's strings onto the gourd: but water would glide down off it back into the river. She stayed there [trying] from noon time till sunset; and, still, to no avail. At the end of the day she headed home in utmost vexation.

Meanwhile, Faṭmah awakened her mates, and said to them, "Girls, this is our chance to escape! Let us go in a hurry!" All of them got up, except the idiot girl. She said to Faṭmah, "I am staying here! The food is good and plenty, and I have to do no chores!" Faṭmah warned her, "This is the ogress! You have eaten her mash and have become crazy! Come with us!" The idiot girl refused, and went back to sleep; but Faṭmah would not leave her behind and said to her, "You are coming with us," and dragged her along.

Before leaving the ogress's house, Faṭmah got the ogress's daughters: seven [of them], and placed them in their own sleeping places, and said to them, "Cover yourselves well, for the cold of the night goes straight to the bones!"

The ogress returned home and arrived; she was vexed at Faṭmah and said [to herself], "I am not going to let her speak again!" She went directly to where the girls were asleep. With her axe, she went: "*Huh, Huh, Huh, Huh!*" [i.e., chop, chop, chop!] She killed all the seven [who were asleep]. Then she, of course, wanted to have some supper. She lifted the cover off the first: her mind flew away. She saw that it was her own daughter, then the second, then the third: all seven. She ran after Faṭmah and her companions; but they were too far [ahead of her]. She yelled, "By the Lord, may you, O Faṭmah, run across ankle bracelets (*ḥujûl*), one on top of the other, and you separate them!"

Immediately, before Faṭmah and her mates there appeared a heap of ankle bracelets. They sat down on the ground, and began to pick and choose. (That was a ruse by the ogress to catch up with them.) When they sat down to sort out the ankle bracelets, the ogress came closer. Faṭmah looked and saw her coming at a distance. She said to the girls [in a commanding tone], "Girls, give up the ankle bracelets. The ogress is about to catch up with us!" All of them ran behind Faṭmah, except for that girl who was an idiot. The ogress caught up with her—while she was still picking and choosing—and ate her up. Then she said, "I must catch up with Faṭmah and her mates!" [And she resumed the pursuit.]

Then she yelled, "By the Lord, may you, Faṭmah, run across earrings, one on top of the other, and you separate them!"

Immediately, before the girls there appeared a heap of earrings. They sat down on the ground, and began to pick and choose. When they sat down to sort out the earrings, the ogress came closer. Again, Faṭmah looked and saw her coming at a distance. She said to the girls, "Girls, give up the earrings. The ogress is about to catch up with us!" Faṭmah ran, and the girls ran behind Faṭmah.

When the ogress realized that they did not linger around, she yelled, "By the Lord, may you, Faṭmah, come across a sea: its beginning is in the east, and its end is in the west!" Immediately, a sea appeared before them; they could not cross it. [Narrator speaks in a tone denoting despair.] They sat down waiting for the ogress.

Faṭmah saw a crocodile in the water. She said to him [in an imploring tone], "Father crocodile, would you take us across to the other bank, and [in return] we give you a good catch?"[780] He said "Yes! What is the catch?" Faṭmah replied, "Your catch will be one of us!" He was happy and said, "Ride on my back." They got on his back, and he swam until he ferried them to the other side. Before reaching the other bank, Faṭmah saw the ogress on the other side [that they had just left]. She [the ogress] called, "O, Fair Faṭmah! Why do you do this to your mother [the ogress]! I went to get you the water from the seventh sea; I prepared mash for you! And you run away like this! Come back!"

Faṭmah pretended to believe her! She yelled back, "You come with us." Then she said to the crocodile, "We forgot our grandmother (*ḥabbûba-tnâ*) behind! Would you ferry her to us, and [then] we will give you your fare!" The crocodile let them [the girls] off, and went back to get their grandmother. She got on the crocodile's back, and he swam back towards the other bank. While [it was] in the middle of the sea, Faṭmah yelled at him, "Father crocodile! Your catch is with you!" Immediately, the crocodile turned around [thus dumping the ogress off its back], and snatched her between its jaws: the ogress was finished!

The girls found themselves on an island. They lived there in God's safekeeping; Faṭmah was their chieftainess [commanding them:] "Do this!" and "Don't do that!" and they would listen to her. They found a cave and dwelt in it.

One day, the camels of Wed-al-'Amîr[781] came to pasture near the cave; an old man was their herder. All the girls hid [in the cave], except Faṭmah. She went to the old man and asked him, "Father, how does one flay a human being?" He answered her, "With the thorn of the *kitir*[782] tree!" She got a thorn from a *kitir* tree, and hid it in her head [i.e., hair]. When the old man came again, she said to him, "Let me louse you." As she was lousing him, she reached for the *kitir* thorn and stuck it into his head: his hide fell off him—just like the skin of a [ripe] palm date. She wore it, and looked like an old man a hundred years old.

When neither the camels nor the old man who was with them did return, the prince [Wed-el-'Amîr] became worried. He took some of his friends and went out to look for them. They followed their tracks; the tracks took them to the cave. The camels were scattered with no one to look after them. One [of the prince's companions] said [exclaiming], "There are people in this cave!" Another said, "Those in the cave are women!" A third said, "The females in the cave are maidens!" All rushed into the cave, and each carried out one beautiful girl; only Wed-al-'Amîr had remained outside. When he entered the cave he found only that old man: every one [had] said, "I do not want him," and left him there.

Wed-al-'Amîr let his companions marry the girls; [as for himself], he said to [the disguised] Faṭmah, "What are we going to do with you, grandfather!? Would you shepherd those camels?"

She answered, "I am old; I cannot pasture camels."

"Would you pasture the cows?"

"I am too old to pasture cows!"

"Would you pasture the geese!"

"With God's help! I will try!"

Every day Fair Faṭmah would take out the geese to pasture, around the house, and would go to the spot in the garden with the spring. She would take off the old man's skin and bathe in the spring water; afterwards, when she was done, she would put the skin back on and, again, would look like the old man. One day a slave saw her in the water. He [happened to be speechless], he went: "'Aa-a-a-a-a!"

Faṭmah got out quickly, put the old man's skin on, and said:

> The foot is a pigeon's [small, pretty], O speechless one!
> The hair is ostrich's down, O speechless one!
> The eyes are gazelle's, O speechless one![783]

The slave went to Wed-al-'Amîr, [being unable to talk, he could only make the sound]: "'Aa-a-a-a! 'Aa-a-a-a!"

Wed-al-'Amîr asked Faṭmah, "Old man, what is the slave saying?"

She answered, "Prince, no one knows but God!"

The same thing happened the following day, and the following day, and the following day. Wed-al-'Amîr decided to follow the slave and see for himself what was causing him to say: "'Aa-a-a-a-a! 'Aa-a-a-a-a!" [and act in such a strange manner].

The following morning, after dawn prayers, he said to his mother, "I am going to look around. [Let no one know where I have gone.]" She answered him, "Peace be with you." He hid in the bushes, and saw: a maiden as beautiful as the [full] moon of the fourteenth [day of the lunar month] get out of the old man's skin. She took her clothes off, and placed them beside the well. He took one of her rings, and left [in the same manner] as he came [without being seen].

When Faṭmah got out, she found that her rings were one less; she counted them [on her fingers]: "This finger has one, this finger has one, this finger has one, but this one has none!"

Then she would count once more: "This finger has one, this finger has one, this finger has one, but this one has none!" Then she would count once more. She suspected the slave [who cannot speak]. She got hold of him: "Where is my ring!?" [But all he could say is:] "'Aa-a-a-a-a! 'Aa-a-a-a-a!"

The following day, Wed-al-'Amîr said to Faṭmah, "Old man, take a rest from herding today. All my friends are married and are with their brides. [Only I am lonely.] Come play checkers[784] with me: the winner may slit the garment of the loser!"

[They played:] Faṭmah won, but she did not slit his garment; Faṭmah won again, and she did not slit his garment. She won seven times, and each time she would forgive him [from having his garment slit]. Finally, at sunset-prayer-time, he won once. He insisted on slitting her dress.

"I forgave you seven times!" [she protested.]

"Even though!"

"I am an old man!"

"Even though!"

"I am a sick man!"

"Even though!"

Then Wed-al-'Amîr, with his sword, slit Faṭmah's garment. He cut deeply and her old man's skin [also] fell off: a maiden as beautiful as the moon of the fourteenth emerged! He married her.

And that is the tale of Fair Faṭmah.

46-1

"IF I AM YOUR SISTER, I CAN'T BECOME YOUR WIFE"

(EGYPT)

NARRATED IN MAY 1982 BY 'OMM EL-¿IZZ (SEE INFORMANT NOTE TO TALE NO. 19). SHE HAD HEARD THIS TALE WHEN A GIRL FROM OTHER GIRLS.

Available data indicate that the "normal form" of this tale in Egypt is incomplete and fragmentary.[785] *Yet, all the texts have maintained the incestuous themes of a sister's exposure, and a brother's desire to marry his sister. The name of the brother in the present variant suggests that this rendition is associated with (or perhaps derived from) the same "incomplete" narrative tradition presented as Tale No. 46-2.*

The formulaic ending constitutes another incident of reorganization of the social system in favor of the brother and sister remaining together.[786]

ONCE there was a boy named Ḥesain and he had a sister named Sit-el-Ḥusn w-el-Gamâl.[787] One day Ḥesain was returning from school, hungry. He went to the oven room and found his sister, Sit-el-Ḥusn w-el-Gamâl, sitting in front of the oven baking bread. He said to her, "I am hungry. Give me a loaf of bread." She replied, "Wait, it is not done." Ḥesain waited, then when she took out the first batch, she handed him a hot loaf. He took a bite and found a long hair in his mouth. He pulled the hair; it was a very long hair. Then he said, "Look at this hair: it comes from [the head of] a girl with beautiful hair. I must marry the girl from whose [head] this hair came!" He looked at his sister, sitting in front of the oven; she had a long braid of hair thrown over her back. He said to her, "I must marry you."

His sister, Sit-el-Ḥusn w-el-Gamâl, answered, "If I am your sister, I may not become your wife!" But Ḥesain replied, "No, I must marry you!"

She left the dough and the baking and ran away. She went and climbed a sesban tree[788] and commanded, "O sesban tree, get higher, get higher. My brother wants to marry me! If I'm his sister, I could not become his wife! And rise, rise, O sesban tree!" [The tree got higher and higher.]

Her father heard that his daughter was on top of the tree. He went to her and said, "O daughter, why don't you come down off that tree?" She answered, "My brother, Ḥesain, wants to marry me. If I am your daughter, you could not become my father-in-law! And O sesban tree, rise, rise!!"

Her mother heard that her daughter was on top of the tree. She came saying, "My daughter is on the sesban tree! O sesban tree, get shorter, get shorter!"

She replied, "If I am your daughter, you could not become my mother-in-law. And, O sesban tree, rise, rise!!"

Her sister heard that her sister, Sit-el-Ḥusn, was on top of the tree. She came running, saying, "My sister is on the sesban tree. O tree, get shorter, shorter!!"

She replied, "If I am your sister, I could not become your brother's wife. And, O sesban tree, rise, rise!!"

Her brother, Ḥesain, came, saying, "My sister is on the tree. O [sesban] tree, get shorter, get shorter!"

She replied, "If I am your sister, I could not become your wife. And, O sesban tree, rise, rise!!"

He said to her, "Come down, and I will not marry you."

She said, "If I am your sister, I can't become your wife. And, O sesban tree, get shorter, get shorter until you become as high as my pinkie!!"

The tree got shorter and shorter and shorter until it was as small as her little finger. She got down and went home.

And they lived in prosperity and stability and begot boys and girls.

❖ 46-2 ❖

ḤASANAIN AND 'ÛLIYYA

(EGYPT)

RENDERED IN WRITING IN MARCH 1965, BY MAḤMÛD M.M.S.¿A., A FIRST-YEAR PUPIL IN RELIGIOUS JUNIOR HIGH SCHOOL, WHO WAS PRESUMABLY BETWEEN ELEVEN AND FOURTEEN, FROM KAFR EL-SHAIKH GOVERNORATE, NORTHWESTERN EGYPT. THIS TEXT WAS SUBMITTED TO MR. ¿U. KHIḌR AS PART OF HIS TALE-COLLECTING PROJECT.[789]

The sister's name ('Awâ'ilah, or 'Ûliyyah [??]) in this fragmentary rendition, coarsely written down, is atypical; it suggests the word 'ûlâ *which denotes Alpha, the foremost, or the first.*

Also noteworthy is the intrusive element ("and he married her") included in the multiple formulaic endings for this rendition.

THERE was a boy named Ḥasanain and a girl named 'Ûliyya. [One day] 'Ûliyya was kneading the dough and Ḥasanain was standing [by her]; she was beautiful with thick long hair. As she was kneading the dough her hair fell in it. Ḥasanain says to her, "Take a loaf [out of the oven for me] to eat because I am hungry." She took out a loaf so that he may eat; the hair entered his mouth. He kept on pulling the hair out of the bread [that was already in his mouth] for an hour [for it was extraordinarily long], meanwhile he [was] saying to her, "I will marry you!" She became afraid and went out of her home in order to mount [the peak of] the hill.

The father came saying, "My daughter 'Ûliyya is on the top of the hill. Hill! Get shorter, get shorter [so that I may reach her]!"

['Ûliyya replied,] "If I were your daughter, I may not become the wife of your son. Hill, get higher, get higher!"

The mother came saying, "My daughter 'Ûliyya is on the top of the hill. Hill, get shorter, get shorter!"

['Ûliyya replied,] "If I were your daughter, I may not become the wife of your son. Hill, get higher, get higher!"

Her brother Ḥasanain [came] saying, "My sister 'Ûliyya is on top of the hill. Hill, get shorter, get shorter!"

[She replied,] "If I am your sister, I may not become your wife. Hill, get higher, get higher!"

[He said to her,] "Okay, I will not marry you! Hill, get shorter, get shorter!"

'Ûliyya says, "Hill, get lower, get lower!"

And they lived in prosperity, and he married her, and they lived in prosperity and distributed it among the girls. And bit by bit, the tale is over.

❖ 46-3 ❖

[THE SISTER'S SHOE]

(EGYPT)

NARRATED BY ¿AZÎZAH M., AGED ABOUT SIXTY-FIVE, MOSLEM, BORN IN EL-ḤILMIYYA DISTRICT OF CAIRO. THE COLLECTOR DESCRIBED THE NARRATOR IN ENGLISH AS "AN OLD MAID," WHICH COULD MEAN THAT SHE WAS NEVER MARRIED, OR THAT SHE IS AN ELDERLY PERSON WORKING AS A MAIDSERVANT. THE NARRATOR COULDN'T REMEMBER WHEN OR WHERE SHE LAST HEARD [THE TALE], "BUT IT WAS LONG AGO." THIS TEXT WAS COLLECTED AND TRANSCRIBED IN ARABIC BY MISS SHARÎFAH MAẒLÛM.[790]

The first part of this narrative typically appears as an introductory episode in "the Brother and Sister" tale (Type 872§). The overtly incestuous latter part of this text tends to substantiate the argument on behalf of the existence of a similar deviant desire in other variants, where that urge is expressed less explicitly.[791]

❖ Brother and Sister ❖

ONCE there was a man and a woman who were married and [had] begotten a girl and a boy. The girl is [i.e., was] older than the boy. The two [parents] died and left a lot of money for their children but no one knows [i.e., knew] where the money was because they had it hidden.

One day the girl was cleaning the house. She came across the money in a hidden spot inside the wardrobe. So, she said to her brother, "Suppose someone told you about [the whereabouts of] the money. What would you do?" He answered her and said, "I'd purchase a drum and a pipe and I would roam about singing in the neighborhood." She realized that he was still [too] young and that it was not necessary [for her] to tell him about the money.

Days and years passed on and the boy grew up. One day his sister asked him, "If someone were to tell you about the whereabouts of the money, what would you do?" He replied to her, "I'd marry, establish a home, work well, and do benevolent deeds." The sister realized that the boy had grown up and [that it was] possible to tell him about the money. [So], she told him.

He decided that he must marry; when she asked him, "Whom will you marry?" he said to her, "You!" She said to him, "[This is] not possible!!! It happens that I am your sister." He answered her that it was not possible for him to marry except a good girl like her.

His sister thought. She gave him a single shoe from a pair of shoes (*fardit gazmah*) of hers so that he may go and look for a girl whose foot would fit into the shoe[792] and he would marry her.

The boy traveled and kept on searching in all the cities [or countries]; it was not possible for him to find a [female] person "into whom the shoe would enter" [i.e., could fit]. So, he returned to his sister and said to her, "I must marry you."

The girl ran away from the home; during the night she left and walked through the hill[s]. She laid down on the ground when she got tired.

The sultan's son was promenading through the hills and found the girl lying down on the ground. He woke her up and asked her about herself; so, she told him the story. He fell in love with her and told her to come with him into [his] palace. She went with him and lived in the palace. The sultan's son called in her brother and told him that he was going to marry her because it is sinful for someone to marry his [own] sister, and indeed, he married her.

And they lived in stability and prosperity and begot boys and girls.

❖ 47 ❖

WDAI¿AH

The Sister of the Seven[793]

(LIBYA; EGYPT, WESTERN DESERT)

NARRATED IN JUNE 1970 BY THE DAUGHTER OF ZÎNAH (OR, ZAINAH) D. (SEE INFORMANT NOTE TO TALE NO. 38), AGED ABOUT THIRTY YEARS, MARRIED, AND LIVING IN TOBRUK, LIBYA. SHE HAD HEARD THE TALE WHEN A GIRL FROM HER MOTHER.

The importance of the existence of a sister for a brother is overtly stated in the present tale: "We need a sister."[794] *Conflict between a presumably white girl—in her role as sister to a brother—and a female rival for the brother's attention is the affective core of this fantasy-tale. The severity of punishment dealt to the rival—a black girl—is indicative of the degree of resentment that characterizes the attitudes of "white" females toward such a female adversary.*[795] *The emphasis placed on the nature of the hair of the two young females reflects the significance of hair as part of a woman's "privates" (*¿awrah*) in Islamic worldviews.*

THERE was, from olden times, that man. He had a wife and seven boys, young men. They had seven guns and seven horses and everything else in sevens—seven this, seven this, and seven that. Their mother became pregnant. They went to her and said, "We need a sister. If you bring forth another boy, we will leave. If you bring forth a girl, we will stay. We will go out to the mountains [and await]. If you bring forth a boy, raise a red flag so that we would know that there's a [new] boy and we will not return. If it is a girl, raise a green flag so that we may know that we have a sister and then we will come back home." And they left.

They went out to the hills and lived by hunting. Every day they would look toward their house to see. When the woman's time came she gave birth to a baby girl and she said to an old servant, an old woman servant, "Go raise the green flag so that my sons will know that they have a sister and come back home." The woman went and raised the red flag. When the seven boys saw the red flag they said, "There is no living for us in this country" and they went far into the hills. The woman, their mother, waited for them to return and she waited and waited; they did not come back. She named the little girl Wdai¿ah.

The girl grew up as an only child; she had neither brother nor sister. When she came of age, she said to her mother, "Mother, all the girls go out to gather firewood and I am staying at home. Let me go with them." Her mother said, [in an imploring tone], "Daughter, you are my only child. The house has neither a son nor a daughter [of mine] in it. Something might happen to you." The girl replied, "All the neighbor girls go and return; nothing happens to them." Finally, she [the mother] said to her, "Peace be with you, [go]!"

The following day, with sunrise, Wdai¿ah went out with the neighborhood girls—seven or eight or nine girls—all of the same age. They went to gather firewood—the girl was from a big house [of notables] and was not used to this sort of work. She followed the other girls and went wherever they went. After a while, when they were far away from their homes, they started saying to her [in a twitting tone], "You little Wdai¿ah, you who have evicted the little seven."[796] The girl went home and said to her mother, "The girls were saying to me, 'You Wdai¿ah, who have evicted the seven.' What does that mean?" Her mother said to her, "Daughter, you have seven brothers who said, 'We need a sister. If you bring forth a boy, raise a red flag so that we would know that there's a boy and we will not return. If it is a girl, raise a green flag so that we may know that we have a sister and then we will come back home.' You came to us, but your brothers have not returned. To where did they go, I do not know. Where they are, I do not know. You are the only thing that I have left."

When the girl heard that, and that her seven brothers had left home because of her, she said, "I must go find my brothers." Her mother implored her, "O daughter, you are the only one who is left for me. Don't go. The hills are wild and you are still young." But the girl insisted. Due to her persistence, her mother finally said to her, "Peace be with you." She (the mother) prepared rations for her and gave her a little bead (*kharazah*) and said to her, "If you want to talk to me, talk to this bead, and then listen to it." She also gave her a black slave-girl (*¿abdah*) to serve her. The girl, Wdai¿ah, mounted a horse and set out searching for her seven brothers.

She went from town to town and from country to country looking for her brothers until they—[she and the slave-girl]—became very tired. The slave-girl said to her, "Mistress, dismount so that I can ride for a while." Because she [Wdai¿ah] was good-hearted, she was going to let her ride while she would walk behind the horse. Wdai¿ah remembered the bead that her mother had given her. She took it out and spoke to it, "Mother, the slave-girl wants to ride." Her mother's voice came through the bead, "No, no, don't you dare. You are the mistress. You stay mounted." She went on. After a while the slave-girl said, "Mistress, mistress, why don't you dismount and let me ride for a while." Again Wdai¿ah asked her mother, "Mother, the slave-girl wants to ride." Her mother's voice came through the bead, "No, no, you are the mistress, you stay mounted." This went on many times until they reached a spot. In that spot, there were two springs: a spring for . . . (No! There was one spring only.) . . . [The spring was] called "Slaves' Spring" (*¿ain el-¿abîd*);[797] whoever would bathe in it, would change: if one happened to be white, he would become black; and if one happened to be black, he would become white. The slave-girl knew that but she was wily; she did not tell her mistress. She said, "Mistress, mistress, let us rest here. We have been traveling in the desert and now we have become dirty and covered with dust. Let us bathe in this spring!" Wdai¿ah was not suspecting treachery; she said, "All right, but I'll ask my mother first!" But the slave-girl said, "Let us dismount first and get comfortable and then you ask permission [of your mother]." While they were preparing a spot under the palm trees so as to rest, the slave-girl hid the bead. When Wdai¿ah could not find it, she thought, "There is no harm in bathing." She went into the spring and came out black—a piece of coal. The slave-girl went in, and she came out as white as milk. Wdai¿ah began shouting, "Mother, mother;" her mother could still hear her and would say, "Don't bathe in this spring. Don't bathe in this spring," but the voice was very faint, and Wdai¿ah could not make it out. She looked for the bead and when she could not find it, the slave-girl said, "Mistress, let us leave. Your brothers are waiting [to be found]." Wdai¿ah left her affairs up to God, mounted the horse, and the two of them left.

After a while, the slave-girl said, "Mistress, mistress, dismount so that I may ride for a while; I am tired." Because she was not expecting treachery, she thought: "Poor girl, I'll let her ride." Of course her mother's voice could not reach her. Wdai¿ah dismounted and the slave-girl rode, and they went on—the two of them—the slave-girl: ladylike, on the horseback, and the lady: slavelike, trailing after her on foot. When Wdai¿ah, the mistress, got tired, she said to the slave-girl, "Dismount, I will ride!" but the slave-girl refused and kept on going. They kept on going like this and it chanced that they came to the place where Wdai¿ah's seven brothers were [living]. Wdai¿ah recognized them and exclaimed, "These are my seven brothers!" As soon as the slave-girl heard that, she leaped off the horse and ran toward the seven young men, yelling, "My brothers, my dear brothers! I am your sister! The servant woman raised the red flag by mistake. You left because of me and now God has reunited us." They hugged and kissed one another.

Meanwhile Wdai¿ah was standing by astonished. She said, "I am your sister. This is a slave-girl." The slave-girl said, [to the brothers], "This is a treacherous slave-girl. All the way she has been trying to kill me and she claims to be your sister. See: I am white; she is black." And then she got a stick and beat up Wdai¿ah and told the brothers, "Put her to pasturing the animals." The oldest one said to her [the slave-girl], "True, you are our sister, dear to us. You stay with us in our home and manage our affairs. As for the slave-girl, you dispense with her as you wish." So the black slave became the lady, and the lady became a black slave looking after sheep, goats, and camels. Every morning Wdai¿ah would sit among the animals and bemoan her situation:

> Wondrous are my traits, wondrous are my traits!
> Go tell my father,
> "Wdai¿ah was a dear one.
> Wdai¿ah has become a slave-girl.
> She drives the cows, she drives the water buffaloes,
> she tends to the water wheel!"[798]

The animals would hear her say so and would cry along with her. She would cry and the animals would cry [along]. The animals, due to their sadness, ceased pasturing; they neither ate nor drank. After that day they became very thin. Her brothers noticed that the cows, the water buffaloes, and the camels were getting shriveled—all except one she-camel who was deaf. That she-camel, who could not hear Wdai¿ah's talk, kept on eating and was well. The eldest brother said, "The animals are sick! O Aḥmad . . . " —(that is the youngest one [of her brothers)—" . . . go and see what is the matter!" Their sister—(who was actually the slave-girl)—said, "The slave-girl who is tending them must be stealing the fodder. Beat her up!" Now, that Aḥmad, their youngest, went to the hills [pasture] and hid somewhere in order to find out what was causing the animals to be sick, but he saw nothing. The next day he came closer [to the slave-girl and the flocks]. He heard her moaning:

> Wondrous are my traits, wondrous are my traits!
> Go tell my father,

"Wdaiʿah was a dear-one.
Wdaiʿah has become a slave-girl.
She drives the cows, she drives the water buffaloes,
she tends to the water wheel!"

He said to himself, there is something [wrong]. He went to the older brother and said, "It seems that this one here in our house is not our sister! We must look for the truth of the matter!" Aḥmad went and brought the slave-girl—(who was their real sister)—from the field and they said to her, "What is your story?" She told them the story. And she told them [about how] the other girls reproached her: "You Wdaiʿah, you who have evicted the seven!" and how she left her home looking for them along with the black slave-girl, and how the slave-girl hid the bead and bathed in the spring and came out white, while she bathed in it and came out black. She told them the whole story. In the meantime, the slave-girl, whom they thought was their sister, was saying, "She is a liar. I am your sister! Your beloved, I genuinely feel for and empathize with you."[799] Aḥmad, her [Wdaiʿah's youngest] brother, pulled the head-scarf off the slave-girl's head; they found her hair kinky and ugly-looking. He pulled the head-scarf off their [real] sister's head; they found her hair [to be] like silk, and long: it rolled down to her waist. [In spite of this evidence] the slave-girl still kept on saying, "I am your sister! I am your sister!"

They took the two to the spring. They dipped the slave-girl in it, and she came out black—[as black as] a piece of coal! [Narrator laughs.] They dipped their sister in it and she came out [as white as] milk! They took her to their bosom [i.e., hugged her] and said, "We do have a sister!"

She said to them, "Let us return to our father and mother." They returned to their home; and [when they got there], they called out: "He who loves the Chosen Prophet would gather firewood for a fire." [They set up a fire and] they threw the slave-girl in it.

And they lived [happily together].

❖ 47-1 ❖

[WE NEED A SISTER]

(ALGERIA, KABYLE)

RENDERED IN WRITTEN ENGLISH IN JULY 1982 BY BELKACEM Z. (SEE INFORMANT NOTE TO TALE NO. 40). HE HAD LEARNED IT FROM "AUNT OUIZA."

This written rendition presented by a young male has maintained all the affective characteristics of this female-bound narrative. The stereotypical role of the wily old woman is assigned to Settût (i.e., old woman), a recurrent title for this character in North African lore.

LET my narrative be beautiful and roll like a long thread. [A] long time ago, in a mountain village, there were seven brothers who gathered together and decided, "If this time, our mother gives birth to a male, we will leave for good." The bad old lady, Settût, who heard them when they made their resolution, went to where they were waiting and announced to them, "Congratulations, your mother had an eighth son." Of course, Settût wanted the brothers away and had lied to them. The mother had borne a daughter. The girl became an adolescent. Once, she went to get water from the source. There she met Settût who told her, "Here is the girl who sent her brothers away." Once home, the girl became sick. Her mother, alarmed, asked her what had happened to her. Then the girl repeated Settût's words. The mother told the girl the truth [about] what her brothers had decided, and why they had gone since she was born. It is her brothers that the girl decided to go search for.

The mother gave her a horse, a slave-[girl], food, and a small grain that would make contact between them. While leaving, her mother told her, "On your way you will find two fountains, one for slaves [(blacks)] and the other for whites; make sure you don't both bathe or drink in the former." After this she left, followed by her slave-girl. They went mountain to valley, again and again. From time to time, the mother would call her daughter using the grain, but now her mother's voice became very weak [due to the distance].

When they saw the two fountains, the slave-girl bathed in the whites' fountain, while the young lady did the same in the slaves' fountain. The girl also lost her grain while bathing.

At a distance from the fountains, the girl could briefly hear her mother; after a while she completely lost contact with her. Meanwhile, the slave-girl was turned white and the girl turned black. Realizing that she had become white, the slave-girl ordered her mistress down from the horse, but the girl refused. After a while the slave-girl became more impatient and forced the girl down from the horse. At last, the two females got to the village where the seven brothers lived. As soon as she saw the brothers the slave-girl rushed toward them and kissed them and told them, "Settût lied to you. I am your sister. I missed you so much, but now you are going to come with me to our parents' house." They answered her, "For now, take some rest, and then we will see." The slave-girl became the mistress of the house and the girl had to serve her and take the seven horses to the fields. As soon as she got to the field, in the middle of the horses, she would start singing this song plaintively:

> Rise up, rise up, rock.
> Let me see my parents' place.
> The slave-girl is mistress of the house.
> And me, I look over [i.e., look after] the horses.
> Cry horses, like I do! Cry!

She stopped eating. Six of the horses cried with her. The seventh, being deaf, ate like usual. While the horses that cried along with the girl became very skinny, the brothers noticed it and one brother decided to follow her secretly. He saw her put her food on the rock and start crying her plaintive song. The youngest brother went up to her and asked, "Who are you, creature?" She answered, "I am your sister," and told him how she had found out about them from Settût, and how she had become black.

The brother went to his brothers and told them what he heard and had seen. To solve this problem, they went to the old man, full of wisdom, and told him what they knew and he answered, "The slave-girl can change her color but she can't change her hair. What you will do is buy some henna (hair coloring powder) and ask them to put it on in front of you. Your true sister has long silky hair." The brothers bought the henna and ordered both of the girls to take off their head covers and put it on. The girl took off hers and her long silky hair covered her back until her waist. The slave-girl refused, saying, "I can't do that in front of my brothers; it is disrespectful." The youngest reached to her head and removed her head cover to reveal her ugly short hair, looking like a shrub. The brothers asked their sister what would satisfy her. She answers, "I would like her head over the fire, her foot as log." Then he killed the slave-girl, and followed his sister's orders. They went to the whites' fountain and brought back some water with which she washed and then became white again. They all returned to their parents' home.

My narrative is like a river. I narrated it to nobles.

BROTHER AND BROTHER

❖ 48 ❖

THE MONKEY WIFE

(SUDAN, EGYPT)

NARRATED IN MAY 1982 BY ḤAMÎDAH ?, AGED FIFTY-SEVEN, BORN IN THE SUDAN OF A SUDANESE MOTHER AND AN EGYPTIAN FATHER WHO WORKED THERE FOR MANY YEARS. SHE IS MARRIED TO AN EGYPTIAN, A NATIVE OF QINÂ GOVERNORATE, SOUTHERN EGYPT, HER FATHER'S HOMETOWN; SHE STATED THAT SHE HAD HEARD THE TALE FROM WOMEN IN HER FAMILY, BOTH IN THE SUDAN AS WELL AS IN EGYPT.

A children's play rhyme (from Qinâ Governorate), that is also used as a lullaby, states:

The boss's box, O mother,
is full of brides, O mother!
No one is beautiful, O mother,
except my brother's wife, O mother!
She went to swim, O mother,
the necklace is cast by her side, O mother!
And I want a bride, O mother,
who would dance before me, O mother;
and would untie my belt, O mother!
My belt is woolen, O mother:
stacked gold, O mother!
I stacked it well, O mother,
And nobody felt [anything], O mother!"[800]

When chanted by a female, the song may be a simple expression of admiration or jealousy of a woman's sister-in-law; but when the chanter is a male—as in this text, the song is an expression of adulterous desire (paralleling tendencies).

Rivalry among wives of brothers (silfât/salâyif)[801] *provides the affective core for this fantasy-tale. The narrative does not express overt conflict among brothers (the husbands), yet latent dissociative feelings are present. These feelings stem from wishing to have the brother's wife for oneself and resentment of one's own wife.*

Although fraternal rivalry is a central theme in folk traditions, tales that are demonstrably narrated predominantly by women seem not to express this aspect as the organizing element. In such female-bound tales, brother-brother rivalry commonly occurs as details.[802] *As indicated elsewhere, with reference to Type 303B§* (Six Jealous Brothers against their Youngest . . .)*, "In most cases where the informant is a female, the punishment of the culprit brothers is either not included in the story or is extremely weak."*[803]

Other significant themes include conflict between sons and father over payment of bride-wealth (mahr)*,*[804] *marriage and kismet* (qismah, *i.e., one's lot in life, or fate), and the supernatural power of a saint's spittle.*

A king had three sons. These three sons became grown up, and they were staying with their father at his home. They wanted to marry, but their father told them, "You are still too young for marriage. Wait for another year." The following year their father told them, "Still, you are too young for marriage. Wait for another year." Whenever they would go to their father and say, "Father, we would like to marry!" He would reply, "Still, you are too young for marriage. Wait for another year."

Finally, they became desperate. The eldest of the brothers said, "Our father does not want to give us money for our marriage—[bride-wealth, *mahr*]! The only way for us to get wives is to leave home and set out on our own through the lands of [the kingdom of] our father." That night they relied on God, and the three of them left their parents' home and went a-traveling: [roaming aimlessly in the manner of] dervishes.

After their horses had galloped some distance, they came to a fakir's abode at a deserted spot. They greeted the fakir, "Peace be upon you!"

"And upon you be peace, Sultan's sons! What brings you here?" [he replied].

"We are going through the world in search of our kismet [lot in life]! Our father refuses to marry us; so, we set out to find wives for ourselves!"

He, that hermit said to them, "Spend the night here. Tomorrow, if God wills, each one of you will find his kismet."

They spent their night there. In the morning, the hermit said, "You eldest! Hand me your spear." He [the eldest brother] handed his spear over to the hermit. The man spat on it, and returned it back to the boy and said, "Go! Throw this spear in the air as hard as you can, then follow it. Wherever it will land will be the place where your kismet is." The boy took his spear and left. Then he turned to the middle one, "You middle one! Hand me your spear." He handed his spear over to the hermit. He did with him as he had done with the eldest. And the middle boy took his spear and left. The same thing happened with the youngest. All three headed back to their father's town.

They reached the town, and halted their horses on its outskirts. The first boy got hold of his spear and hurled it into the air—in the direction of the houses—as hard as he could. The spear traveled upward as high as the eye can see, then began to descend. He followed it from street to street, and from house to house until it landed into the door of a big house, the house of the vizier. The vizier's daughter opened the door. He saw that she was beautiful and married her. Then, the middle boy hurled his spear into the air and followed it until it landed into the door of a big house: the house of the biggest and richest merchant in the country. The daughter of the biggest merchant opened the door. He saw that she was beautiful and married her.

The turn was now the youngest of the three. He got hold of his spear and hurled it into the air—and like his brothers aimed in the direction of the houses—as hard as he could. The spear traveled upwards as high as the eye can see, then began to descend. But instead of going to a house, it veered toward the wilderness, and finally landed in the sand in front of a cave. He entered the cave and found a cage; in the cage there was a she-monkey. When he saw her his heart folded. Meanwhile the she-monkey kept on jumping up and down inside the cage. He said [sadly, but in a tone denoting resignation], "This is my kismet!" He carried the cage home with the she-monkey in it. He went in at night so that no one would see him or her.

When the elder boy arrived home with his wife, his father and mother welcomed them very much. The king was pleased because his eldest son has married well, and the mother was very happy when she saw her son's wife because she was beautiful. And when the middle boy arrived home with his wife, they also welcomed them—but not [as much] as their first son. The king was pleased because his middle son has married well; and the mother was very happy when she saw her son's wife because she was also beautiful. But, when the youngest boy arrived home with his wife and they saw what he has brought back, they could not utter a word. The boy's mother cried, for her youngest son married an animal: a she-monkey! The king also wept—because his little son did not do as well as his brothers. But they said [in resignation], "Marriage is a kismet and [one's predestined] lot!"[805]

The youngest put the she-monkey in his room and locked the door with the key. He would leave at dawn and would return only to fall asleep.

Now the wife of the eldest wanted to make a big feast and invite her *silfât* (the wives of her husband's brothers), and everyone else so as to show them her cleverness in cookery. She went into her kitchen and prepared a great feast. Before dinnertime, the she-monkey was preparing food too; she sent her maidservant to her sister-in-law—the wife of the eldest [brother], and said to her, "Go and ask for some hot pepper. When she asks 'What for?' tell her 'My mistress is preparing pudding.'" The maidservant went to the wife of the eldest:

"My mistress says, 'By God, give us some hot pepper.'"

"What for?"

"My mistress is preparing pudding."

"Do people put hot pepper in pudding!? I don't have any!"

She [the sister-in-law] thought: "Why should I give her my hot pepper! I'll use my own hot pepper in my own pudding!" Then she got hold of the [hot pepper] can and dumped whatever it contained into the pudding.

When the guests came, and ate the food that she [the she-monkey] had prepared, they exclaimed [in admiration], "'All-â-â-â-h!" But when they tasted the desert made by the other, they exclaimed [in disgust], "Yuk-k-k-k! Is there anyone who would put hot pepper in pudding!" The wife of the eldest went back to her room in great shame.

Meanwhile, the she-monkey got out of her monkey skin—she was a beautiful human being but in monkey's skin. Her hair was [so long that it reached all the way] down to her ankle. She put on a pretty dress and went down from her room to the dinner. No one knew who she was. When the elder brother saw her, he said [to himself], "I wish this girl were my wife, instead of that loser (*khâybah*)[806] I married!" Before the dinner ended, she returned to her room without anyone noticing, and got back into her monkey skin. When the middle brother saw her he [also] said, "I wish this girl were my wife!"

Now it was the turn of the wife of the middle [brother] to cook and show everyone. She went into her kitchen and she also prepared a bigger feast. Before dinnertime, the she-monkey was preparing food too; she sent her maidservant to the wife of the middle [brother], and said to her, "Go and ask for some sugar, and when she asks you 'What for?' tell her 'My mistress is preparing fried fish.'"

The maidservant went to the wife of the eldest:

"My mistress says, 'Please give us some sugar.'"

"What for?"

"My mistress is frying fish."

"Do people fry fish with sugar? I don't have any!"

She thought: "Why should I give her my sugar! I'll use my own sugar with my own fish!" Then she got hold of the [sugar] can and dumped whatever it contained into the frying pan, along with the oil and the fish!

When the guests came, and ate the food she [the she-monkey] had prepared, they exclaimed, "Very tasty!" But when they tasted the fish they exclaimed, "Yuk-k-k-k! Is there anyone who would put sugar on fish!" And the wife of the middle one also went back to her room in great shame.

Like the first time, the she-monkey got out of her monkey skin, and put on a dress prettier than the previous one; she went down from her room to the dinner. Still no one knew who she was. When the middle brother saw her he lamented, "I wish this girl were my wife, instead of my wife, the loser!" And as before, she returned to her room without anyone noticing, and got back into her monkey skin.

Now it was the turn of the wife of youngest, the she-monkey, to cook and show everyone. She prepared the greatest feast. Her two sisters-in-law decided to avenge themselves on her over the pudding with red pepper and the fish with sugar [tricks]. They went to her room to see what she had done. When they got there she, before their very eyes, took off her monkey skin. They saw beauty second to none. They asked her, "How did you do that? You are a she-monkey!" She answered them, "If you fleece off your old skins, immediately new prettier skin grows in its place." The two of them did not suspect this bit of news. They ran to their rooms and each got her [heel-rubbing] stone and descended on her own face: scrape, scrape, scrape, until her face became like a piece of liver.

Meanwhile, she put a pretty dress—prettier than the previous two—and went down from her room to the dinner. Still no one knew who she was. When the elder brother thought, "I wish this girl were my wife, instead of that loser I married!" And the middle brother thought, "I wish this girl were my wife, instead of that loser I married!" When the guests ate the food she had prepared, they exclaimed, "Very tasty!" When they ate the desert, they exclaimed, "Very tasty!" When they drank the fruit punch, they exclaimed, "Very tasty! Very tasty!"

Before the dinner ended, she returned to her room without anyone noticing. But this time the youngest brother followed her. She got into her room and as she was getting back into her monkey skin, he came into the room. He got hold of that skin and threw it into the fire. It burned, and she remained in her human form. When his father and mother saw her, they became very happy, because their youngest son really knew how to choose [a wife]. When his two elder brothers saw what their wives have done to themselves, they couldn't bear looking at their [skinned] faces. They divorced them and sent them back to their fathers' homes.

The king put his youngest son in charge of all the affairs of the kingdom.

D. BOY AND MOTHER'S BROTHER

❖ 49 ❖

¿AZÎZ SON OF HIS MATERNAL-UNCLE[807]

(BAHRAIN, QATAR)

NARRATED IN THE SUMMER OF 1986 BY ¿AYSHAH/'OMM Ḥ., A SEVENTY-YEAR-OLD, NONLITERATE GRANDMOTHER (SEE INFORMANT NOTE TO TALE NO. 11). FOR THE NARRATOR, THE STORY IS "TRUE."

THIS NARRATIVE WAS COLLECTED WITH THE ASSISTANCE OF MRS. KALTHAM AL-Ḥ.

In oral nonreligious folk traditions, the character of Abu-Zaid the Hilalite is, perhaps, unsurpassed in terms of significance and recurrence. In contemporary folk traditions, Abu-Zaid seems to have acquired the status of culture hero; his sîrah *(life history, in the form of an epiclike romance)*[808] *is very popular throughout the Middle East and in numerous communities in sub-Saharan Africa.*

The salient folk theme of a young hero being an offspring of brother-sister incest harks back to the ancient traditions of the region. In ancient Egypt, for example, "Anubis . . . was, according to some legends, the son of Naphthous and Osiers, who mistook that goddess for Isis [his wife and twin sister]."[809] *Similarly, among pre-Islamic Arabs, a legendary character with a similar experience is Luqmân the Wise, whose sister conceived through tricking him into sexual intercourse with her; she gave birth to Luqaym (i.e., Little Luqmân).*[810]

Less explicit allusions to this theme occur in contemporary lore; an insult in Egypt, for example, states, "His mother begot him by the maternal-uncle [i.e., her brother]"; a universal Arab adage, with no overt erotic implications, states "A maternal-uncle is [a] father."[811]

While the majority of narratives expressing excessive intimacy between brother and sister do so covertly, the brother-sister incest in this "true story" is overt and graphic. Significantly, the brother-sister incest incurs no punishment.[812] *By contrast, the punishment of an incestuous mother (as in the case of Tale No. 5) is ever present and very severe.*

Of special interest here is the murderous and seemingly incongruent attitude of the maternal-uncle, who is ideally perceived as loving, toward the grown-up sons of his sister. This theme occurs also in other contexts when the sister's son is allied with (or is linked to) his own father.[813] *In all instances, the sister still sides with her brother, and both the brother and his sister remain together after the reorganization of the social milieu.*

The final episode in this true story—a historical legend—represents the ideal of great love in Arab cultures: it is nonsexual love; typically such a sentiment is concluded with the death of both lovers. This theme gives rise to the etiological ending—a belief legend—of the present text.

PRAY on behalf of the Prophet.

No one has come to you except[814] ¿Azîz Son of His Maternal-uncle. His maternal-uncle is [A]bû-Zaid, the hero of the arena, and the horseman of the horsemen. That Bû-Zaid has [i.e., had] a sister whose husband was simple-minded. She had begotten children by him, but she wanted a boy who would be like her brother Bû-Zaid. [She thought], "I want a son in the likeness of my brother, who would elevate my name among the tribes."[815] That Bû-Zaid had concubines but he did not father any children by them: he was extremely careful [not to ejaculate in them]. She [his sister] went to one of those concubines, the one whose turn it was that night, and gave her some gold necklaces and said to her, "Go away." She replied, "Your brother would kill me." She [the sister] replied, "Do not be concerned! He is my brother; leave this matter to me!"[816]

His sister entered upon him[817] during the night! She did not say a word! He entered upon her and had coition with her!![818] As he was having intercourse with her, she had a needle with her—when he was about to ejaculate,[819] she pricked him with the needle [in the loins]. When she pricked him with the needle, he could not control himself and the semen surged into her.[820] [After that], she exited. He did not suspect anything. The Lord willed it and she brought forth that ¿Azîz. She called him, ¿Azîz Son of His Maternal-uncle (¿Azîz-*ben-khâluh*).

Bû-Zaid's sister had six boys and a girl [by her own husband]. Bû-Zaid heard of ¿Alyâ—a maiden from one of the Arab tribes. She was a king's daughter. Her name was ¿Alyâ. She was affianced to her paternal-cousin (*'ibn-¿amm*). He [Bû-Zaid] fell in love with her only through hearing about her. He went to his sister and said to her, "I will take along your eldest son [on my trip to fetch ¿Alyâ]." He went to his young she-camels . . . ; he had raised three young she-camels; he fed them the best fodder in order to have them grow strong. They had matured. He got hold of the first one and pressed on its back [with his elbow]. Its back snapped. He left it and went to the second; its back also snapped. The third one howled and its back got bloody, but its back did not snap. He exclaimed, "This is the one!"

He and the eldest son of his sister went into the desert. After several days the rations and water ran out. Bû-Zaid said to his sister's son, "Serve me coffee (*qahwînî*)."[821] They had neither water nor fire. Bû-Zaid went to sleep. He woke up. He found nothing. He got angry. He hit him [the boy]. He killed him. He returned to his sister [and said],

"I will take your second son."

"Where is the eldest?" [she asked].

"He left!" [Bû-Zaid answered].

He took her second son. He took the second, and as he did with the eldest, he did with his brother. He returned to his sister.

"I will take your [next] son."

"Where are the eldest and his brother?"

"They left!"

He took her third son. As he did with the eldest and his brother, he did with the middle one [i.e., the third]. He kept on doing that until all the six were gone. There remained only ¿Azîz. He took him, [and gave him the same treatment until he reached the point where he said to him], "Make me coffee!" and he [Bû-Zaid] went to sleep.

Neither was there water nor firewood. It was midday. The boy took his own she-camel and ran it until it sweated. He gathered the sweat and placed it in the coffee pot. He cut off the saddle ropes and set them afire. He made the coffee. His maternal-uncle woke up and found the coffee ready. He realized that ¿Azîz was unlike the other six and that he was the man for hard times. They packed up and headed toward ¿Alyâ's land. After much laborious travel they reached her country. They entered the king's town. They entered at dusk. They found drumming and dancing in the streets. That day ¿Alyâ, the sultan's [king's] daughter, was to marry her paternal-cousin:

"How is reaching her to be achieved?" [Bû-Zaid wondered.]

"Maternal-uncle, you have grown old. I will bring her for you!" [¿Azîz stated].

"How will you bring her from the depth of the palace?" [Bû-Zaid asked].

¿Azîz was very handsome. He said to his maternal-uncle (who was black), "We make ourselves into [wandering] poets." They dressed as poets. They stood under her window and chanted. The sultan's soldiers came [and inquired], "What do you seek?" ¿Azîz replied, "We are poets!" And he sang. His voice was beautiful. He sang aloud. People gathered around him. His eye was fixed on [¿Alyâ's] window. ¿Alyâ looked out the window. She was in her wedding attire. She fell in love with him. She nodded at them to enter. The guards prevented them. She said to her father, "Father, allow the poets to enter. These are poets: No confining conditions imposed upon them [by religion], and there is no fear of them."[822] He [her father] consented that only one, but not the other, would enter. ¿Azîz entered.

[¿Azîz, evidently, managed to enlist the aid of an old woman—¿Alyâ's hairdresser.]

The old woman said [in chant]:

> O ¿Alyâ's playmates, depart away from her;
> [for] a lion came for her, from the farthest distance.
> Around her are gazelles [??], and by her sides are partridges,
> and the chest, O ¿Alyâ, is the resting place for the [fatigued] riders.[823]

[So, ¿Alyâ's playmates did leave her.]

[Meanwhile], his maternal-uncle stood outside. He [¿Azîz] said to him, "I will lower her [with a rope] to you."

¿Azîz entered into the harem quarters—(in these older times, men had their hair long).

¿Azîz said [to the old woman], "We will take her with us."

She [¿Alyâ] had become enamored with him. She said, "What about my paternal-cousin and my father's soldiers?"

¿Azîz answered, "I will sit in your place."

He took off his clothes. She put on his clothes and gave him her bridal costume. He put it on. He lowered ¿Alyâ [with ropes] to his maternal-uncle, Bû-Zaid. As for himself, he laid down on the bed in her stead. Her paternal-cousin—that is the groom—entered her room. He sat next to him on the bed. He [¿Azîz] turned his back to him. The groom turned to the other side of the bed. ¿Azîz turned his back to him. The groom would go to one side and ¿Azîz would turn his back; then he [the groom] would go to the other side, and ¿Azîz would turn his back again. They did that for some time. ¿Azîz dozed off. The groom lifted the veil [and saw the bride's face]; ¿Azîz was beardless (*'amrad*).

"This is a man with long braided hair!!!" exclaimed the groom. He went out shrieking [in chant],

> You, ¿Alyâ's family, [help me]: this is not ¿Alyâ.
> This [woman] is a Hilalite man with long claws![824]

The bride's mother came in a hurry. [She wondered,] "What is the matter, man!"

He yelled, "This is not your daughter. This is a Hilalite-man, with long claws!"

She replied, "Do not tread on our honor!" [and chanted],

> This is ¿Alyâ, and all people know of her [honor]:
> chaste [. . .], not a trodden door's thresholds.
> Wound ¿Alyâ, with an injury that wouldn't maim [??],
> and clip off [one of] ¿Alyâ's long hair-braids.[825]

Then, she [calmly] said, "Wait until morning, [we will have examined the matter]; [meanwhile], chop off one of her hair-braids; and make a cut on her left thigh. In the morning we will see!" He went and chopped off a braid; and with his dagger, he made a cut on the left thigh. Then he went out.

¿Azîz woke up to find his thigh bloody and his hair-locks chopped off; he realized what had happened. He lowered himself [through the window] to the ground and hurried to his maternal-uncle, Bû-Zaid. He said, "The secret has been uncovered [we must remedy the situation]: Chop off one of ¿Alyâ's braids and make a cut on her [left] thigh." [They did so] and took her back to her room in her father's palace.

¿Alyâ's father, the king, had said to the groom, his brother's son, "If what you have said is true, I will kill her, but if a lie, I will kill you!" In the morning they entered the bridal chamber. They found ¿Alyâ still in bed: her hair chopped off and the blood from [the wound on] her thigh on her bridal gown. Her father killed the groom. And she remained.

During the night ¿Azîz came back to her. They lowered themselves out of the palace [to the ground]. They reached the valley where Bû-Zaid, his maternal-uncle, was [awaiting them].

When he reached the spot, ¿Azîz chanted,

> Come to me, you have been asleep at night. Get up! Awaken!
> In front of you is the morning, that had been absent.
> You spent the night at Ṣa¿dah and Jalîlah's spring,
> while I spent the night bandaging my wounds.
> ¿Alyâ's wound is one that will not get the best of her [??],
> for, it has clipped off ¿Alyâ her long hair-braids [i.e., honor].[826]

They packed up and left, heading for their home. [On their way] they reached a spring; it was old and deserted. They wanted some water. Bû-Zaid lowered his bucket but it fell. He wanted to go down into the spring after it. ¿Azîz said to him, "Maternal-uncle, you have grown old. I will go down." ¿Azîz [apparently ill from his wound] went down. His wound [was supposed] not to come in contact with water. He went into the spring, got the water. The water fell on the wound. His illness increased. He died. Bû-Zaid wept and was extremely sad. He buried ¿Azîz. He slaughtered his [¿Azîz's] she-camel, and broke his sword and drove it [the broken sword] into his grave [so as to mark it].

He reached home and went to his sister. She asked, "Where are my sons?" She loved ¿Azîz [more than her other sons]. He said to her, "[Before I tell you], I need [first] to cook in a pot fetched from a home whose walls have not been touched by grief. Go look for one!"

She went out and toured the tribal homesteads. She was gone for months and returned. He asked her, "Did you find a household that has not been touched by grief? Did you get the pot?" She replied, "There is no household that has not been visited by sorrow!" He said, "'May long life be yours.' Your six [elder] sons died."

"And what about ¿Azîz??" [she asked, in agony].

"In Iraq, buying and selling," [he answered, unconvincingly].

The boy's [¿Azîz's] sister exclaimed, "Maternal-uncle, you speak while your mouth is dry and your tears are flowing underneath the veil."

He [broke down and] said, "¿Azîz died and is buried at the spring."

¿Azîz's sister heard that; she gasped and dropped dead.

He [Bû-Zaid] said to his sister, "May long life be yours. ¿Azîz died and your daughter has died. Arise, wash your daughter, and bury her."

¿Alyâ heard what he had said. She mounted her she-camel and headed for ¿Azîz's grave, with the broken sword driven into it. She hurled herself off the saddle onto the sword: she hurled herself on the broken sword and died on the spot.

Bû-Zaid and his sister remained. She lived [the remainder of her life] with the grief of the loss of her children.

ASIDE

A woman listener gives the following sequel as a commentary on the main narrative:

(The story does not end like this; there is more:)

Out of their graves, [¿Azîz's and ¿Alyâ's], two trees grew: a henna tree out of ¿Alyâ's, and a thorn-tree out of ¿Azîz's. A camel came and ate all the leaves off the henna tree; he left nothing. (Our Master) al-Khiḍr uttered a prayer against the camel.[827] [It happened that] he came by and saw the stripped henna tree; he cursed the camel with having a split [upper] lip and with never getting filled.

[And that is why a camel has a split upper lip, and eats constantly.]

❖ 50 ❖

TO WHOM DOES THE GOOD FOOD GO?

(EGYPT, EASTERN DESERT)

NARRATED IN THE SPRING OF 1972 BY MABRÛKAH Ṭ., AGED FIFTY, A PEASANT FROM MUNÛFIYYAH GOVERNORATE. SHE HAD HEARD THIS HUMOROUS NARRATIVE—WHICH SHE LABELED *ḤADDÛTAH* (FANTASY-TALE)—WHEN A CHILD FROM HER MOTHER. THIS TALE WAS COLLECTED JOINTLY BY EL-SHAMY AND MRS. F. TAMMÛM, WHO WROTE DOWN THE TEXT IN ARABIC.[828]

The strong affectionate bond between a man and his sister's son is inherently linked to that man's role as a brother to that sister. Here, the man's maligned sister is, typically, innocent and kind; additionally, she is blessed with benevolent supernatural powers.[829] Conversely, the man's wife is assumed to be treacherous and unfaithful; thus resorting to legal trickery by the husband so as to suspend her and render her unable to remarry is deemed justifiable in the tale. Yet, Islamic jurisprudence prohibits such "suspension."[830]

Consistent with this negative attitude toward the man's wife is her role toward the children of her husband's sister. The perception of the relationship between a maternal-uncle's wife and the children of her husband's sister is always negative.[831]

The implicit end result of the tale's plot is the reorganization of the familial unit: a sister whose husband seems to be missing and a brother whose wife is justifiably disposed of are together again.[832] This is the affective experience characteristic of the Brother-Sister Syndrome in Arab cultures.

THERE was a man; every day his wife fed him [only unappetizing] bran-bread (*¿aish senn*). Whenever he would ask her, "But where is the white flour?"[833] she would reply to him, "Your sister took it." He became very vexed with his sister. [Whenever] he would wonder, "But why don't I see her [my sister when she comes]!?" she [his wife] would say to him, "She comes, takes the white flour, the clarified butter (*samn*), and the honey, then leaves immediately."

He said [to himself], "By God, I am going to get even with her; she is like a bad deed [always present]."[834] So, he filled one of the saddlebags with snakes and went to her. She welcomed him very much when she saw him. He gave her the saddlebag and told her to take it [inside her home]. When she opened it, she found it full of the Lord's boon. [The snakes were supernaturally transformed into money.] She said to him [in amazement], "But, brother! What have you kept for yourselves! You bring [me] all this money!" He was very amazed and said to her, "Where is that money?" She showed him the saddlebag; he looked and, indeed, he found money. He said to her, "Sister, may you find contentment in what you have been granted [by God]!" He also said to her, "Actually, I had brought snakes, not money." She replied [in astonishment], "Why, brother!? What is the reason?" He said to her, "Because whenever we grind [the wheat or maize], you come, take the flour, and leave the bran for us; you stay around like a bad deed for us!" She replied, "This did not happen! If you wish to learn the secret [truth], take this scabby-headed son of mine. He is wily (*nâṣiḥ*);[835] he will unveil the [real] story (*el-ḥikâyah*) for you." He returned [to his home] along with his sister's son and said to his wife [apologetically], "The boy clung to me, so I brought him along."

Every morning, he [the boy] pretended to leave along with his maternal-uncle (*khâl*), [but actually] he would go to spy on her from the top of the house. He saw that she slaughtered a goose, cooked it, and prepared strudel-leaves meat pie (*ruqâq*).[836] She placed these under a [pottery] kneading tub (*magûr*) [turned upside down, so as to conceal them].[837] He went out and met his maternal-uncle and said to him, without her being aware [of his act], "I will pretend to know the language of cats. Let us see whether she is going to serve us the food she has prepared or she will not."

When they got home they asked her, "Where is the food?" She answered them, "I am tired and was unable to do a thing! Eat anything!" Meanwhile, a [real] cat came: drawn by the smell of the [hidden] food. The boy pretended to be talking to her [the cat] and said to her, "Is this true? You say, 'There is a goose! And strudel leaves, too!' "

"Mew!" [the cat replied].

"Where?"

"Mew!"

"Under the kneading-tub?"

The woman was confounded. She said to her husband [in a contrived tone of absentmindedness], "O-o-o-h! I forgot, due to my fatigue. The goose fell off the top of the house and I could barely [get to it in time to] slaughter it [according to Islamic law, otherwise it would have been inedible] (*feṭîṣ*)."[838] Due to her vexation, she refused to eat with them.

The boy kept on spying on her until the man—who is her paramour (*mirâfiq-hâ*)[839] and for whom she had been preparing the food—came; he [the boy] heard him ask her, "But where is the food?" She replied, "It happened that this damn one, his sister's son, turned out to know the language of cats. They [the boy and his maternal-uncle] ate the food [I had prepared for you]."

The following day she prepared a chicken, and what happened in the case of the goose happened in the case of the chicken. The boy went and told the story to his maternal-uncle.

Later on, he heard the woman conspiring with the man [her lover] to kill him [the husband]. The boy dressed himself like a *maghrabî*-[magician];[840] he pounded dried egg yolk [into powder] and walked beside the house while crying out, "We foretell fortune, and open the Book!" She did not recognize him, and she called him in. He said to her, "Cast down the fee."[841] [She did.] He said to her, "In your household there is a boy who knows the language of cats and you have done nothing about that!"

"True," [she replied].

"For him, I have [potent, yellow] poison that no one can detect; but you must pay plenty for it!"

[She agreed and handed him the money.] He gave her the egg yolk[-powder] and told her to sprinkle it over a [fried] tom-duck (*ḍakar-baṭṭ*),[842] then feed it to him [the boy].

The important thing is that she followed the advice. She drowned the tom-duck in the egg yolk—which she understood to be poison. When her husband returned from his work she said to him, "I have prepared a tom-duck for [the two of] you because I know that you have come back home exhausted." When she served the food, they invited her to eat with them but she did not agree at all. After they finished eating the man cried out, "Oh, my tummy!" The boy kept on moaning, "Oh, my tummy!" She thought they were finished and about to die. She called that man with whom she had been going. [When he arrived and saw the two seemingly dead bodies], he asked her, "Aren't you going to shriek [in grief over their deaths]?"[843] [in a contentious manner], "Shriek!? [Why should I shriek and wail so soon?] Come on! Come on and let us play till morning, and then I'll wail over their deaths." She pretended to be a filly and he a stallion,[844] and they kept on chasing each other around the dead bodies.

The boy said [sarcastically] to his maternal-uncle, "Get up, maternal-uncle, lest the stallion kick you!" Thus, her husband got up and seized the two of them while they were naked. He sent her to her father's home. He refused to divorce her so that she should remain suspended [unable to remarry] in order to avenge himself on her.

At this [point], the tale ends.

IV

NOTES TO THE TALES

1. *el-mi¿zah el-mi¿zâwiyyah, 'omm qurûn ḥadîdiyyah;* lit.: The "goaty" nanny goat, the one with [. . .]. The word *'omm* (lit.: mother of) may signify "the female with" such and such a quality. The masculine form, *'Abu* (lit.: father of), is used in the same manner to describe a male.

2. On a mother's protective roles, cf. Tales No. 4, 20, 24, and 30. Cf. the role of mother as provider in Tales No. 7 and 24; also cf. informant note to Tale No. 19, where the divorced mother is the provider.

For factual accounts (i.e., personal experience narratives) illustrating a mother's protective roles with reference to a case of mental illness in the narrator's own family, see El-Shamy, "Belief Characters," pp. 14–21, and note 14, pp. 32–33. The situation involved her eldest son's conflict with his father—with her in the middle as mother and as wife; Mot. P7.1§, "Role strain (role conflict). . . . "

For other fantasy-tales by the present narrator, see Tale No. 37, and El-Shamy, *Folktales of Egypt,* No. 9, pp. 63–71.

3. (Mot. P204§). For an example of how a father's role is perceived, see informant note to Tale No. 9, note 149; also cf. a brother's role in Tale No. 1–2.

4. Designated as Type 123C§, *Ogre (Wolf) Gains Access to Children's Home on Treetop.* They are rescued by their brother (father). See Tale No. 1–2.

5. *el-'omm t¿ashshish, we-l-'abb yiṭaffish,* lit.: [As with birds' young], a mother nests, but a father causes running away from home (Mot. P230.0.5§). Compare the role of a "nagging" mother in Tale No. 7.

6. In our present case, the pool is '*en-nash¿*' (lit.: the seepage); it is a small swamp (*birkah*) with tall reeds, formed on the village's lowland by seepage (from lavatories and some irrigation water).

7. See Introduction, p. 6.

8. *laghwit el-ḥarîm* or *ḥadît[h] en-niswân,* and *laghwit eṣ-ṣughâr,* respectively; Mot. T604.4.1.1§, "Baby talk (by an adult)"; cf. P611.3§, "Women's conversation"; W202.1.1.1§, "Indicator of femininity: women's speech tone (soft, low-key)." See also Tale No. 24, note 501.

Mot. Z66.4.1§, "Endearment: to be referred to (or addressed) in the diminutive"; this stylistic feature is depicted in Mot. Z53, "The animals with queer names: as hen (henny-penny), cock (cocky-locky), goose (goosey-poosey);" (Type 2010 IA, bearing the same title).

9. These names suggest: *ḥâ'iz-un, bâzz-un,* and *ḍârib-un bi al ¿ukkâz,* which denote: "Attainer," "Outstanding," and "Striker-with-the-staff" (i.e., "Fighter," "Defender"), respectively.

10. *'ifta-a-a-ḥûlî yâ-wlâdâ-â-â-tî:*
el la-a-aban fe bzâ-â-â-tî,
we l-ḥa-a-shîsh ¿alâ qrûnâ-â-â-tî!

11. *bâbhum maqfûl ¿alaihum, wi kafyîn khairhom sharrohom,* lit.: Their door is closed on them, and their good deeds spare them the bad ones. Cf. 'mastabah-porch' and 'open door,' (Mot. Z70.5.1§, and P3.3.4.2§) in Section II (Profile), note 77.

12. *khafîf we-ḥilw.* Cf. Tale No. 32, note 640.

13. *f-ḥanak wâḥid bal¿uh ẓalṭ.*

14. The lower compartment of a country-style mud oven, where fire is built at the floor level.

15. The passage for hot air between an oven's lower fire chamber and the *¿arṣah* (upper baking chamber).

16. *yâ ¿amm yâ zayyât,*
[ma-]shuftish dîb ¿addâ w-fât
we-f-kirshuh saba¿ mi¿zât?

Note the use of the title "paternal-uncle," Mot. Z67.5.1§, "Esteem: man addressed as '*¿amm* (paternal-uncle)' "; also cf. Tales No. 24, 26, 33, and 42.

The use of "seven kids" here is an allusion to a children's play-rhyme (Type 2330, *Game Tale;* Mot. Z19.1.0.1§, "The fox passed by, seven loops in his tail; . . . "), which speaks of seven *laffât* (loops):

Leader:	*et-ta¿lab:*	(The fox:)
Chorus:	*fât fât!*	(passed by, passed by!)
Leader:	*we-f-dailuh:*	(And in his tail:)
Chorus:	*saba¿ laffât!*	(there were seven loops!)
Leader:	*we-d-debbah:*	(And the she-bear:)
Chorus:	*wiq¿it fi-l-bîr!*	(fell in the well!)
Leader:	*we-ṣâḥibhâ:*	(And its owner:)
Chorus:	*wâḥid khanzîr!*	(is a pig of a person!)

. . . .

The number of goats swallowed is two, but the colloquial Arabic words *'itnain* (two) or *gidyain/mi¿zitain* (two kids/goats) would not rhyme. Thus, the Narrator seems to have creatively introduced the illogical but rhyming: "*saba¿ mi¿zât*"; Mot. Z108§, "Sound (name) symbolism: association based on sound similarities (homophony)."

For another case of creativity exercised "within the limitations set by an established text," see El-Shamy, *Folktales of Egypt,* p. 192.

Note also that the word *kirsh* (huge potbelly, usually on a human male) is often used in vernacular as synonym for the word *baṭn,* which may signify "stomach," "belly," "tummy," "womb," or "one pregnancy." Cf. note 631.

17. *mîn illî bi-ykhabbaṭṭ ¿alâ ṭurbiṭî*
w-anâ b-antish fî ḥitit laḥmitî!?

18. Mot. P801.9.1§, "Wrestling (mainly outdoors)."

19. *'Omm el-¿anzain,* Mother of the two billy goats; (Mot. Z183.6§).

20. For a similar situation with reference to a trickster, see El-Shamy, *Folktales of Egypt,* No. 50, pp. 292–93.

21. *'omm-el-ḥuṣṣain,* lit.: Mother of the Ḥuṣṣain; i.e., a she-fox. Note the rhyming of the names of the two mothers.

22. Cf. Tale No. 30, where the reunion between co-wives and their husband is non-exclusive.

For further information on the contents of this subtype especially in sub-Saharan Africa, see H. El-Shamy, "Vom Fisch geboren (AaTh 705)."

23. For an elaboration on this negative role of a maternal aunt, see Tale No. 35.

24. A parallel situation, where the family persists without the father, is portrayed in Tale No. 24.

25. See El-Shamy, "The Demographic Factor," pp. 92–97.

26. Mother's sister.

27. Although the word used in the original is *¿afrît,* i.e., afrit, the context indicates that the being is a jinni.

28. The idea that *as-sa¿luww* (the ogre) "is the king of the jinn" represents an inconsistency, and seems to be an individualistic notion on the part of the narrator-writer of this text. As the first part of the story indicates, a jinni is perceived as capable of killing a human being; however, the role of being a man-eater is typically reserved for ogres (*sa¿âlî, ghîlân*). Two additional renditions from Saudi Arabia corroborate this argument. In one the predator is a "beast (Qâṭ-Qâṭ)"; in the other it is an "*¿afrît,*" (see al-Juhaymân, Vol. 1, No. 16, pp. 245–54, and Vol. 5, No. 2, pp. 25–36, respectively).

29. Lit., proverb, story of wisdom, example, or model to be emulated.

30. *qalbî ¿alâ waladî infaṭar, we-qalb waladî ¿alayya ḥagar;* i.e., he is cruel, unyielding.

31. *'illi yakhudhâ taḥt minnuh, ma-tibqâsh zayy 'ommoh w-ukhtuh.* Mot. T9.1§, "The power of sex: female's influence."

32. I.e., '*dunaydish*'—diminutive of '*mu-dandash*' (adorned in an elaborate and loud style): "The little adorned one"—a Saudi euphemism for vagina. This statement, made by the wife in the tale, is the title assigned to that Saudi text (al-Juhayman, Vol. 2, pp. 245–67). Mot. T283, "Wife withholds [sexual] intercourse from husband to enforce demand"; J226, "Difficult choices between relatives"; T9.1§, "The power of sex: female's influence."

33. Lit.: his mother's child; i.e., a weakling. Cf. Tale No. 20. For a description of the ideal conduct of a son toward his aged mother, see Tale No. 22.

34. *'itrammillit ¿alaih.*

35. Lit.: in the state of being a *sit* (lady), i.e., like a chieftainess, or bigshot.

36. Lit.: yeast for ill-humor; i.e., to be a source of ever-increasing sourness.

37. *baḥbaḥah* may denote physical space, or loosening of social restrictions.

38. In the layout of a country-style house, an oven room is typically located in a remote corner. It is thought to be inhabited by jinn (who are believed to dwell in fireplaces, among other habitats); Mot. F499.3.5.2§, "Jinn dwell with humans (in such odd places as bathroom, oven room, under staircase)." Yet an oven room may be used for sleeping at night, especially in winter, when the flat surface of the top of a warm oven would be used as a bed.

39. *hiyya ḥa-tâkhod zamanha we-zaman ghairha!?* (lit.: Is she going to take her time and the time[s] of others, i.e., she is due to die); *mawwit-ha w-rayyaḥnâ,* (lit.: Make her die, and . . .).

40. Mot. C434§, "Names of dangerous things (animal, disease, murder, etc.) are not to be uttered at a person without use of precautionary measures (e.g., 'Distant one,' 'Away from you')"; Z13.9.1§, "Speaker wards off evil effects of own speech (words)." Also cf. note 643.

On the use of this and other precautionary measures, see "Formulas in Tales," in El-Shamy, *Folktales of Egypt,* pp. liii–lv.

41. Also called *ballâṣ;* cf. Tale No. 6, note 84. Since the sort of jar specified has a

relatively narrow mouth (approximately four to five inches), placing a cut-up human body into it would not be an easy task. The overall image portrayed in the situation is quite savage and dramatic.

42. Lit.: "O my liver! May God's name. . . . "

43. Cf. the mother-daughter relationship in Tale No. 7.

44. The word *rakk* is often associated with the word *'asâs* (i.e., foundation); here it denotes "the crucial factor."

45. *'ikfi-l-garrah ¿alâ fummahâ, tiṭla¿ el-bint l-ommahâ.* See also introductory note to Tale No. 6.

46. *man shâbaha 'abâhu famâ ẓalam,* (Mot. U121.0.3.1§); i.e., has not done anything that was not expected.

47. Also called *mathal* (proverb, example).

48. *bi-yqûlû-lak,* lit.: They say to you.

49. *¿alâ qadd ḥâlhom,* lit.: they were the size of their condition.

50. Lit.: you who are the soul of your mother. Cf. note 461.

51. I.e., growth stages.

52. A camel is the proverbial largest booty; cf. Mot. J220.1§, "'If you [have to] fall in love, fall in love with a moon[-like beauty]; and if you [have to] steal, steal a camel['s worth].'"

53. The implication is that he became a petty thief or burglar.

54. *min quṭṭâ¿ eṭ-ṭarîq,* lit.: a road cutter, or road blocker—a more brazen crime.

55. I.e., *mansar [luṣûṣ].*

56. A famous hangman in Egypt, during the 1940s and 1950s; his name has become synonymous with the classical noun *gallâd* (executioner, hangman), which is infrequently encountered in folk speech.

57. Mot. U121, "Like parent, like child."

58. Type 950:I *Theft from the Treasury.*

59. Lit.: your female parent, a formal honorific for "your mother"; also see Tale No. 14, notes 320–21.

60. *bitta aṭ-ṭair al-khuddârî:* dialectical Sudanese-Arabic for *bint al-ṭayr al-'ukhayḍir;* the word *khuddârî* signifies semi-green, or greenish.

61. Mot. P611.3§, "Women's conversation."

62. Compare the negative attitude toward female offspring in the introductory note to Tale No. 9; also see Tale No. 12, note 253.

63. For examples of such males' renditions see al-Juhaymân, Vol. 4, p. 382, and Sha¿lân, pp. 29–31.

64. Lit.: purification, circumcision, or [female] clitoridectomy. Often performed on a group of young adults in one ceremony; consequently, members of that group would be referred to as circumcision-mates ("circumcised together").

65. Mot. T405.3§, "Sister's nakedness or exposure." See Tale No. 39; also cf. Tale No. 38, note 720, and Tale No. 42, where the theme is expressed indirectly. Also see El-Shamy, *Brother and Sister: Type 872**, esp. pp. 39–43; and El-Shamy, "Maḥfouẓ's Trilogy," esp. pp. 60–61, notes 48–52.

66. See Tale No. 49, note 812. Also cf. Tale No. 44.

67. I.e., *qibâb,* lit.: domes.

68. *sakhkharr lahâ ṭayrah.*

69. *jiddan,* lit.: Very.

70. Lit.: Son-of-Nimair. Also spelled Nimêr; see introductory note to Tale No. 46, and notes 774, and 781.

71. Lit.: Eve (Ḥawwâ') is a fertile birth-giver; i.e., [as long as there are fertile women], there will always be someone who is better than a certain person who claims to be unique, the best, or to possess the utmost of . . . (Mot. Z63.5.1§).

72. I.e., *zaghârîd:* trellises of joy made by women (Mot. P790.1.2.1§).

73. *¿arrasû,* i.e., performed the consummation of marriage.

74. *¿alaiki en-nabî.*

75. *Corchorus olitorius* (Jew's weed): a dark green summer plant (similar in appearance to fresh mint), with which a favorite souplike food is made; it is also an ingredient in other dishes (e.g., bean mash; see Tale No. 24, note 496). In family life, *molokhiyyah* and its accompaniments constitute a cognitive system that provides stable frames of reference, or proverbial similes (e.g., the crescent-shaped chopper with which it is finely minced, the female's body posture assumed in this mincing act, the sizzling sound and aroma signaling that it is ready to be eaten, its slippery consistency). Cf. Mot. K638.9.1§, "Escape by making self slippery: by covering self with soap, grease, slippery plant (e.g., *molokhiyyah*), etc."; Z186.4.2§, "Symbolism: rubbing (stroking) an object—erotic act"; Z186.9.3.1.1§, "Female in indecent posture 'allows her dish's sizzling aroma to spread'." On the cooking sound associated with this dish, see note 363.

76. *yâ sittanâ, yâ sittanâ,*
. . . [pause]
ti¿tîna . . . molokhiyyah
li-l-waḥîma-l-¿indanâ.

77. Hesitations and pauses indicate the narrator's attempts to recall the rhyme.

78. *bayy! bayy!*
'ommi-twḥḥammat-fiyy wa-bûy ḥimil biyy.
Wad-an-Nimair *ḥabbal 'ommah;*
we-waḥmetḥa tâjî ¿alayy!
ya magaṣṣ guṣṣ lisân el-¿abd,
we-ta¿âla layy!

79. *fi 'amân-Illâh.*

80. See Tale No. 31; also see El-Shamy, *Folktales of Egypt,* No. 50, and "The Trickster Cycle," pp. 219–21.

81. *'ibtikfi l-jarrah ¿â-timhâ, 'ib-tiṭla¿ el-bunyya l-immha*—as pronounced in the dialect of the narrator's region (Mot. U121.0.2.1§). Cf. introductory note to Tale No. 4.

82. On the matter of a wife's clandestine financial contributions to her own family, at the expense of her husband, see El-Shamy, *Folktales of Egypt,* No. 41. Also cf. introduction to Tale No. 19.

83. *¿âr, ¿irḍ,* respectively; in vernacular, the latter is typically pronounced: "*¿arḍ.*" See also Tale No. 9, note 155.

84. A small pottery jar (approximately two feet high, one foot wide at the base, and with a narrow mouth), used for carrying water on one's head. Cf. Tale No. 4, note 41.

85. *rûḥ yâ yoam, ta¿â yâ yoam.* Addressing inanimate objects and abstracts directly is a stylistic trait—Mot. Z122, "Time personified." Cf. the use of the imperative

in lieu of the descriptive, Mot. Z13.5§, "Character prompting: tale teller addresses tale character directly;" also see Tale No. 11, note 242.

86. Henceforth, the narrator refers to the jar in terms of being a girl named Baṭṭiyyah.

87. *wahabnâ es-satr,* lit.: [He] granted us being-shielded; i.e., that our bad or shameful affairs be unexposed to others; Mot. V57.0.1§, "Prayers are to supreme supernatural being (The God, a deity, holy personage, etc.) to solicit help (or to offer thanks)"; cf. M519.2§, "Supplication: being shielded from infamy or public disgrace (*es-satr*); cf. notes 222–24, and 428.

88. *'inshallâ khair,* i.e., *'in shâ'a Allâh. . . .*

89. *khayrât Allâh.*

90. Clearly, the narrator has abridged the tale so as to eschew the indecent episode.

91. *w-ṭâr eṭ-ṭair; yimsîkû bi-l-khair.*

92. ¿Aṣfûrah, *ḥârsah ek-kammûn.*

93. Mot. D950.21§, "Magic tamarisk tree (shrub)"; D1393.1.2§, "Tree grows around object (person) and encloses it (him)."

On the possible connection between this narrative cycle and the Isis "myth," see El-Shamy, "Belief and Non-belief," p. 16.

94. *shîl 'îdak, [ga]tak gaṭ¿ 'îdak!*
foaqak taḥtak, we-taḥtak foaqak,
'inta w-sîdak!

Cf. the chant in Tale No. 31, note 628; Mot. M431.4.1, "Curse: hand of person cursed to drop off." On the theme of being turned upside down, cf. Mot. M443.6.1§, "Curse: one's affairs turned upside down."

95. *baṣṣ laqâ . . . :* an idiom denoting immediacy and/or surprise.

96. *yâ-mmuh ma-tiḥsibîsh 'inn-anî ḥarsa ek-kammûn.*
d-anî f-'îd el-bâshâ, rayḥah Isṭambûl.

97. *ṭarbûsh,* headdress, worn by urban effendis; currently not in use; Mot. P751.3.0.1.2§, "Attire (apparel) of effendis class: (fez, pants, necktie, etc.)."

98. *tûta tûta, khulṣit el-ḥaddûtah.*

99. Fuṭmah *we râs el-fesîkhah.* The heroine's name represents one of the numerous dialectical pronunciations of the recurrent name, "Fâṭimah." Also see Tales No. 9, 18, and 46.

100. *baladî,* as opposed to imported, frozen meats.

101. *dallâlât,* sing., *dallâlah,* fem. of *dallâl,* lit.: teller or guide; a middle-person in business deals involving goods or services (e.g., marketing products, finding household help); a "teller" (man or woman) receives a fee for services rendered; see informant note to Tale No. 9, note 144. Occasionally, a she-teller may act as *khâṭbah* (matchmaker, lit.: an engager, or affiancer), (Mot. P434.5§); see Tale No. 17, note 402.

102. *bint-balad,* lit.: daughter of the town, i.e., native urban and urbane: having more freedom and independence than her bedouin, peasant, and other urban middle-class counterparts; in addition to characteristic liberty in garb, parlance, and native expressive arts (Mot. P726.5§). Also see introductory note to Tale No. 9, note 143.

103. *'akl-¿aish bi-l-ḥalâl,* lit.: bread eating by legitimate means.

With reference to buying and selling and being a woman merchant (Mot. P431.0.1§),

Saʿdiyyah considered this occupation *sharîfah* (honorable, blessed) "ever since the days of . . . The Prophet [Mohammad]" (Mot. A1471.8.1§, "Being a merchant [buying and selling]: an occupation blessed by God").

104. *kalâm fârigh,* lit.: empty talk; cf. Mot. P611.3.1.1§, "Women's talk. . . . "

105. I.e., improper, indelicate, or shameful conduct, and therefore must be stopped.

106. Examples of this approach by a father are illustrated in Tales No. 33 and 40.

107. She is twenty-six years old, a university graduate, and a researcher in the field of traditional music; she heard the tale from a fourteen-year-old maidservant, who hails from Bani-Swaif, middle southern Egypt. (Depository: HE-S: Cairo, 69-3A, No. 1.)

108. *minashshah,* a flyswatter, part of a gentleman's apparel until the 1950s.

109. See informant note to Tale No. 19.

110. See El-Shamy, *Folktales of Egypt,* No. 10, esp. pp. 78–79, and No. 14, esp. p. 105; also see El-Shamy, *Brother and Sister: Type 872*,* p. 45, esp. note 34; cf. Mot. T109.1.1§, "Bride's troubles at in-laws' home."

111. Lit.: O my eye; see also Tale No. 7, note 163.

112. *ḥelyit fi-ʿnaih,* i.e., he found her appealing.

113. *lâ 'aṣl wa-lâ faṣl.*

114. *rabbinâ yewaffaq,* a phrase typically used to wish for a successful venture.

115. *zann,* lit.: buzzing.

116. *ed-diḥk [ḍaḥik] min ghair sabab, qillit 'adab:* a truism.

117. *'aṣlik we-faṣlik, zayy. . . .*

118. *lûlî ḥorr.*

119. AUC: 32, Pt. 2, No. 2.

120. Mot. J20§, "Conditioning: effects associated with past experience cause man (animal) to respond accordingly (conditioned response)."

121. Mot. U248§, "Mental set, (thematic apperception): readiness to perceive in a particular manner (or, certain things)." Cf. the concept of "latent folk traditions" in introductory note to Tale No. 45. On the issue of forgetting, cf. Tale No. 33-1, esp. note 659. Also see "Loss of Folkloric Responses," in El-Shamy, "Folkloric Behavior," pp. 174–93.

122. Cf. Tale No. 22.

123. Lit.: nature, i.e., character trait, second nature.

124. Or, perhaps, to someone else's home. The text is ambiguous.

125. AUC: 14, No. 6.

126. Cf. Tale No. 13, note 288.

127. *al-'amîr,* (i.e., emir). It may be noted that this scene seems atypical of folk narration; also a "prince" is more often referred to as "king's son," "sultan's son," or "emir's son." Cf. Tale No. 12, note 264, where the writer—a university student—felt the need to clarify the folk utterance "the king's son," by parenthetically adding: ("*al-'amîr*") ("the prince").

128. *ṣuʿbit ʿalaih,* lit.: he found her [condition] too hard for him [to take].

129. *tiʿazzî 'ikhwâthâ,* lit.: extend condolences to her brothers.

130. *'aṣlan,* lit.: origin-wise.

131. I.e., that he would reinstate her.

132. *ma ṭaqsh ṣabr.* However, it is not clear as to what the prince could no longer live without.

133. "*khurrâfit lalla ¿Ayshah el-Khaḍrah: 'ajmal m-el-qamar,*" lit.: "The nonsensical (i.e., fairy-)tale of mistress ¿Ā'ishâh-the-green: more beautiful than the moon." The heroine's name signifies "Felicitous Lady ¿Ā'ishâh."

134. These include the present text, and another in which a mother sacrifices her life for her daughter; then the daughter—in her role as a sister to a brother—helps the two of them acquire riches. See note 137.

135. The lingua franca of North Africa.

136. Cf. the reaction of the narrator's son, cited in the informant note to Tale No. 7.

137. *moshsh* is a regional dialectical appellation for "cat." The tale, as a whole, is designated as Type 327L§, *Brother and Sister Possess Supernatural Animal's (Cat's) Treasure;* Mot. K1037§, "Dupe (supernatural cat) made to believe that his anus has been stealing food: beats it to death"; Q205§, "Part of body involved in offense punished"; P253.0.3§, "A sister's sacrifices (sufferings) for her brother's welfare"; P254.0.1§, "Household composed of only brother and sister(s)." The initial episode is tale Type 312F§, *Sister Rescues Infant (Fetus) Brother with Help from Kindly Animal;* see introductory note to Tale No. 40, note 734, and its types and motifs. The ending belongs to Type 15, *The Theft of Butter.* The following is the tale's outline, as I reconstructed it from memory about a day after hearing it:

> A little girl inadvertently released a pet partridge that her father owned. Her mother, due to fear [of her husband—the girl's father], ran away from home with the girl. They spent the night in a tree. Wild beasts killed the mother, who happened to be pregnant. The fetus, a boy, was saved by a kindly animal and given to the sister to care for. With the sister's prayers, the infant grew up [to adolescent age] with miraculous speed.
>
> In the wilderness, the sister found a palace that seemed abandoned. They dwelt in it. Actually, the palace was owned by a [supernatural tom] cat named Moshsh. In the evening, the cat arrived with cattle, sheep, and goats which he was herding. The sister and her brother went into hiding. Moshsh ordered the cows to milk themselves, and then make butter and cheese; they did as ordered. The sister stole the butter and ate it with her brother. The cows tried to warn Moshsh of the theft, but he was deep asleep. The sister smeared some butter on the sleeping cat['s rear]. In the morning, the cat looked for the butter but did not find any; he suspected that his rear stole the butter. He beat it (i.e., himself) as punishment. The same thing happened the following day; the cat beat his rear to death. The sister and her brother stayed in the cat's palace.

138. *yâ qamar, man 'ashabb minnayy?,* lit.: O moon, who is more youthful than me?

139. *w-'aish dhanbhâ! hâdî khilqat mawlây! kaif ṭiflah zayy hâdhihi tindhibiḥ.*

140. *¿alâ sunnat Allâh wa rasûluh.*

141. I.e., judged them at a distance by their blurry profiles. The word *shabaḥ* denotes: ghost, specter.

142. *wa-mashaina wejaina, raḥmat-Allah ¿alâ wâlidainâ, fîmâ qulnâ 'aw nasînâ;* Mot. Z13.10§, "Tale-teller begs God's forgiveness for lying."

143. See Tale No. 7, note 102.

For another narrative by this narrator, see El-Shamy, *Folktales of Egypt,* No. 45.

144. Mot. P434§; see informant note to Tale No. 7, note 101.

145. I.e., has been around, too experienced; Mot. W160§, "Being street-bound (market-bound)."

146. Mot. W188.2§; may also mean a chatterbox, Mot. W141, "Talkativeness."

147. Lit.: her eye is strong, i.e., does not shy away, or is lacking in bashfulness; Mot. W170.1§, "Lack of bashfulness (*ḥayâ'*)"; Z94.5.1.3§, "Rude stare."

148. Mot. F385.2.2§, "Possessing *zâr*-jinn (*'asyâd*) placated by sacrifice;" cf. V11.11§, "Sacrifice to a spirit (jinni)."

The narrator, in a remorseful and self-reprimanding frame of mind, stated, *talâtah tikhrib ed-dâr: ¿irs [¿urs], w-maytam, w-zâr* (Three [things] ruin [i.e., bankrupt] a household: a wedding [celebration], a funeral, and a *zâr*-[exorcism, or jinn-appeasing ritual]). She also added, *'illi m¿âh qirsh we-mḥayyaroh, yishtirî bîh ḥamâm we-yeṭayyroh* (He who has an [extra] penny that is making him restless, buys with it pigeons and lets them loose), i.e., excess money leads to wasteful spending. Both sayings are folk truisms. Cf. Mot. J2199.4, "Short-sighted economy"; W116.2, "Expenditure of money for vanity [(*fangarah*)]"; and P760.6.1§, "Surplus (wealth) invites the needless (decorative, unnecessary)." Also cf. informant note to Tale No. 29.

With reference to wedding expenses, cf. *mahr* (bride-wealth), note 677.

149. *er-râgil yigîb, we-s-sit tidabbar,* (Mot. P204.1§). Cf. Tale No. 1, note 3, where the mother is the provider.

It may be noted here that Nabawiyyah did not apply this principle wisely; she seems to have mismanaged her husband's earnings by spending extravagantly ("hundreds of pounds") on each *zâr* ritual she held. For similar devices employed by wives against potentially polygynist husbands (Mot. T145.10§, "Behavior of a polygynist's wife"), see introductory note to Tale No. 29.

150. *¿aish sûqî,* lit.: market bread, that is, store-bought. Nabawiyyah believes that the male bakers of store-bought bread (pocket bread) place a hex on their product, thus causing a consumer to become addicted to it and *mazghûf* (i.e., too anxious, or showing withdrawal symptoms when deprived of it). She insisted that bakers cast the following spell [addressing bread]: *lûf, lûf: 'illî yaklak yu¿ûd ¿alaik mazghûf* ([Be a] mate, [be a] mate: [may] he who eats you come back to you anxiously!). Mot. D1359.4.1§, "Bewitched food causes gluttony"; cf. G82.3§, "Cannibal's fodder (fattening). [. . .]" On the various grades of bread, see note 698.

It may be pointed out in this regard that most traditional women view eating "from the market" (i.e., at a restaurant) "from a stranger's hands," as an act that lessens a person's moral worth and akin to betrayal (Mot. W160.1§). Also cf. Mot. P785§, "'*ṣaghranah*' (unseemly behavior): committing acts which reduce one's communal standing (worth)."

151. See El-Shamy, "Folkloric Behavior," pp. 67, 86, 96. Also cf. informant note to Tale No. 13.

152. See also Tales No. 5, 7, 9, 11, 12, and 16; also cf. Tales No. 20, 34, and 35.

153. See introduction to Tale No. 11.

154. Lit.: "paternal-uncle's son," i.e., father's brother's son.

155. Cf. Mot. H611.1.1§, "Eggs' fragility analogous to girls ready for marriage;" T594.1.1§, "Infant daughter: her mother's 'enemy.'" See also Tale No. 6, note 83.

156. It is not clear whether the following two stanzas represent one or two poems; they are, however, thematically interconnected. Recorded in April 1970 from Mr. M. A.

Ṭilib, aged forty-five, a janitor in Cairo, who came from el-Bargî village, el-Minya Governorate, southern Egypt.

157. *el-lail kamâ el-waḥsh wi kull en-nâs tikhâf minnuh:*
we-l-bint qâlit l-abûhâ walâ 'ikhtashit minnuh,
"et-toab dâb yâ-bâ, we-n-nahd bân minnuh!"

yâ bû-l-banât baddar we shûf-lak sûq.
we-bî¿ bi-'arkhaṣ taman, yiksab me¿âk es-sûq.
khalaf el-banât sharr, yiglib-lak ma¿arrah w-sû'.

Cf. Mot. T610.2.1§, "Girl's puberty"; and W170.1§, "Lack of bashfulness (*ḥayâ'*)." For a case in which begetting female offspring ("five girls in a row") seems to have contributed to a man's mental illness, see El-Shamy, *Folktales of Egypt,* No. 41, p. 176.

158. *'illi yis¿idha zamânha, tigîb banâthâ qabl ṣubyânhâ.* Cf. Mot. N134.0.1.2§, "Birth of a daughter brings good luck;" and P232.0.3§, "Little daughter as mother's helper." See introductory note to Tale No. 5, where a mother's negative attitude toward female offspring is expressed; also cf. Tale No. 12, note 253.

159. Mot. T463.0.1§. Cf. pseudo-lesbian attraction in Tale No. 17.

160. Mot. C140, H1578.1.8§.

161. Depository: AGSFC: QTR 87-3ff., 686-x-No. 5; narrator: (f, 56, had concluded Qur'ân, heard it from her mother). This theme reflects the scarcity of paper and other writing implements in most households, especially in rural and desert communities.

162. *wilâd ṣubyân:* a form of repetition; also may be interpreted as, "children [who are] sons."

163. *yâ ¿ainî.* See Tale No. 7, note 111.

164. *ṣabâḥ el-khair, yâ-bu es-saba¿ farḥât.*

165. *ṣabâḥ en-nûr* (lit.: Morning of light): the common reply to *ṣabâḥ el-khair* (lit.: morning of good); cf. the mostly feminine greeting: *yis¿id ṣabâḥak* (May He [the Lord] make your morning blissful), see this tale, note 231; also see Tale No. 14, note 328.

166. *yâ-bu es-saba¿ waksât,* i.e., O father of seven relapses!

167. *lâ ḥawla [walâ quwwata 'illâ b]-Illâh.*

168. *yishîl fi-nafsuh,* lit.: carry within himself.

169. *bâbâ:* appellation for father among urban middle and upper classes; typically not used by *baladî* nor by rural categories of the populations, who typically use the words "*'âbúh*" (my father) and "*'ummúh*" (my mother).

170. *niṭawwil raqabtak,* lit.: lengthen your neck. Mot. Z94.3.1.1§, "Pride: with one's neck lengthened (held upright)."

171. I.e., Fâṭimah. See Tale No. 7, note 99.

172. *rabbina yustur ¿ala-l-gamî¿:* i.e., everyone has a skeleton in the closet. Mot. C434.3§, "Scandal (defamation, infamy) must not be spoken of (spread)."

173. *deh-deh-deh!!:* a nonlexical expression of astonishment.

174. *khaddim w-kallif.*

175. *'âdi ez-zîr, we-'âdi ghaṭâh,* lit.: Here is the *zîr,* and here is its lid. The *zîr* is a sort of vat: it is a barrellike pottery water tank and cooler; typically, it is three to five feet high, with a conical lower half and slightly tapered upper, thus giving the impression

of having a big belly. A *zîr* is usually fitted into a three- or four-legged stand, with a bowl underneath to receive filtered water (which is consumed by household animals and birds). Cf. Tale No. 46, note 778.

176. *'Omm Fulân, wi 'Omm-Fulânah, wi-li Bint-¿Illân, wi-Bint ¿Illânah;* the translation of *¿illân* is approximate.

177. *shirîk fi-l-maksb, we-mish fi-l-khusârah.* It is worth noting that such an arrangement is incongruent with Islamic legal edicts concerning business ventures and profits: a legitimate arrangement is one in which the investor stands the chance of incurring either a gain or a loss. An a priori guarantee of profit is considered sinful (illicit, tabu); Mot. C787.1.1§, "Tabu: guarantee of profits in business venture."

178. On the cash value of cooking utensils, see El-Shamy, *Folktales of Egypt*, No. 36.

179. *rismâl,* i.e., *ra's mâl* (cash money).

180. *hinâ haiṣah w-hullailah, wi-hnâk ¿a-s-sukkaitî.*

181. *sikkit es-salâmah, w-sikkit en-nadâmah, w-sikkit 'illî-yurûḥ ma-yirga¿sh,* respectively.

182. *tarzî baladî,* tailor of native, country-style clothes; as compared to *tarzî 'afrangî:* Western-style tailor handling suits, *tayyair-ât* (ladies' jacket-and-skirt suits), collared shirts, etc.

183. *kîs:* characteristic apparel of rural, non-Westernized groups.

184. *futtak b-el-kalâm,* i.e., I did not get the opportunity to tell you that. . . .

185. The name "Bahbahânî" suggests being from a city called Bahbahân; in some variants the name is "el-Baḥbaḥanî," denoting a person who is *me-baḥbaḥ* (lit.: roomy, plenty), i.e., being openhanded, extravagant, or generous, (cf. Mot. P3.1.1§, Family (personal) name as indicator of social status).

186. *[mashrûb] et-taḥayyah,* a customary hospitality practice.

187. *khair 'in-shallah!?,* i.e., . . . *'in shâ'a Allâh.*

188. *kattar [Allâh] khairak,* lit.: May He [God] increase your boon.

189. *buqgah:* a large cloth bag; typically, a bedspread or tablecloth turned into a carrying device (cf. carpetbag).

190. *el-ḥîlah: w-mafîsh ghairoh,* lit.: the trick, or feat . . . ; i.e., the sole feat one has managed. Such a child is presumed to be spoiled, and all his demands are to be met. Mot. T603.1§, "Pampered son(s)."

191. *'oaḍit el-misâfrîn,* i.e., *ghurfat al-musâfirîn;* lit.: the travelers' room; may also be referred to among the urban middle class as *'oaḍit el-gilûs* (sitting room), or *eṣ-ṣâloan* (the salon, parlor).

192. A derivative of *'ibnah* (daughter), lit.: a little daughter, i.e., a [precious] maiden; the word in the diminutive denotes endearment; cf. Mot. Z66.4.1§.

193. The manner in which she looks (with her eyes) at objects and persons; or the eye's mannerisms.

194. *kul 'akl el-gimâl, we qûm qabl er-rigâl:* a traditional saying designating the table manners of a he-man; Mot. P634.0.1.2.1.1§.

195. *ẓafarr—([. . .], w-alladhî minnuh),* lit.: [. . .] and that which is of the same [sort]. Cf. "etc., etc.," in Tale No. 45, note 770.

196. *melaḥlaḥah,* lit.: fast-moving, mobile, a go-getter.

197. The colloquial word '*ḍakar*' (i.e., *dhakar*) denotes maleness or being a '*faḥl*' (stud). It may also indicate, as in this text, that the bird is a male, and, thus, is more

substantial and plentiful when cooked (Mot. W201.2.2§, "Indicator of maleness: being large"). Cf. "male duck" in note 842, and in El-Shamy, *Folktales of Egypt,* No. 40, p. 173. Also cf. "male gum," in note 502.

Similarly, with reference to "*dîk-rûmî*" (lit.: Roman rooster or cock), the word *dîk* is usually grouped with traits commonly attributed to "maleness"; cf. Mot. Z193.3.1§, "Cocklike (roosterlike) man."

198. *'intî ta¿âlî.*

199. *'inta ta¿âlâ.* It is not clear whether this correction is made by the mother as a character in the tale, or by the narrator.

200. *doam* (doum: *Hyphæne thebaica*) is a palm-nut fruit which has a thin fibrous exterior, with a sugary taste and a woodlike consistency. Typically, it is of an irregular round shape. Its size ranges in diameter from about 5 cm. (two inches) to 10 cm. (four inches); its color ranges from light hazel to dark tan.The analogy drawn here is between these nuts and a man's testicles; Mot. Z105§, "Shape (form, color, etc.) symbolism: association based on similarities of visually perceived properties of object"; and Z166§, "Fruit symbolism." See El-Shamy, "The Demographic Factor," p. 80, n. 95.

201. Usually containing dozens of stalks: a heavy load.

202. *baḥr,* lit.: sea. In colloquial Egyptian Arabic this word is used to designate a major river; usually, the sea is referred to as *el-baḥr el-mâliḥ* (the salty sea), or simply the salty.

203. *ṭâḥit; we huwwâ ṭawwaḥ nafsuh warâhâ,* lit.: it flung itself away, and he flung himself after it.

204. *yâ* Ḥasan, *yâ* Bahbahâni: this form of address denotes emphasis or warning (as in addressing a personal friend by using his or her full name in the English language).

205. Cf. body profile or silhouette, especially a female's.

206. Pertaining to women, womanlike.

207. Lit.: [monthly] custom or habit; i.e., period.

208. *madnîl ḥarîmî bi-'ûyah.* For the consequences of menses on a woman's performance of her duties (baking), see El-Shamy, *Folktales of Egypt,* No. 16, esp. p. 112; cf. Mot. J1661.1.3.1§, "Deduction: bread made by a menstruous woman. Hair found in bread."

209. I.e., *rayḥân:* considered flowerlike because of its fragrance.

210. "*tishâhruh,*" i.e., she would cause *mushâhrah* (supernaturally induced barrenness) to occur. Mot. C141.1, "Tabu: menstruous woman not to go near any cultivated field or crop will be ruined [*mushâhrah*]"; C145, Tabu: [touching] certain things during menses. . . . "

211. *'anâ ghulob ḥomârî,* lit.: [As for] me, my donkey gave up; Mot. Z63.7.2§, "Exasperation: 'one's donkey baffled.' "

212. Feeling comfortable due to living together intimately for a long time (Mot. P605.0.1§).

213. *shabandar et-tuggâr:* i.e., *shâhbandar. . . .*

214. *fi-raqabtî,* lit.: around my neck. Cf. *dhimmah,* in this tale, note 225.

215. Lit.: A world! I.e., some otherworld in and by itself!

216. *fulânah bint-fulân.*

217. A large movable tentlike pavilion of patchwork, decorated cloth, typically set up for large public receptions (e.g., weddings, funerals, political rallies).

218. *ḥâgah 'ubbahah!*

219. Mot. C434§; see Tale No. 3, note 40.

220. *kân m¿âyâ boḍâ¿ah: yâmâ!*

221. *el-hals we-l-mashy el-baṭṭâl.*

222. *yallâh baqâ! rabbina yustor ¿alâ walayâna.* (Mot. M519.2§), see Tale No. 6, note 87. Allusion here is made to *¿irḍ* (sexual honor): i.e., she may be in an unnameable location, a place too dishonorable to be mentioned (e.g., a whorehouse, or the like); see introductory note to this tale. On the unspeakable (Mot. C434§), see Tale No. 32, note 643.

223. *¿a-s-sukkaitî, zayy 'illî ¿âmil ¿amalh.*

224. *khallî eṭ-ṭâbiq mastûr,* lit.: Let that which is folded remain concealed. Cf. note 222, this tale; also see note 87, this section.

225. Mot. W37.8§, "*dhimmah:* economic, political, or governmental conscientiousness and honesty." Cf. *¿irḍ:* sexual honor, see this tale, note 214.

226. *yâ fadîlet el-qâdî,* lit.: your virtuousness, the judge; *ṣâhib al-faḍîlah* (possessor of virtue) is a title for addressing higher clergymen (judges).

227. Some variants of the tale cite the buttocks or testicles as the spot where the seal was placed.

228. *'akhkh lazam,* i.e., not just a relative, such as a cousin, who may be labeled brother.

229. *kull 'adab we kamâl.*

230. *we-qâmo el-'afrâḥ we-l-layâli l-milâḥ.*

231. *yis¿id ṣabâḥak, . . . :* feminine style of an answer to the morning greeting; a less routine, more incremental, and more friendly response to the greeting, "Good morning." See this tale, note 165; also see Tale No. 14, note 328.

232. Cf. Mot. L350, "Mildness triumphs over violence."

233. Although the narrator specified that her tale is known in her community as "The Tale of the Cow," other traditional titles are also recurrent: "Gulaidah ([The Girl inside the] Animal Hide)" and "Khushayshibân ([The Girl inside the] Wooden Enclosure)."

234. See for example, Tale No. 14; also see Text "o" in El-Shamy, *Brother and Sister: Type 872**, pp. 6–8.

235. Mot. J1063.0.1§, "Projection: attributing to others one's own shortcomings (defects)."

236. Contrast with Tale No. 38, where the sister marries a person who may be viewed as a paternal figure.

237. *fardit kholkhâl,* a single [of a pair of]. . . .

238. Maryam [Mary], *'omm ed-dill we-d-dalâl.*

239. On the difference between fear and anxiety, see H. El-Shamy, "Emotionskomponente," esp. p. 1392; and "Sentiment, Genre and Tale Typology," p. 43, note 7. With reference to "anxiety" as a sociocultural factor in Arab psychiatry, see H. El-Shamy, "The Brother-Sister Syndrome in Arab Family Life," p. 314.

240. Cf. the relationship between the "white" mistress and "black" servant/slave in Tales No. 28 and 47.

241. This tale (plot) also occurs with reference to a stallion or camel falling in love with the owner's sister; it is designated as Type 313K§.

242. Using the imperative in lieu of the descriptive (i.e., She got up, opened the door, . . . etc.) is a stylistic trait found in various contexts of Arab folk expressions. See

El-Shamy, *Folktales of Egypt*, No. 55, esp. p. 214; also see Tale No. 6, note 85, and Tale No. 20, note 453. Available data indicate that this feature seems to be a female specialty.

243. *¿ammatî,* lit.: my (fem.) paternal-aunt. Note the social distance implied in this kinship term when used by a female.

244. *l-awwal, 'anâ Maryam: 'omm ed-dill we-d-dalâl,*
wa-l-yoam, 'anâ Maryam ra¿¿âyit li-ymâl!
yabbib yâ khoakh, w-ṣaffig yâ rummân,
¿alâ Maryam bint ibn es-ṣulṭân!

In numerous Gulf Region dialects the *j* is pronounced as a *y;* hence the final word of the second line of Maryam's chant is *al-jimâl.*

245. *yâtik sakkîn ṭûl el-bâ¿*
la tkhallî fîki i¿ẓâmah w-la krâ¿.

bâ¿ is the span between the tip of the thumb and that of the little finger of outstretched arms (i.e., two arms and a chest's span).

246. *timlikû-lî ¿alaih,* lit.: you [pl.] give me ownership of him; see Tale No. 16, note 381. Cf. Mot. T463.0.1§, "Pseudo-homosexual (male) attraction: man falls in love with another man who turns out to be a woman in disguise"; also see Tale No. 13, note 285.

247. *lâ titshayṭan ma¿î,* lit.: Do not act like Satan with me.

248. *tabârak al-khallâq fî-ma khalaq;* i.e., the Creator's glory is in His creation. See also note 690.

249. *malakû-lah ¿alaihâ, ¿alâ sunnit Allâh wa rasûluh.* See this tale, note 246.

250. *wa-qa¿adû,* lit.: And they sat.

251. *sit* Kân. The name is atypical.

252. AUC: 11, No. 4.

253. *wa'd* (female infanticide by burying alive; Mot. S302.5§) was reported as a common practice of pre-Islam Arabs. The Qur'ân draws a profoundly moving picture of the trial and punishment that await the murderer, and links this crime to the folding up of the sun, vanishing of mountains, rupturing of the sky, boiling over of the oceans, and kindling of the fires of Hell (Qur'ân, 81:8; cf. 6:151, and 17:31). Clearly, this sacred approach (of reward and punishment) proved successful in stamping out this custom, whereas its secular counterparts in the contemporary world (esp. in such countries as China and India) have been ineffective. See also introductory note to Tale No. 5, note 62, and Tale No. 9, note 157. On the meeting on the Day of Judgment, see Aside, p. 211.

254. Mot. T405.4.1§, "Daughter's nakedness or exposure." The theme is seldom expressed, even in tales concerning father-daughter incest; e.g., Types 510B, *The Dress of Gold, of Silver, and of Stars* (see Tale No. 10); and Type 931B§, *A Father Rapes His Daughter.*

255. Mot. P7.1§. See notes 2, 588, and 713, this section.

256. *ṣu¿bit ¿alaiha.*

257. *yuḥibb,* the word may also mean "love."

258. *al-fatâh aṣ-ṣaghîrah;* may also mean "the young maiden."

259. This classical Arabic phrase may also mean "I've begun to love. . . . "

260. The idea here is that she was dressed in various colors; since blue had already been cited, probably the writer meant a color other than blue.

261. *yanqalib zawjuhâ kamâ kân fi-l-mâḍî.*

262. *tafkîrihâ,* lit.: her thinking, or fears.

263. *'a¿mil zayy en-nâs,* lit.: do as people do. Mot. W44.2§, "Proper bashfulness (*ḥayâ'/khafar, kusûf/khajal*). [. . .]"; cf. J895§, "Consolation by thought of not being alone in misfortune."

264. Cf. the use of "prince" and "king's son," in Tale No. 7-2, note 127.

265. *buhir bi-jamâlihâ el-fattân* (Mot. F575.1.6§).

266. Normally, as rules of modesty require, a woman would be asked to ride (or walk) behind a man in order to lessen her exposure to visual scrutiny by him. The origin of this practice is usually attributed to Prophet Moses; Mot. A1557.3.1.1§, "Moses walks ahead of female guide so as not to observe her posterior (body); she directs (by nonverbal sign)." Also see El-Shamy, *Folktales of Egypt,* No. 44.

267. *shâbbah jamîlah mamshûgat al-qawâm.*

268. *shubbaikî, lubbaikî: es-sa¿d bain 'idaikî.*

269. *khâtim el-mulk,* another label for Solomon's Ring.

270. I.e., *'amân [yâ rabbî];* lit.: [O Lord, grant us] Safety! This exclamation in Arabic is held to be a Turkish expression of astonishment; it is pronounced in supposed Turkish style (with "dark sounds") as: *'umâ-â-â-n.* Also, cf. note 537.

271. *'anâ es-sit, sit* Kân.
'itruk el-'ahl w-el-'aw*ṭân,*
we-ilḥaq bi-s-sit, sit Kân.

272. *yâ qamar, yoam ma-tmût, 'amût.*
wa arûḥ sûq el-khashab wa-'anaggar tabût:
mismâr min lûlî wi-mismâr min yâqût.
yit¿ajjibu 'ahl el-mamlakah: "ḥabîbain fî tabût!"

273. *Furṭ-er-rommân fî ṣawânî dahab,* lit.: loose [kernels of] pomegranates, [placed] on gold trays. The adjective *furṭ,* used here as a noun, refers to fruits separated from their cobs, bunches, or pods; it is typically applied to corn (maize), grapes, peas, etc. The commercial value of such produce depends on the item in question (e.g., loose grapes are cheaper, but loose peas are more expensive). The association between a pomegranate and precious metals and stones is also reflected in the image generated via a true riddle:

> *ṭâṣah; fi-l-baḥr ghaṭṭâsah:*
> *min guwwah lûlî, we-min barrah nḥâsah.*
> (A skillet [bowl]; in water she [it] sinks:
> pearls on the inside, copper on the outside.)

Copper, or brass, is often linked to gold, the color of the surrounding inner skin of a pomegranate (Mot. Z105§). See "multiplexity of cognitive connotations," section I, note 21. Also cf. the image of "Pearls-on-Vines" (masc.) in Tale No. 33.

274. Lit.: My sire, or Our master, i.e., Moslem cleric; cf. reverend. Also see note 429.

275. Lit.: our father, i.e., reverend.

276. *na¿am, we hâḍir.*

277. *yi¿milû-luh ḥisâb.*

278. An affect generated in a person; cf. *haybah* (note 467, this section), a quality

assigned to a powerful person as part of his appearance. Mot. F580§, "Person of awe-inspiring appearance."

The narrator, like many members of the older generations, viewed these practices as belonging to the "good old days"; cf. El-Shamy, *Folktales of Egypt*, p. 54. Mot. J318.1§, "Better things in the past (golden times, 'good old days,' etc.)."

279. AUC: 08, No. 2; transcribed and translated by H. El-Shamy.

280. Religious, traditional, elementary school (or preschool) for children, where basic skills in reading, writing, and arithmetic are taught as a secondary curriculum to memorizing the contents of the scripture (Qur'ân, or Bible); many graduates went on to higher levels of schooling. Typically, such a school consists of one room, has one low-ranking cleric as teacher and owner—sometimes assisted by another male or female instructor—and is occasionally annexed to a mosque or church. Fees were mostly paid in kind (food, clothes), at intervals corresponding to a pupil's completion of a segment of the curriculum. Graduation followed a threefold memorization process: *khatam, we-¿âd, we-samma¿* (i.e., memorizing every chapter in the Holy Book, relearning or repeating, and reciting—all from memory). In this religious context, progress at school is reckoned by passages reached in the Holy Book (Mot. J1487).

281. Especially through the use of "the bow and cudgel/rod" (*el-falkah we-l-maqra¿ah*—a stringed bowlike device for holding the feet upwards so that boys may be struck with a rattan rod on the bottoms of their feet), or *¿abṭ* (i.e., being hugged by a stronger person so that a boy may be paddled on his buttocks).

282. Lit.: the one who knows, i.e., instructor; also labeled '*shaikh*,' or '*fiqî*' (lower cleric). Cf. the character of "parson" in Western lore; also cf. Tale No. 32, note 635.

283. Mot. J20§, "Conditioning: effects associated with past experience cause man (animal) to respond accordingly (conditioned response)."

This negative attitude toward teachers is expressed in other situations. A literary poem assigned in secular schools states:

> *qum li-l-mu¿allimi wa waffihi at-tabgîlâ,*
> *kâda al-mu¿allimu 'an yakûna rasûlâ.*
> (Stand up *for* the teacher and give him his full due of exaltation,
> [since] a teacher could almost be [as venerable as] a prophet.)

A parody by pupils states:

> *qom li-l-mu¿allimi wa waffihi at-talṭîshâ,*
> *kâda al-mu¿allimu 'an yakûna shawîshâ.*
> (Stand up *to* the teacher and give him his full due of slaps across the face,
> [since] a teacher could almost be [as cruel as a police] sergeant.)

Mot. Q50§, "Reward for educating the uneducated"; Q113.5.1§, "Educator (teacher) revered ('as if messenger of God')"; P143.2§, "Abuse of power (authority) by police"; S92§, "Cruel policeman (jailor, executioner, etc.)."

A policeman is a character that is often associated in lore with abuse of power, dishonesty, and inflicting physical pain.

284. See informant note to Tale No. 8, in El-Shamy's *Folktales of Egypt;* also compare

a nomad's negative view of an urban judge's supposed wisdom acquired through punishment, in Tale No. 10 of that work.

285. Cf. Tale No. 9 (Mot. T28, and T463.0.1§); also see Type 570A, *The Princess and the Magic Fish-skin* (abstract), in El-Shamy, "The Demographic Factor," p. 82, and p. 109, note 91.

286. Mot. P199§, "*bitûꜥ-ꜥiyâl, lawâṭî, lûṭiyyah* (homoerotic sodomites, the pedophilic)"; T472.0.1§, "Pedophilia. An adult's abnormal sexual desire for children." Cf. Mot. X360§, "Humor concerning lecherous teacher(s)."

287. Mot. T92.9.1, "Parricide because of father-son rivalry for girl's love"; W195.9.1§, "Father envies son's beautiful wife (wives)."

In folk narrative traditions, a tale revolving around this theme has been designated as Type 303D§/516H§, *The Father Who Wanted a Share of His Son's Beautiful Wives. . . .* Significantly, this tale is narrated mostly by adult men.

288. On triads, see El-Shamy, *Brother and Sister: Type 872**, esp. pp. 68–73; with reference to the reorganization of the social system, see pp. 67, 70, 76, 79; also see H. El-Shamy, "Maḥfouẓ's Trilogy," pp. 67–68. Cf. Tales No. 36 (esp. note 696), 37, and 50. This facet is also applicable to narrator's "errors." See this Tale, note 309, Tale No. 41, note 741, and Tale No. 50, note 830.

289. *gamâꜥah mutawassiṭîn el-ḥâl,* lit.: a group/family of medium standing (condition).

290. The pronoun "her" refers to the word *gamâꜥah* (fem., i.e., group). As a family member interacts with outsiders, it is a matter of etiquette that a lady of the house is not to be referred to by her name, nor directly (e.g., "My wife," "Your wife," etc.). Typically she is only to be alluded to as: *el-gamâꜥah,* (lit.: the group, i.e., the family).

291. *feṭîrah* (i.e., *faṭîrah, pl. fiṭîr/faṭî mishaltit*): a round, multilayered, turnover-like, sugarless, fat-rich pastry, usually without any filling; eaten plain, or with sweet or salty additives (e.g., honey, pickled-cheese); and considered one of the delicacies of countryside cuisine.

292. *ḥâḍir:* lit.: present (i.e., [consider it] done!), a very polite response.

293. *dhuhûl,* state of shock.

294. *bilâd,* sing. *balad,* denotes a town or a country.

295. *bint nâs ṭayyibîn,* lit.: daughter-of-good-hearted-people.

296. *ꜥarûsah,* a bride, a doll.

297. *lâ hiyya min maqâmak walâ min markazak;* i.e., she is not your social match.

298. *teṭâḥin fîh,* lit.: grind against him.

299. *'inta ḥorr,* lit.: you are free; i.e., do what you want, but at your own risk.

300. *dakhal ꜥalaiha,* lit.: entered upon her. See introductory statement to Tale No. 1-1.

301. *yâ Furṭ-er-rommân fi ṣawâni dahab,*
'aish ra'aiti ꜥagab,
lamma futti [fardit] kholkhâlik taḥt el-ꜥatab?

302. *yâ mawlây, kont bi-tꜥallim eṣ-ṣobyân we-l-banât:*
bitꜥallimhum el-ꜥilm we-l-'adab.

303. *ed-dawlah,* the state, the government.

304. *ṣu¿bit ¿alaih.*

305. *yerâ¿îha,* lit.: shepherding or looking after her; i.e., make her feel less hurt.

306. *ḥann-e-lhâ,* i.e., *ḥanna lahâ.*

307. Narrator is avoiding indecent words such as: *yi¿âshir* (cohabit), *yinâm ma¿* (sleep with).

308. *'anâ* Shaddâd, *w-akhûya* Raddâd *w-ukhtî* Boghdâd!
we-ḥyât râs 'abûya el-malik,
el-¿arûsa ma-tkhoshshish el-lailah ¿ala-ommî we-tza¿¿alhâ!

Other texts offer a rhyming last line:

"...
walâ t-hawwib ganb el-bâb!"
(. . . would not enter upon my mother,
or [even] approach the vicinity of the door.)

309. The heroine, unlike her children, is not the daughter of the king; otherwise, she would have been married to her brother. This "error" is congruent with the Brother-Sister Syndrome. On the congruence of such errors with the affective components of tales, cf. Tale No. 13, note 288, and El-Shamy, *Brother and Sister: Type 872**, pp. 50–51.

310. *ḥarâm ¿alayyah we ḥalâl ¿alâ* . . . , .i.e., it would be sinful for me to marry this bride, but. . . .

311. *we radd es-sit beta¿tuh:* the latter phrase is a polite appellation for *mirâtoh* (his wife).

312. I.e., *ḍarâ'ir.* See Tales No. 30 and 31. Cf. rivalry among wives of brothers (i.e., sisters-in-law) in Tale No. 48; also cf. Tale No. 25.

313. *na¿¿âmah:* perceived in feminine terms. Mot. T257.1.2§, "King's pet bird (animal) becomes jealous of king's wife-to-be (fiancée)."

314. An ethnic-racial Mongolian and Turkic people associated with barbaric practices, especially during their invasion of the region during the Middle Ages. Cf. El-Shamy, *Folktales of Egypt,* No. 24.

315. The significance of these planets may be part of a past and forgotten solar mythological belief system.

316. The gender of the word is feminine.

317. I.e., *'ibrîq* (masc.).

318. See "multiplexity of cognitive connotations," section I, note 21. The erotic nature of a pitcher's spout is overtly expressed in other categories of lore; for example, a riddle states: "*qâ¿id ¿alâ basṭituh, wi-mdaldil zubrituh*" ("Sitting on his platform, while dangling his little penis"). Answer: pitcher (AUC: 32, Pt. 1, No. IV-28, informant: same as narrator of Tale No. 7-1). Also compare the role of the pitcher in Tale No. 18, note 418.

319. See "life space," Introduction, p. 6.

320. *wâlidhum 'ittwaffâ,* i.e., . . . *tuwffiyâ,* lit.: their male-parent became deceased. The narrator is attempting to present the tale in a "respectable" style through using elements of formal speech (classical Arabic). Cf. this tale, note 327. Also cf. the style in Tale No. 12.

321. *wâldithum,* lit.: their female parent. Cf. note 59.

322. Lit.: family, relatives. Mot. V293.0.1§, "The afflicted (the weak, the persecuted, the orphaned, etc.) as God's favorite." Cf. "orphan" in Tale No. 32, Aside, p. 259.

323. *ghaṣb ¿annâ*, lit.: in spite of us.

324. *shâshât:* head-scarves made of chiffon material, also used as a partial veil.

325. Deep pottery tub or bowl. It is pinkish and of round semi-conical shape, with the narrow end as base; usually it is about two to three feet deep, and about three feet wide at the mouth. Turned upside down, it also serves as a safe place for keeping food (or hiding other objects). It is often associated with feminine (and erotic) functions and organs. Mot. H888§, "Allegorical riddle: what would an object (utensil, implement, fruit, etc.) say in a given situation?"; H888.1§, "What would say [to a female]: 'Part your thighs wide and take me [in], and then make vocal manifestations of sexual enjoyment (*'ighnughî*) and let me hear [them]'? Answer: kneading tub (*magûr el-¿agîn*)"; cf. Mot. Z186.4.2.1§. See "multiplexity of cognitive connotations," section I, note 21.

326. *'ince mish mi-l-gince.*

327. *bâbâ-hâ:* Narrator is using modern speech, characteristic of urban middle and upper classes. See this tale, notes 320–21.

328. *yis¿id ṣabâḥik:* feminine reply to the greeting, "Good morning." See Tale No. 9, note 165.

329. Narrator switches from indirect to direct speech.

330. *qubqâb:* [A pair of] wooden slippers with leather or rubber straps, to be worn at home in wet areas (e.g., the bathroom); they are, however, frequently worn in the streets, and are thought of as a woman's weapon.

331. *tâkul fi-nafsahâ*, lit.: eat into herself.

332. *yâ sit* Ṭaṭar, *yâ sit* Maṭar,
yâ-llî-ommik esh-shams w-abûki l-qamar,
el-qullah kasaret bazbûzî.

333. *yâ sit* Ṭaṭar, *yâ sit* Maṭar,
yâ-llî-ommik esh-shams w-abûki l-qamar,
ruddî ¿alayya laḥsan qalbi-nfaṭar.

334. *banât el-fawwâl.* Fava beans (*fûl*) are the staple food for breakfast. They require prolonged boiling (usually overnight), and are served with oil, lemon juice, and a variety of spices (e.g., black pepper, cumin, etc.); they are eaten with bread. Vendors of cooked beans and cooked wheat—with their characteristic wobbly handcarts, pottery or copper bean jars, and clients holding bowls in which to carry the family breakfast home—used to be a morning scene at almost every main street corner in residential areas; cf. the image in Mot. H581.2, "Arrested man tells who he is: the hospitable fire of his father is sought (bean merchant)." However, the introducing into homes of appliances for slow cooking has reduced the demand for the bean vendor's commodity.

For other foods with fava beans as an ingredient, see Tale No. 24, note 501.

335. *kuttâb.* See Tale No. 13, note 280.

336. A *¿îd* ("bairam") is a religious holiday associated with festivities and celebrations (comparable to Christmas). Two such bairams are recognized (Mot. V76§, "*¿îd:* Moslem bairam"). The first is *¿îd al-fiṭr* (Bairam of Breaking the Fast) which celebrates the end of the fasting Month of Ramadan; it is also labeled: "Little-Bairam" (because it lasts for only three days), *¿îd el-khalaq* (the Bairam for [wearing new] clothing), and

also the "cookies bairam." The second is *¿îd al-'aḍḥâ* (Bairam of the Sacrifice) which commemorates the deliverance of Ishmael from being sacrificed (Mot. V544§, "God furnishes substitute [. . .] for human sacrifice"); it is also labeled "Big-Bairam" (because it lasts for four days), and *¿îd el-maraq* (the "Bairam for [meat] broth," due to association with mutton).

337. I.e., *gilbâb:* ankle-length, shirtlike garment, worn indoors and outdoors.

338. Also used often as a street garment.

339. Lit.: would machine [it]; i.e., by applying a sewing machine's tight stitching.

340. Typically, "conversational narratives." Cf. Tale No. 20, note 448. On this category of narrating, see "*kalâm,*" "*ḥaky*" (narration or talk), and "Classifications of Traditions," in El-Shamy, *Folktales of Egypt,* pp. xliv–xlvi.

341. *el-ḥittah,* lit.: the piece, or the site.

342. *'ib¿id ¿annak;* Mot. C434§; see Tale No. 3, note 40.

343. *wi-n-nabî yâ 'ubluh . . . , 'ubluh* being an honorific title used in urban areas for female teacher, master craftswoman, etc.; may also denote big sister or aunt. There is no masculine counterpart for the word.

344. *tiḥkî ginân.*

345. Lit.: teasing, annoying—a man placing himself in the path of a female and speaking love at her, addressing her in offensive sexual terms, or even rubbing against her so as to get her attention. See also Tale No. 24, note 489. On clandestine meetings, see introductory note to Tale No. 17.

346. *gawâz ¿ind, gawâz niḥâs,* etc.; latter label signifies marriage for the purpose of causing *naḥs* (misery, ill omen). See Tale No. 28, note 573.

347. *khadsh ḥayâ' al-'unthâ,* lit.: scratching (wounding) of. . . .

348. Mot. J6§, "'Ideal culture'. [. . .]"; and T10.0.2§, "Falling in love may occur only after marriage (with one's spouse)."

349. *mâsiknî min el-'îd illî tiwga¿,* lit.: by the hand which would cause hurt. For a case of marriage with the intent of controlling the bride's family, cf. Tale No. 28.

350. *¿arûsit mûlid-en-nabî:* a doll made from molten sugar, cast into stylized human form with elaborate paper and food coloring decorations; commercially produced, displayed along with other sugar statuettes, and sold on the occasion of celebrating Prophet Mohammad's Birthday. Mot. F855.7.1§, "Sugar puppet (doll)"; P634.0.3.3§, "Sweets eaten on given occasion."

351. Puppet folk theater or comedy, where little puppets mounted on the puppeteer's fingers are made to move and speak in falsetto.

352. Compare Tales No. 10 and 11, where some Oedipal factors seem to exist.

353. *blîlah* (i.e., *balîlah*); breakfast cereal, served with sugar and milk; unlike fava beans, it is infrequently consumed. See this Tale, note 334.

354. *fûl 'abûya ṭâb, ṭâb;*
we-kalo mennoh el-'ahl we-l'aḥbâb!

355. *yâ maḍrûbah,* lit.: stricken one.

356. *fûl abûya ṭâb, ṭâb;*
we-kalo-menno-el-'ahl we-l-aḥbâb!
w-inta mâlak, yâ-bn fardit el-qubqâb!?

357. *yâ 'aṭ'ûṭah,* i.e., *qaṭqûṭah;* lit.: little kitten. Cf. Mot. Z66.4.1§.

358. *yâ m¿allemtî, 'aih dah 'illi-b-yoḥḍon we-ybûs.*

359. *nâmi, nâmi, mafîsh ḥâgah; da-l-kabûs.*

360. *'itshâhidd ¿alâ roaḥak:* i.e., state, "There is no god but God, and Muḥammad is His Prophet," a death ritual (Mot. V28.0.1§).

361. A nonlexical expression signifying deep sorrow, or shock.

362. *min ¿inayyah,* lit.: out of my own eyes.

363. They caused the sizzling splattering sound of adding cold minced onions or garlic to very hot ghi (clarified butter), oil, etc. in a frying pan, thus generating the sound: "*ṭish-sh-sh-sh*"; i.e., sizzling. This sound is linked to the preparation of tasty foods; it elicits mouth watering—a conditioned response; Mot. J20§, "Conditioning: effects associated with past experience cause man (animal) to respond accordingly [. . .]." On some erotic symbolism associated with this sound, see note 75, this section.

364. *'itlahat fîh.*

365. *'anâ ¿awazah figlah ḍakar, mazrû¿ah f-qalb el-ḥagar;* the word *mazrû¿ah* (planted) suggests certain images and actions (from outside inward) not conveyed by the English word: grown (from the inside outward).

The variety of radish commonly consumed in Egypt has an ivory-colored root; more frequently, it is the leaves that are eaten. On the erotic significance of the shape of a radish, cf. carrot in Tale No. 9; also cf. "radish" in Tale No. 28, note 578.

366. *we-tibqâ-nta ez-zây ¿âwiz el-banât el-bikr teḥbal min ghair ḍakar.*

367. *lissah f-lahwit-hum.*

368. *kabasituh,* lit.: she compressed him.

369. *'aksar nifsahâ.*

370. *'agîb manakhirhâ el-'arḍ;* i.e., cause her to lower her head, or rub her nose in dirt. Mot. Z188.5.2§.

371. *'anâ ṭâlib el-qurb minnak fî . . . ,* lit.: I am requesting closeness to you through. . . . Cf. "*nasîbak*" in Tale No. 31, p. 249.

372. *ḥalawânî:* seller of sweet stuffs, mostly sweet pastry.

373. I.e., *karra lahâ,* as if unwinding thread off a spool in a free fall (by holding the thread's tip and rolling away the spool). This semantic aspect reflects a seamstress's worldview; cf. Mot. U248.6§, "Profession (occupation) affects perception."

374. These mannerisms are typical of a female flirt; Mot. T55.6.3§, "Coquette: exhibitionist from vanity."

375. *'awwiltik ¿adâwah, we-'akhritik ḥalâwah;* lit.: Your beginning is enmity. . . .

376. '*khad esh-sharr w-râḥ*'; Mot. N107.2.1§, "An accident 'takes evil and goes away [with it].'" However, since the conflict (or friction) between the heroine and her husband may not be seen as an accident—which must be an unexpected occurrence—the narrator seems to be applying this belief in a very broad sense. A folk truism that is more relevant to this situation is expressed in the Mot. P311.1.1§, "'No love except after enmity' [. . .]."

377. *el-mikhaddah ma-tshilsh 'itnain* (Mot. T202.1.1§).

378. Cf. Tales No. 13, 23, and 28. Also see El-Shamy, *Brother and Sister: Type 872**, p. 70; and El-Shamy, "Belief Characters," pp. 22–23, esp. note 28.

379. *yâ malik ez-zamân,* lit.: O king of the time.

380. *we ¿amal we-sawwâ,* lit.: and he did and straightened out.

381. *'imlikû-lî ¿alâ bint al-malik,* lit.: give me ownership of the king's daughter; see Tale No. 11, note 250.

382. *kalâm el-mulûk lâ yuradd,* lit.: words of kings may not be taken back. Cf. Mot. P525.0.1, "It is a debt if it is promised," and M203, "King's promise irrevocable."

383. *dahbûb:* a small loaf of bread made of leftover dough, scraped off the walls of the kneading tray; usually it turns out to be ill-shaped and of poor quality.

384. *qûmi ta-[ni]nâm, yâ qiffat-i-¿¿âm*
ya-ḥasrat qalbî ¿al-bîḍ es-simân.

385. *'intaẓir tâ 'afîq,*
yâ qiffat ¿aqîq!
yâ ḥasrat qalbî ¿a-sh-shâbb ar-raqîq!

386. *waḥdah min makhâliq rabbinâ,* i.e., some female person who could have been anyone.

387. *el-balad 'illi faqasûk fîha en-niswân ma-lak bihâ ¿aish. faqasûk,* lit.: hatched you out, i.e., see through you.

388. *yifḍaḥik, we-lisânik yitbarrâ minnik.*

389. *kharsah:* dumb, tongue-tied.

390. *min banât al-mulûk,* lit.: one of the daughters of kings, i.e., a princess.

391. Pronounced "Sa¿idd," in the Syrian dialect.

392. *ṭuhog,* i.e., *ṭahuqa.*

393. *'atjawwaz ¿a-l-kharsah,* lit.: marry over the dumb one.

394. *'ekh-kh-kh!! mâ-â-âliḥ-ḥ-ḥ-ḥ!*

395. *yiqta¿ el-kharsah w-yeqta¿ i-¿yâlhâ.*

396. *'anâ jibet* Sa¿d, *w-*Sa¿îd, *w-*Sa¿diyyah,
¿umir 'ibn el-malik ma-simi¿ minnî kilma radiyyah!

397. *w-ṭâr eṭ-ṭair; yemsîku be-l-khair.*

398. AUC: 34, No. 9.

399. Also called *dallâyah* (lit.: that which hangs down); Mot. Z105§, and Z95.0.1§. These words appear in a number of pseudo-erotic riddles evoking stark sexual images but giving manifestly nonerotic ("innocent") answers (Mot. Z13.0.1.1§); e.g., H888.2§, What would say: "Belly on belly, meanwhile that which is dangling knows what to do?—(water-*zîr,* and person with cup trying to reach down for water=sexual intercourse"). See "multiplexity of cognitive connotations," section I, note 22.

400. Mot. K1321.1; also Mot. J1149.3.1§, "Detection of man masking as woman by ordering all to disrobe." Cf. Type 517A§, *Enigmatic Apparition (Dream, Laughing Fish, Speaking Skull) Leads to Detection of Adultery;* see El-Shamy, *Folktales of Egypt,* Tale No. 2 (introductory part), pp. 14–15. Cf. introductory note to Tale No. 15.

401. Mot. T462.0.1§, "Pseudo-lesbian attraction (love): woman falls in love with another woman who turns out to be a man in disguise"; and T28, "Princess falls in love with a man disguised as a woman." Cf. pseudo-homosexuality between males, in Tale No. 9.

402. *dallâlah,* a marriage broker, Mot. P434.5§, "*khâṭibah:* professional matchmaker (marriage broker)"; cf. T380.3.1§, "Certain (nonthreatening) males are viewed as un-

worthy of woman's modesty (e.g., slave, singer, etc.)"; more commonly referred to as '*khâṭbah*.' See Tale No. 7, note 101. Note the use of the title "maternal-aunt," Mot. Z67.5.2§, "Esteem: woman addressed as '*khâlah* (maternal-aunt)'"; cf. note 485.

403. I.e., *hadhr*. With reference to "lovers' play" (Mot. T59.1§), cf. "Sex games" (Mot. T60§) in Tale No. 50, note 844.

404. *shâhbandar et-tuggâr;* see Tale No. 9, note 213.

405. *'ahhilit we-sahhilit,* i.e., said: "*'ahlan wa sahlan.*"

406. I.e., lack of pretense.

407. *baqit be-ẓ-ẓalṭ*. Cf. Mot. K1303.1§, "Seduction by progressive disrobing dancing (striptease, 'searching for the bee,' etc.)."

408. I.e., a pendant, or a penis.

409. May also mean nighttime party (e.g., singing party, chatting party).

410. *ḥabbituh min qalbahâ;* lit.: loved him from her heart.

411. The text does not make clear how the bride recognized that her groom is in fact her former incognito "female" companion "with the dangler." However, it may be assumed that the recognition was by the groom's sexual member. Mot. H79.9§, "Recognition by sex organ."

412. *qiṣṣah min ed-dîn,* lit.: a story from religion; i.e., an exemplum; cf. note 748, this section.

413. Also, see informant note to Tale No. 31.

414. On the issue of a wife's responsibility to disobey, see *Al-Azhar,* II (1931), p. 650.

415. For examples see Basset, *Mille,* III, Nos. 305 and 306.

416. *'aḥsan biyyah, mû bi-l-gharîb,* lit. Better [done] to me than to a stranger. Mot. F956.7.7§, "Venting anger or frustration (*fashsh el-ghill*). Dissipation of negative emotions through strenuous behavior (acts)"; F956.7.7.1.1§, "Invitation to anger venting: person presents self as target for anger venting by another"; F956.7.7.1.1.1§, "Wife awaits husband's return with stick in her hand, in case he is angry and needs to vent his anger: 'Better at me than at a stranger'"; and Z43.7.1§, "Pecking order: chain of aggressive actions and displaced reactions, started against the weak and ending with the weakest."

417. Mot. V301.1§, "Deeds are [judged] according to intent"; A661.1.1.1§, "Inhabitants of Paradise divided into strata."

418. Also see Tale No. 14, note 318.

419. *bayt al-faqîrât,* an institution comparable to a nunnery.

420. The practice was reported by Taqiyy al-Dîn al-Maqrîzî (1364–1422); see Sa¿îd ¿A. ¿Āshûr, *al-Sayyid Aḥmad al-Badawi: shaykh wa ṭarîqah* (Al-Sayyid Aḥmad al-Badawî: A Sheikh and [His Sufi] Brotherhood), p. 223.

421. On the name Fâṭimah, See Tale No. 7, note 99.

422. *¿alaih eṣ-ṣalâtu we-s-salâm.*

423. Gatherer and vendor of brushwood used as fuel.

424. Commonly used to denote "The Lady," i.e., the female descendant of the Prophet or the she-honorable; i.e., Zaynab.

425. E.g., sandals, slippers, etc.

426. *tiwizzahâ ¿alâ râjilhâ.*

427. *¿oartî makshûfah ¿alaih,* i.e., *¿awratî. . . .*

428. Lit.: shielding me. Cf. Mot. T594.2.

429. I.e., *sayyidunâ;* an adjective used to designate one of God's prophets or one of the cardinal angels such as Gibrîl (Gabriel); cf. *sîdî* (my master) used to refer to a saint. Also cf. *rabbanâ* (Our Lord, i.e., God, or The Lord), and note 274, this section.

430. Mot. T199.2.1.1§, "Divorced woman allowed to take away only the garment she is wearing." For a similar situation where a widow becomes the family provider, see informant note to Tale No. 41 in El-Shamy, *Folktales of Egypt.*

431. *kharah 'ibn kharah 'illî yikûn m¿âh w-yiḥwig el-marah* (Mot. W153.0.1.1§). Cf. introductory note to Tale No. 9, note 149; also see El-Shamy, *Folktales of Egypt,* No. 41, where a husband makes his wife take an oath on the Qur'ân not to take anything from his house and give it to her needy mother (p. 177).

432. *'aftikr-lik 'aih, yâ safargalh, we-kull ¿aḍḍah b-dim¿ah,* (Mot. Z166.4.3.3.1§); T201.1.0.1§, "Marriage: 'like [an inviting] quince, [but] every bite produces a tear.'"

433. Cf. Tale No. 24, where the heroine, a widowed mother, does not remarry; cf. Mot. T201.1§, "Marriage: disappointing (only bad memories)"; T311.7§, "Aversion to remarriage (only bad memories)."

434. Both words in this phrase denote edibles, rations, stored foods, etc.; a form of idiomatic repetition.

435. Lit.: that which is stored, i.e., rations for the year.

436. I.e., caused me to be disgraced in the community.

437. *'idda 'amân,* lit.: gave trust.

438. I.e., *ṣawma¿ah.*

439. *layyis-hâ bi-ṭ-ṭîn:* a sealing technique. Cf. introductory note to Tale 38.

440. *lailah l-'ahl-Illâh,* lit.: an eve for God's people; i.e., for saint's sake and/or the poor—a religious celebration usually held at night, where rituals are performed, and food and soft drinks served; Mot. J1347.2.4§, "An eve for God's sake, or for God's people (Sufi occasion, '*khatmah*'): food provided."

441. *we-hibâb 'aih!?,* lit.: and what suit!?

442. Or ghi: the preferred fat for cooking, frying, baking, etc.; typically prepared during the winter months and stored in ceramic jars (without preservatives, e.g., periodic boiling, pickling, refrigeration, etc.) as part of a household's stored rations.

443. *faḍlet khairak,* lit.: leftovers (overflow) from your own boon; Mot. Z13.9.2§, "Speaker ensures that no accusation (taunting) seems to be aimed at listener."

444. Bread cut into morsels, soaked in meat broth, topped with rice and meat (Mot. F849.1.1§, "The basic meat delicacy [. . .]"). Often served at religious celebrations and perceived to be the favorite of, and the target of quests for food by, lower clerics (*fiqî*s) at banquets; Mot. X420.2.0.1§, "Glutton as messy eater ('*fattagî*')"; see H. El-Shamy, "The Story of El-Sayyid Aḥmad El-Badawî with Faṭma Bint Birry, An Egyptian Folk Epic, part II, text and explanatory notes," *Folklore Forum,* Vol. 9, No. 3–4 (1976), pp. 152–53.

445. *maḥshî, min kull ṣanf w-loan.*

446. *yâ marah! yâ marah!*
saba¿ gudûr-e-tfûr;
min shaqqit el-¿aṣfûr!!

447. *shahag w-ṭabb (el-'ab¿ad) ¿a-l-'arḍ sâkit.*

448. *yisawlafn,* (i.e., talk mostly about past events, family affairs, and the like; con-

versational narratives); cf. Tale No. 15, note 340. The nostalgic reflection on more satisfying times in the past is a recurrent theme in contemporary social life marked by radical changes. Mot. J318.1§, "Better things in the past (golden times, good old days, etc.)."

449. Mot. Z292.0.1.1§. Cf. Tale No. 49.

450. *'hâdhî' ḥurmah: ¿azîzah ¿ind râjilhâ* ("This is" a woman . . .); Mot. Z13.5.1§, "Speaker uses show-and-tell style: 'Here is/are. . . . ' "

451. See "life space," Introduction, p. 6; also cf. introductory note to Tale No. 1, and opening formulas in Tales No. 34-1, 38, and 49.

452. *bi-khâṭirhâ.* The wife's name is cited only in a poem below (see note 459, this section).

453. On the use of the imperative as descriptive, see Tale No. 11, note 245.

454. I.e., *¿iqâl.*

455. I.e., *muṭawwi¿¿,* lit.: the one who mellows or softens dour people; i.e., a preacher.

456. *al-maylis,* i.e., *majlis,* public parlor.

457. *mashmûm,* lit.: things to be sniffed, i.e., fragrant things.

458. *naẓartak li-'an ta'assaf el-yalb w-inṭawâ,*

w-ḍawâ min el-ru¿yân kul bakûr.

in kân bik ḍayf w-mlahhîk ¿anna:
'anâ bint man yijurr li-ḍ-ḍuyûf ¿udhûr.

w-in kân bik wâshî sa¿â-l-yoam bennâ;
we-shû: sa¿y-el-wâshî bainâ ybûr.

459. Feminine diminutive of *ghuṣn* (twig); lit.: Little-twig; i.e., "Twiggy." This is the first mention of the wife's name in this text.

460. *yâ*-l-Ghuṣainah, *ya-lli khuntî w-bugtî:*

*kidâdin ¿alaiki yâ-l-*Ghusain[ah] *khusûr.*

'iṭla¿î ¿annâ, ṭal¿it esh-shams bâkir.
wala yonṭor ¿alaiki f-eṣ-ṣabâḥ en-nûr.

461. I.e., *yâ 'ommak,* lit.: O you who are your mother; probably meaning: you who are your mother['s beloved], or the like. Cf. Tale No. 4, note 50.

462. I.e., *wuliydiyy* ('sonny'); (Mot. Z66.4.1§).

463. *'aṭhar min ḥamâm Makkah.*

464. I.e., free of any ritual contaminants, virtuous, irreproachable.

465. *yâ râ¿i l-yûd, illi ṣâr moaj,*

'iftak[??]-Allâh, yoam ma-shûm ṭâl bukâk.

in kân madyûn, daynak ¿indanâ;
w-in kân madmi[yy]in, najalnâ-dimâk.

w-in kân tibghinî ¿alâ ¿âd l-awwal,
waṭarak 'itnaḥḥâ we-l-khalîl yâfâk!

466. This text was published; see El-Shamy, "[Arab Tales]," in *Tales Told around the World,* pp. 166–68. All four Arab texts in that anthology were collected, translated, annotated, and edited by the present writer.

467. *mâ-thâbak,* i.e., *mâ tahâbu-ka.* Cf. *rahbah,* note 278.

468. *kunnah wa-law ¿aṣâ:* "[A] son's wife [is injurious], even when [she happens to be only] a stick." See Tale No. 44, Aside, p. 317.

469. Cf. Tale No. 7-1; also cf. Tale No. 3.

470. *'ibn bârr,* lit.: charitable son.

471. See "cognitive map," and "life space," Introduction, pp. 6–7.

472. Lit.: I will raise her; i.e., I'll discipline, or punish her.

473. A Nubian rendition of the Arabic: Fâṭimah; see Tale No. 7, note 99.

474. See El-Shamy, *Folktales of Egypt,* Nos. 7, 10, 16, and 50.

475. Although the word *nûbî* may denote "Nubian language," the narrator used the word: *ruṭân,* lit.: gibberish, or rattling. See El-Shamy, *Folktales of Egypt,* p. 108.

476. Cf. Mot. J148.2.1§, "One word (phrase, sentence) evokes another associated with it." This phenomenon is related to what Edward L. Thorndike labeled the principle (sublaw) of "polarity," according to which recall occurs in the same order (direction) the material was learned. See Ernest R. Hilgard, *Theories of Learning,* p. 29; also cf. El-Shamy, "Folkloric Behavior," p. 27, which cites a similar concept developed independently by a European folklorist.

A "true" humorous anecdote reprimanding thoughtless rote memorization provides an example of this "principle":

> As an external examiner was entering the oral examination hall at al-'Azhar University (where English had recently been made part of the curriculum), he noticed a student standing at the doorway trying to memorize the English-Arabic words of "animal-(*ḥayawân*)," through numerous repetitions (with eyes closed, and head swaying): "Animal-(*ḥayawân*)," "Animal-(*ḥayawân*)," "Animal-(*ḥayawân*)" [. . .]. Immediately, the examiner called in the student, and asks him: "What is *ḥayawân* [in English]?" The student promptly replied, "We were not given this word!"

(Heard by the present writer from Professor M. Allâm, Dean of the College of Arts, Ain-Shams University, Egypt, as he told it to a freshman class in 1955–56.) Cf. "*'inshâ,*" Introduction, notes 41–43.

477. For information on this narrator, see El-Shamy, *Folktales of Egypt,* No. 50, pp. 196–97.

478. Cf. Tale No. 18. Also see Tale No. 33, note 653.

479. See El-Shamy, "Maḥfouẓ's Trilogy," p. 59; also cf. Nos. 36–47 in the present work.

480. Given under the title: "*bitâ¿ et-tirmis we-l-ghûlah*" (The Lupine-man [i.e., vendor] and the Ogress). Lupine is a beanlike seed of the legume family, of amber color and very bitter taste; it is soaked and washed overnight in running water, then eaten as a snack.

481. *er-râgil ibn er-râgil illi ¿umruh ma-yshâwir marah* (lit.: A man son of a man is he who . . .). Motif.: W201.1.1.1.1.1§, "Indicator of manliness: slighting women's opinion."

482. A Prophet's saying is reported as stating, *shâwirûhun wa khâlifûhun* (Seek their counsel, but do the contrary).

483. See Tales No. 1 and 4. The exception in this regard are Types: 315, *The Faithless Sister;* 315A, *The Cannibal Sister;* and 590/315C§, *The Prince and the Arm Bands.* [Faithless mother conspires with lover against her son.] Cf. Tale No. 50, note 829.

484. Cf. "co-wife," and "stepmother" in Tale No. 30.

485. Cf. Tale No. 35, (Mot. Z67.5.2§); also see note 402, this section.

486. See Tales No. 1 and 2; also cf. Tale No. 19, where the widowed "heroine" does not remarry.

487. Typically made of palm fronds, and with palm-fiber rope handles.

488. *'Abu-esh-Shawârib,* lit.: the one with the moustaches. It is a euphemism for a bearded nomad, a raider, or a dreaded man; comparable to Bluebeard (Mot. S62.1). Mot. P731.0.3.1§, "Bedouins (tribe) as raiders (robbers): they attack village, caravan, traveler, etc. to get booty"; cf. Mot. Z183.5.1§, "Father-of- . . . " (*'Abu- . . .*).

489. *Tilapia nilotica:* a type of fish similar to a bluegill, typically of the shape and size of *'mishṭ el-'îd'* (i.e., the palm of the hand), or the old-fashioned *mishṭ* (comb); the large size is labeled: "*bulṭî.*" A single *bulṭî* fish is labeled *bulṭiyyah;* which is also a female's proper name, and may denote a hefty (pretty) woman; cf. Z191.2.5§, "Fish (certain types, e.g., *bayâḍah, binniyyah, bulṭiyyah*)—beautiful female."

In another text of the introductory part of the tale (Type 1696), the confusion is over the use of the call: "*bulṭî*" and "*bulṭiyyah,*" where an urban community's strongman, who happened to be walking with his hefty wife, thinks that the vendor is alluding to her; he beats the vendor for his "verbal sexual harassment." Cf. Tale No. 15, note 345. Also see "Baṭṭah (Duck)" in introductory note to Tale No. 7-1.

490. *bi-r-rafâ'i wa-l-banîn.*

491. *nâmû ¿alâ laḥm baṭnohom,* lit.: [went to] sleep on the flesh of their stomachs; i.e., the stomach walls stuck together due to being empty.

492. *tannak warâ el-kaddâb li-ḥadd bâb ed-dâr,* lit.: follow the liar until the door of the house.

493. *tikhnû w-lazẓlaẓû.*

494. The fatty extremity of the tail of a cooked fowl; also used humorously to refer to a human's buttocks. Cf. Mot. Z170§, "Food (cooked, processed) symbolism."

495. *el-meḥammar we-l-meshammar.*

496. *biṣârah/buṣârah/bîsârah:* a jellylike meatless dish of greenish-yellow color. It is prepared of fava beans (see Tale No. 15, note 334) and dried *molokhiyyah* (see Tale No. 5, note 75), served with minced fried onions sprinkled on top; typically, it is an unwelcome dish of hard times—usually, shortly before payday when cash is scarce. It and similar vegetable dishes are also viewed as remedies that harshen up overworked, sluggish stomachs. Mot. F956.7.3.3§, "Vegetarian diet (no meat) promotes good health"; F850.2.3§, "Hated bean mash."

497. *tizaghghaṭ*: to give mouth-to-beak feeding; typically, by blowing corn or bean kernels from one's mouth into that of a fowl, then squeezing the kernels down its throat to the gizzard. Applied so as to fatten a bird for slaughter.

498. *badâ el-fâr yil¿ab fi-¿ibbahâ,* lit.: The rat/mouse began to play within her bosom, i.e., she began to suspect foul play.

499. This word is used mostly to denote young chickens that have not yet laid eggs.

500. *ẓarwaṭ roaḥoh: ¿amalhâ fi-l-libâs.* Cf. Mot. U248.0.2§, "'It' taken to mean what listener has in mind."

501. *kulînî min 'widanâtî' [widânî], 'illî ma-sim¿itsh kalâm 'miratâtî' [mirâtî].* On the use of the diminutive form, see introductory note to Tale No. 1, note 8.

502. Lit.: male-gum (or, perhaps, tom-gum), natural chewing gum that is bitter-tasting, as opposed to *libân nitâyah* (female gum, i.e., not bitter; Mot. W202.1§, "Indicators of femaleness"). Cf. tom-turkey, etc. in Tale No. 9, note 197.

503. Large platelike tray, made of dried cotton-plant stalks, typically associated with women bearing foodstuffs (e.g., bread).

504. The span from the tip of the index finger to that of the little finger of a fully stretched out hand.

505. See El-Shamy, *Folktales of Egypt,* informant note to Tale No. 50, pp. 196–67.

506. See informant note to Tale No. 23.

507. Mot. U300§, "Relativity of perception: 'adaptation level' [. . .]"; and U304§, "Relativity of perceiving quality." Cf. "cleansed" data in Section II ("Profile"), notes 73–75.

508. On Batu and Anubis, see William K. Simpson, ed., *The Literature of Ancient Egypt,* pp. 92–93. On the "seven Hathors," see Simpson, p. 101, note 15. Also compare "the four women," in Tale No. 34, note 667. On "the shadow," cf. Mot. Z125, "Virtue personified"; see Aside, pp. 214–15.

509. I.e., *¿adâ'il:* husbands whose wives are sisters. This rivalry is a major theme in Types 314, *The Youth Transformed to a Horse* (Goldner); and 551, *The Sons on a Quest for a Wonderful Remedy for Their Father.* See El-Shamy, *Folktales of Egypt,* No. 4, p. 29.

510. Designated as Type 880A§, *Husband's Indiscreet Boast about his Wife's Beauty Brings about her Destruction.* Motifs: N104§, "Unfortunate beauty: beauty of innocent woman causes communal conflicts (wars). She is blamed"; F575.1.5.1.1§, "Remarkable beauty: woman with buttocks so high that a pomegranate (apple, orange, watermelon, etc.) rolls through underneath small of her back as she lies on floor"; T306§, "Wife's nakedness or exposure"; P601.1§, "'Customs are as compulsory as religious services'"; K2020.2§, "Person secures promise that wish will be granted and then demands the impossible"; M223, "Blind promise (rash boon). Person grants wish before hearing it"; F1041.8.1, "Madness from seeing beautiful woman"; T24.2.1, "Fainting away for love (or sexual desire)"; F1041.8.1.0.1§, "War waged to procure beautiful woman"; and A1617, "Origin of place-name."

The following is a summary of the story of Tâjûj, also labeled "al-Muḥalliq and Jamjûm." It is based on a rendition narrated in 1968 to El-Shamy by Mr. Maḥmûd ¿Alî Sulaymân, aged fifty-five, teacher and tale collector, from the city of Sinnar; he had heard it from "tribal" men.

> A head of a band of cattle robbers (named al-Muḥalliq) married an extremely beautiful girl named Tâjûj. He gave in to a demand by his best friend (named

Jamjûm) to enforce an ancient tribal marriage custom of permitting spying on the bride while she is "naked," and asked his wife (bride) to allow the spying. The wife, in disgust, refused to grant her husband's request. But faced with his insistence, she finally relented with the condition that he would fulfil for her one wish to be specified afterwards. He agreed and she disrobed (usually only partly). The friend was spying on the wife from a treetop, and was crazed by her beauty; he fell and was seriously injured (or died). As for the wife's wish: she demands divorce. The husband felt deceived, but he had to fulfil his promise. He tried repeatedly to remarry her, but she refused.

Tâjûj was subsequently wed to one chieftain or powerful man after another; but each marriage ended with her abduction by another powerful man, and consequent war of rescue. Finally, a band of robbers attacked a caravan in which she was traveling. The robbers fought over her. An elder robber, who wanted to spare his group and the community the havoc her beauty had wreaked on everyone, killed her. She was buried on the spot where she fell. That site came to be called Tâjûj.

511. *mashâyikh min eṣ-ṣi¿îd . . .* (presumed to be more potent than local ones). Also cf. Tale No. 50, note 837. Although the recording of this text took place in Cairo, the narrator is perceiving events from the perspective of placing himself in his birthplace in Nubia, at the extreme southern end of Egypt, from which the character in the tale travels northward to Cairo, and southward to Sudan. See "cognitive map" and "life space," Introduction, pp. 6–7.

512. A humorous paradox; Mot. M147§, "Conditional 'divorce-vow': oath that divorce will have occurred unless certain matter is brought to pass;" Z98§, "Contradictions (oxymoron)."

513. *¿uḍwuh et-tanâsulî,* lit.: his procreative organ.

514. Lit.: the story (or the tale).

515. *yâ khâlah:* a title for addressing a woman stranger while maintaining social distance (Mot. Z67.5.2§); cf. *¿amm* for a man stranger (Mot. Z67.5.1§), see Tales No. 1, 24, 26, 33, and 42.

516. *salâyif:* Women whose husbands are brothers. In the present tale, they are also sisters.

517. I.e., your brother-in-law.

518. Narrator is providing the details of the plot agreed upon by the king and his other sons-in-law. This episode should have been given prior to the act of the helpful youngest sister.

519. *khayâl;* see Aside, pp. 214–15; cf. "the four women," in Tale No. 34.

520. I.e., *labu'ah,* lit.: lioness; thought of as having an insatiable sexual appetite; Mot. Z84.4.5§, "Insult: nymphomania ("Lioness!" i.e., whore)."

521. *'sâ¿it el-ḥuẓẓ ma-tit¿awwaḍsh,'* lit.: An hour of luck. . . .

522. See H. El-Shamy, "Einigkeit macht stark (AaTh 910F)," in *Enzyklopädie des Märchens,* III (1981): 4–5, pp. 1256–261, esp. note 11. Also see, "The Teachings of the Vizier Kagemni," in Simpson, ed., *The Literature of Ancient Egypt,* pp. 178–79.

523. Mot. U281.1§. Cf. balance in Tale No. 32, note 633.

524. *'Allâhumma 'ig¿luh khair;* Mot. D1812.5.1.33§, "Too much laughter (happiness) a bad omen;" C51.9.2§, "Tabu: dealing with omens (dreams) without saying, 'Good, if God wills.' "

525. *hâtî yâ 'ibrah, waddî yâ midrah,* lit.: O Needle, bring; O pitchfork, take away! (Mot. J2199.4.6.1§).

526. *mishannah;* see Tale No. 24, note 503.

527. *bi-gimlit!* i.e., *bi al-gumlah.*

528. At the time of recording this tale (1971), such a bill had been withdrawn from circulation for more than twenty years.

529. *ḥabîbak 'illî tḥibb wa-laww ¿abd Nûḥî.*

530. *we 'intâ sîd el-¿ârfîn.*

531. *w-en-nabî! w-el-walî!*

532. *gamâlhâ ma-yitwiṣfish.*

533. *hunnît bi-mâ 'u¿tîṭ.*

534. I.e., *sharbât;* fragrant sweet drink, made with rose or fruit flavoring, typically served at joyous occasions (Mot. J1347.2.1.3§, "Circumcision procession (celebration): foods provided to guests"), usually accompanied by trellises of joy (Mot. P790.1.2.1§).

535. *min "ṭaqṭaq" li "salâmu ¿alaikum."*

536. *'aqâbil rabb karîm,* lit.: to meet a Lord who is Generous, i.e., prepare for my end.

537. E.g., pronouncing the *g* as *j,* the *q* (*qâf*) as *g,* rather than as *'a,* and the *l* as a light *l* (as in "less") rather than a dark *l* (as in "luck"); the latter pronunciations characterize the dialects of the neighboring peasants. Also, cf. note 270, this section.

538. Diminutive of *ḥujwah.*

539. I.e., a humorous narrative.

540. Riddle; i.e., a verbal puzzle, where the emphasis is on the ability to perform the intricate verbal formulae.

541. See Tale No. 45; also cf. Tale No. 2.

542. Mot. P529.0.1§, "Only husband has right to instant divorce (by mere oath);" T196§, "Wife divorced because of a trifle."

543. *gamlit-el-bukkâr,* i.e., *qamlat al-'abkâr:* "Maidens' Louse."

544. *ḥallat sha¿raha,* lit.: untied; a sign of grief.

545. *shaggat toabhâ,* i.e., *shaqqat thawbahâ.*

546. *yâ-â-â lahwitî-î-î! yâ kharâ-â-â-â-bî-î.*

547. *'anâ qamlit-el-bukkâr,*
ḥâlila l-'ash¿âr;
¿a-l-ḥajj Abu-¿Ammâr,
faṭṭ wija¿ [waqa¿a] fi-n-nâr!

548. *ghurâb el-bain,* lit.: crow-of-separation.

549. *mâlik yâ gamlit-el-bukkâr,*
ḥâlila al-'ash¿âr.

550. *'anâ gamlit-el-bukkâr,*
ḥâlila al-'ash¿âr;
¿a-l-ḥajj Abu-¿Ammâr,
faṭṭ wija¿ fi-n-nâr!

551. *mâlak yâ ghurâb-el-bain,*
nâtif ed-dailain?

552. *'anâ ghurâb el-bain,*
nâtif ed-dailain;
¿alashân gamlit-el-bukkâr,
ḥâlila al-'ash¿âr.
we-l-ḥajj Abu-¿Ammâr,
faṭṭ wija¿ fi-n-nâr!

553. *'ijrâr, 'ijrâr!,* i.e., *jarrâr, . . . :* (dragging, . . .). Thus, the palm tree's *sa¿af* (branches) and their *khûṣ* (fronds) become droopy.

554. *mâlik yâ nakhlet el-'atmâr,*
sa¿afik i-jrâr-i-jrâr?

555. *'anâ nakhlet-el-'atmâr,*
w-sa¿afî jrâr i-jrâr;
¿alâ ghurâb el-bain,
nâtif ed-dailain.
we-gamlit el-bukkâr,
ḥâlila al-'ash¿âr.
we-l-ḥajj Abu-¿Ammâr,
faṭṭ wija¿ fi-n-nâr!

556. *¿ukâr,* i.e., *¿akir.*

557. *mâlik yâ moayit [mâ'] el-bayyâr;*
bagaiti [baqaiti]-¿ukâr-u-¿kâr?

558. *'anâ moayit el-bayyâr,*
bagait-i-¿ukâr-l-¿ukâr;
¿alâ nakhlet el-'atmâr,
w-sa¿fhâ jrâr-i-jrâr;
¿alâ ghurâb-el-bain,
nâtif ed-dailain.
we-gamlit-el-bukkâr,
ḥâlila al-'ash¿âr.
wel-ḥajj Abu-¿Ammâr,
faṭṭ wija¿ fi-n-nâr!

559. *mâlkum yâ ghanamât, iṣghâr?*
ṣirtun niḥâl i-nḥâl [naḥîlah]!

560. *niḥna ghanamât iṣghâr-i-ṣghâr,*
ṣirna nḥâl-i-nḥâl;
¿alâ moayit el-bayyâr,
bagat-i-¿ukâr-i-¿ukâr;
we-nakhlet el-'atmâr,
w-sa¿afhâ jrâr-i-jrâr;
¿alâ ghurâb-el-bain,

nâtif ed-dailain.
we-gamlit-el-bukkâr,
ḥâlila al-'ash¿âr.
we-l-ḥajj Abu-¿Ammâr,
faṭṭ wija¿ fi-n-nâr.

561. *mâlak yâ khûy, yâ* Naṣṣâr?
¿aṣâtak 'i-ksâr-i-ksâr!

562. *'anâ khayyik Naṣṣâr,*
we-¿asâṭi-ksâr-i-ksâr,
we-ghanamât i ṣghâr-i-ṣghâr,
ṣirna nḥâl-i-nḥâl.
wi-moayit el-bayyâr,
bijat ¿ukâr-i-¿ukâr.
we nakhlit-el-'aṭmâr,
sa¿af ha jrâr-i-jrâr;
¿alâ ghurâb el-bain,
nâtif ed-dailain.
we gamlit-el-bukkâr,
ḥâlila l-'ash¿âr.
we-l-ḥajj Abu-¿Ammâr.
faṭṭ wija¿ fi-n-nâr.

563. I.e., *biṣâr[ah].*
564. *mâlik yâ-binti, yâ* Zahrat an-Nawwâr (i.e., Blossom's Flower)?
¿aliki-i-bṣâr i-bṣâr!

565. *'anâ bintik* Zahrat an-Nawwâr,
¿alayya i-bsâr-i-bsâr;
¿ala-khûy, Naṣṣâr,
¿asâtu-ksâr-i-ksâr.
w-ghanâmat u ṣghâr-i-ṣghâr,
ṣirn a-nḥâl-i-nḥâl.
we-moayit el-bayyâr,
bajit ¿ukâr-i-¿ukâr.
we nakhlit-el-'atmâr,
sa¿af ha jrâr-i-jrâr;
¿alâ ghurâb el-bain,
nâtif ed-dailain.
we gamlit-el-bukkâr,
ḥalila al-'ash¿âr.
we-l ḥajj Abu-¿Ammâr,
faṭṭ wija¿ fi-n-nâr!

566. *ṣaffat-ha,* lit.: drained it out.
567. *mâlik, yâ waliyyah:*
'itnî ¿uwâr-i-¿uwâr!?

568. *'anâ maratak,* Ḥamâmit el-'Asḥâr [Dawn's Dove],
ṣirt ¿uwâr-i-¿uwâr.
wa-bitti Zahrat-an-Nawwâr,
¿alaiha bṣâr i-bsâr.
we khayyaha Naṣṣâr,
¿asâtu ksâr-i-ksâr.
we ghanamâtu ṣghâr-i-ṣghâr,
ṣirna nḥâl i-nḥâl.
we-moayit el-bayyâr,
bijat ¿ukâr i-¿ukâr.
we nakhlit el-'atmâr,
sa¿afha jrâr-i-jrâr;
¿al a ghurâb el-bain,
nâtif ed-dailain.
we gamlit el-bukkâr,
ḥâlila l-ash¿âr.
we-l-ḥajj Abu-¿Ammâr,
faṭṭ wija¿ fi-n-nâr!

569. *fî sittîn dâhyah,* lit.: in sixty catastrophes.

570. *'illi ma-ḥaddish yizill b-¿aqlahâ,* lit.: she whom no one can slip with her mind.

571. AUC: 44, No. 17.

572. Mot. P558.3§, "Battle cry: sister's name."

573. See also Tale No. 15, note 346.

574. Cf. Tale No. 47. Also cf. Tale No. 26, where a black female is preferred to a white one. This theme recurs as an episode in Types 403:IVc (*The Substituted Bride*), and 408:III (*The Substitution of a Negress for the Orange Princess*), both of which are female-bound.

575. *ghâlî,* lit.: dear.

576. *we-ḥyât 'ukhtî . . . ,* i.e., *bi ḥayât 'ukhtî. . . .* On the construction of this sentence, see Tale No. 20, note 570.

577. *ṣubâ¿ 'idhâ,* as opposed to a toe ("foot-finger").

578. Lit.: Roman radish. With reference to foods—especially produce (e.g., pepper, carrots, eggplant, etc.), the adjective *rûmî* means large, light-colored, and mild-tasting; as opposed to *baladî* (country[-style]), which usually signifies being smaller, dark-colored, and of hot or tangy taste. Thus, the finger looked large, plump, and light-complected. Cf. radish in Tale No. 15, note 365.

579. To be like the foliage, or sprouts—not yet blossomed—of palm-tree fronds, or sugarcane leaves; i.e.: of light color, soft, firm and plump, yet crisp; eaten as a delicacy.

580. *kamarairah 'afrangiyyah:* Western female personal attendant; presumably light-complected. Cf. Mot. F575.0.1§, "Remarkably beautiful face."

581. *ḥalâwithâ,* lit.: her sweetness.

582. *en-noamah fî ḥoḍnahâ.* Cf. Mot. Z55.3§, "Social (interactional) process carried to its climax."

583. The assumption is that the paramour may recognize her accent. Mot. H38.3, "Slave recognized by his conversation, habits, and character."

584. *'inbasat,* lit.: unfolded, i.e., had fun, became content, was pleased (Mot. K1843.1.2§). In *The Arabs* (New York, 1964), p. 117, Anthony Nutting reports that al-¿Abbasah, sister of Caliph Hârûn al-Rashîd (d. 809 A.D.), used the same trick to consummate her marriage and conceive from her Persian husband, Ja¿far al-Barmakî (Mot. T131.11.1.1§), to whom she had been wedded in a nonsexual marriage (Mot. P529.6.3.1§). This act allegedly caused rage in al-Rashîd to the extent that he had his sister killed together with her husband and children. He also ordered the decimation of the entire Barmakî family (Mot. L410.9§), thereby deepening the rift between Arabs and Persians. (Cf. Types 315, and 891F§/1379; also cf. Tale No. 49, note 816, below.)

585. *yâ-shaikh 'itlihi,* lit.: Sheik, get immersed in total absorption; cf. Tale No. 15.

586. *shîl henâ, ḥoṭṭ henâ!* (Mot. Z95.0.1§, "Double meaning. . . . " Also cf. Mot. U248.0.2§, U248.4§.)

587. AUC: 25, No. 2.

588. AUC: 33, No. 7. (Narrator is a housemaid and literate. She gave her age as twenty-eight, but collector thinks she is forty.) On role strain (Mot. P7.1§), see notes 2, 255, and 713, this section.

589. *¿amal:* i.e., there is a magical incantation that would render him impotent with, or cause him to lose interest in, another woman! Mot. T591.0.2§. See El-Shamy, *Folktales of Egypt,* No. 42.

590. *'yâ-me'âmanh li-r-rigâl, yâ ma'mnah li-l-mayyah f-il-ghurbâl'* (Mot. J2756.1.1§); cf. Mot. W256.6.8.1§, "Men cannot resist temptation." These and the following proverbs were used by Mrs. Nabawiyyah M.Y. (see informant note to Tale No. 9).

591. *qaṣqṣî ṭairik la-ylûf bi-ghairik* (Mot. T145.10.1§).

592. *el-maḥamal:* the appellation for this official caravan. However, what is meant here is: howdah, mounted on a camel.

593. Fanning with one's garment is done with an angular, rapid, up-and-down movement, usually to generate a draft of air to cool off one's face or to ignite a fire.

594. Idiomatic for *yi¿mil faṣl fî:* lit.: to play (or do) an unexpected, embarrassing trick on someone; i.e., a gag.

595. *yallâh,* i.e., quickly, get with it. Here, it is accompanied by a hand motion to signal: "Out!" Cf. Mot. Z63.10.2.3§, "'Get road-bound' ('hit the road!')"

596. Al-Basra (al-Baṣrah) is a city in southeastern Iraq—not in esh-Shâm (the Levant Coast countries) as the narrator seems to think; the city's name suggests the Arabic word: *baṣar,* i.e., eyesight.

597. *surrit el-balad,* lit.: the town's navel.

598. *milâyah laff,* lit.: a wrapping-sheet, i.e., a black mantle that would lightly wrap a woman from head to upper ankle except for her face—the typical attire of urban *baladî* (country-style) native women.

599. *'ahl-Illâh,* lit.: God's people, i.e., saints and/or the poor.

600. *ḥilwah wallâ maltûtah?*

601. *'ibn es-sab¿ah.*

602. *zayy eḍ-ḍarâyir.*

603. *markib eḍ-ḍarâyir sârit, w-markib es-salâyif ghârit* (Mot. P264.0.1.2§).

604. Also see introductory note to Tale No. 38.

605. On the co-wife, see tale No. 31. With reference to the cruelty of a maternal-

aunt, see Tale No. 35; also cf. Tale No. 34, note 672. Cf. how a wife perceives husband's "sister" (who would be the children's paternal-aunt) in Tale No. 24.

606. Cf. Tale No. 24, note 483.

607. *riyâẓ*, i.e., *riyâdh*.

608. *el-¿uhdah ¿a-r-râwî*, i.e., if any blame is to be assigned, it should go to the source from whom I had heard the tale; cf. "Don't blame me," "no offense," etc.

609. "*Si-¿Lây-ed-Dîn*," i.e., Mr. ¿Alâ'-ad-Dîn.

610. *khâlâtuh*. See introductory note to this tale, note 605.

611. *ejnainet el-lûlî we-l-mirjân, 'illi fi-blâd el-ghîlân*.

612. *'akbar minnî b-shahr, we 'a¿lam minnî b-dahr*.

613. *raḍa¿t ibzâzik, wi-ṣirt mitil [mithl]-awlâdik*.

614. *'omminâ el-ghûlah*, lit.: Our Mother the Ogress. Henceforth, Mother Ogress.

615. "*'incî bain 'iḍrâsak, we-s-saif yiqta¿ râsak*."

616. In the romance of Delhimah, the name Jundubah (the Foundling) is given to the male hero as a result a swarm of locusts providing him with a cover (Mot. B486.1.1§); see E. W. Lane, *The Modern Egyptians*, p. 417.

617. *nâyim sanah, qâyim sanah*.

618. *tannî* i.e., *thannî*, lit.: second [it].

619. *mâ ¿allamtni-ommî* (Mot. Z18.3§).

620. *yâ qaṣr ḥanḥan ejrâsah*
w-raḥal w-raḥalat nâsah.

621. *mayy el-muḥâyâh* (i.e., *mâ' al-'iḥyâ'*); Mot. E80.

622. *su¿adâ w-masrûrîn, w-teslamu yâ-sam¿în*.

623. *'el-ḥichâya ḥachainâha, we-b-¿ibkun dashshainâha*.

624. *¿Uglit eṣ-Ṣubâ¿*.

625. The narrator is the less favored wife. Her husband stated that despite his misery with two wives, he has not divorced her out of kindness to her ("Who is going to provide for her?") and consideration for her own family's feelings ("Her parents are very old and her father is my paternal-uncle"); Mot. T199.3.1§, "First wife not divorced out of kindness to her," and T199.3.2§, "First wife not divorced due to her family's power (influence)."

This is the only case known to the present writer where a husband has openly admitted that his wife tells him *ḥawâdit* (fantasy-tales); also see informant note to Tale No. 18 (told by the narrator's mother-in-law). For additional information on this tale and its narrator, see El-Shamy, "Belief and Non-belief," pp. 9–15; also see El-Shamy, *Folktales of Egypt*, No. 55.

626. Mot. D1716, "Magic power of the infirm;" cf. W256.8.1§, "The tyranny by (might of) the infirm (physically handicapped)."

627. Cf. rivalry among wives of brothers (sisters-in-law) in Tale No. 48; also cf. Type 898:IV ("The Prince's Marriage"), Tale No. 14. On the trickster cycle, see El-Shamy, *Folktales of Egypt*, pp. 219–21.

628. *shîlî 'îdik,*
[ja]tek gaṭ¿ 'îdik!
da-nâ ḍorritik, we-jâya-kîdik!

Mot. M431.4.1, "Curse: hand of person cursed to drop off." Cf. the chant in Tale No. 6-1, note 94.

629. *wiggah,* i.e., *'uqqah:* approx. 2.75 pounds; the standard weight measure in Egypt until it was replaced by the kilogram in the 1950s.

630. The sounds made to call cats and dogs, respectively.

631. *baṭnahâ ¿abbat;* on the meanings of the word *baṭn,* see Tale No. 1, note 16.

632. The name Zlaizlah, i.e., Slaislah, is probably a diminutive of *selsilah* (a chain), and may be in reference to a girl with long chainlike hair—a mark of beauty. The name *'Omm*-Zaba¿ba¿ suggests a female with a character that resembles a *zawba¿ah* (duststorm). However, a number of women in the audience began to giggle at the name; I learned later that the actual name in the tale is: *'Omm-zabarbar* (the female with a little penis), which suggests a female who had not undergone clitoridectomy (i.e., an uncircumcised female)—a trait considered disgraceful especially among tradition-bound groups (Mot. Z84.4.5.1§). Also cf. T329§, "Clitoridectomy (excision of girls): so as to insure future chastity"; V82.0.1§, "Circumcision is required for cleanliness (of male or female)."

633. Cf. "blackness" in Tale No. 26, note 523.

634. See also Tales No. 24 and 34.

635. I.e., *faqîh:* a religious savant. In vernacular, a *fiqî*/"*fi'î*" denotes a low-ranking cleric (e.g., preacher, parson). Cf. the role of such a cleric in Tale No. 13, esp. note 282.

636. *ghirbâl,* i.e., *ghurbâl.*

637. *kirbâl:* the narrator did not know exactly the meaning of this word and explained: "Some sort of thing, and that is all;" probably: *kirbâj/kurbâg,* i.e., whip.

638. *salâsil el-jabbâr.*

639. *ligâḥ,* i.e., *liqâḥ.*

640. *yij¿al shahdî f-lsânik, walâ yij¿alsh zabânî f-kalâmik.* Allusion is being made to proverbial images: "honey-dripping tongue" and "poison-dripping tongue," respectively. Cf. Tale No. 1, note 12.

641. *'Allâhumma ṣallî ¿a-n-nabî:* supplication believed to aid memory.

642. *waffagget bainhom.*

643. *ya-llî ma-tissammîsh.* It is believed that the mere mention of an evil entity causes it to occur. Consequently, unnameable signifies being too evil to be mentioned. Cf. Tale No. 3, note 40, and Tale No. 9, note 222.

644. Mot. P503.3.3§, "Dodging responsibility"; cf. J894.2§, "Consolation: *'anâ-mâlî* ('None of my business')."

645. *jîb w-ḥuṭṭ,* lit.: bring and place (put); i.e., heap upon. Cf. Mot. M440.2.1§, "'May He bring [calamities] and heap [them] upon . . . [someone].'"

646. Mot. T137.5, "Bride (and party) fetched by groom and party after wedding."

647. *el-lûlî f-¿anâqîduh,* lit.: The pearls on their own vines. Henceforth "Pearls-on-Vines."

648. For example, see El-Shamy, "Belief Characters," pp. 13–14; also see El-Shamy, *Folktales of Egypt,* Nos. 3, 41, and 44.

649. For example, see Tale No. 47.

650. *salamtak, w-laff ¿imamtak, w-qa¿ditak fi-l-bait zayy ¿awâydak.*

651. *'intî 'illî fîhom.*

652. *es-Sind we-l-Hind.*

653. In the context of belief accounts, it is believed that one of the conditions a supernatural spouse or lover sets is that the affair with the human companion be kept a secret (Mot. C645§ and F300.0.1§). On keeping a husband's (lover's) secret, see Tale No. 23, note 478.

654. *balad tishilhâ w-balad teḥuṭṭahâ.*

655. *yamâmtain;* sing., *yamâmah:* mourning dove, turtledove.

656. *sammat ¿alaihom:* an Islamic requirement for killing a bird or animal so as to use its meat for food (Mot. C229.7.1§). Cf. Tale No. 50, note 838.

657. *mâ-kaddibûsh khabar;* i.e., took the news instantly at face value.

658. AUC: 44, No. 11.

659. Cf. the information on (remembering) memory given in Tale No. 7-1, note 121.

660. On resocialization and the retention of lore, see El-Shamy, *Brother and Sister: Type 872**, p. 51; and El-Shamy, *Folktales of Egypt*, pp. lii, 75.

661. *gittituh,* i.e., *guththatihi.* The classical Arabic word *guththah* denotes a corpse or cadaver; the vernacular word '*gittah*' may denote also body, physique, figure, etc.

662. *es-Sind we-l-Hind we-blâd tirkab el-'afyâl.*

663. *bishwaish, bishwaish.*

664. *w-in khaff ¿alâ 'idaikî [(yadaykî)], ḥaykûn mulkî taḥt reglaikî.* Lit.: . . . under your feet.

665. *wa¿d el-ḥurr dain,* lit.: A free-man's promise. . . .

666. Type 409B§, *Youth Marries Wild Animal; She Proves to be a Beautiful Maiden. A Relative Imitates: Disastrous Results.* Cf. Tale No. 48.

667. *al-arba¿ niswân.* Cf. "the shadow" in Tale No. 25, note 508. These beings appear also in another context (Type 318A§) as man-eaters (ogresses), with their breasts thrown over their shoulders (Mot. F531.1.5.1), and as mothers of four children; see D. H. Müller, *Südarabische Expedition, Mehri- und Soquri-Sprache,* Vol. 6, No. 16, pp. 89–95; esp. p. 91.

668. According to Mr. ¿Ali ¿A. Ghulûm, then of the Arab Gulf States Folklore Center, and a native of Bahrain.

669. See also Tales No. 2, 8, 32, and Nos. 35, 36, and 37.

670. *ghaḍḍah baḍḍah, 'idhâ mishi el-barghûth ¿alâ khaddahâ qaḍḍah* (Mot. F574.9.1.1§). This is a regional opening formula; it is used here in addition to a variation on the standard, Pray on behalf of the Prophet.

671. From a classical Arabic perspective, the word *ḥût* denotes a whale, '*ḥawwât*' signifies a whaler; used here as fisherman.

672. *khâlah,* lit.: maternal-aunt. On the use of this term to denote "stepmother," see introductory note to Tale No. 30, note 605.

673. *bayt en-nâr,* lit.: fire-house; cf. kitchen.

674. *la¿b,* lit.: play, i.e., party, fun.

675. *lûlû w-mirjân,* i.e., *lu'lu' wa marjân;* the latter being "[sea] coral," designating a red precious stone, similar to *yâqût 'aḥmar* ("red ruby").

676. Lit.: Do you have his [its] brother? i.e., the second of the pair.

677. Money paid by the groom to the bride's family. It is meant as a gift to the bride-to-be, to be used for furnishing the residence for the newlywed couple. This practice

often appears in academic literature as "bride-price." (Cf. Mot. T52.3, "Bride purchased for her weight in gold.") With reference to wedding expenses, cf. *¿urs* (wedding), in note 148, this section.

678. *shoarhâ ¿ind 'ommhâ.*

679. *qatalû-ha,* lit.: they killed her.

680. *mâ jâkû 'illâ. . . .* On the significance of this formulaic beginning see informant note to Tale No. 20.

681. *yadkhul fîhâ al-ḥidhâ';* lit.: the shoe enters in/into her. Cf. Tale No. 46-3, note 792. On the symbolic significance of the act of inserting a foot into a shoe (Mot. Z186.4.3.1§), see El-Shamy, "Beide?" pp. 55–64.

682. *nrîd ¿alaihâ 'irwaid, we-¿oam, we-tamr.* According to Mrs. K. al-Ḥ. (see informant note to Tale No. 11): *'irwaid* is a radishlike plant, and *¿oam* is a tiny fish caught in abundance then salted for preservation; these were basic dietary items before the oil boom. (Cf. Mot. F561.10§, "People who live on salt-cured (pickled) foods.")

683. *lam yuḥâlif hâ al-ḥaẓẓ*: a literary cliché.

684. On the theme of eyes lost and then restored, see El-Shamy, *Folktales of Egypt,* pp. 262–63; also see El-Shamy, "Vom Fisch geboren (AaTh 705)," pp. 1211–18.

685. *hân hân; we ¿alâ-Allâh et-tuklân.* This formula may also mean: Things get easier, [if] one's reliance is on God.

686. *'Allâhu huwa al-mâniḥ al-mâni¿.*

687. *'l-Illâh' (li-Allâh), yâ muḥsinîn.*

688. *¿alâ sunnit Allâh we rasûluh: b-el-ḥalâl.*

689. *'anta al-mâniḥ al-mâni¿;* Mot. V52, "Miraculous power of prayer"; cf. N190.0.1§, "'God grants whomsoever He pleases without limit'"; A102.0.1§, "God's names (99 attributes)"; A102.14.2§, "Generosity of God."

690. *tabârak al-khallâq fî-ma khalaq;* also see note 248, this section.

691. *al-yasmîn b-el-¿ain al-yamîn.*

692. *al-'azhâr b-el-¿ain el-yasâr.*

693. M224.1§, "Kerchief of safety (*maḥramat al-'amân*): cloth given to the accused indicating promise of immunity from punishment."

694. *wa-hâdhi hi[ya] el-hichâyah, wa-laww baytanâ qarîb l-jibt-ilkum ḥiml zabîb.*

695. See V. Ions, *Egyptian Mythology,* p. 57, where a photograph of an ancient Egyptian relief depicting this act is provided.

696. J. Rivière, *Djurdjura,* p. 70. Also see Tales No. 13, note 288, and 38, note 715. On the significance of the formulaic ending, see Tale No. 37, note 701.

697. *yâ-baqaret nenetna yâ-ḥallâbah,*
ya-ḥamyân a me-n-nâr w-ed-diyâbah,
'iddîna men khairek, da-ḥna yatâmah rhalâbah!

698. Bread made from *'adhrah* (maize) flour is considered inferior to that made of wheat (*qamḥ*) flour; typically, it has a rougher texture and less malleability. Softness, thinness, and malleability are necessary for using a morsel of bread as a spoon (labeled cat's ear) to scoop up souplike stews (labeled *ghumûs,* i.e., dip), which is the standard style for eating. Cf. note 833, this section; also see Tale No. 9, note 150.

699. See El-Shamy, "Belief Characters," p. 21ff. Mot. P236.3, "Not daring to curse father directly, son does so indirectly."

700. On Isis and Osiris, see "Plutarch's Mythological History of Isis and Osiris," cited in E. A. Budge, *The Gods of the Egyptians,* pp. 186–94; Ions, *Egyptian Mythology,* pp. 50–63; see also E. Spence, *Myth and Legends of Ancient Egypt,* pp. 68–69.

Also cf. Tale No. 39 where a sister is reincarnated.

701. Cf. note 288, this section. Also see tale 46-2, note 789. On the affective significance of such formulaic endings, see El-Shamy, *Brother and Sister: Type 872**, p. 74.

702. *sit el-Ḥusn [we-l-gamâl],* Mistress of Comeliness [and Beauty]: a recurrent heroine's name in folktales. See also Tale No. 46-1, note 787.

703. *esh-shâṭir.* Typical title for a hero in fantasy-tales.

704. *faḥl,* lit.: stud, out of which smaller branches go to water a field.

705. *qarmûṭ*: *Clarias anguillaris;* a variety of catfish.

706. *ghaiẓ* (i.e., *ghayẓ*): quiet ire or wrath.

707. *'ana-l-¿aṣfûr l-akhḍa-a-ar, l-akhḍa-a-a-ar!*
'amshi ¿al-ḥaiṭ 'aṭmakhṭa-a-a-ar, 'aṭmakhṭa-a-a-ar!
marat 'abûya dabaḥit nî-î-î-î, dabaḥit nî-î-î!
wa 'abûya l-¿arṣ kal laḥmî-î-î, kal laḥmî-î-î!
w-ukhti l-¿azîzah dafanit ¿iḍmî-î-î, ¿iḍmî-î-î!

708. *lâ ḥawla [walâ quwwata 'illâ bi] Allâh.* Cf. Mot. V90§, "Miraculous effects of invoking God's attributes (*basmalah, ḥasbanah, ḥawqalah,* etc.)."

709. *bàss! (we khulṣit ¿alâ kidah).*

710. See this tale, note 701.

711. *el-'akhkh el-ghazâl,* lit.: the deer brother.

712. On the narrator's relatives in Egypt, see informant note to Tale No. 37 in El-Shamy, *Folktales of Egypt,* p. 164.

713. This strain (Mot. P7.1§) is dramatically illustrated in Tale No. 45. Cf. the nearly identical statement by the Sayyidah D., the narrator of Tale No. 9 (Type 707) in El-Shamy's *Folktales of Egypt,* p. 63. Also see Tales No. 1, and 37 in the present work.

714. Mot. Z66.4.1§. It should be noted that Aarne-Thompson, *The Types of the Folktale* labels this tale type (450) "*Little Brother and Little Sister.*"

715. Mot. K1843.5§, T415, and N365.3; cf. Type 932A§, Tale No. 49. Also cf. introductory note to Tale No. 36, note 696. On the theme of a wife sharing her husband with other co-wives, see introductory note to Tale No. 30, note 604.

716. *el-khalâ,* i.e., *al-khalâ',* lit.: the open space. This statement may also mean sleeping outside the privacy of one's own home.

717. *yiktib ¿alaiha.*

718. *dakhal ¿alaiha, shâlit minnuh,* lit.: he entered upon her, she carried from him.

719. *yâ-khayyitî, yâ* Bdûr!
ya-khayyitî, yâ Bdûr!
sannain es-sakâkîn,
we-ḥammai n el-qudûr;
¿alashân khuwayyi k Ṣûr!

720. *yâ-khuwayyî, yâ* Ṣûr!
ya-khuwayyî, yâ Ṣûr!
sha¿rî maḥlûl w-mḥalainî [??],

w-ibn es-sulṭân fe-ḥaḍainî.
w-mâ-lî 'ilak wusûr [wusûl]!

The Arabic *mḥalainî* constitutes a phrase that suggests *muḥallin-lî* (pronounced: *miḥallî-nî*), i.e., makes me beautiful (lit.: sweetens me). Translated here as covering me up in congruence with the general message of the poem. Cf. Mot. T405.3§, "Sister's nakedness or exposure"; also see Tale No. 5, note 65.

721. *maskûnah,* lit.: inhabited. Cf. note 727, this section.

722. *'anâ 'inciyyah min khiyâr el-'unûce.*

723. *mîn yiṭûl!,* lit.: Who [can] reach! This statement may mean: It would be so fortunate if one were to become [as pretty as] a deer; or, perhaps: It would be fortunate if a woman were to be able to keep her brother with her all the time (even in a deer form).

724. *qa¿¿âdah ¿âj we qa¿¿âdah zjâj.*

725. *samâmî an-niswân,* lit.: women's chatter [yarn]. Mot. W202.1.1.3§, "Women's superstitious ways (old wives' tales, old wives' medicine, etc.)."

726. El-Shamy, *Brother and Sister: Type 872**, p. 57 (emphasis added); for other characteristics of this subtype, see pp. 40–41.

727. I.e., inhabited by jinn. Cf. note 721, this section.

728. *tunshur laish yâ-nashshâr?*
b-tunshur ¿aẓhmî b-el-minshâr.

729. *tabâraka al-khallâq [fî-mâ khalaq];* see note 248, this section.

730. *bi-llâhî, yâ 'ommî;* i.e., respectable lady, please. . . .

731. *yirûḥ 'et-tawalitt;* probably a modernized aspect of the narrator's speech.

732. *mahr;* see Tale No. 34, note 677.

733. *qa¿¿âda ¿âj w-qa¿¿âda zjâj:*
kaif-yaḥill bain el-'akhkh w-ukhtu zwâj!

734. Mot. W28, "Self-sacrifice." Cf. Mot. P7.1§, "Role strain"; see Tale No. 1, note 2. Also see Tale No 8, note 137.

735. AUC: 11, No. 1.

736. In a case of supernatural illness (possession), a young bride miscarries due to mistreatment by the trouble-making sister of her husband. The bride's cure begins when the husband's sister gets married and moves out of the extended family home to join the household of her own husband, thus sparing her brother's wife from further aggravation. See El-Shamy, "Belief Characters," p. 25.

On the theme of blind trust and forgiveness by a brother toward his sister, see El-Shamy, *Brother and Sister: Type 872**, p. 53; and this tale, note 740.

737. Also see this tale, note 741.

738. *muwashshâh bi-l-qaṣab.*

739. *yâ sit el-milâḥ, yâ sit el-milâḥ,*
el-lail rawwaḥḥ we-l-fajr lâḥ.
'imt-an yiṣîr er-rawâḥ?

740. *'ed-dunyâ titshabbih,* lit.: the world [has many things that may be] matched. It is significant to note in this context that the brother does not verify his sister's false

claim by asking his wife, who looks exactly like his sister and has a dress exactly like hers, about her own dress. Also see introduction to this tale, note 736.

741. See introductory note to this tale, note 737; also cf. Tale No. 13, note 288.

742. *shâlit rijil, wi-ḥaṭṭat rijil, wi-jâbat walad zayy el-¿ijil,* i.e., she went through what should have been a difficult birth with ease (presumably a mark of a good fertile woman).

743. A major episode is missing from this rendition of the tale. In the Gulf Region, where this narrative seems to have its widest recurrence, the brother's wife arranges for the child to be adopted by his real father, then for the mother to be hired as a wet nurse for the infant.

744. *raḍî¿,* lit: he-suckling; i.e., a newborn boy still in the breast-feeding stage.

745. *yâ-bn lailah wi-talt layâlî:*
yâ illî 'awwal lailah min el-layâlî rabaṭ fustânî bi-fustânuh!
yâ illî tânî lailah min el-layâlî laff sha¿rî ¿alâ drâ¿uh!
yâ illî tâlit lailah min el-layâlî dahan rasrâs fî qubqâbî!

746. *yâ ṭairah ṭârit min 'ibrajkum li-brâjna.*
eṭ-ṭairah khallift wi-frâkhhâ ¿indanâ.
tilqu eṭ-ṭairah ¿alâ eṭ-ṭair,
wallâ tâkhdû frâkhkum ¿anannâ?

Cf. Mot. Z189§, "Symbolism concerning virginity and defloration." Also see Tale No. 50, note 826.

747. *'esh-shaikh bi-maṣriyyitain.*
'we-l-waraqa bi-rub¿iyytai n [??].
'we-b-nilqâ eṭ-ṭairah ¿a-ṭ-ṭair.'

The meaning of this seemingly incomplete enigmatic statement is not clear. However, it seems to suggest that since the bride is not a virgin, her bride-wealth (*mahr*) will be small and easy to pay; consequently, the two birds (lovers) would be properly united.

748. *giṣṣah dîniyyah,* i.e., *qiṣṣah. . . .* See exemplum, Tale No. 18, note 412.

749. *'illi mâ-luh 'ukht yatîm.* Also see Tale No. 47, note 794. This truism was also used by a Sudanese (male) folklorist, during a conference held in Doha, Qatar in 1986.

750. *qamîṣ*: an ankle-length, light-weight garment.

751. *khoṣṣ*: an enclosurelike hut, usually without a roof; built of branches and reeds.

752. *¿azza wa jall.*

753. *Allâh—(subḥânahu wa ta¿âlâ),* also: '*rabbinâ/rabbunâ . . . ,*' i.e., *rabbanâ* (lit.: Our Lord, Our God).

754. *al-ḥamdu li-llâh, 'alladhî lâ yuḥmadu ¿alâ makrûhin siwâh,* lit.: whom no one but He may be thanked for an affliction (Mot. V318.2§).

755. Lit.: senior-woman, i.e., woman saint ("saintess"). In the Arabian Peninsula and among Bedouins, this title denotes "chieftainess," i.e., princess, or matriarch. See introductory note to Tale No. 34-1.

756. *taḥt râs-oh ¿alâ ṭûl,* lit.: under his head directly; i.e., the immediate younger, and closest to him in age.

757. Lit.: forbearance or mercy [from God]; i.e., mild insanity.

758. *marfû¿ ¿anhâ el-ḥigâb;* Mot. D1820.0.1§, "Clairvoyance (*raf¿/kashf al-ḥijâb*):

supernatural power (ability) to see that which is out of sight (hidden, unknown, unseen, etc.)"; V223.0.2§, "Clairvoyance of madmen (fools, the insane, *magâdhîb*)."

759. During the early stages of field research on the Brother-Sister Syndrome, the present writer formulated an interview questionnaire that included the following questions: "If religion were to allow marriage between brother and sister, would you marry your brother?" and "If you were an ancient Egyptian princess, would you have married your brother?" Of eleven young university women students, only one answered emphatically "No!" and affirmed that she would marry a man like her father (which is the case in actual life, for her husband was considerably older than she, and known for his authoritarian paternalistic character).

See note 768, this section; also, cf. Tales No. 41, and 49.

760. *tigawwiz el-'ukht li 'akhûhâ.*

761. *khair ma-¿amaltî.*

762. *minhon fîhon,* i.e., *minhom/minnahom wa fîhom,* i.e., very intimate with them, one of the family.

763. *'Allâhumma ṣallî ¿alâ sayyidinâ Muḥammad:* supplication believed to aid memory.

764. *subḥân Allâh,* lit.: praise be to God.

765. *el-wajih wajih bintî, we-l-'affah 'affat marat-'ibnî.*

766. Mot. U248§, "Mental set. . . . " Also see introductory note to Tale No. 7-1, note 121, and Tale No. 33-1.

767. *el-wild mawlûd we-l-baww mawjûd, we-nâr al-khaww tish¿al bilâ waqûd.* On the viewpoint that a husband is replaceable, see Tale No. 27, note 541.

768. Mot. P7.1§, "Role strain." A text (from the Bete of western Africa) presents a dilemma of a man who must choose among his "sister, wife, and mother-in-law"; see William Bascom, *African Dilemma Tales,* no. 82:2, p. 93. On the possible association between a dilemma tale in sub-Saharan Africa and its nondilemma counterparts north of the Sahara, see El-Shamy, *Folktales of Egypt,* p. 250; also see El-Shamy, "Dilemma Tales," in *Folklore: An Encyclopedia of Forms, Methods, and History,* Thomas A. Green, gen. ed., Vol. 1, pp. 188–89.

Some informal experimentation using this narrative (Type 985) as a dilemma tale in a cross-cultural context involving Americans in the United States may be of interest. Two demographically distinct, broadly defined, social groups rendered starkly different results:

> Category I: A large class of about 300 students, predominantly white, nineteen to twenty-three years of age, in a Midwestern town.
> Category II: A comparatively small class of African Americans (38 women, 1 man, and 1 white woman); mostly middle-aged (thirty-five to fifty), in a small southern town, teachers attending a summer (1978) seminar on the use of folklore in education.

As a classroom lecture device, the story (Type 985) was told, followed by the question: "If you happened to be that woman, whom would you choose: son, husband, or brother?" Respondents indicated their choice by raising their hands:

Category I: Regardless of the order in which the choices were presented, the following pattern seems to be the recurrent choice of the younger students:

- The clear majority of young women chose "son" (with a ratio of female:male of about 10:1).
- Relatively small number of young women chose "husband" (with a ratio of female:male of about 1:5).
- More men than women chose "husband."
- A very small number of either gender chose "brother" (about 4–5 percent).
- More women than men chose "brother."

Category II: The following pattern was the choice of the professional *African American* adults:

- Of the 38 black women 37 chose "brother" (a seemingly unbelievable uniformity).
- 1 black woman chose (with visible hesitation) "husband."
- The one black man chose "husband."
- The one white woman chose "son."

Note: The main instructor for the course (and the present writer's host, Prof. A. S. Zuhrul Haque) explained: the black woman who chose "husband," was married to the man who also chose "husband," and that he was "looking at her to find out whom she was going to choose."

Addendum: During the numerous times this poll has been informally used in class with Category I (between 1974 and 1996), only once did a fourth (new) choice surface: the woman should offer herself in lieu of her captive relatives, and free all three men. Notably, this solution was proposed by a young male.

For a similar situation, in which female Egyptian university students projected a pattern of sentiments comparable to that of African Americans, see note 759, this section.

On "Experimental folklore," see El-Shamy, "Folkloric Behavior," pp. 36–41; and "Behaviorism and the Text," pp. 150–54.

769. *'âlâf mu'allafah.*

770. "*'ilakhkh, 'ilakhkh*": i.e., "*'ilâ 'âkhirih, . . .* "; lit.: "to the end of . . . , to the end . . . "; a literary acronym that does not occur in folk narration (cf. "and the like," in Tale No. 9, note 195). Mot. J2519.5§, "Intemperance in mourning"; P681.1.1§, "Accompaniments of mourning."

771. *al-'ibn mawlûd, wa-z-zoaj mawjûd, wa-l-'akhkh mafqûd.*

772. *ḥujwat* Fâṭmah *es-samḥah.* The adjective *samḥah* is commonly translated as "beautiful." On the name Fâṭimah, see Tale No. 7, note 99.

773. Mot. T461.0.1§, "Erotic fetishism." Cf. Tale No. 11, where a girl flees from her father's stallion.

774. S. Hurreiz, *Ja¿aliyyîn Folktales,* No. 8., pp. 83–85; cf. this tale, note 781, and Tale No. 5, note 70.

775. *nâr es-sa¿luwwah.*

776. *'aḥabâb, yâ-mmuh es-sa¿luwwah,* lit.: [We are] friends, Mother Ogress.

777. *¿aṣîdat es-sa¿luwwah.*

778. *zîr:* see Tale No. 9, note 175.

779. *gar¿ah,* i.e., *qar¿ah,* dried gourd or pumpkin.

780. *ṣaydah:* i.e., game, prey.

781. I.e., *walad al-'amîr:* the prince's son; used here as a given name. Cf. Tale No. 5, note 70.

782. *kittir* thorny tree, a sort of acacia.

783. *el-gadam, gadam ḥamâm yâ baykam!*
esh-sha¿ir, rîsh na¿âm, yâ baykam!
we ¿uyûn, ¿uyûn ghuzlân, yâ baykam!

784. *bangâb:* a game similar to checkers.

785. Cf. introductory notes to Tales No. 7-1, 13, and 14.

786. On the significance of this formulaic ending in the brother-sister context, see Tale No. 37, note 701.

787. Mistress of Comeliness and Beauty; see Tale No. 37, note 702.

788. *sasabânah,* i.e., *saysabân: Sesbania aegyptica,* Danchi plant; a shrub that typically grows only to twig size.

789. CFMC: ¿UKH-I, No. 295. An abstract of this tale was published in El-Shamy's "Mental Health in Traditional Culture," p. 16; the tale was reported there, in error, to be from Upper Egypt.

790. AUC: 17, No. 1.

791. See El-Shamy, *Brother and Sister: Type 872*,* pp. 35–43, esp. p. 42.

792. *tidkhul fîha fardit eg-gazmah,* lit.: into whom that one shoe [can] enter. Cf. Tale No. 34-1, note 681.

793. *Wdai¿ah . . . ,* i.e., *Wuday¿ah . . . :* probably a diminutive of *wada¿ah,* (conch, seashell); may also be a diminutive of *wadî¿ah,* (something entrusted to someone, or a female who is meek).

794. See informant note to Tale No. 42, note 749. Also see El-Shamy, *Brother and Sister: Type 872*,* p. 33.

795. For examples of such gender-bound hostility, see Tales No. 11, and 28; also cf. Tales No. 33, 47, and 47-1. On the severity of punishment as a component of an attitude, see El-Shamy, *Brother and Sister: Type 872*,* pp. 67–68. Cf. the supernatural punishment dealt the brother's wife in Tale No. 40.

796. *yâ* Wudai¿ah, *yâ megalliyya es-sabai¿ah.* Note the use of the diminutive form (Mot. Z66.4.1§).

797. Other renditions from the same region speak of two springs: Free-[persons'] Spring (*¿ain el-'aḥrâr*), and Slaves' Spring.

798. *jalla ma-bî, jalla mâ-bî!*
rûḥû qûlû l-a-abî,
"kânet Wodai¿ah ghâliyah.
"ṣabaḥit Wodai¿ah jâryah,

"tisûq el-baqar we-tsûq el-jamûs,
"ṣabaḥet tesûq es-sâqiyah!"

It is interesting to note that the image portrayed in this rhyme is of a rural setting, perhaps northern Egyptian, rather than nomadic.

799. *qalbî ¿alaikum,* lit.: my heart is on you.

800. *ṣandûg er-rayis, yâ-mmuh,*
malyân ¿arâyis, yâ-mmuh!
walâ waḥdah ḥilwah, yâ-mmuh,
ghair marat-'akhûyâ, yâ-mmuh!
nizlit tissabbaḥḥ, yâ-mmuh,
we-l-¿igd mlaggaḥḥ, yâ-mmuh!
wa-nâ biddî ¿arûsah, yâ-mmuh!
tirguṣ giddâmî, yâ-mmuh?
we-tḥill ḥizâmî, yâ-mmuh!
we-ḥizâmî ṣûf, yâ-mmuh:
dahab marṣûṣ, yâ-mmuh!
raṣṣait uh raṣṣ, yâ-mmuh!
we mâ-ḥaddish ḥass, yâ-mmuh!

See El-Shamy, "Mental Health in Traditional Culture," p. 15. This childhood rhyme expresses the younger brother's erotic impulse toward the wife of his elder brother. It was collected from a seven-year-old child in Upper Egypt. (In Arabic, the word *¿arûsah* is used to mean both doll and bride; it has been translated as bride in this song.)

801. I.e., sisters-in-law; cf. co-wives, in Tales No. 14, and 31.

802. See Tale No. 34; Type 409B§, *Youth Marries Wild Animal; She Proves to be a Beautiful Maiden. A Relative Imitates: Disastrous Results;* cf. Tale No. 9.

803. See: El-Shamy, *Folktales of Egypt,* p. 240.

804. See Tale No. 34, note 677.

805. *eg-gawâz qismah wa naṣîb,* i.e., *al-zawâj. . . .*

806. I.e., clunker or maladroit; opposite of clever or adroit.

807. ¿Azîz *ben-khâluh* (Mot. L111.5.1§). The latter part of the tale is also entitled "Bu-Zaid *yijîb* (Fetches) ¿Alyâ."

808. On the *sîrah,* see M. C. Lyons's comprehensive survey: *The Arabian Epic: Heroic and Oral story-telling.* Also cf. "Genres of the Folk Narrative," Appendix, p. 511.

809. E. A. Wallis Budge, *The Mummy,* p. 279.

810. Mot. L111.5.1§.

On the Luqmân legend, see for example al-Jâḥiẓ, *al-Ḥayawân,* Vol. 1, pp. 21–22. Also see Maḥmûd Taymûr, *muḥâḍarât fî al-qaṣaṣ fî 'adab al-¿Arab: mâḍîhi wa ḥâḍirh (Lectures on Narratives in Arabs' Literature: Its Past and Present),* pp. 34, 76.

811. *'ommoh gaybâh m-el-khâl*—Mot. Z84.4§, "Insult concerning sexual conduct"; cf. Mot. H795.1§, "Riddle: 'Your father is from your father (or, 'Your father! Who is your father?'); your father is your maternal-uncle.'"

The adage states *el-khâl wâlid,* lit.: a birth giver (i.e., a maternal-uncle is a father [to his sister's child] [Mot. P297.2.2§]); see El-Shamy, *Brother and Sister: Type 872*,* p. 79.

812. For a hypothetical incestuous brother-sister marriage, see Tale No. 44, especially note 759. On the phenomenon that brother-sister incest seems to be "free of gross

personality disorder, neurosis or psychosis," see El-Shamy, "The Brother-Sister Syndrome in Arab Family Life," pp. 319–20; also see N. Lukianowicz, "Incest," in *British Journal of Psychiatry,* 120 (1972), 301–13, esp. p. 309.

813. Mot. K2217.0.3§, "Treacherous maternal-uncle." For another example of this incongruity, where a maternal-uncle treacherously murders his nephew, see Anonymous, *qiṣṣat ez-Zîr Sâlim, Abu-Lailah al-Muhalahal al-kabîr (The Story of ez-Zîr Sâlim, Abu-Lailah al-Muhalahal, Senior),* pp. 65–66, 119–22. Cf. Type 315B§, *The Cannibal Son: Diabolic Son of Ogre Betrays Sister (Brother) of His Devoured Human Mother.* Also, cf. Tale No. 45.

814. *mâ-jâkû 'illâ;* see Tale No. 34-1, note 680; on the significance of this formulaic beginning see introductory note to Tale No. 20.

815. *yiẓhir nashmî f-el-qabâyil, mithl 'akhûy.*

816. *'itrukî,* i.e., "Leave!" "Depart!" or "Let be!" This statement could also mean: "Leave him *for* me!" Cf. Tale No. 28, note 584, above.

817. *dashshat ¿alaih 'ukhtoh.*

818. *dashsh ¿alaihâ w-¿âshirhâ.*

819. *jâtuh ash-shahwah,* lit.: when his lust came.

820. *ṭâḥat fîhâ an-najâsah,* lit.: the ritual-contaminant flung [itself] into her.

821. Lit.: "Coffee me"; the word "coffee" is used as a verb.

822. *lâ ḥaraj ¿alaihum, walâ khawf minhom.* In this respect, bards (poets) are placed on the same level as the blind, the feebleminded, etc., who may enter into women's quarters (Mot. T380.3.1§).

823. *yâ-¿akayrabât ¿Alyâ gûmû tfâyṭu ¿anhâ;*
yâhâ sab¿ min 'agṣâ al-ba¿âyid.
ḥawâlay hâ al-ghaẓâ [??] we-ynûbîha al-gaṭâ,
we-el-sidr, yâ-¿Alyâ, huwwâ manâkh er-rakâyib.

824. *¿alayya, yâ-ahl* ¿Alyâ: *mâ-hâdhî bi-*¿Alyâ.
hâdhî hilâlî ṭawîl el-makhâlib!

825. *hâdhî* ¿Alyâ *we-¿ind en-nâs ¿ilmhâ:*
¿afîfat dhail, ma-doas el-¿atâyibb.
'ijraḥ ¿Alyâ *jurḥ ma-yejûd-hâ [??]*
we-guṣṣ min ¿Alyâ iṭwâl el-basâyil.

826. *¿alayya yâ râgidîn el-lail. gûmu! tanabbahû!*
juddâmk um eṣ-ṣubḥ illî kân ghâyibb.
*'intû bittû bi-*Sa¿dah *we-¿ain* Jalîlah,
wa-na bitt aḥuṭṭ ¿alâ jurḥi el-¿aṣâyibb.
jariḥ ¿Alyâ *jarîḥ ma-yjûd-hâ [??],*
we-qaṣṣ min ¿Alyâ *'aṭwâl es-sabâyil.*

On the significance of a woman's clipped-off hair, see Mot. H806.1§, "Riddle: bird flew out of its nest on two wings but flew back on only one—(braid of hair, loss of chastity)," in Type 851, *The Princess Who Cannot Solve the Riddle;* see El-Shamy, *Folktales of Egypt,* No. 11, esp. pp. 85–86. Cf. Tale No. 41, note 746.

827. "*sayyidnâ* al-Khudhr *da¿â ¿alâ ey-yamal (jamal) . . . ,*" lit.: prayed [to God] against the camel; i.e., cursed it. Mot. F440.3§, "al-Khiḍr (the Green-one): benevolent

spirit associated with vegetation and water"; A2342.3§, "Why camel's lip is split"; A2499.2.1§, "Why animal eats constantly (is a glutton)"; M416.1.1§, "Curse: gluttony (being controlled by dictates of the stomach)"; cf. A2542, "Why animal is cursed."

828. AUC: 25, No. 11.

829. On the sister in this positive role, see Tale No. 24, note 483.

830. *mit¿allaqah* (lit.: dangling down). On the prohibition of this and similar unfair practices, see Qur'ân, 4: 129. Mot. P529.0.1.4§, "Wife is to be retained with kindness (*ma¿rûf*), or released (divorced) with kindness."

831. Mot. S75.3§, "Cruel maternal-uncle's wife (*marat-khâl*)." See El-Shamy, *Brother and Sister: Type 872**, pp. 26, 48, 52, and 67.

832. On the symbolic reorganization, see Tale No. 13, note 288.

833. On the various grades of bread, see note 698.

834. *'zayy el-¿amal er-raḍiyy*, i.e., *al-radî'* (bad, evil); Mot. Z63.10.1.1§, "To be like a bad deed—ever present."

835. Lit.: advice giver; denotes a person who is shrewd, alert, and witty, usually in an aggravating manner; cf. *shâṭir* (clever).

836. Baked meat cake; made from layers of very thin bread soaked in broth, with a filling of browned ground meat. Usually a bairam meal, Mot. F849.1§, "Loved meat (fowl, fish) dishes"; J1347.2.2.2§, "Big-bairam: meat (mutton) provided."

837. See Tale No. 14, note 325.

838. Lit.: suffocated, smothered; i.e., God's name was not mentioned at the time of the slaughtering, thus eating it would be sinful (Mot. C229.7.1§). Cf. Tale No. 33, note 656.

839. Lit.: the man who has her for a comrade.

840. Magicians from Maghreb (North African) are presumed to be potent. See El-Shamy, *Folktales of Egypt*, No. 6. Also cf. Tale No. 25, note 511.

841. *'irmî bayâḍik*. May also mean: "Cast the shells," [in the manner dice are thrown, so that I may be able to tell your fortune from the pattern they form]. Mot. D1812.3.2.1§, "Fortune told by reading seashells (*wada¿*)."

842. On the significance of the bird's gender, see note 197, this section.

843. *mish ḥa-tṣawwaṭî?;* Mot. P681.1§, "Publication of a death (mourning)"; P681.1.1.1§, "Mourning: verbal expressions (wailing, dirge)"; P790.3.1§, "Shrieking for grief (*'ṣuwâṭ'*). (Typically voiced by women at a calamitous occurrence such as a death, serious injury, receiving a prison sentence, etc.)"

844. Mot. T60§, "Sex games"; cf. horsing around by lovers (Mot. T59.1§), in Tale No. 17, note 403.

V.

TALE TYPES, MOTIFS, AND OCCURRENCES

The rationale for the inclusion of this segment in *Tales Arab Women Tell* is given in the Introduction (see p. 13). In conformity with the system adopted in El-Shamy, *Folk Traditions of the Arab World,*[1] the data in this section are presented in the order in which the culture regions are listed here:

PEN: Arabian Peninsula (Bahrain, the Emirates, Oman, Qatar, Saudi Arabia, Yemen including Hadhramout, and Arabic-speaking groups in Zanzibar, Eritria, and Somalia)

MSP: Mesopotamia (Iraq)

SHM: *esh-Shâm* (or the Levant Coast: Syria, Lebanon, Palestine, Jordan, and indigenous groups in Israel)

NLE: Nile Valley—Egypt (including Berber-speaking Siwa—culturally belonging more to the Maghreb)

NLĐ: Nile Valley—Sudan

MGH: Maghreb (Libya, Tunisia, Algeria, and Morocco).

Archival Materials

Unpublished materials used in the present work were kept to a minimum; the materials are either field recordings on magnetic sound tapes, or written manuscripts. They are on deposit at public facilities (archives, university libraries) or are privately owned. The archival materials are designated as follows:

AGSFC Arab Gulf States Folklore Center, Ministry of Information, Doha, Qatar

AUC The American University in Cairo. Field collections undertaken by students during the academic years 1971 and 1972, and submitted to H. El-Shamy, in partial fulfillment of the requirements for "Anthropology 206: Folklore."

CFMC Center for Folklore, Ministry of Culture, Cairo, Egypt

HE-S: Hasan El-Shamy's collections, private archives[2]

IUFTL Indiana University Folklore Tape Library (Folklore Archives), Bloomington, Indiana.

With reference to tape-recorded data, citations of specific items are given as follows:

1. Depository (AGSFC, AUC, CFMC, HE-S, IUFTL).
2. Region where item was collected.

1. See "Note on data presentation, abbreviations, and archival materials," Vol. 1, pp. xxiii–xxiv.

2. Including the American University in Cairo: Student's Collections, and "Miscellaneous Manuscripts." El-Shamy's fieldwork and materials he collected as an official member of the CFMC are cited as archival holdings of that governmental agency.

3. Date item was collected (which is also used here as the call number for the tape); the first hyphenated set of figures represents the last two digits of the year the field trip was undertaken and the month: 71-3 means March 1971.

4. The second set of three hyphenated figures refers to the number of the reel in the collection, followed by the track number on the tape, then by the number of the item on that track. When the item number is undetermined (usually due to incomplete cataloging of the exact contents of a tape), an *x* is used.

For example,

CFMC: Oases 71-3, 3-1-1, stands for: the Oases/New Valley collection, trip undertaken in March 1971, reel number 3, track number 1, item number 1.

AGSFC: QTR 87-3, 700-2-No. 3, stands for: Qatar collection, trip undertaken in March 1987, reel number 700, track number 2, item number 3.

AUC: The American University in Cairo (1971–72). The figure immediately following AUC refers to the serial number of the collection, while the ensuing figure refers to the number of the tale in that collection.

For example,

AUC: 3, No. 3 stands for paper (collection) number three in the American University in Cairo collections, tale number 3.

Other Abbreviations and Marks

AT	Tale Type Number (in Aarne-Thompson, *The Types of the Folktale*)
NK	Ursula Nowak ("Beiträge")
Ranke	Kurt Ranke (in Kronenberg)
Uther	H. Uther (in Daum)
—:	partition; end bibliography, begin typology
< >	types and motifs identifications
≡	partition; additional types, motifs follow
Σ:	partition within < >, commentary on the text follows
()	information on narrator, collector
{}	remarks

The syntax of the annotation line is as follows:

⟨serial no. of item in list of texts⟩ author, ref. title {remarks on ref., reprints, etc.} —: <tale type≡, other types and motifs. Σ: additional info.> (information on narrator, collector).

For example,
⟨3⟩ Muḥammad ¿Alî Nâṣir, *Turâth* XI:11/12, 189–92 {*q.sh.¿i.* I, 385–89} —: <676A§≡, 834A,-cf. + Q2.1§. Σ: local subtype> (f, 67)

⟨1⟩ al-Bâṭinî, *al-ḥikâyât,* 106–9, No. 19 —: <123≡+ 327F, K1832 + K1832.2§> (f, auth.-col., from f kin)

⟨2⟩ Stevens, *Iraq,* 246–52, No. 43 —: <545F§≡, B422+F857.1, 545H§,-cf., {NK58a}> (f, youth—Kurd, in Ar.; col. f, Euro.).

1. The Nanny Goat with the Iron Horns (Egypt)

TYPE: **123, *The Wolf and the Kids.* + 327F, *The Witch and the Fisher Boy.* [Tongue (voice) made thin.]**

Motifs: P200.1.1§, "Mother as head of single-parent family"; P209.1§, "Mother as provider"; K1832, "Disguise by changing voice"; K1839.1, "Wolf puts flour [(lime, etc.)] on his paws to disguise himself"; K1832.2§, "Disguise by changing color of feet (paws)"; F556.2, "Voice changed by work of silversmith (goldsmith)"; P771.3.1§, "Food for service (e.g., ear of corn for a shave, an egg for knife sharpening, etc.)"; G413, "Ogre disguises voice to lure victim"; W48§, "Being sweet-tongued"; J144, "Well-trained kid does not open door to wolf"; R263§, "Chase in and out of oven. Pursuer (wolf, ogre) tires: intended victim escapes"; R319.0.1§, "Predator (wolf, hyena, etc.) lives in graveyard"; K1991.1§, "Mother goat masks her sharp horns by covering them with mud (dough, wax)"; R153.4.3§, "Mother goat rescues her sons (kids)"; K82, "Deceptive drinking contest"; G522, "Ogre persuaded to drink pond dry bursts"; F913, "Victims rescued from swallower's belly."

1-1. The Mother-of-the-two-kids (Saudi Arabia)

TYPE: **123.**

Motifs: K1832.1§, "Disguise by changing texture of skin (hide, fur)"; K1839.1.1§, "She-fox (vixen) applies egg yolk to her tail so as to make it smooth and disguise herself."

Occurrences: 53 additional texts are available. The ratio of f:m narrators is 23:6. The following renditions were narrated by females (or children):

PEN: ⟨1⟩ al-Bâṭinî, *al-ḥikâyât,* 106–9, No. 19 —: <123≡+ 327F, K1832 + K1832.2§> (f, auth.-col., from f kin); ***MSP:*** ⟨2⟩ ¿Abd-Allâh A. Aghâ, *Turâth* X:11, 115–18 {*q.sh.¿i.* II, 208–10} —: <123≡> (f, 55, from mo and elder sisters); ⟨3⟩ ¿U. Abu-Ṭâlib, *al-bî'ah,* 134–38 {*q.sh.¿i.* II, 253–56} —: <123≡> (f, 80s); ⟨4⟩ Stevens, *Iraq,* 205–9, No. 38 —: <123≡+ 327G-1119,-cf.> (f, mid-age, Chr, non-litr., col. f, Euro.); ***SHM:*** ⟨5⟩ Gh. al-Ḥasan, "al-'urdunî," 303–5, No. 59 —: <123≡> (f, 42); ⟨6⟩ ¿Abd-al-Hâdî, *kharârîf,* 24–26, No. 5 —: <123≡+ 327F> (f, 70, unwed/"Miss"); ⟨7⟩ Muhawi-Kanaana, *Speak,* 281–83, No. 38 —: <123≡+ 2032,-pt.> (f, 55); ***NLE:*** ⟨8⟩ Sulaymân, 140, No. III-C-1/6 —: <123≡+ 136,-cf., W151 + K891.1.2§/327-fin. ∑: transformed, moral.> (f, 62, non-litr., wed, w/6 children); ⟨9⟩ Ammar, *Silwa,* 168–69, No. 3 —: <123≡,-cf./no-mother. ∑: transformed> (m/c, presum., 11–14?, pupil); ***NLĐ:*** ⟨10⟩ Hurreiz, *Ja¿aliyyîn,* 113, No. 34 —: <123≡+ [327F], F556.2,

K638.9.1§, 333,-cf. ∑: "ḥujwa," abstr.> (m/c, pupil); ***MGH:*** ⟨11⟩ Bouhdiba, *maghrebin,* 5–6, Fr. tr, 25/, No. 1 —: <123≡> (f, adult, tells to children, col. m); ⟨12⟩ Houri-Pasotti, *Ghazala,* 177–80, No. 84 —: <123≡> (f, J, elder, to f col., gr-dgh); ⟨13⟩ Amrouche, *Le grain,* 85–89, No. 9 —: <303≡, P251.5.2 + 300 + F913.3§, R155, G551.4, 123/333,-cf./fin-theme> (f, adult, Chr-presum., auth.-col., from mo); ⟨14⟩ Amrouche, *Le grain,* 111–13, No. 12 —: <333≡/123,-cf., P291/Z292.0.1.1§, F556.1.2.1§, A2611, A2681.2,-cf. + G512.3> (f, adult, Chr-presum., auth.-col., from mo); ⟨15⟩ Légey, *Marrakech,* 257–58, No. 74 —: <123≡> (f, presum. adult).

Other Rendition(s): ***NLĐ:*** ⟨16⟩ CFMC: N-Nubia 69–10A, 3-1-06 —: <327B≡+123, K638.9.1§ + 124 + 327F + 136 + 1119 + 1180> (m, 33, litr., bi-ling., bank clerk, lives in Alex., col. m); ***MGH:*** ⟨17⟩ Frobenius, *Kabylen* II, 227–29, No. 27 —: <123≡,/333,-cf./as-intro., P252,/four, K1832, N303.1§, F1041.9.9.1§ + 886A§,-cf./theme + 873B§,-cf. ∑: legend?, human actors> (); ⟨18⟩ Scelles-Millie, *paraboles,* 101–8, No. 10 —: <123≡> (??—"F.Kh.").

1-2. Zaynabu, 'Omm-Zmayyim, and Their Brother (Sudan)

TYPE: **123C§, *Predator (Ogre, Wolf, etc.) Gains Access to Children's Home on Tree-top.* They are rescued by their brother (father);** Cf. **333C§, *Children Swallowed and then Delivered;*** and **312A, *The Brother Rescues his Sister from the Tiger* [(Hyena, Ogre, etc.)].**

Motifs: P204§, "Patriarch ('man of the house': husband, father, elder brother, etc.) as family provider"; F562.2, "Residence in a tree"; P254.0.1§, "Household composed of only brother and sister(s)"; G415§, "Ogre (predator) poses as relative of intended victim (prey)"; R311.4, "Stretching tree refuge for fugitive"; D481§, "Supernatural stretching and contraction of an object (tree, cliff, etc.)"; D482.1, "Transformation: stretching tree. A tree magically shoots upward"; F556.1.2.1§, "Voice (ogress's) made smooth by having ants seeking sunlight travel from one end of body to the other (anus to mouth): they clear away impurities"; D2136.4.3§, "All water in lake (well) supernaturally put into small container (water skin)"; D1641.12.1, "Lake is drunk dry"; R156, "Brother rescues sister(s)"; G551.1, "Rescue of sister from ogre by brother"; F913.3§, "Ogre's belly (toe) cut, all victims come out and repopulate town (nation, village)"; cf. P798.1.1§, "Conflict within a triad: one party is removed so as to restore stability (balance)."

Occurrences: 4 additional texts are available. The ratio of f:m narrators is 4:0. The following renditions were narrated by females (or children):

NLĐ: ⟨1⟩ Hurreiz, *Ja¿aliyyîn,* 113, No. 35 —: <123C§≡+ [327F, F556.1.2.1§, Z292.0.1.1§]. ∑: "ḥujwa," abstr., "123"> (m/c, pupil, from gr-mo); ⟨2⟩ Kronenberg, *Nubische,* 183–87, No. 39 —: <123C§≡, + 327F + 315,-B-S, + J229.16.1§> (f, 35); ⟨3⟩ al-Zayn, *Musabba¿ât,* 85–88 —: <123C§≡+ F562.2, D481.1§,-cf. + 327F + 312A> (f, presum. adult, non-litr.).

Other Rendition(s): ***NLĐ:*** ⟨4⟩ ¿A. al-Ṭayyib, *sûdâniyyah,* 89–92, No. 11 —: <123C§≡+ 312A,-cf. ∑: **drawing shows goats, not humans, suggesting that artist had in mind the plot of Type 123**> ().

2. The Two Sisters and the Ogre's Treasure (Saudi Arabia)

TYPE: **676A§, *Two Mothers (Sisters) and the Ogre's Treasure.* The rich but unkind mother imitates: she is killed.**

Motifs: P252.1.0.1§, "Two sisters as contrast"; K2212, "Treacherous sister"; S73.0.1§, "Sister cruel to her sister"; P200.0.2.1§, "Father is powerless"; S72.2§, "Cruel maternal-aunt (*khâlah*)"; K2216.1§, "Treacherous maternal-aunt (*khâlah*)"; F401.6, "Spirit in human form"; F301, "Fairy lover"; S160.3, "Fairies [(jinn, etc.)] mutilate mortals"; F399.5§, "Jinni (fairy) envious of human"; F361.17.11§, "Jinni (fairy, etc.) kills human husband of the human woman he secretly loves"; F451.4.5.2§, "Jinn (afrits, etc.) tribunals and courts of law"; F386.5, "Fairy imprisoned as punishment"; N511, "Treasure in ground"; D2101.0.1§, "Blood opens treasure"; F1041.17.3§, "Fainting from fear (horror)"; N478, "Secret wealth betrayed by money left in borrowed money-scales"; J2401, "Fatal imitation"; S166.7§, "Mutilation by skinning (flaying)."

Occurrences: 8 additional texts are available. The ratio of f:m narrators is 4:2. The following renditions were narrated by females (or children):

PEN: ⟨1⟩ al-Bâṭinî, *al-ḥikâyât,* 74–77, No. 13 —: <676A§≡, K2212> (f, auth.-col., from f kin); ⟨2⟩ El-Shamy, "The Demographic Factor," 98–99 —: <676A§≡, K2211> (f, 20, from mo); ***MSP:*** ⟨3⟩ Muḥammad ¿Alî Nâṣir, *Turâth* XI:11/12, 189–92 {*q.sh.¿i.* I, 385–89} —: <676A§≡, 834A,-cf. + Q2.1§. Σ: local subtype> (f, 67).

Other Rendition(s): ***PEN:*** ⟨4⟩ al-Juhaymân, *Jazîrat al-¿arab* V, 25–36, No. 2 —: <676A§≡480,-cf./kind-unkind pattern> (m, adult); ***MGH:*** ⟨5⟩ Frobenius, *Kabylen* I, 130–33, No. 29 —: <676A§≡,-cf.> ().

3. Mother's Liver (Egypt)

TYPE: **980H§, *A Mother's Heart (Liver): still Looks after Son who had just Murdered her.***

Motifs: P231.3, "Mother-love"; W254.2§, "Empathy in sorrow (pity, compassion) resides in liver (also in eye, soul, or heart—especially woman's)"; T316.1§, "Widowed mother chooses to remain unwed for child's sake"; S54, "Cruel daughter-in-law"; K961.2, "Flesh (or vital organ) of certain person alleged to be only cure for disease"; K961.2.3§, "Wife demands flesh (heart, liver, etc.) of husband's relative (son, mother) as medicine"; D1248, "Human liver as medicine"; P231.3.1§, "Mother lovingly allows son to kill her so that he may be happy"; E422.1.10, "Dismembered corpse"; E786.1§, "Severed heart (liver) speaks"; E783.5, "Vital head speaks"; P231.3.2§, "Heart (liver, etc.) of murdered mother still loves son who had murdered her."

Occurrences: 5 additional texts are available. The ratio of f:m narrators is 2:1. The following renditions were narrated by females (or children):

MSP: ⟨1⟩ al-Bâzargân, *'amthâl,* 323, No. 242 —: <980H§≡,-cf. Σ: prov.> (); ***MGH:*** ⟨2⟩ Amrouche, *Le grain,* 217–18, No. 22 —: <980H§≡, Σ: etiol. legend> (f, adult, Chr-presum., auth.-col., from mo).

Other Rendition(s): ***MGH:*** ⟨3⟩ Chimenti, *Morocco,* 115–17 **—:** <980H§≡> (m, professional "relig-bard", col. f).

4. The Mother's Tongue (Egypt)

TYPE: **838, *The Bad Rearing.* Son on gallows bites his mother's (father's) nose [(tongue)] off: punishment for neglect in youth.**

Motifs: P200.1.1§, "Mother as head of single-parent family"; U121.0.1§, "Bad parents, bad children"; J10.5§, "Persistence of early acquired knowledge, during childhood"; P463§, "Executioner (hangman)"; P243§, "The bad rearing: parent(s) blamed for child's misconduct"; Q410.1.1§, "One wish granted before execution"; Q586, "Son on gallows bites his mother's (father's) nose [(tongue)] off: punishment for neglect in youth"; P202.1.3§, "Parent(s) reproached for child's misconduct"; Q405§, "Punishment of parents for children's offense."

4-1. The Tongue of the Shrouds-thief Mother (Somalia)

TYPE: **838. + 950, *Rhampsinitus.*** Pt. I: *The Theft from the Treasury.*

Motifs: P475.0.1.1§, "Shroud thief"; P305.1.1.1§, "'The Prophet recommended [caring for neighbors] as far as the seventh [house away]'"; K301, "Master thief"; K315, "Thief enters treasury through secret passage"; N884.2.1§, "Robber (thief) steals from the rich and gives to the poor"; S24.2§, "Son kills his mother"; N328§, "Death from non-lethal (non-mortal) wound or blow"; J702, "Necessity of work"; T604.3.1§, "The mother is the school (*el-'omm [hiyyah el-] madrasah*)"; J1010, "Value of industry"; J1014§, "Making a living (by earning wages)"; J142, "Lack of proper education regretted."

Occurrences: 5 additional texts are available. The ratio of f:m narrators is 3:0. The following renditions were narrated by females (or children):

NLE: ⟨1⟩ AUC: 12, No. 15 **—:** <883B≡,-cf. + 838,-cf.> (f, 36, shop-owner, widow, from mo 25 yrs earlier, col. f); ***MGH:*** ⟨2⟩ Houri-Pasotti, *Ghazala,* 46–7, No. 6 **—:** <838≡-tongue-mot-missing> (f, J, elder, to f col., gr-dgh).
Other Rendition(s): ***MSP:*** ⟨3⟩ al-Bâzargân, *'amthâl,* 102–4, No. 71 **—:** <838≡, Σ: prov.> (); ***SHM:*** ⟨4⟩ al-Aswad, *shâmiyyah,* 365 **—:** <838≡> ().

5. The Daughter of the *Khuddârî*-bird (Sudan)

TYPE: **705A§, *Born from a Pregnant Man; Raised by a Bird (Animal): the Falcon's (Kite's) Daughter.* + Cf. 554B*, *The Boy in the Eagle Nest.* + 860A*, *Finding the Hidden Princess.* + 870C*, *Stepmother Makes Love to Stepson,* the king.**

Motifs: T578, "Pregnant man"; P232.0.2.1§, "Mother-to-be (stepmother) to pregnant husband: 'Abandon it if it is a girl, bring it home if it is a boy'"; B32, "Phoenix"; B535.0.5.1§, "Abandoned infant girl raised by falcon in nest"; V82.2§, "Clitoridectomy: female excision (circumcision)"; P609.1§, "Homosocial rites: group rituals for members of same sex (prayers, circumcision, etc.)"; B535, "Animal nurse"; B535.0.7.3§, "Falcon (hawk) as nurse for child"; F562.2, "Residence in a tree"; R351.0.1§, "Maiden in tree discovered by her reflection in water"; T11.5, "Falling in love with reflection in water"; P274.3§, "Prince marries maiden found, and then raised as his foster sister"; S51, "Cruel mother-in-law"; K512.1.2§, "Compassionate executioner: animal's (bird's) blood in bottle as proof"; K1895§, "False proof: grave containing buried animal (sheep) as evidence of someone's death"; D1664, "Summer garden and winter garden"; H936, "Task assigned because of longings of pregnant woman [(craving)]"; K1843.6§, "Mother masks as her son's wife and sleeps with him"; T412, "Mother-son incest"; N365.1, "Boy unwittingly commits incest with his mother"; T571, "Unreasonable demands of pregnant women [(craving)]"; T570.1§, "Pregnant woman's wish (craving)"; H1212.4, "Quest assigned because of longings of pregnant woman"; D1183, "Magic scissors (shears)"; D2021.2§, "Dumbness caused by magic scissors cutting off tongue"; Q242, "Incest punished"; S22, "Parricide"; S24.2§, "Son kills his mother"; Q416, "Punishment: drawing asunder by horses."

Occurrences: 67 additional texts are available. The ratio of f:m narrators is 41:6. The following renditions were narrated by females (or children):

PEN: ⟨1⟩ al-Bâṭinî, *al-ḥikâyât,* 32–35, No. 4 —: <705A§≡+ T412> (f, auth.-col., from f kin); ⟨2⟩ al-Duwayk, *Qaṭar* I, 147 —: <450≡705A§:I/709A:I/860A* + 450. Σ: abstr., atypical combo> (f, 30, emply.); ***SHM:*** ⟨3⟩ Bergsträsser, *Neuaramäische/,* 2–5, No. 2 {NK194V: AT400 [??]} —: <705A§≡+ 403:IV/408:IV> (f, Chr—wife and mo); ***NLE:*** ⟨4⟩ HE-S: Basatîn, 69–64, No. 3 {El-Shamy, "The Falcon's Daughter," *Around the World,* 159–63} —: <705A§≡+ 706> (f, 38, non-litr., Bdw, co-wife, hus-32); ⟨5⟩ Farag, *Daqahliyyah,* 114–17 —: <705A§≡+ 706> (f/c, 12, non-litr., maid, from pat-aunt); ⟨6⟩ ¿U. Khiḍr, *al-Masâ',* 7-8-1965 {S. Jahn, *Arabische,* p. 132, No. 17—"0705 + 403:IV,-cf."} —: <705A§≡+ H604.1§> (f, elder, from f kin); ***NLĐ:*** ⟨7⟩ Kronenberg, *Nubische,* 162–65, No. 35 —: <705A§≡[= + 706] {Ranke: "705/Nowak194"}> (f, 65); ***MGH:*** ⟨8⟩ Hejaiej, *Tunis,* 149–53, No. I-8 —: <705A§≡,-pt.1, + K778.5§, T145.1.0.1§ + 405, K2222 + F975, Q432.0.1§> (f, 63, edu./litr., wed., racont.; col. f); ⟨9⟩ Légey, *Marrakech,* 34–37, No. 6 {NK194d: AT400 [??]} —: <705A§≡, B535, B443.4, B535.0.3.1§ + 405, K2222, T257.2.2.1§, D765.1.2 + S139.2.0.1§. Σ: from Légey> (f, presum. adult).

Other Rendition(s): ***NLE:*** ⟨10⟩ von Massenbach, *Nubische,* pt. A.II, 27, No. 18 —: <705A§≡-pt1 + 860A*. Σ: incompl.> (); ***MGH:*** ⟨11⟩ Shâkir, *maghribî* I, 331–35 —: <705A§≡+ 405 + 301> (m, 50, peasant).

6. "Mother, See What I've Got for You!" (Palestine)

TYPE: **591, *The Thieving Pot.***

Motifs: U121.0.2.1§, "'Upset a jar on its mouth, a daughter turns out like her mother'"; T569.3§, "Woman gives birth to a pot"; D1605.1, "Magic thieving pot"; Z139.9.3§,-{formerly-Z0139.7.3§}, "Pot (jar) as symbol of female"; P209.3§,

"Daughter as provider"; T117.7.1§, "Marriage to a pot (jug)"; D1412.2, "Magic pot draws person into it"; D1605.1.1§, "Magic thieving pot steals penis: pot broken."

Occurrences: 11 additional texts are available. The ratio of f:m narrators is 7:3. The following renditions were narrated by females (or children):

PEN: ⟨1⟩ al-Duwayk, *Qaṭar* I, 79–80 —: <591≡> (f, 60); ***SHM:*** ⟨2⟩ Gh. al-Ḥasan, "al-'urdunî," 211–12, No. 38 —: <591≡= 1655,-cf.> (f, 55); ⟨3⟩ Schmidt-Kahle, *Palästina* I, 76–81, No. 32 —: <591≡, Σ: "Shwank"> (f, adult); ⟨4⟩ Muhawi-Kanaana, *Speak*, 55–59, No. 1 —: <591≡> (f, 55).

Other Rendition(s): ***PEN:*** ⟨5⟩ al-Duwayk, *Qaṭar* I, 80–81 —: <591≡+ D1605.1.1§> (); ⟨6⟩ al-Duwayk, *Qaṭar* I, 81 —: <591≡+ D1605.1.1§> (m, 28, emply.); ***NLE:*** ⟨7⟩ von Massenbach, *Nubische*, pt. A.II, 36, No. 22 —: <591≡, Σ: frag.> (m); ***MGH:*** ⟨8⟩ Loubignac, *Zaër*, Pt. I, 262–64, No. 14 {NK448a: AT 700} —: <700≡+ 591,-cf./fin> (m, presum.).

6-1. She-sparrow: The Cumin Guard (Egypt)

TYPE: **591A§, *The Thieving Starling.***

Motifs: T554.10, "Woman gives birth to bird"; P232.0.3§, "Little daughter as mother's helper"; D1565.3, "Magic song causes plowed ground to become unplowed"; D2072.6, "Paralysis by singing magic song"; D2072.6.1§, "Magic song (formula) causes man to be turned upside down."

Occurrences: 20 additional texts are available The ratio of f:m narrators is 12:2. The following renditions were narrated by females (or children):

PEN: ⟨1⟩ Daum, *Jemen*, 169–74, No. 19 —: <591A§≡+ 402,-cf. {Uther:409A}. Σ: fragment> (f, 75, widow, non-litr.); ***NLĐ:*** ⟨2⟩ Kronenberg, *Nubische*, 137–42, No. 31 —: <591A§≡+ K1335/400,-cf.-pt./feathers-stolen + 402,-cf. + 1442§,-cf./898,-fin {Ranke: "409A"}> (f, 35); ⟨3⟩ Kronenberg, *Nubische*, 132–37, No. 30 —: <591A§≡-lizard + 402-fin, T26.1> (f, 35); ***MGH:*** ⟨4⟩ Bouhdiba, *maghrebin*, 19–22, Fr. tr, 85/, No. 6 —: <715A≡+ 620,-cf. + 591A§,-cf./pt.?> (f, adult, tells to children, col. m); ⟨5⟩ Houri-Pasotti, *Ghazala*, 101–7, No. 46 —: <591A§≡,-cf. + 215§,/as-intro> (f, J, elder, to f col., gr-dgh).

Other Rendition(s): ***NLE:*** ⟨6⟩ von Massenbach, *Nubische*, pt. A.II, 43, No. 25 —: <591A§≡+ 1442§> (); ⟨7⟩ Spitta, *Grammatik*, 472–81 {NK211b} —: <871A≡+ 591A§,-cf., 400:I/407A + 898:V,-cf.-fin, H13.2.5> (m, pres. adult, shopkeeper); ***MGH:*** ⟨8⟩ Basset, *Contes pop. berb.* 83–89, No. 42 —: <715A≡+ 715A + 591A§,-cf., 620A§,-cf. Σ: closer to tale type> (m, son of mayor).

7. Fuṭmah and the Pickled Fish Head (Egypt)

TYPE: **545H§, *Grateful Animal (Dog) Furnishes Poor Runaway Woman with Riches that Surpass her Husband's: Broom of Pearls and Gold.* + Cf. 545D*, *The Bean King.* [Poor youth aided by ghost.]**

Motifs: P209.1§, "Mother as provider"; P232.0.3§, "Little daughter as mother's helper"; S12.8§, "A mother's cruel nagging drives child insane"; S12, "Cruel

Mother"; S24§, "Matricide"; S24.1§, "Daughter kills her mother"; E222, "Dead mother's malevolent return"; E222.0.1, "Mother haunts daughter"; E631, "Reincarnation in plant (tree) growing from grave"; F535.0.2§, "Remarkably small woman (girl)"; N456, "Enigmatic smile (laugh) reveals secret knowledge"; T258.1.1, "Husband insists upon knowing wife's secret"; K1952.2, "Better things at home"; N457§, "Reason for smiling needlessly is demanded"; B391, "Animal grateful for food"; B421, "Helpful dog"; F857.1, "Golden besom (broom)."

Occurrences: 22 additional texts are available. The ratio of f:m narrators is 17:3. The following renditions were narrated by females (or children):

PEN: ⟨1⟩ al-Duwayk, *Qaṭar* II, 239–40 {see also Vol. 1, p. 169, 192} **—:** <545H§≡545H§ + 886A§ + 285B*. Σ: atypical combo, fantasy-tale, not "animal tale" [??], {see Bashmî, *ḥikâyât*, 85–89}> (f, 50); ⟨2⟩ Noy, *Jefet*, 84–86, No. 26 **—:** <545H§≡:I + 537:II,IV + "537**f {Hansen}" + [545H§, B435.1, K1952.2, F857.1]> (f, 66, J); ***SHM:*** ⟨3⟩ Gh. al-Ḥasan, "al-'urdunî," 116–21, No. 19 **—:** <545H§≡> (f, 35); ⟨4⟩ al-Sârîs, *al-filisṭînî*, 183–85 **—:** <545H§≡> (f, elder); ⟨5⟩ al-Aswad, *shâmiyyah*, 223–27 **—:** <545H§≡,-fin. Σ: frag., distorted> (f, elder, from old f-kin).

Other Rendition(s): ***NLE:*** ⟨6⟩ Hassan, *In-Nâs*, 1–8 **—:** <545H§≡, Σ: matricide lacking> (m, élite, narrator-writer, replicating fem. style); ***MGH:*** ⟨7⟩ Panetta, *Bengasi*, 24–26 {NK108b: xx} **—:** <545H§≡, Σ: 545D*> ().

7-1. The Pickled Fish Head (Egypt)

TYPE: **920F§, *Beggar Cannot Give up Eating Habits.* + Cf. 545H§, *Grateful Animal (Dog) Furnishes Poor Runaway Woman with Riches that Surpass her Husband's: Broom of Pearls and Gold.***

Motifs: U130, "The power of habit"; U135.3.2§, "Beggar girl married to a rich man is unable to give up old beggars' habits"; Q432.0.1§, "Divorce as punishment"; H38.2.6§, "Young beggar-girl married to gentleman betrays old trade by enacting begging scenes at meal-times"; U61.0.2.1§, "A poor person remains poor, even when he has money."

Occurrences: 13 additional texts are available. The ratio of f:m narrators is 9:1. The following renditions were narrated by females (or children):

PEN: ⟨1⟩ AGSFC: QTR 87-3ff., 676-1-133-66 **—:** <920F§≡> (f, 70, wed to Qatari, col. f); ***SHM:*** ⟨2⟩ ¿Abd-al-Hâdî, *kharârîf*, 162–65, No. 39 **—:** <920F§≡, P736.1§> (f, 70s).

Other Rendition(s): ***PEN:*** ⟨3⟩ ¿Abduh, *yamaniyyah*, 131–36 **—:** <920F§> (); ***SHM:*** ⟨4⟩ al-Aswad, *shâmiyyah*, 371 **—:** <920F§≡> (); ⟨5⟩ Ṭaḥḥân, *al-ḥalabî* II 7–10 **—:** <920F§≡, U120, U135.3.2§> ().

7-2. [The Pot of Meat] (Kuwait)

TYPE: **545F§, *The Monkey (Dog, Fox, Jackal, etc.) Tests the Fidelity (Gratitude) of its Master.* + Cf. 545H§.**

Motifs: B182.1.0.2, "Magic dog transformed person"; V21.8§, "Deathbed confession: made so as to meet God with clear conscience"; P239.0.1§, "Deathbed confession concerning son or daughter"; P239.1§, "Man declares his paternity of heretofore unacknowledged child"; K1952.4.3§, "Poor girl poses as daughter of noble person"; H1556.1.2§, "Monkey (fox, jackal, dog, etc.) feigns death (illness) to test master's gratitude (fidelity)"; H1556.1, "Test of fidelity by feigning death"; H1565, "Test of gratitude"; W154.24.1§, "Man fails to treat his benefactor animal kindly when it is sick (dead)"; B299.1, "Animal takes revenge on man"; K2201.1§, "Secret betrayed out of spite (or for revenge)"; P210.0.2§, "Husband as his wife's disciplinarian"; Q441.3§, "Punishment: demotion, reduction in rank"; Q263.4§, "Suppression of truth punished"; Q482.1.2§, "Kitchen work as punishment for noble person (woman)"; P605.9.2§, "Upper floor(s): desirable (preferred, honorific) living quarters"; P605.9.3§, "Basement (kitchen, hearth, stable, etc.): undesirable living quarters"; W154.4.1§, "Wife is still grateful to helpful animal when it becomes sick, husband ungrateful: animal does not retaliate against husband"; Q281, "Ingratitude punished"; P213.3§, "Husband forgives culprit wife"; D422.2.1, "Transformation: dead dog to money [(jewels)]."

Occurrences: 19 additional texts are available. The ratio of f:m narrators is 4:2. The following renditions were narrated by females:

MSP: ⟨1⟩ Noy, *Israel*, 45–46, No. 20 —: <545F§≡,-cf./theme, B103.1.1, 751C*,-cf.> (f, J, Iraqi, to gr-dgh col.); ⟨2⟩ Stevens, *Iraq*, 246–52, No. 43 —: <545F§≡, B422+F857.1, 545H§,-cf., {NK58a}> (f, youth—Kurd, in Ar.; col. f, Euro.); ***NLE:*** ⟨3⟩ AUC: 19, No. 22 —: <545F§≡> (f, 22, u. grad., Chr, from gr-mo; col. f);

Other Rendition(s): ***PEN:*** ⟨4⟩ Kamâl, *kuwaytiyyah*, 398–403 —: <545F§≡, B441.1> (); ***SHM:*** ⟨5⟩ Aḥmad ¿A. al-Ḥusayn, *Turâth* X:9, 125–30 —: <545F§≡=J2132, K1047, 47A,-cf., 1900,-cf./as-intro.> (m/f??—"Muntahâ", from Aleppo, Syr., 55); ***NLE:*** ⟨6⟩ AUC: 10, No. 1 —: <545F§≡> (m, 46, servant, from old man; col. f); ⟨7⟩ Aḥmad, al-*Nûbah*, 65–70, [No. 6] —: <545F§≡> (); ***MGH:*** ⟨8⟩ Panetta, *Bengasi*, 96–98 —: <160≡:I+ 545F§,-cf., {NK52: AT160 + 545B}> (); ⟨9⟩ Desparmet, "maures," *RTP*, 28, 511–15, No. 20 —: <545F§≡, B435.2> (m, cleric); ⟨10⟩ de Pétigny, *algériens*, 157–69, [No. 9] —: <545F§≡> (); ⟨11⟩ Frobenius, *Kabylen* III, 86–97, No. 26 —: <545F§≡> (); ⟨12⟩ Mouliéras-Lacoste, *Kabaylie*, 420–25, No. 64 —: <545F§≡> (); ⟨13⟩ Mouliéras-Lacoste, *Kabaylie*, 426–34, No. 65 —: <545F§≡> (); ⟨14⟩ Nacib, *Djurjura*, 23–29, No. 2 —: <545F§≡> (); ⟨15⟩ Rivière, *Djurdjura*, 99–104 —: <545F§≡> (); ⟨16⟩ Rivière, *Djurdjura*, 135–36 —: <545F§≡, B435.2> (); ⟨17⟩ Savignac, *Kabylie*, 98–100, No. 9 —: <545F§≡> (m??, x); ⟨18⟩ Laoust, *Chenoua*, 192–93, No. 22 —: <545F§≡, [??]> (); ⟨19⟩ Laoust, *Maroc*, 256–57, No. 123 —: <545F§≡> ().

8. More Beautiful Than the Moon (Algeria)

TYPE: **709, *Snow-White.* [Mother Jealous of her daughter's beauty.]**

Motifs: P232, "Mother and daughter"; D1311.6.1, "Moon (stars) answer[s] questions"; D1311.2, "Mirror answers questions"; S12, "Cruel mother"; S322.2, "Jealous mother casts daughter forth"; S118.0.1§, "Butcher as executioner"; K512.1.2§,

"Compassionate executioner: animal's (bird's) blood in bottle as proof"; S143, "Abandonment in forest"; G90.5§, "Hate to be quenched by drinking blood of hated person"; N831.1, "Mysterious housekeeper"; F567, "Wild man. Man lives alone in wood like a beast"; G38§, "Abused person becomes ogre-like"; F1041.16.8.1§, "Person bursts from anger (frustration)"; K288.2§, "Girl will marry a man only if fitting certain description: she arranges for the terms never to occur"; F451.5.1.2, "Dwarfs adopt girl as sister"; T92.5.0.1§, "Brothers as rivals in love"; P253.10.2§, "Brothers compete for their sister's love (affection)"; M139.2§, "Vow to marry only the man with the most rosy (red) henna-colored hands"; B17.1.5.1§, "Hostile (mischievous) cat extinguishes fire by urinating on it"; G400, "Person falls into ogre's power"; K321.1, "Girl made to carry shell from which ashes fall: she is thus followed"; D582, "Transformation by sticking magic pin into head"; S111, "Murder by poisoning"; V68.2, "Dead washed and hair combed"; P253.11.2§, "Sister's corpse is placed on horse's (camel's) back to wander, awaiting vivification"; F852.1, "Glass coffin"; E21, "Resuscitation by withdrawal of wounding instrument"; D765.1.2, "Disenchantment by removal of enchanting pin (thorn)"; H1381.2.2.3§, "Boy twitted with rootlessness seeks unknown *khâl* (maternal-uncle)"; H11, "Recognition through story telling"; Z71.5.8, "Seven brothers marry seven sisters."

Occurrences: 36 additional texts are available. The ratio of f:m narrators is 21:2. The following renditions were narrated by females (or children):

PEN: ⟨1⟩ AGSFC: QTR 87–3ff., 700-2-No. 7 —: <709≡:I + F451.5.1.2, F302.0.4.1§> (f, 53, non-litr., widow, col. f); ⟨2⟩ ¿Abd-al-Hâdî, *kharârîf,* 39–43, No. 11 —: <709≡> (f, 75); ***NLE:*** ⟨3⟩ ¿Adlî Ibrâhîm, "Cairo," 112–16, No. 10A —: <709≡> (f/c, 10); ⟨4⟩ Ammar, *Silwa,* 176–77, No. 12 —: <709≡+ 894:III> (f-presum., 11–14?, pupil); ⟨5⟩ CFMC: Oases 71-3, 3-2-[7] —: <451A≡+ 709:III + 405. Σ: patterned combo> (f, 20, "still mademoiselle", col. f); ⟨6⟩ al-Baqlûṭî, *Tûnis,* 66–67, Fr. tr. p. 95 —: <709≡> (f, adult); ***MGH:*** ⟨7⟩ Amrouche, *Le grain,* 39–45, No. 4 —: <709≡+ 894> (f, adult, Chr-presum., auth.-col., from mo); ⟨8⟩ Delheure, *Ouargla,* 218–25 —: <709≡> (f, old, col. in 1976); ⟨9⟩ Légey, *Marrakech,* 78–82, No. 17 —: <709≡+ T92.5.0.1§> (f-presum. adult, and f, elder, notable racont. to upper-class women).

Other Rendition(s): ***MGH:*** ⟨10⟩ Khemir, *L'Ogress,* 179?-84 —: <327K§≡, B17.1.5.1§,-sister, 327H§,-cf./sister + 709:I + 311C§,-cf.> (); ⟨11⟩ El-Fasi-Dermenghem, *fasis* I, 114–25 —: <709≡, K2258.1§, P251.6.3.1§, T92.5.0.1§, M139.2§,-cf. Σ: individ.> (); ⟨12⟩ Laoust, *Chenoua,* 155, No. 3 —: <709≡:I. Σ: frag.> ().

9. Father of Seven Joys and Father of Seven Sorrows (Egypt)

TYPE: **923C§,** ***Girl Wins against Boy (usually, her Eldest Paternal-cousin) in a Contest of Worth.***

Motifs: P234, "Father and daughter"; P234.0.1§, "Father of daughter(s) less powerful"; P234.0.3.2§, "Seven daughters"; P251.5.3, "Hostile brothers [(jealous, in conflict)]"; P431.0.1§, "Woman (girl) merchant—businesswoman"; N122.0.2§, "The choice of roads: Road of Safety, Road of Sorrow, or Road of No-return"; K1837, "Disguise of woman in man's clothes"; P335.1§, "Shabby hospitality (inhospitality) betrays host's bad character"; N411.4, "Salt in saltless land sold for fortune"; L252§, "Girl with modest capital realizes large profits"; J708.1§, "Little money (capital) invested becomes wealth"; T463.0.1§, "Pseudo-homosexual (male) attraction: man falls in love with another man who turns out to be a woman in disguise"; P231, "Mother and son"; P231.3, "Mother-love"; H1578.1, "Test of sex of girl masking as man"; P3.1.1§, "Family (personal) name as indicator of social status"; H1578.1.9.2§, "Detection of a person's sex: psychological means (mental set, etc.)"; U248.5§, "Gender affects perception: males and females perceive different things (and view the same thing differently); P634.0.1, "Customs connected with eating and food"; W201.1.1.2§, "Indicator of manliness: powerful manners (being assertive, firm, resolute)"; P634.0.1.2.1.1§, "'Eat in the manner of camels, and quit ahead of [the other] men'"; W202.1.1.2§, "Women's non-assertive ways"; H1578.3§, "Test of sex: bathing (swimming) in the nude"; H1578.1.3§, "Test of sex of girl masking as man: guns and jewels; men take notice of guns"; P779.1.2§, "Imported fine weapons (sword, spear, etc.)"; H1578.1.8§, "Test of sex of girl masking as man: flowers (plant) near her will wither, if she is menstruous"; H1578.1.7§, "Test of sex of girl masking as man: climbing a tall tree. Male genitals will be visible"; P171.0.1§, "Seal of slavery (humiliation)"; L153§, "Girl succeeds where boy fails (they are paternal-cousins)"; W41§, "Resolve (determination, willpower, endurance, 'grit')"; W164.1.7.1§, "Girl's (woman's) willpower as source of self-esteem (self-concept)"; P523, "Bringing suit in law courts"; H55, "Recognition through branding"; K2211.4§, "Treacherous paternal-cousin(s)"; W183.1.2§, "Brother pleased with his brother's failure"; Z63.3.3.6.3§, "To say, 'O earth, open up and swallow me'"; L143.3§, "Poor brother surpasses rich brother"; L178§, "Despised brother wins wager (contest) against arrogant brother."

9-1. Seven Girls and Seven Boys (Algeria, Berber)

TYPE: **923C§.**

Motifs: J1129§, "Female trickster"; P431.2§, "Merchant as trickster (cheat)"; K145.1§, "Valuable animal (dog, horse) sold repeatedly; always escapes to join original master (owner)."

Occurrences: 44 additional texts are available. The ratio of f:m narrators is 23:10. The following renditions were narrated by females (or children):

PEN: ⟨1⟩ al-Duwayk, *Qaṭar* II 301 —: <923C§≡, Σ: novella, "belief tale" [??]> (f, 25, u. stu.); ***NLE:*** ⟨2⟩ Sulaymân, 143–44, No. IV-01 —: <923C§≡> (f, 62, non-litr., wed, w/6 children); ***NLĐ:*** ⟨3⟩ Hurreiz, *Ja¿aliyyîn*, 89, No. 12 —: <923C§≡,-tasks + 879:II-as-intro + 884B*. Σ: "ḥikâya," distorted/transformed> (f, 50, widow, social focal point).

Other Rendition(s): ***SHM:*** ⟨4⟩ al-Sârîs, *al-filisṭînî*, 103–5 —: <923C§≡> (m, adult, from mo); ***NLE:*** ⟨5⟩ Hassan, *In-Nâs*, 33–37 —: <923C§≡> (m, élite, narrator-writer, replicating fem. style); ***MGH:*** ⟨6⟩ Mouliéras-Lacoste, *Kabaylie*, 267–69, No. 30 —: <923C§≡> ().

10. The Girl inside the Golden Cow (Egypt)

TYPE: **510B, *The Dress of Gold, of Silver, and of Stars.* [Girl flees from her father who wants to marry her.]**

Motifs: H363, "Deceased wife marriage test"; H366§, "Father unwittingly qualifies as bridegroom of daughter in test"; T411.1, "Lecherous father"; M139.1§, "Vow to marry only a girl whom a certain object (shoe, bracelet, etc.) would fit"; M139§, "Vow to marry only a person fitting certain description (size, color, etc.)"; T461.0.1§, "Erotic fetishism"; K1891.1§, "Person hides inside statue and then arranges for it to be sold to the beloved"; J1144.3§, "Owner takes notice of missing food: intruder detected."

Occurrences: 46 additional texts are available. The ratio of f:m narrators is 27:7. The following renditions were narrated by females (or children):

PEN: ⟨1⟩ AGSFC: Doha 85-4, 2-No. 11 —: <510B≡> (f, adult, to son-col.); ⟨2⟩ Noy, *Jefet,* 121–24, No. 39 —: <706D§≡510B,-cf., [510B:I,-cf. + 450,-cf.,-lacks Motif D114.1.1]. Σ: abstr.> (f, 66, J); ***MSP:*** ⟨3⟩ Kh. ¿Abd-al-Amîr, *Turâth* X:3/4, 157–62 {*q.sh.¿i.* I, 283–89} —: <510B≡> (f, 70); ***SHM:*** ⟨4⟩ ¿Abd-al-Hâdî, *kharârîf,* 147–50, No. 34 —: <510B≡+ 870A> (f, 30s); ⟨5⟩ ¿Abd-al-Hâdî, *kharârîf,* 84–90, No. 21 —: <510B≡+ K2212.2.1§, E781.2> (f, 30s, unwed); ⟨6⟩ al-Sârîs, *al-filisṭînî,* 161–63 —: <510B≡/313E*,-cf./psych.-pattern, T411.1, R223§, K551.16 + 1600A§ + 313E*,-cf. + G90.5§,-cf., K512.1.2§, K1874.1§ + S22, P254.1.2§, Q242.2.1§, J1913.1§, K812, K955.1, K891.1.1§,-cf. Σ: patterned combo> (f, ??); ⟨7⟩ al-Aswad, *shâmiyyah,* 249–55 —: <510B≡+ 533A§> (f, elder, from old f-kin); ⟨8⟩ Bergsträsser, *Neuaramäische,* 47–49, No. 14 —: <510B≡{NK104V: AT510B + 516B} > (f, Chr—wife and mo); ⟨9⟩ Bergsträsser, *Neuaramäische,* 101–2, No. 33 —: <510B≡> (m/c, 13, Chr, presum. from mo, col. H. Stumme); ***NLÐ:*** ⟨10⟩ Hurreiz, *Ja¿aliyyîn,* 83–85, No. 8 —: <313E*≡, Σ: "ḥujwa," "510B"—actually, 313E*> (f, 50, widow, social focal point); ***MGH:*** ⟨11⟩ Légey, *Marrakech,* 202–5, No. 54 —: <510B≡+ 533A§> (f, elder, slave, from f-slave); ⟨12⟩ Légey, *Marrakech,* 206–10, No. 55 —: <510B≡> (f, elder, notable, racont. to upper-class women).

Other Rendition(s): *NLE:* ⟨13⟩ Blackman, *Upper Egypt,* 272–74 —: <510B≡+ 949*, P51> (m, elder, racont.); ***MGH:*** ⟨14⟩ Scelles-Millie, *algériennes,* 15–26, No. 1 —: <510B≡> (??—"F.Kh."); ⟨15⟩ El-Fasi-Dermenghem, *fasis* II, 140–50, [No. 18] —: <923C§≡> ().

11. Maryam, of Cool and Coquetry (Bahrain)

TYPE: **510D§, *Daughter Flees to Escape Passion of her Father's Stallion (Bull-Camel or Horse).* + 533A§, *Beautiful Maiden in Hideous Disguise. She is detected by the prince [. . .].***

Motifs: T381.0.3§ (formerly T381.2§), "Virgin imprisoned to prevent riding-animal from desiring (falling in love with) her"; S215.2§, "Daughter promised to a riding-animal (stallion, camel)"; T311.1, "Flight of maiden (bridegroom) to escape marriage"; D1183.1§, "Magic scissors (shears) kill monster"; K1891.2§, "Fugitive escapes pursuer by hiding in animal carcass"; P185§, "Faithful slave-woman"; P180.1.1§, "Slave addresses master (mistress) as paternal-uncle (paternal-aunt)"; Z67.5§, "Esteem: to be addressed as respected relative (with social distance kept)"; G412.3§, "Ogre's (ogress's) fire lures person"; S166.7§, "Mutilation by skinning (flaying)"; P187§, "Inherent rivalry between mistress and young female slave"; K521.1.4, "Escape by putting on old woman's skin"; K1941, "Disguised flayer. An imposter dresses in the skin of his victim"; T463.0.1§, "Pseudo-homosexual (male) attraction: man falls in love with another man who turns out to be a woman in disguise"; T112§, "Marriage of person to another of same sex (proves to be of opposite sex)."

Occurrences: 10 additional texts are available. The ratio of f:m narrators is 8:2. The following renditions were narrated by females (or children):

PEN: ⟨1⟩ AGSFC: BHR 86-4, 2-1-110/1 —: <510D§≡+ 881> (f, 38, lit., col. f); ⟨2⟩ al-Bâṭinî, *al-ḥikâyât,* 62–67, No. 11 —: <510D§≡> (f, auth.-col., from f kin).
Other Rendition(s): *PEN:* ⟨3⟩ Kamâl, *kuwaytiyyah,* 187–91 —: <510D§≡> (); ***NLĐ:*** ⟨4⟩ ¿A. Khiḍr, *ḥawâdît* I, 96–102 —: <311D§≡+ 510D§,-cf./pat.-uncle + 533A§, S71.2§, R152> ().

12. Lady Kân (Syria)

TYPE: **931C§, *The Father who Hates his Daughters, and Kills them.* One is spared, and he falls in love with her; she flees and eventually marries her rescuer. + 883§, *Innocent Slandered (Suspected) Female.* + Also cf. Types: 705A§, 510B.**

Motifs: S302.4§, "All newborn daughters to be slaughtered"; G90.5§, "Hate to be quenched by drinking blood of hated person"; T645.2.1, "'Kill it if it is a girl'"; K512.1.2§, "Compassionate executioner: animal's (bird's) blood in bottle as proof"; P272, "Foster mother"; S351, "Abandoned child cared for by mother secretly"; P605§, "Living (sleeping) arrangements within the household"; N365.2.1, "Father unwittingly falls in love with daughter"; K1227.1.1§, "Lover (seducer) put off until girl attends to call of nature"; T405.4.1§, "Daughter's nakedness or exposure"; K551.16, "Woman escapes by ruse: must go defecate [(to toilet)]"; K539§, "Escape by cutting off restraint (rope, garment, etc.) held by captor"; R351.0.1§, "Maiden in tree discovered by her reflection in water"; N711, "King (prince) accidentally finds maiden and marries her"; F575.1.6§, "Beauty that disorients (dazzles) the beholder"; T55.6.4§, "Fashion display (fashion show): body exhibited in various complimentary dresses (costumes)"; T91.4.1.2§, "Girl thought by older man to be too young for marriage is raised and then taken for a wife (by him)"; T196§, "Wife divorced because of a trifle"; D1470.1.15, "Magic wishing-ring. [Solomon's Ring]"; P324.0.1.1.1§, "Ground covered with carpet, flowers, etc. for guest ('red-carpet treatment')"; Z169.0.1§, "Symbolism: thorny and thornless flowers"; Z169.0.1.1.2§, "Tamarisk as symbol of tenderness"; T81, "Death from love"; F1041.1.1, "Death from a broken heart"; T86.2, "Lovers die at the same time"; T86, "Lovers buried in same grave"; Z292.0.1.1§, "Tragic ending of a story (tale): all die."

Occurrences: 3 additional texts are available. The ratio of f:m narrators is 1:0. The following renditions were narrated by females (or children):

SHM: ⟨1⟩ AUC: 11, No. 4 —: <931C§≡, 510:I,-cf. = + 705A§,-cf./implicit + 883§ + 970,-cf.> (f, 70s, Chr, in Aleppo from Syr mo; col. f).

Other Rendition(s): *NLĐ:* ⟨2⟩ Shahi-Moore, *Nile,* 165–68, No. 36 —: <931C§≡,-cf. + 363,-cf./510B:I,-cf./transformed, S302.4§= + R245.1.1§,-cf. Σ: wrt.> (col. pupil); ***MGH:*** ⟨3⟩ Scelles-Millie, *Maghreb,* 162–65, No. 18 —: <931C§≡+ 510B:I,-cf. Σ: Oedipal?> (??—"A.A.").

13. Pomegranate Kernels on Gold Trays (Egypt)

TYPE: **894, *The Ghoulish Schoolmaster and the Stone of Pity.*** + **874A§, *Estranged Couple are Reunited by their Children.***

Motifs: P340, "Teacher and pupil"; P426.0.3§, "Cleric (*¿arrîf, fi'î, muṭawwi¿, 'abûnâ,* father, etc.) as children's school-teacher"; G11.3, "Cannibal witch"; G11.9, "Ogre schoolmaster"; L162, "Lowly heroine marries prince (king)"; D1932.1§, "Wall opens to let in being with supernatural power (afrit, ogre, magician, etc.) and then closes after he exits"; G261, "Witch steals children"; K2155.1, "Blood smeared on innocent person brings accusation of murder"; K2116.1.1.1, "Innocent woman accused of eating her newborn children"; S451, "Outcast [(cast-out)] wife at last reunited with husband and children"; F994, "Object expresses sorrow"; F956.7.6§, "Catharsis (*faḍfaḍah*): relief from mental troubles through talking about them"; F956.7.6.1§, "Publication of secrets to 'stone of pity,' 'box of patience,' etc.)"; F994.3§, "Stone bursts out of pity for persecuted heroine"; D1318.1.1, "Stone bursts as sign of unjust judgment"; Q62, "Reward for ability to keep secrets"; G443.2§, "Ogre abducts woman's children, raises them and then returns them to their mother"; S451.1§, "Children bring about reunion between their father and outcast mother"; P230.5§, "Children spoil their father's wedding to a new bride-to-be and bring about reinstatement of their own mother"; T92.9, "Father and son as rivals in love"; T92.9.2§, "Son is given in marriage the bride-to-be intended for his father."

Occurrences: 52 additional texts are available. The ratio of f:m narrators is 31:4—mostly under age 20. The following renditions were narrated by females (or children):

PEN: ⟨1⟩ AGSFC: QTR 87-3ff., 684-1-No. 2 —: <894≡,-cf.-pt. Σ: completely transformed text> (f, 45, wed, elem. relig. ed., but non-litr., col. f); ⟨2⟩ al-Duwayk, *Qaṭar* I, 254 —: <894≡> (f, 25, stu.); ⟨3⟩ Noy, *Israel,* 117, No. 48 —: <894≡> (f, pupil?, J, recorded by f pupil, J); ***SHM:*** ⟨4⟩ Gh. al-Ḥasan, "al-'urdunî," 97–101, No. 16 —: <403≡:IV, 451A,-cf./pattern + 408:III + 894:IV,-cf./candleholdr, H76§. Σ: atypical, wrt.> (f, 50); ⟨5⟩ Gh. al-Ḥasan, "al-'urdunî," 102–9, No. 17 —: <894≡+ 891:III> (f, 50); ⟨6⟩ Muhawi-Kanaana, *Speak,* 261–67, No. 35 —: <894≡+ 874A§> (f, 65); ⟨7⟩ al-Sârîs, *al-filisṭînî,* 127–33 —: <894≡> (f, 40); ***NLE:*** ⟨8⟩ Farag, *Daqahliyyah,* 148–49 —: <894≡> (f/c, 12, non-litr., maid, from pat-aunt); ⟨9⟩ von Massenbach, *Nubische,* pt. A.II, 37, No. 23 —: <894≡> (f/c, 12); ***NLĐ:*** ⟨10⟩ Kronenberg, *Nubische,* 20–29, No. 6 —: <894≡, eats girl's brother>

(f, 35); ***MGH:*** ⟨11⟩ Bouhdiba, *maghrebin*, 28–29, Fr. tr, 115/, No. 9 —: <894≡, Σ: frag.> (f, adult, tells to children, col. m); ⟨12⟩ Amrouche, *Le grain*, 39–45, No. 4 —: <709≡+ 894> (f, adult, Chr-presum., auth.-col., from mo); ⟨13⟩ Légey, *Marrakech*, 100–3, No. 23 —: <894≡> (f, elder, notable, racont. to upper-class women); ⟨14⟩ Légey, *Marrakech*, 143–47, No. 32 —: <894≡,-cf./gen.,/363,/621:I,-cf., Mot. H522.1.1,/missing,/363, G81, G565§ + 884B*, K1826.0.1§ + K2117, 706,-cf./elem. Σ: composite, transformed rendition, retained psych. pattern> (f, elder, notable, racont. to upper-class women).
Other Rendition(s): ***PEN:*** ⟨15⟩ al-Duwayk, *Qaṭar* II, 271–72,—see Vol. 1, p. 254 —: <894≡, Σ: fantasy-tale, not "belief tale"> (m, 20, stu., from gr-mo); ⟨16⟩ A. Jahn, *Mehri: SAE* III, 62–71, No. 11 —: <883A≡+ 894:I,-cf.> (m, adult, Swh blck, b. in Ghayḍah); ***MGH:*** ⟨17⟩ Dermenghem, *kabyles*, 21–29 —: <894≡> (m, presum. adult).

14. The Ostrich of the Sultan's Son (Egypt)

TYPE: **898, *The Daughter of the Sun. (The Speechless Maiden; the Puppet Bride.)***

Motifs: P252.0.1§, "Sisters in conflict"; K2212, "Treacherous sister"; L215.1§, "Unpromising object (item) in inheritance division proves best"; L215, "Unpromising magic object chosen"; B312.6.1§, "Hen (chicken) as sole inheritance"; B103.2.1.1§, "Treasure-laying chicken (hen)"; B103.2.1, "Treasure-laying bird"; S322.0.2§, "Elder siblings deprive younger of inheritance"; K963, "Rope cut and victim dropped"; G443§, "Ogre adopts human child"; C611, "Forbidden chamber"; P14.22.1§, "King keeps ostrich as pet"; T257.1.2§, "King's pet bird (animal) becomes jealous of king's future wife (fiancée)"; S139.2.0.1§, "Ghoulish trophy: part of enemy's corpse kept and displayed (or put to use)"; N482.3.1§, "Secret learned by threatening to have person (mother, daughter, etc.) dipped in boiling water"; T115.1§, "Ogre's (ogress's) consent to daughter's marriage to man is given"; T115, "Man marries ogre's [(ogress's)] daughter"; C400, "Speaking tabu"; C406§, "Tabu: answering (responding to) call or question"; C438.1§, "Tabu: responding unless addressed by correct name (title)"; H323, "Suitor test: learning girl's name"; D1935.3§, "Magic ability to perform any task"; J2401, "Fatal imitation"; Z186.5§, "Symbolism: pitcher's spout—phallus"; Z139.9.3§,-{formerly-Z0139.7.3§}, "Pot (jar) as symbol of female—(general)"; D1620, "Magic automata"; D1607§, "Self-performing chore: (cooking, cleaning, etc.) gets itself done"; D1171.4, "Magic pitcher"; H13.2.5, "Recognition by overheard conversation with cups (or other utensils)"; M119.8.1, "Swearing by one's father and mother"; P208.3§, "Bilineal descent (double descent): child identified by both father's and mother's lines."

Occurrences: 58 additional texts are available. The ratio of f:m narrators is 35:9. The following renditions were narrated by females (or children):

PEN: ⟨1⟩ al-Bâṭinî, *al-ḥikâyât*, 54–57, No. 9 —: <652A≡,-cf. + 898:IV + P295.1.2§. Σ: frag.??> (f, auth.-col., from f kin); ⟨2⟩ al-Duwayk, *Qaṭar* II, 93–94 —: <1442§≡, P252.3, Z71.5.8, 898:IV,-cf. + F969.7, 1442§, K944.1§. Σ: realistic, prob. transformed 898, "folktale [!]" ?> (f, 90); ***SHM:*** ⟨3⟩ al-Sârîs, *al-filisṭînî*, 141–44 —: <327J§≡,-cf., S322.6.3.0.1§, S72.2§ + 898:III, 710,-cf., C911.1§,-silver finger + 533A§, D712.5,-cf. + 409B§> (f, 40); ⟨4⟩

¿Abd-al-Hâdî, *kharârîf,* 241–48, No. 59 —: <402≡+ 465 + 898:IV,/1442§> (f, 65); ⟨5⟩ ¿Abd-al-Hâdî, *kharârîf,* 267–70, No. 64 —: <898≡, Σ: incompl.> (f, 60); ⟨6⟩ Lewin, *Hama,* 28–37, No. 4 —: <898≡, {NK78b: "123 + 311", NK231b}> (f, 50s-b. 1909, non-litr., mid-class, when girl, from maid); ***NLE:*** ⟨7⟩ Gamal, *Miṣr,* 70–73, No. 12 —: <898≡> (f, col. ??); ***NLĐ:*** ⟨8⟩ Kronenberg, *Nubische,* 68–74, No. 14 —: <898≡= + B103.1.7§, cat instead of hen + 1739A* [J2321.2], {Ranke: "879-subtype," NK58: [545, only mot.]}> (f, 35); ***MGH:*** ⟨9⟩ al-Baqlûṭî, *Tûnis,* 29–33, Fr. tr. p. 61 —: <327K§≡+ 327H§,-cf.-not listen to si + 898:IV, P14.22.1§,-cow> (f, adult); ⟨10⟩ Hejaiej, *Tunis,* 154–63, No. I-9 —: <898≡, M209§ + C438.1§, C406§, M119.8.2,/P208.1§, Z159.2.1§ + K2222, 1442§,-cf., Z186.5§> (f, 63, edu./litr., wed., racont.; col. f); ⟨11⟩ Galley, *Badr az-Zên,* 207–25, No. 6 —: <898≡+ 327K§,/as-intro +> 898 (f, mid-aged, lit., col. Euro. f); ⟨12⟩ Scelles-Millie, *Souf,* pt. V, 299–304, No. 4 —: <898≡+ 327K§,/as-intro + 898> (f, 15).

Other Rendition(s): ***PEN:*** ⟨13⟩ al-Juhaymân, *Jazîrat al-¿arab* III, 179–92 —: <898≡,-cf., 872§,-as intro + 898. Σ: full text—atypical intro, male's rendition of female's theme> (m, adult, from friend); ⟨14⟩ Daum, *Jemen,* 24–38, No. 3 —: <898≡{Uther: cf. 331 + cf. 400}. Σ: incompl.> (m, 80); ⟨15⟩ Sengo, "Kiswahili," 1027–50, No. 44 —: <737A*≡/923B + 898, P14.22.1§. Σ: {Sengo:934D}> (m, 70, ret. seaman); ***SHM:*** ⟨16⟩ Bushnaq, *Arab,* 201–5 —: <898≡> (); ⟨17⟩ Muhawi-Kanaana, *Speak,* 178–81, No. 20 —: <898≡> (m, 70s); ⟨18⟩ Sâ¿î, *Lâdhiqiyyah,* 99–103, No. 15[+1] —: <898≡> (); ***NLE:*** ⟨19⟩ Hassan, *In-Nâs,* 9–12 —: <652A≡,-cf., 407A,/652A,-cf., V11.12.1§, K2375.1§, N641.0.1§ + 898:IV,/1442§/. Σ: frag., atypical: author's preface: V74§, J1347.2.2.1§> (m, élite, narrator-writer, replicating fem. style); ⟨20⟩ Hassan, *In-Nâs,* 67–70 —: <898≡:I, T52.0.1.2§ + D1652.5.1.1§, D1651.16§ + . Σ: frag.> (m, élite, narrator-writer, replicating fem. style); ⟨21⟩ Spitta, *Grammatik,* 472–81 —: <871A≡+ 591A§,-cf. 400:I/407A + 898:V,-cf./fin, H13.2.5, {NK211b}> (m, pres. adult, shop-keeper); ***MGH:*** ⟨22⟩ El-Fasi-Dermenghem, *fasis* II, 184–92, [No. 22] —: <898≡+ 1442§,-cf.> ().

15. The Daughters of the Bean Vendor (Egypt)

TYPE: **879,** ***The Basil Maidens (The Sugar Puppet, Viola).***

Motifs: P169.1.3§, "Poor peddler (vendor)"; P452, "Dressmaker (milliner, [seamstress], etc.)"; L61, "Clever youngest daughter"; L63, "Youngest daughter avoids seducer"; J1251.1, "Humiliated lover in repartee with disdainful [(scornful)] mistress"; K1214.1.1, "Importunate lover is induced to undergo a series of humiliations"; P234.0.1§, "Father of daughter(s) less powerful"; K1590.2§, "Embracing and kissing, felt by maiden in the dark, explained to her as dream (nightmare)"; H1054.1, "Task: coming neither naked nor clad. (Comes wrapped in a net or the like)"; H1027§, "Task: bringing pregnant virgins. (Girls fed gas-giving food, stomach becomes swollen)"; F851.9.1.1.1§, "Gas-giving foods eaten: beans, onions, leeks, taro [. . .]"; H1064, "Task: coming laughing and crying at once. (Rubs eyes with a twig [(onion)] to simulate crying)"; H1053, "Task: coming neither on horse nor on foot (riding nor walking)"; H1049.2.1§, "Task: bringing pregnant virgins. Countertask: bringing radish grown in rock"; H1334§, "Quest for radish grown in rock";

J1163, "Pleading for accused by means of parable"; J99, "Wisdom (knowledge) taught by parable"; T72.0.1§, "Man loses battle of wits with (is humiliated by) girl (his paternal-cousin) then marries her for spite"; T72.2.1, "Prince marries scornful girl and punishes her"; K1833, "Disguise as ghost"; K1828.1.1, "Woman disguised as angel of death [(Azrael)]"; K525, "Escape by use of substituted object. The object is attacked rather than the intended victim"; J1525, "Poor girl outwits prince in fright contest"; P311.1.1§, "'No love except after enmity' (i.e., friendship that comes after enmity is strong)."

Occurrences: 56 additional texts are available. The ratio of f:m narrators is 31:7. The following renditions were narrated by females (or children):

PEN: ⟨1⟩ AGSFC: QTR 87-3ff., 687-x-484-549 —: <879≡, Σ: fragment> (f, 48, non-litr., unwed, col. f); ***MSP:*** ⟨2⟩ Qaṣiy ¿A. ¿Askar, *Turâth* X:5, 131–34 {*q.sh.¿i.* II, 105–10} —: <879≡+ 891. Σ: fragment> (f, auth.'s mo and f—mat-unc.'s wf and other old f); ⟨3⟩ Gh. al-Ḥasan, "al-'urdunî," 277–84, No. 51 —: <879≡:III–IV + 891. Σ: supernatural elements: atypical, wrt.> (f, 35); ***SHM:*** ⟨4⟩ ¿Abd-al-Hâdî, *kharârîf,* 52–53, No. 14 —: <879≡:IV. Σ: frag.> (f, 50, from mo); ***NLE:*** ⟨5⟩ Farag, *Daqahliyyah,* 336–37 —: <879≡:II,VI> (f/c, 10, pupil, from neighbor m, lit.); ***NLĐ:*** ⟨6⟩ Hurreiz, *Ja¿aliyyîn,* 90, No. 13 —: <879≡+ 875. Σ: "ḥikâya"> (f, 50, widow, social focal point); ***MGH:*** ⟨7⟩ Galley, *Badr az-Zên,* 182–99, No. 5 —: <879≡> (f, mid-aged, lit., col. Euro. f); ⟨8⟩ Galley, *Badr az-Zên,* 152–99, No. 4 —: <879≡> (f, mid-aged, lit., col. Euro. f); ⟨9⟩ Laoust, *Maroc,* 162–65, No. 99 —: <879≡>+ 315A:IVb-hus killd= + 1530*,-cf.> (f, adult); ⟨10⟩ Légey, *Marrakech,* 7–13, No. 1 —: <879≡> (f, elder, Sultan's concubine, "Little Sheherezade," from f-slave).

Other Rendition(s): ***PEN:*** ⟨11⟩ al-Juhaymân, *Jazîrat al-¿arab* I, 329–38, No. 24 —: <879≡:I–II,-cf. + 1353,-cf. Σ: transformed, unusual fin.> (); ⟨12⟩ al-Juhaymân, *Jazîrat al-¿arab* V, 160–72, No. 12 —: <879≡:I–II. Σ: intro. distorted, supposed fa telling to son—drawing: man and three female children> (); ⟨13⟩ A. Jahn, *Mehri: SAE* III, 112–16, No. 22 —: <879≡> (m, adult, Swh blck, b. in Ghayḍah); ***SHM:*** ⟨14⟩ al-Aswad, *shâmiyyah,* 301–4 —: <879≡:I,IV> (m, adult, from mo); ***NLE:*** ⟨15⟩ Hassan, *In-Nâs,* 46–48 —: <879≡,-pt.> (m, élite, narrator-writer, replicating fem. style); ***NLĐ:*** ⟨16⟩ Basset, *Nouveaux,* 156–61, No. 116 —: <879≡, Σ: atypical fin> (m, presum.-adult).

16. The Speechless [Bride] (Syria)

TYPE: **886A§, *The Speechless (Dumb, Tongue-tied) Wife is Obliged to Retort.* + 621, *The Louse-Skin.***

Motifs: F983.2, "Louse fattened"; H511, "Princess offered to correct guesser"; H522.1.1, "Test: guessing the nature of certain skin—louse-skin"; P529.0.4.1.1§, "Wife is to follow husband (wherever he goes)"; W31, "Obedience"; T121.9.1§, "Beautiful girl weds ugly husband"; T253.1.1§, "Nagging husband"; T215.1, "Wife carries mutilated husband on her back so that he may beg"; R227.2, "Flight from hated husband"; S146.1.3§, "Wife abandons cruel husband in a well"; T192.0.1§, "Misery brought about by forced marriage"; M411.20.1§, "Curse by husband"; M439§, "Curse: infamy or public disgrace (*faḍîhah*)"; D1610.5.1, "Magic speaking tongue"; K523.3§, "Dumbness feigned to escape telling the truth"; T272.2§, "Silent wife brought to speak by husband's impending remarriage"; Q477.1§, "Ridiculing by mimicking as punishment"; P230.5§, "Children spoil their father's wedding to a new bride-to-be and bring about reinstatement of their own mother"; S451.1§, "Children bring about reunion between their father and outcast mother"; T144.3.1§, "One wife divorced, another (new) acquired."

Occurrences: 11 additional texts are available. The ratio of f:m narrators is 9:1. The following renditions were narrated by females (or children):

PEN: ⟨1⟩ al-Bâṭinî, *nisâ'iyyah,* 55–57, No. 11 —: <886A§≡,-cf. ∑: fragment?, fin.- "possibly altered"-if violent> (f, 70s, col. f); ⟨2⟩ al-Duwayk, *Qaṭar* II, 239–40 {See also Vol. 1, p. 169, 192} —: <545H§≡545H§ + 886A§ + 285B*. ∑: atypical combo, fantasy-tale, "animal tale" [?]> (f, 50); ***MSP:*** ⟨3⟩ Ms [.??]/Batûl S. Dâwûd, *Turâth* X:3/4, 163–64 {*q.sh.¿i.* I, 290–92} —: <886A§≡> (f?, col.-auth., heard 40 yrs earlier); ***SHM:*** ⟨4⟩ Gh. al-Ḥasan, "al-'urdunî," 110–15, No. 18 —: <886A§≡≡ + 621 + 891:III = 874A§,-cf., 886> (f, 45); ***MGH:*** ⟨5⟩ al-Baqlûṭî, *Tûnis,* 98–99, Fr. tr. p. 127 —: <886A§≡+ F950.5/921N§,-cf. ∑: individ> (f, adult).

Other Rendition(s): ***PEN:*** ⟨6⟩ Bashmî, *ḥikâyât,* 85–89 —: <545H§≡545H§ + 886A§ + 285B*-cat. ≡: atypical combo, prob. altered duplicate of al-Duwayk's> ().

17. The Girl with a Dangler (Palestine)

TYPE: **884E§, *The Boy Disguised as Girl is Wooed by another Girl.***

Motifs: H360, "Bride test"; T101.1§, "Bride qualities"; T101.1.2.0.1§, "Bride quality: sex naivety (innocence)"; T452, "Bawds. Professional go-betweens"; P434§, "Service broker: middleman, or middle-woman (*dallâlah*)"; T61.9§, "Betrothal of the veiled female (unseen)"; K1836, "Disguise of man in woman's dress"; K1349.1, "Disguise to enter girl's (man's) room"; K1321.1, "Man disguised as woman admitted to women's quarters: seduction"; T59.1§, "Lovers' play (foreplay): embracing, kissing, necking, etc."; K1321, "Seduction by man disguised as woman"; H389.3§, "Bride test: total ignorance of men (sex naivety)"; J1807.3§, "Penis mistaken for an object (finger, pin, etc.)"; J1919.8.1§, "Simpleton led to believe that woman (actually man masking as woman) has a penis"; T462.0.1§, "Pseudo-lesbian attraction (love): woman falls in love with another woman who turns out to be a man in disguise"; T28, "Princess falls in love with a man disguised as a woman"; L162, "Lowly heroine marries prince (king)"; H79, "Recognition by physical attributes—miscellaneous"; H79.9§, "Identification (recognition) by sex-organ."

Occurrences: 6 additional texts are available. The ratio of f:m narrators is 3:0. The following renditions were narrated by females (or children):

SHM: ⟨1⟩ AUC: 34, No. 09 —: <884E§≡> (f, 36, litr., clerk, Turk. fa and Plstn. mo; col. f); ⟨2⟩ AUC: 11, No. 05 —: <884E§≡> (f, 70s, Chr, Syrian, learned in Egypt, 50 yrs earlier; col. f); ⟨3⟩ AUC: 34, No. 08 —: <884E§≡> (f, 80, Chr—col.'s gr-mo, in Aleppo, Syria from mo; col. f).

Other Rendition(s): ***NLÐ:*** ⟨4⟩ Frobenius, *Kordofan,* 44–49, No. 4 —: <884E§≡,-cf., K2107.3§, T100.0.9.2§, J414, K1321.1, H360, T101.1.2.0.2§/W4§,-cf.> (); ⟨5⟩ Kâmil, *soudaniyyah,* 46–50 {S. Jahn, *Arabische,* 281–84, No. 39, "cf. 1458"} **—:** <884E§≡,-cf., K2107.3§, T100.0.9.2§, J414, K1321.1, H360, T101.1.2.0.2§/W4§,-cf.> (); ***MGH:*** ⟨6⟩ Laoust, *Maroc,* 238–40, No. 119 **—:** <726A§≡+ 884E§,-cf.> ().

18. "Who Will Enter Paradise First?" (Egypt, Eastern Desert)

TYPE: **756D§, *The Most Devout will Enter Paradise First: Obedient Wife.***

> Motifs: V250.0.1§, "*as-sayyidah* Zaynab: supreme saint (culture-heroine, 'The Lady,' 'The Chieftainess,' etc.)"; P169.1.4§, "Poor firewood (underbrush) garnerer"; Q172, "Reward: admission to heaven"; P529.0.4.1§, "Wife (bride) is to obey her husband (except in sin)"; W31, "Obedience"; J2460, "Literal obedience"; W31.1§, "Blind obedience: mark of the good wife"; T306.1.1§, "Woman's (wife's) modesty and water pitcher: too modest to be exposed to a pitcher's spout"; J80, "Wisdom (knowledge) taught by parable"; V231.6, "Angel in the form of an old man"; V246.4.1§, "Angel in human form induces mortal to decide wisely."

Occurrences: 6 additional texts are available. The ratio of f:m narrators is 3:1. The following renditions were narrated by females (or children):
SHM: ⟨1⟩ HE-S: Plstn/Qatar 86-5, No. xx **—:** <756D§≡, Σ abstr., Informant: "I hate it. Women here [. . .] always cite it to justify their husbands' excesses!"> (f, 28, wed, one son, u. grad.); ***NLE:*** ⟨2⟩ HE-S: Basâtîn/Maadi 72-6, No. xx **—:** <756D§≡, Σ instructive, exemplum> (f, 48–50, non-litr., Bdw, from mo); ⟨3⟩ CFMC: Aswan 70-12B, 8-1-3 **—:** <756D§≡> (f, adult, w/3 children; col. f).
Other Rendition(s): ***PEN:*** ⟨4⟩ Müller, *Soqoṭri: SAE* VI, 104–6, No. 22 **—:** <756D§≡> (m, 36, non-litr., Ar.-Afr., Ar mo, sailor-fisher); ***SHM:*** ⟨5⟩ al-Sârîs, "al-filisṭînî," 1972, 367–68, No. 128 **—:** <756D§≡> (); ***MGH:*** ⟨6⟩ Dwyer, *Images,* 48–49, No. 5 **—:** <756D§≡> (col. Euro. f).

19. "Seven Overboiling Cauldrons from a Sparrow's Side!" (Egypt)

TYPE: **1407, *The Miser.* [Spies on his wife: he falls, or is punished.]**

> Motifs: T53.0.3§, "Inquiring about family of spouse-to-be [. . .]"; S62, "Cruel husband"; S132, "Murder by starvation"; W153.2, "Miserly husband spies on wife to see that she does not eat too much"; S51.2§, "Wife starved (by mother-in-law, sister-in-law, etc.)"; T144.3§, "Serial monogamy: successive monogamous marriages"; P263.1, "Widower marries wife's sister. [Sororate]"; T144.4§, "Serial sororal marriages: marrying one sister after another (from a group of sisters)"; S60.0.1§, "Uxoricide (wife-killing)"; T142.4§, "Compensation-bride (girl—usually sister of executed wife—given to wronged husband as restitution)"; K1984.2.2§, "Starved wife steals miserly husband's money, prepares a grand feast and claims: 'All seven cauldrons are from half a sparrow (sparrow's side)'"; K1984.2.1, "Girl claims to have overeaten on a nightingale's thigh"; F849§, "Remarkably delicious (liked) dishes—(ordinary foods)"; Q272, "Avarice punished"; N383.5§, "Miser falls dead when he realizes that his treasure has been discovered (stolen)."

Occurrences: 19 additional texts are available. The ratio of f:m narrators is 7:3. The following renditions were narrated by females (or children):

PEN: ⟨1⟩ AGSFC: QTR 87-3ff., 798-x-No. 1 —: <1407≡,-cf.> (f, 60-b. 1927, non-litr., widow, col. f); ***MSP:*** ⟨2⟩ Jamali, *Domes,* 13–17 {NK346} —: <1407≡> (f, elderly, to col. Euro. dgh-in-law); ⟨3⟩ Kh. ¿Abd-al-Amîr, *Turâth* III:10, 162–64, No. 2 —: <1407≡> (f, adult, col.'s mo); ***SHM:*** ⟨4⟩ Bergsträsser, *Neuaramäische,* 53[not 2]-54, No. 16 {NK204V: xx} —: <1407≡,-cf., = + 903C*,-cf.> (f, Chr—wife and mo); ***MGH:*** ⟨5⟩ Légey, *Marrakech,* 183–86, No. 47 —: <1407≡/955,-cf.> (f, elder, slave, from f-slave).

Other Rendition(s): ***PEN:*** ⟨6⟩ Kamâl, *kuwaytiyyah,* 314–18 —: <1407≡,-cf.> (); ***SHM:*** ⟨7⟩ Littmann, *al-Quds,* 264–65, Gr. tr., 408–12 {NK345} —: <1407≡,-cf.> (col. m, from kin); ***MGH:*** ⟨8⟩ Stumme, *Tamazratt,* 71–2, No. 25 —: <1305≡,-cf., 1407,-cf.> (); ⟨9⟩ Frobenius, *Kabylen* III, 102–8, No. 28 —: <1407≡,-cf. + 1407,-cf./miserly-fa. Σ: legend> ().

20. ¿Ali al-¿Abdalî (Oman)

TYPE: **883E§,** ***The Innocent Slandered Wife: Falsified Evidence (by Mother-in-law, Sister-in-law).*** **+ 971§,** ***Despairing Lover Commits Suicide or Becomes Insane.*** **+ Cf. 971A§,** ***Insanity and Death from Unrequited Love.*** **(Qays and Lylâ.)**

> Motifs: T200, "Married life"; T105§, "Preferred Marriages"; T98§, "Mother opposed to son's marriage"; J226.4§, "Choice: whether to marry from father's or mother's family"; T105.1.2§, "Descending scale of preferred endogamous marriages"; T107§, "Maternal-cousin is preferred as spouse"; P230.0.1.1§, "Misery of childlessness"; K2218.1, "Treacherous mother-in-law accuses wife"; K2112.2.2.1§, "Female confederate (maidservant, daughter, sister, etc.) masked as man is introduced into a girl's room as ruse so as to slander her"; K2212.2, "Treacherous sister-in-law"; P610.1.1§, "Men meet at communal parlor (*majlis, dawwâr,* guest-house, etc.)"; K2112, "Woman slandered as adulteress (prostitute)"; Q432.0.1§, "Divorce as punishment"; T145.2, "Second wife taken because first is barren"; T198§, "Return to parents' (father's) home after end of marital relations (divorce, or death of spouse)"; T298.1§, "Wrongly (hastily) condemned wife refuses reconciliation"; T81.7, "Woman dies on hearing of lover's or husband's death"; T211.9.1, "Wife dies of grief for death of husband"; T211.2, "Wife's suicide at husband's death"; T81.3, "Girl falls dead on lover's body"; Z292.0.1.1§, "Tragic ending of a story (tale): all die."

Occurrences: 21 additional texts are available. The ratio of f:m narrators is 16:2. The following renditions were narrated by females (or children):

PEN: ⟨1⟩ AGSFC: BHR 86-4, 13-x-149 —: <883E§≡,-cf., 883C*. Σ: legend, realistic> (f, 55, lit., col. f); ⟨2⟩ al-Bâṭinî, *nisâ'iyyah,* 66–71, No. 16 —: <883E§≡, Σ: fin. "possibly altered"-if violent> (f, 70s, col. f); ⟨3⟩ AGSFC: QTR 87-3ff., 678-x-188–213 —: <883E§≡+ 895B§,-cf., P325> (f, ?, div., col. f).

Other Rendition(s): ⟨4⟩ al-Juhaymân, *Jazîrat al-¿arab* IV, 231–43 —: <883E§≡,-cf. K2212.2 + P325, 895B1§> (m, as auth.'s source, adult); ***PEN:*** ⟨5⟩ al-Juhaymân, *Jazîrat al-¿arab* IV, 244–57 {Fadel, No. 26} —: <883E§≡+ K2212.2 + 874A§> ().

21. The Cruel Mother-in-law (Iraq)

TYPE: **903C*, *Mother-in-law and Daughter-in-law.*** + **Cf. 1618A§, *Lying Mother-in-law (Daughter-in-law, or Co-wife) Nonplussed: the Biting Dummy (Doll, Stick).***

> Motifs: T109.1.1§, "Bride's troubles at in-laws' home"; P207§, "There can be only one matriarch within a household"; S51, "Cruel mother-in-law"; S51.2§, "Wife starved (by mother-in-law, sister-in-law, etc.)"; H1582.5.1§, "Inability to laugh indicates sickness (hunger, starvation)"; P783.1§, "Breaking wind in public: disgraceful"; J1144, "Eaters of stolen food detected"; J1141.1, "Guilty person deceived into gesture (act) which admits guilt"; F559.3, "Extraordinary excrements"; J1141.1.13§, "Gold coins said to be from feces found in wife's bed: woman (mother-in-law) admits she is the one who has been wetting the bed all along"; J215.5§, "Present daughter-in-law proved better than a new, more 'evil' one."

Occurrences: 14 additional texts are available. The ratio of f:m narrators is 11:1. The following renditions were narrated by females (or children):

PEN: ⟨1⟩ al-Juhaymân, *Jazîrat al-¿arab* II, 323–32 {Fadel, No. 71} —: <903C*≡+ J1919.8.1§> (f, as source, auth.'s wife); ***MSP:*** ⟨2⟩ Jamali, *Domes*, 37–43 {NK198a} —: <903C*≡> (f, elderly, to col. Euro. dgh-in-law); ***SHM:*** ⟨3⟩ Sirḥân, *filisṭîniyyah*, 174–77, No. 14 —: <903C*≡> (f, ??); ⟨4⟩ Lewin, *Hama*, 20–27, No. 3 {NK198c} —: <903C*≡, S51> (f, 50s-b. 1909, non-litr., mid-class, when girl, from maid); ⟨5⟩ Bergsträsser, *Neuaramäische*, 53–54, No. 16 {NK204V: xx} —: <1407≡,-cf., = + 903C*,-cf.> (f, Chr—wife and mo); ***MGH:*** ⟨6⟩ Hejaiej, *Tunis*, 301–3, No. II-21 —: <903C*≡, T131.1.2.6.1§, T109.1.1§, J215.5§+ P780§> (f, 55, non-litr., widow, racounteur, col. f); ⟨7⟩ Houri-Pasotti, *Ghazala*, 199, No. 91 —: <1406A§≡,-cf.-theme?? + 903C*,-cf.?> (f, J, elder, to f col., gr-dgh).

Other Rendition(s): ***NLE:*** ⟨8⟩ Hassan, *In-Nâs*, 63–64 —: <903C*≡> (m, élite, narrator-writer, replicating fem. style); ***NLĐ:*** ⟨9⟩ Shahi-Moore, *Nile*, 207–8, No. 62 —: <903C*≡,-cf. (co-wives), T109.1.1§, P268§, T257.2, P268.2§, K2310.1§ + 1397§,-cf.> (col. pupil).

22. "A Son's Wife, Even When a Stick" (Syria)

TYPE: **1618A§, *Lying Mother-in-law Nonplussed (Daughter-in-law, or Co-wife): the Biting Dummy (Doll, Stick).***

> Motifs: P240§, "Dutiful children"; P262.1, "Bad relations between mother-in-law and daughter-in-law"; K2218.1, "Treacherous mother-in-law accuses wife"; J1141.11.1§, "Liar nonplussed: truth detected through trap-doll. The biting mother-in-law (daughter-in-law, co-wife): proves to be a dummy (doll, stick)"; P240.3.1§, "Dutiful son punishes nagging (impossible-to-please) mother."

Occurrences: 4 additional texts are available. The ratio of f:m narrators is 1:1. The following renditions were narrated by females (or children):

SHM: ⟨1⟩ ¿Abd-al-Hâdî, *kharârîf*, 204–6, No. 48 —: <1618A§≡/903C* ??> (f, 60).

Other Rendition(s): ***SHM:*** ⟨2⟩ Jason, *Israel*, 117, No. 36 —: <1618A§≡/903C*,-cf.> (m, J); ⟨3⟩ Sâ¿î, *Lâdhiqiyyah*, 376–79, No. 86[+1], 290–91, No. C-36] —: <1618A§≡/903C* ??> (); ***MGH:*** ⟨4⟩ Shâkir, *maghribî* II, 232–42 —: <1618A§≡> ().

23. The Sultan of the Underwater (Egypt, Nubia)

TYPE: **425L, *The Padlock on the Enchanted Husband.* [Wife punished for discovering supernatural husband's secret.]**

Motifs: F133, "Submarine otherworld"; T111, "Marriage of mortal and supernatural being"; T135.3, "Wedding by proxy [(surrogate)]"; Q341, "Curiosity punished"; T258.2, "Wife insists upon knowing husband's secret"; F521.3.5§, "Man with padlock and key on his chest (thigh, or other parts of the body)"; F133.6§, "Otherworld inside body of a person"; B147.2.2.1, "Crow as bird of ill-omen"; J21.47.1, "'Do not send wife for a long visit to her parents'"; W155, "Hardness of heart"; S55, "Cruel sister-in-law"; P264.3§, "Kindly sister-in-law: aids her brother's wife"; P264.3.1§, "Only youngest sister-in-law is kindly to (aids) her brother's cast-off wife"; T318.0.1§, "Legitimacy of child established through similarities between its physical characteristics (color, race) and father's"; S451.1.1§, "Husband reinstates his outcast wife due to her giving birth to his child (son)."

Occurrences: 18 additional texts are available. The ratio of f:m narrators is 7:2. The following renditions were narrated by females (or children):
MSP: ⟨1⟩ ¿U. Abu-Ṭâlib, *al-bî'ah,* 108–18 {*q.sh.¿i.* II, 234–42} **—:** <425L≡> (f, 80s); ***SHM:*** ⟨2⟩ al-Sârîs, *al-filisṭînî,* 167–68 **—:** <425L≡, padlock> (f, 40); ***MGH:*** ⟨3⟩ Amrouche, *Le grain,* 223–29, No. 23 **—:** <425L≡,-cf. + 433,-cf.> (f, adult, Chr-presum., auth.-col., from mo).
Other Rendition(s): ***MSP:*** ⟨4⟩ ¿Abd-Allâh A. Aghâ, *Turâth* XI:8, 185–90 {*q.sh.¿i.* II, 196–203} **—:** <425L≡> (m, col.-auth., from gr-mo, repeatedly when child); ***NLE:*** ⟨5⟩ HE-S: Minya 69–64, No. 13 **—:** <425L≡,-fin missing + 425A + 874A§> (m, 19, non-litr., no sibling, custodian of M.D.'s office, from f Chr, mid-age, friend's mo); ***MGH:*** ⟨6⟩ Panetta, *Bengasi,* .87–89 {NK97a: AT425L} **—:** <425L≡> (); ⟨7⟩ Panetta, *Bengasi,* 157–61 {NK97b: AT425L} **—:** <425L≡> (); ⟨8⟩ Frobenius, *Kabylen* II, 281–93, No. 33, **—:** <425≡+ 425L> (); ⟨9⟩ El-Fasi-Dermenghem, *fasis* I, 48–59 **—:** <425G≡+ 870/870A*,-as intro + 425L,-pt.,-P264.2§, F911.4, P253.2.0.1§, P253.12.2§ + K2258.1§, K1816.13.1§, Q416> (); ⟨10⟩ El-Fasi-Dermenghem, *fasis* I, 225–47 **—:** <425L≡, K2212, F521.3.5§, P790.2.3§, D1266, T24.1, W30.0.1§, J2218§,-cf. + 227/122Z. Σ: individ., incompl.> ().

24. The Ears That Didn't Heed the Wife's Fears (Egypt)

TYPE: **327H§, *Foolish Husband Ignores his Wife's Advice and Leads her and the Children to Ogress.* He is Devoured. + 1696, *What Should I Have Said (Done)?***

Motifs: J2461, "What should I have done (said)?"; J2461.2, "Literal following of instructions about greetings. [Wrong conditions (circumstances)]"; P773.1§, "Peddlers' cries"; G376.0.3§, "Ogress in form of woman (girl)"; G415.1§,-{formerly G415§}, "Ogress poses as man's sister and invites him to live in her house"; K2011.3.1§, "Ogress poses as man's sister and feigns affection for his children"; J2301.4§, "Gullible husband believes ogress, but not his own wife"; T255, "The obstinate wife or husband"; G11.3, "Cannibal witch"; G82, "Cannibal fattens victim";

J490§, "Young (tender) preferred to old (tough)"; K551.4.5, "Escape by pretending to go to river and wash clothes"; F851.9.1.1.1§, "Gas-giving foods eaten: beans, onions, leeks, taro [. . .]"; K523.0.1.2§, "Escape by shamming illness: food (paste, mash, porridge, etc.) smeared on intended victim's posterior and claimed to be the effects of diarrhea"; K537§, "Escape by leaving behind object (bracelet, drum, etc.) that makes noise when wind blows"; G121.3§, "Ogre's (ogress's) eyes emit sparks"; F1041.17.4§, "Involuntary defecation (urination) from fear"; J229.16.5.1§, "Captive man to ogress: 'Devour me beginning with my little ears (beard), which did not heed my wife's fears (advice)'"; K1817.4.1.2§, "Disguise as peddler so as to gather news (usually about escaped or missing person)"; G512.4.1§, "Ogress persuaded to crawl underneath door: she is burned"; N538.3.1§, "Prosperity from living in slain ogress's dwelling"; P209.1§, "Mother as provider"; P798.1§, "Unbalanced (unstable) triads."

Occurrences: 31 additional texts are available. The ratio of f:m narrators is 15:3. The following renditions were narrated by females (or children):

PEN: ⟨1⟩ al-Duwayk, *Qaṭar* I, 68 —: <327H§≡, Σ: abstr.> (f, 80); ***MSP:*** ⟨2⟩ ¿Alî S. ¿Inâd, *Turâth* X:6, 127–28 {*q.sh.¿i.* I, 281–82} —: <327H§≡> (f, 60); ⟨3⟩ Stevens, *Iraq*, 27–29, No. 7 {NK61a} —: <327K§≡,-cf. + 327H§,-cf.> (f, mid-age, Chr, non-litr., col. f, Euro.); ***SHM:*** ⟨4⟩ Gh. al-Ḥasan, "al-'urdunî," 260–64, No. 48 —: <327H§≡> (f, 40); ***NLE:*** ⟨5⟩ HE-S: IUFTL: N.Y. 61–66, 124, No. 5 —: <327H§≡, J229.16.5.1§> (f, 30–35?, lit.); ⟨6⟩ Sulaymân, 54–55, No. I-03 —: <327H§≡> (f, 74, non-litr., widow); ***NLĐ:*** ⟨7⟩ Kronenberg, *Nubische,* 78–83, No. 16 —: <327H§≡+ 1696 {Ranke: "G10"}> (f, 35); ⟨8⟩ al-Zayn, *Musabba¿ât,* 65–68 {Eng. Abstr., Ibrahîm-1991, No. 1} —: <327H§≡,-cf.? + 1442§,-mot. Σ: etiol., origin of fire> (f, presum. adult, non-litr.); ***MGH:*** ⟨9⟩ al-Baqlûṭî, *Tûnis,* 29–33, Fr. tr. p. 61 —: <327K§≡+ 327H§, P253.6.2§ + 898:IV, P14.22.1§,/cow> (f, adult); ⟨10⟩ Desparmet, *Blida* I, 206–21 —: <327H§≡,-cf.> (f, wife); ⟨11⟩ Légey, *Marrakech,* 129–30, No. 29 —: <327H§≡> (f, elder, slave, from f-slave).

Other Rendition(s): ***MGH:*** ⟨12⟩ Belamri, *La rose,* 73–79 —: <327K§≡+ 327H§,-cf. Σ: Oedipal fin> ().

25. The Man Who Severed His Own Thing (Egypt, Nubia)

TYPE: **318A§, *The Man who Lost his Organ and then Regained it.* The ungrateful wife.**

Motifs: T101.1.3.1.2§, "Bride quality: plainness (absence of sex-appeal or loud beauty)"; J482.2, "Better to marry ugly than fair wife. Less hard to satisfy"; H492.3.1§, "Dying wife asks husband to prove his faithfulness by severing his genitals"; M135.3§, "Spouse no-remarriage pact: each of husband and wife vows never to remarry if the other dies first"; S176.1, "Mutilation: emasculation"; T333.4.1§, "Husband severs own genitals so as to persuade his dying wife that he will remain celibate"; T261, "The ungrateful wife"; W154.0.1§, "Perfidy: repayment of good deeds with evil ones"; S160.1.1§, "Self-mutilation to express grief"; P264.0.1.3§, "Sisters as *salâyif* (sisters-in-law)"; H171.2.1§, "Bird (dove) selects new king: by alighting on his shoulder or head"; T315.2, "The continent husband"; T210.1,

"Faithful wife"; M295, "Bargain to keep secret"; T210.1.1§, "Wife keeps husband's secret(s)"; H493, "Virility test for husband"; N813, "Helpful genie (spirit)"; D2161.3.2.4§, "Severed penis supernaturally restored"; E782.6§, "Severed genitals replaced"; J679.5§, "Truth-speaking meddler fails to prove his report (claim): punished for 'slander'"; Q297, "Slander punished."

Occurrences: 9 additional texts are available. The ratio of f:m narrators is 1:8. Only one (No. 9), in which the central theme of loss and subsequent restoration of phallus is implicit, was narrated by a female. That text seems to be derived from literary works. Texts given by males include the following:

PEN: ⟨1⟩ al-Ja¿far, No. 10 —: <705B§≡, H271§/ + 449 + 318A§ + H271§ + D11 + D12 + T578.2 + E782.6§ + E780.5§,-cf./black penis on white man +> (m, b. 1923, blacksmith); ⟨2⟩ Müller, *Mehri-und Soqoṭri: SAE* IV, 125–34, No. F —: <318A§≡= 318A§, 516B,-cf. + 516C,-cf. +> (m and/or his Bdw mo); ⟨3⟩ Müller, *Soqoṭri: SAE* VI, 89–95, No. 16 —: <318A§≡+ 516C,-cf.> (m, 36, non-litr., Ar.-Afr., Ar mo, sailor-fisher); ⟨4⟩ Müller, *Shḥauri: SAE* VII, 102–10, No. 22 —: <315≡, K2287.1§, B515, B422 + 516B + 318A§ + 516C,-cf. + H1213.1, + S176.1> (m, adult, Bdw, herb-garnerer); ***SHM:*** ⟨5⟩ Ritter, *Ṭûr ¿Abdîn* I.1.2, 606–37, No. 78 —: <318A§,-tstcls≡> (m, b. 1913, Chr, fa was in Turk. Army and in Russ. prison); ⟨6⟩ Ritter, *Ṭûr ¿Abdîn* I.1.3, 478–81, No. 110 —: <318A§,-pt. 1≡+ 844A§,/as-intro> (m, b. 1928, Chr, factory-worker, lived in Constantinople); ***NLE:*** ⟨7⟩ HE-S: Cairo-Qulali 69-3A, No. 2 —: <318A§≡> (m, 30s, teacher-folklorist, from f); ⟨8⟩ CFMC: N-Nubia 69-10A, 2-2-8 —: <318A§≡+ T333> (m, 61–63, litr., bi-ling., ret'd chief guard, racont.); ***MGH:*** ⟨9⟩ Galley, *Badr az-Zên*, 258–62, No. 7 —: <318≡,-cf. + 318A§,-implicit. ∑: lit.> (f, mid-aged, litr., col. Euro. f).

26. "A Lost Hour of Fun Cannot Be Made Up For" (Egypt)

TYPE: **910K1§, *A Lost Hour of Fun (Merriment) Cannot be Made-up for.***

Motifs: W131.1, "Profligate [(heir)] wastes entire fortune before beginning his own adventures"; J2199.4.6.1§, "Earnings by the needle, expenditure by the pitchfork (deficit spending)"; J163.4, "Good counsels bought"; J21.53§, "'A lost hour of fun (merriment) cannot be made-up for'"; J21.54§, "'Beauty is in the eye of the beholder'"; J21.54.1§, "'The beauty is the one whom you love even if a Noah's crow (bear).' Which of two women is the pretty one: the black or the white?"; J21.30.1§, "'Betray not a trust even if you happened to be a betrayer'"; T5§, "Sexual attractiveness (sex-appeal) is relative"; F771.4.5.1§, "Mill (factory) haunted by a demon (jinni, afrit, etc.)"; G100.1, "Giant ogre (Fomorian)"; G307.3, "Jinni kills whoever tries to occupy house he has chosen to live in"; D1932.1§, "Wall opens to let in being with supernatural power (afrit, ogre, magician, etc.) and then closes after he exits"; J1014§, "Making a living (earning wages)"; P771.3.5§, "Hireling works in exchange for subsistence (food, lodging)"; V532, "Pilgrimage to Mecca"; T331, "Man unsuccessfully tempted by woman. [Chaste man]"; K2111, "Potiphar's wife [and Joseph]"; K978, "Uriah letter. [Message of death fatal to sender]"; K978.1, "Message of death"; K1612, "Message of death fatal to sender"; P963.1§, "Public procession (feast) for a boy's circumcision"; S118.0.1§, "Butcher as executioner"; N338, "Death as result of mistaken identity: wrong person killed"; Q72, "Loyalty rewarded"; Q87, "Reward for preservation of chastity."

Occurrences: 39 additional texts are available. The ratio of f:m narrators is 10:19; a decidedly male-bound pattern that contradicts the present writer's early view (based on male informants' assertions) that the tale is female-bound (see informant's note to this tale, section III, above). The following renditions were narrated by females (or children):

PEN: ⟨1⟩ AGSFC: QTR 87-3ff., 694-x-103-203 —: <910K1§≡> (f, 70, non-litr., widow, col. f); ⟨2⟩ HE-S: Somalia/Qatar 1973, No. 3 —: <910K1§≡+ 992A-449/1511 . Σ: composite> (f, 22, litr., nurse, from mo in Somalia, written down in Ar.); ***NLE:*** ⟨3⟩ Sulaymân, 132–34, No. III-B-02 —: <910K1§≡, Σ: mrlstc-prov> (f, 72, non-litr., wed-); ***MGH:*** ⟨4⟩ Bouhdiba, *maghrebin,* 16–18, Fr. tr, 73, No. 5 —: <1438§≡+ 910k1§,-pt. + 1353C§,-cf.> (f, adult, tells to children, col. m).
Other Rendition(s): ***SHM:*** ⟨5⟩ al-Jarâjrah, *¿ishq,* 118–21 —: <923B≡= + 896,/as-intro + 910K1§,-pt., J21.54.1§> (); ⟨6⟩ al-Bustânî, *lubnâniyyah,* 283–90 {NK284a, Assaf 18, S. Jahn 38} —: <923B≡= + /737A* + 923B,-cf. 896 + 910K1§,-cf./pt., J21.54.1§. Σ: fatalistic> (); ***NLÐ:*** ⟨7⟩ Hurreiz, *Ja¿aliyyîn,* 114, No. 36 —: <910K1§≡, Σ: "ḥujwa," abstr.> (m, 60, racont., Egypt'n links); ⟨8⟩ ¿A. ¿A. Ibrâhîm, "Rubâṭâb," No. 4 —: <910K1§≡> (f, 45–47, co-wife, farmer).

27. The Virgins' Louse (Egypt, Eastern Desert)

TYPE: **2021*, *The Louse Mourns her Spouse, the Flea.* + 2022A, *The Death of the Little Hen Described with Unusual Words.***

Motifs: J2519§, "Absurd extreme mourning"; J2519.1§, "Animal (bird, insect) foolishly mourned"; P681.1.1§, "Accompaniments of mourning"; Z32.2, "Chains involving a death: animal actors"; P681.1.1.2.2§, "Mourning: self-injury"; P681.1.1.2§, "Mourning: physical manifestations"; P681.1.1.2.1§, "Mourning: baring head (face) in public"; P681.1.1.2.1.1§, "Mourning: tearing garment"; P681.1.1.1§, "Mourning: verbal expressions (wailing)"; B299.5.2, "Animal fasts to express sympathy"; S160.1.1§, "Self-mutilation to express grief"; B299.5, "Sympathetic animals"; B299.5.1, "Animal mutilates self to express sympathy"; F994, "Object expresses sorrow"; F819§, "Sympathetic plant(s)"; F979.15, "Tree sheds all of its leaves out of sympathy"; Z32.2.1, "The death of the little hen described with unusual words [(neologism)]"; F932.6.2, "River dries up its waters out of sympathy"; J1701, "The stupid [(foolish)] wife"; Q432.0.1§, "Divorce as punishment."

Occurrences: 22 additional texts are available. The ratio of f:m narrators is 11:3. The following renditions were narrated by females (or children):

PEN: ⟨1⟩ al-Bâṭinî, *al-ḥikâyât,* 114–17, No. 21 —: <2021*≡+ 2022A . Σ: off focus, not "animal tale"> (f, auth.-col., from f kin); ⟨2⟩ Gh. al-Ḥasan, "al-'urdunî," 176–78, No. 31 —: <2021*≡+ 2022A,-cf.> (f, 55); ⟨3⟩ Muhawi-Kanaana, *Speak,* 288–90, No. 41 —: <2021*≡> (f, 70s); ***NLE:*** ⟨4⟩ Gamal, *Miṣr,* 62–65, No. 10 —: <2021*≡> (f, col. f.); ⟨5⟩ Farag, *Daqahliyyah,* 379–80 —: <2021*≡> (m/c, 14, pupil, fa is blacksmith, mo is grain trader, from fa, pat-aunts and gr-fa); ***NLĐ:*** ⟨6⟩ Kronenberg, *Nubische,* 251–52, No. 52 —: <2021*≡, 2022,-cf. [+]. Σ: "animal," formula> (f, 65){Ranke: 2022}; ***MGH:*** ⟨7⟩ Houri-Pasotti, *Ghazala,* 126–29, No. 60 —: <2021*≡+ 2022A> (f, J, elder, to f col., gr-dgh); ⟨8⟩ Amrouche, *Le grain,* 173–76, No. 18 —: <2021*≡,-cf. + 2022A> (f, adult, Chr-presum., auth.-col., from mo); ⟨9⟩ Légey, *Marrakech,* 221–23, No. 59 —: <2021*≡+. Σ: formula> (f, presum. adult).

28. She Whose Reason Couldn't Be Made to Slip (Egypt)

TYPE: **1379/891F§, *Wife Deceives Husband with Substituted Bedmate.***

Motifs: N15, "Chastity wager"; N15.3§, "Wager on sister's chastity"; N2.6.1, "Sister as wager"; P610.1.2§, "Men meet at drinking (smoking) shop (coffeehouse, tavern, bar, etc.)"; T455.8§, "Princess (beautiful woman) allows men to see her for a fee (pay)"; K2112.1.1, "Fingers as false token of wife's unfaithfulness. [Prove to be the maidservant's]"; J32.0.2§, "'If her finger (hand, heel, etc.) is that beautiful, then how the rest of her body must be!'"; T296, "Wife buys (sells) privilege of sleeping one night with husband"; K1843, "Wife deceives husband with substitute bedmate"; K1843.2.2, "Wife takes mistress's place in bed but is deceived in turn"; K1843.1.2§, "Disguised wife sleeps in her husband's bed as his bedmate (lover, slave-girl): she conceives"; T562, "White woman bears black child"; P187§, "Inherent rivalry between mistress and young female slave"; T318.0.1§, "Legitimacy of child established through similarities between its physical characteristics (color, race) and father's"; P180.5§, "Treatment of slave's children in relationship to master's"; S451.1.1§, "Husband reinstates his outcast wife due to her giving birth to his child (son)."

Occurrences: 15 additional texts are available. The ratio of f:m narrators is 11:3. The following renditions were narrated by females (or children):

PEN: ⟨1⟩ AGSFC: BHR 86-4, 28-x-x —: <1379≡879:III + 1379> (f, 40, non-litr., col. f); ⟨2⟩ Noy, *Jefet,* 181–83, No. 75 —: <1379≡,-cf. [actually: 873-pt.,-cf., or 1379,-cf.]> (f, 66, J); ⟨3⟩ Noy, *Jefet,* 188–91, No. 79 —: <875B≡[+ 1379] + 879 + 1441 + 920:II> (f, 66, J); ***SHM:*** ⟨4⟩ al-Sârîs, *al-filisṭînî,* 282–84 —: <1379≡≡ + 425,-intro + 1379 + 892,-cf., 874,-cf.> (f, adult); ⟨5⟩ ¿Abd-al-Hâdî, *kharârîf,* 11–15, No. 1 —: <1379≡,-cf./pt. + 983,-cf.??> (f, 70); ***NLĐ:*** ⟨6⟩ Kronenberg, *Nubische,* 172–81, No. 37 —: <1379≡+ P293.0.1§ {Ranke: 0}> (f, 35).

Other Rendition(s): *PEN:* ⟨7⟩ A. Jahn, *Mehri: SAE* III, 14–21, No. 6 —: <1379≡+ 879:III,-cf.> (m, adult, Swh blck, b. in Ghayḍah); ***NLĐ:*** ⟨8⟩ Shahi-Moore, *Nile,* 205–7, No. 61 —: <1379≡+ 890:III, N15.3§, T563 + 879,-cf. Σ: wrt.> (col. pupil).

29. The Lovesick Husband (Egypt)

TYPE: **516A1§, *The Body Talk by the Princess,* interpreted for the love-sick husband (by his wife, fiancée). + 861, *Sleeping at the Rendezvous.***

Motifs: T55, "Girl as wooer. Forthputting woman"; V532, "Pilgrimage to Mecca"; N711.7§, "Lover sees beloved first while she is a-traveling"; H607, "Discussion by symbols"; H607.3, "Princess declares her love through sign language, not understood"; Z175, "Sign language. Message delivered by means of the fingers, etc."; H611.2, "Sign message sent by girl to enamored prince. Interpreted by prince's friend [(cousin-wife)]"; T24.1, "Love-sickness"; P295.1.2§, "Marriage between *'ibn-¿amm* and his *bint-¿amm* (paternal-cousin)"; T416§, "Paternal-cousin (*bint-¿amm*) as substitute for sister"; Z63.9.2§, "Brother (sister) or paternal-cousin: what is the difference!? [None!]"; T100.0.9.2§, "Marriage as treatment (cure) for unhappiness (immaturity)"; H611.2.1§, "Prince's wife (who is also his cousin) interprets for him girl's love message"; Z100, "Symbolism"; Z188.2§, "Symbolism: eye—sight"; Z188.1.1§, "Symbolism: arms, legs—children"; Z188.1§, "Symbolism: head of animal or fowl—chief or family patriarch"; Z166.1.1§, "Symbolism: pomegranate (apple, orange)—breast"; Z188.3§, "Symbolism: navel—the center of city"; T35, "Lovers' rendezvous"; T30, "Lovers' meeting"; T36, "Girl sleeps in garden to meet lover"; T35.0.2.1§, "Lover falls asleep and misses rendezvous"; D1972, "Lover's magic sleep at rendezvous"; K528, "Substitute in ordeal"; K626, "Escape by bribing the guard"; K649.9, "Confederate causes confusion so that prisoner can escape"; K527, "Escape by substituting another person in place of the intended victim"; K528.2.2§, "Wife substitutes self for maiden with whom her husband is in love—(maiden accused of unchastity)"; H461.1, "The clever wife in disguise wins a second wife for her husband"; T193§, "Marriage through threatening girl (woman) with disgrace (scandal)"; T145.0.4§, "Happy polygynous marriage."

Occurrences: 17 additional texts are available. The ratio of f:m narrators is 6:7. The following renditions were narrated by females (or children):
PEN: ⟨1⟩ AGSFC: QTR 87-3ff., 712-x-No. 2 —: <516A≡+ K2293> (f, 65, non-litr., wed, head of "folk-art-troupe", col. f); ***NLE:*** ⟨2⟩ AUC: 33, No. 7 —: <516A≡, taped> (f, 28–40, litr., maid, col. f); ⟨3⟩ CFMC: Oases 71-3, 4-2-[4] —: <516A≡:II–III, legend, "happened surely-truly 7–8 yrs ago"> (f, 55, heard in Cairo, col. f).
Other Rendition(s): ***PEN:*** ⟨4⟩ AGSFC: QTR 87-3ff., 712-x-No. 2 —: <516A≡+ K2293> (f, 65, non-litr., wed, head of "folk-art-troupe", col. f); ⟨5⟩ al-Duwayk, *Qaṭar* II, 87–88 —: <516A≡,-cf.> (m, 20, stu., from his gr-mo); ***SHM:*** ⟨6⟩ ¿Abd-al-Hâdî, *kharârîf*, 216–23, No. 52 —: <1538A§≡, M155.5§ = 1750A + 1525W§/1526,-cf./dead infant + 516A,-cf./pt., K527.3.1§> (f, 49); ⟨7⟩ al-Sârîs, *al-filisṭînî*, 64–66 —: <516A≡> (m, h.-sch. pupil, from kin); ⟨8⟩ al-Sârîs, *al-filisṭînî*, 118–22 —: <516A≡> (m, h.-sch. pupil, from kin); ⟨9⟩ Ritter, *Ṭûr ¿Abdîn* I.1.2, 664–75, No. 83 —: <516A≡+ P293.2> (m, ?, Chr, building-contractor in Beirut); ***NLĐ:*** ⟨10⟩ Ṭ.M. al-Ṭayyib et al., *al-Manâṣîr*, 50–54 —: <516A≡:II, H607.3. Σ: fragment?> (m).

30. The Son of Seven [Mothers] (Syria)

TYPE: **462, *The Outcast Queens and the Ogress Queen.***

Motifs: G264, "La Belle Dame San Merci. Witch entices men with offers of love and then deserts or destroys them"; T9.1§, "The power of sex: female's influence";

S413.1, "Ogress wife orders raja to turn out [(cast-off)] his six wives"; P529.0.8§, "Declaration (publication) of divorce (a necessary condition for its actualization)"; R41.3, "Captivity in dungeon"; S438, "Abandoned queen blinded"; K961.2.2, "Ogress wife demands eyes of six wives of raja or she will die"; T581.2.2, "Blind wives fall [(are cast)] in pool where they give birth to children"; G78.1, "Cannibalism in times of famine"; G72.2, "Starving woman abandoned in cave eats newborn child"; L71, "Only youngest of group of imprisoned women refuses to eat her newborn child"; Z215, "Hero 'Son of seven mothers'"; N842.1, "Cook as foster father"; S31, "Cruel stepmother"; K1996.2§, "Feigning illness by shamming physical symptoms: saffron dye on face to simulate 'yellowness' (paleness) of death"; H1212, "Quest assigned because of feigned illness"; H1211, "Quests assigned in order to get rid of hero"; N825.2, "Old man helper"; N122.0.2§, "The choice of roads: Road of Safety, Road of Sorrow, or Road of No-return"; G123, "Giant ogress with breasts thrown over her shoulders"; T671, "Adoption by suckling. Ogress who suckles hero claims him as her son"; D211.2, "Transformation: man (woman) to pomegranate"; N812, "Giant or ogre as helper"; C742, "Tabu: striking monster twice"; Z18.3§, "Ogre to man: 'Repeat [your blow]!' Man to ogre: 'My mother did not teach me [to do this]!'"; E11.1, "Second blow resuscitates. First kills"; G634.4.1§, "Ogre is asleep for a year, then is awake for a year"; D2136.2, "Castle [palace] magically transported"; D1505.14, "Animal liver cures blindness"; D2161.3.1.1, "Eyes torn out magically replaced"; E781.2, "Eyes bought back and replaced"; E80, "Water of Life. Resuscitation by water"; E125.3.1§, "Resuscitation by stepbrother"; L13.1, "Youngest wife's son restores eyesight to blinded six wives of raja and reinstates his mother."

Occurrences: 14 additional texts are available. The ratio of f:m narrators is 6:3. The following renditions were narrated by females (or children):

SHM: ⟨1⟩ Sirḥân, *min Filisṭîn,* 41–47 —: <462≡> (f); ⟨2⟩ Schmidt-Kahle, *Palästina* I, 160–65, No. 44 {NK189} —: <462≡, Σ: "Märchen"> (f, adult); ⟨3⟩ Muhawi-Kanaana, *Speak,* 237–41, No. 30 —: <462≡> (f, 65); ***MGH:*** ⟨4⟩ al-Baqlûṭî, *Tûnis,* 102–4, Fr. tr. p. 131 —: <462≡> (f, adult).

Other Rendition(s): ***SHM:*** ⟨5⟩ al-Sârîs, *al-filisṭînî,* 240–42 —: <462≡> (??); ***NLE:*** ⟨6⟩ Spitta, *modernes,* 12–29, No. 2 {NK177, Budge, *Tales,* pt. 3, 306–19, No. 2} —: <462≡> (m, cook, from f-"aunts"); ***NLĐ:*** ⟨7⟩ Ṭ. M. al-Ṭayyib et al., *al-Manâṣîr,* 24–25 —: <462≡> (m, presum. adult).

31. Finger Joint (Egypt, Eastern Desert)

TYPE: **1442§, *Stupid Woman (Co-wife) is Deceived into Imitating Foolishly:* she kills her child. + Cf. 1387*, *Woman Must Do Everything Like her Neighbors.* Absurd results.**

Motifs: T553.1§, "*ṭulbah:* Thumbling born in answer to prayer"; F535.0.2§, "Remarkably small woman (girl)"; F535.1.1.10, "Thumbling hides in a small place"; J1701, "The stupid [(foolish)] wife"; K2222, "Treacherous co-wife (concubine)"; M431.4.1, "Curse: hand of person cursed to drop off"; D1935.3§, "Magic ability to perform any task"; J2303, "Gullible mother"; K992§, "Misleading advice";

P741.2.1§, "Chaos (disorder) from absence of commander (chief)"; S342, "Mother induced by rival to kill her children"; J2401, "Fatal imitation"; T145.0.3§, "Polygyny brings misery (trouble)"; Q432.0.1§, "Divorce as punishment."

Occurrences: 31 additional texts are available. The ratio of f:m narrators is 20:3. The following renditions were narrated by females (or children):

PEN: ⟨1⟩ al-Duwayk, *Qaṭar* II, 93–94 —: <451A≡+ 1442§,-pt. Σ: "folk-tale [!]"> (f, 90); ***MSP:*** ⟨2⟩ ¿Alî Ḥaydar Ṣâliḥ, *Turâth* III:5/6, 46 —: <1442§≡= G72.2.1§> (f, attributed to "Baghdadi mothers"); ***SHM:*** ⟨3⟩ Gh. al-Ḥasan, "al-'urdunî," 130–36, No. 22 —: <1442§≡,-cf., G72.1.1§. Σ: wrt.> (f, 50); ***NLE:*** ⟨4⟩ Abu-Lughod, *Bedouin,* 104–6 —: <1442§≡> (f, "Dateefa"/[??, prob. Laṭîfa], co-wife, col. f); ***NLĐ:*** ⟨5⟩ Kronenberg, *Nubische,* 119–23, No. 26 —: <1442§≡,-cf. = + T145.0.4§, P268.2§ {Ranke: "0"}> (f, 35); ⟨6⟩ al-Zayn, *Musabba¿ât,* 65–68 {Eng. Abstr., Ibrahîm-1991, No. 1} —: <327H§≡,-cf.? + 1442§,-mot. Σ: etiol., origin of fire> (f, presum. adult, non-litr.); ⟨7⟩ Kronenberg, *Nubische,* 137–42, No. 31 —: <591A§≡+ K1335/400,-cf./feathers-stolen + 402,-cf. + 1442§,-cf./898,-cf./fin {Ranke: 409A}> (f, 35).

Other Rendition(s): ***PEN:*** ⟨8⟩ Shalabî, *Ṣûmâl,* 31–32 —: <1442§≡+> (); ***NLE:*** ⟨9⟩ Sha¿lân, "al-nawâdir," 370 —: <1442§≡,-cf.-pt. = + 620,-cf. Σ: male's rendition> (m); ***NLĐ:*** ⟨10⟩ von Massenbach, *Nubische,* pt. B.VIII, 150, No. 38 —: <402≡+ 1442§/1387*:I> (m, presum. adult).

32. Zlaizlah and 'Omm-Zaba¿ba¿ (Egypt, Western Desert)

TYPE: **480, *The Spinning-Women by the Spring.* The Kind and Unkind Girls. + 511A, *The Little Red Ox.* [Cow helps orphans.]**

Motifs: Z84.4.5.1§, "Insult: uncircumcised woman (nymphomaniac, unclean)"; T548.1, "Child born in answer to prayer"; M117.0.1§, "*nadhr/'nadr':* conditional vow: pledge to perform certain (good) act if prayer is answered (request is granted)"; S24.1.1§, "Widow induces girl to kill her mother and persuade father to marry the widow"; S121, "Murder by slamming down chest-lid"; S24.1§, "Daughter kills her mother"; B115, "Animal with horn of plenty"; B411, "Helpful cow"; B335.2, "Life of helpful animal demanded as cure for feigned sickness"; S34, "Cruel stepsister(s)"; Q2, "Kind and unkind"; P252.0.1§, "Sisters in conflict"; D1860, "Magic beautification"; D1658.4§, "Grateful object bestows its own good attribute(s) upon helper"; D1658.1, "Objects repay kindness"; Z65.3§, "White as milk (cheese)"; W48§, "Being sweet-tongued"; U280§, "Balance between merits and demerits, advantages and disadvantages, good and evil"; U280.1§, "Everything found to have merit"; U281.1§, "Merits and demerits of color (black, white)"; N825.3.2, "Old woman by spring [(well)] as helper"; H935, "Witch [(ogress)] assigns tasks"; H580.1, "Girl given enigmatic commands must do the opposite"; B392.1, "Animals grateful for being given appropriate food"; G466, "Lousing as task set by ogress"; K874.3§, "Sesame (being eaten) said to be 'Ogress's sweet-tasting lice!'"; W31.1.1§, "Obedience to seniors mark of good girl"; Q41.2, "Reward for cleaning loathsome person"; X1505.1.1§, "Reward for carrying out orders by contraries"; D1470.1.35, "Magic wishing-well"; D926, "Magic well"; D1659.3§, "Angry plant inflicts its bad attribute(s) upon unkind person"; Q2.1§, "Flattering lies rewarded, unflattering truth punished"; J268§, "Flattery of authority or seniors rewarded"; D1870, "Magic hideousness"; T137.5, "Bride (and party) fetched by groom and party after wedding [(*esh-shailah*)]"; K1911, "The false bride (substituted bride)"; K1911.3.1, "Substitution of false bride revealed by animal"; N458§, "Overheard animal's (bird's) chant reveals commission of crime (deception)"; N458.1§, "Cat's chant betrays substitution of bride"; K1911.3, "Reinstatement of true bride"; Q414, "Punishment: burning alive."

Occurrences: 76 additional texts are available. The ratio of f:m narrators is 53:9. The following renditions were narrated by females (or children):

PEN: ⟨1⟩ AGSFC: BHR 86-4, 15.1-x-x —: <480≡:VI–VIII. Σ: fragment> (f, 40, col. f); ⟨2⟩ al-Duwayk, *Qaṭar* II, 233–34 —: <480≡,-cf. + 409C§. Σ: not "animal tale"> (f, 60); ⟨3⟩ al-Duwayk, *Qaṭar* II, 235–36 —: <480≡+ 409C§. Σ: "animal tale," narrator: "this *sâlifah* [true story] . . . , happened a long time ago," incompl.> (f, 60); ⟨4⟩ Sengo, "Kiswahili," 593–601, No. 19 —: <480≡,-cf. Σ: didactic, moral.> (f, 19, h.-sch. pupil); ***MSP:*** ⟨5⟩ Stevens, *Iraq,* 187–93, No. 36 {NK63} —: <511A≡, no brother + T671 + 480:VI–VII + 510:IV–V> (f, mid-age, Chr, non-litr., col. f, Euro.); ***SHM:*** ⟨6⟩ Muhawi-Kanaana, *Speak,* 301–6, No. 43 —: <620≡, = + 480,-cf./pt.> (f, 55); ⟨7⟩ ¿Abd-al-Hâdî, *kharârîf,* 191–95, No. 45 —: <480≡, Σ: incompl.> (f, 50); ⟨8⟩ ¿Abd-al-Hâdî, *kharârîf,* 265–67, No. 63 —: <476*≡+ 480-pt. ??> (f, 65); ⟨9⟩ al-Aswad, *shâmiyyah,* 29–34 —: <480≡+ E323.2.4§/as-intro> (f, elder); ***NLE:*** ⟨10⟩ Sulaymân, 155–56, No. V-02 —: <480≡+ 511A-pt. + D447.8.1§. Σ: -bones become cats, kill st-mo., supernatural beings> (f/c, 13, pupil); ⟨11⟩ Gamal, *Miṣr,* 66–69, No. 11 —: <480≡> (f, col. f); ⟨12⟩ Farag, *Daqahliyyah,* 238–42 —: <511A≡,-one girl + 480> (f, pupil, fa butcher, from gr-mo and pat-aunt); ⟨13⟩ Abu-Lughod, *Bedouin,* 154–59 —: <511A≡+480> (f, ??, col. f); ***NLÐ:*** ⟨14⟩ Shahi-Moore, *Nile,* 98–101, No. 15 —: <480≡,-cf. + 327D,-cf./mot., G530. Σ: wrt.> (Funj, col. pupil); ⟨15⟩ S. M. ¿Abd-Allâh, *Sukkût,* 251–54, No. 7 —: <480≡> (f, 65, widow); ***MGH:*** ⟨16⟩ al-Baqlûṭî, *Tûnis,* 22–28, Fr. tr. p. 54 —: <480≡+ 510/elements> (f, adult); ⟨17⟩ Hejaiej, *Tunis,* 245–50, No. II-9 —: <480≡, S31.5, S24.1.1§, K289§> (f, 55, non-litr., widow, racounteur, col. f); ⟨18⟩ Légey, *Marrakech,* 104–11, No. 24 —: <432≡+ 884B* + 480,-pt.> (f, elder, slave, from f-slave); ⟨19⟩ Shâkir, *maghribî* I, 304–10 —: <480≡, S24.1.1§,/as-intro + 620 + 569A§. Σ: local pattern> (f, elder-gr-mo).

Other Rendition(s): ***PEN:*** ⟨20⟩ Sengo, "Kiswahili," 425–51, No. 8 —: <480≡+ B108.1, B112, 561:II,-cf. Σ: {Sengo:328}> (m, 26, careener's apprentice, under Talib Chum); ⟨21⟩ Sengo, "Kiswahili," 601–17, No. 20 —: <480≡+ K1039§. Σ: {Sengo:512*}> (m?, 60); ⟨22⟩ Sengo, "Kiswahili," 826–54, No. 34 —: <480≡/511A, S24§ + 405, K2211.1 + 720B§,-intro,-cf. {Sengo: 891A}> (m, 29, elem.-sch. dropout, wed, 2 sons, farmer); ***SHM:*** ⟨23⟩ AUC: 2, No. 10 —: <480≡> (m, 20, u. stu. in Cairo, col. f); ***NLE:*** ⟨24⟩ Hassan, *In-Nâs,* 18–20 —: <480≡:pt. + 511A,-pt.> (m, élite, narrator-writer, replicating fem. style); ***MGH:*** ⟨25⟩ Desparmet, *Blida* II, 265–78 —: <480≡, P251.5.3,-as intro, P264.0.1§ + P295.1.7.1.1§. Σ: male's rendition of a female's theme> (m).

33. Pearls-on-Vines (Egypt)

TYPE: **432, *The Prince as Bird.* [In snake's (serpent's) form, visits heroine and is wounded by her jealous sisters]; + 973, *Placating the Storm.* [Man thrown overboard.]**

Motifs: L221, "Modest request: present from the journey. [Present from father's proves difficult]"; P252.0.1§, "Sisters in conflict"; K2212, "Treacherous sister"; V532, "Pilgrimage to Mecca"; H151.14, "Tears fall on person below and indicate presence of those above"; N825.3, "Old woman helper"; Q41, "Politeness rewarded"; D1254.3.1§, "Magic mortar and pestle: audible from great distance"; F821.1.5, "Dress of gold, silver, color of sun, moon and stars"; F1381.8§, "Quest for unknown bridegroom (lover) for daughter (sister)"; J1805.2.1, "Daughter says 'Sobur' (wait [patience]) to her father when he asks what to bring from the journey. Father finds prince Sobur"; D1318.10.1, "Ship refuses to move with guilty man aboard"; S264.1, "Man thrown overboard to placate the storm"; D641.1.0.1§, "Lover as snake visits mistress"; B640.1, "Marriage to beast by day and man by night"; S181, "Wounding by trapping with sharp knives (glass)"; W181, "Jealousy"; W195.9.3§, "Sister envies sister's handsome husband (suitor, lover)"; K919.1§, "Broken glass (placed by jealous sisters) to wound and detect sister's lover"; K1565, "Blades (broken glass) to wound and detect wife's [(sister's)] lover"; D791.1.1, "Disenchantment at end of seven years"; K1837, "Disguise of woman in man's clothes"; H1385.5, "Quest for vanished lover"; H1385.4, "Quest for vanished husband"; K1825.1.4, "Girl masks as doctor to find departed lover"; B517§, "Overheard conversation of birds (turtledoves, pigeons) reveals that some of their own organs are the only medicine to cure hero: they are caught and killed for the cure"; C434.1§, "Effect of spoken evil words [to be] averted by spitting"; J571.5.1§, "Promise secured not to act till story is told in full"; N681.1, "Wife finds lost husband just as he is to marry another"; Q94, "Reward for cure"; Q261, "Treachery punished"; Q414, "Punishment: burning alive."

33-1. Without a Title (Egypt)

TYPE: **432.**

Motifs: Q94, "Reward for cure"; H388.3§, "Prince given to woman who can heal him"; T67.2, "Marriage to prince as reward for curing him"; J414, "Marriage with equals or with unequals"; M203, "King's promise irrevocable"; P525.0.1, "It is a debt if it is promised"; T121.6.1§, "Master marries slave-girl."

Occurrences: 46 additional texts are available. The ratio of f:m narrators is 22:9. The following renditions were narrated by females (or children):

PEN: ⟨1⟩ AGSFC: BHR 86-4, 3-x-No. 1 **—:** <432≡,-cf.> (f, 47, in literacy program, from mo, col. f); ***MSP:*** ⟨2⟩ Stevens, *Iraq,* 20–26, No. 6 {NK245} **—:** <432≡> (f, youth, col. f, Euro.); ⟨3⟩ Ms. Lylâ Ibrâhîm al-Samâwî, *Turâth* IV:10, 123–26 **—:** <425A≡, K919.1§ + 425D + 425K> (f, 63, auth.'s gr-mo, from her mo, col. f); ***SHM:*** ⟨4⟩ ¿Abd-al-Hâdî, *kharârîf,* 78–81, No. 19 **—:** <432≡/325. Σ: frag.> (f, 60); ***NLĐ:*** ⟨5⟩ Kronenberg, *Nubische,* 112–18, No. 25 **—:** <432≡+ {Ranke: 425}> (f, 35); ⟨6⟩ Kronenberg, *Nubische,* 123–25, No. 27 **—:** <432≡, Σ: incompl.> (f, 40); ***MGH:*** ⟨7⟩ Scelles-Millie, *Souf,* pt. V, 291–97, No. 3 **—:** <432≡> (f, 15); ⟨8⟩ Légey, *Marrakech,* 104–11, No. 24 **—:** <432≡+ 884B* + 480,-pt.> (f, elder, slave, from f-slave).

Other Rendition(s): ***PEN:*** ⟨9⟩ Hein-Müller, *Mehri-Ḥaḍramî: SAE* IX 37–41, No. 20

{NK86b} —: <432≡> (m, youth, soldier); ***SHM:*** ⟨10⟩ al-Bustânî, *lubnâniyyah,* 128–39 {NK86a; Assaf 5} —:<425≡+ 432 + 884B*,-theme> ().

34. The Fisherman's Daughter (Oman)

TYPE: **510,** ***Cinderella and Cap o' Rushes.***

Motifs: F574.9.1.1§, "Skin so soft that it will not support a flea's weight (formulaic)"; S31, "Cruel stepmother"; S34, "Cruel stepmother(s)"; P252.0.1§, "Sisters in conflict"; P200.0.2.1§, "Father is powerless"; L55, "Stepdaughter heroine"; Z71.5, "Formulistic number: seven"; H1091.1, "Task: sorting grains: performed by helpful ants"; P963.1§, "Public procession (feast) for a boy's circumcision"; N813, "Helpful genie (spirit)"; N711.6, "Prince sees heroine at ball and is enamored"; K626.1, "Escape by throwing money (treasure) so that guards [(pursuers)] fight over it"; D1002, "Magic excrements"; H36.1, "Slipper test: identification by fitting of slipper"; K2212.1, "Treacherous stepsisters"; D1454.5, "Treasure from excrements [(anus)]"; F559.3.2§, "Jewels as extraordinary excrements"; W181, "Jealousy"; W195.4§, "Wealth (material possessions) envied"; W195.9.2§, "Brother envies brother's beautiful wife (wives)"; J2400.1§, "Foolish imitation of brother by brother"; J2411.6.2§, "Unsuccessful imitation by stepsister (sister-in-law) to produce treasure from excrements."

34-1. Fsaijrah (Qatar)

TYPE: **510.**

Motifs: B375.1, "Fish returned to water: grateful"; B470.1, "Small fish as helper."

Occurrences: 48 additional texts are available. The ratio of f:m narrators is 30:5. The following renditions were narrated by females (or children):

PEN: ⟨1⟩ AGSFC: BHR 86-4, 1-x-5-65 —: <510≡> (f, 66, non-litr., col. f); ⟨2⟩ al-Bâṭinî, *al-ḥikâyât,* 14–19, No. 1 —: <510≡> (f, auth.-col., from f kin); ⟨3⟩ al-Duwayk, *Qaṭar* II, 133–34 —: <510≡> (f, 47, div., sch. custodian, from paternal gr-mo); ⟨4⟩ al-Duwayk, *Qaṭar* II, 135–36 —: <510≡+> (f, 90); ⟨5⟩ al-Duwayk, *Qaṭar* II, 137–38 —: <510≡+> (f, 105); ⟨6⟩ al-Duwayk, *Qaṭar* II, 139–40 —: <510≡+> (f, 25); ⟨7⟩ al-Duwayk, *Qaṭar* II, 143–44 —: <510≡> (f, 80); ⟨8⟩ al-Duwayk, *Qaṭar* II, 185–86 —: <923≡:I + 510,-cf. + K512 + 510:Ic. Σ: atypical> (f, 60); ⟨9⟩ Noy, *Jefet,* 81–83, No. 24 —: <511A≡,-cf. + 510 + 403,-pt., D150, D582> (f, 66, J); ***MSP:*** ⟨10⟩ Stevens, *Iraq,* 187–93, No. 36 {NK63} —: <511A≡, no brother + T671 + 480:VI–VII + 510:IV–V> (f, mid-age, Chr, non-litr., col. f, Euro.); ***MGH:*** ⟨11⟩ al-Baqlûṭî, *Tûnis,* 22–28, Fr. tr. p. 54 —: <480≡+ 510-elements> (f, adult).

Other Rendition(s): ***PEN:*** ⟨12⟩ Kamâl, *kuwaytiyyah,* 115–24 —: <510≡> (); ***NLĐ:*** ⟨13⟩ Shahi-Moore, *Nile,* 118–20, No. 22 —: <313E*≡+ 510,-cf./dancing. Σ: wrt.> (col. pupil); ***MGH:*** ⟨14⟩ Mouliéras-Lacoste, *Kabaylie,* 246–54, No. 27 —: <450≡, =511A:I,-cf. + 510 + 450 + 403D§,-cf., S72.1§> (); ⟨15⟩ Laoust, *Chenoua,* 181–83, No. 16 —: <720≡511A:I/as-intro + 720/720A§= + 318B§ + 510:III–IV + 403:IVc> ().

35. The Maternal-aunt (Iraq)

TYPE: **403D§, *The Cruel Maternal-aunt Blinds her Niece and Substitutes her own Daughter as Bride.***

Motifs: J551.6.2§, "Only youngest daughter tells king (her father) that it is not him but destiny (God) who controls a human's fortune: she is banished"; P761.1§, "Division of inheritance causes conflict"; S73.0.1§, "Sister cruel to her sister"; T69.6§, "Daughter [sister] given to beggar (as alms)"; T570.1§, "Pregnant woman's wish (craving)"; S72.2§, "Cruel maternal-aunt (*khâlah*)"; K2216.1§, "Treacherous maternal-aunt (*khâlah*)"; P200.0.2.1§, "Father is powerless"; P271.2, "Fisherman as foster father"; D1454.2, "Treasure falls from mouth"; D1454.2.1, "Flowers fall from lips [(mouth)]"; F971.5, "Flowers bloom in winter"; V222.12.1§, "Blessedness of a person restores a garden to bloom"; N859§, "Fisher as helper"; F960.11§, "Extraordinary nature phenomena at a person's smiling"; M225, "Eyes exchanged for food"; K1911, "The false bride (substituted bride)"; E781.2, "Eyes bought back and replaced"; D2161.3.1.1, "Eyes torn out magically replaced"; E782, "Limb successfully replaced"; H71.4.1§, "Flowers from lips (mouth, footprint) as proof of heroine's identity"; H94.1, "Identification by ring baked in cake"; J1675.9§, "King's promise of safety secured before breaking news to him"; Q261, "Treachery punished"; Q411, "Death as punishment. [Execution.]"

Occurrences: 16 additional texts are available. The ratio of f:m narrators is 5:3. The following renditions were narrated by females (or children): Of the remaining 11 texts, men were cited as the source of the tale in only 3.

MSP: ⟨1⟩ Stevens, *Iraq*, 14–19, No. 5 {NK91} —: <403D§≡> (f, youth, lit., col. f, Euro.); ⟨2⟩ Kh. ¿Abd-al-Amîr, *Turâth* III:10, 165–70 {*q.sh.¿i.* I, 339–47, Bushnaq, 75–79} —: <403D§≡923:I + 403D§ + 533A§> (f, ad, col.'s mo); ***NLĐ:*** ⟨3⟩ Kronenberg, *Nubische*, 142–51, No. 32 —: <403D§≡+ P253, P263.1 {Ranke: 403}> (f, 35); ***MGH:*** ⟨4⟩ Shâkir, *maghribî* I, 128–34 —: <403D§≡+ 425G1§,/as-intro + 403D§. Σ: solar mythololological> (f, 25, maid, of peasant orig.).

Other Rendition(s): ***PEN:*** ⟨5⟩ Müller, *Shḥauri: SAE* VII, 63–69, No. 16 —: <403D§≡, Q2> (m, adult, Bdw, herb-garnerer); ***MSP:*** ⟨6⟩ Khalaf H. ¿Abbûd, *Turâth* X:7, 173–74 {*q.sh.¿i.* II, 79–81} —: <403D§≡> (m, 71); ***NLE:*** ⟨7⟩ *Ṣabâḥ el-Khair*, No. 492 —: <403D§≡> (); ⟨8⟩ Farag, *Daqahliyyah*, 177–88 —: <403D§≡, P208.7.7§, + 1379, K1843 + 403/403D§,-cf./stp-mo, S31, B491.1. Σ: composite> (m, 20–22, u. stu., during childhood from maid); ***MGH:*** ⟨9⟩ Rivière, *Djurdjura*, 51–56 —: <403≡, P253, P253.1.1§,-cf., P426.0.3§, T17.5§, 403D§,-cf., K2212.1, M225, B451.4, E670 + G61 + B-S> (col. m).

36. The Cow of the Orphans (Egypt)

TYPE: **511A, *The Little Red Ox.* [Cow helps orphans (brother and sister).]**

Also see Type 480, Tale No. 32.

Motifs: M341.0.5§, "Person knows time of own death"; P253, "Sister and brother"; E323.2.1, "Dead mother (in animal [cow] form) returns to aid persecuted children"; B411, "Helpful cow"; B313.3§, "Helpful cow out of mother's grave"; B132.1§,

"Cow speaks to orphans"; B132, "Truth speaking cow"; B535.0.1, "Cow as nurse cares for children"; B733.0.1§, "Animals perceive supernatural beings (spirits) and supernatural acts"; K2056, "Hypocritical stepmother [. . .]"; P252.0.1§, "Sisters in conflict"; D830.1, "Attempt to learn about magic object by spying"; M295, "Bargain to keep secret"; K2212.1, "Treacherous stepsisters"; B115, "Animal with horn of plenty"; B335.2, "Life of helpful animal demanded as cure for feigned sickness"; K1514.11, "Illness feigned to call physician paramour"; K1996.1§, "Feigning illness by shamming physical symptoms: crackling bread under mattress to simulate crackling bones"; K1996.2§, "Feigning illness by shamming physical symptoms: saffron dye on face to simulate 'yellowness' (paleness) of death"; D1601.25.3.1§, "Cow cooks self"; D1318.7.3§, "Animal's flesh obeys only owner's commands"; E670.2§, "Repeated reincarnation: person (woman, mother, man) becomes cow, then tree, then fruit, etc."; D1472.1.3, "Magic tree supplies food."

Occurrences: 62 additional texts are available. The ratio of f:m narrators is 42:4. The following renditions were narrated by females (or children):

PEN: ⟨1⟩ al-Duwayk, *Qaṭar* I, 95–96 —: <511A≡+> (f, 105); ⟨2⟩ al-Duwayk, *Qaṭar* I, 97 —: <511A≡+ 1761*/1418,-cf., K1514.11, K1517.2, K451.3,-cf. + Q411.0.2. Σ: indiv., elements from Type 1418> (f, 25, u. stu.); ⟨3⟩ Noy, *Jefet,* 60–63, No. 17 —: <511A≡,-[511A,-cf. + 327A + 312E§,-cf., J226 + T9.1§ + E323 + D1610.6.4, R231 + 1121]:IIa, III + 327:IIc,d + 313:IIIa + 314A*> (f, 66, J); ⟨4⟩ Noy, *Jefet,* 83–84, No. 25 —: <511A≡,-cf. + B413> (f, 66, J); ***MSP:*** ⟨5⟩ Stevens, *Iraq,* 187–93, No. 36 {NK63} —: <511A≡,/no brother + T671 + 480:VI–VII + 510:IV–V> (f, mid-age?, Chr, non-litr., col. f, Euro.); ***SHM:*** ⟨6⟩ Gh. al-Ḥasan, "al-'urdunî," 225–26, No. 40 —: <511A≡, Σ: wrt> (f/c, 10); ⟨7⟩ Muhawi-Kanaana, *Speak,* 89–93, No. 7 —: <450≡+ 511A,/as-intro> (f, 70s); ***NLE:*** ⟨8⟩ Sulaymân, 155–56, No. V-02 —: <480≡+ 511A-pt. + D447.8.1§. Σ: -bones become cats-kill st-mo, supernatural beings> (f/c, 13, pupil); ⟨9⟩ Farag, *Daqahliyyah,* 238–42 —: <511A≡,-one girl + 480> (f, pupil, fa butcher, from gr-mo and pat-aunt); ⟨10⟩ Farag, *Daqahliyyah,* 189–98 —: <510≡/510A + F234.1.1, 511A:I,/jinni-cow. Σ: lit. influence> (f, 30s ?, non-litr., racont., wife of musician); ⟨11⟩ Abu-Lughod, *Bedouin,* 154–59 —: <511A≡+480> (f, ??, col. f); ***NLḌ:*** ⟨12⟩ Hurreiz, *Ja¿aliyyîn,* 117, No. 46 —: <511A≡, Σ: "ḥujwa," abstr.> (m/c, 10, pupil); ⟨13⟩ al-Zayn, *Musabba¿ât,* 80–84 —: <511A≡> (f, presum. adult); ***MGH:*** ⟨14⟩ Amrouche, *Le grain,* 55–62, No. 6 —: <511A≡+ 450> (f, adult, Chr-presum., auth.-col., from mo); ⟨15⟩ Légey, *Marrakech,* 19–23, No. 3 —: <510A≡+ 511A,/as-intro + 403,-cf., D40.2> (f, presum. adult and f, elder, slave).

Other Rendition(s): ***NLE:*** ⟨16⟩ Hassan, *In-Nâs,* 18–20 —: <480≡:pt. + 511A,-pt.> (m, élite, narrator-writer, replicating fem. style); ***MGH:*** ⟨17⟩ Rivière, *Djurdjura,* 67–70 —: <511A≡, M256.0.4§, P263.2§,-cf., P17.0.5.1§, P798.1.0.5§> (col. m); ⟨18⟩ El-Fasi-Dermenghem, *fasis* II, 69–73, [No. 7] —: <510A≡> (); ⟨19⟩ Laoust, *Maroc,* 140–42, No. 93 —: <154A§≡+ 511A:I/as-intro> (m, adult).

37. The Green He-sparrow (Egypt)

TYPE: **720, *My Mother Slew Me; My Father Ate Me. The Juniper Tree.* The boy's bones transformed into a bird.**

Motifs: P253, "Sister and brother"; S31, "Cruel stepmother"; S31.4.1§, "Stepmother (co-wife) kills co-wife's son"; D950, "Magic tree"; E607.1, "Bones of dead collected and buried. Return in another form directly from grave"; K1856.1.2§, "Wife serves her husband flesh of his (or, her) own son"; G61, "Relative's flesh eaten unwittingly"; G61.1.2§, "Sister evades eating her brother's flesh"; E631, "Reincarnation in plant (tree) growing from grave"; E613.0.1, "Reincarnation of murdered child as bird"; S22, "Parricide"; E232.1, "Return from the dead to slay own murderer"; S20.5§, "Child kills both parents"; P200.0.2.1§, "Father is powerless"; Z84.4.6§, "Insult: pimp"; E326, "Dead brother's friendly return."

Occurrences: 46 additional texts are available. The ratio of f:m narrators is 19:5. The following renditions were narrated by females (or children):

MSP: ⟨1⟩ Muḥammad I. ¿Abd-al-Ḥamd, *Turâth* IV:7, 113–14, No. 3 —: <136A*≡+ 1442§ + 720, E63> (f, 70, col., M.I. ¿Abbûd); ***SHM:*** ⟨2⟩ Gh. al-Ḥasan, "al-'urdunî," 227–28, No. 41 —: <720≡872§,-cf./psych.-pattern + 318B§/405-fin, E21,-cf., D765.1.2> (f/c, 10, pupil-currently in Libya); ⟨3⟩ Muhawi-Kanaana, *Speak,* 98–102, No. 9 —: <720≡> (f, 55); ⟨4⟩ Schmidt-Kahle, *Palästina* I, 186–89, No. 49 {NK314} —: <720≡, Σ: "Märchen"> (f, adult); ⟨5⟩ Bergsträsser, *Neuaramäische,* 101, No. 31 —: <720≡> (m/c, 13, Chr, presum. from mo, col. H. Stumme); ***NLE:*** ⟨6⟩ Sulaymân, 154, No. V-01 —: <720≡+ Σ: social-supernatural beings> (f/c, 13, pupil); ***MGH:*** ⟨7⟩ Amrouche, *Le grain,* 107–109, No. 11 —: <720≡+ W125.2 + S12.2.0.1§ + P230.10.1§, P230.7.1§, P140.0.3§, Q171.0.1.1§> (f, adult, Chr-presum., auth.-col., from mo).

Other Rendition(s): ***MSP:*** ⟨8⟩ K. Sa¿d-al-Dîn, *¿Irâqiyyah,* 34 —: <136A*≡+ 720. Σ: abstr.> (); ***SHM:*** ⟨9⟩ al-Aswad, *shâmiyyah,* 345–47 —: <720≡> (); ⟨10⟩ Sâ¿î, *Lâdhiqiyyah,* 219–21, No. 51[+1], =[173, No. C-1] —: <720≡> (); ***NLE:*** ⟨11⟩ AUC: 1, No. 2 —: <720≡> (m, 22, gardener, from mo ten yrs earlier, col. f).

38. Brother Deer (Libya)

TYPE: **450, *Little Brother and Little Sister.* [Brother transformed into deer (he-goat, kid).]**

Motifs: P253, "Sister and brother"; Z66.4.1§, "Endearment: to be referred to (or addressed) in the diminutive"; S10, "Cruel parents"; S272.3§, "Flight of brother and sister from home to avoid being sacrificed"; N773.2, "Adventure from returning for forgotten comb"; D114.1.1, "Transformation: man to deer"; D134, "Transformation: man to goat (he-goat, she-goat, kid, etc.)"; D555.3§, "Transformation by drinking from well (spring)"; P253.2, "Sister faithful to transformed brother"; T52.11.1§, "Sister marries to save brother(s)"; K2222, "Treacherous co-wife (concubine)"; K832.1.2§, "Victim persuaded to sit in position of honor at center. Seat is on mouth of well concealed with mat: victim falls in"; S432.1§, "Pregnant woman cast into well by jealous rivals"; F555.3.4, "Rapid growth of hair as protection against being seen nude"; S453.1§, "Exposed woman helped by clergyman"; T581.2.0.1§, "Child born of woman abandoned in well; she nurses him in water"; B313, "Helpful animal an enchanted person"; B335.2, "Life of helpful animal demanded as cure for feigned sickness"; P253.2.1, "Brother faithful to persecuted sister"; R141, "Rescue from well"; P253.2.3§, "Transformed brother (deer) about to be slaughtered pleads with sister for help; she had been exposed and is helpless"; Q432.0.1§, "Divorce as punishment"; P529.3.0.1§, "Triple (three-fold) divorce oath: one oath intended to be irrevocable"; Q171.0.2§, "Attempted murder unpunished (forgiven)."

Occurrences: 36 additional texts are available. The ratio of f:m narrators is 17:5. The following renditions were narrated by females (or children):

PEN: ⟨1⟩ al-Bâṭinî, *al-ḥikâyât,* 36–41, No. 5 —: <450≡, K2212.2.1§> (f, auth.-col., from f kin); ⟨2⟩ al-Duwayk, *Qaṭar* I, 147 —: <450≡+ 705A§:I/709A:I/860A* + 450. Σ: abstr., atypical combo> (f, 30, emply.); ⟨3⟩ al-Duwayk, *Qaṭar* II, 260–61 —: <450≡, Σ: fantasy-tale, not "belief tale"> (f, 25, u. stu.); ⟨4⟩ al-Duwayk, *Qaṭar* II, 262–63 —: <450≡,-cf.-elements. Σ: not "belief tale"> (f, 105); ***SHM:*** ⟨5⟩ Muhawi-Kanaana, *Speak,* 89–93, No. 7 —: <450≡+ 511A,/as-intro> (f, 70s); ⟨6⟩ al-Sârîs, *al-filisṭînî,* 137–41 —: <450≡+ 705A§:pt.-2, mother-son incest> (f, 40); ***NLE:*** ⟨7⟩ Sulaymân, 63–64, No. I-06 —: <450≡, D134,/he-goat. Σ: "khurâfiyyah"/nonsense> (f, 72, non-litr., wed-); ***MGH:*** ⟨8⟩ Amrouche, *Le grain,* 55–62, No. 6 —: <511A≡+ 450> (f, adult, Chr-presum., auth.-col., from mo); ⟨9⟩ Laoust, *Chenoua,* 173–78, No. 13 —: <450≡511A + 450> (m/c, 13).

Other Rendition(s): ***PEN:*** ⟨10⟩ Hein-Müller, *Mehri-Ḥadramî: SAE* IX 99–105, No. 39 {NK138b} —: <450≡> (m, youth, soldier); ***MSP:*** ⟨11⟩ K. Saʿd-al-Dîn, *Turâth* III:10, 17 —: <450≡+ N365.3, T415 + 932C§,-cf., K1843.5§. Σ: abstr.> (); ***NLĐ:*** ⟨12⟩ Shahi-Moore, *Nile,* 71–75, No. 7 —: <872A§≡= B441.1 + 545,-cf. + 450,-pt./in-well. Σ: wrt.> (col. pupil); ***MGH:*** ⟨13⟩ Cohen, *Tunis,* 85–89 {NK138a: AT450} —: <450≡+ 409B§,-elem.> ().

39. An Ivory Bed and a Glass Bed (Yemen)

TYPE: **872B§, *The Murdered Sister is Reincarnated and Betrothed to her Brother: the Talking Bed.* + 318B§, *Murdered Person (Lover, Husband, Brother) Brought Back to Life through Repeated Reincarnations (Transformations).* + 674A§, *Brother-sister Incest Averted: Talking Bed (or other Bedroom Items) Warns.***

Motifs: P253, "Sister and brother"; T591.5§, "Pregnancy induced by abnormal means (magic, philtre, potion, etc.)"; K2212.2.0.1§, "Magic pregnancy induced by treacherous sister-in-law to discredit husband's sister"; K2178§, "Virgin made to look pregnant. Magic potion (snake's eggs, etc.) used"; K2112.0.1§, "Innocent (chaste) maiden slandered"; P253.1.1§, "Brother as guardian of his sister's chastity (sexual-honor)"; Q411.0.3.1§, "Brother kills unchaste sister"; E631.0.5, "Tree from innocent man's blood"; E631, "Reincarnation in plant (tree) growing from grave"; D1648.1, "Tree bends to certain person"; E631.0.4, "Speaking and bleeding trees"; D481§, "Supernatural stretching and contraction of an object (tree, cliff, etc.)"; E670.2§, "Repeated reincarnation: person (woman, mother, man) becomes cow, then tree, then fruit, etc."; N365.3.1, "Brother and sister unwittingly in love with each other"; T111.3, "Marriage of man with woman who has come from an egg"; H175, "Recognition by force of nature. Unknown member of family immediately and magically [(mystically)] recognized"; H175.7§, "Blood-relative mystically recognized: 'Blood's yearning,' 'Blood's howling'"; T160, "Consummation of marriage"; D1610.17, "Speaking bed"; N681.3.2, "Man in love with his sister accidentally learns her identity"; N681.3.0.2§, "Incest accidentally averted: talking bed"; T415.4, "Two lovers give each other up when they learn that they are brother and sister"; Q432.0.1§, "Divorce as punishment."

Occurrences: 5 additional texts are available. The ratio of f:m narrators is 3:0. The following renditions were narrated by females (or children):

PEN: ⟨1⟩ al-Duwayk, *Qaṭar* II 182 —: <872B§≡+ E600. ∑: fragment, "khurâfiyyah"/nonsense> (f, 25, u. stu.); ⟨2⟩ Noy, *Jefet*, 129–31, No. 41 —: <872B§≡[] + 408:V,VI + 622 + S55, D1610.17, T415.4> (f, 66, J); ⟨3⟩ Sengo, "Kiswahili," 919–36, No. 38 —: <408≡+ 310,-cf.,-as intro + 872B§,/318B§,-cf. ∑: transformed> (f, sch. dropout, wed).
Other Rendition(s): *PEN:* ⟨4⟩ ¿Abduh, *yamaniyyah*, 111–17 —: <872B§≡+ 318B§,-cf. +> (); ⟨5⟩ Shahâb, *al-yamanî*, 111–15 —: <872B§≡+> ().

40. Snakes in the Sister's Belly (Algeria, Berber)

TYPE: **872A1§, *Snakes in the Sister's Belly.*** + **312F§, *Sister Rescues Infant (Fetus) Brother with Help from Kindly Animal.*** + **285B*, *Snake Enticed out of Man's Stomach.* Patient fed salt: animal comes out for water.**

Motifs: S11, "Cruel father"; S62, "Cruel husband"; R226§, "Flight from home so as to escape wrath of patriarch (father, husband)"; F956.7.7.1.1.2§, "Mother places self between her child (son, daughter) and father's (her husband's) wrath"; F1045, "Night spent in tree"; N382.3§, "Fugitive in tree urinates thus betraying hiding place"; R351.1.2§, "Urine drops from fugitive on lion (wild beast) and reveals fugitive's hiding place in tree"; G443.1.1§, "Ogre kills pregnant woman, spares fetus and adopts it"; G72.3.1§, "Sister raises infant brother on slain mother's marrow (flesh)"; P253.0.3§, "A sister's sacrifices (sufferings) for her brother's welfare"; P254.0.1§, "Household composed of only brother and sister(s)"; P263.2§, "Bad relations between brother and his sister's husband (brother-in-law)"; K2212.2.0.1§, "Magic pregnancy induced by treacherous sister-in-law to discredit husband's sister"; K2178§, "Virgin made to look pregnant. Magic potion (snake's eggs, etc.) used"; T511.7.2.1§, "Conception from swallowing snake egg"; N711, "King (prince) accidentally finds maiden and marries her"; B784.2.1, "Patient fed salt: animal comes out for water"; H1381.2.2.3§, "Boy twitted with rootlessness seeks unknown *khâl* (maternal-uncle)"; H11.1, "Recognition by telling life history"; F942.3.1, "Earth opens at woman's bidding to enclose her"; Q552.2.3.5§, "Treacherous person sinks into earth (swallowed by earth)"; R219.3§, "Person sinking into earth pulled out by rescuer"; P253.8, "Clever sister saves life of brother."

Occurrences: 12 additional texts are available. The ratio of f:m narrators is 4:2. The following renditions were narrated by females (or children):

NLE: ⟨1⟩ Sulaymân, 65–66, No. I-07 —: <872A1§≡, ∑: "khurâfiyyah"/nonsense> (f, 74, widow, from Plstn, w/6 children, farmer/herb-healer); ***MGH:*** ⟨2⟩ al-Baqlûṭî, *Tûnis*, 92–97, Fr. tr. p. 122 —: <327H§≡+ 872A1§. ∑: atypical combo> (f, adult); ⟨3⟩ Amrouche, *Le grain*, 139–48, No. 15 —: <872A1§≡+ 312F§ + 285B*> (f, adult, Chr-presum., auth.-col., from mo); ⟨4⟩ Galley, *Badr az-Zên*, 30–59, No. 1 —: <872A1§≡+ 285B*/as-intro + 451A> (f, mid-aged, lit., col. Euro. f).

41. Clever Ḥasan's Sister (Syria)

TYPE: **872X§, *The Pregnant Girl (Sister) is Aided by her Brother's Wife (Sister-in-law) in Finding the Father of her Illegitimate Child.* + Cf. 850*, *Through the Girl's Mistake the Youth Comes to her Room at Night.***

Motifs: P253, "Sister and brother"; P779.1.1§, "Imported fine textile (cloth)"; T101.1.6.1.1§, "Bride in the likeness of groom's sister"; K1523, "Underground passage [(tunnel)] to paramour's house. (Inclusa.) Woman goes from one to the other"; N770, "Experiences leading to adventures"; N793§, "Adventures from entering pit, hole, cave, or crack (in ground)"; T475, "Unknown (clandestine) paramour"; T35, "Lovers' rendezvous"; T400, "Illicit sexual relations"; T59.2.1§, "Accidental defloration (impregnation)"; T640, "Illegitimate children"; H51, "Recognition by scar"; H56, "Recognition by wound"; H111, "Identification by garment"; P264.2§, "Kindly brother's wife (sister-in-law): aids husband's sister"; S351, "Abandoned child cared for by mother secretly"; T192.3§, "Marriage due to girl's (premarital) pregnancy."

Occurrences: 17 additional texts are available. The ratio of f:m narrators is 13:1. The following renditions were narrated by females (or children):

PEN: ⟨1⟩ AGSFC: BHR 86-4, 13-x-xxxx **—:** <872X§≡> (f, 55, lit.); ⟨2⟩ AGSFC: QTR 87-3ff., 680-?-119-49 **—:** <872X§≡> (f, 70, wed to Qatari); ***SHM:*** ⟨3⟩ AUC: 11, No. 1 **—:** <872X§≡,-cf.> (f, 70s, Chr, in Aleppo from f friend, col. f); ***MGH:*** ⟨4⟩ al-Baqlûṭî, *Tûnis,* 56–61, Fr. tr. p. 86 **—:** <872X§≡+ 850*,-cf.> (f, adult).

Other Rendition(s): *PEN:* ⟨5⟩ al-Bâṭinî, *nisâ'iyyah,* 94–95, No. 24 **—:** <872X§≡> (); ⟨6⟩ al-Bâṭinî, *nisâ'iyyah,* 96–98, No. 25 **—:** <872X§≡,-pt. 1. ∑: fragment> (); ***NLE:*** ⟨7⟩ Littmann, *Ägypten,* pt. I, 56–60, No. 10 {NK87a} **—:** <872X§≡+ 850*,-cf. + 1419E,-cf. ∑: wrt.> (m, adult, after his gr-mo).

42. One Garment for a Man and His Sister (Sudan)

TYPE: **751H§, *Only One Garment (Shirt) in the Household: to be Worn Alternately.* + Cf. 461A, *The Journey to the Deity for Advice or Repayment.* [Sick beast is to eat brain of a stupid man for cure.]**

Motifs: P253.2.0.1.1§, "'He who has no sister is an orphan'"; P254.0.1§, "Household composed of only brother and sister(s)"; T405.3§, "Sister's nakedness or exposure"; N131, "Acts performed for changing luck"; V214§, "Moses as prophet (founder)"; H1263, "Quest to God for fortune"; H1388, "Quest: answer to certain question"; Q68.2, "Honesty rewarded"; P253.6.1§, "Sister always consulted by her brother and her counsel sought"; N534.1.1§, "Treasure discovered by following an animal"; W25.1, "Equanimity of the enslaved unfortunate. Does not complain when beset by series of misfortunes"; U62.1.2§, "Brother and sister so poor that they own only one shirt"; U62.1.1§, "Husband and wife so poor that they own only one shirt"; Q64, "Patience rewarded"; Q22.1§, "Placing one's faith in God alone rewarded"; V318.2§, "'Only God is to be thanked for an affliction (*makrûh:* a disliked matter, seeming harm).'"

Occurrences: 3 additional texts are available. The ratio of f:m narrators is 1:1. The following rendition was narrated by females (or children):

NLE: ⟨1⟩ CFMC: Ṣawâm¿ah 71-1, 8-2-2 —: <751H§≡, P210 + 461A:I–II> (f, 50s).

Other Rendition(s): ***NLE:*** ⟨2⟩ Ḥ. El-Khoalî, "al-furûq al-rîfiyyah-al-ḥaḍariyyah," 334–40 —: <971C§≡,-cf. + 751H§,-cf./brother-sister = P253.9, E405§, T405.3§, T24.3. Σ: local saint's legend> (); ⟨3⟩ CFMC: Ṣawâm¿ah 71-1, 8-1-2 —: <751H§≡, P253 + 461A:I–II> (m, 61, fruit vendor).

43. The Death of *Shaikhah* Shafîqah's Brother (Egypt)

TYPE: **971C§, *Insanity (Death) from Death of Beloved Sibling (Brother, Sister).* + Cf. 751H§, *Only One Garment (Shirt) in the Household: to be Worn Alternately.***

> Motifs: V220.0.4§, "Woman saint"; Z183.6§, "'Mother-of- . . . '" (*'Omm/'Umm- . . .*); F1041.8.2, "Madness from grief"; E405.1§, "Vanishing (elusive) corpse"; P253.3.1§, "Sister favors brother over her husband"; P253.9.1§, "Sister becomes insane due to death of brother"; T405.3§, "Sister's nakedness or exposure"; N384.0.2§, "Insanity (loss of senses) due to calamity or fright."

Occurrences: 3 additional texts are available from contemporary traditions. The ratio of f:m narrators is 1:2.

NLE: ⟨1⟩ Ḥ. El-Khoalî, "al-furûq al-rîfiyyah-al-ḥaḍariyyah," 334–40 —: <971C§≡,-cf., 751H§,-cf./brother-sister = P253.9, E405§, T405.3§, T24.3. Σ: local saint's legend> (); ***MGH:*** ⟨2⟩ Noy, *Moroccan*, 33, No. 2 —: <971C§≡, V374§ +, {Noy: "1824*E"}. Σ: legend> (m, J, from m-fisher).

Other Rendition(s): ***SHM:*** ⟨3⟩ HE-S: Plstn 69-3, No. 7 —: <971C§≡+751H§,-cf., Σ: saint's legend> (m, adult). Cf. ⟨4⟩ Basset, *Mille* III, 466–67, No. 283 —: <971C§≡,-cf., P254.0.1§, P253.9, M341.0.5§ + P486§, P253.11.5§, V68.4.2§, V68.7§, V61.12.1§ Σ: memorate, lit., {after al-'Ibshîhî}> (m, pres. adult, from male, undertaker).

44. My Daughter Is My Son's Wife (Syria)

TYPE: **932B§, *A Mother's own Daughter as her Daughter-in-law; Bride Behaves as a Daughter-in-law.* Brother-sister marriage (sister as wife).**

> Motifs: T415.5, "Brother-sister marriage"; T415.5.1.1§, "Mother weds own daughter to own son"; P262.2§, "Even when a woman's very own daughter becomes her daughter-in-law, she is hostile to her mother-in-law (her own mother)"; P262.1, "Bad relations between mother-in-law and daughter-in-law."

Occurrences: 5 additional texts are available. The ratio of f:m narrators is 2:1. The following renditions were narrated by females (or children):

SHM: ⟨1⟩ ¿Abd-al-Hâdî, *kharârîf*, 202–4, No. 47 —: <932B§≡/, -make believe> (f, 40s).

Other Rendition(s): ***MSP:*** ⟨2⟩ Ms.?/Ni¿mah Mahdî al-Sâ¿idî, *Turâth* IV:11, 110–18 —:

<936A§≡= 932B§,-cf., 470E§,-cf., R224.1§ + 973 + 612B§ + R212.1.1, 1900,-cf. Σ: frame> (col. f?).

45. Son, Husband, or Brother? (Yemen)

TYPE: **985, *Brother Chosen Rather than Husband or Son.***

Motifs: P12.2.2.1§, "al-Ḥajjâj as tyrant"; P12.2.2§, "Tyrannical viceroy (or minister)"; P506.3§, "Rebellion against government"; Q218.1§, "Rebellion against government (ruler, king, etc.) punished"; J226, "Difficult choices between relatives"; P253.3, "Brother chosen rather than husband or son"; P798.1.0.5§, "Triads revolving around brother and sister as unbalanced (Sethian syndrome)"; P798.1.1§, "Conflict within a triad: one party is removed so as to restore stability (balance)"; Z19.3§, "Etiological tales: 'That-is-why'-tales."

Occurrences: 3 additional texts are available. The ratio of f:m narrators is 1:1. The following renditions were narrated by females (or children):

NLÐ: ⟨1⟩ Kronenberg, *Nubische*, 196–206, No. 42 **—:** <857§≡/516F§ = T257.0.2§, T562 + H506.9 + 884C§ + 985,-cf. {Ranke: "00"}> (f, 35).

Other Rendition(s): *NLE:* ⟨2⟩ Taymûr, *al-'amthâl*, 186, No. 986 **—:** <985≡, Σ: folk prov., lit. narrative, abstract> (); ⟨3⟩ HE-S: Cairo 1985 **—:** <985≡, Σ: lit.> (m, 28, engin., read in magazine).

46. Fair Fâṭmah (Sudan)

TYPE: **313E*, *Girl Flees from Brother who Wants to Marry her.* + 1180, *Catching Water in a Sieve.* + 1119, *The Ogre Kills his Own Children.* Places changed in bed—(nightcaps). + 533A§, *Beautiful Maiden in Hideous Disguise:* She is detected by the prince. (Khushayshibûn, Kashabân, Galadânah, Gulaidah, etc.)**

Motifs: T11.4.1, "Love through sight of hair of unknown princess"; F555.3, "Very long hair"; H75, "Identification by hair"; T415.1, "Lecherous brother"; T415.2.1§, "Sister repels incestuous brother"; H310.2, "Brother unwittingly qualifies as bridegroom of sister in test"; N365.3.3§, "Boy finds a woman's hair and decides to marry the person to whom it belongs: it is his sister's"; M139§, "Vow to marry only a person fitting certain description (size, color, etc.)"; T311.1, "Flight of maiden (bridegroom) to escape marriage"; T415.5.1§, "Parents approve (arrange) marriage between their son and daughter (brother-sister)"; R224, "Girl flees to escape incestuous brother"; Z41.11§, "Climax of relatives. (Ascending series of relations)"; G412, "Children lured into ogre's house"; G412.3§, "Ogre's (ogress's) fire lures person"; G82.3.1§, "'Ogress's mash'. Fodder made of ground bones and ogress's milk, used to fatten victims"; G634.3.1§, "Open eyes as indication of ogre's deep sleep"; G565§, "Escape from ogre (ogress, witch, etc.)"; K550.3§, "Captor busied with performing task while captive escapes"; H1023.2, "Task: carrying water in sieve"; K605, "Cannibal sent for water with vessel full of holes: victim escapes"; K1611,

"Substituted caps [sleeping places] cause ogre to kill his own children"; R232§, "Lure flight: pursuer causes precious objects to appear before fugitive which the fugitive stops to pick up"; R245.1.1§, "Crocodile ferry. Fugitives are carried across the water on crocodile"; K455.4.4§, "Fugitives promise predator (crocodile) one of them as payment for helping them escape pursuer: predator deceived into eating pursuer as fee"; G519.6§, "Ogre (ogress) delivered as food to another predator (ogre)"; K1941, "Disguised flayer. An imposter dresses in the skin of his victim"; K1816.5, "Disguise as goose-girl (turkey-girl)"; F575.1.5.9.1§, "Remarkably small foot"; K521.1.4, "Escape by putting on old woman's skin"; T194§, "Marriage by abduction (or raid)"; H151.12, "Geese tell of beauty of their mistress and bring about recognition"; K780.2§, "Winner of game is to disrobe loser: person masking as of other sex is thus discovered"; K2010.4§, "Treacherous one-time winner. Loses repeatedly and is forgiven, but refuses to yield when finally wins."

46-1. "If I Am Your Sister, I Can't Become Your Wife" (Egypt)

TYPE: **313E***.

Motifs: Z41.11.1§, "That which a kin-woman may not be: 'If I'm your daughter, [O father,] I cannot be your son's wife!' 'If I'm your daughter, [O mother,] I cannot be your son's wife!' 'If I'm your sister, [O sister,] I cannot be your brother's wife!' 'If I'm your sister, [O brother,] I cannot be your wife!'"; T405.3§, "Sister's nakedness or exposure"; Z186.4.2.1§, "Symbolism: kneading—erotic act"; R311, "Tree refuge"; D481.1§, "Mountain (hill, tree, etc.) stretches to put fugitive beyond pursuers' reach"; H1385.6, "Quest for lost sister"; D1576.1, "Magic song causes tree to rise to sky"; Z41.11§, "Climax of relatives. (Ascending series of relations)"; Z10.2, "End formulas."

46-2. Ḥasanain and 'Ûliyya (Egypt)

TYPE: **313E***.

Motifs: Z183.0.1§, "Meaning of a name"; cf. Z119.3.2§, "Rules of grammar as symbols of erotic action."

46-3. [The Sister's Shoe] (Egypt)

TYPE: **313E***.

Motifs: T101.1.6.1.1§, "Bride in the likeness of groom's sister"; H365.1§, "Bride test: size of feet to match sister's"; M139.1§, "Vow to marry only a girl whom a certain object (shoe, bracelet, etc.) would fit"; H36.1, "Slipper test: identification by fitting of slipper"; Z186.4.3§, "Symbolism: wearing (putting on) garment or shoe—sexual intercourse."

Occurrences: 30 additional texts are available. The ratio of f:m narrators is 12:4. The following renditions were narrated by females (or children):

PEN: ⟨1⟩ AGSFC: QTR 87-3ff., 679-?-237-63 —: <313E*≡,-cf. + T145.0.3§ + R156 + 312,-cf. Σ: likely: transformed rendition, incestuous theme missing> (f, 30, u grad, wed, teacher, col. f); ***SHM:*** ⟨2⟩ al-Sârîs, *al-filisṭînî,* 161–63 —: <510B≡/313E*,-cf./psych.-pattern, T411.1, R223§, K551.16 + 1600A§ + 313E*,-cf. + G90.5§,-cf., K512.1.2§, K1874.1§ + S22, P254.1.2§, Q242.2.1§, J1913.1§, K812, K955.1, K891.1.1§,-cf. Σ: patterned combo> (f, ??); ***NLĐ:*** ⟨3⟩ Kronenberg, *Nubische,* 44–50, No. 10 —: <313E*≡/510C§ + H522.1.1,/mot.-only + G82.3.1§ + R245.1.1§ + 1119 + 533A§ + {Ranke: + "621 + 327B + 533"}> (f, 35); ⟨4⟩ Kronenberg, *Nubische,* 50–54, No. 11 —: <313E*≡/510C§ -Ring + 1180 + 1119 + R231,-cf. + 533A§, K1941 {Ranke: 327B + 1180 + 533}> (f, 65); ⟨5⟩ Hurreiz, *Ja¿aliyyîn,* 83–85, No. 8 —: <313E*≡, Σ: "ḥujwa," "0510B" [??]> (f, 50, widow, social focal point); ⟨6⟩ ¿A. ¿A. Ibrâhîm, "Rubâṭâb," No. 07 —: <313E*≡+ 318B§,-cf.,/990*,-cf., S139.2, E422.1.10, E1.3.1§, T510.1.1§ + 706,-cf.+ 705A§,-cf./pt.2, K2222, D454.1.3§. Σ: abstr.> (f, 45–47, co-wife, farmer); ***MGH:*** ⟨7⟩ Houri-Pasotti, *Ghazala,* 95–97, No. 42 —: <313E*≡+ T415,/implicit. Σ: lgnd?> (f, J, elder, to f col., gr-dgh).

Other Rendition(s): ***NLE:*** ⟨8⟩ Aḥmad, *al-Nûbah,* 21–32 —: <313E*≡,-??> (); ***NLĐ:*** ⟨9⟩ von Massenbach, *Nubische,* pt. B.VIII, 163–65, No. 42 —: <313E*,-cf./cousin≡+ 533A§ + K1941. Σ: defensively told??, Oedipal?> (m, presum. adult); ⟨10⟩ ¿A. al-Ṭayyib, *sûdâniyyah,* 58–68, No. 8 —: <313E*≡313H*,-cf.> (); ⟨11⟩ S. Jahn, *Arabische,* 166–78, No. 21 —: <313E*≡+ 313H*> ({Ṭayyib, pt. 5, p. 25}); ⟨12⟩ Shahi-Moore, *Nile,* 110–14, No. 20 —: <313E*≡, Σ: wrt.> (col. pupil); ⟨13⟩ Shahi-Moore, *Nile,* 114–18, No. 21 —: <313E*≡, Σ: wrt.> (col. pupil); ⟨14⟩ Shahi-Moore, *Nile,* 118–20, No. 22 —: <313E*≡+ 510,-cf.-dancing. Σ: wrt.> (col. pupil); ⟨15⟩ Shahi-Moore, *Nile,* 120–25, No. 23 —: <313E*≡, Σ: wrt.> (col. pupil); ***MGH:*** ⟨16⟩ Delheure, *Ouargla,* 68–73 —: <313E*≡+ 706C> (??, 15, col. in 1950); ⟨17⟩ Frobenius, *Kabylen* III, 118–21, No. 30 —: <313E*≡+ 706C + B451.5 + D2064.5, M424.1§, 713A§,-cf.> (); ⟨18⟩ Savignac, *Kabylie,* 159–61, No. 23 —: <313E*≡+ 872*,-cf.> (m?, x); ⟨19⟩ Galley-Sinaceur, *marocains,* 15–17, Fr. tr. 85, No. 3. —: <313E*≡/"510B", N365.3.3§, T11.4.1 + N134.0.1.3§, 713A§,-cf., Q552.3.0.5§,-cf. + 450, D555.3§, D113.4, P253.2.3§, T101.1.6.1.1§. Σ: composite, hero's name typically associated with AT 310> (col. Euro., Mr. G. S. Colin).

47. Wdai¿ah: The Sister of the Seven (Libya; Egypt, Western Desert)

TYPE: **451A, *The Sister Seeking her Nine Brothers.* [Substitute sister.]**

Motifs: P253.0.1.2§, "Brother(s) need(s) a sister (be born)"; Z71.5, "Formulistic number: seven"; T595, "Sign hung out informing brothers whether mother has borne boy or girl"; N344.1, "Wrong sign put out leads to boys' leaving home"; K2293, "Treacherous old woman"; S272.1.1§, "Flight of brothers from home due to treachery"; Z141.3.1§, "Red as symbol of evil (danger, drought, etc.)"; S73.0.3.3§, "Flight of brother(s) from home due to reported birth of another brother, rather than a sister"; Z71.5.1, "Seven brothers and one sister"; D1312.5§, "Magic bead gives advice from mother"; H1385.8, "Quest for lost brother(s)"; K2261.0.1§, "Treacherous [black woman]"; K1934, "Imposter forces heroine to change places with her";

D591, “Transformation by immersing in magic well”; D30, “Transformation to person of different race”; D31, “Transformation: white person to Negro”; D32§, “Transformation: black person to white”; D766.1, “Disenchantment by bathing (immersing) in water”; H12, “Recognition by song”; B299.5.2, “Animal fasts to express sympathy”; H1587§, “Test of race: black person has kinky hair”; H76§, “Black woman turned white supernaturally is recognized: she still has kinky hair”; Z65.3§, “White as milk (cheese)”; Q414, “Punishment: burning alive.”

47-1. [We Need a Sister] (Algeria, Kabyle)

TYPE: **451A.**

Motifs: S139.2.0.1§, “Ghoulish trophy: part of enemy’s corpse kept and displayed (or put to use)”; S139.2.1.1, “Head of murdered man taken along as trophy”; Q491, “Indignity to corpse as punishment.”

Occurrences: 23 additional texts are available. The ratio of f:m narrators is 9:3. The following renditions were narrated by females (or children):

SHM: ⟨1⟩ ¿Abd-al-Hâdî, *kharârîf,* 29–34, No. 8 **—:** <451A≡> (f, 60); ⟨2⟩ ¿Abd-al-Hâdî, *kharârîf,* 15–18, No. 2 **—:** <451A≡, Σ: out of focus> (f, 70); ⟨3⟩ ¿Abd-al-Hâdî, *kharârîf,* 18–19, No. 3 **—:** <451A??≡,-cf. Σ: frag.> (f, 70); ⟨4⟩ Sirḥân, *min Filisṭîn,* 71–74 **—:** <451≡+ B17.1.5.1§, G332.1, E11.1, P253.5,-ogress + 451A, D133.3 + 450,-oxen, F911.4 + 405, D154.1> (f, 55); ***NLE:*** ⟨5⟩ Sulaymân, 52–53, No. I-02 **—:** <451≡+ 451A,-pt., H12. Σ: frag., distorted> (f, 74, non-litr., widow); ***NLÐ:*** ⟨6⟩ ¿A.¿A. Ibrâhîm, “Rubâṭâb,” No. 15 **—:** <451A≡> (f, 45–47, farmer); ⟨7⟩ al-Baqlûṭî, *Tûnis,* 85–87, Fr. tr. p. 115 **—:** <451A≡> (f); ***MGH:*** ⟨8⟩ Galley, *Badr az-Zên,* 30–59, No. 1 **—:** <872A1§≡+ 285B*/as-intro + 451A> (f, mid-aged, lit., col. Euro. f).

Other Rendition(s): ***MGH:*** ⟨9⟩ Stumme, *Tripolis,* 81–93, No. 2 {NK139:709 + 451A} **—:** <451A≡, K2218.5.1§, K252.4§, N464§, N464.1§ + B17.1.5.1§ + P253.11.2§, D765.1.2, 709:II–III, N730.1§,-(weep), Z71.5.1,-(united)> (); ⟨10⟩ Frobenius, *Kabylen* III, 129–33, No. 34 **—:** <451≡+ 451A> (); ⟨11⟩ Frobenius, *Kabylen* III, 133–37, No. 35 **—:** <451≡+ 451A> (); ⟨12⟩ Galley-Sinaceur, *marocains,* 11–14, Fr. tr. 75, No. 2. **—:** <451A≡, Σ: {“451B [??]”}> (??, col. Euro., Mr. G. S. Colin); ⟨13⟩ Laoust, *Chenoua,* 165–68, No. 10 **—:** <872A1§≡+ 451A,/as-intro + 285B*> (); ⟨14⟩ Laoust, *Maroc,* 159–61, No. 98 **—:** <451A??≡> (m, ?); ⟨15⟩ Rivière, *Djurdjura,* 45–49 **—:** <451A≡, K2216§, C106§ + S139.2.0.1§> (col. m).

48. The Monkey Wife (Sudan, Egypt)

TYPE: **402, *The Mouse (Cat, Frog, etc.) as Bride.* [Three brothers seek wives; youngest marries a she-monkey, (tortoise).] + Cf. 898:IV, *The Prince’s Marriage.* + 1442§, *Stupid Woman (Co-wife) is Deceived into Imitating Foolishly:* she kills her child.**

Motifs: H1301.1, “Quest for the most beautiful bride”; H1381.3.1.2, “Quest for bride for oneself”; T54.1§, “Choosing bride by lot (shooting arrow, throwing ball, etc.)”; N844, “Dervish as helper”; D1001, “Magic spittle”; B641.7, “Marriage to person in monkey form"; B601.7, "Marriage to monkey"; B601.7.1§, "Man marries female monkey"; L54.2§, "Youngest son agrees to marry monster; later the brothers are jealous"; P264.0.1§, "*salâyif* (women whose husbands are brothers, sisters-in-law)"; P264.0.1.1§, "Rivalry between a woman and her *silfah* (wife of husband's brother, sisters-in-law)"; U118.1§, "One's own spouse seems less attractive"; W195.9.2§, "Brother envies brother's beautiful wife (wives)"; D1935.3§, "Magic ability to perform any task"; H504.4§, "Contest in cooking (baking)"; K1045, "Dupe induced to oversalt (overpepper) food"; J2400, "Foolish imitation"; T55.6.4§, "Fashion display (fashion show): body exhibited in various complimentary dresses (costumes)"; D700, "Person disenchanted"; F575.1.6§, "Beauty that disorients (dazzles) the beholder"; T26.1, "Finger cut because of absorption in the charm of the beloved"; Q432.0.1§, "Divorce as punishment."

Occurrences: 30 additional texts are available. The ratio of f:m narrators is 17:2. The following renditions were narrated by females (or children):

PEN: ⟨1⟩ AGSFC: QTR 87-3ff., 699-1-No. 3 **—:** <402≡, Σ: fragment> (f, 53, non-litr., widow, col. f); ⟨2⟩ Daum, *Jemen,* 169–74, No. 19 **—:** <591A§≡+ 402,-cf. Σ: fragment, {Uther: 409A}> (f, 75, widow, non-litr.); ***SHM:*** ⟨3⟩ ¿Abd-al-Hâdî, *kharârîf,* 241–48, No. 59 **—:** <402≡+ 465 + 898:IV,/1442§> (f, 65); ***NLĐ:*** ⟨4⟩ Kronenberg, *Nubische,* 132–37, No. 30 **—:** <591A§≡,-lizard + 402-fin, T26.1> (f, 35); ⟨5⟩ Kronenberg, *Nubische,* 137–42, No. 31 **—:** <591A§≡+ K1335/400,-cf./feathers-stolen + 402,-cf. + 1442§,-cf./898,-fin {Ranke: 409A}> (f, 35); ***MGH:*** ⟨6⟩ Légey, *Marrakech,* 48–52, No. 9 **—:** <402≡,-cf. + 465A-pt., D361.1,-cf. N803.2§ + 516H§,-cf., W195.9.1§, 513C:II/467,-cf.> (f, elder, slave, from f-slave).

Other Rendition(s): ***NLE:*** ⟨7⟩ Artin, *Nil,* 103–14, No. 6 {NK173d, NK249a} **—:** <402≡+ 898:IV,-cf.> (); ⟨8⟩ Spitta, *modernes,* 43–60, No. 4 {NK252b, Budge, *Tales,* pt. 3, 328–39, No. 4} **—:** <402≡?> (m, cook, from f-"aunts"); ***NLĐ:*** ⟨9⟩ von Massenbach, *Nubische,* pt. B.VIII, 150, No. 38 **—:** <402≡+ 1442§/1387*:I> (m, presum. adult).

49. ¿Azîz Son of His Maternal-uncle (Bahrain, Qatar)

TYPE: **857§, *Nephew Wins a Bride for his Maternal-uncle: Abu-Zaid Gets ¿Alyâ.* + 932A§, *The Sister who Desires a Son Sired by her Brother Achieves her Goal: the Unsuspecting Brother.* + 970 (formerly 966**), *The Twining Branches.* + 844A§, *Search for Household not Touched by Grief (has not Known Sorrow).***

Motifs: L111.5.1§, "Child of brother-sister incest as hero: 'Son of own maternal-uncle' "; L113.1.8§, "Black man (black-slave) in 'white' nation (tribe) as hero. (¿Antar, Abu-Zaid, etc.)"; T415.8§, "Sister who desires a son sired by her brother achieves her goal: the unsuspecting brother"; K1315.5.2§, "Noble woman poses as prostitute"; K1843.5§, "Sister masks as her brother's wife and sleeps with him"; N365.3, "Unwitting brother-sister incest"; N365, "Incest unwittingly committed"; A511.1.3.2, "Demigod [culture hero] son of king's unmarried sister by her brother"; T296.1§, "Sister buys privilege of sleeping one night with her own brother"; T504.2.1§, "Pulling out at ejaculation to avoid impregnation"; F611.3.3.5§, "Strong hero tests riding-animals (horses, camels). Breaks backs of many"; H506.9, "Test of resourcefulness: to cook rice without fire"; P297.2.1§, "Bond between mother's brother (*khâl*) and sister's son"; H506.9.1§, "Test of resourcefulness: making coffee (tea) without water"; K514, "Disguise as girl to avoid execution"; K649.4.1§, "Son disguised as daughter in order to spare his life"; S71.3.4.1§, "A woman's brother kills her son(s) but spares daughter"; T11.1.1, "Beauty of woman reported to king causes quest for her as his bride"; K1817.3, "Disguise as harper (minstrel)"; T380.3.1§, "Certain (non-threatening) males are viewed as unworthy of woman's modesty (e.g., slave, singer, etc.)"; T380.3.1.1§, "Male singer allowed to perform for women in women's quarters"; K1349.1, "Disguise to enter girl's (man's) room"; K1371, "Bride-stealing"; F575.2, "Handsome man"; Z257, "Beardless hero"; T28, "Princess falls in love with a man disguised as a woman"; K1915, "The false bridegroom (substitute bridegroom)"; K1310, "Seduction by disguise or substitution"; K1371.1.2, "Lover's foster brother (friend) steals bride from wedding with unwelcome suitor"; K1321, "Seduction by man disguised as woman"; K1836.3, "Disguised man takes bride's place"; K1321.2, "Man disguised as woman abducts princess"; H51, "Recognition by scar"; H56, "Recognition by wound"; R225, "Elopement"; S71.3§, "Cruel maternal-uncle (*khâl*)"; T81, "Death from love"; T81.7, "Woman dies on hearing of lover's or husband's death"; S115.5.1§, "Suicide by falling on erect sword (dagger)"; H1394, "Quest for person who has not known sorrow"; J886§, "Greater grief: person seeks consolation in adversity"; J836§, "Man (woman) who loses all his (her) seven (forty, ninety-nine) sons at once seeks comfort"; H1394.1§, "Quest for person who has had more grief (chagrin, sorrow)"; E631.0.1, "Twin branches grow from graves of lovers"; A2324.3§, "Why camel has split lip"; A2701§, "Origin of plant name"; Z292.0.1.1§, "Tragic ending of a story (tale): all die."

Occurrences: 22 additional texts are available. The ratio of f:m narrators is 14:7. The following renditions were narrated by females (or children):

PEN: ⟨1⟩ AGSFC: BHR 86-4, 11-x-89 —: <857§≡932A§ + 857§,-cf. +> (f, 45, semi-litr., col. f); ⟨2⟩ AGSFC: Doha 85-4, 1-No. 9 —: <857§≡+ 884C§,-cf. + 844A§> (f, adult, to son-col.); ⟨3⟩ AGSFC: QTR 87-3ff., 748-x-No. 2 —: <857§≡+ 932A§ + 884C§ + 844A§. Σ: full text> (f, 42, elem. relig. ed. -but prob. non-litr., col. f); ⟨4⟩ al-Duwayk, *Qaṭar* II, 28 —: <857§≡+ 844A§. Σ: "folk-tale [!]" ?> (f, 25, u. stu.); ***NLĐ:*** ⟨5⟩ Kronenberg, *Nubische*, 196–206, No. 42 —: <857§≡/516F§ = T257.0.2§, T562 + H506.9 + 884C§ + 985,-cf. {Ranke: "00"}> (f, 35).

Other Rendition(s): ***PEN:*** ⟨6⟩ Müller, *Mehri-und Soqoṭri: SAE* IV, 60–68, No. A —: <850A*§≡,-cf./857§= 1545 + 1525U§ + 926E§/1617A§, J123 + H41.5 + P35 + 1525U§/1542:V. Σ: trickster> (m and/or his Bdw mo); ⟨7⟩ Rhodokanakis, *Ẓfâr: SAE* VIII, 50–52, No. 13 {NK105} —: <857§≡+ 932A§,/implicit + 884C§,-cf. + 970, K639§> (m, adult, Bdw, herb-garnerer); ***SHM:*** ⟨8⟩ Ritter, *Ṭûr ¿Abdîn* I.1.3, 250–305, No. 96 —: <315A1§≡/650A:I + 301 + A725/D2146 + 956 + 326 + 302 + 516 + 857§,-cf. Σ: composite> (m, b. 1910, Chr, farmer-shepherd).

49. TYPE: **932A§, *The Sister who Desires a Son Fathered by her Brother Achieves her Goal: the Unsuspecting Brother.***

Motifs: A511.1.3.2.1§, "Culture-hero son of sister by her brother"; T415, "Brother-sister incest"; T415.8§, "Sister who desires a son sired by her brother achieves her goal: the unsuspecting brother"; T504.2.1§, "Pulling out at ejaculation to avoid impregnation"; N365.3, "Unwitting brother-sister incest"; T471.1, "Man unwittingly ravishes his own sister"; K1315.5.2§, "Noble woman poses as prostitute"; K1310, "Seduction by disguise or substitution"; K1390.1§, "Man deceived into impregnating woman (fathering a child)"; K1843.5§, "Sister masks as her brother's wife and sleeps with him"; T296.1§, "Sister buys privilege of sleeping one night with her own brother"; K1390.1.2.1§, "Man tricked into ejaculating inside woman (by causing him to lose control)"; T59.2.1§, "Accidental defloration (impregnation)"; L111.5.1§, "Child of brother-sister incest as hero: 'Son of own maternal-uncle' "; P256§, "Brother forgives his (seemingly) culprit sister(s)"; P297.2.1§, "Bond between mother's brother (*khâl*) and sister's son"; Z183.2.1§, "Child's name reveals inexorable fate."

Occurrences: 4 additional texts are available. The ratio of f:m narrators is 2:2. The following renditions were narrated by females (or children):

PEN: ⟨1⟩ AGSFC: BHR 86-4, 11-x-89 —: <932A§≡+ 857§,-cf. Σ: implicit> (f, 45, semi-litr., col. f); ⟨2⟩ AGSFC: QTR 87-3ff., 748-x-No. 2 —: <857§≡+ 932A§ + 884C§,-cf. + 884A§> (f, 42, elem. relig. ed. -but prob. non-litr., col. f); ⟨3⟩ Rhodokanakis, *Ẓfâr: SAE* VIII, 50–52, No. 13 {NK105} —: <857§≡+ 932A§ implicit + 884C§,-cf. + 970> (m, adult, Bdw, herb-garnerer); ⟨4⟩ al-Duwayk, *Qaṭar* II, 26–27 —: <857§≡+ 932A§ + 884C§,-cf. + 844A§. Σ: "folk-tale [!]" ?> (m, 70); ***MSP:*** ⟨5⟩ K. Sa¿d-al-Dîn, *Turâth* III: 10, 17 —: <450≡+ N365.3, T415 + 932C§,-cf., K1843.5§. Σ: abstr.> ().

+ TYPE: **932C§,** ***Paternal-cousins (or Foster Brother and Sister) Commit Adultery (Fornication).***

Motifs: T416.8§, "Adultery (sexual liaison) between *'ibn-¿amm* and his *bint-¿amm* (paternal-cousins)."

Occurrences: 5 additional texts are available. The ratio of f:m narrators is 0:3. The following renditions were narrated by males or unspecified informants:

PEN: ⟨1⟩ al-Juhaymân, *Jazîrat al-¿arab* II, 351–63 {Fadel, No. 32 } —: <932C§≡, Σ: legend> (); ⟨2⟩ Rhodokanakis, *Ẓfâr: SAE* VIII, 5–20, No. 2 {NK160} —: <513D§≡,-gen.= 300 + 932C§, T416.8§ + 1000,-cf. + M139§, H310.2,-cf. + 510:IV, H36.1 + 934A,-cf. Σ: composite, *sîrah*> (m, adult, Bdw, herb-garnerer); ⟨3⟩ al-Juhaymân, *Jazîrat al-¿arab* IV, 166–75 {Fadel, No. 34} —: <932C§≡,-cf. + 993§. Σ: local legend?> (m, as auth.'s source, cleric).

50. To Whom Does the Good Food Go? (Egypt, Eastern Desert)

TYPE: **1358C,** ***Trickster Discovers Adultery: Food Goes to Husband Instead of Paramour.*** **+ Cf. 834A,** ***The Pot of Gold and the Pot of Scorpions.*** **+ Cf. 1380,** ***The Faithless Wife.*** **Asks God how she can fool her husband.**

Motifs: K2212.2, "Treacherous sister-in-law"; J1144, "Eaters of stolen food detected"; K1550.1.2, "Adulteress detected by food she prepares for paramour"; P293.2.3§, "Nephew helps mother's brother catch adulteress wife and lover"; P297.2.1§, "Bond between mother's brother (*khâl*) and sister's son"; L112.7.2§, "Scabby-head (*'aqra¿*) as hero"; K1969.5.1§, "Person pretends to know language of animals (birds, insects, etc.)"; J1341.10, "Hungry student gets meat [by telling mewing cat that he got only bone]"; C229.7.1§, "Tabu: eating flesh of animal killed without mentioning God's name"; N182.1§, "Snakes and scorpions turn into gold"; K1571, "Trickster discovers adultery: food goes to husband instead of lover"; K149.5§, "Egg yolk (powdered) sold as potent (yellow) poison"; K1553, "Husband feigns blindness and avenges himself on his wife and her paramour"; T60§, "Sex games. Lovers pretend to be animals, objects, etc."; T60.1.1§, "Lovers pretend to be copulating stallion and mare (filly)"; Q432.0.2§, "Divorce withheld as punishment"; P798.1.0.5§, "Triads revolving around brother and sister as unbalanced (Sethian syndrome)"; P798.1.1§, "Conflict within a triad: one party is removed so as to restore stability (balance)."

Occurrences: 23 additional texts are available. The ratio of f:m narrators is 11:7. The following renditions were narrated by females (or children):

PEN: ⟨1⟩ AGSFC: QTR 87-3ff., 685-x-No. 6 —: <1358C≡> (f, 45, wed, elem. relig. ed., but non-litr., col. f); ***SHM:*** ⟨2⟩ al-Sârîs, *al-filisṭînî,* 144–46 —: <315≡, S166.7.1§ + 315A1§,-pt. + 1358C,-pt., K1613.5§. Σ: influenced by Type 315A> (f, 40); ***NLE:*** ⟨3⟩ Sulaymân, 172–74, No. VIII-01 —: <1358C≡,-cf., N884.3§, N884.2§ + 1359A,-cf., K1210.0.1§. Σ: merry> (f, 62, non-litr., wed, w/6 childrn); ⟨4⟩ Farag, *Daqahliyyah,* 251–57 —: <1358C≡> (f, 22, non-litr., singer, from mo); ⟨5⟩ Ammar, *Silwa,* 175–76, No. 11 —: <1358C≡> (m/c, presum., 11–14?, pupil).

Other Rendition(s): ***MSP:*** ⟨6⟩ Mâjid K. ¿Alî, *Turâth* X:1/2, 249–53 {*q.sh.¿i.* II, 99–104} —: <1358C≡, K2211.4§ + 1535:V> (m, 38, teacher); ***SHM:*** ⟨7⟩ Sâ¿î, *Lâdhiqiyyah,* 357–59, No. 78[+1], =[277, No. C-28] —: <1358C≡,-pt., J1341.10. Σ: frag.> ().

REGISTER OF TALE TYPES

All *new* tale types added to the Aarne-Thompson tale-type system, and new motifs added to the Thompson motif system are marked by the sign (§) at the end of the number.[1] A double dagger sign (‡) indicates a *newer* tale type or motif, added or developed after the publication of my *Folk Traditions of the Arab World: A Guide to Motif Classification* in 1995. (See Appendix I, "Locations of Tale-types in the Arab World," pp. 415–42.)

1. Normally, a newly generated tale-type (or motif) number is indicated by an asterisk (*) to the left of an addition. In computer-managed programs (as is the case with the present work), such an arrangement would be disruptive and dysfunctional. Additionally, the asterisk is used in several other applications in type and motif indexes. See H. El-Shamy, "A Response [to Jason's Review of *Folk Traditions of the Arab World* . . .]," esp. pp. 351–52.

318A§	*The Man who Lost his Organ and then Regained it.* The ungrateful wife.	434, 435.
318B§	*Murdered Person (Lover, Husband, Brother) Brought Back to Life through Repeated Reincarnations (Transformations).*	442, 446, 447, 448, 453.
325	*The Magician and his Pupil.*	442.
326	*The Youth who Wanted to Learn What Fear Is.*	26 n. 50, 456.
327	*The Children and the Ogre.*	57 n. 91, 445.
327A	*Hansel and Gretel.*	445.
327B	*The Dwarf and the Giant.* [Nuṣṣ-Nuṣaiṣ (Halved-half), Ḥdaydûn (Little Iron Person), etc.]	453.
327D	*The Kiddlekaddelkar.* [Ogre's wife (daughter) protects his victims-to-be.]	441.
327F	*The Witch and the Fisher Boy.* [Tongue (voice) made thin.]	413–14.
327G	*The Boy at the Devil's (Witch's) House.* The Daughters are to cook him, but are killed by him.	57 n. 91, 414.
327H§	*Foolish Husband Ignores his Wife's Advice and Leads her and the Children to Ogress.* He is Devoured.	421, 427, 433, 434, 440, 448.
327J§	*Girl Abandoned by Jealous Playmates (or by her Sisters).* She falls into the power of an ogre.	426.
327K§	*Ogre Gains Access into the Children's House after Persuading most of them to Kill their Guarding Pet (Dog).* (Only one escapes.)	421, 427, 434.
327L§	*Brother and Sister Possess Supernatural Animal's (Cat's) Treasure.*	20 n. 4, 25 n. 46, 368 n. 137.
328	*The Boy Steals the Giant's Treasure.* Jack and the Beanstalk.	441.
331	*The Spirit in the Bottle.* [Jinni released, then tricked back into captivity.]	427.
333	*The Glutton (Red Riding Hood).*	414.
333C§	*Children Swallowed and then Delivered.*	414.
363	*The Vampire.* [Bridegroom (husband) eats corpses, then tests his wife's ability to keep secret.]	425, 426.
400	*The Man on a Quest for his Lost Wife.* [Supernatural (fairy) wife departs for own home.]	418, 427, 440.
402	*The Mouse (Cat, Frog, etc.) as Bride.* [Three brothers seek wives; youngest marries a she-monkey, (tortoise).]	418, 427, 440, 454.
403	*The Black and the White Bride.* [Ugly bride substituted for beautiful bride.]	444, 393 n. 574, 425, 442, 444, 445.

470C§	*Man in Utopian Otherworld Cannot Resist Interfering: He is Expelled.* ("It Serves me Right!")	57 n. 85.
470E§	*Man in Utopian Otherworld Punished for his Desire to Marry Foster-sister(s).* The forty.	451.
476*	*In the Frog's House.* [Helpful person given garbage which turns into gold.]	441.
480	*The Spinning-Women by the Spring. The Kind and Unkind Girls.*	58 n. 95, 440, 441, 442, 445.
510	*Cinderella and Cap o' Rushes.*	425, 441, 442, 445, 453, 457.
510A	*Cinderella.*	271–72, 445.
510B	*The Dress of Gold, of Silver, and of Stars.* [Girl flees from her father who wants to marry her.]	208, 374 n. 254, 423, 424, 425, 453.
510D§/ 313K1§	*Daughter Flees to Escape Passion of her Father's Stallion (Bull-Camel or Horse).*	423, 424.
511A	*The Little Red Ox.* [Cow helps orphans (brother and sister).]	57 n. 92, 440, 441, 442, 444, 445, 447.
512*	*The Sister is Driven from Home.* [Cruel older sister.]	441.
513C	*The Son of the Hunter.* [King assigns tasks: one present fetched calls for another.]	455.
513D§	*The Tribal Hero (Abu-Zaid, Antar, etc.) and his Companion(s).* (Focus.)	457.
516	*Faithful John.*	27 n. 60, 456.
516A	*The Body Talk by the Princess,* [and the misunderstood true friend].	438.
516A1§	‡*The Sign Language of the Princess,* interpreted for the love-sick husband (by his wife, fiancée).	436.
516B	*The Abducted Princess* (Love Through Sight of Floating Hair).	423, 435.
516C	*St. James of Galicia.* [Hero's child is to be sacrificed, or given away so as to save hero's friend.]	435.
516F§	‡*Nephew Wins a Bride for his Maternal-uncle.* (Abu-Zaid Gets ¿Alyâ.)	451, 456.
516H§	*The Father who Wanted a Share of his Son's Beautiful Wives.* He is killed with the help of the hero's friend.	27 n. 60, 377 n. 287, 455.
517A§	*Enigmatic Apparition (Dream, Laughing Fish, Speaking Skull, etc.) Leads to Detection of Adultery.*	382 n. 400.
533	*The Speaking Horsehead.* [It reveals substitution of bride by her waiting-maid.]	453.
533A§	*Beautiful Maiden in Hideous Disguise.* She is detected	

850A*§	*Rape for Rape: the Brother Avenges Violation of his Sister.* "My Father Aggressed; My Maternal-uncle Redressed."	456.
851	*The Princess who Cannot Solve the Riddle.*	406 n. 826.
857§	*Nephew Wins a Bride for his Maternal-uncle: Abu-Zaid Gets ¿Alyâ.*	451, 455, 456, 457.
860A*	*Finding the Hidden Princess.*	447.
861	*Sleeping at the Rendezvous.*	436.
870	*The Princess Confined in the Mound.* [Digs her way out, and eventually marries her sweetheart to whom she had been betrothed.]	433.
870A	*The Little Goose Girl.* [Poor girl woos the prince, and her place usurped by substitute bride.]	423.
870A*	‡*The Enclosed Girl Follows her Lover.* [Glass enclosure broken; elopement, separation then.]	433.
870C*	*Stepmother Makes Love to Stepson,* the king.	416.
871A	*The Unfaithful Queen.* [The Maiden Puts out Eye of Cat's (Bird's) Adulterous Wife.]	418, 427.
872§	*Brother and Sister: Separation and Reunion.*	330, 427, 446.
872*	*Brother and Sister.* [Brother's wife calumniates his sister.]	453.
872A1§	*Snakes in the Sister's Belly.*	448, 454.
872A§	*The Pregnancy of the Virgin Sister by Treachery.*	58 n. 99, 447.
872B§	*The Murdered Sister is Reincarnated and Betrothed to her Brother: the Talking Bed.*	447, 448.
872X§	*The Pregnant Girl (Sister) is Aided by her Brother's Wife (Sister-in-law) in Finding the Father of her Illegitimate Child.*	449.
873	*The King Discovers his Unknown Son.* [Token found at son's execution.]	436.
873B§	*Boy Twitted with Rootlessness (Illegitimacy) Seeks Unknown Maternal-uncle.*	414.
874	*The Proud King is Won.*	436.
874A§	*Estranged Couple are Reconciled (Reunited) by their Children.*	425, 429, 431, 433.
875	*The Clever Peasant Girl.* [Performs impossible tasks, marries king, and selects him as dearest.]	428.
875B	*The Clever Peasant Girl and the King.* [For each impossible task she gives countertasks.]	436.
879	*The Basil Maidens (The Sugar Puppet, Viola).*	422, 427, 428, 436.
880A§	*Husband's Indiscreet Boast about his Wife's Beauty Brings about her Destruction.*	388 n. 510.
881	*Oft-proved Fidelity.*	424.
883§	*Innocent Slandered (Suspected) Female.*	424, 425.

883A	*The Innocent Slandered Maiden.*	57 n. 87, 57 n. 90, 426.
883B	*The Punished Seducer.* [Only One Sister Resists Seduction.]	416.
883C*	*The Innocent Slandered Maiden: Alleged Pregnancy.*	431.
883E§	*The Innocent Slandered Wife: Falsified Evidence (by Mother-in-law, Sister-in-law).*	431.
884A§	‡*The Girl Disguised as Man is Wooed by the Queen.*	457.
884B*	*Girl Dressed as a Man Deceives the King.*	422, 426, 441, 442.
884C§	*The Boy Disguised as Girl is Wooed by another Boy (Prince, King, etc.).*	451, 456, 457.
884E§	*The Boy Disguised as Girl is Wooed by another Girl.*	429.
885**	*The Foster Children.* ['Brother and sister' Fall in Love with each other. They learn that one is adopted. They get married.]	107.
886	*The Girl Who Could Not Keep the Secret.*	429.
886A§	*The Speechless (Dumb, Tongue-tied) Wife is Obliged to Retort.*	419, 428, 429.
890	*A Pound of Flesh.*	436.
891	*The Man who Deserts his wife and Sets Her the Task of Bearing Him a Child.*	425, 428, 429.
891A	*The Princess from the Tower Recovers her Husband.* (Frequently mixed with 891.)	441.
891F§/1379	‡*Wife Deceives Husband with Substituted Bedmate.*	394 n. 584, 436.
892	*The Children of the King.* [Sister slandered by a man, but she vindicates her self.]	436.
894	*The Ghoulish Schoolmaster and the Stone of Pity.*	421, 425, 426.
895B1§	*Husband Divorces his Chaste Wife so that she may be Reunited with her First Love.* (Khaḍrah.)	431.
895B§	*Host Surrenders his Wife (Sister) to Guest.*	431.
896	*The Lecherous Holy Man and the Maiden in a Box.*	436.
898	*The Daughter of the Sun. (The Speechless Maiden; the Puppet Bride.)*	56 n. 72, 395 n. 627, 418, 426, 427, 434, 454, 455.
903C*	*Mother-in-law and Daughter-in-law.*	431, 432.
904§	‡*Tender Persuading of the Shy (Innocent) Maiden (Bride, Girl, Virgin).*	24 n. 42.
910F	*The Quarreling Sons and the Bundle of Twigs.*	389 n. 522.
910K1§	*A Lost Hour of Fun (Merriment) Cannot be Made-up for.*	435, 436.
911*	*The Dying Father's Counsel.*	26 n. 50.
920	*The Son of the King (Solomon) and of the Smith.* [Traits of Character are Inborn.]	436.

983	*The Dishes of the Same Flavor.* Man thus shown that one woman is like another [. . .].	436.
985	*Brother Chosen Rather than Husband or Son.*	314, 402 n. 768, 451, 456.
986	*The Lazy Husband.*	57 n. 89.
990*	*A Merchant's Son Finds the Princess Wounded in a Coffin.* He helps her in her revenge and marries her.	453.
992A	*The Adulteress's Penance.*	436.
993§	*Adultery (Faithlessness, Attempted Seduction) Revealed and Punished.*	457.
1000	*Bargain Not to Become Angry.*	457.
1119	*The Ogre Kills his Own Children.* Places changed in bed (night-caps).	57 n. 91, 451, 453.
1121	*Ogre's Wife Burned in his Own Oven.*	445.
1180	*Catching Water in a Sieve.*	451, 453.
1305	‡*The Miser's Gold.*	431.
1313D§	*Death Feigned to Discover who had Consumed the Food.* [. . .].	57 n. 93.
1353	*Old Woman as Trouble Maker.* Beats the devil.	428.
1353C§	*Old Woman beats the Devil: "Close this Crack [Vagina]!"*	436.
1358C	*Trickster Discovers Adultery: Food Goes to Husband Instead of Paramour.*	457, 458.
1359A (formerly 1406*)	*Hiding the Lover.*	458.
1379/891F§	*Wife Deceives Husband with Substituted Bedmate.*	436, 444.
1380	*The Faithless Wife.* Asks God how she can fool her husband.	457.
1387*	*Woman Must Do Everything Like her Neighbors.* Absurd results.	439, 440.
1397§	*Troubles for the Polygynist Man.*	432.
1406A§	*Youth (Man) Learns about the Wiles of Women.*	432.
1407	*The Miser.* [Spies on his wife: he falls, or is punished.]	429, 431, 432.
1407B§	*Wife Escapes her Miserly Husband to Find her New Fiancé More Miserly; she Returns to the First.*	183.
1418	*The Equivocal Oath.* [Adulteress wife exposes her privates: evades detection of perjury.]	445.
1419E	*Underground Passage to Paramour's House.* (Inclusa.)	449.
1438§	*Wife Prepares herself for the Spiraling Promises Made by her Foolish Husband: Accidentally Fulfilled.*	436.
1441	*Respite from Wooer while he Brings Clothes all Night.*	437.
1442§	*Stupid Woman (Co-wife) is Deceived into Imitating Foolishly:* she kills her child.	418, 426, 427, 434, 439, 440, 446, 454, 455.

1511	*The Faithless Queen.* [Wife prefers loathsome paramour.]	436.
1525U§	*Giving Trap-name (Catch-name).*	456.
1525W§	*Leaving Infant (Corpse, Hireling) with Merchant as Security.*	438.
1526	*The Beggar and the Robbers.* [Beggar dressed up as gentleman: goods received on his credit (or an infant is used as surety).]	438.
1530*	*The Man and his Two Dogs.* [Calling the animals scares away robber(s).]	428.
1535	*The Rich and the Poor Peasant.* (Unibos.)	458.
1538A§	*Female Master Thief.* Woman (girl) performs series of tricks (for revenge, or to fulfill a pledge).	438.
1542	*The Clever Boy.*	456.
1545	*The Boy with Many Names.*	456.
1563	*"Both?"* [Seduction by bearing false order.]	27 n. 60.
1600A§	*The False Grave as Evidence of the Death.* Buried sheep claimed to be the corpse of an absent.	423, 453.
1617A§	*Other Tricks (Subterfuges) to Recover Usurped Money.*	456.
1618A§	*Lying Mother-in-law (Daughter-in-law, or Co-wife) Nonplussed: the Biting Dummy (Doll, Stick).*	432.
1653A*	*Pretended Corpse at Practice Funeral.* [Priest kills pretender.]	57 n. 93.
1655	*The Profitable Exchange.*	418.
1696	*What Should I Have Said (Done)?*	433, 434.
1739A*	*Man Thinks he has Given Birth to a Child by Letting Wind.*	427.
1750A	*Sending a Dog to be Educated.* [Trickster claims he may not repeat what the animal said.]	438.
1761*	*Imposter Hiding in Holy Image Beaten.*	445.
1900	*How the Man Came out of a Tree Stump (Marsh).*	420, 451.
2010 I A	*The Animals with Queer Names:* as hen (henny-penny), cock (cocky-locky), goose (goosey-poosey).	361 n. 8.
2021*	*The Louse Mourns her Spouse, the Flea.*	436.
2022	*The Death of the Little Hen.*	436.
2022A	*The Death of the Little Hen Described with Unusual Words.*	436.
2036	*Drop of Honey Causes Chain of Accidents.* [Bloody feud between villages ensues.]	xvii.
2330	*Game-tales.* (Used in games.)	362 n. 16.
2335	*Tales Filled with Contradictions.*	xvii.
2412§	*Unclassified Formula Tales.*	xvii.

REGISTER OF MOTIFS

A. MYTHOLOGICAL [AND RELATED BELIEF] MOTIFS

A6.3.1§	‡Eve created to relieve Adam's loneliness.	24 n. 40.
A63.5.1	Satan seduces Adam to sin because he is jealous of him.	24 n. 40.
A63.5.3§	Eblis vows to corrupt Adam's descendants.	23 n. 40.
A63.6	Devil in serpent [(viper)] form tempts first woman (Satan and Eve).	24 n. 40.
A102.0.1§	God's names (99 attributes).	398 n. 689.
A102.14.2§	‡Generosity of God.	398 n. 689.
A132.17.1§	‡Goddess in form of frog (Heket).	25 n. 44.
A511.1.3.2	Demigod [culture hero] son of king's unmarried sister by her brother.	455.
A511.1.3.2.1§	Culture-hero son of sister by her brother.	456.
A661.1.1.1§	Inhabitants of Paradise divided into strata.	383 n. 417.
A725	Man controls rising and setting of sun.	456.
A1231.3§	Adam and Eve descend from sky.	24 n. 40.
A1275.1	Creation of first woman from man's rib. [Adam's rib.]	24 n. 40.
A1332§	‡Accompaniments of Paradise lost.	24 n. 40.
A1332.1§	‡Violation of food tabu in paradise results in need to defecate; (assimilation of forbidden food is incomplete).	24 n. 40.
A1332.4§	‡The forbidden paradise food (drink).	24 n. 40.
A1335.1.1	Origin of death: wrong messenger goes to God.	58 n. 97.
A1371.5§	Deviant women from Adam's 'crooked rib.'	24 n. 40.
A1372.9	Why women are subservient to men.	24 n. 40.
A1386.1.1§	‡Eve serves Adam liquor till drunk (he obeys her sinful instigation).	24 n. 40.
A1471.8.1§	‡Being a merchant (buying and selling): an occupation blessed by God.	367 n. 103.
A1557.3.1§	‡Moses walks ahead of female guide so as not to observe her posterior (body); she directs (by non-vocal signs).	375 n. 266.
A1617	‡Origin of place-name.	388 n. 510.
A1622.1§	‡People rescued from monster form a community (village, town, etc.) on the spot of their deliverance.	72.
A1650.5.1.1§	‡Punishment of Adam: God's reconciliatory-reprimand (*¿itâb*).	24 n. 40.
A1650.5.1.10§	‡Punishment of Adam: toiling and misery: the first to have his brow sweat from labor fatigue.	24 n. 40.

B. ANIMALS

B313.3§	Helpful cow out of mother's grave.	444.
B335.2	Life of helpful animal demanded as cure for feigned sickness.	440, 445, 446.
B375.1	Fish returned to water: grateful.	443.
B391	Animal grateful for food.	419.
B392.1	Animals grateful for being given appropriate food.	440.
B411	Helpful cow.	440, 444.
B413	Helpful goat.	445.
B421	Helpful dog.	419.
B422	Helpful cat.	420, 435.
B435.1	Helpful fox.	419.
B435.2	Helpful jackal.	420.
B441.1	Helpful monkey.	420, 447.
B443.4	‡Helpful gazelle.	417.
B451.4	Helpful crow.	444.
B451.5	Helpful raven.	453.
B470.1	Small fish as helper.	442.
B486.1.1§	‡Swarm of locusts protects exposed newborn infant.	395 n. 616.
B491.1	Helpful serpent ([snake]).	444.
B515	Resuscitation by animals.	435.
B517§	Overheard conversation of birds (turtle-doves, pigeons) reveals that some of their own organs are the only medicine to cure hero: they are caught and killed for the cure.	442.
B535	Animal nurse.	417.
B535.0.1	Cow as nurse cares for children.	445.
B535.0.3.1§	‡Gazelle as nurse for child.	417.
B535.0.5.1§	Abandoned infant girl raised by falcon in nest.	417.
B535.0.7.3§	Falcon (hawk) as nurse for child.	417.
B601.7	Marriage to monkey.	455.
B601.7.1§	Man marries female monkey.	455.
B640.1	Marriage to beast by day and man by night.	442.
B641.7	Marriage to person in monkey form.	454.
B733.0.1§	Animals perceive supernatural beings (spirits) and supernatural acts.	445.
B778.1.2§	Mouse (rat) as thief.	26 n. 46.
B784.2.1	Patient fed salt: animal comes out for water.	448.
B789.0.1§	‡Bat fastens self with its fangs to victim's face.	25 n. 44.
B789.1.1.1.1.1§	‡Bat releases victim upon hearing zebra's braying.	25 n. 44.
B789.1.1.1.3.1§	‡Bat releases victim only upon hearing country-style drumming.	25 n. 44.

C. TABU

C22§	‡"Pearls on their Vine!": jinni's name uttered. He appears.	265, 375 n. 273, 396 n. 647.

C51.9.1§	Tabu: planning for the future without saying, "*'in-shâ'-Allâh* (If God wills)."	25 n. 44.
C51.9.2§	Tabu: dealing with omens (dreams) without saying, "Good, if God wills."	390 n. 524.
C106§	‡Tabu: woman going (seen) unveiled in public—(*sufûr*).	454.
C140	**Tabu connected with menses.**	370 n. 160.
C141.1	Tabu: menstruous woman not to go near any cultivated field or crop will be ruined [*mushâhrah*].	372 n. 210.
C145	Tabu: [touching] certain things during menses [*mushâhrah*].	372 n. 210.
C229.7.1§	Tabu: eating flesh of animal killed without mentioning God's name.	397 n. 656, 407 n. 838, 458.
C400	**Speaking tabu.**	426.
C406§	‡Tabu: answering (responding to) call or question.	426, 427.
C434§	Names of dangerous things (animal, disease, murder, etc.) are not to be uttered at a person without use of precautionary measures (e.g., 'Distant one,' 'Away from you').	363 n. 40, 373 n. 219, 373 n. 222, 380 n. 342.
C434.1§	Effect of spoken evil words [to be] averted by spitting.	442.
C434.3§	‡Scandal (defamation, infamy) must not be spoken of (spread).	370 n. 172.
C438.1§	‡Tabu: responding unless addressed by correct name (title).	426, 427.
C611	Forbidden chamber.	426.
C645§	The one forbidden thing: revealing secret of being married to fairy (jinniyyah, jinni).	397 n. 653.
C742	Tabu: striking monster twice.	439.
C787.1.1§	‡Tabu: guarantee of profits in business venture.	371 n. 177.
C911.1§	‡Silver finger as sign of opening forbidden chamber.	426.

D. MAGIC [AND SIMILAR SUPERNATURAL OCCURRENCES]

D11	Transformation: woman to man.	435.
D12	Transformation: man to woman.	435.
D30	**Transformation to person of different race.**	454.
D31	Transformation: white person to negro.	454.
D32§	Transformation: black person to white.	454.
D40.2	Transformation to likeness of another woman.	445.
D113.4	‡Transformation: man to jackal.	453.
D114.1.1	Transformation: man to deer.	423, 446.
D133.3	Transformation: man to ox.	454.
D134	‡Transformation: man to goat (he-goat, she-goat, kid, etc.).	446, 447.

D2072.6	Paralysis by singing magic song.	418.
D2072.6.1§	Magic song (formula) causes man to be turned upside down.	418.
D2101.0.1§	Blood opens treasure.	417.
D2136.2	Castle [palace] magically transported.	439.
D2136.4.3§	‡All water in lake (well) supernaturally put into small container (water skin).	414.
D2146	Magic control of day and night.	456.
D2161.3.1.1	Eyes torn out magically replaced.	439, 444.
D2161.3.2.4§	Severed penis supernaturally restored.	435.

E. THE DEAD

E1.3.1§	‡Murdered (dismembered) woman comes back to life—(supernaturally).	453.
E11.1	Second blow resuscitates. First kills.	439, 454.
E21	Resuscitation by withdrawal of wounding instrument.	421, 446.
E63	Resuscitation by prayer.	446.
E80	**Water of Life. Resuscitation by water.**	395 n. 621, 439.
E125.3.1§	‡Resuscitation by stepbrother.	439.
E222	Dead mother's malevolent return.	419.
E222.0.1	Mother haunts daughter.	419.
E232.1	Return from the dead to slay own murderer.	446.
E323	Dead mother's friendly return.	445.
E323.2.1	Dead mother (in animal [cow] form) returns to aid persecuted children.	444.
E323.2.4§	Only the hand of dead mothers is to be used to punish her children.	441.
E326	Dead brother's friendly return.	446.
E405§	Uncontrollable corpse ('flying bier'): bearers compelled as to speed and route.	450.
E405.1§	‡Vanishing (elusive) corpse.	450.
E422.1.10	Dismembered corpse.	453.
E600	**Reincarnation.**	448.
E607.1	Bones of dead collected and buried. Return in another form directly from grave.	446.
E613.0.1	Reincarnation of murdered child as bird.	446.
E631	‡Reincarnation in plant (tree) growing from grave.	419, 446, 447.
E631.0.1	Twin branches grow from graves of lovers.	456.
E631.0.4	Speaking and bleeding trees.	447.
E631.0.5	Tree from innocent man's blood.	447.
E670	**Repeated reincarnation.**	444.
E670.2§	Repeated reincarnation: person (woman, mother, man) becomes cow, then tree, then fruit, etc.	445, 447.
E780.5§	Transplanted organ retains original characteristics.	435.
E781.2	Eyes bought back and replaced.	423, 439, 444.

F. MARVELS

	sunlight travel from one end of body to the other (anus to mouth): they clear away impurities.	414.
F556.2	Voice changed by work of silversmith (goldsmith).	413.
F559.3	Extraordinary excrements.	432.
F559.3.2§	Jewels as extraordinary excrements.	442.
F561.10§	People who live on salt-cured (pickled) foods.	398 n. 682.
F562.2	Residence in a tree.	414, 417.
F567	‡Wild man. Man lives alone in wood like a beast.	421.
F574.9.1.1§	‡Skin so soft that it will not support a flea's weight (formulaic).	397 n. 670, 442.
F575.0.1§	‡Remarkably beautiful face.	393 n. 580.
F575.1.5.1.1§	Remarkable beauty: woman with buttocks so high that a pomegranate (apple, orange, watermelon, etc.) rolls through underneath small of her back as she lies on floor.	388 n. 510.
F575.1.5.9.1§	‡Remarkably small foot.	452.
F575.1.6§	‡Beauty that disorients (dazzles) the beholder.	375 n. 265, 424, 455.
F575.2	Handsome man.	456.
F580§	Person of awe-inspiring appearance.	376 n. 278.
F611.3.3.5§	Strong hero tests riding-animals (horses, camels). Breaks backs of many.	455.
F771.4.5.1§	‡Mill (factory) haunted by a demon (jinni, afrit, etc.).	435.
F787.3	‡Ivory bed.	303–4.
F787.5§	‡Glass (crystal) bed.	303–4.
F819§	‡Sympathetic plant(s).	436.
F821.1.5	‡Dress of gold, silver, color of sun, moon and stars.	442.
F849§	‡Remarkably delicious (liked) dishes—(ordinary foods).	430.
F849.1§	‡Loved meat (fowl, fish) dishes.	407 n. 836.
F849.1.1§	‡The basic meat delicacy. (Meat on top of rice, broth-soaked bread, stuffing, or a similar starchy food; labeled: *fattah,* "meat and potatoes," or the like).	384 n. 444.
F850.2.3§	‡Hated bean mash.	387.
F851.9.1.1.1§	‡Gas-giving foods eaten: beans, onions, leeks, taro (*qulqâs:* Colocasia esclenta), etc.	427, 434.
F852.1	Glass coffin.	421.
F855.7.1§	‡Sugar puppet (doll).	380 n. 350.
F857.1	Golden besom (broom).	419, 420.
F911.4	Jonah [(Yûnus)]. Fish ([whale], or water monster) swallows a man.	433, 454.
F913	Victims rescued from swallower's belly.	413, 414.
F913.3§	Ogre's belly (toe) cut, all victims come out and repopulate town (nation, village).	414.
F932.6.2	River dries up its waters out of sympathy.	436.
F942.3.1	Earth opens at woman's bidding to enclose her.	448.
F950.5	Extreme fear [(horror)] as cure for sickness.	429.

F951.3.2.1§	‡Watching mating between lovebirds (pigeons, doves) arouses sexual desire.	25 n. 42.
F956.7.3.3§	‡Vegetarian diet (no-meat) promotes good health.	387 n. 496.
F956.7.6§	‡Catharsis (*faḍfaḍah*): relief from mental troubles through talking about them.	425.
F956.7.6.1§	‡Publication of secrets to "stone of pity," "box of patience," etc.).	425.
F956.7.7§	‡Venting anger or frustration (*fashsh el-ghill*). Dissipation of negative emotions through strenuous behavior (acts).	383 n. 416.
F956.7.7.1.1§	‡Invitation to venting anger: person presents self as target for anger-venting by another.	383 n. 416.
F956.7.7.1.1.1§	‡Wife awaits husband's return with stick in her hand, in case he is angry and needs to vent his anger: "Better at me than at a stranger."	383 n. 416.
F956.7.7.1.1.2§	‡Mother places self between her child (son, daughter) and father's (her husband's) wrath.	448.
F960.11§	Extraordinary nature phenomena at a person's smiling.	444.
F969.7	Famine.	426.
F971.5	Flowers bloom in winter.	444.
F975	‡Garden becomes wilderness.	417.
F979.15	Tree sheds all of its leaves out of sympathy.	436.
F981.9.1§	‡Animal kills self (commits suicide).	26 n. 46.
F983.2	Louse fattened.	428.
F994	Object expresses sorrow.	425, 436.
F994.3§	Stone bursts out of pity for persecuted heroine.	425.
F1041.1.1	Death from a broken heart.	424.
F1041.8.1	Madness from seeing beautiful woman.	388 n. 510.
F1041.8.1.0.1§	War waged to procure beautiful woman.	388 n. 510.
F1041.8.2	Madness from grief.	450.
F1041.9.9.1§	Dumbness from horror.	414.
F1041.16.8.1§	‡Person bursts from anger (frustration).	421.
F1041.17.3§	‡Fainting from fear (horror).	415.
F1041.17.4§	‡Involuntary defecation (urination) from fear.	434.
F1043§	Reaction to sensory deprivation.	25 n. 42.
F1045	Night spent in tree.	448.
F1381.8§	‡Quest for unknown bridegroom (lover) for daughter (sister).	442.

G. OGRES [AND SATAN]

G10	Cannibalism.	434.
G11.3	Cannibal witch.	425, 433.
G11.9	Ogre schoolmaster.	425.
G38§	Abused person becomes ogre-like.	421.

G61	Relative's flesh eaten unwittingly.	444, 446.
G61.1.2§	‡Sister evades eating her brother's flesh.	446.
G72.1.1§	Ill-advised mother eats (cooks) own child.	440.
G72.2	Starving woman abandoned in cave eats newborn child.	439.
G72.2.1§	Pleiades deceives Scorpio into eating her own children.	440.
G72.3.1§	Sister raises infant brother on slain mother's marrow (flesh).	448.
G78.1	Cannibalism in times of famine.	439.
G81	Unwitting marriage to cannibal.	426.
G82	Cannibal fattens victim.	433.
G82.3§	Cannibal's fodder (fattening). Fodder causes gluttony and insanity: victim fattened.	369 n. 150.
G82.3.1§	"Ogress's mash." Fodder made of ground bones and ogress's milk, used to fatten victims.	451, 453.
G90.5§	‡Hate to be quenched by drinking blood of hated person.	421, 423, 424, 453.
G100.1	Giant ogre (Fomorian).	435.
G121.3§	‡Ogre's (ogress's) eyes emit sparks.	434.
G123	Giant ogress with breasts thrown over her shoulders.	439.
G261	Witch steals children.	425.
G264	La Belle Dame San Merci. Witch entices men with offers of love and then deserts or destroys them.	438.
G307.3	Jinn kills whoever tries to occupy house he has chosen to live in.	435.
G332.1	Ogre sucks victim's finger and drinks all his blood.	454.
G376.0.3§	‡Ogress in form of woman (girl).	433.
G400	Person falls into ogre's power.	421.
G412	‡Children lured into ogre's house.	451.
G412.3§	‡Ogre's (ogress's) fire lures person.	424, 451.
G413	‡Ogre disguises voice to lure victim.	413.
G415§	‡Ogre (predator) poses as relative of intended victim (prey).	414.
G415.1§ (formerly G415§)	Ogress poses as man's sister and invites him to live in her house.	433.
G443§	Ogre adopts human child.	426.
G443.1.1§	Ogre kills pregnant woman, spares fetus and adopts it.	448.
G443.2§	Ogre abducts woman's children, raises them and then returns them to their mother.	425.
G466	Lousing as task set by ogress.	440.
G512.3	‡Ogre burned to death.	414.
G512.4.1§	Ogress persuaded to crawl underneath door: she is burned.	434.
G519.6§	‡Ogre (ogress) delivered as food to another predator.	452.

G522	Ogre persuaded to drink pond dry bursts.	413.
G530	**Ogre's relative aids hero.**	441.
G551.1	Rescue of sister from ogre by brother.	414.
G551.4	‡One brother rescues another from ogre.	414.
G565§	Escape from ogre (ogress, witch, etc.).	426, 451.
G634.3.1§	Open eyes as indication of ogre's deep sleep.	451.
G634.4.1§	Ogre is asleep for a year, then is awake for a year.	439.

H. TESTS

H11	Recognition through story-telling.	421.
H11.1	‡Recognition by telling life history.	448.
H12	Recognition by song.	454.
H13.2.5	Recognition by overheard conversation with cups (or other utensils).	271, 418, 426, 427.
H36.1	Slipper test: identification by fitting of slipper.	442, 452, 457.
H38.2.6§	Young beggar-girl married to gentleman betrays old trade by enacting begging scenes at meal-times.	419.
H38.3	Slave recognized by his conversation, habits, and character.	393 n. 583.
H41.5	Unknown prince shows his kingly qualities in dealing with playmates.	456.
H51	Recognition by scar.	449, 456.
H55	Recognition through branding.	422.
H56	Recognition by wound.	449, 456.
H71.4.1§	Flowers from lips (mouth, footprint) as proof of heroine's identity.	444.
H75	Identification by hair.	451.
H76§	Black woman turned white supernaturally is recognized: she still has kinky hair.	425, 454.
H79	Recognition by physical attributes—miscellaneous.	429.
H79.9§	‡Identification (recognition) by sex-organ.	383 n. 411, 429.
H94.1	Identification by ring baked in cake.	444.
H111	Identification by garment.	449.
H151.12	Geese tell of beauty of their mistress and bring about recognition.	452.
H151.14	Tears fall on person below and indicate presence of those above.	442.
H171.2.1§	Bird (dove) selects new king: by alighting on his shoulder or head.	434.
H175	Recognition by force of nature. Unknown member of family immediately and magically [(mystically)] recognized.	447.
H175.7§	Blood-relative mystically recognized: "Blood's yearning," "Blood's howling."	447.

H271§	Contest in telling the strangest (most bizarre) life experience (story).	435.
H310.2	Brother unwittingly qualifies as bridegroom of sister in test.	451, 457.
H323	Suitor test: learning girl's name.	426.
H360	**Bride test.**	429.
H363	Deceased wife marriage test.	423.
H365.1§	Bride test: size of feet to match sister's.	452.
H366§	Father unwittingly qualifies as bridegroom of daughter in test.	423.
H388.3§	‡Prince given to woman who can heal him.	442.
H389.3§	Bride test: total ignorance of men (sex-naivety).	429.
H461.1	The clever wife in disguise wins a second wife for her husband.	438.
H492.3.1§	Dying wife asks husband to prove his faithfulness by severing his genitals.	434.
H493	Virility test for husband.	435.
H504.4§	‡Contest in cooking (baking).	455.
H506.9	Test of resourcefulness: to cook rice without fire.	451, 455, 456.
H506.9.1§	Test of resourcefulness: making coffee (tea) without water.	456.
H511	Princess offered to correct guesser.	428.
H522.1.1	Test: guessing the nature of certain skin—louse-skin.	426, 428, 453.
H580.1	Girl given enigmatic commands must do the opposite.	440.
H581.2	Arrested man tells who he is: the hospitable fire of his father is sought (bean merchant).	379 n. 334.
H604.1§	Symbolic meaning of animal (lamb) without heart, liver, brain, eyes, etc. served at dinner: so was guest's behavior.	417.
H607	Discussion by symbols.	438.
H607.3	Princess declares her love through sign language, not understood.	438.
H611.1.1§	Eggs's fragility analogous to girls ready for marriage.	369 n. 155.
H611.2	Sign message sent by girl to enamored prince. Interpreted by prince's friend [(cousin-wife)].	438.
H611.2.1§	Prince's wife (who is also his cousin) interprets for him girl's love message.	438.
H631.4.1§	‡What is strongest? Woman's resolve.	24 n. 41.
H795.1§	Riddle: "Your father is from your father (or, Your father!: Who is your father?); your father is your maternal-uncle." (Son of girl raped by her brother.)	405 n. 811.
H806.1§	Riddle: bird flew out of its nest on two wings but flew back on only one—(braid of hair, loss of chastity).	406 n. 826.
H888§	‡Allegorical riddle: what would an object (utensil, implement, fruit, etc.) say in a given situation?	379 n. 325.
H888.1§	‡What would say [to a female]: "Part your thighs wide	

	and take me [in], and then make vocal manifestations of sexual enjoyment (*ghang*) and let me hear [them]"? Answer: kneading tub (*magûr el-¿agîn*).	379 n. 325.
H888.2§	‡What would say: "Belly on belly, meanwhile that which is dangling knows what to do"? Answer: wide-bellied water-tank (*zîr*), and person with cup trying to reach down for water (=sexual intercourse).	382 n. 399.
H915.1.1§	‡Task assigned because of a brother's boast of sister.	230.
H935	Witch [(ogress)] assigns tasks.	440.
H936	Task assigned because of longings of pregnant woman [(craving)].	417.
H947.1§	‡Task: fetch unknown "pearls on their vine" (or the like)—prove(s) to be a jinni (elfin) prince.	264.
H1023.2	Task: carrying water in sieve.	451.
H1027§	Task: bringing pregnant virgins. (Girls fed gas-giving food, stomach becomes swollen.)	427.
H1049.2.1§	Task: bringing pregnant virgins. Countertask: bringing radish grown in rock.	427.
H1053	Task: coming neither on horse nor on foot (riding nor walking).	427.
H1054.1	Task: coming neither naked nor clad. (Comes wrapped in a net or the like.)	427.
H1064	Task: coming laughing and crying at once. (Rubs eyes with a twig [(onion)] to simulate crying.)	427.
H1091.1	Task: sorting grains: performed by helpful ants.	442.
H1211	Quests assigned in order to get rid of hero.	439.
H1212	Quest assigned because of feigned illness.	439.
H1212.4	Quest assigned because of longings of pregnant woman.	417.
H1213.1	Quest for princess caused by sight of one of her hairs dropped by a bird (or floating on river).	435.
H1263	Quest to God for fortune.	449.
H1301.1	Quest for the most beautiful bride.	454.
H1334§	Quest for radish grown in rock.	427.
H1381.2.2.3§	Boy twitted with rootlessness seeks unknown *khâl* (maternal-uncle).	421, 448.
H1381.3.1.2	‡Quest for bride for oneself.	454.
H1385.4	Quest for vanished husband.	442.
H1385.5	Quest for vanished lover.	442.
H1385.6	Quest for lost sister.	452.
H1385.8	Quest for lost brother(s).	453.
H1388	Quest: answer to certain question.	449.
H1394	Quest for person who has not known sorrow.	456.
H1394.1§	Quest for person who has had more grief (chagrin, sorrow).	456.
H1556.1	Test of fidelity by feigning death.	420.
H1556.1.2§	Monkey (fox, jackal, dog, etc.) feigns death (illness) to test master's gratitude (fidelity).	420.

H1565	Test of gratitude.	420.
H1578.1	Test of sex of girl masking as man.	422.
H1578.1.3§	Test of sex of girl masking as man: guns and jewels; men take notice of guns.	422.
H1578.1.7§	Test of sex of girl masking as man: climbing a tall tree. Male genitals will be visible.	422.
H1578.1.8§	Test of sex of girl masking as man: flowers (plant) near her will wither, if she is menstruous.	370 n. 160, 422.
H1578.1.9.2§	‡Detection of a person's sex: psychological means (mental set, etc.).	422.
H1578.3§	Test of sex: bathing (swimming) in the nude.	422.
H1582.5.1§	‡"Inability to laugh indicates sickness (hunger, starvation)."	432.
H1587§	Test of race: black person has kinky hair.	454.

J. THE WISE AND THE FOOLISH

J6§	‡"Ideal culture." (Learned ways and values for social living as they are supposed to be: good, bad, or neutral.)	53 n. 24, 380 n. 348.
J10.5§	Persistence of early acquired knowledge, during childhood.	416.
J20§	Conditioning: effects associated with past experience cause man (animal) to respond accordingly (conditioned response).	367 n. 120, 376 n. 283, 381 n. 363.
J21.30.1§	"Betray not a trust even if you happened to be a betrayer."	435.
J21.47.1	"Do not send wife for a long visit to her parents."	433.
J21.53§	"A lost hour of fun (merriment) cannot be made-up for."	435.
J21.54§	"Beauty is in the eye of the beholder."	435.
J21.54.1§	"The beauty is the one whom you love even if a Noah's crow (bear). Which of two women is the pretty one: the black or the white?"	435, 436.
J29.2.1§	‡Learning to overcome childhood fear.	25 n. 44.
J32.0.2§	"If her finger (hand, heel, etc.) is that beautiful, then how the rest of her body must be!"	436.
J80	**Wisdom (knowledge) taught by parable.**	429.
J99	Wisdom (knowledge) taught by parable—[miscellaneous].	428.
J123	Wisdom of child decides law suit.	456.
J133.9§	Kindness learned from example of animal's (bird's) kind behavior: imitated.	25 n. 42.
J142	Lack of proper education regretted.	416.

J144	Well-trained kid does not open door to wolf.	413.
J148.2§	‡Memorization.	23 n. 35.
J148.2.1§	‡One word (phrase, sentence) evokes another associated with it. ("Principle of polarity": stability of syntax, word sequence, word order.)	386 n. 476.
J163.4	Good counsels bought.	435.
J215.5§	Present daughter-in-law proved better than a new, more "evil" one.	432.
J220.1§	‡"If you [have to] fall in love, fall in love with a moon [-like beauty]; and if you [have to] steal, steal a camel['s worth]"	364 n. 52.
J226	Difficult choices between relatives.	363 n. 32, 445, 451.
J226.4§	Choice: whether to marry from father's or mother's family.	431.
J229.16.1§	Ogre gives captive girl choice: marriage to him, or death (to be eaten, etc.).	414.
J229.16.2.1§	Choice: becoming ogre's daughter.	153.
J229.16.2.2§	Choice: becoming ogre's sister.	109, 153.
J229.16.5.1§	Captive man to ogress: "Devour me beginning with my little ears (beard) which did not heed my wife's fears (advice)."	434.
J268§	Flattery of authority or seniors rewarded.	441.
J318.1§	"Better things in the past (golden times, good old days, etc.)."	376 n. 278, 385 n. 448.
J414	Marriage with equals or with unequals.	429, 442.
J482.2	Better to marry ugly than fair wife. Less hard to satisfy.	434.
J490§	‡Young (tender) preferred to old (tough).	434.
J551.6.2§	Only youngest daughter tells king (her father) that it is not him but destiny (God) who controls a human's fortune: she is banished.	444.
J571.5.1§	‡Promise secured not to act till story is told in full.	442.
J679.5§	‡Truth-speaking meddler fails to prove his report (claim): punished for "slander."	435.
J702	Necessity of work.	416.
J706	Acquisition of wealth.	55 n. 65.
J707.1§	‡Property preferred to marital amity (peace in marriage).	55 n. 65.
J708.1§	‡Little money (capital) invested becomes wealth.	422.
J708.2§	‡Acquisition of property (real estate) leads to wealth.	55 n. 65.
J836§	Man (woman) who loses all his (her) seven (forty, ninety-nine) sons at once seeks comfort.	456.
J885	Clever person's defeat pleases inferior [*shamâtah*].	53 n. 26.
J886§	Greater grief: person seeks consolation in adversity.	456.
J894.2§	Consolation: "*'anâ-mâlî*" ("None of my business").	396 n. 644.

J895§	‡Consolation by thought of not being alone in misfortune.	375 n. 263.
J960.1§	‡Man tries to persuade woman that elongated shadow of his limb (organ) on wall is indicative of his prowess.	23 n. 39.
J1010	**Value of industry.**	416.
J1014§	‡Making a living (by earning wages).	435.
J1063.0.1§	Projection: attributing to others one's own shortcomings (defects).	373 n. 235.
J1129§	Female trickster.	422.
J1141.1	Guilty person deceived into gesture (act) which admits guilt.	432.
J1141.1.13§	Gold coins said to be from feces found in wife's bed: woman (mother-in-law) admits she is the one who has been wetting the bed all along.	432.
J1141.11.1§	Liar nonplussed: truth detected through trap-doll. The biting mother-in-law (daughter-in-law, co-wife): proves to be a dummy (doll, stick).	432.
J1144	Eaters of stolen food detected.	432, 457.
J1144.3§	Owner takes notice of missing food: intruder detected.	423.
J1149.3.1§	Detection of man masking as woman by ordering all to disrobe.	382 n. 400.
J1163	Pleading for accused by means of parable.	428.
J1215§	‡Know-it-all person (*'Abu-el-¿urraif'*): a talkative fool.	26 n. 47.
J1251.1	Humiliated lover in repartee with disdainful [(scornful)] mistress.	427.
J1341.10	Hungry student gets meat [by telling mewing cat that he got only bone].	458.
J1347.2.1.3§	‡Circumcision procession (celebration): foods provided to guests.	390 n. 534.
J1347.2.2.1§	‡Ramadan-fasting: rich foods (especially pastries) are prepared.	427.
J1347.2.2.2§	‡Big-bairam: meat (mutton) provided.	407 n. 836.
J1347.2.4§	‡An eve for God's sake, or for God's people (Sufi occasion, '*khatmah*'): food provided.	384 n. 440.
J1487	Progress at school. [Reckoned by passages reached in Holy Book.]	376 n. 280.
J1525	Poor girl outwits prince in fright contest.	428.
J1661.1.3.1§	Deduction: bread made by a menstruous woman. Hair found in bread.	372 n. 208.
J1675.9§	King's promise of safety secured before breaking news to him.	444.
J1701	The stupid [(foolish)] wife.	436, 439.
J1805.2.1	Daughter says "sobur" (wait [patience]) to her father when he asks what to bring from the journey. Father finds prince Sobur.	442.
J1807.3§	Penis mistaken for an object (finger, pin, etc.).	429.

J1913.1§	Exposure of teeth from pain (anger, death) thought to be a smile.	423, 453.
J1919.8.1§	Simpleton led to believe that woman (actually man masking woman) has a penis.	429, 432.
J2132	Numskull dragged.	420.
J2199.4	Short-sighted economy.	369 n. 148.
J2199.4.6.1§	‡Earnings by the needle, expenditure by the pitchfork (deficit spending).	390 n. 525, 435.
J2218§	The effect of group-opinion: clearly false statement held as true outweighs physical evidence.	433.
J2301.4§	Gullible husband believes ogress, but not his own wife.	433.
J2303	‡Gullible mother.	439.
J2321.2	Man thinks he has given birth to a child by letting wind.	427.
J2400	Foolish imitation.	455.
J2400.1§	Foolish imitation of brother by brother.	442.
J2401	Fatal imitation.	426, 440.
J2411.6.2§	Unsuccessful imitation by stepsister (sister-in-law) to produce treasure from excrements.	442.
J2460	**Literal obedience.**	429.
J2461	What should I have done (said)?	433.
J2461.2	Literal following of instructions about greetings. [Wrong conditions (circumstances).]	433.
J2519§	‡Absurd extreme mourning.	436.
J2519.1§	‡Animal (bird, insect) foolishly mourned.	436.
J2519.5§	‡Intemperance in mourning.	403 n. 770.
J2756.1.1§	‡"A woman trusting men['s fidelity] is a woman trusting water [to remain] in a wide-meshed sieve!"	394 n. 590.

K. DECEPTIONS

K82	Deceptive drinking contest.	413.
K145.1§	Valuable animal (dog, horse) sold repeatedly; always escapes to join original master (owner).	422.
K149.5§	Egg yolk (powdered) sold as potent (yellow) poison.	458.
K252.4§	Person painted black and sold (kept) as slave.	454.
K288.2§	Girl will marry a man only if fitting certain description: she arranges for the terms never to occur.	421.
K289§	Artificial (deceptive) compliance: one party to a bargain arranges for the terms (conditions, stipulations) to occur.	441.
K289.1§	Artificial (deceptive) compliance: "Wait until fat (parsley) has oozed out of the ram's anus (ear)."	57 n. 93.
K301	Master thief.	416.
K315	‡Thief enters treasury through secret passage.	416.
K321.1	Girl made to carry shell from which ashes fall: she is thus followed.	421.

K322	Theft of gold hoard by spying on secret hiding place.	185, Tale No. 19.
K451.3	Concealed confederate as unjust witness.	445.
K455.4.4§	‡Fugitives promise predator (crocodile) one of them as payment for helping them escape pursuer: predator deceived into eating pursuer as fee.	452.
K477.0.1.1§	‡Attention drawn by mischief (obnoxious acts).	150.
K512	Compassionate executioner.	442.
K512.1.2§	Compassionate executioner: animal's (bird's) blood in bottle as proof.	420, 423, 424, 453.
K514	Disguise as girl to avoid execution.	456.
K521.1.4	Escape by putting on old woman's skin.	424, 452.
K523.0.1.2§	Escape by shamming illness: food (paste, mash, porridge, etc.) smeared on intended victim's posterior and claimed to be the effects of diarrhea.	434.
K523.3§	Dumbness feigned to escape telling the truth.	428.
K525	Escape by use of substituted object. The object is attacked rather than the intended victim.	428.
K527	Escape by substituting another person in place of the intended victim.	438.
K527.3.1§	Exchange of clothes between hero's female confederate (wife, paternal-cousin) and imprisoned princess.	438.
K528	Substitute in ordeal.	438.
K528.2.2§	‡Wife substitutes self for maiden with whom her husband is in love—(maiden accused of unchastity).	438.
K537§	Escape by leaving behind object (bracelet, drum, etc.) that makes noise when wind blows.	434.
K539§	Escape by cutting off restraint (rope, garment, etc.) held by captor.	424.
K550.3§	‡Captor busied with performing task while captive escapes.	451.
K551.4.5	Escape by pretending to go to river and wash clothes.	434.
K551.16	Woman escapes by ruse: must go defecate [(to toilet)].	423, 424, 453.
K605	‡Cannibal sent for water with vessel full of holes: victim escapes.	451.
K626	‡Escape by bribing the guard.	438.
K626.1	Escape by throwing money (treasure) so that guards [(pursuers)] fight over it.	442.
K638.9.1§	‡Escape by making self slippery, by covering self with soap, grease, slippery plant (e.g., *molokhiyyah*), etc.	365 n. 75.
K639§	Escape by disabling pursuer's (companion's) means of transportation.	456.
K649.4.1§	Son disguised as daughter in order to spare his life.	456.
K649.9	Confederate causes confusion so that prisoner can escape.	438.

K1315.5.2§	Noble woman poses as prostitute.	455, 457.
K1321	Seduction by man disguised as woman.	429, 456.
K1321.1	Man disguised as woman admitted to women's quarters: seduction.	382 n. 400.
K1321.2	Man disguised as woman abducts princess.	456.
K1335	Seduction (or wooing) by stealing clothes [(feathers)] of bathing girl (swan maiden).	418, 440, 455.
K1349.1	‡Disguise to enter girl's (man's) room.	429, 456.
K1371	Bride-stealing.	456.
K1371.1.2	Lover's foster brother (friend) steals bride from wedding with unwelcome suitor.	456.
K1390.1§	‡Man deceived into impregnating woman (fathering a child).	457.
K1390.1.2.1§	‡Man tricked into ejaculating inside woman (by causing him to lose control).	457.
K1514.11	Illness feigned to call physician paramour.	445.
K1517.2	Paramour poses as doctor.	445.
K1523	Underground passage [(tunnel)] to paramour's house. (Inclusa.) Woman goes from one to the other.	449.
K1550.1.2	Adulteress detected by food she prepares for paramour.	457.
K1553	Husband feigns blindness and avenges himself on his wife and her paramour.	458.
K1565	Blades (broken glass) to wound and detect wife's [(sister's)] lover.	442.
K1571	Trickster discovers adultery: food goes to husband instead of lover.	458.
K1590.2§	‡Embracing and kissing, felt by maiden in the dark, explained to her as dream (nightmare).	427.
K1611	‡Substituted caps [sleeping places] cause ogre to kill his own children.	451.
K1612	Message of death fatal to sender.	435.
K1613.5§	Turning the plate around: would-be poisoner poisoned with his own poison.	458.
K1816.5	Disguise as goose-girl (turkey-girl).	452.
K1816.13.1§	Disguise as black salve-woman.	433.
K1817.3	Disguise as harper (minstrel).	456.
K1817.4.1.2§	‡Disguise as peddler so as to gather news (usually about escaped or missing person).	434.
K1825.1.4	Girl masks as doctor to find departed lover.	442.
K1826.0.1§	‡Posing as cleric-schoolteacher (instructor).	426.
K1828.1.1	Woman disguised as angel of death [(Azrael)].	428.
K1832	Disguise by changing voice.	413, 414.
K1832.1§	Disguise by changing texture of skin (hide, fur).	413.
K1832.2§	Disguise by changing color of feet (paws).	413.
K1833	Disguise as ghost.	428.
K1836	Disguise of man in woman's dress.	429.

K1836.3	Disguised man takes bride's place.	456.
K1837	Disguise of woman in man's clothes.	422, 442.
K1839.1	Wolf puts flour [(lime, etc.)] on his paws to disguise himself.	413.
K1839.1.1§	She-fox (vixen) applies egg yolk to her tail so as to make it smooth and disguise herself.	413.
K1843	Wife deceives husband with substitute bedmate.	436, 444.
K1843.1.2§	Disguised wife sleeps in her husband's bed as his bedmate (lover, slave girl): she conceives.	394 n. 584, 436.
K1843.2.2	Wife takes mistress's place in bed but is deceived in turn.	436.
K1843.5§	Sister masks as her brother's wife and sleeps with him.	399 n. 715, 447, 455, 457.
K1843.6§	Mother masks as her son's wife and sleeps with him.	417.
K1856.1.2§	‡Wife serves her husband flesh of his (or, her) own son.	446.
K1874.1§	‡Truth-telling and lie-telling agents give testimony (simultaneously).	423, 453.
K1891.1§	Person hides inside statue and then arranges for it to be sold to the beloved.	423.
K1891.2§	Fugitive escapes pursuer by hiding in animal carcass.	423.
K1895§	False proof: grave containing buried animal (sheep) as evidence of someone's death.	417.
K1911	The false bride (substituted bride).	441, 444.
K1911.3	Reinstatement of true bride.	441.
K1911.3.1	Substitution of false bride revealed by animal.	441.
K1915	The false bridegroom (substitute bridegroom).	456.
K1934	Imposter forces heroine to change places with her.	453.
K1941	Disguised flayer. An imposter dresses in the skin of his victim.	424, 452, 453.
K1952.2	Better things at home.	419.
K1952.4.0.1§	‡Imposter son or daughter.	104.
K1952.4.3§	‡Poor girl poses as daughter of noble person.	420.
K1969.5.1§	‡Person pretends to know language of animals (birds, insects, etc.).	457.
K1984.2.1	Girl claims to have overeaten on a nightingale's thigh.	429.
K1984.2.2§	Starved wife steals miserly husband's money, prepares a grand feast and claims: "All seven cauldrons are from half a sparrow (sparrow-side)."	429.
K1991.1§	Mother goat masks her sharp horns by covering them with mud (dough, wax).	413.
K1996.1§	Feigning illness by shamming physical symptoms: crackling bread under mattress to simulate crackling bones.	445.
K1996.2§	Feigning illness by shamming physical symptoms: saffron dye on face to simulate "yellowness" (paleness) of death.	439, 445.
K2010.4§	‡Treacherous one-time winner. Loses repeatedly and is forgiven, but refuses to yield when finally wins.	452.

K2011.3.1§	‡Ogress poses as man's sister and feigns affection for his children.	433.
K2020.2§	‡Person secures promise that wish will be granted and then demands the impossible.	388 n. 510.
K2056	Hypocritical stepmother [. . .].	445.
K2092§	Spirit possession feigned in order to gain pity (sympathy).	55 n. 67.
K2107.3§	‡Rumor mongering. False report concocted and spread.	187, 429.
K2111	Potiphar's wife [and Joseph].	435.
K2112	Woman slandered as adulteress (prostitute).	431.
K2112.0.1§	‡Innocent (chaste) maiden slandered.	447.
K2112.1.1	Fingers as false token of wife's unfaithfulness. [Prove to be the maidservant's.]	436.
K2112.2.2.1§	Female confederate (maidservant, daughter, sister, etc.) masked as man is introduced into a girl's room as ruse so as to slander her.	431.
K2116.1.1.1	Innocent woman accused of eating her newborn children.	425.
K2117	Calumniated wife: substituted letter (falsified message).	426.
K2155.1	Blood smeared on innocent person brings accusation of murder.	425.
K2178§	Virgin made to look pregnant. Magic potion (snake's eggs, etc.) used.	447, 448.
K2201.1§	‡Secret betrayed out of spite (or for revenge).	420.
K2211.1	Treacherous brother-in-law.	441.
K2211.4§	Treacherous paternal-cousin(s).	422, 458.
K2212	Treacherous sister.	426, 433, 442.
K2212.1	Treacherous stepsisters.	442, 444, 445.
K2212.2	Treacherous sister-in-law.	431, 457.
K2212.2.0.1§	Magic pregnancy induced by treacherous sister-in-law to discredit husband's sister.	447, 448.
K2212.2.1§	Treacherous husband's *bint-¿amm* (paternal-cousin, wife's in-law).	423, 447.
K2216§	Treacherous aunt.	454.
K2216.1§	Treacherous maternal-aunt (*khâlah*).	444.
K2217.0.3§	Treacherous maternal-uncle.	406 n. 813.
K2218.1	Treacherous mother-in-law accuses wife.	431, 432.
K2218.5.1§	‡Treacherous paternal-uncle's wife.	454.
K2222	Treacherous co-wife (concubine).	427, 439, 446, 453.
K2250.2§	‡Treacherous (dishonest) workman (hireling).	26 n. 47.
K2258.1§	‡Treacherous peasant woman (girl).	421, 433.
K2261.0.1§	Treacherous black woman [. . .].	453.
K2287.1§	A *kâfir* ("disbeliever") as villain.	435.
K2293	Treacherous old woman.	438, 453.
K2310.1§	‡Deception by literal following (misconstruction) of instructions.	432.

K2375.1§	White liquid (soap-water, milk) said to be milk-white from bathing person (girl) in it.	427.

L. REVERSAL OF FORTUNE

L13.1	Youngest wife's son restores eyesight to blinded six wives of raja and reinstates his mother.	439.
L54.2§	Youngest son agrees to marry monster; later the brothers are jealous.	455.
L55	Stepdaughter heroine.	443.
L61	Clever youngest daughter.	427.
L63	Youngest daughter avoids seducer.	427.
L71	Only youngest of group of imprisoned women refuses to eat her newborn child.	439.
L111.5.1§	Child of brother-sister incest as hero: "son of own maternal-uncle."	405 n. 807, 405 n. 810, 455, 457.
L112.7.2§	‡Scabby-headed person (*'aqra¿*) as hero.	457.
L113.1.8§	Black man (black-slave) in 'white' nation (tribe) as hero (¿Antar, Abu-Zaid, etc.).	455.
L143.3§	Poor brother surpasses rich brother.	422.
L153§	Girl succeeds where boy fails (they are paternal-cousins).	422.
L162	Lowly heroine marries prince (king).	271, 425, 429.
L178§	Despised brother wins wager (contest) against arrogant brother.	422.
L215	Unpromising magic object chosen.	426.
L215.1§	Unpromising object (item) in inheritance division proves best.	426.
L221	Modest request: present from the journey. [Present from father's journey proves difficult.]	442.
L252§	Girl with modest capital realizes large profits.	422.
L350	**Mildness triumphs over violence.**	373 n. 232.
L405§	Rich (high) becomes poor (low).	52 n. 17.
L410.9§	Barmecide Catastrophe: noble family destroyed	394 n. 584.

M. ORDAINING THE FUTURE

M117.0.1§	*nadhr/'nadr'*: conditional vow: pledge to perform certain (good) act if prayer is answered (request is granted).	440.
M119.8.1	Swearing by one's father and mother.	426.
M119.8.2	Swearing by life of father [(or ancestors)].	427.
M135.3§	Spouse no-remarriage pact: each of husband and wife vows never to remarry if the other dies first.	434.
M139§	Vow to marry only a person fitting certain description (size, color, etc.).	423, 451, 457.
M139.1§	Vow to marry only a girl whom a certain object (shoe, bracelet, etc.) would fit.	423, 452.

M139.2§	Vow to marry only the man with the most rosy (red) henna-colored hands.	421.
M147§	Conditional "divorce-vow": oath that divorce will have occurred unless certain matter is brought to pass.	389 n. 512.
M155.5§	Vow to perform certain acts of trickery.	438.
M203	King's promise irrevocable.	382 n. 382, 442.
M209§	Reminder of unfulfilled (forgotten) vow: recipient must execute own part of pledge (bargain).	427.
M223	‡Blind promise (rash boon). Person grants wish before hearing it.	388 n. 510.
M224.1§	‡Kerchief of safety (*maḥramat al-'amân*): cloth given to the accused indicating promise of immunity from punishment.	398 n. 693.
M225	Eyes exchanged for food.	444.
M256.0.4§	‡Promise to dying wife broken.	445.
M295	Bargain to keep secret.	435, 445.
M341.0.5§	Person knows time of own death.	444, 450.
M411.20.1§	Curse by husband.	428.
M411.20.2§	Curse by wife.	55 n. 70.
M416.1.1§	Curse: gluttony (being controlled by dictates of the stomach).	407 n. 827.
M424.1§	‡Incestuous brother cuts his sister's hand off, she curses him (to becoming crippled); he recovers when her hand is restored.	453.
M431.4.1	Curse: hand of person cursed to drop off.	366 n. 94, 396 n. 628, 439.
M439§	‡Curse: infamy or public disgrace (*faḍîhah*).	428.
M440.2.1§	‡"May He bring [calamities] and heap [them] upon . . . [someone]."	55 n. 69, 396 n. 645.
M443.6.1§	‡Curse: one's affairs turned upside down.	366 n. 94.
M519.2§	‡Supplication: being shielded from infamy or public disgrace—(*es-satr*).	366 n. 87, 373 n. 222, 383 n. 428.

N. CHANCE AND FATE

N2.6.1	Sister as wager.	436.
N15	Chastity wager.	436.
N15.3§	Wager on sister's chastity.	436.
N104§	"Unfortunate beauty: beauty of innocent woman causes communal conflicts (wars). She is blamed."	388 n. 510.
N107.2.1§	‡An accident "takes [a coming] evil and goes away [with it]."	381 n. 376.
N122.0.2§	The choice of roads: Road of Safety, Road of Sorrow, or Road of No-return.	421, 439.

N131	Acts performed for changing luck.	449.
N134.0.1.2§	Birth of a daughter brings good luck.	370 n. 158.
N134.0.1.3§	‡A sister brings good luck (prosperity) to her brother.	453.
N182.1§	Snakes and scorpions turn into gold.	458.
N190.0.1§	‡Inexplicable inequality in possessions (wealth, power, etc.).	398 n. 689.
N303.1§	‡Only one family member survives calamity.	414.
N338	Death as result of mistaken identity: wrong person killed.	435.
N339.18§	‡Accidental killing when part of body (organ) containing soul is severed (wounded).	16.
N342.1.2§	‡Virtuous woman (maiden) hastily condemned as adulteress (unchaste).	189, Tale No. 20.
N344.1	Wrong sign put out leads to boys' leaving home.	453.
N353§	‡Bird (animal) steals precious object from person and accidentally brings it to the attention of another person: search for owner of object follows.	272.
N365	Incest unwittingly committed.	455.
N365.1	Boy unwittingly commits incest with his mother.	417.
N365.2.1	Father unwittingly falls in love with daughter.	424.
N365.3	Unwitting brother-sister incest.	399 n. 715, 447, 455, 457.
N365.3.1	Brother and sister unwittingly in love with each other.	447.
N365.3.3§	Boy finds a woman's hair and decides to marry the person to whom it belongs: it is his sister's.	451, 453.
N382.3§	Fugitive in tree urinates thus betraying hiding place.	448.
N383.5§	Miser falls dead when he realizes that his treasure has been discovered (stolen).	429.
N384.0.2§	Insanity (loss of senses) due to calamity or fright.	450.
N411.4	Salt in saltless land sold for fortune.	422.
N456	Enigmatic smile (laugh) reveals secret knowledge.	419.
N457§	Reason for smiling needlessly is demanded.	419.
N458§	Overheard animal's (bird's) chant reveals commission of crime (deception).	441.
N458.1§	Cat's chant betrays substitution of bride.	441.
N464§	‡Secret discovered during physical closeness (contact) with another person.	454.
N464.1§	‡Secret discovered while lousing person.	454.
N478	Secret wealth betrayed by money left in borrowed money-scales.	415.
N482.3.1§	Secret learned by threatening to have person (mother, daughter, etc.) dipped in boiling water.	426.
N511	Treasure in ground.	415.
N534.1.1§	Treasure discovered by following an animal.	26 n. 46, 449.
N538.3.1§	Prosperity from living in slain ogress's dwelling.	434.
N641.0.1§	Patient laughs so hard at comic actions (scenes) about	

	him, thus abscess breaks (object in throat dislodged) and he is healed.	427.
N681.1	Wife finds lost husband just as he is to marry another.	442.
N681.3.0.2§	Incest accidentally averted: talking bed.	448.
N681.3.2	Man in love with his sister accidentally learns her identity.	447.
N711	King (prince) accidentally finds maiden and marries her.	424, 448.
N711.6	Prince sees heroine at ball and is enamored.	442.
N711.7§	‡Lover sees beloved first while she is a-traveling.	438.
N730.1§	‡Expression of affection (love) at meeting of separated family members.	454.
N770	**Experiences leading to adventures.**	449.
N773.2	Adventure from returning for forgotten comb.	446.
N793§	‡Adventures from entering pit, hole, cave, or crack (in ground).	449.
N803.2§	‡Jinni-woman receives help from her mother.	455.
N812	Giant or ogre as helper.	439.
N813	Helpful genie (spirit).	435, 443.
N825.2	Old man helper.	439.
N825.3	Old woman helper.	442.
N825.3.2	Old woman by spring [(well)] as helper.	440.
N831.1	Mysterious housekeeper.	421.
N842.1	Cook as foster father.	439.
N844	Dervish as helper.	454.
N859§	Fisher as helper.	444.
N884.2§	Chivalrous (gallant) robber (thief).	458.
N884.2.1§	Robber (thief) steals from the rich and gives to the poor.	416.
N884.3§	Robber helps person he had intended to rob.	458.

P. SOCIETY

P3.1.1§	‡Family (personal) name as indicator of social status.	371 n. 185, 422.
P3.2§	‡Social connections (friends) as indicator of social status.	51 n. 4.
P3.2.1§	‡Name-dropping: frequently mentioning names of famous persons in a familiar manner so as to impress listener.	51 n. 4.
P3.3.4§	‡Owning own dwelling (house) as "status symbol."	53 n. 31.
P3.3.4.2§	‡Living in house with "open door" as indicator of social status.	56 n. 77, 361 n. 11.
P7.1§	‡Role strain (role conflict): effects of difficult choices between conflicting obligations.	22 n. 26, 54 n. 38, 55 n. 57, 361 n. 2, 374 n. 255, 394 n. 588, 399 n. 713, 400 n. 734, 402 n. 768.
P12.2.2§	Tyrannical viceroy (or minister).	451.

P253.2.0.1§	Great love of sister for brother(s).	433.
P253.2.0.1.1§	"He who has no sister is an orphan."	311, 450.
P253.2.1	Brother faithful to persecuted sister.	446.
P253.2.3§	Transformed brother (deer) about to be slaughtered pleads with sister for help; she had been exposed and is helpless.	447, 453.
P253.3	Brother chosen rather than husband or son.	55 n. 58, 451.
P253.3.1§	‡Sister favors brother over her husband.	55 n. 57, 450.
P253.5	Sister avenges brother's death.	454.
P253.6.1§	Sister always consulted by her brother and her counsel sought.	449.
P253.6.2§	‡Trouble from ignoring sister's advice.	434.
P253.8	Clever sister saves life of brother.	448.
P253.9	Woman dies of sorrow for death of brother.	450.
P253.9.1§	Sister becomes insane due to death of brother.	450.
P253.10.2§	Brothers compete for their sister's love (affection).	421.
P253.11.2§	Sister's corpse is placed on horse's (camel's) back to wander, awaiting vivification.	421, 454.
P253.11.5§	Brother and sister buried together.	450.
P253.12.2§	‡A brother must be equitable with (fair to) all his sisters.	433.
P253.13.2§	‡A caring sister between her two feuding brothers.	54 n. 38.
P254.0.1§	‡Household composed of only brother and sister(s). They live alone in palace (house, cave, etc.).	29 n. 75, 368 n. 137, 448, 449, 450.
P254.1.2§	‡Sister and brother kill their father.	423, 453.
P256§	Brother forgives his (seemingly) culprit sister(s).	457.
P261.1.1§	‡Man fearful (distrustful) of daughter's husband (suitor).	160, 380 n. 349.
P262.1	Bad relations between mother-in-law and daughter-in-law.	432, 450.
P262.1.1§	‡"A mother-in-law is a fever, a husband's sister is a deadly scorpion."	54 n. 50.
P262.2§	Even when a woman's very own daughter becomes her daughter-in-law, she is hostile to her mother-in-law (her own mother).	450.
P263.1	Widower marries wife's sister. [Sororate.]	429, 444.
P263.2§	Bad relations between brother and his sister's husband (brother-in-law).	445, 448.
P263.3.1§	‡Bad relations between a man and his cousin-sister's husband.	28 n. 71.
P264.0.1§	*salâyif* (women whose husbands are brothers, sisters-in-law).	441, 455.
P264.0.1.1§	Rivalry between a woman and her *silfah* (wife of husband's brother, sisters-in-law).	455.

P264.0.1.2§	Accommodation is not possible between a woman and her *silfah* (wife of husband's brother, sisters-in-law), but possible between co-wives.	394 n. 603.
P264.0.1.3§	Sisters as *salâyif* (sisters-in-law).	434.
P264.1§	Bad relations between wife and husband's sister.	53 n. 37.
P264.2§	Kindly brother's wife (sister-in-law): aids husband's sister.	449.
P264.3§	Kindly sister-in-law: aids her brother's wife.	433.
P264.3.1§	Only youngest sister-in-law is kindly to (aids) her brother's cast-off wife.	433.
P268§	Co-wives (*ḍarâyir*).	432.
P268.2§	Accommodation between co-wives.	432, 440.
P271.2	Fisherman as foster father.	444.
P272	Foster mother.	424.
P274.3§	Prince marries maiden found, and then raised as his foster sister.	417.
P291	Grandfather.	414.
P293.0.1§	Maternal-uncles (*'akhwâl, khu'ûlah*) as source of power.	436.
P293.2	Mother's brother as helper.	438.
P293.2.0.1§	‡Kind maternal-uncle (mother's brother, *khâl*).	53 n. 25.
P293.2.3§	Nephew helps mother's brother catch adulteress wife and lover.	457.
P294.0.1.2.2.1§	‡Paternal-aunt reserved (cool) toward her brother's daughter: thinks niece is allied with her own mother (i.e., the wife of the aunt's brother).	54 n. 38.
P295.1.2§	Marriage between *'ibn-¿amm* and his *bint-¿amm* (paternal-cousin).	426, 438.
P295.1.7.1.1§	‡Female paternal-cousins as rivals in love (marriage).	441.
P297.2.1§	Bond between mother's brother (*khâl*) and sister's son.	456, 457.
P297.2.2§	‡"A maternal-uncle is a father [to his sister's child]" (*'el-khâl wâlid*).	405 n. 811.
P305.1.1.1§	‡"The Prophet recommended [caring for neighbors] as far as the seventh [house away]."	416.
P305.6§	‡Weak relations between neighbors.	55 n. 59.
P311.1.1§	"No love except after enmity" (i.e., friendship that comes after enmity is strong).	381 n. 376, 428.
P320	**Hospitality. Relation of host and guest.**	56 n. 77.
P324.0.1.1.1§	‡Ground covered with carpet, flowers, etc. for guest ("red-carpet treatment").	424.
P324.0.2§	‡Providing welcome (conversation, entertainment, "greetings") is host's responsibility.	53 n. 33.
P325	Host surrenders his wife to his guest.	431.
P335.1§	‡Shabby hospitality (inhospitality) betrays host's bad character.	422.
P340	**Teacher and pupil.**	425.
P410.1§	‡"Unskilled laborer."	55 n. 60.

P779.1.1§	‡Imported fine textile (cloth).	449.
P779.1.2§	‡Imported fine weapons (sword, spear, etc.).	422.
P780§	**Shameful (disgraceful) acts.**	432.
P783.1§	‡Breaking wind in public: disgraceful.	432.
P785§	'*ṣaghranah*' (unseemly behavior): committing acts that reduce one's communal standing (worth).	369 n. 150.
P790.0.1.1§	‡Having a conversation (interesting social talk).	56 n. 77.
P790.0.1.2§	‡Invitation to have "conversation."	56 n. 78.
P790.1.2.1§	‡Trellis (ululation) of joy ('*ẓaghrûṭah*'/*zaghrûdah*). (Typically voiced by women at a joyous occasion such as a wedding, pilgrimage, winning at law-court, release from prison, etc.)	25 n. 44, 365 n. 72, 390 n. 534.
P790.2.3§	‡Refusal to eat or drink (at host's) as signs of displeasure (anger).	433.
P790.3.1§	‡Shrieking for grief ('*ṣuwâṭ*'). (Typically voiced by women at a calamitous occurrence such as a death, serious injury, receiving a prison sentence, etc.)	407 n. 843.
P798.1§	Unbalanced (unstable) triads.	434.
P798.1.0.5§	Triads revolving around brother and sister as unbalanced (Sethian syndrome).	445, 451, 458.
P798.1.1§	Conflict within a triad: one party is removed so as to restore stability (balance).	451, 458.
P801.9.1§	‡Wrestling (mainly outdoors).	362 n. 18.
P963.1§	Public procession (feast) for a boy's circumcision.	435, 442.

Q. REWARDS AND PUNISHMENTS

Q2	Kind and unkind.	440, 444.
Q2.1§	Flattering lies rewarded, unflattering truth punished.	440.
Q22.1§	Placing one's faith in God alone rewarded.	449.
Q41	Politeness rewarded.	442.
Q41.2	Reward for cleaning loathsome person.	440.
Q50§	‡Reward for educating the uneducated.	376 n. 283.
Q50.1§	‡Reward for teaching the non-literate how to read and write.	54 n. 47.
Q62	Reward for ability to keep secrets.	425.
Q64	Patience rewarded.	449.
Q68.2	Honesty rewarded.	449.
Q72	‡Loyalty rewarded.	436.
Q87	‡Reward for preservation of chastity.	436.
Q94	Reward for cure.	442.
Q113.5.1§	‡Educator (teacher) revered ("as if messenger of God").	376 n. 283.
Q171.0.1.1§	Murder unpunished (forgiven).	446.
Q171.0.2§	‡Attempted murder unpunished (forgiven).	447.
Q172	Reward: admission to heaven.	54 n. 47, 429.

R. CAPTIVES AND FUGITIVES

R212.1.1	Man buried alive escapes from tomb when thief tries to rob it.	451.
R219.3§	‡Person sinking into earth pulled out by rescuer.	448.
R223§	‡Girl flees to escape her incestuous father.	423, 453.
R224	Girl flees to escape incestuous brother.	451.
R224.1§	Foster-brother flees to escape incestuous foster-sister.	451.
R225	Elopement.	456.
R226§	Flight from home so as to escape wrath of patriarch (father, husband).	448.
R227.2	Flight from hated husband.	428.
R231	Obstacle flight—Atalanta type. Objects are thrown back which the pursuer stops to pick up while fugitive escapes.	445, 453.
R232§	‡Lure flight: pursuer causes precious objects to appear before fugitive which the fugitive stops to pick up.	452.
R245.1.1§	Crocodile ferry. Fugitives are carried across the water on crocodile.	425, 452, 453.
R263§	Chase in and out of oven. Pursuer (wolf, ogre) tires: intended victim escapes.	413.
R311	Tree refuge.	452.
R311.4	‡Stretching tree refuge for fugitive.	414.
R319.0.1§	‡Predator (wolf, hyena, etc.) lives in graveyard.	413.
R319.1.2.1.1§	‡Incestuous brother and sister live inside closed tomb so as to hide their illicit love.	28 n. 67.
R351.0.1§	Maiden in tree discovered by her reflection in water.	424.
R351.1.2§	Urine drops from fugitive on lion (wild beast) and reveals fugitive's hiding place in tree.	448.

S. UNNATURAL CRUELTY

S10	**Cruel parents.**	446.
S11	Cruel father.	448.
S12	Cruel mother.	418, 420.
S12.2.0.1§	Mother kills her own son.	446.
S12.8§	A mother's cruel nagging drives child insane.	418.
S20.5§	Child kills both parents.	446.
S22	Parricide.	423, 446, 453.
S24§	Matricide.	419, 441.
S24.1§	Daughter kills her mother.	419, 440.
S24.1.1§	Widow induces girl to kill her mother and persuade father to marry the widow.	440, 441.
S24.2§	Son kills his mother.	416.
S31	Cruel stepmother.	439, 442, 444, 446.
S31.4.1§	Stepmother (co-wife) kills co-wife's son.	446.

S31.5	Girl persuades her father to marry a widow who has treated her kindly.	441.
S34	‡Cruel stepsister(s).	440, 442.
S51	Cruel mother-in-law.	432.
S51.2§	Wife starved (by mother-in-law, sister-in-law, etc.).	429, 432.
S54	Cruel daughter-in-law.	415.
S55	Cruel sister-in-law.	433, 448.
S57§	‡Husband cast out of wife's home by his in-laws.	57 n. 85.
S60.0.1§	Uxoricide (wife-killing).	429.
S62	Cruel husband.	429, 448.
S62.1	Bluebeard. Girl marries murderous husband.	387 n. 488.
S71.2§	Cruel paternal-uncle (*¿amm*).	53 n. 25, 424.
S71.3§	Cruel maternal-uncle (*khâl*).	456.
S71.3.4.1§	A woman's brother kills her son(s) but spares daughter.	456.
S72.1§	Cruel paternal-aunt (*¿ammah*).	442.
S72.2§	Cruel maternal-aunt (*khâlah*).	426, 444.
S73.0.1§	Sister cruel to her sister.	444.
S73.0.3.3§	‡Flight of brother(s) from home due to reported birth of another brother, rather than a sister.	453.
S75.3§	Cruel maternal-uncle's wife (*marat-khâl*).	407 n. 831.
S92§	‡Cruel policeman (jailor, executioner, etc.).	376 n. 283.
S111	Murder by poisoning.	421.
S115.5.1§	‡Suicide by falling on erect sword (dagger).	456.
S118.0.1§	Butcher as executioner.	420, 435.
S121	Murder by slamming down chest-lid.	440.
S132	‡Murder by starvation.	429.
S139.2	Slain person dismembered.	453.
S139.2.0.1§	‡Ghoulish trophy: part of enemy's corpse kept and displayed (or put to use).	426, 454.
S139.2.1.1	Head of murdered man taken along as trophy.	454.
S143	‡Abandonment in forest.	421.
S146.1.3§	Wife abandons cruel husband in a well.	428.
S160.1.1§	Self-mutilation to express grief.	434, 436.
S160.3	Fairies [(jinn, etc.)] mutilate mortals.	415.
S166.7§	Mutilation by skinning (flaying).	424.
S166.7.1§	‡Face skinning.	458.
S176.1	Mutilation: emasculation.	434, 435.
S181	Wounding by trapping with sharp knives (glass).	442.
S215.2§	Daughter promised to a riding-animal (stallion, camel).	423.
S264.1	Man thrown overboard to placate the storm.	442.
S272.1.1§	Flight of brothers from home due to treachery.	453.
S272.3§	Flight of brother and sister from home to avoid being sacrificed.	446.
S302.4§	All newborn daughters to be slaughtered.	424, 425.
S302.5§	Newborn daughters buried alive (*wa'd*).	374 n. 253.

S322.0.2§	Elder siblings deprive younger of inheritance.	426.
S322.2	Jealous mother casts daughter forth.	420.
S322.6.3.0.1§	‡Hardhearted maternal-aunt refuses to shelter niece (nephew).	426.
S342	Mother induced by rival to kill her children.	440.
S351	Abandoned child cared for by mother secretly.	424, 449.
S403.1§	‡Enchanted person (in form of animal) about to be slaughtered begs for mercy (help).	297.
S413.1	Ogress wife orders raja to turn out [(cast-off)] his six wives.	439.
S432.1§	Pregnant woman cast into well by jealous rivals.	446.
S438	Abandoned queen blinded.	439.
S451	Outcast [(cast-out)] wife at last reunited with husband and children.	425.
S451.1§	Children bring about reunion between their father and outcast mother.	425, 429.
S451.1.1§	Husband reinstates his outcast wife due to her giving birth to his child (son).	433, 436.
S453.1§	Exposed woman helped by clergyman.	446.

T. SEX

T5§	Sexual attractiveness (sex-appeal) is relative.	435.
T9.0.1§	‡Sexual frustration (deprivation).	24 n. 41.
T9.1§	The power of sex: female's influence.	363 n. 31, 363 n. 32, 438, 445.
T10.0.2§	‡Falling in love may occur only after marriage (with one's spouse).	380 n. 348.
T11.1.1	Beauty of woman reported to king causes quest for her as his bride.	456.
T11.4.1	Love through sight of hair of unknown princess.	451, 453.
T11.5	Falling in love with reflection in water.	417.
T17.5§	‡Child induced to describe a female relative (child's mother, sister).	444.
T24.1	Love-sickness.	433, 438.
T24.2.1	‡Fainting away for love (or sexual desire).	388 n. 510.
T24.3	Madness from love.	450.
T26.1	Finger cut because of absorption in the charm of the beloved.	418, 455.
T28	Princess falls in love with a man disguised as a woman.	377 n. 285, 382 n. 401, 429, 456.
T30	**Lovers' meeting.**	438.
T35	Lovers' rendezvous.	438, 449.
T35.0.2.1§	Lover falls asleep and misses rendezvous.	438.
T36	Girl sleeps in garden to meet lover.	438.

T52.0.1.2§	‡Ghoulish (bloody) bride-price: life (organ) of person (or pet animal) demanded.	427.
T52.3	Bride purchased for her weight in gold.	398 n. 677.
T52.11.1§	Sister marries to save brother(s).	446.
T53.0.3§	‡Inquiring about family of spouse-to-be [. . .].	429.
T53.7.2.1.1§	‡Sister "marries her brother [to girl(s) of her choosing]."	300.
T54.1§	Choosing bride by lot (shooting arrow, throwing ball, etc.).	454.
T55	Girl as wooer. Forthputting woman.	438.
T55.6.3§	‡Coquette: exhibitionist from vanity.	381 n. 374.
T55.6.4§	‡Fashion display (fashion show): body exhibited in various complimentary dresses (costumes).	424, 455.
T59.1§	‡Lovers' play (foreplay): embracing, kissing, necking, etc.	383 n. 403, 407 n. 844, 429.
T59.2.1§	‡Accidental defloration (impregnation).	449, 457.
T60§	‡Sex games. Lovers pretend to be animals, objects, etc.	383 n. 403, 407 n. 844, 458.
T60.1.1§	‡Lovers pretend to be copulating stallion and mare (filly).	458.
T61.9§	‡Betrothal of the veiled female (unseen).	429.
T63.1§	‡Emasculated man accidentally selected as groom (husband).	212.
T63.2§	‡Woman masking (disguised) as man selected as groom (husband).	136.
T67.2	Marriage to prince as reward for curing him.	442.
T69.6§	Daughter [sister] given to beggar (as alms).	444.
T72.0.1§	Man loses battle of wits with (is humiliated by) girl (his paternal-cousin) then marries her for spite.	428.
T72.2.1	Prince marries scornful girl and punishes her.	428.
T81	Death from love.	424, 456.
T81.3	‡Girl falls dead on lover's body.	431.
T81.7	Woman dies on hearing of lover's or husband's death.	431, 456.
T86	Lovers buried in same grave.	424.
T86.2	Lovers die at the same time.	424.
T91.4.1.2§	‡Girl thought by older man to be too young for marriage is raised and then taken for a wife (by him).	424.
T92.5.0.1§	Brothers as rivals in love.	421.
T92.9	Father and son as rivals in love.	425.
T92.9.1	Parricide because of father-son rivalry for girl's love.	377 n. 287.
T92.9.2§	Son is given in marriage the bride-to-be intended for his father.	425.
T98§	Mother opposed to son's marriage.	431.
T100.0.9.2§	‡Marriage as treatment (cure) for unhappiness (immaturity).	429, 438.

T144.3.1§	‡One wife divorced, another (new) acquired.	429.
T144.4§	‡Serial sororal marriages: marrying one sister after another (from a group of sisters).	429.
T145.0.3§	Polygyny brings misery (trouble).	440, 453.
T145.0.4§	Happy polygynous marriage.	438, 440.
T145.1.0.1§	Marriage to four women.	417.
T145.2	Second wife taken because first is barren.	431.
T145.10§	Behavior of a polygynist's wife.	369 n. 149.
T145.10.1§	"Clip your bird's wings lest he mate with another." Wife is to keep husband poor.	394 n. 591.
T149.1§	Mother's name required for supernatural (magic, religious) ritual.	55 n. 70.
T160	**Consummation of marriage.**	52 n. 6, 447.
T160.0.5§	‡Tender defloration (first sexual intercourse).	25 n. 42.
T164.2.1§	‡Loss of daughter's income (labor) as an obstacle to consummation of marriage.	52 n. 6.
T183§	Wife (woman) tired of coition.	169.
T192.0.1§	Misery brought about by forced marriage.	428.
T192.3§	‡Marriage due to girl's (premarital) pregnancy.	449.
T193§	Marriage through threatening girl (woman) with disgrace (scandal).	438.
T194§	Marriage by abduction (or raid).	452.
T196§	Wife divorced because of a trifle.	390 n. 542, 424.
T197§	Wife's relatives (father, brother, etc.) force her divorce from husband without her consent.	57 n. 85.
T198§	Return to parents' (father's) home after end of marital relations (divorce, or death of spouse).	29 n. 75, 431.
T198.2§	‡Man returns to parents' home after end of his marriage.	57 n. 85.
T198.3.1§	‡Angered wife (*ghaḍbânah*): leaving husband's home for own family's (father's, brother's, etc.).	51 n. 4.
T198.3.4§	‡Unhappy (angered) husband leaves marital home.	55 n. 64.
T199.2.1.1§	‡Divorced woman allowed to take away only the garment she is wearing.	384 n. 430.
T199.3.1§	‡First wife not divorced out of kindness to her.	395 n. 625.
T199.3.2§	‡First wife not divorced due to her family's power (influence).	395 n. 625.
T200	**Married life.**	431.
T201.1§	Marriage: disappointing (only bad memories).	384 n. 433.
T201.1.0.1§	‡"Marriage: 'like [an inviting] quince, [but] every bite produces a tear—[because the fruit is actually bitter-tasting]'."	384 n. 432.
T201.1.1§	Marriage fatigue: decreasing value of (affection for) a spouse with passage of time.	24 n. 41.
T202.1.1§	‡"A pillow would not carry two [of a kind]."	381 n. 377.
T205.1§	Wife-beating.	55 n. 68.

T329§	"Clitoridectomy (excision of girls): so as to insure future chastity."	396 n. 632.
T331	Man unsuccessfully tempted by woman. [Chaste man.]	435.
T333	Man mutilates himself to remove temptation.	435.
T333.4.1§	Husband severs own genitals so as to persuade his dying wife that he will remain celibate.	434.
T351	Sword of chastity	17, 28
T380§	Heterosociality	160
T380.3.1§	Certain (non-threatening) males are viewed as unworthy of woman's modesty (e.g., slave, singer etc.).	382 n. 402, 406 n. 822, 456.
T380.3.1.1§	Male singer allowed to perform for women in women's quarters.	456.
T381.0.3§ (formerly T381.2§)	Virgin imprisoned to prevent riding-animal from desiring (falling in love with) her.	423.
T400	**Illicit sexual relations.**	449.
T405.3§	Sister's nakedness or exposure.	364 n. 65, 400 n. 720, 449, 450, 452.
T405.4.1§	Daughter's nakedness or exposure.	374 n. 254, 424.
T411.1	Lecherous father.	423, 453.
T412	Mother-son incest.	417.
T415	Brother-sister incest.	399 n. 715, 446, 453, 457.
T415.1	Lecherous brother.	451.
T415.2.1§	Sister repels incestuous brother.	451.
T415.4	Two lovers give each other up when they learn that they are brother and sister.	448.
T415.5	Brother-sister marriage.	450.
T415.5.1§	‡Parents approve (arrange) marriage between their son and daughter (brother-sister).	451.
T415.5.1.1§	‡Mother weds own daughter to own son.	450.
T415.8§	Sister who desires a son sired by her brother achieves her goal: the unsuspecting brother.	455, 456.
T416§	Paternal-cousin (*bint-¿amm*) as substitute for sister.	438.
T416.5§	Aversion to cousin-marriage: incest-like. Cousin (paternal or maternal) refuses marriage to cousin.	54 n. 49.
T416.8§	Adultery (sexual liaison) between *'ibn-¿amm* and his *bint-¿amm* (paternal-cousins).	457.
T452	Bawds. Professional go-betweens.	429.
T455.8§	Princess (beautiful woman) allows men to see her for a fee (pay).	436.
T461.0.1§	‡Erotic fetishism.	403 n. 773, 423.
T462.0.1§	Pseudo-lesbian attraction (love): woman falls in love with another woman who turns out to be a man in disguise.	382 n. 401, 429.

U. THE NATURE OF LIFE

	ment depends on circumstances, objects of comparison, frame of reference, or context).	56 n. 73, 388 n. 507.
U303.4§	Distance is relative.	52 n. 5.
U304§	Relativity of perceiving quality.	56 n. 73, 388 n. 507.
U315.1§	Seeking a conversation (social interaction).	25 n. 42, 56 n. 77.

V. RELIGION [AND RELIGIOUS SERVICES]

V11.11§	Sacrifice to a spirit (jinni).	369 n. 148.
V11.12.1§	‡Milk poured out for spirit(s).	427.
V21.8§	‡Deathbed confession: made so as to meet God with clear conscience.	420.
V28.0.1§	‡*tashahhud* (uttering testimony: "No god but God, and Mohammed is His Messenger"): Moslem's last rite.	381 n. 360.
V52	Miraculous power of prayer.	398 n. 689.
V57.0.1§	‡Prayers are to supreme supernatural being (The God, a deity, holy personage, etc.) to solicit help (or to offer thanks).	366 n. 87.
V61.12.1§	‡Burial (death) with face toward the *Qiblah* (Mecca).	450.
V68.2	Dead washed and hair combed.	421.
V68.4.2§	‡Dead wrapped in shrouds.	450.
V68.7§	‡Corpse of female prepared for burial by female (undertaker's assistant).	450.
V74§	Ramadan-fasting.	427.
V76§	*¿îd:* Moslem bairam(s).	379 n. 336.
V82.0.1§	"Circumcision is required for cleanliness (of male or female)."	396 n. 632.
V82.2§	Clitoridectomy: female excision (circumcision).	417.
V85.1.0.1§	‡*al-maḥmal:* ceremonial sending of drapes ("veil") for The Black Stone (in Mecca).	234 n. 592.
V90§	Miraculous effects of invoking God's attributes (*basmalah, ḥasbanah, ḥawqalah,* etc.).	399 n. 708.
V214§	Moses as prophet (founder).	449.
V220.0.4§	Woman saint.	450.
V222.12.1§	‡Blessedness of a person restores a garden to bloom.	444.
V223.0.2§	Clairvoyance of madmen (fools, the insane, *magâdhîb*).	402 n. 758.
V231.6	Angel in the form of an old man.	429.
V233.5§	‡Azrael's assistant(s): help(s) when innumerable souls must be extracted (seized) simultaneously.	163.
V246.4.1§	‡Angel in human form induces mortal to decide wisely.	429.
V250.0.1§	*as-sayyidah* Zaynab: supreme saint (culture-heroine, "The Lady," "The Chieftainess," etc.).	429.
V293.0.1§	‡The afflicted (the weak, the persecuted, the orphaned, etc.) as God's favorite.	379 n. 322.

V301.1§	‡"Deeds are [judged] according to intent."	383 n. 417.
V318.2§	‡"Only God is to be thanked for an affliction (*makrûh:* a disliked matter, seeming harm)."	401 n. 754, 449.
V374§	‡Jewish traditions about Moslems.	450.
V384.1§	‡Extreme interpretations of religious dogmas concerning females (social category).	25 n. 43.
V384.1.1§	‡Counter-belief (counter-interpretation): "A woman is of sound faith, honor, and heart, [. . .], unless urged by lust [. . .]."	24 n. 42.
V532	Pilgrimage to Mecca.	435, 438, 442.
V544§	God furnishes substitute (ram) for human sacrifice.	380 n. 336.

W. TRAITS OF CHARACTER

W4§	‡Religiosity (piety): most favorable trait of character.	429.
W10.3.3§	‡Poor arrangement (deal) tolerated so as not to injure pride of the other party.	54 n. 52.
W14.8§	‡Right to a woman (girl) surrendered or claimed as an act of gallantry.	248.
W25.1	Equanimity of the enslaved unfortunate. Does not complain when beset by series of misfortunes.	449.
W27.2.2.1§	‡"I would [willingly] become a slave for him who would teach me [even] a letter."	376 n. 283.
W28	Self-sacrifice.	400 n. 734.
W30.0.1§ (formerly W129.3§)	‡Intolerance to cognitive dissonance.	433.
W31	Obedience.	428, 429.
W31.1§	Blind obedience: mark of the good wife.	429.
W31.1.1§	Obedience to seniors mark of good girl.	440.
W37.8§	‡*dhimmah:* economic, political, governmental conscientiousness and honesty.	373 n. 225.
W41§	‡Resolve (determination, willpower, endurance, "grit").	422.
W44§	‡Proper bashfulness (*ḥayâ'/khafar, kusûf/khajal*). A person's modesty (social sensitiveness, shyness, or decency).	121.
W44.2§	‡Bashfulness at indecent (obscene) words.	121, 375 n. 263.
W48§	Being sweet-tongued.	440.
W111.4.1§	‡Wife punishes (beats, refuses to feed) lazy husband.	55 n. 63.
W116.2	‡Expenditure of money for vanity [(*fangarah*)].	369 n. 148.
W125.2	Gluttonous wife eats all the meal while cooking it.	446.
W129.1§	‡Person who doubts a prediction (belief, claim, etc.) fails to see that he is living proof of its validity.	29 n. 75.
W131	Profligacy.	53 n. 18.
W131.1	Profligate [(heir)] wastes entire fortune before beginning his own adventures.	435.
W141	Talkativeness.	369 n. 146.

W142.1.1§	‡Person cannot bring himself to say: "I do not know."	26 n. 47.
W151	Greed.	75, 413.
W153.0.1.1§	‡"Shit Son-of-shit is he who can provide but renders the woman (wife) needy!"	384 n. 431.
W153.2	Miserly husband spies on wife to see that she does not eat too much.	429.
W154.0.1§	Perfidy: repayment of good deeds with evil ones.	434.
W154.4.1§	Wife is still grateful to helpful animal when it becomes sick, husband ungrateful: animal does not retaliate against husband.	420.
W154.24.1§	Man fails to treat his benefactor animal kindly when it is sick (dead).	420.
W155	Hardness of heart.	433.
W155.0.1§	‡Apathy (social insensitiveness, indifference to the plight of others).	54 n. 45.
W160§	‡Being street-bound (market-bound).	369 n. 145.
W160.1§	‡Eating from the market (at a restaurant) reduces one's worth.	369 n. 150.
W164.1.3§	‡Display of wisdom (knowledge) as promoter of self-esteem.	51 n. 4.
W164.1.7.1§	‡Girl's (woman's) willpower as source of self-esteem (self-concept).	422.
W164.2§	Injured pride.	54 n. 52.
W165.0.1§	‡Improper pride (pomposity).	52 n. 10.
W165.2§	Man ashamed of working woman, though her honest earnings support him (or feed family).	52 n. 10.
W170.1§	‡Lack of bashfulness (*qillat ḥayâ'*).	369 n. 147, 370 n. 157.
W171	Two-facedness.	53 n. 37.
W181	Jealousy.	54 n. 40, 442.
W183§	‡Pleasure (rejoicing) at another's misfortune (*shamâtah*).	53 n. 26.
W183.1.2§	‡Brother pleased with his brother's failure.	53 n. 26, 422.
W188.2§	‡Argumentativeness (*ghalabah*—fondness of arguments—being too clever with words; speciousness, sophistry).	369 n. 146.
W195	Envy.	54 n. 40.
W195.4§	Wealth (material possessions) envied.	442.
W195.6§	Social status (influence, authority) envied.	54 n. 42.
W195.9.1§	Father envies son's beautiful wife (wives).	377 n. 287, 455.
W195.9.2§	Brother envies brother's beautiful wife (wives).	442, 455.
W195.9.3§	Sister envies sister's handsome husband (suitor, lover).	442.
W201.1.1.1§	‡Indicator of manliness: controlling women.	52 n. 10.
W201.1.1.1.1.1§	‡Indicator of manliness: slighting women's opinion.	387 n. 481.
W201.1.1.2§	‡Indicator of manliness: powerful manners (being assertive, firm, resolute).	51 n. 1, 422.
W201.2.1§	‡Roughness of physical constitution (appearance) as indicator of maleness.	70.

W201.2.2§	‡Indicator of maleness: being large.	372.
W202.1§	‡Indicators of femaleness.	388 n. 502.
W202.1.1.1§	‡Indicator of femininity: women's speech tone (soft, low-key).	361 n. 8.
W202.1.1.2§	‡Indicator of femininity: women's non-assertive ways.	422.
W202.1.1.3§	‡Indicator of femininity: women's superstitious ways ("old-wives' tales," "old-wives' medicine," etc.).	25 n. 44, 400 n. 725.
W254.2§	‡Empathy in sorrow (pity, compassion) resides in liver (also in eye, soul, or heart—especially woman's).	416.
W256.6.1§	"Women are lacking in mind and religion."	23 n. 40.
W256.6.8.1§	‡Men cannot resist temptation.	394 n. 590.
W256.8.1§	‡The tyranny by (the might of) the infirm (physically handicapped).	395 n. 626.

X. HUMOR

X360§	‡Humor concerning lecherous teacher(s).	377 n. 286.
X365§	‡Humor concerning pupils and their answers.	23 n. 35.
X420.2.0.1§	‡Glutton as messy eater (*'fattagî'*).	384 n. 444.
X1321	Lies about snakes.	26 n. 47.
X1321.3	‡Lies about remarkable kinds of snakes.	26 n. 47.
X1370	Lies about imaginary animals.	26 n. 47.
X1505.1.1§	Reward for carrying out orders by contraries.	440.

Z. MISCELLANEOUS GROUPS OF MOTIFS

Z1.0.1§	‡*'inshâ*-style literary composition: constituted mainly from copied (memorized) famous quotations.	22 n. 34.
Z10.2	End formulas.	452.
Z12.3§	‡Account (of happenings) skips (shortens) certain events, and prolongs others—("leaping and lingering").	200.
Z13.0.1.1§	‡Pseudo-erotic riddle (joke).	382 n. 399.
Z13.5§	Character-prompting: speaker (tale-teller) addresses tale-character directly.	366 n. 85.
Z13.5.1§	‡Speaker uses show-and-tell style: "Here is/are. . . . "	385 n. 450.
Z13.8§	‡Speaker disclaims responsibility for offensive contents.	242, 394 n. 608.
Z13.9.1§	‡Speaker wards off evil effects of own speech (words).	54 n. 53, 363 n. 40.
Z13.9.2§	‡Speaker ensures that no accusation (taunting) seems to be aimed at listener.	384 n. 443.
Z13.10§	‡Tale-teller begs God's forgiveness for lying (speaking untruth).	368 n. 142.
Z18.0.1§	‡Narrative's dramatic dialogue—(told as drama, as opposed to mere description).	23 n. 39.

Z18.3§	‡Ogre to man: "Repeat [your blow]!" Man to ogre: "My mother did not teach me [to do this]!"	395 n. 619, 439.
Z19.1.0.1§	‡The fox passed by, seven loops in his tail; the she-bear fell in the well, etc. (chasing game).	362 n. 16.
Z19.1.0.3§	‡Fingers (toes) counted, touched: child tickled. "This is the egg, this is the one who roasted it, this is the one who peeled it, this is the one who ate it, and this is the one who cried out: Me too! Me too!" (Catch-tale: tickling, touching.)	64.
Z19.3§	Etiological tales: "That-is-why"-tales.	451.
Z32.2	Chains involving a death: animal actors.	436.
Z32.2.1	The death of the little hen described with unusual words [(neologism)].	436.
Z41.11§	Climax of relatives. (Ascending series of relations.)	451, 452.
Z41.11.1§	‡That which a kin-woman may not be: "If I'm your daughter, [O father,] I cannot be your son's wife!" "If I'm your daughter, [O mother,] I cannot be your son's wife!" "If I'm your sister, [O sister,] I cannot be your brother's wife!" "If I'm your sister, [O brother,] I cannot be your wife!"	452.
Z43.7.1§	‡Pecking order. Chain of aggressive actions and reactions, started against the weak and ending with the weakest.	383 n. 416.
Z53	‡The animals with queer names: as hen (henny-penny), cock (cocky-locky), goose (goosey-poosey).	361 n. 8.
Z55.3§	‡Social (interactional) process carried to its climax.	293 n. 582.
Z62.0.1§	"Khurâfah's report, [mythical, but it is the truth]."	23 n. 38.
Z63.3.3.6.3§	‡"To say, 'O earth, open up and swallow me.'"	422.
Z63.5.1§	"Eve is fertile," "A womb brings forth": formulas signifying futility of conceit.	365 n. 71.
Z63.7.2§	‡Exasperation: "one's donkey baffled."	372 n. 211.
Z63.9.2§	‡Brother (sister) or paternal-cousin: what is the difference!? [None!]	438.
Z63.10.1.1§	‡To be like a bad deed—ever present.	407 n. 834.
Z63.10.2.3§	‡"Get road-bound" ("Hit the road!").	394 n. 595.
Z65.3§	White as milk (cheese).	440, 454.
Z66.4.1§	‡Endearment: to be referred to (or addressed) in the diminutive.	371 n. 192, 381 n. 357, 385 n. 462, 399 n. 714, 404 n. 796, 446.
Z67.5§	‡Esteem: to be addressed as respected relative (with social distance kept).	424.
Z67.5.1§	‡Esteem: man addressed as "*¿amm* (paternal-uncle)."	362 n. 16, 389 n. 515.

Z166§	Fruit (vegetable) symbolism.	372 n. 200.
Z166.1.1§	Symbolism: pomegranate (apple, orange)—breast.	438.
Z166.4.3.3.1§	"O quince, what shall I remember of you: a tear for every bite!"	384 n. 432.
Z169.0.1§	‡Symbolism: thorny and thornless flowers.	424.
Z169.0.1.1.2§	‡Tamarisk as symbol of tenderness.	424.
Z170§	Food (cooked, processed) symbolism.	387 n. 494.
Z175	Sign language. Message delivered by means of the fingers, etc.	438.
Z183.0.1§	Meaning of a name.	452.
Z183.2.1§	‡Child's name reveals inexorable fate.	457.
Z183.5.1§	"Father-of-" (*'Abu-*).	387 n. 488.
Z183.6§	"Mother-of-" (*'Omm/'Umm-*).	362 n. 19, 450.
Z186.4.2§	Symbolism: rubbing (stroking) an object—erotic act.	365 n. 75.
Z186.4.2.1§	Symbolism: kneading—erotic act.	379 n. 324, 452.
Z186.4.3§	Symbolism: wearing (putting on) garment or shoe —sexual intercourse.	452.
Z186.4.3.1§	Symbolism: wearing (slipping on, pounding "it" into, etc.) a shoe or garment—sexual intercourse.	398 n. 681.
Z186.5§	Symbolism: pitcher's spout—phallus.	56 n. 75, 426, 427.
Z186.9.3.1.1§	‡Female in indecent posture "allows her dish's sizzling aroma to fill the air."	365 n. 75.
Z188.1§	Symbolism: head of animal or fowl—chief or family patriarch.	438.
Z188.1.1§	Symbolism: arms, legs—children.	438.
Z188.2§	Symbolism: eye—sight.	438.
Z188.3§	Symbolism: navel—the center of city.	438.
Z188.5.1§	‡Arrogance: to place one's own nose in the sky.	167.
Z188.5.2§	‡Humiliation: to bring down someone's nose to the ground.	381 n. 370.
Z189§	Symbolism concerning virginity and defloration.	401 n. 746.
Z193.3.1§	‡Cock-like (rooster-like) man.	372 n. 197.
Z215	Hero "Son of seven mothers."	439.
Z257	‡Beardless hero.	456.
Z292.0.1.1§	‡Tragic ending of a story (tale): all die.	385 n. 449, 424, 431, 456.
Z356.4.2§	‡Only a pair of a group of siblings survives—(usually brother and sister).	18 n. 75.

APPENDIX

Genres of the Folk Narrative

In introducing the texts of narratives included in the present work, a term indicating the genre(s) to which the story belongs is given (e.g., fantasy-tale: *sabḥûnah, ḥujwah;* religious story: *qiṣṣah min ed-dîn,* exemplum, saint's legend; humorous narrative: humorous anecdote, joke; etc.). To help the reader in relating a given genre term to the broader folk narrative system, the following general chart is provided. It outlines the various generic categories of the folk narrative as applied in this book and other works by the present writer.[1] The genre to which a story is assigned is reckoned in terms of a patterned combination of several factors that include form, style, structure, contents, medium and direction of communication, and the story's manifest function according to the narrator's intent.

Many stories manifest characteristics of more than one genre, and the genre to which a story belongs can be transformed into another through the narrator's intent and the context in which narration occurs:

I. Genres of the *prose* folk narrative:

1. Fantasy narratives (*ḥaddûtah, khurraifah, ḥujwah, ḥikâyah*)
   Märchen/magic-tale, cf. fairy-tale
   Novella/romanistic tale
   Animal tale (cf. fable)
   Formula tale (*ḥizr, fazzûrah, nuktah*): Cumulative, Catch, Endless, Rounds (clock)

2. Humorous narratives (*nuktah, nâdirah, ḥaddûtah*)
   Merry tale/humorous tale
   Humorous anecdote/*Schwank (nâdirah, qafshah)*
   The joke/*Witz (nuktah)*

3. Knowledge, narratives expressing (*qiṣṣah, 'usṭurah, sîrah, târîkh*)
   The legend (*'usṭûrah, qiṣṣah*)
      Historical legend/*Sage;* life history
      Historical anecdote (cf. etiologic tale)
      Migratory legend
      Memorate, personal experience legend,
      Urban legend, etc.

1. See El-Shamy, *Folktales of Egypt,* pp. xliv–xlv.

4. Didactic narratives (*mathal, ḥikmah, qiṣṣah*)
   Dilemma tale: (*ḥizr, fazzûrah*)—scarce in Arabic lore.
   Riddle tales
   Fable (cf. exemplum, animal tale)

5. Belief narratives (*qiṣṣah, maw¿iẓah, 'usṭurah, . . .*)
   Sacred belief story (cf. "religious legend"), religious story
   "Myth," (*khurâfah qaṣaṣiyyah*) [mislabeled *'usṭûrah* by most Arab writers]
   Exemplum (*wa¿ẓ/'irshâd, qiṣṣah dîniyyah*)
   Belief legend: local legend, migratory legend, personal experience legend/memorate, urban legend.

II. Genres of the versified (poetry) narrative:

Epic: *malḥamah,* poetic *qaṣîdah* (ode)—typically a versified religious belief or quasi-religious belief account, a historical-legendary account[2]
Cante fable (*sîrah,* narrative in prose and poetry, ballad)—labeled "epic" in recent academic literature
The ballad (*mawwâl qaṣaṣî*)—typically a "legend" or "belief" account[3]

2. On the characteristics of the "true" epic, see H. El-Shamy, "The Story of El-Sayyid Aḥmad El-Badawî with Faṭma Bint Berry, part I, An Introduction," *Folklore Forum,* Vol. 10, No. 1, pp. 1–13, esp. p. 5.

3. For an overview of the subject matter of this genre, see Appendix III: "The Egyptian Folk Ballad and Related Lyric Narrative-Songs, 1900?–1982," in El-Shamy, *Folk Traditions of the Arab World,* Vol. 1, pp. 445–48.

BIBLIOGRAPHY

¿Abd-al-Hâdî, Tawaddud, *kharârîf sha¿biyyah: al-qiṣaṣ al-shas¿biyyah* (*Folk Fairy Tales: Folk Narratives [from Palestine]*) (Beirut, 1980).

¿Abd-Allâh, Sayyid M., *ḥayât wa-turâth al-Nûbah bi-minṭaqat al-Sukkût* (*Nuba's Life and Traditions in the Sukkât Region*) (Khartoum, 1973).

¿Abduh, ¿Alî Muḥammad, *ḥikayât wa 'asâṭîr yamaniyyah* (*Yemeni Tales and Legends*) (Beirut, Sanaa, 1978).

¿Āshûr, Sa¿îd ¿A., *al-Sayyid Aḥmad al-Badawi: shaykh wa ṭarîqah (Al-Sayyid Aḥmad al-Badawî: A Sheikh and [his Sufi] Brotherhood*) (Cairo: al-Dâr al-Miṣriyyah, n.d.; preface dated 1966).

Aarne, Antti, and Stith Thompson, *The Types of the Folktale: A Classification and Bibliography* (Helsinki, 1961, 1964).

Abu-Lughod, Lila, *Writing Women's Worlds: Bedouin Stories* (Berkeley: University of California Press, 1993).

AGSFC: Arab Gulf States Folklore Centre, Doha, Qatar; currently: "G.C.C. Folkore Center."

Aḥmad, Gamâl Muḥammad, col., *ḥikâyât min al-Nûbah (Tales from Nubia)* ¿Abd-al-Ḥamîd Yûnus, tr. (Cairo, 1987).

Ammar, Hamed, *Growing Up in an Egyptian Village: Silwa, Province of Aswan* (London, 1954, 1966).

Amrouche, Marguerite Taos, *Le grain magique: contes, poèmes et proverbes berbères de Kabylie* (Paris: François Maspero, 1966).

Anonymous, *'alf laylah wa laylah* (*Thousand Nights and a Night*), 4 vols. (Cairo, Muḥammad Ṣubaiḥ, n.d.).

Anonymous, *qiṣṣat ez-Zîr Sâlim, Abu-Lailah al-Muhalahal al-kabîr (The Story of ez-Zîr Sâlim, Abu-Lailah al-Muhalahal, Senior)* (Cairo, n.d.).

Artin, Yacoub, *Contes populaires inédits de la vallée du Nil* (Paris, 1893, 1968).

Aswad (al-), Nizâr, *al-ḥikâyât al-sha¿biyyah al-shâmiyyah* (*The Syrian Folktale*) (Damascus, 1985).

AUC, American University in Cairo, Students' Collections. (Manuscripts are in El-Shamy's Archives.)

AUC: 1, "Folklore Collection," ¿Allâm, Miss Bahîga, col., MS., Cairo, 1971–72.

AUC: 2, "Folklore Collection," ¿Abd-al-Ghaffâr, Mrs. ¿Aliyyah, col., MS., Cairo, 1971–72.

AUC: 8, "Folklore Collection," Boqṭor, Miss Hodâ, col., manuscript, Cairo, 1971–72.

AUC: 10, "Folklore Collection," Sharîf ["Cherîf"], Miss Djenân, col., manuscript, Cairo, 1971–72.

AUC: 11, "Folklore Collection," Fahmî, Miss Monâ Ḥannâ, col., manuscript, Cairo, 1971–72.

AUC: 12, "Folklore Collection," Ghunaim, Miss Firyâl, col., manuscript, Cairo, 1971–72.

AUC: 14, "Folklore Collection," Khalîl, Miss Ilhâm, col., manuscript, Cairo, 1971–72.

AUC: 17, "Folklore Collection," Maẕlûm, Miss Chérîfa, col., manuscript, Cairo, 1971–72.

AUC: 19, "Folklore Collection," Na¿was, Miss Ḥanân, col., manuscript, Cairo, 1971–72.

AUC: 25, "Folklore Collection," Ṭammûm, Mrs. Fâṭimah, col., manuscript, Cairo, 1971–72.

AUC: 32, "Folklore Collection," El-Bakrî, Miss Zaynab Bashîr, col., manuscript, Cairo, 1971–72.

AUC: 33, "Folklore Collection," Bîkar, Miss Rânda, col., manuscript, Cairo, 1971–72.

AUC: 34, "Folklore Collection," Fahmî, Miss Hodâ Ḥannâ, col., manuscript, Cairo, 1971–72.

AUC: 44, "Folklore Collection," Zuhdî, Miss Mâgda, col., manuscript, Cairo, 1971–72.

Azhar (al-)/Nûr al-Islâm, (*mashyakhat* al-Azhar, Cairo, 1930ff.).

Baqlûṭî (al-), al-Nâṣir, ed., tr., *ḥikâyât sha¿biyyah min Tûnis (Contes populaires de Tunisie)* (Sfax, 1988).

Bâṭinî (al-), Bazzah, *al-ḥikâyât al-khurâfiyyah al-sha¿biyyah* (*The Folk Fairy Tales*) (Kuwait, 1988).

———, *ṭarâ'if wa-ḥikâyât nisâ'iyyah min al-turâth al-sha¿bî al-kuwaytî* (*Women's Anecdotes and Tales from Kuwaiti Folk Traditions*) (Kuwait, 1987).

Bascom, William, *African Dilemma Tales* (The Hague, Chicago: Mouton, 1975).

Bashmî, Ibrâhîm, ed., *ḥikâyât sha¿biyyah* (*Folktales*) (Bahrain, 1986).

Basset, René, *Contes populaires berbères* (Paris, 1887).

———, *Mille et un contes, récites & légendes arabes,* 3 vols. (Paris, 1924–26).

———, *Nouveaux contes berbères* (Paris, 1897).

Bâzargân (al-), Ra'ûf, *'amthâl sha¿biyyah lahâ ḥikâyât* (*Folk Proverbs with Tales*) (Baghdad, 1983).

Belamri, Rabah, *La rose rouge* (Paris, 1982).

Bergsträsser, Gotthelf, ed., *Neuaramäische Märchen und andre Texte aus Ma¿lûla, hauptsächlich aus der Sammlung E. Prym's und A. Socin's* (Leipzig, 1915).

Blackman, Winifred S., *The Fellahin of Upper Egypt* (London 1927).

Bouhdiba, Abdelwahab, *L'imaginaire maghrebin: étude de dix contes pour enfants* (Tunis: Maison Tunisienne, 1977).

Budge, E. A. Wallis, *The Gods of the Egyptians* (London, 1904).

———, ed., tr., *Egyptian Tales and Romances* (London: T. Butterworth, 1931).

———, *The Mummy,* 2nd ed. (New York, 1894, 1974).

Bushnaq, Inea, ed., tr., *Arab Folktales* (New York, 1986).

Bustânî (al-), Karam, *ḥikâyât lubnâniyyah* (*Lebanese Tales*) (Beirut, 1961).

CFMC: Center for Folklore, Ministry of Culture, Cairo, Egypt.

Chauvin, Victor, *Bibliographie des ouvrages arabes ou relatifs aux arabes,* 12 vols. (Liège, 1892–1922).

Chimenti, Elisa, *Tales and Legends of Morocco,* Aaron Benami, tr. (New York, 1965).

Cohen, David, *Le parler arabe des juifs de Tunis: Textes de dolinguistique et ethnographiques* (La Haye-Paris, 1964).

Climo, Shirley, *The Egyptian Cinderella* (New York: HarperCollins, 1989, 1993).

Crowley, Daniel J., Review of *Folktales of Egypt,* in *Research in African Literatures,* Vol. 12, No. 3 (1981): 398–400.

Daum, Werner, *Märchen aus dem Jemen* (Düsseldorf, Köln, 1983).

Delheure, Jean, *Contes et légendes berbères de Ouargla* (Paris, 1989).

Dermenghem, Emile, *Contes kabyles* (Algiers: Charlot, 1945).

Desparmet, Jean, "Contes maures recueillis à Blida et traduit." *RTP,* 28 (1913).

Despármet, J., *Contes populaires sur les ogres recueillis à Blida et traduits*, 2 vols. (Paris, 1909–10).
Dundes, Alan, "Foreword" in Ibrahim Muhawi and Sharif Kanaana, *Speak, Bird, Speak Again: Palestinian Arab Folktales* (Berkeley, 1989), pp. ix–xiii.
Duwaik (al-), Muḥammad Ṭâlib, *al-qaṣaṣ al-sha¿bî fî Qaṭar* (*Folk Narratives in Qatar*), 2 vols. (Doha, 1984).
Dwyer, Daisy H., *Images and Self-Images, Male and Female in Morocco* (New York, 1978).
Farag, Fattûḥ A., *al-qaṣaṣ al-sha¿bî fî al-Daqahliyya (Folk Narratives in Daqahliyya [Governorate, Egypt])* (Cairo, 1977).
Fasi (el-), Mohammed, and Émile Dermenghem, *Contes fasis*, [I], *recueillis d'après la tradition orale* (Paris: F. Rieder, 1926).
——, *Nouveau contes fasis*, [II] (Paris, 1928).
Frobenius, Leo, *Volksmärchen der Kabylen, Atlantis*, Vols. 1–3 (Jena, 1921–22).
——, *Märchen aus Kordofan, Atlantis*, Vol. 4 (Jena, 1923).
Galley, Micheline, *Badr az-Zîn, et six contes algériens* (Paris: Arman Collin, 1971).
Galley, Micheline, and Zakia Iraqui Sinaceur, eds., trs., *Dyab, Jha, La'âb a. . . . Le triomphe de la ruse. Contes marocains du fonds [George S.] Colin, traduits et présentés par. . . .* Classiques africaines, 26 (Paris, 1994).
Gamal (al-), ¿Abd-al-Fattâḥ, ed., *ḥikâyât sha¿biyyah min Miṣr* (*Folktales from Egypt*) (Cairo, 1985).
Green, Thomas A., gen. ed., *Folklore: An Encyclopedia of Forms, Methods, and History*. 2 vols. (Santa Barbara, Calif: Abc-Clio, 1997).
Ḥasan (al-), Ghassân Ḥ. A., "al-ḥikâyah al-khurâfiyyah fî al-'adab al-sha¿bî al-'urdunî" ("The Fairy-tale in Jordanian Folk Literature"), 2 vols., master's thesis, Cairo University, 1973.
Hassan, Motie I., inform., tr., *In-Nâs Wil-Malik* (*The People and the King [Folktales from Egypt as Narrated by the Author]*) (Copenhagen, 1971).
Hein, Wilhelm, and David H. Müller, *Mehri- und Ḥaḍrami-Texte. Gesammelt im Jahre 1902 in Gischin von Dr. Wilhelm Hein, bearbeitet und hrsg., Südarabische Expedition*, Vol. 9 (Vienna, 1909).
Hejaiej, Monia, *Behind Closed Doors: Women's Oral Narratives in Tunis* (New Brunswick, N.J: Rutgers University Press, 1996).
Hilgard, Ernest R., *Theories of Learning* (New York, 1956).
Hill, Winfred F., *Learning, A Survey of Psychological Interpretation* (New York, 1977).
Houri-Pasotti, Myriam, *Contes de Ghazala* (Paris, 1980).
Hurreiz, Sayyid H., *Ja¿aliyyîn Folktales* (Bloomington: Indiana University, Research Center for Language and Semiotic Studies, 1977).
Ibrâhîm, ¿Abd-Allâh ¿Alî, col., "*min 'aḥâjî al-Rubâṭâb*" ("From Rubâṭâb Folktales, [Sudan, collected in May 1985]"). Résumés, unpublished. Bloomington, 1987.
Ibrâhîm, ¿Adlî, "An Annotated Collection of Folktales Collected in Cairo," unpublished master's thesis, unfinished, Bloomington, Indiana, 1966.
'Ibshîhî (al-), Muḥammad 'ibn Ahmad, *al-Mustatraf fî kull fann mustaẓraf* (That Which Is Thought of as Quaint in Every Art That Is Considered Cute), 2 vols. (Cairo: al-Ḥalabî, 1952).
Ions, Veronica, *Egyptian Mythology* (Middlesex: Hamlyn, 1968).
IUFTL: Tapes Nos. 123–38. Hasan El-Shamy, col., Collection from Brooklyn, New York

(Informants from: Egypt: Cairo, Suez, Alexandria, Asyut, Suhâg, Nubia [Kunûzî]; Iraq; Palestine; Yemen) May-September, 1961.

Ja¿far (al-), ¿Alî ¿Ā., col., transcriber, "ḥikâyât sh¿biyyah min al-Kuwayt, bi-ruwâyat al-sayyid Y. ¿. al-Ḥaddâd" ("Folktales from Kuwait, as Narrated by Mr. . . . " [with the collaboration of narrator's son]), MS., Bloomington, Indiana, 1993.

Jâḥiz (al-), 'Abû-¿Uthmân ¿Amr ibn Baḥr, *al-ḥayawân* (Animal[s]), ¿Abd-al-Salâm Muḥammad Hârûn, ed., 7 vols. (Cairo: al-Ḥalabî, 1938–45).

Jahn, Alfred, *Die Mehri-Sprache in Südarabien, Südarabische Expedition,* Vol. 3 (Vienna, 1902).

Jahn, Samja, ed., tr., *Arabische Volksmärchen* (Berlin: Academie-Verlag, 1970).

Jamali, Sarah Powell, *Folktales from the City of Golden Domes* (Beirut, 1965).

Jarâjrah (al-), ¿Îsâ, *¿ishq ḥattâ al-mawt, dirâsah naẓariyyah wa qaṣaṣ sha¿bî 'urdunî* (*Love Till Death, A Theoretical Study and [Texts of] Jordanian Folk Narratives*) (Amman, 1985).

Jason, Heda, ed., *Märchen aus Israel* (Düsseldorf, 1976).

Johnson, Allen, and Douglas Price-Williams, *Oedipus Ubiquitous: The Family Complex in World Folk Literature* (Stanford, Calif.: Stanford University Press, 1996).

Joseph, Roger, Review of *Folktales of Egypt* in *Arab Studies Quarterly,* Vol. 4 (Summer 1982): 272–74.

Juhaymân (al-), ¿Abd-al-Karîm, *min 'asâṭîrina al-sha¿biyyah* (*From Our Folk Legends*), and *'asâṭîr sha¿biyyah min qalb jazîrat al-¿arab* (*Folk Legends from the Heart of the Arabian Peninsula*), 5 vols. (Beirut and Riyadh, 1967–84).

Kamâl, Ṣafwat, *al-ḥikâyât al-sha¿biyyah al-kuwaytiyyah: dirâsatun muqâranah* (*The Kuwaiti Folktale: A Comparative Study*) (Kuwait, 1986).

Kâmil, Murâd, *qiṣaṣ sûdâniyyah* (Sudanese [Folk-]Stories) (Cairo, 1963).

Khemir, Nacer, *L'ogresse* (Paris: F. Maspero, 1975).

Khiḍr, ¿Abbâs, *ḥawâdît ¿arabiyyah* (*Arab Folktales*), 2 vols. (Cairo, 1960–64).

Khoalî (el-), Ḥasan A., "al-furûq al-rîfiyyah-al-ḥaḍariyyah fî ba¿ḍ ¿anâṣir al-turâth al-sha¿bî" ("Urban-Rural Differences in Some Elements of Folk Traditions"), doctoral dissertation, Cairo University, 1981.

Krech, David, R. S. Crutchfield, and E. L. Ballachey, *Individual in Society* (New York, 1962).

Kronenberg, Andreas, and Waltraud Kronenberg, *Nubische Märchen* (Düsseldorf, Köln, 1978).

Lacoste, Camille, ed., *Légendes et contes merveilleux de la grande Kabylie: recueillis par Auguste Moulieras* (Paris: Imprimerie Nationale, 1965).

Lane, Edward William, *An Account of the Manners and Customs of the Modern Egyptians* (New York, 1973).

Laoust, Emile, *Contes berbères du Maroco,* 2 vols. (Paris, 1949–50).

———, *Étude sur le dialecte berbère du Chenoua* (Paris: Ernest Leroux, 1912).

Légey, Françoise, *Contes et légendes populaires du Maroc, recueillis à Marrakech* (Paris, 1926).

Lewin, Bernhard, *Arabische Texte im Dialekt von Hama* (Beirut, 1966).

Littmann, Enno, "Alflaylah wa-Layla," in *Encyclopaedia of Islam,* 2nd ed., Vol. 1 (Leyden: Brill, 1960).

———, *Modern Arabic Tales [from al-Quds]* (Leyden, 1905). German translation and annotation: *Arabische Märchen* (Leipzig, 1935).

——, "Arabische Märchen und Schwänke aus Ägypten," *Akademie der Wissenschaften und der Literatur. Abhandlungen der Klasse der Literatur,* No. 2 (Wiesbaden, 1955).

Loubignac, Victorien, *Textes arabes des Zaërs* (Paris, 1952).

Lukianowicz, N., "Incest," in *British Journal of Psychiatry,* 120 (1972), pp. 301–13.

Lyons, M. C., *The Arabian Epic: Heroic and Oral Story-telling,* 3 vols. (Cambridge University Press, 1995).

Ma'thûrât (al-) al-Sha¿biyyah (*Folk Traditions*) (Doha, Qatar: The G. C. C. Folklore Center, 1986ff).

Massenbach (Von), Gertrude, *Nubische Texte im Dialekt der Kunûzi und Dongolawi: Abhandlungen für die Kunde des Morgenlandes,* 34, No. 4 (Wiesbaden, 1962).

Muhawi, Ibrahim, and Sharif Kanaana, *Speak, Bird, Speak Again: Palestinian Arab Folktales* (Berkeley, 1989).

Müller, David H., *Die Mehri- und Soquṭri-Sprache,* Pt. I, *Texte, Südarabische Expedition,* Vol. 4 (Vienna, 1902).

——, *Die Mehri- und Soquṭri-Sprache,* Pt. II, *Soqoṭri Texte, Südarabische Expedition,* Vol. 6 (Vienna, 1905).

——, *Die Mehri- und Soquṭri-Sprache,* Pt. III, *Shḥauri Texte, Südarabische Expedition,* Vol. 7 (Vienna, 1907).

Nacib, Youssef, *Contes algériens du Djurdjura* (Paris: Publisud, 1982).

Nowak, Ursula, "Beiträge zur Typologie des arabischen Volksmärchens," doctoral dissertation, Freiburg, 1969.

Noy, Dov, ed., *Folktales of Israel* (Chicago: University of Chicago Press, 1963).

——, ed., *Jefet Schwili Erzählt: Hundertneunundsechsich jemenitische Volkserzählungen aufgezeichnet in Israel 1957–60* (Berlin: Walter de Gruyter, 1963).

——, ed., *Moroccan Jewish Folktales* (New York, 1966).

Nutting, Anthony, *The Arabs: A Narrative History from Mohammed to the Present* (New York, London, 1964).

Panetta, Ester, *L'arabo parlato a Bengasi* (Rome, 1943).

Paz, Francis X., Review of *Folktales of Egypt,* in *Journal of the American Oriental Society,* Vol. 102, No. 1 (1982), pp. 219–20.

Pétigny (de), Clara Filleul, *Contes algériens* (Paris, 1951).

Prym, Eugene, and Albert Socin, *Der Neue-Aramaeische Dialect des Tûr 'Abdîn: Syrische Sagen und Märchen,* 2 vols. (Göttingen: Vanderhoech, 1881).

q.sh.¿i.: qiṣas sha¿biyyah ¿iraqiyyah (*Iraqi Folktales* [Previously Published by various writers in *al-Turâth al-Sha¿bî*]), Ṣabrî Ḥammâdî, and Dawûd Sallûm, compil., eds., 2 vols. (Doha, Qatar, 1987).

Qur'ân (al-): The Glorious Kur'an, translation and commentary by Abdallah Yousuf Ali (Libyan Arab Republic: The Call for Islam Society, 1973).

Rhodokanakis, Nikolaus, *Der vulgärarabische Dialekt im Ḍofâr (Ẓfâr), Südarabische Expedition,* Vol. 8 (Vienna, 1908).

Ritter, Helmut, *Ṭûrôyo: die Volkssprache der syrischen Christen des Ṭûr ¿Abdîn, A: Texte,* 3 vols. (Beirut, 1967, 1969, 1971).

Rivière, Joseph, *Recueil de contes populaires de la Kabylie du Djurdjura* (Paris: E. Leroux, 1882).

RTP: Revue des Traditions populaires (Paris, 1886–1917).

Sâris (al-), ¿Umar, "al-ḥikâyah al-sha¿biyyah fî al-mujtama¿ al-filisṭînî" ("The Folktale in Palestinian Society"), 2 vols., master's thesis, Cairo University, 1972, under the name ¿Umar ¿A. "Yûsuf."

——, *al-ḥikâyah al-sha¿biyyah fî al-mujtama¿ al-filisṭînî* (*The Folktale in Palestinian Society*) (Amman, 1984).

Ṣabâḥ al-Khair, weekly magazine, Enclosures for Young Readers (Cairo, 1960s).

Sa¿d-al-Dîn, Kâẓim, *al-ḥikâyah al-sha¿biyyah al-¿irâqiyyah* (*The Iraqi Folktale*) (Baghdad, 1979).

Sâ¿î, Aḥmad Bassâm, "al-ḥikâyât al-sha¿biyyah fî al-Lâdhiqiyyah" ("Folktales in Latakia"), 2 vols, master's thesis, Cairo University, 1970.

Savignac, Pierre H., *Contes berbères de Kabylie* (Québec: University of Québec, 1978).

Scelles-Millie, Jeanne, *Contes arabes du Maghreb* (Paris, 1970).

——, *Contes sahariens du Souf* (Paris, 1963).

——, *Paraboles et contes d'Afrique du Nord* (Paris, 1982).

——, *Tradition algériennes* (Paris, 1979).

Schmidt, Hans, and Paul Kahle, *Volkserzählungen aus Palästina*, 2 vols. (Göttingen, 1918, 1930).

Schultz, Duane, *A History of Modern Psychology* (New York, 1975).

Sengo, Tigiti Shaaban Yusuf, "The Indian Ocean Complex and the Kiswahili Folklore: The Case of Zanzibarian Tale-Performance," 2 vols., doctoral dissertation, Khartoum University, 1985.

Shahâb, Mnḥammad. A., *min al-turâth al-sh¿bî al-yamanî: al-ḥikâyât al-sha¿biyyah* (*From Yemeni Folk Traditions: The Folktales*) (Beirut, 1980).

Shahi (al-), Ahmad, and F. C. T. Moore, *Wisdom from the Nile* (Oxford, 1978).

Shâkir, Yusrî, *ḥikâyât min al-folklore al-maghribî* (*Tales from Maghribian Folklore*), 2 vols. (al-Dar al-Bayda: Dar al-nashr al-maghribiyyah, [1978], 1985).

Shalabî, Ḥusain Aḥmad, *'aqâṣîṣ min al-ṣûmâl* (*Short [Folk-]Narratives from Somalia*) (Cairo: al-Maarif, 1962).

Shamy (el-), Hasan, "African World View and Religion," in *Introduction to Africa*, P. Martin and P. O'Meara, eds. (Bloomington: Indiana University Press, 1977), pp. 208–20.

——, "An Annotated Collection of Egyptian Folktales, Collected from an Egyptian Sailor in Brooklyn, New York," master's thesis, Indiana University, 1964.

——, "[Arab Tales: collected, translated, annotated, and edited]," in *Tales Told around the World*, R. M. Dorson, gen. ed. (Chicago: University of Chicago Press, 1975), pp. 149–68.

——, "Behaviorism and the Text," in *Folklore Today: A Festschrift for Richard M. Dorson*, Linda Dégh, Henry Glassie, and Felix Oinas, eds. (Bloomington, Indiana, 1976), pp. 145–60.

——, "'Beide?' AaTh 1563," in *Enzyklopädie des Märchens*, Nos. 1–2 (1977), pp. 55–64.

——, "Belief and Non-Belief in Arab, Middle Eastern and Sub-Saharan Tales: The Religious–Non-Religious Continuum. A Case Study," in *al-Ma'thûrât al-Sha^c biyyah*, Vol. 3, No. 9 (Doha, January 1988): 7–21.

——, "Belief Characters as Anthropomorphic Psychosocial Realities: The Egyptian Case," with a résumé in Arabic, in *al-kitâb al-sanawî li-^c ilm al-'igtimâ^c* (*Annual Review of Sociology*), published by Department of Sociology, Cairo University, Vol. 3 (1982), pp. 7–36; Arabic Abstract, pp. 389–93.

——, *Brother and Sister, Type 872*: A Cognitive Behavioristic Text Analysis of a Middle*

Eastern Oikotype, Folklore Monograph Series, Vol. 8, Folklore Publications Group, Bloomington, Indiana, 1979.

——, "The Brother-Sister Syndrome in Arab Culture: A Preliminary Report," in *IX International Congress of Anthropological and Ethnological Sciences, Supplement II, Plan of Congress and Résumés of Contributions,* Abst. No. 1717 (Chicago, 1973).

——, "The Brother-Sister Syndrome in Arab Family Life. Socio-cultural Factors in Arab Psychiatry: A Critical Review," in *International Journal of Sociology of the Family,* Special Issue, *The Family in the Middle East,* Mark C. Kennedy, ed., Vol. 11, No. 2 (July-December 1981): pp. 313–23.

——, "d. Ḥasan al-Shamî yuwaḍḍiḥ" ("Dr. Hasan El-Shamy Clarifies"), in *al-Qabas,* No. 5594 (Kuwait, Dec. 9, 1987).

——, "Einigkeit macht stark (AaTh 910F)," in *Enzyklopädie des Märchens* (Göttingen), Vol. 3 (1981), Nos. 4–5, pp. 1256–61.

——, "Emotionskomponente," in *Enzyklopädie des Märchens,* Vol. 3, Nos. 4–5, pp. 1391–95.

——, "Folkloric Behavior: A Theory for the Study of the Dynamics of Traditional Culture," Ph.D. dissertation, Indiana University, 1967.

——, *Folktales of Egypt: Collected, Translated and Edited with Middle Eastern and African Parallels* (Chicago: University of Chicago Press, 1980).

——, *Folk Traditions of the Arab World: A Guide to Motif Classification,* 2 vols. (Bloomington, Indiana: Indiana University Press, 1995).

——, "Foreword," in *The Tradition of Moses and Mohammed: Jewish and Arab Folktales,* Blanche L. Serwer-Bernstein, ed. (Northvale, New Jersey, London, 1994), pp. 171–77.

——, "Mental Health in Traditional Culture: A Study of Preventive and Therapeutic Folk Practices," in *Psychiatry and the State,* Mark C. Kennedy, ed., *Catalyst* (Petersborough, Ontario: Trent University Press, 1972), pp. 13–28.

——, "Oral Traditional Tales and the *Thousand Nights and a Night:* The Demographic Factor," in *The Telling of Stories: Approaches to a Traditional Craft,* Morton Nøjgaard et al., eds. (Odense, Denmark: Odense University Press, 1990), pp. 63–117.

——, "Psychologically-based Criteria for Classification by Motif and Tale-type," in *Journal of Folklore Research,* Vol. 34, No. 3, (1997): 233–43.

——, "radd ¿alâ maqâl (A Reply to an Essay), in *al-Mujtama*ᶜ, No. 855, pp. 40–41 (Kuwait, Feb. 9, 1988).

——, "A Response [to Jason's Review of *Folk Traditions of the Arab World: A Guide to Motif Classification*]," in *Asian Folklore Studies,* Vol. 57, No. 2 (Nagoya, Japan, 1998), pp. 345–55.

——, "Sentiment, Genre, and Tale Typology: Meaning in Middle Eastern and African Tales," in *Papers III.* [Proceedings of] the 8th Congress for the International Society for Folk Narrative Research, R. Kvideland and T. Selberg, eds. (Bergen, Norway, 1985), pp. 255–83. Also (revised and expanded) in *al-Ma'thûrât al-Sha*ᶜ*biyyah,* Vol. 1, No. 3 (Doha, Qatar, 1986): 41–52.

——, "The Story of El-Sayyid Aḥmad El-Badawî with Faṭma Bint Birry, An Egyptian Folk Epic, Part II, Text and Explanatory Notes," in *Folklore Forum,* Vol. 9, No. 3–4 (Bloomington, 1976): 140–63.

——, The Story of El-Sayyid Aḥmad El-Badawî with Faṭma Bint Berry," Part I, "An Introduction," in *Folklore Forum,* Vol. 10, No. 1 (Bloomington, 1976): 1–13.

——, "tawḍîḥ ḥawla naẓariyyatih ¿an râbiṭat al-'akhkh wa al-'ukht min al-doktôr

al-Shâmî (Clarification Concerning His Theory about the Brother and Sister Bond, by Dr. El-Shamy)" in *al-Qabas*, No. 5621 and No. 5622 (Kuwait, Jan. 6 and 7, 1988).
——, "Towards a Demographically-Oriented Type Index for Tales of the Arab World," in *Cahiers de Littérature Orale*, No. 23: *La tradition au présent (Monde arabe)*, Praline Gay-Para, ed. (Paris, 1988), pp. 15–40.
——, "The Traditional Structure of Sentiments in Maḥfouẓ's Trilogy: A Behavioristic Text Analysis," in *Al-ᶜArabiyya: Journal of the American Association of Teachers of Arabic*, Vol. 9 (October 1976): 53–74.
——, "A Type Index for Tales of the Arab World," in *Fabula*, Vol. 29, No. 1–2 (Berlin, New York, 1988): 150–63.
——, "Vom Fisch geboren (AaTh 705)," in *Enzyklopädie des Märchens*, Vol. 4, No. 4–5, (1984): 1211–18.
Sherif, C., M. Sherif, and R. Nebergall, *Attitude and Attitude Change* (Philadelphia, 1967).
Sherif, Muzafar, "Social Psychology: Problems and Trends," in *Psychology: A Study of a Science*, Vol. 6: *Investigation of Man as Socious: Their Place in Psychology and Social Sciences*, Sigmund Koch, ed. (New York: McGraw Hill, 1963).
Simpson, William K., ed., *The Literature of Ancient Egypt* (New Haven: Yale University Press, 1972).
Sirḥân, Namir, *al-ḥikâyah al-sha¿biyyah al-filisṭîniyyah* ([The] Palestinian Folktale) (Beirut, 1974).
——, col., ed., *ḥikâyât sh¿biyah min Filisṭîn* (Folktales from Palestine) (Cairo, Beirut, 1987).
Spence, E., *Myth and Legends of Ancient Egypt* (New York, 1927).
Spitta, Wilhelm, col., tr., *Contes arabes modernes* (Leiden, 1883).
——, *Grammatik des arabischen Vulgärdialektes von Ägypten* (Leipzig, 1880).
Stevens, Ethel S., *Folk-tales of Iraq* (Oxford, 1931).
Stumme, Hans, *Märchen der Berber von Tamazratt in Südtunisien* (Lepzig 1900).
——, *Märchen und Gedichte aus der Stadt Tripolis in Nordafrika* (Leipzig: Hinrichs, 1898).
Sulaymân, Ṣâliḥ A. I., "al-ḥikâyât al-sha¿biyyah fî rîf muḥâfaẓat al-Sharqiyyah" ("Folktales in Rural Sharqiyyah Governorate [Egypt]"), diploma thesis, Arts Academy, High Institute for Folk Arts, Ministry of Culture, Cairo, 1992.
Ṭâlib (al-), ¿Umar, *'athar al-bî'ah fî al-ḥikâyah al-sha¿biyyah* (*The Influence of Environment on the Folktale*) (Baghdad, 1981).
Talmoudi, Fathi, *Texts in the Arabic Dialect of Sûsa (Tunisia)*, transcription, translation, notes, and glossary (Acta Universitatis Gothoburgensis, Sweden, 1981).
Ṭaḥḥân, Samîr, *al-qaṣṣâṣ al-ḥalabî* [II] (*The Aleppo-narrator*) (Aleppo, 1982).
Taymûr, 'Aḥmad, *al-'amthâl al-¿âmmîyyah* (*Vernacular Proverbs*) (Cairo, 1956).
Taymûr, Maḥmûd, *muḥâḍarât fî al-qaṣaṣ fî 'adab al-¿Arab: mâḍîhi wa ḥâḍirih (Lectures on Narratives in Arabs' Literature: Its Past and Present)* (Cairo, 1971).
Ṭayyib (al-), ¿Abd-Allâh, *al-aḥaji al-sûdâniyyah (Sudanese Folktales)* (Khartoum, 1978).
Ṭayyib (al-), al-Ṭayyib Muḥammad, ¿A. Sulaymân, and ¿Ali Sa¿d, *al-turâth al-sha¿bî li-qabîlat al-Manâṣîr* (*Folk Traditions of the Manâṣîr Tribe*) (Khartoum, 1969).
Thompson, Stith, *Motif Index of Folk-Literature*. 6 vols. (Bloomington, 1955–58).
Turâth: al-Turâth al-Sha¿bî (*Folk Legacy*) (Baghdad, 1963–64, 1969ff).
Zayn (al-), 'Ādam, *al-turâth al-sha¿bî li-qabîlat al-Musabba¿ât* (*Folk Traditions of the Musabba¿ât Tribe*) (Khartoum, 1970).

AUTHOR INDEX

SUBJECT INDEX

Hasan M. El-Shamy, Professor of Folklore and Near Eastern Languages and Cultures at the Indiana University Folklore Institute (Bloomington), is the author of *Folktales of Egypt* and *Folk Traditions of the Arab World: A Guide to Motif Classification.* Professor El-Shamy has been a member of the African Studies program, a Senior Fulbright Research Fellow, and his work has received numerous honors, including the Ford Foundation Social Science Research Award, the Chicago Folklore Prize, and a National Endowment for the Humanities Award.